FILM NOIR
COMPENDIUM

Other Applause Books/Limelight Editions by the same Authors

More Things Than Are Dreamt Of (1994)
What Ever Happened to Robert Aldrich? (1995)
Film Noir Reader (1996)
Film Noir Reader 2 (1999)
Horror Film Reader (2000)
Film Noir Reader 3 (with Robert Porfirio, 2002)
Film Noir Reader 4 (2004)
Gangster Film Reader (2007)
The Vampire Film from Nosferatu to True Blood (2011)
Film Noir the Directors (2012)
The Zombie Film (2014)
American Neo-Noir (2015)

Other Books

David Lean and His Films (1974)
The Noir Style (1999)
Film Noir (Taschen Film Series, 2004)
L.A. Noir: the City as Character (2005)
Roger Corman: Metaphysics on a Shoestring (2006)
Film Noir the Encyclopedia (4th Edition, 2010)
Film Noir Graphics: Where Danger Lives (2012)
The Film Noir Jigsaw: Critical Perspectives on the Classic Period (2016)

Also by Alain Silver

Robert Aldrich: a guide to references and resources (with Elizabeth Ward, 1979)
The Film Director's Team (with Elizabeth Ward, 1983)
Raymond Chandler's Los Angeles (with Elizabeth Ward, 1987)
The Samurai Film (3rd Edition, 2005)
James Wong Howe The Camera Eye (2010)

Also by James Ursini

The Life and Times of Preston Sturges, An American Dreamer (1976)
The Modern Amazons: Warrior Women on Screen (with Dominique Mainon, 2006)
Cinema of Obsession (with Dominique Mainon, 2007)
Femme Fatale (with Dominique Mainon, 2009)
Directors on the Edge (2011)

FILM NOIR
Compendium

Edited by
Alain Silver
and
James Ursini

Published in 2016 by Applause Theatre and Cinema Books
An Imprint of Hal Leonard Corporation
7777 West Bluemound Road
Milwaukee, WI 53213

Trade Book Division Editorial Offices
33 Plymouth St., Montclair, NJ 07042

Permissions, sources and earlier copyright details may be found in the Acknowledgments, on pages 7-9.

Book and cover design by Alain Silver.

Printed in the United States of America.

Library of Congress Cataloging-in-Publication Data
Names: Silver, Alain, 1947- editor. | Ursini, James, editor.
Title: Film noir compendium : key selections from the Film noir reader series
 / edited by Alain Silver and James Ursini.
Description: Milwaukee, WI : Applause Theatre & Cinema Books, an imprint of
 Hal Leonard Corporation, [2016] | Includes bibliographical references.
Identifiers: LCCN 2016009073 | ISBN 9781495058981 (pbk.)
Subjects: LCSH: Film noir--United States--History and criticism.
Classification: LCC PN1995.9.F54 F555 2016 | DDC 791.43/655--dc23
LC record available at https://lccn.loc.gov/2016009073

www.applausebooks.com

Front cover: *The Killers* with Burt Lancaster and Ava Gardner.
Back cover: *Double Indemnity* with Fred MacMurray and Barbara Stanwyck.
Frontispiece: *Phantom Lady* will Ella Raines and Alan Curtis.
Page 10: *The Big Combo* with Jean Wallace and Cornel Wilde.

Contents

Acknowledgments

The root idea for all of the noir anthologies that we have edited goes back to fall of 1974. At that time we talked to several prospective collaborators—Janey Place, Lowell Peterson, Richard Thompson, and Tim Hunter—some of whom helped to formulate our original outline. That book concept was dropped when Peter Mayer suggested that Alain Silver and Elizabeth Ward undertake *Film Noir: An Encyclopedic Reference to the American Style*. The extensive research done by Elizabeth Ward on that book included acquiring copies of many of the seminal pieces, which became the basis for the first *Film Noir Reader*. After a conversation with our late colleague Bob Porfirio, we refined the idea. To the seminal articles that helped define the movement, we would add key portions of Bob's unpublished dissertation, case studies and even new pieces written especially for the anthology. In 1995 Selise Eiseman, who was then the Special Projects Officer for the Directors Guild of America, suggested several potential contributors; and Adele Field, who was in charge of DGA publications, made suggestions about software and design.

In the actual permissions process, in addition to the individual authors themselves, we are grateful for the assistance of Robin Wood at *CineAction*, James Schwoch at Northwestern University/*Film Reader*, Gary Morris at *Bright Lights Film Journal*, Sayre Maxfield at *Film Comment*, Caroline Beven at *Screen*, Roma Gibson at the B.F.I., Tomm Carroll at the *DGA Magazine*, Jérôme Lindon at Les Éditions de Minuit, Ouardia Teraha at Éditions de l'Étoile, Marci R. McMahon at University of Texas Press, Mary Jaine Winokur at Heldref Publications, Arlene W. Sullivan at The John Hopkins University Press, and Suzanne Regan at *Journal of Film and Video*. New research was done at the Academy of Motion Picture Arts and Sciences Library in Beverly Hills and at the UCLA URL and Theater Arts Libraries and subsequently on the internet.

Most stills are from the collection originally assembled with Elizabeth Ward for *Film Noir: An Encyclopedia*. Janey Place provided illustrations for "Some Visual Motifs of Film Noir" and several other photos/frame enlargements that she assembled with Lowell Peterson. Others are from the Robert Porfirio Collection at Brigham Young University administered by James D'Arc; David Chierichetti; James Paris; Lee Sanders; and Adell Aldrich. Bob Hoover and Linda De Martinez typed portions of the manuscript. Linda Brookover and Glenn Erickson proofread the various *Reader*s; and for this book meticulous work by Elizabeth Ward found all (hopefully) the typographical errors that had slipped through before. And, of course, Mel Zerman at Limelight Editions made the entire *Reader* series possible. With regards to this most recent volume John Cerullo, Carol Flannery, Marybeth Keating, Clare Cerullo, and Lindsay Wagner lent editorial support from Applause Theatre & Cinema Books/Hal Leonard.

Stills are reproduced courtesy of Allied Artists, Cineville, Columbia, ITC, Live, MGM, Miramax, New Line, Orion, Overseas, Paramount, Quinn Martin, RKO, Shapiro-Glickenhaus, Sovereign, TriStar, 20th Century-Fox, United Artists, Universal, and Warner Bros.

While we have attempted to reproduce the original pieces as closely as possible, some formal and/or practical considerations resulted in minor changes. Twenty years ago a few images for "Some Visual Motifs of Film Noir" and "No Way Out: Existential Motifs in the Film Noir" could not be found; but for this book all have been located. Moreover, most the frame enlargements have been redone, so higher resolution DVD frame captures are used rather then analog frame enlargements. In selecting and organizing new stills and keying all photographs to the text, we again have occasionally taken the liberty of injecting our own viewpoint into the captions. While film titles may have been all caps or underlined in the original, for the sake of stylistic consistency we have chosen to use italics and conformed spellings etc. Except as noted, any underlining, boldface or other emphasis in the text is that of the original authors. Most of the authors used end notes, so we have adopted that format for each piece.

1996 by Todd R. Erickson. Printed by permission of the author.

"Son of Noir, the Emergence of Neo-Film Noir and the Neo-B Picture" by Alain Silver, originally published in the *DGA Magazine*, Vol. 17, No. 3, June-July, 1992. Copyright © 1992 by the Directors Guild of America, Inc. Reprinted by permission of the Directors Guild of America, Inc.

"Lounge Time: Postwar Crises and the Chronotope of Film Noir" by Vivian Sobchack, originally published in *Refiguring American Film Genres: Theory and History*, Nick Browne, editor, copyright © 1998 by the author and University of California Press. Reprinted by permission of the author.

"'Lounge Time' Reconsidered: Spatial Discontinuity and Temporal Contingency in Out of the Past" by R. Barton Palmer; "Voices from the Deep: Film Noir as Psychodrama" by J. P. Telotte; and "Manufacturing Heroines: Gothic Victims And Working Women In Classic Noir Films" by Sheri Chinen Biesen—all originally published in *Film Noir Reader 4*, Alain Silver and James Ursini, editors, copyright © 2004 by the authors. Printed by permission of the authors.

"The Strange Case of Film Noir" by Robert G. Porfirio, originally published in *A Companion to Film Noir*, Andrew Spicer and Helen Hanson, editors, copyright © 2012 and 2013 by the author and Blackwell Publishing. Reprinted by permission of Lisa Porfirio/the Estate of Robert G. Porfirio.

"*Kiss Me Deadly*: Evidence of a Style" by Alain Silver, originally published in *Film Comment*, March-April, 1975. Copyright © 1975 by Film Comment Publishing Corporation. Reprinted by permission of the author and the Film Society of Lincoln Center. Revisions and Addendum, copyright © 1994, 1995 by Alain Silver.

"At the Margins of Film Noir: Preminger's *Angel Face*" by Richard Lippe, originally published in *CineAction!*, Nos. 13-14, Summer, 1988. Copyright © 1988 by *CineAction!* Reprinted by permission of the author and *CineAction!*

"*The Killers*: Expressiveness of Sound and Image in Film Noir" and "Dark Jazz: Music in Film Noir," adapted from *The Dark Age of American Film: A Study of American Film Noir (1940-1960)*, a doctoral dissertation, Yale University by Robert G. Porfirio. Copyright © 1979, 1995, and 1999 by Robert G. Porfirio. Printed by permission of the author.

"What is This Thing Called Noir" by Alain Silver and Linda Brookover, originally published in *Film Noir Reader*, Alain Silver and James Ursini, editors, copyright © 1996 by the authors. Printed by permission of the authors.

Phantom Lady, Cornell Woolrich, and the Masochistic Aesthetic" by Tony Williams, originally published in *CineAction!*, Nos. 13-14, Summer, 1988. Copyright © 1988 by *CineAction!* Reprinted by permission of the author and *CineAction!*.

"Noir 101" by Philip Gaines, originally published in *Film Noir Reader 2*, Alain Silver and James Ursini, editors, copyright © 1999 by the author. Printed by permission of the author.

"*Ride the Pink Horse*: Money, Mischance, Murder, and the Monads of Film Noir" by Alain Silver, originally published in *The Philosophy of Film Noir*, Mark T. Conard, editor, copyright © 2005 by the author and University of Kentucky Press. Reprinted by permission of the author.

"Creativity and Evaluation: Two Film Noirs of the Fifties" by Robin Wood, originally published in *CineAction!*, Nos. 21-22 (Summer/Fall, 1990). Copyright © 1990 by the author and *CineAction!*. Reprinted by permission of the author.

"Film Noir, Voice-over, and the Femme Fatale" adapted from *Embattled Voices: the Narrator and the Woman in Film Noir and Women's Films*, doctoral dissertation, University of Illinois at Chicago by Karen Hollinger. Copyright © 1990 and 1995 by Karen Hollinger. Printed by permission of the author.

"The Camouflaged [Unintended] Femme Fatale: *The File on Thelma Jordan* and *Pushover*." by Elizabeth Ward, ASUCLA Program Notes, Spring, 1974. Copyright © 1974, 1996 by Elizabeth Ward. Reprinted by permission of the author.

The Big Combo, photographed by John Alton.

Introduction

Alain Silver

The existence over the last few years of a "série noir" in Hollywood is obvious. Defining its essential traits is another matter.

—Raymond Borde and Étienne Chaumeton, *Panorama du Film Noir Américain*

1.

Sixty years after Borde and Chaumeton defined the above challenge, critical commentators on film noir continue to grapple with it. Ironically, American writers did not immediately take up consideration of this indigenous phenomenon and the question of its "essential traits." Only gradually in a frequently cross-referenced series of essays in the 1970s did they begin to concur on the "obvious existence" of film noir and express themselves about it. Six decades later, there are now scores of full-length books in English concerning film noir and its diverse aspects (with undoubtedly many more to follow).

Past and present commentators have brought and continue to bring to bear on the noir phenomenon a variety of critical approaches, and that was the foundation of the *Film Noir Reader* series. In 1979, the introduction, other essays, and individual entries in *Film Noir: An Encyclopedic Reference to the American Style* were the first published attempt in English to search the entire body of films for "essential traits." I remarked there that the full range of the noir vision depends on its narratives, its characterizations, and its visual style. In fact, that style is a translation of both character emotions and narrative concepts into a pattern of visual usage. No doubt a pop critic such as Barry Gifford, author of the informal survey *The Devil Thumbs A Ride*, who deems such concerns to be "academic flapdoodle," could assert that it is formalist mumbo-jumbo to "detect" alienation lurking beyond the frame line in a vista of the dark, wet asphalt of a city street or obsession in a point-of-view shot that picks a woman's face out of crowd. I would argue that to resist such readings is to deny the full potential of figurative meaning not merely in film noir but in all motion pictures. Obviously none of the various elements of visual style—angle, composition, lighting, montage, depth, movement, etc.—which inform any given shot or sequence are unique to film noir. What sets the noir cycle apart is the unity of its formal vision. As the various essays reprinted in this volume will confirm, there is nothing in the films themselves which precludes or invalidates any established critical method.

Michael Walker's opening comments in the early anthology *The Book of Film Noir* reveal a fairly straightforward auteurist bias. But what can one say about a viewpoint such as French critic Marc Vernet's in his introductory essay, "Film Noir at the Edge of Doom" in the later *Shades of Noir*? Certainly it epitomizes the sort of criticism that Gifford scorns; but Gifford's opprobrium is not the issue. In the third edition of *Film Noir: An Encyclopedic Reference* our review of the literature on film noir included Vernet's previously published conclusion that "a hero cannot be both strong and vulnerable, the woman good and evil." The assertion made there—that his observations were part of a simplistic, structuro-semiological rush to judgment clearly at odds with the narrative position of film noir as a whole—still pertain. Where once Vernet merely puzzled over contradictory icons, in "Edge of Doom" he indulges in pointless deconstruction. On the one hand Vernet now bemoans "complacent repetition" about film noir. On the other hand he presents the ultimate obfuscation by calling it "impossible to criticize." What then is he writing about?

I am used to having my actual name mispronounced and misspelled, as when Vernet changes "Alain" to "Alan"—his is certainly not the first reference with that particular error. While I am not suggesting that the value of critical writing depends on crossing every "t" or including every "i," especially true with commentators on motion pictures, an expressive medium that is the most complex in the history of art. But Vernet's assumption about how a particular name should be spelled is telling in that it reveals his tendency towards pre-judgment and succinctly encapsulates the problem with his critical outlook. Vernet sees a simple contradiction: a French first name like those in the credits of *L'Année Dernière à Marienbad* paired with an English last name right out of *Treasure Island*. "Of course," he deduces, "this must be a mistake." Some unnamed researcher has erred, which Vernet corrects by Anglicizing the spelling. The root of Vernet's outlook is clear: It derives from a solipsistic arrogance that can presume to "correct" anomalies that it does not comprehend and can therefore generate the offhanded observation that film noir is "the triumph of European artists even as it presents American actors."

Aside from its remarkably unembarrassed Eurocentric bias, such a statement completely ignores Paul Schrader's decades-old warning that "there is a danger of over-emphasizing the German influence in Hollywood"; and it typifies many recent attempts both to break down the "myth" of film noir and to relocate its origins. As Borde and Chaumeton realized from the first, there is no easy answer. The noir cycle is an event garmented in the uneasy synthesis of the social turmoil churned up by the greatest war in history and Hollywood. Given its brief history film noir has inspired more than its share of discussion, and sundry critics of film noir have been troubled by its themes and characters, by protagonists who often perish because of an obsessive and/or alienated state of mind. Must it be really so remarkable, when methodologies from Marxism to Freudianism to Existentialism assailed the moral and political status quo, that a movement such as film noir should develop characters with a sense of alienation and despair? It may be unduly simplified to erect such a causality or to cite a fortuitous confluence of factors as responsible for the appearance of the noir movement; but that does not make it incorrect.

Much has been made of the crisis of masculinity in film noir. Much could be made of the crisis in Judeo-Christian patriarchal structures since the mid-point of the 20th Century. The dramatic crisis of film noir is the same as that which drives any convergent group of characterizations. The unprecedented social upheaval of two world wars compounded by economic turmoil and genocides on every continent was globally promulgated by broadcasts and newsreels and all condensed into a thirty year span from 1915 to 1945. Just as the technique and technology of filmmaking has progressed in its hundred year history, the ideological outlook of its artists cannot have been unaffected by the other events in the world during that span of time.

Whatever one may believe about the delimiting factors of film noir, then or now, its first expression in what is generally accepted as "the classic period" was solely in American movies made in America by American filmmakers. Vernet seems to imply that Fritz Lang, Robert Siodmak, Anthony Mann, Otto Preminger, and Billy Wilder were European or, more specifically, German artists. Overlooking the fact that none of these five men was actually German-born,[1] the issue of European expatriates working in the United States does have significance; but not just for film noir. American filmmaking has benefited from foreign talent from the early silent era to the present day. So how can any list of filmmakers at any time be glibly summarized as a "triumph of European artists presenting American actors"? Putting aside for a moment questions of auteurism or whether these filmmakers were more significant to the cycle of noir films than American-born directors from Robert Aldrich to Robert Wise, does the national origin of the directors change the nationality of a film? Did Joseph Losey continue to make American movies even after the blacklist compelled his move to England? Do John Farrow's origins make his films for Paramount and RKO Australian film noir?

When Borde and Chaumeton wrote the first book-length study of the phenomenon in 1955 they called it, naturally enough, *Panorama du Film Noir Américain*. The title itself expresses the second truism of film noir. Vernet and others may have a reason other than Eurocentric bias for stressing the non-American aspects of film noir. The British and French publishers of *Film Noir: An Encyclopedic Reference* probably did not delete "to the American Style" from the title just because they thought it was too long. Still, while many subsequent writers have questioned both specifics and generalities of Borde and Chaumeton's seminal work, none have questioned the very existence of the American phenomenon which they tried to define.

In 1979 I wrote that

> with the Western, film noir shares the distinction of being an indigenous American form. But unlike Westerns, which derive in great part from a preexisting literary genre and a period of American history, the antecedents of film noir are less precise. As a consequence, the noir cycle has a singular position in the brief history of American motion pictures: a body of films that not only presents a relatively cohesive vision of America but that does so in a manner transcending the influences of auteurism or genre. Film noir is not firmly rooted in either personal creation or in the translation of another tradition into movie terms. Rather film noir is a self-contained reflection of American culture and its preoccupations at a point in time. As such it is the unique example of a wholly American film style.

Vernet makes some assertions about film noir's origins, about censorship and prejudices in both America and France from which he concludes that post-World War II French critics "created" film noir. Can anyone seriously contend that critics created anything but the term? As Edgardo Cozarinsky notes "film noir defies translation into English, though its object of study is mainly (and, one may argue, its only legitimate examples are) English-speaking."[2] The suggestion of Vernet and others abrogates the very concept of creation. At the risk of belaboring the obvious, films are made by filmmakers not by critics, whose understanding of the process is necessarily limited. To paraphrase Vernet, the primary consideration is not the technical process nor the financial process, but the expressive process, which relies on the audience—the perceivers of the expression—for completion. This is the fundamental transaction on which Vernet or any critic should concentrate.

> They are, therefore, not revolutionary but conservative. Nay more, they are reactionary, for they try to roll back the wheel of history.
>
> —Karl Marx and Friedrich Engels, *The Communist Manifesto*

In order to see the subject of film noir as it is, one need look no farther than the films. Vernet's revisionism is like any of the neo-Freudian, semiological, historical, structural, socio-cultural, and/or auteurist assaults of the past. Film noir has resisted them all. Why then are critics like Vernet interested in the phenomenon of film noir? Are they at heart all neo-Platonists and *Il Conformista* the film that they watch over and over late at night? Perhaps many of the new European essayists feel a need to tear apart the foundation laid by Borde and Chaumeton in order to build something new. Certainly there is justification in James Damico's lament in "Film Noir: A Modest Proposal" that an "order of breezy assumption seems to have afflicted film noir criticism from its beginnings." Unfortunately, in this latter context, a reactionary commentator like Vernet offers nothing new, but just another brand of breezy assumptions. Actually, he offers a void, a noir hole where there once was a body of films.

Much of *Shades of Noir* progresses from the suggestion made by David Bordwell in *The Classical American Cinema* that film noir is merely an invention of critical commentators. In discussing this concept in *Film Noir: An Encyclopedic Reference*, Bordwell's assertion was cited to the effect that "critics have not succeeded in defining specifically noir visual techniques... or narrative structure. The problem resembles one in art history, that of defining 'non-classical' styles." At first glance there is nothing to dispute in Bordwell's remark. The tautological nature of his position is clearer in a more recent expression by a reviewer: "Genres are invented by critics. When the first film noir—whatever you might consider that to be— was released, nobody yelled, 'Hey, let's go on down to the Bijou! The first film noir is out!' What is at first innovation or anomaly only becomes a genre through repetition and eventual critical classification."[3] Movements are also named by critics, as when a disdainful Louis Leroy used the title of a Monet painting to coin the term "impressionism" in 1874. But while no art historian would claim that the impressionist movement did not exist before Leroy "defined" it (and the most celebrated of its practitioners embraced the term), some film historians have glibly asserted that the noir film movement did not exist until French critics hung a moniker on it.

If nothing else, Klein's is certainly a more cogent expression of the obvious than either Vernet or Bordwell make. So they didn't go down to the Bijou to see *Stranger on the Third Floor* or *Two Seconds* (Vernet's candidate from 1932) because it was the "first film noir." To answer in kind, "So what?" Did the first audiences for

The Great Train Robbery or *Nosferatu* congratulate themselves on attending the first Western or the earliest adaptation of Bram Stoker's *Dracula*? The best answer to anyone's assertion that filmmakers of the classic period never specifically decided to make "a film noir" is still cinematographer John Alton's evocation of the noir milieu in his book *Painting with Light*: "The room is dark. A strong streak of light sneaks in from the hall under the door. The sound of steps is heard. The shadows of two feet divide the light streak. A brief silence follows. There is suspense in the air."

If Bordwell was not aware of Alton's book when he wrote "critics have not succeeded in defining specifically noir visual techniques," he certainly must have known Janey Place and Lowell Peterson's essay on visual motifs in noir. Place and Peterson themselves quoted Higham and Greenberg's 1968 book *Hollywood in the Forties* on the subject of visual style. The visual analysis of film noir was further developed by Janey Place in *Women and Film Noir*, by Robert Porfirio's extensive work in his dissertation *The Dark Age of American Film: A Study of American Film Noir*, and ourselves in *The Noir Style*. In fact, the evocation of a "noir look" goes all the way back to Borde and Chaumeton. In 1979 I first cited the years of production immediately after World War II as the most visually homogeneous of the entire noir cycle. One might still examine the credits to a selection of motion pictures released over an eighteen month period such as *The Big Clock* (Paramount, 1948), *Brute Force* (Universal, 1947), *Cry of the City* (20th Century-Fox, 1948), *Force of Evil* (MGM, 1948), *Framed* (Columbia, 1947), *Out of the Past* (RKO, 1947), *Pitfall* (United Artists, 1948), and *The Unsuspected* (Warner Bros., 1947) and discover that eight different directors, cinematographers, and screenwriters adapted different original stories for different stars at eight different studios. These people of great and small technical reputations created eight otherwise unrelated motion pictures with one cohesive style.[4]

I have previously contended that the noir cycle's consistent visual style is keyed specifically to recurrent narrative patterns and character emotions. Because these patterns and emotions are repeatedly suggestive of certain abstractions, such as alienation and obsession, it may seem that film noir is overly dependent on external constructions, such as Existentialism or Freudianism, for its dramatic meanings. Irrefutably film noir does recruit the ethical and philosophical values of the culture as freely as it recruits visual conventions, iconic notations, and character types. This process both enriches and dislocates the noir cycle as a phenomenon so that it resists facile explanation.

Criticism is often less a search for meaning than for sub-text. In film the dilemma is that narrative is usually explicit and style is usually not. Charts of narrative patterns, icons, and the like are easy to make. For example, one could assign critical allegiances to noir figures:

Alienated characters	< = >	Existentialism
Obsessed characters	< = >	Freudianism
Proletarian characters	< = >	Marxism
Femme fatales	< = >	Feminism
All of the above	< = >	Structuralism

A writer like Gifford might well accuse chart makers of chasing their own tall tales. For him, film noir is more about Lawrence Tierney's sneer than statistics or structures. The real question, as suggested by Bordwell, is noirneo-formalist: if film noir is heavily reliant on visual style, how does that affect meaning?

Opposite (clockwise from top left), the noir style at work in *The Big Clock*, *Out of the Past*, and *Brute Force*.
Below (clockwise from top left): *Pitfall*, *Force of Evil*, and *Cry of the City.*

What I answered in *Film Noir: An Encyclopedic Reference* was that there is no grammar attached to this visual substance because its conventions of expression are not analogous to those of language. Or, as Pasolini put it, "The cinema author has no dictionary."[5] Divergent concepts of "signs and meaning" notwithstanding, the side-lit close-up, the long take, or the foreground object bisecting the frame may imply respectively a character's indecision, a building tension, a figurative separation of the other persons and things in the frame; or they may not. The potential is always there. The specific image may or may not participate in that potential. Without denotation, it is the connotations which film noir repeatedly creates that are telling. The dark streets become emblems of alienation; a figure's unrelenting gaze becomes obsessive; the entire environment becomes hostile, chaotic, deterministic. Some critics have found a conflict between the documentary import of certain police dramas, which are ostensibly realistic, and the low-key style of detective films, which are ostensibly expressionistic. In fact, the issue is really one of convention. Which is more lifelike, a man in a dark alley, his face illuminated by a match as he lights a cigarette or a woman on a veranda built on a sound stage cottage, her body casting three shadows as she shoots her victim? Hollywood reality is by convention. The visual conventions of film noir are, as often as not, actually more naturalistic.

What the essays originally collected in the *Film Noir Reader* series will quickly reveal is the breadth of theories which critics have brought to the noir phenomenon. Whatever one calls it—series, style, genre, movement, school, cycle—none of the seminal essayists on film noir represented in this book have contradicted Borde and Chaumeton's remark that the existence of a noir series is "obvious." Certainly they did not all agree (when have critics ever done that?); but they did address the visual techniques and narrative structures of film noir in dozens of articles.

> History is to take an arbitrarily selected series of continuous events and examine it apart from others, although there is and can be no beginning to any event, for one event always flows uninterruptedly from another.
>
> —Leo Tolstoy, *War and Peace*

It should go without saying that any investigator must first look at the heart of the matter, to the films themselves. How then could Marc Vernet look at those films and conclude that "film noir is a collector's idea that for the moment can only be found in books"? Actually, this may be the most accurate statement that Vernet makes; although, if I may borrow a touch of his condescension, he probably doesn't even know why. Obviously there is nowhere in the literal history of cinema, that is, in the films themselves, a "film noir," any more than there is a Western, a war film, or a screwball comedy. Even straining credibility and accepting Bordwell's assertion that the makers of noir films did not in any way realize what they were doing, is conscious intentionality a prerequisite for creative expression? It can only be assumed that it is Vernet's lack of knowledge about the real process by which films are made which leads to his confusion. Of course, it does not take a rocket scientist to realize that one is hard pressed to make a samurai film without swords or a Western without six-guns.

> Fresh from the translation of Borde and Chaumeton, I am moved to slip for a moment into a free-form, anecdotal, somewhat French style. In 1975, I sit in an almost empty theater in Santa Monica watching Walter Hill's *Hard Times*, the directorial debut of the screenwriter of the remarkable neo-noir *Hickey & Boggs*; and I am somehow reminded of director Kihachi Okamoto's equally remarkable *Samurai Assassin*. Two years later, I sit in a living room in the Hollywood hills, interviewing Walter Hill for *Movie* magazine. In the preliminary banter, I remark that the Charles Bronson character in *Hard Times* is like a Japanese ronin, a masterless samurai. Hill goes to a shelf and brings over two scripts. One is a Western, still unproduced, entitled "The Last Gun." While I flip through, noting that the main character is named Ronin and that the act breaks are marked by quotes from bushido, the code of the warrior, Hill finds a particular page in the *Hard Times* script. As he hands it to me, his thumb indicates a line of stage direction in which the street fighter "crouches in the corner like a samurai."

Is *Hard Times* a samurai film? Of course not. No more than the elements borrowed even more extensively in

Hill's *The Warriors* can make it a samurai film. Neither Hill nor Clint Eastwood nor John Milius nor George Miller, as much as they might admire the genre, have made anything more than allusions to samurai films; just as reciprocally Akira Kurosawa could never make a John Ford Western. Styles of films have more than requisite icons to identify them. Filmmakers know this when the films are made. Contemporary filmmakers understand, as actor Nick Nolte asserts, that "film noir is putting a style over the story."[6] "Collectors," as Vernet brands them, only realize it after the fact. In the end, does it matter what the filmmakers of the classic period of film noir thought about the films they were making? Film noir is a closed system. To some extent, it is defined after the fact. How could it be otherwise? Was the Hundred Years War, something else after only fifty years of fighting? So when did film noir become what it is? For those more interested in the phenomenon than the phenomenology, the answer must be from the first, when that first noir film opened at the Bijou. But perhaps a more eloquent answer is a question. Consider the photograph that we reproduce again below. Why did Robert Aldrich, producer/director of *Kiss Me Deadly*, pose with a copy of the first edition Borde and Chaumeton's book, in which he is not even mentioned, as he stood on the set of *Attack!* in 1956?

2.

A fact thus set down in substantial history cannot easily be gainsaid. Nor is there any reason it should be.

—Herman Melville, *Moby Dick*

Questions of phenomenology aside, film history is as clear now about film noir as ever: it finds its existence as obvious as Borde and Chaumeton did sixty years ago. If observers of film noir agree on anything, it is on the boundaries of the classic period that begins in 1941 with *The Maltese Falcon* and ends less than a score of years later with *Touch of Evil*. Issues of pre-noir or neo-noir aside, we the editors of the *Reader* series and *Film Noir the Encyclopedia* along with many other commentators have long considered film noir to be more than a traditional film movement. Exactly what Borde and Chaumeton claim to mean by their term "series"—which they define as a group of "motion pictures from one country sharing certain traits (style, atmosphere, subject matter...) strongly enough to mark them unequivocally and to give them, over time, an unmistakable character"—is not clarified by their lists of analogies to film noir that include both genres and movements. Because so many of the essayists on the noir phenomenon in the 70s were still deliberating the question of "essential traits" posed by Borde and Chaumeton in 1955, there is no consensus on film noir to be found in this or any compendium of critical thought.

Beginning with Borde and Chaumeton's first chapter, "Towards a Definition of Film Noir," Part One of *Film Noir Reader* contained eight Seminal Essays. *Film Noir Reader 2* added seven more. Taken altogether they represented the proliferation and divergence of significant published opinions on film noir through 1983, just a few years after the first edition of *Film Noir: An Encyclopedic Reference* appeared in 1979. Since then, not only has the movement's first encyclopedic reference undergone a major revision, but a dozen variants by diverse hands have followed.

It's just that producers have got hep to the fact that plenty of real crime takes place every day and that it makes a good movie. The public is fed up with the old-fashioned melodramatic type of hokum. You know, the whodunit at which the audience after the second reel starts shouting, "We know the murderer. It's the butler. It's the butler. It's the butler."

—James M. Cain

James M. Cain also told *New York Times* writer Lloyd Shearer in 1945 that he had "never written a murder mystery in my life. Some of the characters in my novels commit murder, but there's no mystery involved in them. They do it for sex or money or both." Like the filmmakers who defined the classic period of film noir and some of its prototypes, Cain never uses the word noir. This seems natural enough for an English-speaking writer; but no doubt some could interpret this as more proof that film noir was invented by a bunch of Frenchmen catching up on American movies in the Parisian cinemas of 1946. In fact, with or without a copy of Borde and Chaumeton in hand, with or without the term, Cain, Aldrich, and all the filmmakers of the classic period were hep to the concept of film noir.

In part one of this introduction, classic period cinematographer John Alton is quoted on the subject of style. That same perception of a style clearly underlies Cain's comments. Writing in 1945 and disdainful of a noir cycle, which he calls "hard-boiled, gut-and-gore crime stories, all fashioned on a theme with a combination of plausibly motivated murder and studded with high-powered Freudian implication," Lloyd Shearer certainly perceives the existence of the noir style more than a year before either Nino Frank or Jean-Pierre Chartier thought of giving it a name. Many years later, it is chilling to realize that some readers of the *Times* may have been digesting their evening meal alongside Shearer's comments deploring Hollywood violence at the exact moment that, half a world away, much of Hiroshima was being vaporized. What might Shearer have made of the theory that audiences were numbed to violence by World War II, had his article appeared just one day later?

The underpinning of Shearer's dismissal of noir is old-fashioned, New York style Hollywood bashing that begins with his anecdote about Producer Joe Sistrom and *Double Indemnity*. At the end of the article, Shearer also quotes Raymond Chandler about the Hays office and escapist entertainment. For our purposes, a more useful quote from Chandler is found in his letter to Joe Sistrom, written two years after the Shearer piece:

> Back in 1943 when we were writing *Double Indemnity* you told me that an effective motion picture could not be made of a detective or mystery story for the reason that the high point is the revelation of the murderer and that only happens in the last minute of the picture. Events proved you wrong, for almost immediately the mystery trend started, and there is no question but that *Double Indemnity* started it.... The thing that made the mystery effective on the screen already existed on paper, but you somehow did not realize just where the values lay. It is implicit in my theory of mystery story writing that the mystery and the solution to the mystery are only what I call "the olive in the martini," and the really good mystery is one you would read even if you knew somebody had torn out the last chapter.[7]

While Chandler's prose is typically hyperbolic and may overreach with his comment about tearing out the last chapter, clearly what defines for him the "mystery trend" that the noir movement is its style.

While Shearer's antagonism towards Hollywood makes him use Cain and Chandler like literary cudgels, Nino Frank understood what Cain and Chandler were saying when he wrote about the old and new kind of American police dramas. The sensibilities of Hammett, Cain, and Chandler were integral to what Frank called a "new kind" of film, which he was the first to dub "noir." Frank probably never read Shearer's piece and the Cain quote and certainly could not know what Chandler wrote to Joe Sistrom; but he was clearly on the same wavelength as them in discussing an outdated style of novel and film when he affirmed that "I don't know of any enlightened devotees of the genre who could not nowadays plumb the mystery from the first fifty pages or the first two reels..." For Cain, Chandler, Frank, and others to follow, plot mysteries were old hat, stale and predictable long before creaking to an end. Style and character were now the key.

They still are. There are plenty of plot twists in classic period noir and the best of neo-noir as well, but those twists are designed to surprise the protagonist not the viewer. The self-assured deductions of Holmes and his ilk still have no place in the noir sensibility. The definition of that sensibility is the purpose of the essayists collected herein. And as always the writers herein may approach that definition either directly (what film noir is) or indirectly (what it is not). Either way, the range of their opinions derives from a common perception that goes back to Shearer, Frank. and Jean-Pierre Chartier, whichever they may be and whatever makes them so, some films are noir.

The journals in which Frank, and Chartier first called noir films noir are long defunct. And it may seem that, other than the fact that they coined the term, their insights into film noir are limited. But, as with Shearer, their perspective and their significance as seminal articles is unique in that it is contemporaneous with the height of the classic period. And there is a key perception, that Shearer either does not see or does not care about, which Frank and Chartier simultaneously have: that these films are something new, not mysteries in the detective tradition going back to Poe and Doyle, but psychological dramas, grimly naturalistic, sordid, despairing, and exciting to watch.

As the classic period wound down, Claude Chabrol and others writing for *Cahiers du Cinéma* and *Positif* sustained the critical discussion of film noir culminating with Borde and Chaumeton's book-length, French-language study in 1955. It was in the 1983 Afterword to the reprint of *Panorama du Film Noir Américain*, which was based on an article about film noir in the 70s, where Borde and Chaumeton asserted that "film noir had fulfilled its role, which was to create a specific malaise and to drive home a social criticism of the United States." Whether the authors were injecting the issue of "social criticism" in hindsight is unknown; but it underlines the second main theme which many of the seminal essayists also consider: the relationship of the noir cycle to the socio-cultural history of the United States.

As Borde and Chaumeton wrestle through lists of films, considering plot points and character types, they also make a telling observation about the style of film noir. In their subsequent chapter on the "sources" of film noir, they introduce not only the obvious influence of hard-boiled fiction but also the prevalence of psychoanalysis in the 1940s as a popular treatment of nervous disorders. The original edition of *Panorama* had a unique perspective being not merely the first but also the only study of film noir written contemporaneously with the classic period. From this position, Borde and Chaumeton's initial attempt at definition of film noir cannot be superseded as the benchmark for all subsequent work making the same attempt.

By 1962, French film historian George Sadoul was offhandedly remarking in his *Histoire du Cinéma* that film noir "was a school,...where psychoanalysis was applied [so that] a childhood trauma became the cause of criminal behavior just as unemployment explained social unrest." Both the term and the concept took longer to gain acceptance with English-language critics, and it is still remarkable that no English-language critics would enter the discussion for more than a decade after *Panorama*. The first extensive discussion of film noir in English appeared in the chapter, "Black Cinema," of Charles Higham and Joel Greenberg's *Hollywood in the Forties*. Beginning with an evocative and oft-cited paragraph about the dark wet streets and flashing neon signs that create the "ambience of film noir," what follows is an overview of what Higham and Greenberg consider "a genre," but no usable definition of film noir emerges from this impressionistic piece.

In 1970, an article by Raymond Durgnat appeared in the British magazine *Cinema*. "Paint It Black: the Family Tree of the Film Noir" is the first structural approach to film noir which asserts that "it is not a genre as the Western or gangster film is, and takes us into the realms of classification by motif and tone." As Durgnat rambles through scores of titles in less than a dozen pages the branches of his family tree twist around and entangle themselves with each other. In the end Durgnat has no time, and perhaps no inclination, to plot these intertwinings. Ironically, Durgnat's "family tree" is better known in a truncated version stripped down to a two-page chart of just categories printed by *Film Comment* in 1974. Curiously, Vernet claims that Durgnat's self-professed "imperfect schematizations" helped "to paralyse reflection on film noir."

Paul Schrader's "notes on film noir" originally appeared in a program accompanying a retrospective of noir films at the first Los Angeles Film Exposition. When it was published in *Film Comment* in 1972, it was the first analysis of film noir many American readers had ever seen. If any single essay had the possibility of "paralyzing reflection on film noir," it was this one. Schrader cited and embraced Durgnat's assertion that film noir is not a genre. Rather than charting his own types, Schrader summarizes the mediating influences on the noir phenomenon and then discusses its style and themes. Schrader steps over the question of definition with a disclaimer about subjectivity: "Almost every critic has his own definition of film noir, and a personal list of film titles.... How many noir elements does it take to make a film noir *noir*?" While he is the first to summarize succinctly four "causes"—(1) World War II and post-War disillusionment; (2) post-War realism; (3) the German influence; and (4) the hard-boiled tradition emerging from 1930s pulp fiction—Schrader considers the "uneasy, exhilarating combination of realism and expressionism" to be contradictory; and, surprisingly, he never considers how oneirism or nightmarish images can reflect a psychological truth as mentioned by Borde and Chaumeton. The ground-breaking aspect of Schrader's article is the outline of film noir style and characterization. For Schrader the classic period ends early but still produces a plethora of chiaroscuro and an multitude of haunted protagonists. The stylistic discussion carries over as the piece ends tellingly on the question of film noir and auteurism: "Auteur criticism is interested in how directors are different; film noir criticism is interested in what they have in common."

While he warns that he "in no way attempts to trace the limits of film noir," Tom Flinn's 1972 piece is one of the first in-depth articles on particular aspects of noir. Two years later, Stephen Farber's social analysis appeared in a special film noir section of *Film Comment* in 1974. Earlier in that year, *Film Comment* published another article as influential as and perhaps even more widely cited than the Durgnat and Schrader pieces: Janey Place and Lowell Peterson's "Some Visual Motifs of Film Noir." "Visual Motifs" is actually two separate pieces. In the first part, Place and Peterson introduce the concept of what they call "anti-traditional elements," that is, a mise-en-scène by directors and a lighting scheme by cinematographers that radically diverges from the studio "norm." In doing so, they are the first to attempt a systematic if abbreviated assessment of film noir style. The second part of the article is meant to illustrate the first; but the stills and frame enlargements have detailed annotations which permit them to stand alone as an analysis of the noir form.

Published in *Sight and Sound* in 1976, Robert Porfirio's "No Way Out: Existential Motifs in the Film Noir" was extracted from his dissertation in progress and anticipates the editorial perspective he brought to *Film*

Noir: An Encyclopedic Reference. Before redacting of noir's many instances of alienation and despair, as promised in the piece's title, Porfirio notes that "visual style rescued many an otherwise pedestrian film from oblivion." Porfirio's analytical method is more closely aligned to that of Place and Peterson than to Durgnat or Schrader, as he makes extensive use of frame enlargements to illustrate such prototypical moments of existential angst in film noir as the narrator's lament in *Detour* that "fate or some mysterious force can put the finger on you or me for no reason at all."

James Damico's 1978 "Film Noir: A Modest Proposal" from *Film Reader* makes a case for noir as a genre but also focuses on the limitations of a genre model that is based on "plot structure and character type." Damico's principal alternative concept—his modest proposal—is an archetype based on Northrup Frye's model, largely dependent on the femme fatale, and in many respects reminiscent of Borde and Chaumeton, to whom he frequently refers. Damico's piece has itself often been cited as a first major article to express a viewpoint opposed to Paul Schrader's because of his search for a narrative model. Actually Damico seems to admire Schrader's genealogy of noir even as he decries Durgnat's unfocused and/or too broad categories. Perhaps Damico's most radical assertion is consigned to a note at the very end of the piece. Damico briefly surveys all the preceding essays on noir except Place and Peterson's, yet in his note he casually dismisses the concept of visual style because he can "see no conclusive evidence [of] anything cohesive."

As the title suggests, the aim of Paul Kerr's "Out of What Past? Notes on the B Film Noir." is "to refocus...on one important, industrially-defined, fraction of the genre—the B film noir." Kerr regards film noir as a genre but also accepts that "the curious cross-generic quality of film noir is perhaps a vestige of its origins as a kind of 'oppositional' cinematic mode." He begins a search for a new definition by reviewing past assessments from Borde and Chaumeton to Damico then presents his own digest of observations keyed to economic issues. His most original points, such as low-key lighting being used to mask low-budget sets or night shooting as a strategy to get more set-ups into each production day, are part of a "technological determinism" for film noir. While his use of statistical data is extensive, a few of Kerr's conclusions are marginally backed by the facts. For instance, he asserts that the studios with larger financial reserves, Paramount, Fox, and MGM, made "not only fewer...but also more lavish" noir films. While RKO and United Artists clearly had the highest tally of titles in the classic period, Paramount made almost as many; and Fox's total was equal to Warners. Despite his basically "non-aesthetic" discussion, Kerr's influence on later writers seeking alternatives to the auteurist or structural models still continues.

By 1979—although commentators generally agreed on when the classic period began and ended and which pictures were most significant—what soon emerged as and has remained the key issue is the core definition of film noir, whether it was genre or movement, content or style. Marc Vernet's 1983 article redefines the thrust of French criticism under the influence of semiological and structural methods. Vernet's close inspection of six classic period films (*Maltese Falcon*, *Double Indemnity*, *The Big Sleep*, *The Lady from Shanghai*, *Out of the Past*, and *The Enforcer*) moves from Borde and Chaumeton's concept of ambiguity to the chaos that underlies the noir universe. Because film noir is resistant to a straightforward semiological deconstruction, Vernet concedes that its "sense of disorder and reversal, however, is in every case relative." But when he concludes that "a hero cannot be both strong and vulnerable, the woman good and evil," Vernet seems to fall off the structuro-semiological deep end. His search for oppositions using Vladimir Propp or Claude Lévi-Strauss becomes a search through enclosed texts where "each functions perfectly within the context of its own system"; but this ignores the critical context, that viewer expectations are derived from the emphasis on character over plot, from the evolution of film noir, as first described by Frank, Chartier, and Chabrol. Vernet seems to echo Chartier's analysis of the Dietrichson/Neff dynamic when he types the femme fatale: "the woman is made guilty and, despite her protestations, she is either abandoned or killed by the hero." But Chartier understood that it was Neff's outlook, not Dietrichson's, which was the linchpin of noir, a paternalistic outlook which dichotomizes women into destroyers or saviors. Vernet is seeking designating structures in a film movement that often depicts extreme, even cataclysmic events, what Frank called a "change in background from a vast and novelistic treatment of nature to a 'fantastic' social order." In this context, a superior guiding principle might have been an observation analogous to Frank's by structuralist Maurice Merleau-Ponty: "the dialectic proper to the organism and the milieu can be interrupted by 'catastrophic' behavior."

No anthology would be complete without considering neo-noir, its popularity with contemporary producers and influence on the independent and "neo-B" filmmakers. Todd Erickson coined the term in 1990 and his exploration of the parallels in technological developments which underlie both the classic period and neo-noir reveals how a new generation of filmmakers have transformed a movement into a genre. My piece from 1992 overlays Paul Kerr's concept on neo-noir and finds kinship between the B's of the classic period and new generation of low-budget filmmakers.

In a new addition to the classic text, 1998's "Lounge Time: Postwar Crisis and the Chronotype of Film Noir," Vivian Sobchack uses a prototype—or rather chronotype—derived from diverse precedents, Mikhail Bakhtin in the foreground certainly but with nuances from *Women in Film Noir,* other anthropo/cultural studies going back to Barbara Deming and perhaps even a soupçon of Proust's "temps perdu" thrown into the mix. In her core sampling of noir's narratives, Sobchack suggests an alternative reading of the movement's underlying angst: not existential ennui or emotional alienation caused by mischance or obsession, but the sense of displacement, the loss of home that many of the 20th century's refugees (including so many classic period filmmakers) suffered and that led literally and figuratively to drowning their sorrows in a "world of bars, diners, and seedy hotels." In the first of three pieces written for *Film Noir Reader 4* in 2004, R. Barton Palmer—who has written and edited his own books on noir—reconsiders "Lounge Time" and attempts a reconciliation between Sobchack's approach and a crucial film in the noir canon, *Out of the Past.* J. P. Telotte, who has also written his own volume on noir, examines the elements of depth and darkness, focusing in particular on *Sunset Boulevard* and *Kiss Me Deadly.* Then Sheri Chinen Biesen, distilling from her subsequent book on the movement, considers the female protagonist in noir, particularly its title characters in movies such as *Laura, Mildred Pierce,* and *Gilda.*

As he had first attempted in his introduction to *The Philosophy of Film Noir*, in "The Strange Case of Film Noir" (his last writing on the subject), our late, ground-breaking colleague Bob Porfirio reviews the evolution of noir and its criticism, repeatedly crossing methodological boundaries and attempting to discover the essence of noir in the "nexus between a restrictive aesthetic world and the more accessible social one," a shadow universe where idiolects collide and create something beyond genre, beyond movement, beyond transgressive values, in short, film noir.

As with the *Reader* series, the second section of *Film Noir Compendium* contains "case studies" of individual films, directors, and themes. While most of the writers follow a convention that goes back to Borde and Chaumeton's assertion that they would "deem films to be created by their directors," not all of these case studies are auteurist. In fact, the critical biases and methodologies from Bob Porfirio's visual analysis of *The Killers* to Tony Williams on *Phantom Lady* cover as broad a range as the seminal articles reproduced in Part One. My own *"Kiss Me Deadly*: Evidence of a Style" derives from two earlier close studies of visual usage and work on my first book, *David Lean and his Films.*[7] In fact, it was meant to apply to the graphic style of any film not just noir.

While the distinction may not be as simple as Paul Schrader suggested, film noir has never been "about" auteurism or particular directors, any more than silent Soviet dramas were about Eisenstein or Pudovkin or *neorealismo* about Rossellini or De Sica. But as it is with all of film history, auteurism is part of film noir. For many directors noir provided a "B" context to display his or her talent and make the transition to "A" pictures. For others, as Richard Lippe writes about Preminger ("At the Margins of Film Noir: Preminger's *Angel Face*"), the boundaries of noir are stretched to accommodate what Porfirio calls "personal idiolect."

"What is this Thing Called Noir?" is, not coincidentally, the title of one of the essays that I wrote expressly with Linda Brookover for the original *Film Noir Reader*. Also included are the late Robin Wood's close analysis of creativity and authorship through *The Big Heat* and *Kiss Me Deadly*; Elizabeth Ward's reflection about the impact of *Double Indemnity* on subsequent classic period noir films starring Barbara Stanwyck and Fred MacMurray; my discussion of *Ride the Pink Horse* from underrated actor/director Robert Montgomery; Robert

Porfirio's dual considerations of jazz in classic noir and how the title sequence sets up viewer expectation and a noir mood in a dozen key films including *The Maltese Falcon, Double Indemnity, Kiss Me Deadly, In a Lonely Place, The Killers* and *Touch of Evil;* Karen Hollinger's discourse on narrative structure and the femme fatale; and, mindful of the fact that the first *Reader* was well received as a reference text for survey courses, we have also included Philip Gaines' somewhat irreverent but salient schematic for such a course.

But having now read and reread all these essays, old and new, the most important reason for *Film Noir Compendium* is clearer than ever: the historical and ongoing importance of film noir itself to American motion pictures. Without going as far as Schrader's assertion that "picked at random, a film noir is likely to be a better made film than a randomly selected silent comedy, musical, western, and so on," it is fair to ask how many seventy-year-old movies can still hold the attention of a contemporary average filmgoer? Scores of classic period noir films are as fascinating for current audiences as they were for the French filmgoers who suddenly discovered them en masse after World War II. If there were a critical consensus of the best films from the 40s and 50s, many if not most of them would be noir films. In fact, in the years since Borde and Chaumeton, "noir" itself has so become a part of the American idiom that journalists can now write about a dark aspect of society without fear of misunderstanding: "this is America noir, a moral nether world plumbed by tabloid television and pulp fiction."[8]

Those familiar with our other anthologies or our director or genre studies will know what comes last: the admonition that all these texts are secondary documentation, that what counts most are the films themselves. Having given our usual admonition not to confuse the comments with the artifacts, to refer the reader to the "things themselves" is not to suggest they did or do exist in a vacuum. If we have been rhetorical in this or any past introduction, it is not because we are seeking something akin to Henri Bergson's *élan vital*, nor are we subscribing to Benedetto Croce's anti-fascist polemic that "every true history is contemporary history." If anything we are echoing Samuel Butler's warning in *Erewhon*: "It has been said that though God cannot alter the past, historians can." But ultimately we must agree with what Claude Chabrol wrote in 1955: "successes, popular styles, genres are all mortal. What remains are the works, good or bad."

Notes

1. Preminger was born in the Ukraine; Lang and Wilder, in Austria. Mann came into the world just south of Hollywood in San Diego, California to Austrian/Bavarian parents, and several biographers have asserted that Siodmak was born in Tennessee.

2. "American Film Noir" in *Cinema: A Critical Dictionary* (New York: Viking, 1980), edited by Richard Roud, p. 57.

3. Andy Klein, "Shady Characters, A Fortnight of Noir Nihilism," *Los Angeles Reader*, V. 17, n. 16 (January 27, 1995), p. 15.

4. The particulars: *The Big Clock* directed by John Farrow, photographed by John Seitz, from a script by Jonathan Latimer based on a novel by Kenneth Fearing, and starring Ray Milland and Charles Laughton; *Brute Force* directed by Jules Dassin, photographed by William Daniels, from a script by Richard Brooks based on a story by Robert Patterson, and starring Burt Lancaster and Yvonne DeCarlo; *Cry of the City* directed by Robert Siodmak, photographed by Lloyd Ahern, from a script by Richard Murphy based on a novel by Henry Edward Helseth, and starring Victor Mature and Richard Conte; *Force of Evil* directed and co-scripted by Abraham Polonsky, photographed by George Barnes, co-script by Ira Wolfert based on his novel, and starring John Garfield; *Framed* directed by Richard Wallace, photographed by Burnett Guffey, from a script by Ben Maddow based on a story by Jack Patrick, and starring Glenn Ford and Barry Sullivan; *Out of the Past* directed by Jacques Tourneur, photographed by Nicholas Musuraca, from a script by Daniel Mainwaring [using the pseudonym Geoffrey Homes] and Frank Fenton [uncredited] based on Mainwaring's novel, and starring Robert Mitchum, Kirk Douglas, and Jane Greer; *Pitfall* directed by André de Toth, photographed by Harry Wild, from a script by Karl Lamb based on a novel by Jay Dratler, and starring Dick Powell and Lizabeth Scott; and lastly *The Unsuspected* directed by Michael Curtiz, photographed by Woody Bredell, from a script by Ranald MacDougall based on a novel by Charlotte Armstrong, and starring Claude Rains.

5. *Cahiers du Cinéma* (English), No. 7, p. 36. Pasolini's lecture on "The Cinema of Poetry" (presented at the first New Cinema Festival at Pesaro, Italy in June, 1965 introduced the concept of a "styleme" or a unit of "stylistic grammar." That statement from Pasolini and Umberto Eco's "Articulations of Cinematic Code" delivered the following year at Pesaro are the foundation texts for "Style and Meaning."

5. Nick Nolte interviewed by Jim Brown, NBC *Today* Show, August 31, 1995.

6. Letter of December 16, 1947 to Joseph Sistrom excerpted in *Raymond Chandler Speaking* (London: Hamish Hamilton, 1962), p. 130.

7. The book *David Lean and his Films* in collaboration with James Ursini was originally commissioned for the Movie Paperback series by Ian Cameron and designed to include extensive frame enlargements from eight of Lean's movies. With Janey Place, I had done frame-by-frame analysis of *Thieves' Highway* that was part of a class project in the UCLA doctoral program and a first iteration of the nine elements of style using Aldrich's *World for Ransom.* The editors at *Film Comment* requested the revision using examples from the best-known of Aldrich's noir films.

8. Stephen Braun, "Contract Killings in Suburbia," *Los Angeles Times* (February 10, 1995), p. A1.

Classic Period lines of demarcation from *Maltese Falcon* (opposite) to *Touch of Evil* (below).

Double Indemnity's deadly couple.

Crime Certainly Pays on the Screen

Lloyd Shearer (1945)

The growing crop of homicidal films poses questions for psychologists and producers.

Of late there has been a trend in Hollywood toward the wholesale production of lusty, hard-boiled, gut-and-gore crime stories, all fashioned on a theme with a combination of plausibly motivated murder and studded with high-powered Freudian implication. Of the quantity of such films now in vogue, *Double Indemnity, Murder, My Sweet, Conflict* and *Laura* are a quartet of the most popular which quickly come to mind.

Shortly to be followed by Twentieth Century-Fox's *The Dark Corner* and *The High Window,* MGM's *The Postman Always Rings Twice* and *The Lady in the Lake,* Paramount's *Blue Dahlia* and Warner's *Serenade* and *The Big Sleep,* this quartet constitutes a mere vanguard of the cinematic homicide to come. Every studio in town has at least two or three similar blood-freezers before the cameras right now, which means that within the next year or so movie murder, particularly with a psychological twist, will become almost as common as the weekly newsreel or musical.

Fortunately most of the crime films recently released have been suspense-jammed and altogether entertaining and it is entirely possible that those which follow will maintain the standard, but why at this time are so many pictures of the same type being made? This is a question which the average screen fan would like answered.

Hollywood says the moviegoer is getting this type of story because he likes it, and psychologists explain that he likes it because it serves as a violent escape in tune with the violence of the times, a cathartic for pent-up emotions. These learned men, in a mumbo-jumbo all their own, assert that because of the war the average moviegoer has become calloused to death, hardened to homicide and more capable of understanding a murderer's motives. After watching a newsreel showing the horrors of a German concentration camp, the movie fan, they say, feels no shock, no remorse, no moral repugnance when the screen villain puts a bullet through his wife's head or shoves her off a cliff and runs away with his voluptuous next-door neighbor.

Moreover, the psychologists aver, each one of us at some time or other has secretly or subconsciously planned to murder a person we dislike. Through these hard-boiled crime pictures we vicariously enjoy the thrills of doing our enemies in, getting rid of our wives or husbands and making off with the insurance money.

In short, the war has made us psychologically and emotionally ripe for motion pictures of this sort. That's why we like them, that's why we pay out good money each week to see them and that's why Hollywood is producing them in quantity.

Of course this is just one school of thought and you may skip school or enroll in it, as you like. You may simplify the entire problem and say that you see crime movies simply because they happen to be showing at the time you attend the theatre, and that you enjoy them not because they afford you the opportunity of vicariously murdering your mother-in-law or projecting your own repressed emotions but because they're well paced, exciting and interesting. If you say this, however, you may be admitting at once that the war has not altered your sensitivity to death, that you are not profound, that you are subnormal in homicidal instinct, and, worse yet, you are repudiating the psychologists. And who wants to repudiate psychologists? Let's face it. They have to live too.

Another school of thought (there are always at least two schools of thought about anything in Hollywood) subscribes to the belief that the main reason behind the current crop of hard-boiled, action-packed cinema

Above, Alexis Smith and Humphrey Bogart in *Conflict*.
Opposite, Gene Tierney and Dana Andrews in *Laura*.

murders is the time-honored Hollywood production formula of follow-the-leader. Let one studio turn out a successful detective-story picture and every other studio in the screen capital follows suit. Result: a surfeit of motion pictures of one type.

Take, for example, the Paramount picture *Double Indemnity*, generally accorded the honor of being the first of the new rough, tough murder yarns. How did this movie come to be? Did Paramount's executives confer with one another and say: "These are times of death and bloodshed and legalized murder; these are times when, if an audience can stomach newsreels of atrocities, it can take anything. Therefore let's buy *Double Indemnity*." Or did someone simply say: "This is a fast-moving story. We can buy it cheap. Let's do it!"

Well, these are the facts on how *Double Indemnity* came to be made and started the cinema's cycle of crime.

One afternoon early in 1944 Joe Sistrom, a producer at Paramount, buzzed for his secretary, Miss Thelda Victor, an attractive brunette with blue eyes. He got no reply. He rang again. Still no answer. Mildly irritated, he rose from his desk, stalked out front and asked another secretary where Miss Victor was.

"She's been in the ladies' lounge for the past hour," the girl volunteered, "reading a script."

"On studio time, no doubt," Sistrom sputtered and stalked back to his office.

When he next saw Miss Victor, Sistrom demanded to know what story had kept her away from her desk for more than an hour. Miss Victor was all aglow. Her eyes were rhapsodies in blue. She couldn't contain herself. Her voice shook like a taut rope. "The story is sensational," she began, "simply sensational. It's by James Cain, and it's called *Double Indemnity*, and it's a natural for Billy Wilder to direct. You said Wilder was looking for a story. This is it. It's hot. It's sexy. It's exciting. It's got everything."

And she forthwith launched into a resume of the novel which Cain had written in 1935 and the Hays office had banned for the movies on the ground that it was "a blueprint for a murder."

In Hollywood most opinions of women are considered as interesting as laundry lists and about as important, but Miss Victor's are usually valid. Because he knew this, Sistrom took *Double Indemnity* home with him that night. He read it, liked it and, after several conferences with Billy Wilder, bought it.

Skillfully adapted for the screen by Raymond Chandler and Wilder, the story was filmed last year with Fred MacMurray and Barbara Stanwyck in the leading roles. It was received with outstanding critical acclaim and considerable box-office enthusiasm.

Forever watchful of audience reactions, the rest of the industry almost immediately began searching its

story files for properties like *Double Indemnity*. RKO suddenly discovered it had bought Chandler's novel, *Farewell, My Lovely*, on July 3, 1941. If *Double Indemnity* was so successful, why not make *Farewell, My Lovely*? And make it RKO did, under the title *Murder, My Sweet*. Twentieth Century-Fox followed with *Laura*. Warner's began working on Chandler's *The Big Sleep* for Humphrey Bogart and Lauren Bacall. MGM excavated from its vaults an all-but-forgotten copy of James Cain's *The Postman Always Rings Twice*. The trickle swelled into a torrent and a trend was born.

When will the trend stop? Probably not until the market has been glutted with poorly made pictures of the type. So long as producers turn out interesting and entertaining murder pictures, the public will flock to them. There is nothing new, however, about these tough, realistic homicide yarns, nothing new at all. You can take the word of James Cain for that.

Cain, at 53, has been writing them (*Mildred Pierce, Serenade, The Postman Always Rings Twice*) ever since the death in 1931 of *The New York World*, on which paper he served, and he has sold all but one of his works, *Love's Lovely Counterfeit*, to the movies.

"The reason Hollywood is making so many of these so-called hard-boiled crime pictures," he explains, "is simply that the producers are now belatedly realizing that these stories make good movies. It's got nothing to do with the war or how it's affected the public or any of that bunk. If Billy Wilder, for example, had made *Double*

Philip Marlowe (Dick Powell) with the elegant femme fatale Mrs. Grayle (Clare Trevor) in *Murder, My Sweet*.

Indemnity back in 1935 the picture would have done just as well as it has now.

"It's just that producers have got hep to the fact that plenty of real crime takes place every day and that it makes a good movie. The public is fed up with the old-fashioned melodramatic type of hokum. You know, the whodunit at which the audience after the second reel starts shouting, `We know the murderer. It's the butler. It's the butler. It's the butler.'

"The novels I write are honest and plausible. A lot of people come up to me and say, `I enjoyed your last murder mystery very much.' Now, I've never written a murder mystery in my life. Some of the characters in my novels commit murder, but there's no mystery involved in them. They do it for sex or money or both. Take *Double Indemnity*. There's nothing mysterious about that. As a matter of fact, it's so clear and lucid that the insurance companies are now using it as a text. They're having their agents read it and they're distributing copies of it to some of their clients, just to let them know how thorough their claims department is. I think *Double Indemnity* started the trend toward the production of fast-paced, hard-boiled, life-like pictures, and I think it will last as long as the story supply."

One of the chief sources of this story supply is Raymond Chandler, a reserved, quiet writer with an unusual talent for literary imagery, e.g., "Old men with faces like lost battles... The surf curled and creamed almost without sound... She looked as if she would have a hall-bedroom accent... Dry white hair clung to his scalp like wild flowers fighting for life on a bare rock."

At the moment Chandler is the darling of tough-guy detective story readers and reviewers. He has been called the foremost practitioner of the art since Dashiell Hammett.

An American raised in England who returned to the United States in 1919, Chandler has written four novels, *Farewell My Lovely, The High Window, The Big Sleep,* and *The Lady in the Lake,* all of which have been made into motion pictures. In addition, he has written an original screen play *The Blue Dahlia*, in which Paramount's Alan Ladd will soon star, and in between jobs has worked on the scripts of *Double Indemnity* and *The Unseen*. He is, therefore, well qualified to discuss Hollywood's recent predilection for the hard-boiled murder yarn.

"My own opinion," Chandler says, "is that the studios have gone in for these pictures because the Hays office has become more liberal." (The Hays office denies this.) "I think they're okaying treatments now which they would have turned down ten years ago, probably because they feel people can take the hard-boiled stuff nowadays. Of course, people have been reading about murderers, cutthroats and thieves in the newspapers for the past hundred years, but only recently has the Hays office permitted the movies to depict life as it really is. The Hays office has lost Warner Brothers and United Artists and may be little fearful of antagonizing the remaining studios which support it. Then again it's entirely possible that the studios have become smarter and have submitted story treatments which satisfy the production code.

"In any event, the public likes well-done crime films for the very same reason they like good detective stories. They're escapist and interesting."

So there you have them, the authoritative, expert explanations of the cinema's current cycle of crime. You pays your nickel and you takes your choice!

Effete Waldo Lydecker (Clifton Webb) sniffs disparagingly at Det. Mark McPherson (Dana Andrews) in *Laura*.

A New Kind of Police Drama: the Criminal Adventure

Nino Frank (1946)

Here we are one year after a series of poor quality American movies made it seem that Hollywood was finished. Today another conclusion is needed, because the appearance of half a dozen fine works made in California compels us to write and affirm that American cinema is better than ever. Our filmmakers are decidedly manic depressive.

Seven new American films are particularly masterful: *Citizen Kane, The Little Foxes, How Green Was My Valley,* plus *Double Indemnity, Laura,* and, to a certain extent, *The Maltese Falcon* and *Murder, My Sweet*. The first three are exceptional; but we cannot consider them if we want to focus on typical Hollywood productions. Instead let's look at the other four.

They belong to a class that we used to call the police film, but that from this point on would best be described on by such a term as "about criminal adventure" or, better yet, "about criminal psychology." This is a major class of films which has superseded the Western: and there are wry conclusions to be drawn from the displacement of an on-screen dynamic involving chases on horseback and idylls in coaches by the dynamic of violent death and dark mysteries, as well as the change in background from a vast and novelistic treatment of nature to a "fantastic" social order.

This sort of film has now notably changed in the U.S. following the course of popular literature where the preeminence of S.S. Van Dine has ceded to that of Dashiell Hammett. Since Poe, since Gaboriau, and since Conan Doyle, we've become familiar with the formula for detective stories: an unsolved crime, some suspects, and in the end the discovery of the guilty party through the diligence of an experienced observer. This formula had long been perfected: the detective novel (and film) have substituted for the Sunday crossword puzzle and become overshadowed by boring repetition. I don't know of any enlightened devotees of the genre who could not nowadays plumb the mystery from the first fifty pages or the first two reels.

In motion pictures this handicap was heavier. First problem: long explications coming at the end of the narrative, at the exact moment when a film, its action being over, no longer interests the viewer. Another problem: if most of the characters could be lively and imaginative, the hero, that is to say, the detective, was merely a thinking machine and, even under the best of circumstances (such as Simenon's, Maigret), a thinking machine while sniffing and stuffing his pipe. One might focus on the setting, on some moment of levity or other crimes, anything to spark one's interest.

We are witnessing the death of this formula. Of the four works cited earlier, only *Laura* belongs to this outdated genre; but Otto Preminger and his collaborators forced themselves to renew the formula by introducing a charming study of the furnishings and faces, a complicated narrative, a perverse writer who is prosaic but amusing, and foremost a detective with an emotional life. To sum up, the result is a film lacking in originality but perfectly distracting and, one can say, successful.

For the other three, the method is different. They are to the traditional crime drama what the novels of Dashiell Hammett are to those of Van Dine or Ellery Queen. They are as what one might call "true to life." The detective is not a mechanism but a protagonist, that is the character most important to us: accordingly the heroes of *Maltese Falcon* and *Murder, My Sweet* practice this strange profession of private detective, which (in the U.S.) has nothing to do with bureaucratic function but, by definition, puts them on the fringe of the law,the law as represented by the police and the codes of gangsters as well. The essential question is no longer "who-

Night shooting on a practical location in *Double Indemnity*.

done-it?" but how does this protagonist act? It's not even required to comprehend all the twists and turns of the action in which he is caught up (I would never be able to sum up coherently the sequence of events of which these two films are composed), only the uncertain psychology of one and the other, at once friend and foe. Still more significantly neither the punch in the face nor the gunshot play a major role until the end. And it cannot be by accident that the two films end in the same manner, the cruelest way in the world with the heroines paying full price. These final scenes are harsh and misogynistic, as is most of contemporary American literature.

I would not go so far as to say these films are completely successful. While *Maltese Falcon* is quite exciting (and is taken from a novel by Dashiell Hammett), *Murder, My Sweet* is very uneven and at times vacuous (despite the excellent reputation of the Raymond Chandler novel from which it is adapted).

We rediscover this hardness, this misogyny, in *Double Indemnity*. There is no mystery here, we know everything from the beginning, and we follow the preparation for the crime, its execution, and its aftermath (just as in *Suspicion* which Alfred Hitchcock adapted from a remarkable novel by Francis Iles [pseudonym for Anthony Berekeley] with poor results). Consequently our interest is focused on the characters, and the narrative unfolds with a striking clarity that is sustained throughout. This is because the director, Billy Wilder, has done more than merely transpose the narrative structure offered by the James Cain novel from which the film is adapted. He started by creating, with Raymond Chandler, a peremptorily precise script which deftly details the motives and reactions of its characters. The direction is a faithful rendering of this script.

In this manner these "noir" films no longer have any common ground with run-of-the-mill police dramas. Markedly psychological plots, violent or emotional action, have less impact than facial expressions, gestures, utterances, rendering the truth of the characters, that "third dimension" of which I have already spoken. This is a significant improvement: after films such as these the figures in the usual cop movie seem like mannequins. There is nothing remarkable in the fact that today's viewers are more responsive to this stamp of verisimilitude, of "true to life," and, why not, to the kind of gross cruelties which actually exist and the past concealment of which has served no purpose: the struggle to survive is not a new story.

Concurrently with this internal development, there is another, purely formal, change in expository style, the intervention of a narrator or commentator permits a fragmentation of the narrative, to quickly gloss over the traditional plot elements and to accentuate the "true-to-life" side. It's clear that this method permits the story to be rapidly engaged, but it also permits the insertion of a dynamic element into an otherwise static, psychological portrait.

Sacha Guitry was the first to utilize this technique in *Le Roman d'un Tricheur*. The makers of the films which I have mentioned (except for *The Maltese Falcon*) utilized it also and revealed both its flexibility and the enhanced possibility of adding a deeper layer to the narrative style. I must note, however, that Preminger in *Laura* has the story explained in the beginning by a character who cannot know the succeeding events nor, reason dictates, their conclusion.

Has Hollywood definitively outclassed Paris?

It seems to me that we shouldn't rush precipitously to this conclusion. Doubtless after this sort of film, it won't be easy to construct police stories in the usual manner. Doubtless we'll have to work harder, assiduously refine our scripts, and give up beautiful images, camera tricks, and other technical razzle-dazzle which diminish that "third dimension" on screen by creating visual falsehood and "going Hollywood" (in the bad sense of the term). Certainly we've witnessed the emergence of a new class of authors, the Billy Wilders, the Premingers, the Chandlers, the John Hustons, who promise to leave behind the old guard and the old school, the John Fords, the Wylers, and even the Capras.

But from this, to conclude that French filmmakers should fold up their tents...

There is one point, however, that deserves to be underscored for our own filmmakers: the primacy of the script, and the fact that a film is first and foremost a sober story well constructed and presented in an original manner. I read exactly the opposite of what I've just said from my old friend Georges Charensol writing about *How Green Was My Valley*. Charensol and other reviewers seemed to be nostalgic for the silent movie and to judge a film by the quantity of pretentious flourishes it displays. I'm afraid it would be useless to contradict them: the relentless evolution of motion pictures will settle their case. In motion pictures, the creation of which are more and more a function of the screenplay, one can find today more dramatic energy in a static shot than in a majestic panorama.

The proof? Admirable films such as *How Green Was My Valley* and *The Letter*, admirable and profoundly boring. On the one hand, production value written in capital letters, graphic beauty, paternalistic traveling shots, and dullness precisely distilled by the camera. On the other hand, filmed theater in all its splendor made possible by a special lens, a ballet going nowhere, magnificently rendered, prodigiously breathed to life, that one follows with a yawn. Both are devoid of life, of truth, of depth, of charm, of vitality, of real energy, of that "third dimension" that I prefer. Trompe-l'oeil and filmed theater, these two antiquated and antithetical formulas come together and compel us to assert, sadly, that such magnificent gentlemen as John Ford and William Wyler are already museum pieces. The meaningful glances in *Laura* or *Double Indemnity*, it's sad to say, but it must be said, are more moving than the eloquent compositions of the former or the skilled touch of the latter.

Above all, don't make me say that the future belongs to crime movies told in the first person...

Translated from the French by Alain Silver

Claire Trevor as the deadly Mrs. Grayle in *Murder, My Sweet.*

Americans Also Make Noir Films

Jean-Pierre Chartier (1946)

"She kisses him so that he'll kill for her."

Emblazoned on the movie posters, over a blood stain, is that description of Billy Wilder's *Double Indemnity*. The same line would work just as well for Edward Dmytryk's *Murder, My Sweet*. It would hold true again for *The Postman Always Rings Twice* which is currently a big hit in the U.S. We understood why the Hays Office had previously forbidden film adaptations of James M. Cain's two novels from which *Double Indemnity* and *The Postman Always Rings Twice* are drawn. It is harder to understand, given this censor's moral posture, why this interdiction was lifted, as it's hard to imagine story lines with a more pessimistic or disgusted point of view regarding human behavior.

Doubtless the crime film has its genre conventions: one needs a dead victim, and no society condones murder. But with a detective as protagonist and a few innocent bystanders in support, human nature's tendency to do right can still be reaffirmed. In *Double Indemnity*, as in *Murder, My Sweet*, all the characters are more or less venal. And while there is a pure young girl in both films, which permits some hope about future generations, the females are particularly monstrous. Practically every scene reveals a new evil created by Barbara Stanwyck portraying Phyllis Dietrichson in *Double Indemnity*. As the film opens, she flirts with the young insurance salesman who has come to close a deal with her husband; two meetings later she asks him to kill her husband after insuring his life; she cold-bloodedly takes part in the murder; we then learn that she had previously poisoned Dietrichson's first wife; when things get complicated, she tries to kill her insurance agent accomplice; and the film hasn't yet reached its climax before we further learn that, while all this was going on, she was having an affair with her step-daughter's fiancé.

Claire Trevor in *Murder, My Sweet* has no less charming a role. Despite having married into respectability, she acts like a cheap hooker: after committing murder to cover up her sordid past, the least she can do, as naturally as drawing breath, is to offer her favors to a private detective in exchange for helping with a second killing.

We can see how significant sexual attraction is in the through line of these narratives. It's a sort of contradiction that, from convention, the film censors, insensitive to the pessimism and despair which radiates from these characters, forbids putting the real emphasis on the sexual drive that dooms them. The result is that the actions of all these figures seems conditioned by an obsessive and fatal attraction to the crime itself. The sexual entrapment that Phyllis Dietrichson exercises over the free will of Walter Neff (Fred MacMurray), if it were underscored even more, would make his character even more hapless, as he actually is while under her spell, and this would be a sort of relief for the viewer.

As with many new films from the U.S., *Double Indemnity* and *Murder, My Sweet* are told in the first person. This choice of a specific point of view is used in both films but with very different results.

The narrator of *Murder, My Sweet* is a private detective. He is catapulted into a shadowy scheme without knowing either the principals nor their intentions. The ambiguity of the film, that the viewer is immersed in an imbroglio, this is a desired effect. *Murder, My Sweet* is no ordinary crime drama where from scene to scene more of the mystery is revealed: the script is not a whodunit designed to draw the viewer into guessing the outcome, it aims not to intrigue but to create an atmosphere of fright. Precisely because we don't understand them, we sense the menace of unknown dangers. *Murder, My Sweet* genuinely deserves the label of thriller,

Sexual entrapment by means of "a honey of an anklet" in *Double Indemnity*.

as the first person narrative is used to make the viewer shudder with the thrill of fear. This forced perspective is uncompromising. Several times in the course of the film, the detective is rendered unconscious, and each time the screen tries to render the experience of someone being knocked out: a play of twisted shapes, which makes us think of the experiments of "pure cinema," of the presentation of a nightmare and disturbed vision in the manner of the old school of avant-garde filmmakers. *Double Indemnity* used the narrative progression for psychological ends: as the guilty man is telling the story, there is no formal mystery; on the contrary, it is the psychological mechanism by which Walter Neff is dragged unrelentingly into the criminal action that unwinds before our eyes. The action doesn't spring from exterior causes: the seduction of law-abiding young man by a calculating bitch, the appeal of the perfect crime, the gauntlet thrown down to the friend in charge of investigating fraud have a verisimilitude that draws us personally into this sordid tale.

Raymond Chandler is the author of the source material for *Murder, My Sweet* and the co-screenwriter of *Double Indemnity*; and one can sense the same influence on both films. *Double Indemnity* doubtless owes its superiority to the source material of James Cain. But the hand of director Billy Wilder is clearly evident, particularly in the first person narrative which is used as well in his other "noir" film *The Lost Weekend*. In that film, the development of the story is extremely stylized and Wilder's success is even more telling: Ray Milland, who portrays the protagonist, is in every frame and often alone. It's almost a case study: as per its tag line, the film is "the diary of an alcoholic." The entire story is restricted to the memories of a pathological drunk. Usually in the care of his brother, Milland, left alone for a weekend takes a drink and starts to talk, takes another drink and resumes his monologue, sleeps for awhile and then drinks some more. The impressions of insanity, of a senseless void, left by the drama of a young man in the grip of singular addiction, makes *The Lost Weekend* one of the most depressing movies I have ever seen. Certainly a charming young lady helps our alcoholic hero sober up and permits the film to end with a kiss. But the impression of extreme despair persists despite this upbeat ending.

Women as insatiable as the Empress Messalina, animalistic or senile husbands, young guys ready to kill for the sexual favors of a femme fatale, unrepentant alcoholics, these are the charming types from the films we've discussed. There's been talk of a French school of film noir, but *Le Quai des Brumes* and *L'Hotel du Nord* contain some glimmer of resistance to the dark side, where love provides at least the mirage of a better world, where some re-vindication of society opens the door for hope, and even though the characters may despair they retain our pity and our sympathy. There is none of that in the films before us now: these are monsters, criminals and psychopaths without redemptive qualities who behave according to the preordained disposition to evil within themselves.

Translated from the French by Alain Silver

Anne Shirley as Ann Riordan, the bespectacled opposite of the imperious Mrs. Grayle with Marlowe (Dick Powell) in *Murder, My Sweet*.

All eyes (except the dead woman's, of course) are on the camera in director Robert Montgomery's "first-person" adaptation of Raymond Chandler's *Lady in the Lake*.

The Evolution of the Crime Film

Claude Chabrol (1955)

I. In Memoriam

Success creates fashion, which defines genre. At the height of popularity for the crime novel between the two world wars there was a correspondent event in American films, poorly imitated by many others, the creation of a genre which quickly lapsed, as often happens, into mediocrity and low-budget versions. The earliest examples, taken from the successful fiction of S.S. Van Dine and Earl Derr Biggers, were a smattering of movies which were, if not admirable, at least compelling and well turned out like the celebrated *Canary Murder Case*, unforgettable for a reason not directly related to this discussion.[1] The immense success of these movies gave merchandisers the bright idea of an endless array of inexpensive knock-offs cheaply packaged by Smith, Jones...or Dupont, in which Charlie Chan, Perry Mason, Philo Vance and Ellery Queen returned periodically in new adventures, usually putting on the same face (that of Warner Oland, Warren Williams, or other character actors), all in order, it would seem, to give their not-terribly-demanding viewers an experience akin to following the Sunday funnies.

There was a similar occurrence with gangster films, which were born from the complex social, economic, and political alliances of the 1930s. Certainly the early examples were masterpieces; they were drawn from the exploits of the Prohibition era's celebrated Italian bootleggers and, as they say, "ripped from today's headlines." But those quickly became yesterday's headlines and were gone as a source of inspiration. The knock-offs, which are never embarrassed by their own low quality, then had the field to themselves.

Curiously, although they were already running out of steam in 1935, there are practically no examples of either genre before 1929. The attempts to adapt the novels of Dashiell Hammett had no results other than to bring the protagonists of *The Thin Man* to the screen in a series of films which persisted through increasingly fatigued, forlorn, and flat examples until near the end of the War. Accordingly the status of the crime genre, the expressions of crime in books and in cinema, was hardly promising in 1940. The straight-forward mystery novel was stumbling and becoming untranslatable into movies. Prohibition had long since been repealed by the proponents of strong drink and the persistence of organized crime had not been generally perceived. The related movies were becoming sinister cop stories effectively restricted to small budgets and even smaller talent.

Then an abrupt rediscovery of Dashiell Hammett, the appearance of the first Chandlers and favorable social atmosphere suddenly gave the hard-boiled genre acclaimed status[2] and opened the doors of the studios to receive it. The popularity of these films from Raoul Walsh's *High Sierra* and Huston's *Maltese Falcon* continued to grow until 1948. The concept of the movement underwent important modifications: they were still mining a rich vein based on the preestablished plot lines, but the new works were nonetheless different from each other due, in the best instances, to their tone or style; and if the same character appeared in several movies, it was merely by chance or on account of similar literary sources: no one but a fool would mistake the Marlowe of *Murder, My Sweet* for the one in *Lady in the Lake*. Many of these releases were of exceptional quality, often much better than one would expect from their directors (I'm thinking of Dmytryk, Hathaway, and Daves). In this regard, there are two reasons: these films were drawn from the work of talented writers, specialists in the genre such as Chandler, Burnett, Jay Dratler or Leo Rosten;[3] and the filmmakers had perfected a standard style, extremely suitable and rich in visual effects, which was just right for a type of film in which refinement acted as a counterpoint.

As fate would have it, this movement carried within itself the seeds of its own destruction. Based on shocking and surprising the viewer, it could offer even the most imaginative of screenwriters and the most diligent directors, a limited number of dramatic situations, which, after a few repetitions, could no longer achieve either shock or surprise. If the noir crime films, and with them, the novels, held on for eight years, it was thanks to two qualities which began as external elements: suspense[4] and documentary reality. These elements were, once again, snares. Suspense introduced a new, extremely hazardous mood, the achievement of which was appropriate to only a few situations and which concealed the problem without resolving it. As for documentary reality, its multitude of possibilities were muzzled by the nature of the genre, which soon rendered it dull and monotonous. Thus trapped in a generic prison of its own construction, in searching for a way out, the crime film could do nothing but hit its head against a wall like a frenzied fool. The gratuitous use of subjective camera such as that of Robert Montgomery in *Lady in the Lake*, the inappropriate shift to period in Sam Wood's *Ivy*, the sophomoric and distorted surrealism of Robery Florey in his tale of an amnesiac [*The Crooked Way*], all this resounded like a knell. One day, Ben Hecht, to put an end to it, hacked out, from a very bad novel by Eleazar Lipsky, a remarkable script that included to the nth degree all the archetypes of the crime genre. And as if to underscore the strengths and the weaknesses of such an enterprise, *Kiss of Death* was directed by a capable technician with a trace of individuality, Henry Hathaway (who turned out one of the finest examples of the genre in the first half of *Dark Corner*); and *Kiss of Death* was a swan song for a formula, for a recipe, for a mother lode which exploded in one's face with a few rich nuggets but soon played out.

2. Noblissima Visione

The crime film is no longer, nor by the way is there still a crime novel. The source is dried up, and renewing it is impossible. What's left, now that it has run its course? In the wake of all the other genres that made up the best of the American cinema of yesteryear, the crime film, while in itself gone, remains a marvelous concept.

Inside civilized society, of which Valéry took the measure, successes, popular styles, genres are all mortal. What remains are the works, which may be good or bad but are the sincere expression of the ideas and pre-occupations of their authors. In the matter before us, another historical panorama reveals itself and offers for our review *Lady of the Pavements* [Griffith, 1929], *Underworld* [Von Sternberg, 1927], *Scarface* [Hawks, 1932], a wide, mournful, and protracted long shot, until at last a few films from today predict the crime film of tomorrow.

It is out of the question for these films to renew a genre by widening its scope or intellectualizing it in some manner. It is, effectively, out of the question to renew anything but simply to express oneself by mediating any

Opposite, "giving the hard-boiled genre acclaimed status," Roy Earle (Humphrey Bogart) menaces Babe (Alan Curtis) as Red (Arthur Kennedy) and Marie (Ida Lupino) look on in *High Sierra*. Below, the classic period work on "a capable technician," stolid District Attorney Louis D'Angelo (Brian Donlevy) questions the manic Tommy Udo (Richard Widwark, center) and the hapless Nick Bianco (Victor Mature) in *Kiss of Death* directed by Henry Hathaway.

misguided mythologizing. Are not the best criteria of a work's authenticity most often its complete ingenuous-ness and its perfect spontaneity? Is it forbidden after considering the ably constructed *Dark Passage* with its cunning use of the camera in the opening sequences and its wry, surrealistic ending, to prefer the barely deci-pherable plot, the freshness and wit of *Out of the Past* directed by Jacques Tourneur from an awkward but per-fectly earnest script by Geoffrey Homes [Daniel Mainwaring]? By what virtue, one can ask, is this latter film more sincere than the other? By virtue of its very awkwardness! The perfect sublimation of a genre usually comes down to its complete submission to this: to make a crime film, what's required is that it be conceived as such and no more; or, otherwise stated, that it be made from the components of a crime film. The genre demands a certain inspiration, which it hems in with its strict rules. So what is needed, one must concede, is the uncommon talent to be true to one's self while in the embrace of this rather odd enterprise (that's the won-der of *The Big Sleep)*; or at least an inspiration, an aspiration, a world view in communion with the rules of the genre (exemplified by another miracle, *Laura*; and as well, from a certain point of view, by the cases of Lang and Hitchcock).

Certainly the superiority of *The Big Sleep* proves the case of function over form for which writers and direc-tors strive. The central intrigue of this film is a model of the crime film equation with three variables (the black-mailer, the killer, the avenger) so simple and so subtle that its first expression is incomprehensible. In truth, nothing could be easier to follow, in its second rendering, than this film's line of inquiry. The only difference between the viewer and Bogart as Marlowe is that the character understands and picks up clues from the first.

It would seem that this film resembles others of its type only in the measure by which it dominates them but that its deepest roots and strongest ties relate back to the total output of director Howard Hawks. It's no accident that the private detective in this instance is more perceptive and more competent than we are, and, more palpably than elsewhere, is confronted by the brutal strength of his antagonists. *The Big Sleep* is closer to *Scarface,* to *The Thing*, and even to *Monkey Business* than to Robert Montgomery's *Lady in the Lake*. One must also admit that in this instance function subordinates creation, that it markedly displaces it once and for all, because the "Hawksian" model of the hard-boiled film could never be reconstructed without creating in its turn a sterile and flaccid knock-off.

Matters present themselves somewhat differently in the case of Otto Preminger's *Laura*: here the element of pure crime drama is completely subsumed by the preselected narrative style which markedly transmutes it. The novel of Vera Caspary, from which the film is taken, is a crime fiction of the classic sort, or more precisely neo-classic, that is to say based on a less stereotyped and realistic story. In any case, it's a perfect example of a formula worn down to the bone. It's on the character plane that the distinct features of the film take off, as the writers (Preminger and Jay Dratler) push them to their logical extremes and thus create personas intrinsically attractive to the viewer, so that the course of events in which they are caught up seems to be the only one possible. Here things happen as if these people had existed before the crime (given that the opposite is usually true), as if they themselves were creating the intrigue, were transposing it to a place where no one

Sources of wonder for Chabrol (and, it would seem, for visually entrapped characters in the center also: *The Big Sleep* (opposite) and *Laura* (below).

dreamed of being. To underscore this effect, Preminger devised an original narrative progression (which incidentally gives his film a significant historical importance): long sequences shot with a dolly that accompanies the movements of the key characters in various scenes, in such a way that these figures are trapped in the frame (usually a medium close shot or an American plan [medium shot from head to ankle]) and must watch their surroundings mutate and alter according to their actions. We have demonstrated here that a crime story, done well and with depth, can simultaneously be a matter of style and conviction. Vera Caspary wrote a crime novel, Preminger shot a character piece that was closer to his heart. Laura remains nonetheless an atypical work, because its success relies on a pre-existing mystery that fits well enough with the director's style, or, more exactly, compels the director to integrate his vision into a given crime story. Here again the filmmaker takes the first step and adapts himself to the genre. And is the result, which we find admirably done, worth infinitely more than the principal of self-expression, of which we get but a half measure?

Meanwhile we can easily understand how these films were decisive stages in the peaceful struggle for the liberation of the genre and the destruction of its formulas: if deficient as prototypes they were catalysts. Accordingly we can perceive a group of films that were daring, at times falling short, but mostly remarkable, and in all cases earnest and personal, for which the crime theme was but a pretext or a means but, in any case,

Another trapped figure: Gene Tierney as Ann Sutton in Premindger's *Whirlpool*.

not an objective, I would quickly cite Welles' *Lady from Shanghai*, Nick Ray's *On Dangerous Ground* and *In A Lonely Place*,[5] Joseph Losey's *The Prowler*, Preminger's *Where the Sidewalk Ends* and *Whirlpool*, and assorted other titles which made the crime film worthy of accolades, movies which would not adhere to absurd guidelines or arbitrary classifications. On the surface we can surely see little in common between *Lady from Shanghai* and *In a Lonely Place*. For what they have in common in their very difference, is the striking honesty, face to face with their own visions, of Welles and Nicholas Ray. Rewards don't come from mining a vein but from prospecting to find it.

I can see an objection here: all the films mentioned, and they were specifically selected, derive their most obvious merit from pulling the wings off the genre; they hang from it by the slenderest of threads, which has nothing to do with their best qualities. It is not a bit dishonest to fortell the future of the crime film from this, from the very diminution of the criminal elements in these films, because, to push this thing forward to its paradoxical conclusion, could one not easily conceive an ideal evolution in which this element is purely and simply eliminated?

In truth, what may seem a diminution is, in reality, development. All these filmmakers have one thing in common: they no longer consider the crime or all the other criminal appurtenances as dramatic situations leading to variations that are more or less adroit, but see them from an ontological (in the case of Ray, Losey, or Dassin) or metaphysical (in the case of Welles, Lang, and Hitchcock) point of view.

It may be a valid approach to focus on one theme, as Proust tried to do with time or [Marcel] Jouhandeau with homosexuality. In the realm of motion pictures, this can be accomplished through the actual direction of the film, as is the case with Preminger, or through the refinement of the script in anticipation of a certain direction (Hitchcock and Welles). It can also be accomplished, if I dare say, in an autonomous fashion, in the pure refinement of the script. And, as written description is the easiest, I will take my example from this final category.

Consider Robert Wise's *Born to Kill*, which came and went without much notice. Here is an instance of the script itself embodying the value and complete originality. The flaw in the armor is in fact the direction, technically beyond reproach and occasionally powerful but, alas, terribly ordinary and typical of the genre, which the aim of the film should have been precisely to avoid being, if not to grind the genre's remains under its heel. The script is a faithful adaptation, even if the times require it to be a bit simplistic, of a novelist named James Gunn. This young man wrote his book as "an exercise for a creative writing class." The curriculum gave him the initial impulse; but in the next moment he pared away the useless elements and then was exceptionally astute in selecting, as the framework of his narrative, two well-worn themes from a dying genre: a woman more monstrous than a male monster (*Deadlier than the Male* is the original title, *Tender Female* is the French title) and an old woman who becomes an amateur detective to avenge a murdered friend. These are stereotypes which he literally blows up in front of our eyes. By the mediation of a freely developed plot and an absolutely extraordinary tone, pushing each scene towards a violent, ironic, and macabre paroxysm, he succeeds in giving all these elements an unexpected dimension, a poetic depth, and, at the same time, in validating his chosen themes, because they alone are capable of driving the characters to their own ends, they alone are capable of distilling their essences, they alone are capable of justifying the tone, the style, and the subject matter. Ignorant to a fault, Wise did not know how to, or simply could not, take the reins, and *Born to Kill* could not quite live up to its potential as either a complete masterpiece or as a manifesto.

Whatever it may be, spanning successes and failures, this evolution is undeniable; and no one, I think, would pine for *The Thin Man* or *Murder, My Sweet* of yesteryear while watching today's *In A Lonely Place* or *The Prowler*. For those who remain unconvinced by the strength of my argument, I've kept an ace up my sleeve. Here it is, the crime film of tomorrow, free from all restraints and its own roots, illuminating with its powerful vision the unspeakable abyss. To make it harder, they chose the worst material imaginable, the most pitiful and sickening product of a genre fallen into putrefaction: a novel by Mickey Spillane. From a crushed, discolored, and chewed-up sow's ear, Robert Aldrich and A.I. Bezzerides[6] have violently and sure-handedly fashioned a silk purse embellished with elaborate and fanciful patterns. In *Kiss Me Deadly* the usual aspects of the

A "bleached blonde killer " with a shiny gun, Lily Carver (Gaby Rodgers) in *Kiss Me Deadly*.

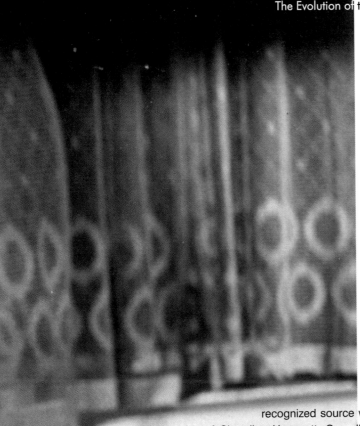

crime film aren't even on screen, but merely lurks in the undercurrent for the unenlightened. It's about something more profound and unveils alluring images of Death, Fear, Love, and Horror. Still all the elements are there: the tough detective with a familiar name, atomic age gangsters with glass jaws, cops, beauties in bathing suits, and a bleached blonde killer. Who would not recognize them, who would be embarassed not to recognize them, unmasked, their measure taken, these sinister acquaintances from the past?

Crisis in the genre, proclaims the straightforward observer! As if the genre was not what its authors made it!

Translated from the French by Christiane Silver and Alain Silver

Notes

1. It's called Louise Brooks.

2. Although the genre had existed for some time, its recognized source was the pulp magazine *Black Mask* which published the first short stories of Chandler, Hammett, Cornell Woolrich, and Raoul Whitfield. Moreover, *The Maltese Falcon* and *The Glass Key* had already been made into very low budget movies around 1933.

3. Editors' Note: W.R. Burnett, novelist and screenwriter (*The Asphalt Jungle, Beast of the City, High Sierra, I Died A Thousand Times, Nobody Lives Forever, The Racket, This Gun for Hire*); Jay Dratler, screenwriter (*Call Northside 777, The Dark Corner, Laura, Pitfall*); Leo Rosten, screenwriter (*The Dark Corner, Sleep My Love, Where Danger Lives*).

4. It is very difficult to define clearly the boundaries of the "suspense" film and those of the "thriller." In a literary context, the former is closer to William Irish [Cornell Woolrich], and the latter to Chandler. In actuality they have always been intermingled.

5. It appears that Ray chose to adapt some of the most highly regarded writers in the genre. *On Dangerous Ground* is taken from a good novel by Gerald Butler, *Mad with Much Heart*. As for *In a Lonely Place*, it is very, very loosely drawn from an excellent work by Dorothy B. Hughes (to whom we owe the story for *Ride the Pink Horse*) also entitled *In a Lonely Place*.

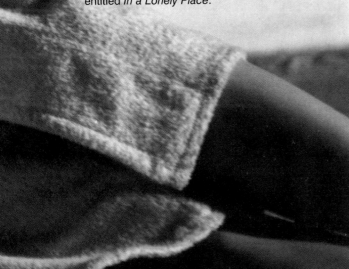

6. Bezzerides is currently one of Hollywood's best screenwriters: breaking in with the adaptation of his novel *Thieves' Market* for Jules Dassin (*Thieves' Highway*). He has since been screenwriter and adapter on *Beneath the Twelve Mile Reef, On Dangerous Ground*, and other solidly crafted films rich in original ideas. The character of "Nick" in *Kiss Me Deadly* is a typical Bezzerides creation... One can get an idea of the physical aspect of this fascinating personality in the beginning of *On Dangerous Ground:* he's the second tempter of Robert Ryan (who wants to bribe him).

Barry Fitzgerald (center) as a traditional "brave and imcorruptible hero," Lt. Muldoon, "the diminuitive Irish detective of *The Naked City* who believes in God and works on his own time to see justice done." His short stature is emphazied when flanked by his much taller young partner Halloran (Don Taylor, left) and a medical figure (Russ Conway) but in his dark suit Muldoon nonetheless dominates the scene.

Towards a Definition of Film Noir

Raymond Borde and Étienne Chaumeton (1955)[1]

It was during the summer of 1946 that French moviegoers discovered a new type of American film. In the course of a few weeks, from mid-July to the end of August, five movies flashed one after the other across Parisian screens, movies which shared a strange and violent tone, tinged with a unique kind of eroticism: John Huston's *The Maltese Falcon*, Otto Preminger's *Laura*, Edward Dmytryk's *Murder, My Sweet,* Billy Wilder's *Double Indemnity*, and Fritz Lang's *The Woman in the Window.*

Long cut off from the United States, with little news of Hollywood production during the war, living on the memory of Wyler, of Ford and Capra, ignorant even of the newest luminaries in the directorial ranks, French critics could not fully absorb this sudden revelation. Nino Frank, who was among the first to speak of "dark film" and who seemed to discern from the first the basic traits of the noir style, nonetheless wrote of *The Maltese Falcon* and *Double Indemnity* that "[these films] belong to a class that we used to call the police film, but that from this point on would best be described on by such a term as 'about criminal adventure' or, better yet, 'about criminal psychology.'" [see page 33 above][2] This was also the reaction of genre critics who, it must be said, failed to grasp the full impact of these releases.

But a few months later Frank Tuttle's *This Gun for Hire*, Robert Siodmak's *The Killers*, Robert Montgomery's *The Lady in the Lake*, Charles Vidor's *Gilda*, and Howard Hawks' *The Big Sleep* imposed the concept of film noir on moviegoers. A new "series" had emerged in the history of film.

A series can be defined as a group of motion pictures from one country sharing certain traits (style, atmosphere, subject matter...) strongly enough to mark them unequivocally and to give them, over time, an unmistakable character. Series persist for differing amounts of time: sometimes two years, sometimes ten. To some extent, the viewer decides on this. From the point of view of "filmic evolution," series spring from certain older features, from long-ago titles. Moreover they all reach a peak, that is, a moment of purest expression. Afterwards they slowly fade and disappear leaving traces and informal sequels in other genres.

The history of film is, in large part, a history of film cycles. There are, of course, certain titles that resist classification: Welles' *Citizen Kane* or Clifford Odets' *None But the Lonely Heart* are among these. Often a remarkable film cannot be classified because it is the first in a new movement and the observer lacks the necessary perspective. *Caligari* was unclassifiable before it engendered "Caligarism."

Since the start of talkies, one could cite many examples: in the United States, social realism, gangster films; in Germany, the farces from 1930 to 1933 which inspired a like movement in American comedy; in the USSR, films dedicated to the October Revolution; in France, the realism of Carné, Renoir, and Duvivier.

More recently, we have seen British comedies, a French series dealing with mythic evasions (from *L'éternal Retour* to *Singoalle and Juliette*), the social documentaries of Daquin, Rouquier and Nicole Védrès. From the USSR come paeans to the glory of collective labor and the Kolkhoz cycle. In the United States: the crime documentary (Hathaway, Kazan, Dassin), the psychological melodrama, and the new school of the Western: so many types of films, each having its particular locales, traditions, and even fans.

The existence over the last few years of a "série noir" in Hollywood is obvious. Defining its essential traits is another matter.

One could simplify the problem by assigning to film noir qualities such as nightmarish, weird, erotic, ambivalent, and cruel. All these exist in the series; but at one moment, reverie may dominate and the result is

Shanghai Gesture, at another, eroticism comes to the fore in *Gilda*. In still other titles, the cruelty of some bizarre behavior is preeminent. Often the noir aspect of a film is linked to a character, a scene, a setting. *The Set-up* is a good documentary on boxing: it becomes a film noir in the sequence when scores are settled by a savage beating in a blind alley. *Rope* is a psychological melodrama which attaches itself to film noir through its intriguing sadism. Alternately, *The Big Sleep, This Gun for Hire*, and *The Lady in the Lake* seem to be typical "thrillers." We will begin by addressing the problem of definition by discussing the pictures which critics have most often dubbed "films noirs."

One last note: by convention we will deem films to be created by their directors. This is a convention because one can never know with regard to American productions whether the director is really the ultimate creator of a work. Sternberg himself said "I work on assignment, that is to say by the job. And each job order, just like those given to a cabinet maker, bookbinder, or cobbler, is for a specific piece of work."3 What is the contribution of the producer, the screenwriter, the editor? Is it coincidental that the late Mark Hellinger produced three such distinctive pictures as *The Killers, Brute Force*, and *The Naked City*? Who can say, other than those who were there, whether Hellinger put his own mark on these films or gave Dassin and Siodmak free rein?

In reality, while there may be few instances of a director who has the final word in Hollywood, his role is certainly a significant one; and his degree of independence will logically enough increase with his commercial success. This could explain the persistence of vision in a given director's work: the theme of failure and adventure in John Huston, the theme of violence with Raoul Walsh, the theme of urban realism with Dassin, and even Sternberg, who has never strayed far from exotic sensuality. By all accounts, this convention of authorship is entirely apt.

"The bloody paths down which we drive logic into dread."[4]

The noir film is black for us, that is, specifically for the Western and American moviegoers of the 1950s. It exists in response to a certain mood at large in this particular time and place. Accordingly one who seeks the root of this "style" must think in terms of an affected and possibly ephemeral reaction to a moment in history. This is what links productions as diverse as The *Shanghai Gesture* and *The Asphalt Jungle*.

From this vantage, the method is obvious: while remaining as scientifically and objectively grounded as possible, one must examine the most prominent characteristics of the films which critics have classed as noir. From these characteristics one may then derive the common denominator and define that unique expressive attitude which all these works put into play.

It is the presence of crime which gives film noir its most constant characteristic. "The dynamism of violent

The very "diverse" milieus of *Shanghai Gesture* (opposite) and *The Asphalt Jungle* (below) are bound together by the "style" of film noir.

death," is how Nino Frank evoked it, and the point is well taken. Blackmail, accusation, theft, or drug traffick-ing set the stage for a narrative where life and death are at stake. Few cycles in the entire history of film have put together in seven or eight years such a mix of foul play and murder. Sordidly or bizarrely, death always comes at the end of a tortured journey. In every sense of the word a noir film is a film of death.

But film noir has no monopoly on death, and an essential distinction must be overlaid. In principle, film noir is not a "crime documentary." We know that since 1946 Hollywood has exported a score of films to France which have as their main themes criminal inquiries supposedly based on actual cases. In fact, a title card or a narrator often alert the viewer at the start of the film that this is a true story which took place in such and such a time at such and such a place. The shots on the screen faithfully reconstruct the start of the process: a call to the homicide bureau, the discovery of a body. Sometimes it may be a seemingly inconsequential incident or some report from a neighborhood police station that sets events in motion. Then comes the tedious "leg" work by the cops: the careful but fruitless searches, ineffective surveillance, and futile decoys. Finally there is a glimmer, some object found, a witness, which leads to a climactic chase and uncovering a den of cutthroats. This series, which has produced interesting pictures (Henry Hathaway's *Call Northside 777* and *The House on 92nd Street*, Elia Kazan's *Boomerang* and *Panic in the Streets*, Laslo Benedek's *Port of New York*, Jules Dassin's *Naked City*, and, testing the limits of the genre, Bretaigne Windust's *The Enforcer*), shares several characteristics with film noir: realistic settings, well developed supporting roles, scenes of violence, and excit-

Realistic detail arrayed behind the main desk at the station in the "police documentary" *House on 92nd Street.*

ing pursuits. In fact, these documentary-style films often have typically noir elements: we won't soon forget the repellent aspect of the head of Murder Inc. in *The Enforcer* or the laconic gangster in *Panic in the Streets*. It sometimes happens that a given director will alternate between the genres. Jules Dassin is credited with *Naked City* and also with *Night and the City*. Joseph H. Lewis produced a classic noir work in 1950 with *Gun Crazy*, while a year earlier he had detailed the work of treasury agents in *The Undercover Man*.

Still there are differences between the two series. To begin with there is a difference in focus. The documentary-style picture examines a murder from without, from the point of view of the police official; the film noir is from within, from the point of view of the criminals. In features such as *The Naked City*, the action begins after the criminal act, and the murderers, their minions, and other accomplices move across the screen only to be followed, marked, interrogated, chased, and killed. If some flashback depicts a scene between gangsters it is to illustrate a disclosure or some testimony, a transcript of which is already in the police file. The police are always present, to act or to overhear. Nothing of this sort occurs in film noir, which situates itself within the very criminal milieu and describes it, sometimes in broad strokes (*The Big Sleep* or *Dark Passage*), sometimes in depth with correlative subtlety (*The Asphalt Jungle*). In any case, film noir posits a criminal psychology which recalls, from another discipline, the popular psychology in vogue at the end of the last century; both delve into forbidden milieus.

The second difference between the series is one of moral determinism, and this may be even more essential. In the police documentary investigators are traditionally portrayed as righteous men, brave and incorruptible. The naval medical officer in *Panic in the Streets* is a hero. So is, if less obviously so, the diminutive Irish detective of *The Naked City*, who believes in God and works on his own time to see justice done. As message film, the American "police documentary" is more accurately a glorification of the police, much as is the French production *Identité Judiciare* or the British *The Blue Lamp*.

This is not the case for the noir series. If police are featured, they are rotten—like the inspector in *The Asphalt Jungle* or the corrupt hard case portrayed by Lloyd Nolan in *The Lady in the Lake*, sometimes even murderers themselves (as in Otto Preminger's *Fallen Angel* or *Where the Sidewalk Ends*). At minimum, they let themselves get sucked into the criminal mechanism, like the attorney in *The File on Thelma Jordon*. As a result of this, it is not haphazardly that screenwriters have frequently fallen back on the private detective. It would have been too controversial always to impugn American police officials. The private detective is midway between lawful society and the underworld, walking on the brink, sometimes unscrupulous but putting only himself at risk, fulfilling the requirements of his own code and of the genre as well. As if to counterbalance all this, the actual law breakers are more or less sympathetic figures. Of course, the old motto of the pre-War shorts from MGM, "Crime does not pay," is still the order of the day, and there must be moral retribution. But the narrative is manipulated so that at times the moviegoer sympathizes, identifies with the criminals. Remember the suspenseful scene of the jewel theft in *The Asphalt Jungle*. What viewer failed to identify with the thieves? And *Gun Crazy*, we dare say, brought an exceptionally attractive but murderous couple to the screen.

As to the unstable alliances between individuals in the heart of the underworld, few films have described them as well as *The Big Sleep* and, in its noir sequence (Rico's testimony), *The Enforcer*. We perceive in this rogue's gallery of suspects and convicts, a complex and shifting pecking order based on bribery, blackmail, organized crime and the code of silence. Who will kill and who will be killed? The criminal milieu is an ambiguous one, where a position of strength can be quickly eroded.

This uncertainty is also manifest in the ambivalence of the characters themselves. The integral protagonist, the elemental figure of the Scarface type, has disappeared from film noir and given way to a crowd of sanctified killers, neurotic gangsters, megalomaniac crime bosses, and their perplexing or tainted cronies. Notable examples are the solitary and scientific serial killer in *He Walked by Night*, the self-destructive loser in *Night and the City*, or the hyperactive gang boss so attached to his mother in *White Heat*. Just as twisted are the vicious, drunken, grub-like henchmen in *The Enforcer*.

There is ambiguity, too, with regard to the victims, who usually are under some suspicion as well. Their ties to the unsavory milieu are what attract the attention of their executioners. Often, they are victims precisely because they cannot be executioners. The decadent partner in *The Lady from Shanghai* is such a type, a man who finds death when he tries to simulate his own murder and who will long remain a prototype of the sham victim. One could also cite the terrorized woman, who seems destined to be killed before the end of Jacques Tourneur's *Out of the Past* but who had already set up her would-be assassin for a fall. This tough guy had no more chance than a steer consigned to the slaughterhouse.

As for the ambiguous protagonist, he is often more mature, almost old, and not too handsome. Humphrey Bogart typifies him. He is also an inglorious victim who may suffer, before the happy ending, appalling abuse. He is often enough masochistic, even self-immolating, one who makes his own trouble, who may throw himself into peril neither for the sake of justice nor from avarice but simply out of morbid curiosity. At times, he is a passive hero who allows himself to dragged across the line into the gray area between legal and criminal behavior, such as Orson Welles in *The Lady from Shanghai*. As such, he is far from the "superman" of adventure films.

"...an unknown breed of men rose up before us. Their lot includes mild-mannered hit men" (Alan Ladd in *This Gun for Hire*).

Finally, there is ambiguity surrounding the woman: the femme fatale who is fatal for herself. Frustrated and deviant, half predator, half prey, detached yet ensnared, she falls victim to her own traps. While the inconstancy of Lauren Bacall in *The Big Sleep* may not cost her her life, Barbara Stanwyck cannot escape the consequences of her murderous intrigues in *The File on Thelma Jordon*. This new type of woman, manipulative and evasive, as hard bitten as her environment, ready to shake down or to trade shots with anyone, and probably frigid, has put her mark on "noir" eroticism, which may be at times nothing more that violence eroticized. We are a long way from the chaste heroines of the traditional Western or historical drama.

Film noir has renovated the theme of violence. To begin with, it abandoned the adventure film convention of the fair fight. A sporting chance has given way to settling scores, beatings, and cold-blooded murders. Bodyguards kick a powerless victim back and forth like football then toss his bloody body on a common thoroughfare (*Ride the Pink Horse*), in a back alley (*The Set-up*), or with the garbage (*I Walk Alone*). Crime itself is performed by the numbers, professionally, by a contract killer who does his job "without anger or hate." The opening of Robert Siodmak's *The Killers*, the celebrated scene in a roadhouse, where two men searching for their victim terrify the other patrons with their callous confidence, will remain one of the most gripping moments in American film, an unforgettable slice of life. Twitching and stigmatized, an unknown breed of men rose up before us. Their lot includes mild-mannered hit men (Alan Ladd in *This Gun for Hire*), indiscriminate brutes (William Bendix), and the clear-eyed menacing organizers (Everett Sloane in *The Enforcer*). It also includes the twisted, corpulent killers, sweating in fear, humiliated by their cronies, who suddenly boil over (Laird Cregar and Raymond Burr).

As for the ceremony of execution itself, film noir has the widest array of examples. Random samplings are the offhanded gesture of a wealthy publisher who sends a bothersome witness who was washing windows down an elevator shaft; all that was needed was to tip over the stool with the handle of his cane while idly chatting (*The High Wall*) or the atrocious death by razor in *The Enforcer*, or a kick to a car jack (*Red Light* [and *Kiss Me Deadly*]). In other films, a paralyzed woman is tied to her wheelchair and hurled down a stairway (*Kiss of Death*); an informer is locked inside a Turkish bath and the steam valve is opened (*T-Men*); a cornered convict is forced under a pile driver by the threat of red-hot irons (*Brute Force*); one man is crushed by a tractor, another drowned in slime (*Border Incident*)... An unparalleled range of cruelties and torments are paraded before the viewer in film noir.

The anxiety in film noir possibly derives more from its strange plot twists than from its violence. A private detective takes on a dubious assignment: find a woman, eliminate a blackmail threat, throw someone off track, and suddenly corpses are scattered across his path. He is followed, beaten, arrested. He asks for some information and finds himself trussed up and bloodied on the floor of a cellar. Men glimpsed in the night shoot at him and run off. There is something of the dream in this incoherent and brutal atmosphere, the atmosphere common to most noir films: *The Big Sleep, Ride the Pink Horse, The Lady in the Lake, Chicago Deadline*. Georges Sadoul remarked in this regard that "The plot is murky, like a nightmare or the ramblings of a drunkard."[5] In fact, one of the rare parodies of the genre, Elliott Nugent's *My Favorite Brunette*, begins exactly this way. Bob Hope wants to play detective and Dorothy Lamour gives him a retainer to tackle one of these vague assignments that only Americans understand, such as "Find my brother" or "Find my sister." Immediately a hail of daggers menaces him, bodies pile up by the roadside, and inexorable gears of mischance drag him towards the electric chair by way of a hospital that doubles as a gangland hide-out.

Usually the mystery is a bit more realistic: an amnesiac tries to discover his past and flushes a crime out of its den. This theme was explored by Robert Florey in *The Crooked Way* and by Joseph Mankiewicz in *Somewhere in the Night*. But in these instances, the context of the narrative dilemma is such that the viewer expects confusion. In a true film noir, the bizarre is inseparable from what might be called the uncertainty of motivations. For instance, what are Bannister and his partner hoping to accomplish with their shadowy intrigues in *The Lady from Shanghai*? All the weirdness of the movie is focused on this: in these mysterious and metamorphosing creatures who tip their hands only in death. Elsewhere does a fleeting figure in a nightclub indicate a possible ally or an enemy? The enigmatic killer, will he be an executioner or a victim? Honor among thieves, an extortion network, unexplained motives, all this verges on madness.

"As for the ambiguous protagonist, he is often more mature, almost old, and not too handsome. Humphrey Bogart typifies him...[and] there is ambiguity surrounding the woman: the femme fatale who is fatal for herself...Lauren Bacall in *The Big Sleep*."

In our opinion, this resounding confusion is at the core of film noir's peculiar oneirism. It is simple to find several titles the action of which is deliberately associated with dreams, such as Fritz Lang's *The Woman in the Window*. The same is true of pictures where the artifice focuses on the symbolic and the imaginary, as with Sternberg's *Shanghai*. But, as a general rule, the perspective of film noir is realistic and each scene in isolation could pass for an excerpt from a documentary. It is the sum total of these realistic snapshots of a weird theme which creates the atmosphere of the nightmare.

As we might have guessed, all the components of film noir yield the same result: disorienting the spectator, who can no longer find the familiar reference points. The moviegoer is accustomed to certain conventions: a logical development of the action, a clear distinction between good and evil, well-defined characters, sharp motives, scenes more showy then authentically violent, a beautiful heroine and an honest hero. At least, these were the conventions of American adventure films before the War.

Now the moviegoer is being presented a less severe version of the underworld, with likable killers and corrupt cops. Good and evil go hand in hand to the point of being indistinguishable. Robbers become ordinary guys: they have kids, love young women, and just want to go home again (*The Asphalt Jungle*). The victim seems as guilty as the hit man, who is just doing his job. The primary reference point of earlier days, the moral center, is completely skewed.

The heroine is depraved, murderous, doped-up or drunk. The hero is under the gun or, as they say in boxing, he absorbs a lot of punishment when accounts are settled up. So the secondary reference point, the myth of Superman and his chaste fiancée, also fades.

The action is confused, the motives are unclear. There is nothing resembling classic dramas or the moral tales from a realistic era: criminals vie against each other (*The Big Sleep*), a policeman arrives on the scene, reveals his criminal intent, and does nothing but enhance the viewer's apprehension (*The Lady in the Lake*); the sober process by which a man's fate is determined concludes in a fun house (*The Lady from Shanghai*). A film takes on the characteristics of a dream and the viewer searches in vain for some old-fashioned logic.

In the end, the chaos goes "beyond all limits." Gratuitous violence, the overweening rewards for murder, all this adds to the feeling of alienation. A sense of dread persists until the final images.

The conclusion is simple: the moral ambivalence, the criminality, the complex contradictions in motives and events, all conspire to make the viewer co-experience the anguish and insecurity which are the true emotions of contemporary film noir. All the films of this cycle create a similar emotional effect: that state of tension instilled in the spectator when the psychological reference points are removed. The aim of film noir was to create a specific alienation.

Translated from the French by Alain Silver

Notes

1. The Authors wish to thank Mr. Freddy Buache, secretary-general of the Cinématheque of Lausanne, who agreed to publish this Introduction in the review *Carreau*.

2. *Écran Français*, No. 61, August 28, 1946.

3. *Le Figaro*, May 8, 1951.

4. Editors' Note: the quote is from Isidore Ducasse, Count Lautréamont, 19th Century pre-surrealistic writer. The French reads: "Les filières sanglantes par oú l'on fait passer la logique aux abois."

5. Review of *The Big Sleep* in *Les Lettres Françaises*.

"..film noir's peculiar oneirism...such as Fritz Lang's *The Woman in the Window*."

Van Heflin (standing), Kirk Douglas, and Barbara Stanwyck in *The Strange Love of Martha Ivers.*

Noir Cinema

Charles Higham and Joel Greenberg (1968)

A dark street in the early morning hours, splashed with a sudden downpour. Lamps form haloes in the murk. In a walk-up room, filled with the intermittent flashing of a neon sign from across the street, a man is waiting to murder or be murdered...the specific ambience of film noir, a world of darkness and violence, with a central figure whose motives are usually greed, lust and ambition, whose world is filled with fear, reached its fullest realization in the Forties. A genre deeply rooted in the nineteenth century's vein of grim romanticism, developed through U.F.A. and the murky, fog-filled atmosphere of pre-war French movies, flowered in Hollywood as the great German or Austrian expatriates (Lang, Siodmak, Preminger, Wilder) arrived there and were allowed more and more freedom to unleash their fantasies on the captive audience.

To that scene of night streets, recurring again and again in the films of the period, most notably in Michael Curtiz's *The Unsuspected*, can be added images of trains: clanking and swaying through storm-swept darkness, their arrival at remote stations signalled by the presence of mysterious raincoated figures, while in the narrow corridors, the antiseptic cramped compartments, assignations are made and, more often than not, a murder is planned. Elevators often figure as well, most notably in *Dark Passage*, where the lift gives an entrance, for the fugitive central figure, to an enclosed world of luxury and safety, where the gates clanging shut on the tear-stained face of the defeated villainess forebode her own incarceration in Tehachapi. Cocktail bars, too, exercise a special fascination: mirrors, stretching to the ceiling, reflect the stew of faces, each one predatory, doomed or afraid, and the glasses are piled in pyramids, often, this was an especial passion of Curtiz's, to be smashed by one of the principals in an outburst of rage. Standard lamps fallen on pile carpets, spilling a fan of light about the face of a corpse; interrogation rooms filled with nervous police, the witness framed at their center under a spotlight; heels clicking along subway or elevated platforms at midnight; cars spanking along canyon roads, with anguished faces beyond the rain-splashed windscreen...here is a world where it is always night, always foggy or wet, filled with gunshots and sobs, where men wear turned-down brims on their hats and women loom in fur coats, guns thrust deep into pockets.

The soundtracks, laced by the minatory scores of Franz Waxman, Max Steiner, Miklós Rózsa or Erich Wolfgang Korngold, also create the flavor: one remembers the whine of Dan Duryea in Fritz Lang's *Woman in the Window* and *Scarlet Street*, the breathlessness and the faked sob in the voice of Mary Astor in *The Maltese Falcon*, the scream of the elevated across the luxurious self-contained world of the threatened woman in *Sorry, Wrong Number* and the cold hard voices on the telephone switchboard; the cry of the train in *The Strange Love of Martha Ivers*, carrying away, in the rain of course, the escaping adolescents to a lifetime of suffering; the rapping of Ella Rainess heels on the platform and the hysterical jangle of the jazz-band in *Phantom Lady*, the shuffle of the husband's feet on the ceiling in *Gaslight* and the dissonant woodwind of Bronislau Kaper's score as the gaslights dim; the sound of "Tangerine" floating from a radio down the street as the lovers enter their death-clinch in the shuttered room in *Double Indemnity*.

And above all, shadow upon shadow upon shadow: Lee Garmes, Tony Gaudio, Lucien Ballard, Sol Polito, Ernest Haller, James Wong Howe, John F. Seitz and the other great cameramen of the era pitched every shot in glistening low-key, so that rain always glittered across windows or windscreens like quicksilver, furs shone with a faint halo, faces were barred deeply with those shadows that usually symbolized some imprisonment of body or soul. The visual mode was intensely romantic, and its precise matching to the stories of fatal women and desperate men, straight out *The Romantic Agony*, gave Forties film noir its completeness as a genre.

A world was created, as sealed off from reality as the world of musicals and of Paramount sophisticated comedies, yet in its way more delectable than either.

Hitchcock's notable film noir of the period, *Shadow of a Doubt* (1943), was pitched in a calm world, its darkness suggested rather than stated. The opening takes place on a sunny, dusty day, Charlie, the widow-mur-
derer, dodging the police, lying wearily back in his walk-up room or standing looking at his pursuers, puffing
proudly at a cigar. Later as he enters the chintzy little world of his small-town Californian relatives, he shows
himself a genuine occupant of film noir: in a cafe, he tells his niece that the universe is a "foul sty," and over
dinner he discloses something of his neurotic, perhaps basically homosexual loathing of women. Joseph
Cotten's performance cleverly suggests the psychotic tension under the bland generous front; here is a creature of the darkness blinking against the light of a very American innocence.

Rope (1948) and *The Paradine Case* (1948) are more firmly centered on a world of evil. In *Rope* two homo-
sexuals murder a "straight" youth, serving his father, aunt and fiancée dinner from the chest he is entombed
in; while in *The Paradine Case* "une belle dame sans merci," the heartless Maddelena Paradine, murders her
blind husband and shows complete contempt for the defense counsel engaged to save her. Hitchcock and his
writers here delineate lives lived without conscience and without love. In *Rope*, the homosexual ambience is
ably suggested: the slightly over-decorated apartment, the "understanding" housekeeper, the elliptical,

wounding and sharp-witted exchanges between the killers, played by Farley Granger and John Dall, and their mutually suspicious and resentful relationship with the dead boy's girl-friend. The gradual breakdown from smooth party badinage to nerves and finally dissolution of the psyche, arrest and ruin, is charted with precision, and the endlessly gliding takes, moving from death-chest to window spangled with New York lights to shifting trays of food, create an atmosphere as stifling as the interior of a coffin.

The Paradine Case has as its center a fatal woman of whom Wedekind would have been proud: as played by Alida Valli, she is a leprous madonna, her lips permanently twisted into a smile of contempt, her hair tightly drawn back, her skin stretched on the delicate skull. The prison scenes are pure film noir: echoing corridors, barred with Lee Garmes's famous shadows, enclose her in a world of stone; the shadows deepen in her face as her foolish, infatuated counsel drones on and on. No less sinister, in Hitchcock's black vision, the judge Lord Horfield (Charles Laughton) smacks his lips over Mrs. Paradine's forthcoming hanging while gobbling a meal, dwelling on the convolutions of a walnut ("they resemble the human brain") while framed through a silver candelabra in his mansion, the reward of a lifetime of judicial murder.

Opposite, Charlie (Joseph Cotten) "lying weariily back" with money nearby in his room in *Shadow of a Doubt.*

Below, Alida Valli (center right) as the fatal woman and "leprous madonna, her lips permanently twisted into a smile of contempt, her hair tightly drawn back, her skin stretched on the delicate skull" in *The Paradine Case.*

Closely allied to Hitchcock, Robert Siodmak , a colleague of Billy Wilder and Fred Zinnemann at U.F.A. in the early 1930s ,expresses a more detached, urbane and less cynical observation of the dark side of human nature. Nevertheless, his Germanic pessimism and fascination with cruelty and violence are not in doubt.

Phantom Lady (1944), produced by Joan Harrison (who also worked with Hitchcock), created, with aid of John Goodman's art direction and Woody Bredell's nocturnal camerawork, a powerful mise-en-scène of squalor and violence. The story—from a pulp novelette about a search for an accused murderer's alibis, most notably a mysterious woman in a bizarre hat met in a bar to the strains of "I Remember April" becomes an excuse for the exploration of the underworld, for a series of descending spirals into hell.

New York is evoked during the toxic heat of midsummer: menace and poetry come together in images of pursuit, as the accused's girl (Ella Raines) tries to break down the bribed witnesses to her lover's innocence. A bartender is tracked across an elevated platform: heels tap on stone, a turnstile groans, a train shrieks to a stop. A tap-drummer sweats through a fog of cigarettes and alcohol in a dive rocking to the sounds of a jazz-band. Behind the suave apartment blocks, Siodmak is telling us, there is a world waiting to pounce in: at the gates of the respectable, the jungle is already thrusting upwards.

"...rocking to the sounds of a jazz band" in *Phantom Lady.*

Christmas Holiday (1944) is no less black: after an opening of gaiety (Robert and Abigail are idyllic newly-weds) Robert is gradually exposed as a crook, squandering the family fortune in gambling. One morning he burns a pair of blood-stained trousers: Abigail finds that he has murdered a bookmaker, hiding the body with his mother's help. Moreover, his relationship with his mother is depicted as incestuous, and his manner suggests homosexual tendencies. Siodmak's elliptical direction and cleverly off-beat casting of Deanna Durbin and Gene Kelly help to create an atmosphere of lightly suggested menace, of wickedness just an inch below the suburban surface.

The Suspect (1945), based on the Crippen case and set in late Victorian London, is equally merciless about human nature: a tobacconist (Charles Laughton), flabby and dominated by a vicious wife (Rosalind Ivan), murders her, but he is made to seem less evil than the inquisitive neighbor (brilliantly played by Henry Daniell) and the cruelly observant detective (Stanley Ridges) who brings about his downfall. In thickly cluttered, stifling sets, full of aspidistras, wax fruit and gewgaws, Siodmak discloses the horror of breakdown, a lifetime of genteelly endured misery collapsing into moral disintegration, ruin and death.

Again, in *Conflict* (1945), from a Siodmak story but not directed by him, a husband is dominated by a vicious wife whom he murders, and is destroyed by a detective—here once more the genteel suburban world is shown to contain cracks which at any moment can bring about its destruction. *The Strange Affair of Uncle Harry* (1945) shows a "nice" New England family: celibate, careful Harry (George Sanders) and his two sisters (Geraldine Fitzgerald and Moyna MacGill). When Harry falls in love, his younger sister Lettie, insane with incestuous jealousy, tries to destroy the relationship and finally goes to the gallows for her pains. The bickering, despair and repressed sexual longing of this tight little clan are exposed in shadows as black as those which blanket the characters' psyches. And in *The Spiral Staircase* (1946), the story of a mute terrified girl in a town haunted by a killer of maimed women, the darkness closes in. A murder in a room above a flickering bioscope display; an eye lurking deep in a cupboard; a face that swims out of focus as the dumb mouth blurs into a hole, watched by the killer: here is direction of the boldest Gothic flair.

The Dark Mirror (1946), about twins, one evil, one good, *The Killers* (1946) and *Criss Cross* (1949) were less successful, although patches of technique, the grim first sequence of *The Killers*, based on Hemingway's story, a robbery sequence in *Criss Cross*, are justly remembered. But in *Cry of the City* (1948), Siodmak returned strongly to form. In this story about a conflict between a sanctimonious policeman (Victor Mature) and an accused killer (Richard Conte), the director evokes a fine range of low-life locales: the sense of a lived-in night city is admirably managed. The gross, six-foot masseuse (Hope Emerson) is a memorable monster, gobbling her breakfast or striding through her house to receive a nocturnal guest, observed by the camera through a glass-topped doorway as she switches on the lights in successive rooms. And so is the furtive shyster of Barry Kroeger, white and plump as a slug. Little scenes like a police interview with abortionists, mostly European refugees, show Siodmak's talent for observing squalor in full display. A tense prison hospital escape matched to an almost imperceptibly swelling drum-beat; a murder in a swinging, creaking office chair, the film is crammed with sequences like these, powerfully realized and charged with an oppressive coldness.

Fritz Lang's *Woman in the Window* (1944) and *Scarlet Street* (1945) were equally rancid portraits of darkness and the city. In both, a weakling played by Edward G. Robinson, sexually unfulfilled, lonely and depressed, becomes the victim of a pretty and ruthless seductress played by Joan Bennett. Lang and his writers disclose without mercy how the beautiful can feed on the ugly, and the films, set in classic surroundings of wet, dark streets, rooms full of hideous knick-knacks, shimmering street lamps, remain memorable for the viciousness of the characterizations, notably Dan Duryea's stripe-suited pimp, and the unblinking look at middle-class life: a retirement party with bawdy jokes accompanying the presentation of a watch, a quarrel across a cluttered flat, a close-up of a clerk's embarrassed face as his fly-by-night asks him for money in a public place.

In *Laura* (1944) and *Fallen Angel* (1945) Otto Preminger made two remarkable contributions to the genre. On the surface, *Laura* looks atypical: from the first shot, a slow left to right pan across a series of shelves filled with objets d'art, the world we are shown is cool, sunlit or filled with the soft light of standard lamps: a world of apartments in the highest brackets of New York. But the characters cast their own shadows: Waldo Lydecker, played expertly by Clifton Webb, is a brittle jealous killer behind the front of a Woollcott-like columnist; Shelby Carpenter (Vincent Price) is a parasite feeding on rich women; his mistress (Judith Anderson) is a purchaser of male flesh. Only Laura herself, played as the Eternal Woman by Gene Tierney, remains beyond reach of the mire. Preminger's direction, calm and detached, and Jay Dratler's and Samuel Hoffenstein's sophisticated dialogue, turn the women's magazine conventions of the story inside out, so that at the end we are given a portrait of the utmost corrosiveness. Elegance and taste are balanced by greed and cruelty, and these endlessly bright rooms, these soft carpets and clocks and screens and china figures express a menace not reduced by the high-key handling.

Conversely, *Fallen Angel* (1945) is set in the lower rungs of the American milieu: this story of a man who marries for money in a small town so he can afford a floozie has an admirable mise-en-scène, evoking the contrast between suburban house and end-of-the-road hotel, a fine Forties range of seedy rooms, neons flashing in the dark, doors opening from dark streets into the cosy vibrant warmth of a cafe or bar.

Below, Preminger's ambitious proletarian women: Linda Darnell (left) in *Fallen Angel* and Gene Tierney in *Laura*.

Much the same atmosphere pervades Michael Curtiz's *Mildred Pierce* (1945) and *The Unsuspected* (1947). *Mildred Pierce*, wittily adapted by Ranald MacDougall from the novel by James M. Cain, charts the rise of a housewife (Joan Crawford) from waitress to owner of a chain of restaurants on the Californian coast, with mayhem along the way. No film has caught so completely the feel of Southern California, and it is not surprising that a restaurant commemorates it in Hollywood, with dishes named after Cain's characters. The coast roads, the plush taut atmosphere of restaurants, and the endless jostling greed of the environment are conveyed with an aficionado's knowledge. The opening is typical Curtiz: a series of shots fired into a mirror, following distant views of a beach-house at night, the murdered lover (Zachary Scott) lurching past his reflected face, gasping a last word "Mildred." The film conveys Curtiz's love of the American night world, of piers shining under rain, dark beaches, the Pacific moonlight seen through a bar's windows, and the tough direction of the players at all times pays dividends. In their respective portrayals of ambition, sisterly humor and brainless lust, Joan Crawford, Eve Arden and Zachary Scott are in splendid form.

The Unsuspected is even more beguiling: here Curtiz surpassed himself with U.F.A.-esque camera effects. As Victor Grandison, superbly hammed by Claude Rains, moves from harmless Waldo Lydecker-like crime story-telling on radio to committing murder himself, Curtiz charts a vivid course of greed and heartlessness. In order to satisfy his desire for possessions, for control of a fortune and his niece's mansion, Grandison murders and risks his life: he is finally arrested while broadcasting to America on a particularly violent murder case.

The images have an unusually massive opulence: the huge house, with its tables covered in black mirrors, pyramids of glasses in the cocktail bar, and a record library which plays a complex role in the action, is a triumph of the Warners art department. A girl's poisoning is seen through the bubbles of a glass of champagne, as though she were drowning in alcohol. A chest containing a body that has to be got rid of in a hurry is lifted high on a crane above a disposal-ground, watched desperately by the murderer's accomplice. And one sequence remains the quintessence of Forties film noir. The camera moves out of a train window, across a narrow street filled with neon signs, and up to a room where a killer lies smoking, terrified in the dark, listening to the story of his crimes related by Victor Grandison on the radio.

Lewis Milestone, in *The Strange Love of Martha Ivers* (1946), also created a striking addition to the lists. An aunt murdered and a getaway on a freight-car at night; the rise of an ambitious woman, definitively played by Barbara Stanwyck, and her no less ruthless mate, the attorney O'Neill; with the aid of her childhood companion, Martha plans her husband's murder. Replete with impressive images of cruelty and destructiveness, this chef d'oeuvre could not have been more persuasively directed. Nor could the similar Joan Crawford vehicle *The Damned Don't Cry* (1949-50) of Vincent Sherman's, made at the very end of the period. Here, the sense of an enclosed world of criminals is masterfully suggested, as the pushing girl played by Crawford moves from a ravishingly photographed *Tobacco Road* setting to furs, luxury, guns and the company of murderers and thieves.

Still more black a portrait of the underworld, but this time of a different kind, is Edmund Goulding's *Nightmare Alley* (1947), based by Jules Furthman on the novel by William Lindsay Gresham. This is the story of a small-town carnival operator, Stanton Carlisle (Tyrone Power) who obtains the secrets of a fake mind-reader and climbs to the big time in Chicago by setting himself up as a spiritualist. On the way, he acquires a partner in crime, Zeena, a sideshow fortune teller, and a remarkably clever accomplice, the psychologist Dr. Lilith Ritter, played brilliantly, with icy, calculating intelligence by Helen Walker. Huge-eyed, sly as a cat, Dr. Ritter's gestures suggest a soulless ambition; the web of hair, the smoothly disciplined face are unforgettable.

Nightmare Alley is a work of great daring, even risking a few shots at human belief in immortality. People are shown as venal, gullible, and hell-bent on success at any cost. Memorable are the portraits of Ezra Grindle (Taylor Holmes), the millionaire determined to materialize his dead mistress Addie so that he can again make love to her; of the alcoholic ex-mind reader (Ian Keith); and of the shrewd and wealthy Mrs. Peabody bamboozled by spiritualism. Joan Blondell is perfect as Zeena, the warm, fleshy, blowsy carny queen out of the sticks; Lee Garmes's photography effectively evokes the circus settings; but the film's greatest triumph lies in its uncompromising portrait of American corruption. As Carlisle rises from hick to ace charlatan and crashes

"Joan Blondell is perfect as Zeena, the warm, fleshy, blowsy carny queen out of the sticks" with Tyrone Power in *Nightmare Alley*.

to become a "geek," a creature tearing the heads off live chickens in a bran-pit, we see a frightening glimpse of life without money or hope in a society that lives by both. Scenes like the one in the cheap hotel when a waiter asks the now stricken Carlisle if he would "like anything else" convey, with the aid of sleazy sets, an ambience of almost unbearable squalor, achieved through the bitter, heartless writing, and through direction of an unusually cutting edge.

Only one director could exceed Goulding in sophisticated observation of greed: Billy Wilder. But whereas Goulding's was an honest understanding, Wilder's was a cynical and corrosive criticism. *Double Indemnity* (1944), one of the highest summits of film noir, is a film without a single trace of pity or love.

A blonde, Phyllis Dietrichson (Barbara Stanwyck), sets out to seduce an insurance man, Walter Neff (Fred MacMurray), so she can dispose of her unwanted husband for the death money. Infatuated, he succumbs, and helps her work out a complicated scheme; this misfires, the couple meet desperately after the killing in super-markets or risk telephone calls; finally, they shoot each other in a shuttered room, with "Tangerine," most haunting of numbers, floating through the windows. As in *Mildred Pierce*, the Californian ambience is all impor-tant: winding roads through the hills leading to tall stuccoed villas in a Spanish style 30 years out of date, cold tea drunk out of tall glasses on hot afternoons, dusty downtown streets, a huge and echoing insurance office, Chinese checkers played on long pre-television evenings by people who hate each other's guts. The film rever-berates with the forlorn poetry of late sunny afternoons; the script is as tart as a lemon; and Stanwyck's white rat-like smoothness, MacMurray's bluff duplicity, are beautifully contrasted. A notable scene is when the car stalls after the husband's murder, the killing conveyed in a single close-up of the wife's face, underlined by the menacing strings of Miklós Rózsa's score.

Lana Turner impersonated a femme fatale not unlike Stanwyck's in a similar story,[2] *The Postman Always Rings Twice* (1946), directed by Tay Garnett, based by Harry Ruskin and Niven Busch on the novel by James M. Cain, already adapted for the screen twice before: as *Le Dernier Tournant* (Pierre Chenal, 1939), and *Ossessione* (Visconti, 1942). Cold and hard in brilliant high-key lighting, Garnett's film captured Cain's atmosphere as perfectly as Curtiz's *Mildred Pierce*: in this story of a girl in a roadside cafe (Lana Turner) who seduced a ne'er do well (John Garfield) and induces him to murder her husband (the estimable Cecil Kellaway) the tension is drawn very tight. Lana Turner, almost always dressed in ironical white, introduced when she drops her lipstick case to the floor in a memorable sequence, is cleverly directed to suggest a soulless American ambition; and Garfield, tense, nervous, unwillingly drawn into a web of crime, makes an excellent foil. This is the perfect film noir, harsh and heartless in its delineation of character, disclosing a rancid evil beyond the antiseptic atmosphere of the roadside diner.

But one should accord an even greater accolade to Welles's *The Lady from Shanghai* (1948); here is a film Shakespearean in the complexity of its response to an evil society. Rita Hayworth, sex symbol of the Forties, is made to play a deadly preying mantis, Elsa Bannister; her husband, Arthur Bannister, the great criminal lawyer, is, as interpreted by Everett Sloane, an impotent and crippled monster whose eyelids are like the freckled hoods of a snake's.

The monstrous Bannisters in
The Lady from Shanghai.

"Lana Turner impersonated a femme fatale not unlike Stanwyck's in a similar story" with John Garfield in *The Postman Always Rings Twice*.

The Fatal Woman theme is reworked in brilliant detail; the fake sex symbol that beamed down from the hoardings along the American highways and glittered from the period's front-of-house is stripped bare, while the husband becomes a no less striking symbol of the emasculated American male. Only Michael, played by Welles himself, the sailor trapped into a charge of murder by his love of Elsa, is made to seem decent and free. At the end of the film, when Elsa and her husband shoot each other to death in a hall of mirrors, Michael walks across a wharf sparkling with early morning sunlight, released from an evil civilization to the clean life of the sea.

Physically, the film is Welles' most mesmerizing achievement. It conjures up the "feel" of the tropics, of the lazy movement of a yacht at sea, of the beauty of marshes and palms, and the misty calm of remote ports-of-call. In the film's most beautiful sequence, when Elsa Bannister lies on her back on deck singing, and Bannister and his partner Grisby exchange wisecracks ("That's good, Arthur!";"That's good, George!") Welles's love of luxury, of relaxation and pleasure, flash through the bitter social comment and show him to be essentially a poet of the flesh.

The soundtrack is no less exhilarating than the images of Charles Lawton, Jr., Heinz Roemheld's menacing arrangements of Latin American themes match the tensions of the yachting holiday, the journey through Mexican backwaters. Woodwinds and castanets echo throughout the preparations for a mammoth party near Acapulco, a commercial jingle on the yacht's radio mockingly underlines the sailor's seduction; and while the wife in a white dress runs through the pillars of an Acapulco street a male chorus sings a primitive song, followed by two startlingly harsh chords from the brass section. Throughout the film, the feral shrieks and neurotic whispers or giggles of the cast, the sneezes, coughs and chatter of the trial scene extras, give the listener the impression of being trapped in a cage full of animals and birds.

From a film loaded with detail, baroque and sumptuous, one can pick out a handful of memorable scenes. The picnic party, lights strung out across an inlet, men wading through water, and the sailor emerging from the darkness to tell his sweating, hammocked employers a symbolic tale about a pack of sharks which tore each other to pieces off the Brazilian coast. A talk about murder high on a parapet above the fjords of Acapulco harbor, interrupted by a gigolo's shrill "Darling, of course you pay me!" A conversation in the San Francisco Aquarium, the wife's fake passion breathed in silhouette against the mindless pouting of a grouper fish. The trial, and the final shoot-out in the mirror hall, the lawyer firing at his wife through layers and layers of deceiving glass panes.

Note

1. In 1968, this chapter was called "Black Cinema," in an attempt to render into English the sense of the French term "film noir." To avoid misunderstanding about the subject, the authors have asked that it be retitled.

2. Editor's Note: "similar" because as a reporter for the *New York World* James M. Cain covered the sensational trial of Ruth Snyder and Judd Gray and used particulars from their conspiracy to murder Snyder's husband in both *The Postman Always Rings Twice* and *Double Indemnity*.

Dana Andrews as Det. Mark Dixon in *Where the
Sidewalk Ends*.

Paint It Black: The Family Tree of the Film Noir

Raymond Durgnat (1970)

In 1946 French critics having missed Hollywood films for five years saw suddenly, sharply, a darkening tone, darkest around the crime film. The English spoke only of the "tough, cynical Hammett-Chandler thriller," although a bleak, cynical tone was invading all genres, from *The Long Voyage Home* to *Duel in the Sun*.

The tone was often castigated as Hollywood decadence, although black classics are as numerous as rosy (Euripides, Calvin, Ford, Tourneur, Goya, Lautréamont, Dostoievsky, Grosz, Faulkner, Francis Bacon). Black is as ubiquitous as shadow, and if the term film noir has a slightly exotic ring it's no doubt because it appears as figure against the rosy ground of Anglo-Saxon middle-class, and especially Hollywoodian, optimism and puritanism. If the term is French it's no doubt because, helped by their more lucid (and/or mellow, or cynical, or decadent) culture, the French first understood the full import of the American development.

Greek tragedy, Jacobean drama and the Romantic Agony (to name three black cycles) are earlier responses to epochs of disillusionment and alienation. But the socio-cultural parallels can't be made mechanically. Late '40s Hollywood is blacker than '30s precisely because its audience, being more secure, no longer needed cheering up. On the other hand, it was arguably insufficiently mature to enjoy the open, realistic discontent of, say, *Hotel du Nord*, *Look Back In Anger*, or Norman Mailer. The American film noir, in the narrower sense, paraphrases its social undertones by the melodramatics of crime and the underworld; *Scarface* and *On the Waterfront* mark its limits, both also "realistic" films. It's almost true to say that the French crime thriller evolves out of black realism, whereas American black realism evolves out of the crime thriller. Evolution apart, the black thriller is hardly perennial, drawing on the unconscious superego's sense of crime and punishment. The first detective thriller is *Oedipus Rex*, and it has the profoundest twist of all; detective, murderer, and executioner are one man. The Clytemnestra plot underlies innumerable films noirs, from *The Postman Always Rings Twice* to *Cronaca di Un Amore*.

The nineteenth century splits the classic tragic spirit into three genres: bourgeois realism (Ibsen), the ghost story, and the detective story. The avenger ceases to be a ghost (representative of a magic order) and becomes a detective, private or public. The butler did it. *Uncle Silas*, *Fantomas*, and *The Cat and the Canary* illustrate the transitional stage between detective and ghost story. For ghosts the film noir substitutes, if only by implication, a nightmare society, or condition of man. In *Psycho*, Mummy's transvestite "mummy" is a secular ghost, just as abnormal Norman is, at the end, a "Lord of the Flies," a Satanic, megalomaniac, hollow in creation. The film noir is often nihilistic, cynical or stoic as reformatory; there are Fascist and apathetic denunciations of the bourgeois order, as well as Marxist ones.

There is obviously no clear line between the threat on a grey drama, the sombre drama, and the film noir, just as it's impossible to say exactly when a crime becomes the focus of a film rather than merely a realistic incident. Some films seem black to cognoscenti, while the public of their time take the happy end in a complacent sense; this is true of, for example, *The Big Sleep*. *On the Waterfront* is a film noir, given Brando's negativism and anguished playing, whereas *A Man Is Ten Feet Tall* is not, for reasons of tone suggested by the title. *Mourning Becomes Electra* is too self-consciously classic, although its adaptation in '40s Americana with Joan Crawford might not be. *Intruder in the Dust* is neither Faulkner nor noir, despite the fact that only a boy and an old lady defy the lynch-mob; its tone intimates that they tend to suffice. The happy end in a true film noir is that the worst of danger is averted, with little amelioration or congratulation. The film noir is not a genre, as the Western and gangster film, and takes us into the realm of classification by motif and tone. Only some crime films are noir, and films noirs in other genres include *The Blue Angel, King Kong, High Noon, Stalag 17, The Sweet Smell of Success, The Loves of Jeanne Eagels, Attack, Shadows, Lolita, Lonely Are The Brave,* and *2001.*

The French film noir precedes the American genre. French specialists include Feuillade, Duvivier, Carné, Clouzot, Yves Allegret and even, almost without noticing, Renoir (of *La Chienne, La Nuit du Carrefour, La Bête Humaine, Woman on the Beach*) and Godard. Two major cycles of the '30s and '40s are followed by a gangster cycle in the '50s, including *Touchez Pas Au Grisbi* (Becker, 1953), *Du Rififi Chez Les Hommes* (Dassin, 1955), *Razzia Sur La Chnouf* (Decein, 1957), *Mefiez-vous Fillettes* (Allegret, 1957), and the long Eddie Constantine series to which Godard pays homage in *Alphaville. Fantomas,* made for Gaumont, inspired their rival Pathé to the Pearl White series, inaugurated by the New York office of this then French firm. *La Chienne* becomes *Scarlet Street, La Bête Humaine* becomes *Human Desire, Le Jour se Leve* becomes *The Long Night,* while *Pepe-le-Moko* becomes *Algiers* ("Come with me to the Casbah") and also Pepe-le-Pew. The American version of *The Postman Always Rings Twice* (1945) is preceded by the French (*Le Dernier Tournant*, 1939) and an Italian (*Ossessione*, 1942). The '50s gangster series precedes the American revival of interest in gangsters and the group-job themes. Godard was offered *Bonnie and Clyde,* before Penn, presumably on the strength of *Breathless* rather than *Pierrot Le Fou.*

The Italian film noir, more closely linked with realism, may be represented by *Ossessione,* by *Senza Pieta, Caccia Tragica, Bitter Rice* (neo-realist melodramas which pulverize Hollywood action equivalents by Walsh, et al.), and *Cronaca di Un Amore,* Antonioni's mesmerically beautiful first feature. The American black Western, which falters in the early '60s, is developed by the Italians. Kracauer's *From Caligari to Hitler* details the profu-

"The criminal hero" and the hostage family in *He Ran All the Way.*

sion of films noirs in Germany in the '20s, although the crime theme is sometimes overlaid by the tyrant theme. *The Living Dead*, a compendium of Poe stories, anticipates the Cormans. The Germans also pioneered the horror film (*Nosferatu* precedes *Dracula*, *Homunculus* precedes *Frankenstein*). German expressionism heavily influences American films noirs, in which German directors (Stroheim, Leni, Lang, Siodmak, Preminger, Wilder) loom conspicuously (not to mention culturally Germanic Americans like Schoedsack and Sternberg).

The English cinema has its own, far from inconsiderable, line in films noirs, notably, the best pre-war Hitchcocks (*Rich and Strange, Sabotage*). An effective series of costume bullying dramas (*Gaslight*, 1940), through *Fanny by Gaslight* and *The Man in Grey* to *Daybreak* (1947), is followed by man-on-the-run films of which the best are probably *Odd Man Out, They Made Me a Fugitive* and *Secret People*. The also-rans include many which are arguably more convincing and adventurous than many formula-bound Hollywood cult favorites. The following subheadings offer, inevitably imperfect schematizations for some main lines of force in the American film noir. They describe not genres but dominant cycles or motifs, and many, if not most, films would come under at least two headings, since interbreeding is intrinsic to motif processes. In all these films, crime or criminals provide the real or apparent centre of focus, as distinct from films in the first category from non-criminal "populist" films such as *The Crowd, Street Scene, The Grapes of Wrath, Bachelor Party, Too Late Blues* and *Echoes of Silence*.

1. CRIME AS SOCIAL CRITICISM

A first cycle might be labelled: "Pre-Depression: The Spontaneous Witnesses." Examples include *Easy Street* (1917), *Broken Blossoms* (1919), *Greed* (1924), *The Salvation Hunters* (1925). Two years later the director of *The Salvation Hunters* preludes with *Underworld*, the gangster cycle which is given its own category below. The financial and industry-labour battles of the '30s are poorly represented in Hollywood, for the obvious reason that the heads of studios tend to be Republican, and anyway depend on the banks. But as the rearmament restored prosperity, the association of industry and conflict was paraphrased in politically innocent melodrama, giving *Road to Frisco* (1939) and *Manpower* (1940). (Realistic variants like *The Grapes of Wrath* are not noir). *Wild Harvest* (1947) and *Give Us This Day* (1949) relate to this genre. The former has many lines openly critical of big capitalists, but its standpoint is ruralist-individualist and, probably, Goldwaterian. The second was directed by Dmytryk in English exile, but setting and spirit are entirely American.

Another cycle might be labelled: "The Sombre Cross-Section." A crime takes us through a variety of settings and types and implies an anguished view of society as a whole. Roughly coincident with the rise of neo-realism in Europe this cycle includes *Phantom Lady, The Naked City, Nightmare Alley, Panic in the Streets, Glory Alley, Fourteen Hours, The Well, The Big Night, Rear Window* and *Let No Man Write My Epitaph*. The genre shades into Chayefsky-type Populism and studies of social problems later predominate. European equivalents of the genre include *Hotel du Nord, It Always Rains on Sunday, Sapphire* and even *Bicycle Thieves*, if we include the theft of bicycles as a crime, which of course it is, albeit of a non-melodramatic nature. The American weakness in social realism stems from post-puritan optimistic individualism, and may be summarised in political terms. The Republican line is that social problems arise from widespread wrong attitudes and are really individual moral problems. Remedial action must attack wrong ideas rather than the social set-up. The Democratic line is a kind of liberal environmentalism; social action is required to "prime the pump," to even things up sufficiently for the poor or handicapped to have a fairer deal, and be given a real, rather than a merely theoretical equality in which to prove themselves. Either way the neo-realist stress on economic environment as virtual determinant is conspicuous by its absence, although the phrase "wrong side of the tracks" expresses it fatalistically. It's a minor curiosity that English liberal critics invariably pour scorn on the phrases through which Hollywood expresses an English liberal awareness of class and underprivilege.

Two remarkable movies, *He Ran All the Way* and *The Sound of Fury*, both directed by victims of McCarthy (John Berry, Cy Enfield) illustrate the slick, elliptic terms through which serious social criticisms may be expressed. In the first film, the criminal hero (John Garfield) holds his girl (Shelley Winters) hostage in her father's tenement. The father asks a mate at work whether a hypothetical man in this position should call in the

Above, Frank Lovejoy as the hapless Howard Tyler restrains Richard Carlson and waits for psycho killer Jerry Slocum (Lloyd Bridges) to decide his next move in *The Sound of Fury* (aka *Try and Get Me!*)

police. His mate replies: "Have you seen firemen go at a fire? Chop, chop, chop!" A multitude of such details assert a continuity between the hero's paranoid streak ("Nobody loves anybody!") and society as a paranoid (competitive) network. Similarly, in *The Sound of Fury*, the psycho killer (Lloyd Bridges) incarnates the real energies behind a thousand permitted prejudices: "Beer drinkers are jerks!" and "Rich boy, huh?" His reluctant accomplice is an unemployed man goaded by a thousand details. His son's greeting is: "Hullo father, mother won't give me 90 cents to go to the movies with the other kids," while the camera notes, in passing, the criminal violence blazoned forth in comic strips. When sick with remorse he confesses to a genteel manicurist, she denounces him. An idealistic journalist whips up hate; the two men are torn to death by an animal mob, who storming the jail, also batter their own cops mercilessly.

Socially critical films noirs are mainly Democratic (reformist) or cynical-nihilistic, Republican moralists tend to avoid the genre, although certain movies by Wellman, King Vidor, and Hawks appear to be Republican attempts to grasp the nettle, and tackle problems of self-help in desperate circumstances (e.g. *Public Enemy, Duel in the Sun, Only Angels Have Wings*).

However, certain conspicuous social malfunctions impose a black social realism. These are mostly connected with crime, precisely because this topic reintroduces the question of personal responsibility, such that right-wing spectators can congenially misunderstand hopefully liberal movies. These malfunctions give rise to various subgenres of the crime film:

(a) Prohibition-type Gangsterism. It's worth mentioning here a quiet but astonishing movie, *Kiss Tomorrow Goodbye* (1949), in which Cagney, as an old-time gangster making a comeback, corrupts and exploits the corruption of a whole town, including the chief of police. His plan, to murder his old friend's hellcat daughter (Barbara Payton) so as to marry the tycoon's daughter (Helena Carter) and cement the dynasty, is foiled only by a personal quirk (his mistress's jealousy). The plot is an exact parallel to *A Place in the Sun* except that Dreiser's realistically weak characters are replaced by thrillingly tough ones. (Its scriptwriter worked on Stevens' film also.) Post-war gangster films are curiously devoid of all social criticism, except the post-war appeal of conscience, apart from its devious but effective reintroduction in *Bonnie and Clyde*.

(b) A Corrupt Penology (miscarriages of justice, prison exposes, lynchlaw). Corrupt, or worse, merely lazy, justice is indicted in *I Want To Live, Anatomy of a Murder,* and *In the Heat of the Night*. Prison exposés range from *I Am a Fugitive from a Chain Gang* to Dassin's brilliant *Brute Force* and Don Siegel's forceful *Riot in Cell Block 11*. Lynching films range from *Fury* (1936) through *Storm Warning* (1951) to *The Chase*, and, of course, *In the Heat of the Night*.

(c) The fight game is another permitted topic, the late '40s springing a sizzling liberal combination (*Body and Soul, The Set-Up, Champion, Night and the City*).

(d) Juvenile delinquency appears first in a highly personalized, family motif concerning the youngster brother or friend whom the gangster is leading astray. The juvenile gang (*Dead End*, 1937) introduces a more "social" motif. *Angels with Dirty Faces* combines the two themes, with sufficient success to prompt a rosy sequel called *Angels Wash Their Faces*, which flopped. The late '40s seem awkwardly caught between the obvious inadequacy of the old personal-moral theme, and a new, sociology-based sophistication which doesn't filter down to the screen until *Rebel without a Cause* and *The Young Savages*. Meanwhile there is much to be said for the verve and accuracy of *So Young So Bad* and *The Wild One*.

Rackets other than prohibition are the subject of *Road to Frisco* (1939), *Force of Evil* (1947), *Thieves' Highway* (1949) and, from *The Man with the Golden Arm* (1955), drugs.

The first conspicuous post-war innovation is the neo-documentary thriller, much praised by critics who thought at that time that a documentary tone and location photography guaranteed neo-realism (when, tardily, disillusionment set in it was, of course, with a British variant, *The Blue Lamp*). In 1945 a spy film (*The House on 92nd Street*) had borrowed the formula from the *March of Time* news-series, to give a newspaper-headline impact. The most open-air movies of the series (*The Naked City, Union Station*) now seem the weakest, whereas a certain thoughtfulness distinguishes *Boomerang, Call Northside 777* and *Panic in the Streets*. The cycle later transforms itself into the *Dragnet*-style TV thriller. Several of the above films are noir, in that, though the police (or their system) constitute an affirmative hero, a realistic despair or cynicism pervade them. A black cop cycle is opened by Wyler's *Detective Story* (1951), an important second impetus coming from Lang's *The Big Heat*. The cop hero, or villain, is corrupt, victimized or berserk in, notably, *The Naked Alibi, Rogue Cop*, and *Touch of Evil*. These tensions remain in a fourth cycle, which examine the cop as organization man, grappling with corruption and violence (*In the Heat of the Night, The Detective, Lady in Cement, Bullitt, Madigan* and *Coogan's Bluff*). Clearly the theme can be developed with either a right or left-wing inflection. Thus the post-*Big Heat* cycle of the lone-wolf fanatic cop suggest either "Pay the police more, don't skimp on social services" or "Give cops more power, permit more phone tapping" (as in *Dragnet* and *The Big Combo*). The theme of a Mr. Big running the city machine may be democratic (especially if he's an extremely WASP Mr. Big), or Republican ("those corrupt Democratic city machines!") or anarchist, of the right or the left. If a favorite setting for civil rights themes is the Southern small town it's partly because civil rights liberalism is there balanced by the choice of ultra-violent, exotically backward, and Democratic, backwoods with which relatively few American filmgoers will identify. *Coogan's Bluff* depends on the contrast of Republican-fundamentalist-small town with

Democratic-corrupt-but-human-big-city. The neo-documentary thrillers created a sense of social networks, that is, of society as organizable. Thus they helped to pave the way for a more sophisticated tone and social awareness which appears in the late '40s.

A cycle of films use a crime to inculpate, not only the underworld, the dead-ends and the underprivileged, but the respectable, middle-class, WASP ethos as well. *Fury* had adumbrated this, melodramatically, in the '30s; the new cycle is more analytical and formidable. The trend has two origins, one in public opinion, the second in Hollywood. An affluent post-war America had more comfort and leisure in which to evolve, and endure, a more sophisticated type of self-criticism. Challengingly, poverty no longer explained everything. Second, the war helped Hollywood's young Democratic minority to assert itself, which it did in the late '40s, until checked by the McCarthyite counter-attack (which of course depended for its success on Hollywood Republicans). These films include *The Sound of Fury*, the early Loseys, *Ace in the Hole*, *All My Sons* (if it isn't too articulate

Below, James Cagney as the old-style gangster Cody Jarrett, facing off against the undercover cop (Edmond O'Brien) that preyed on his juvenile emotions. Right, "executive style gansterism" in *Underworld U.S.A.* where headlines matter and deadly decisions are carefully weighed.

for a film noir), and, once the McCarthyite heat was off, *The Wild One*, *On The Waterfront* and *The Young Savages*. But McCarthy's impact forced film noir themes to retreat to the Western. Such films as *High Noon*, *Run of the Arrow* and *Ride Lonesome* make the 1950s the Western's richest epoch. Subsequently, Hollywood's fear of controversy mutes criticism of the middle-class from black to grey (e.g. *The Graduate*). *The Chase*, *The Detective*, even *Bonnie and Clyde* offer some hope that current tensions may force open the relentless social criticism onto the screen.

2. GANGSTERS

Underworld differs from subsequent gangster films in admiring its gangster hero (George Bancroft) as Nietzschean inspiration in a humiliating world. If *Scarface* borrows several of its settings and motifs it's partly because it's a riposte to it. In fact public opinion turned against the gangster before Hollywood denounced him with the famous trans-auteur triptych, *Little Caesar, Scarface* and *Public Enemy*. To Hawk's simple-minded propaganda piece, one may well prefer the daring pro- and contra-alternations of *Public Enemy*. The mixture of social fact and moralizing myth in pre-war gangster movies is intriguing. Bancroft, like Cagney, represents the Irish gangster, Muni and Raft the Italian type, Bogart's deadpan grotesque is transracial, fitting equally well the strayed WASP (Marlowe) and the East European Jews, who were a forceful gangster element. It's not at all absurd, as NFT audiences boisterously assume, that *Little Caesar* and *Scarface* should love their Italian mommas, nor that in *Angels With Dirty Faces* priest Pat O'Brien and gangster Cagney should be on speaking terms. 1920s gangsters were just as closely linked with race loyalties as today's Black Muslim leaders, the latter have typical gangster childhoods, and without the least facetiousness can be said to have shifted gangster energies into Civil Rights terms. It helps explain the ambivalence of violence and idealism in Black Muslim declarations; dialogues between "priest" (Martin Luther King) and advocates of violence are by no means ridiculous. Disappointed Prohibitionist moralists found easier prey in Hollywood, and the Hays Office, and cut off the gangster cycle in its prime. A year or two passes before Hollywood evolves its "anti-gangster"—the G-Man or FBI agent who either infiltrates the gang or in one way or another beats the gangster at his own game. *Angels With Dirty Faces* (1938) combines the Dead End kids (from Wyler's film of the previous year) with gangster Cagney. When he's cornered, priest Pat O'Brien persuades him to go to the chair like a coward so that his fans will be disillusioned with him. By so doing, Cagney concedes that crime doesn't pay, but he also debunks movies like *Scarface*. In 1940 *The Roaring Twenties* attempts a naive little thesis about the relationship between gangsterism and unemployment.

Between 1939 and 1953 Nazi and then Russian spies push the gangster into the hero position. A small cycle of semi-nostalgic gangster movies appears. A unique, Hays Code-defying B feature *Dillinger* (1945), is less typical than *I Walk Alone* (1947). This opposes the old-fashioned Prohibition-era thug (Burt Lancaster) who, returning after a long spell in jail, finds himself outmoded and outwitted by the newer, nastier, richer operators who move in swell society and crudely prefigure the "organization men" who reach their climax in the Marvin-Gulager-Reagan set-up of Siegel's *The Killers*. *The Enforcer* is another hinge movie, pitting D.A. Bogart against a gang which while actually Neanderthal in its techniques is felt to be a terrifyingly slick and ubiquitous contra-police network. *Kiss Tomorrow Goodbye* and *White Heat* are contemporary in setting but have an archaic feel. *The Asphalt Jungle* is a moralistic variant within this cycle rather than a precursor of *Rififi* and its gang-job imitations (which include *The Killing* and *Cairo,* a wet transposition of Huston's film).

The next major cycle is keyed by various Congressional investigations, which spotlight gangsterism run big business style. "Brooklyn, I'm very worried about Brooklyn," frowns the gang boss in *New York Confidential* (1954); "It's bringing down our average; collections are down 2%." An equally bad sequel, *The Naked Street*, handles a collateral issue, gangster (or ex-gangster?) control of legitimate business (a tardy theme: during the war Western Union was bought by a gangster syndicate to ensure troublefree transmission of illegal betting results). Executive-style gangsterism has to await *Underworld U.S.A.* and *The Killers* for interesting treatment. For obvious reasons, the American equivalent of *La Mani Sulla Citta* has still to be made. *Johnny Cool* is a feeble "sequel" to Salvatore Giuliano.

One of the earliest fugitive couples: Sylvia Sidney and Henry Fonda soon to be on the run in 1937's *You Only Live Once*.

Instead, the mid-'50s see a new cycle, the urban Western, which take a hint from the success of *The Big Heat*. A clump of movies from 1955-1960 includes *The Big Combo, Al Capone, The Rise and Fall of Legs Diamond, Baby Face Nelson, The Phenix City Story* and *Pay Or Die*. Something of a lull follows until the latter-day Technicolor series (*The Killers, Bonnie and Clyde, Point Blank*). With or without pop nostalgia for the past, these movies exist, like the Western, for their action (though the killings relate more to atrocity than heroism). The first phase of the cycle is ultra-cautious, and falters through sheer repetition of the one or two safe moral clichés, while the second phase renews itself by dropping the old underworld mystique and shading Illegal America into virtuous (rural or grey flannel suit) America. The first phase carries on from the blackest period of the Western. The second coincides with the Kennedy assassinations and Watts riots.

3. ON THE RUN

Here the criminals or the framed innocents are essentially passive and fugitive, and, even if tragically or despicably guilty, sufficiently sympathetic for the audience to be caught between, on the one hand, pity, identification and regret, and, on the other, moral condemnation and conformist fatalism. Notable films include *The Informer, You Only Live Once, High Sierra, The Killers, He Ran All The Way, They Live By Night, Cry of the City. Dark Passage* and a variant, *The Third Man. Gun Crazy* (*Deadlier Than The Male*), an earlier version of the Bonnie and Clyde story, with Peggy Cummins as Bonnie, fascinatingly compromises between a Langian style and a Penn spirit, and, in double harness with the later film, might assert itself, as a parallel classic.

4. PRIVATE EYES AND ADVENTURERS

This theme is closely interwoven with three literary figures, Dashiell Hammett, Raymond Chandler and Hemingway. It constitutes for some English critics the poetic core of the film noir, endearing itself no doubt by the romanticism underlying Chandler's formula: "Down these mean streets must go a man who is not himself mean..." This knight errant relationship has severe limitations. The insistence on city corruption is countered by the trust in private enterprise; and one may well rate the genre below the complementary approach exemplified by *Double Indemnity* and *The Postman Always Rings Twice*, in which we identify with the criminals. The genre originates in a complacent, pre-war cycle, the *Thin Man* series (after Hammett) with William Powell, Myrna Loy and Asta the dog, being both sophisticated and happily married (then a rarity) as they solve crimes together. The motif is transformed by Bogart's incarnation of Sam Spade in the misogynistic *Maltese Falcon*, and the bleaker, lonelier, more anxious Hemingway adventurer in *To Have and Have Not*. In the late '40s Chandler's Marlowe wears five faces, Dick Powell's, Bogart's, Ladd's, Robert Montgomery's and George Montgomery's, in *Farewell My Lovely (Murder, My Sweet)*, *The Big Sleep*, *The Blue Dahlia*, *Lady In The Lake* and *The High Window (The Brasher Doubloon)*. An RKO series with Mitchum (sometimes Mature) as a vague, aimless wanderer, hounded and hounding, begins well with *Build My Gallows High (Out of the Past)* but rapidly degenerates. The series seeks renewal in more exotic settings with *Key Largo, Ride the Pink Horse. The Breaking Point,* and *Beat The Devil*, but concludes in disillusionment. In *Kiss Me Deadly, Confidential Agent* and

Dick Powell, one of Marlowe's five faces, is interrogated in *Murder, My Sweet.*

Wendell Corey and Barbara Stanwyck in *The File on Thelma Jordon.*

a late straggler, *Vertigo,* the private eye solves the mystery but undergoes extensive demoralization. In retrospect, films by well respected auteurs like Hawks, Ray, Siegel and Huston seem to me to have worn less well than the most disillusioned of the series; Dmytryk's visionary *Murder, My Sweet* prefiguring the Aldrich-Welles-Hitchcock pessimism. *The Maltese Falcon*, notably, is deep camp. Huston's laughter deflates villainy into the perverted pretension of Greenstreet and Lorre who are to real villains as Al Jolson to Carmen Jones. In the scenes between Bogart and Mary Astor (a sad hard not-so-young vamp with more middle class perm than "it") it reaches an intensity like greatness. Huston's great film noir is a Western (*Treasure of Sierra Madre*).

5. MIDDLE CLASS MURDER

Crime has its harassed amateurs, and the theme of the respectable middle-class figure beguiled into, or secretly plotting, murder facilitates the sensitive study in black. The '30s see a series centering on Edward G. Robinson, who alternates between uncouth underworld leaders (*Little Caesar, Black Tuesday*) and a guilt-haunted or fear-bourgeoisie (in *The Amazing Dr. Clitterhouse, The Woman In The Window, Scarlet Street, The Red House,* and *All My Sons*). Robinson, like Laughton, Cagney and Bogart, belongs to that select group of stars, who, even in Hollywood's simpler-minded years, could give meanness and cowardice a riveting monstrosity, even force. His role as pitiable scapegoat requires a little excursion into psychoanalytical sociology. Slightly exotic, that is, un-American, he symbolized the loved, but repudiated, father/elder sibling, apparently benevolent, ultimately sinister, never unlovable, either an immigrant father (Little Rico in *Little Caesar*) or that complementary bogey, the ultra-WASP intellectual, whose cold superior snobbery infiltrates so many late '40s movies (Clifton Webb in *Laura*). The evolution of these figures belongs to the process of assimilation in America. Robinson's '50s and '60s equivalents include Broderick Crawford, Anthony Quinn, Rod Steiger and Vincent Price. The theme of respectable eccentricity taking murder lightly is treated in *Arsenic and Old Lace, Monsieur Verdoux, Rope,* and *Strangers On A Train.* The theme of the tramp corrupting the not-always-so-innocent bourgeois is artistically fruitful, with *Double Indemnity, The Postman Always Rings Twice, The Woman in the Window, The Woman On the Beach* and, a straggler, *The Pushover. The Prowler* reverses the formula: the lower-class cop victimizes the lonely wife. The theme can be considered an American adaptation of a pre-war European favorite (cf. *Pandora's Box, La Bête Humaine*), and the European versions of *The Postman Always Rings Twice.* The cycle synchronizes with a climax in the perennial theme of Woman: Executioner/Victim, involving such figures as Bette Davis. Barbara Stanwyck, Gene Tierney, Joan Crawford and Lana Turner. Jacques Siclier dates the misogynistic cycle from Wyler's *Jezebel* (1938), and it can be traced through *Double Indemnity, Gilda, Dragonwyck, The Strange Love of Martha Ivers, Ivy, Sunset Boulevard, Leave Her To Heaven, Beyond The Forest, Flamingo Road, The File on Thelma Jordan, Clash By Night, Angel Face, Portrait in Black* and *Whatever Happened To Baby Jane?.* A collateral cycle sees woman as grim heroic victim, struggling against despair where her men all but succumb or betray her (*Rebecca, Phantom Lady*). Many films have it both ways, perhaps by contrasting strong feminine figures, the heroine lower-class and embittered, the other respectable but callous (like Joan Crawford and her daughter in *Mildred Pierce*), or by plot twists proving that the apparent vamp was misjudged by an embittered hero (as Rita Hayworth beautifully taunts Glenn Ford in *Gilda* "Put the blame on Mame, boys..."). The whole subgenre can be seen as a development out of the "confession" stories of the Depression years, when Helen Twelvetrees and others became prostitutes, golddiggers and kept women for various tear-jerking reasons. Replace the tears by a glum, baffled deadpan, modulate self pity into suspicion, and the later cycle appears. Maybe the misogyny is only an aspect of the claustrophobic paranoia so marked in late '40s movies.

Double Indemnity is perhaps the central film noir, not only for its atmospheric power, but as a junction of major themes, combining the vamp (Barbara Stanwyck), the morally weak murderer (Fred MacMurray) and the investigator (Edward G. Robinson). The murderer sells insurance. The investigator checks on claims. If the latter is incorruptible, he is unromantically so; only his cruel Calvinist energy distinguishes his "justice" from meanness. The film's stress on money and false friendliness as a means of making it justifies an alternative title: *Death of a Salesman.* This, and Miller's play all but parallel the relationship between *A Place In The Sun* and *Kiss Tomorrow Good-bye* (realistic weakness becomes wish fulfillment violence).

Lew Ayres with Olivia de Havilland in the dual role in *The Dark Mirror*.

6. PORTRAITS AND DOUBLES

The characteristic tone of the '40s is sombre, claustrophobic, deadpan and paranoid. In the shaded lights and raining night it is often just a little difficult to tell one character from another. A strange, diffuse play on facial and bodily resemblances reaches a climax in Vidor's *Beyond The Forest* (where sullen Bette Davis is the spitting image, in long-shot, of her Indian maid) and, in exile, in Losey's *The Sleeping Tiger*, where dominant Alexis Smith is the spitting image of her frightened maid. A cycle of grim romantic thrillers focused on women who, dominant even in their absence, stare haughty enigmas at us from their portraits over the fireplace. Sometimes the portrait is the mirror of split personality. The series included *Rebecca, Experiment Perilous, Laura, The Woman in the Window, Scarlet Street* and *The Dark Mirror*. Variants include the all-male, but sexually inverted, *Picture of Dorian Gray, Portrait of Jennie* (rosy and tardy, but reputedly one of Buñuel's favorite films), *Under Capricorn* (the shrunken head), and a beautiful straggler, *Vertigo*.

7. SEXUAL PATHOLOGY

In *The Big Sleep* Bogart and Bacall, pretending to discuss horse-racing, discuss the tactics of copulation, exemplifying the clandestine cynicism and romanticism which the film noir apposes to the Hays Office. Similarly, "love at first sight" between Ladd and Lake in *The Blue Dahlia* looks suspiciously like a casual, heavy pick-up. *In A Lonely Place, The Big Heat* (and, just outside the film noir, *Bus Stop*) make another basic equation: the hero whose tragic flaw is psychopathic violence meets his match in the loving whore.

The yin and yang of puritanism and cynicism, of egoism and paranoia, of greed and idealism, deeply perturbs sexual relationships, and films noirs abound in love-hate relationships ranging through all degrees of intensity. Before untying Bogart, Bacall kisses his bruised lips. Heston rapes Jennifer Jones in *Ruby Gentry*, and next morning she shoots her puritanical brother for shooting him. Lover and beloved exterminate each other in *Double Indemnity* and *Out of the Past*. He has to kill her in *Gun Crazy* and lets her die of a stomach wound in *The Lady From Shanghai*.

Intimations of non-effeminate homosexuality are laid on thick in, notably, *Gilda*, where loyal Glenn Ford gets compared to both his boss's kept woman and swordstick. A certain flabbiness paraphrases effeminacy in *The Maltese Falcon* (the Lorre-Greenstreet duo repeated in the Morley-Lorre pair in *Beat The Devil*), and in *Rope* and *Strangers on a Train* (where Farley Granger and Robert Walker respectively evoke a youthful Vincent Price). Lesbianism rears a sado-masochistic head in *Rebecca* (between Judith Anderson and her dead mistress) and *In a Lonely Place* (between Gloria Grahame and a brawny masseuse who is also perhaps a symbol for a coarse vulgarity she cannot escape). Homosexual and heterosexual sadism are everyday conditions. In *Clash By Night* Robert Ryan wants to stick pins all over Paul Douglas's floosie wife (Barbara Stanwyck) and watch the blood run down; we're not so far from the needle stuck through a goose's head to tenderize its flesh in *Diary of A Chambermaid* ("Sounds like they're murdering somebody," says Paulette Goddard).

Slim knives horrify but fascinate the paranoid '40s as shotguns delight the cool '60s. Notable sadists include Richard Widmark (chuckling as he pushes the old lady down stairs in her wheelchair in *Kiss of Death*), Paul Henreid in *Rope of Sand* (experimenting with a variety of whips on Burt Lancaster's behind), Hume Cronyn in *Brute Force* (truncheoning the intellectual prisoner to the strains of the Liebestod), Lee Marvin flinging boiling coffee in his mistress's face in *The Big Heat*; and so on to Clu Gulager's showmanlike eccentricities in *The Killers* and, of course, Tony Curtis in *The Boston Strangler*.

8. PSYCHOPATHS

Film noir psychopaths, who are legion, are divisible into three main groups: the heroes with a tragic flaw, the unassuming monsters, and the obvious monsters, in particular, the Prohibition-type gangster. Cagney's *Public Enemy* criss-crosses the boundaries between them, thus providing the moral challenge and suspense which is the film's mainspring. Cagney later contributes a rousing portrait of a gangster with a raging Oedipus complex in *White Heat*, from Hollywood's misogynistic period. Trapped on an oil storage tank, he cries exultantly: "On top of the world, ma!" before joining his dead mother via the auto-destructive orgasm of his own personal mushroom cloud. The unassuming monster may be exemplified by *The Blue Dahlia*, whose paranoid structure is almost as interesting as that of *Phantom Lady*. Returned war hero Alan Ladd nearly puts a bullet in his unfaithful wife. As so often in late 1940s films, the police believe him guilty of the crime of which he is nearly guilty. The real murderer is not the hero with the motive, not the wartime buddy whom shellshock drives into paroxysms of rage followed by amnesia, not the smooth gangster with whom the trollop was two-timing her husband. It was the friendly hotel house-detective.

On our right, we find the simple and satisfying view of the psychopath as a morally responsible mad dog deserving to be put down (thus simple, satisfying films like *Scarface* and *Panic in Year Zero*). On the left, he is an ordinary, or understandably weak, or unusually energetic character whose inner defects are worsened by factors outside his control (*Public Enemy, The Young Savages*). These factors may be summarized as (1) slum environments, (2) psychological traits subtly extrinsic to character (neurosis) and (3) a subtly corrupting social morality. In Depression America, the first explanation seems plausible enough (*Public Enemy*, with exceptional thoughtfulness, goes for all three explanations while insisting that he's become a mad dog who must die). In 1939, *Of Mice and Men* prefigures a change of emphasis, and in post-war America, with its supposedly universal affluence, other terms seem necessary to account for the still festering propensity to violence. Given the individualism even of Democratic thought, recourse is had to trauma, either wartime (*The Blue Dahlia, Act of Violence*) or Freudian (*The Dark Corner, The Dark Past*). A second group of films, without exonerating society, key psychopathy to a tone of tragic confusion (*Of Mice and Men, Kiss The Blood Off My Hands*). A third group relates violence to the spirit of society (*Force of Evil, The Sound of Fury*). A cooler more domestic tone prevails with *Don't Bother To Knock*, with its switch-casting (ex-psychopath Richard Widmark becomes the embittered, kindly hero, against Marilyn Monroe as a homicidal baby-sitter). This last shift might be described as anti-expressionism, or coolism, with psychopathy accepted as a normal condition of life. Critics of the period scoff at the psychopathic theme, although in retrospect Hollywood seems to have shown more awareness of American undertones than its supercilious critics. *The Killers, Point Blank* and *Bonnie and Clyde* resume the "Democratic" social criticism of *Force of Evil* and *The Sound of Fury*. A highly plausible interpretation of *Point Blank* sees its hero as a ghost; the victims of his revenge quest destroy one another, or themselves. The psychopathy theme is anticipated in pre-war French movies (e.g. *Le Jour Se Leve*) with a social crisis of confidence, a generalized, hot, violent mode of alienation (as distinct from the glacial variety, a la Antonioni). With a few extra-lucid exceptions, neither the French nor the American films seem to realize the breakdown of confidence as a social matter.

9. HOSTAGES TO FORTUNE

The imprisonment of a family, an individual, or a group of citizens, by desperate or callous criminals is a hardy perennial. But a cycle climaxes soon after the Korean War with the shock, to Americans, of peacetime conscripts in action. A parallel inspiration in domestic violence is indicated by *The Petrified Forest* (1938), *He Ran All The Way* and *The Dark Past*. But the early '50s see a sudden cluster including *The Desperate Hours, Suddenly, Cry Terror* and *Violent Saturday*. The confrontation between middle-class father and family, and killer, acts out, in fuller social metaphor, although, often, with a more facile Manicheanism, the normal and abnormal sides of the psychopathic hero.

10. BLACKS AND REDS

A cycle substituting Nazi agents and the Gestapo for gangsters gets under way with *Confessions Of A Nazi Spy* (1939). The cold war anti-Communist cycle begins with *The Iron Curtain* (1948), and most of its products were box-office as well as artistic flops, probably because the Communists and fellow-travellers were so evil as to be dramatically boring. The principal exceptions are by Samuel Fuller (*Pick Up On South Street*) and Aldrich (*Kiss Me Deadly*). Some films contrast the good American gangster with the nasty foreign agents (*Pick Up On South Street*); *Woman On Pier 13* links Russian agents with culture-loving waterfront union leaders and can be regarded as ultra-right, like *One Minute To Zero* and *Suddenly*, whose timid liberal modification (rather than reply) is *The Manchurian Candidate*. *Advise and Consent* is closely related to the political film noir.

11. GUIGNOL, HORROR, FANTASY

The three genres are clearly first cousins to the film noir. Hardy perennials, they seem to have enjoyed periods of special popularity. Siegfried Kracauer has sufficiently related German expressionist movies with the angst of pre-Nazi Germany. Collaterally, a diluted expressionism was a minor American genre, indeterminate as between film noir and horror fantasy. Lon Chaney's Gothic grotesques (*The Unknown, The Phantom of the Opera*) parallel stories of haunted houses (*The Cat and the Canary*) which conclude with rational explanations. Sternberg's *The Last Command* can be considered a variant of the Chaney genre, with Jannings as Chaney, and neo-realistic in that its hero's plight symbolizes the agonies of the uprooted immigrants who adapted with difficulty to the tenement jungles. The Depression sparked off the full-blown, visionary guignol of *Dracula, Frankenstein* (with Karloff as Chaney), *King Kong* (with Kong as Chaney!), *The Hounds of Zaroff, Island of Lost Souls*, etc. (the Kracauer-type tyrant looms, but is defeated, often with pathos). Together with gangster and sex films, the genre suffers from the Hays Office. After the shock of the Great Crash, the demoralizing stagnation of the depressed 1930s leads to a minor cycle of black brooding fantasies of death and time (*Death Takes a Holiday, Peter Ibbetson*). The war continues the social unsettledness which films balance by cozy, enclosed, claustrophobic settings (*Dr. Jekyll and Mr. Hyde, Flesh and Fantasy, Cat People*). A post-war subgenre is the thriller, developed into plain clothes Gothic (*The Spiral Staircase, The Red House, Sorry Wrong Number*). *Phantom Lady* (in its very title) indicates their inter-echoing. A second Monster cycle coincides with the Korean War. A connection with scientists, radioactivity and outer space suggests fear of atomic apocalypse (overt in *This Island Earth, It Came From Outer Space* and *Them*, covert in *Tarantula* and *The Thing From Another World*). *The Red Planet Mars* speaks for the hawks, *The Day The Earth Stood Still* for the doves. *Invasion of the Body Snatchers* is a classic paranoid fantasy (arguably justified). As the glaciers of callous alienation advance, the Corman Poe adaptations create their nightmare compensation: the aesthetic hothouse of Victorian incest. *Psycho* crossbreeds the genre with a collateral revival of plainclothes guignol, often revolving round a femi-nine, rather than a masculine, figure (Joan Crawford and Bette Davis substitute for Chaney in *Whatever Happened To Baby Jane?*). The English anticipate of the Corman Poe films are the Fisher *Frankenstein* and *Dracula*. With *Dutchman*, the genre matures into an expressionistic social realism.

The '60s obsession with violent death in all forms and genres may be seen as marking the admission of the film noir into the mainstream of Western pop art, encouraged by (a) the comforts of relative affluence, (b) moral disillusionment, in outcome variously radical, liberal, reactionary or nihilist, (c) a post-Hiroshima sense of man as his own executioner, rather than nature, God or fate, and (d) an enhanced awareness of social con-flict. The cinema is in its Jacobean period, and the stress on gratuitous tormenting, evilly jocular in *The Good, the Bad and the Ugly,* less jocular in *Laughter in the Dark*, parallel that in Webster's plays. Such films as *Paths of Glory, Eva,* and *The Loved One* emphasize their crimes less than the rottenness of a society or, perhaps, man himself.

Noir style superimposed on sci-fi: Michael Rennie in *The Day the Earth Stood Still..*

Orson Welles as corrupt
detective Hank Quinlan
in *Touch of Evil*.

notes on film noir

Paul Schrader (1972)

In 1946 French critics, seeing the American films they had missed during the war, noticed the new mood of cynicism, pessimism and darkness which had crept into the American cinema. The darkening stain was most evident in routine crime thrillers, but was also apparent in prestigious melodramas.

The French cineastes soon realized they had seen only the tip of the iceberg: as the years went by, Hollywood lighting grew darker, characters more corrupt, themes more fatalistic and the tone more hopeless. By 1949 American movies were in the throes of their deepest and most creative funk. Never before had films dared to take such a harsh uncomplimentary look at American life, and they would not dare to do so again for twenty years.

Hollywood's film noir has recently become the subject of renewed interest among moviegoers and critics. The fascination film noir holds for today's young filmgoers and film students reflects recent trends in American cinema: American movies are again taking a look at the underside of the American character, but compared to such relentlessly cynical films noir as *Kiss Me Deadly* or *Kiss Tomorrow Goodbye*, the new self-hate cinema of *Easy Rider* and *Medium Cool* seems naive and romantic. As the current political mood hardens, filmgoers and filmmakers will find the film noir of the late Forties increasingly attractive. The Forties may be to the Seventies what the Thirties were to the Sixties.

Film noir is equally interesting to critics. It offers writers a cache of excellent, little-known films (film noir is oddly both one of Hollywood's best periods and least known), and gives auteur-weary critics an opportunity to apply themselves to the newer questions of classification and transdirectorial style. After all, what is film noir?

Film noir is not a genre (as Raymond Durgnat has helpfully pointed out over the objections of Higham and Greenberg's *Hollywood in the Forties*). It is not defined, as are the western and gangster genres, by conventions of setting and conflict, but rather by the more subtle qualities of tone and mood. It is a film "noir," as opposed to the possible variants of film gray or film off-white.

Film noir is also a specific period of film history, like German Expressionism or the French New Wave. In general, film noir refers to those Hollywood films of the Forties and early Fifties which portrayed the world of dark, slick city streets, crime and corruption.

Film noir is an extremely unwieldy period. It harks back to many previous periods: Warner's Thirties gangster films, the French "poetic realism" of Carné and Duvivier, Sternbergian melodrama, and, farthest back, German Expressionist crime films (Lang's *Mabuse* cycle). Film noir can stretch at its outer limits from *The Maltese Falcon* (1941) to *Touch of Evil* (1958), and most every dramatic Hollywood film from 1941 to 1953 contains some noir elements. There are also foreign offshoots of film noir, such as *The Third Man, Breathless* and *Le Doulos*.

Almost every critic has his own definition of film noir, and personal list of film titles and dates to back it up. Personal and descriptive definitions, however, can get a bit sticky. A film of urban night life is not necessarily a film noir, and a film noir need not necessarily concern crime and corruption. Since film noir is defined by tone rather than genre, it is almost impossible to argue one critic's descriptive definition against another's. How many noir elements does it take to make film noir noir?

The noir cycle begins and end with the "fat man": opposite, its conclusion with Orson Welles as Hank Quinlan in *Touch of Evil*. Next page, the beginning, Sydney Greenstreet as Kasper Gutman pats the *The Maltese Falcon*.

Rather than haggle definitions, I would rather attempt to reduce film noir to its primary colors (all shades of black), those cultural and stylistic elements to which any definition must return.

At the risk of sounding like Arthur Knight, I would suggest that there were four conditions in Hollywood in the Forties which brought about film noir. (The danger of Knight's *Liveliest Art* method is that it makes film history less a matter of structural analysis, and more a case of artistic and social forces magically interacting and coalescing.) Each of the following four catalytic elements, however, can define the film noir; the distinctly noir tonality draws from each of these elements.

War and Post-war Disillusionment. The acute downer which hit the U.S. after the Second World War was, in fact, a delayed reaction to the Thirties. All through the Depression, movies were needed to keep people's spirits up, and, for the most part, they did. The crime films of this period were Horatio Algerish and socially conscious. Toward the end of the Thirties a darker crime film began to appear (*You Only Live Once, The Roaring Twenties*) and, were it not for the War, film noir would have been at full steam by the early Forties.

The need to produce Allied propaganda abroad and promote patriotism at home blunted the fledgling moves toward a dark cinema, and the film noir thrashed about in the studio system, not quite able to come into full prominence. During the War the first uniquely film noir appeared: *The Maltese Falcon, The Glass Key, This Gun for Hire, Laura,* but these films lacked the distinctly noir bite the end of the war would bring.

As soon as the War was over, however, American films became markedly more sardonic, and there was a boom in the crime film. For fifteen years the pressures against America's amelioristic cinema had been building up and, given the freedom, audiences and artists were now eager to take a less optimistic view of things.

The disillusionment many soldiers, small businessmen and housewife/factory employees felt in returning to a peacetime economy was directly mirrored in the sordidness of the urban crime film.

This immediate post-war disillusionment was directly demonstrated in films like *Cornered, The Blue Dahlia, Dead Reckoning*, and *Ride the Pink Horse*, in which a serviceman returns from the war to find his sweetheart unfaithful or dead, or his business partner cheating him, or the whole society something less than worth fighting for. The war continues, but now the antagonism turns with a new viciousness toward the American society itself.

Post-war Realism. Shortly after the War every film-producing country had a resurgence of realism. In America it first took the form of films by such producers as Louis de Rochemont (*House on 92nd Street, Call Northside 777*) and Mark Hellinger (*The Killers, Brute Force*), and directors like Henry Hathaway and Jules Dassin. "Every scene was filmed on the actual location depicted," the 1947 de Rochemont-Hathaway *Kiss of Death* proudly proclaimed. Even after de Rochemont's particular "March of Time" authenticity fell from vogue, realistic exteriors remained a permanent fixture of film noir.

The realistic movement also suited America's post-war mood; the public's desire for a more honest and harsh view of America would not be satisfied by the same studio streets they had been watching for a dozen years. The post-war realistic trend succeeded in breaking film noir away from the domain of the high-class melodrama, placing it where it more properly belonged, in the streets with everyday people. In retrospect, the pre-de Rochemont film noir looks definitely tamer than the post-war realistic films. The studio look of films like *The Big Sleep* and *The Mask of Dimitrios* blunts their sting, making them seem more polite and conventional in contrast to their later, more realistic counterparts.

The German Influence. Hollywood played host to an influx of German expatriates in the Twenties and Thirties, and these filmmakers and technicians had, for the most part, integrated themselves into the American film establishment. Hollywood never experienced the "Germanization" some civic-minded natives feared, and there is a danger of over-emphasizing the German influence in Hollywood.

But when, in the late Forties, Hollywood decided to paint it black, there were no greater masters of chiaroscuro than the Germans. The influence of expressionist lighting has always been just beneath the surface of Hollywood films, and it is not surprising, in film noir, to find it bursting out in film bloom. Neither is it surprising to find a larger number of German and East Europeans working in film noir: Fritz Lang, Robert Siodmak, Billy Wilder, Franz Waxman, Otto Preminger, John Brahm, Anatole Litvak, Karl Freund, Max Ophuls, John Alton, Douglas Sirk, Fred Zinnemann, William Dieterle, Max Steiner, Edgar G. Ulmer, Curtis Bernhardt, Rudolph Maté.

On the surface the German expressionist influence, with its reliance on artificial studio lighting, seems incompatible with post-war realism, with its harsh unadorned exteriors; but it is the unique quality of film noir that it was able to weld seemingly contradictory elements into a uniform style. The best noir technicians simply made all the world a sound stage, directing unnatural and expressionistic lighting onto realistic settings. In films like *Union Station, They Live by Night, The Killers* there is an uneasy, exhilarating combination of realism and expressionism.

Perhaps the greatest master of noir was Hungarian-born John Alton, an expressionist cinematographer who could relight Times Square at noon if necessary. No cinematographer better adapted the old expressionist techniques to the new desire for realism, and his black-and-white photography in such gritty film noir as *T-Men, Raw Deal, I the Jury, The Big Combo* equals that of such German expressionist masters as Fritz Wagner and Karl Freund.

The Hard-boiled Tradition. Another stylistic influence waiting in the wings was the "hard-boiled" school of writers. In the Thirties, authors such as Ernest Hemingway, Dashiell Hammett, Raymond Chandler, James M. Cain, Horace McCoy and John O'Hara created the "tough," cynical way of acting and thinking which separated one from the world of everyday emotions, romanticism with a protective shell. The hard-boiled writers had their roots in pulp fiction or journalism, and their protagonists lived out a narcissistic, defeatist code. The hard-boiled hero was, in reality, a soft egg compared to his existential counterpart (Camus is said to have based *The Stranger* on McCoy), but he was a good deal tougher than anything American fiction had seen.

When the movies of the Forties turned to the American "tough" moral understrata, the hard-boiled school was waiting with pre-set conventions of heroes, minor characters, plots, dialogue and themes. Like the German expatriates, the hard-boiled writers had a style made to order for film noir; and, in turn, they influenced noir screenwriting as much as the German influenced noir cinematography.

The most hard-boiled of Hollywood's writers was Raymond Chandler himself, whose script of *Double Indemnity* (from a James M. Cain story) was the best written and most characteristically noir of the period. *Double Indemnity* was the first film which played film noir for what it essentially was: small-time, unredeemed, unheroic; it made a break from the romantic noir cinema of [the later] *Mildred Pierce* and *The Big Sleep*.

(In its final stages, however, film noir adapted and then bypassed the hard-boiled school. Manic, neurotic post-1948 films such as *Kiss Tomorrow Goodbye, D.O.A., Where the Sidewalk Ends, White Heat,* and *The Big Heat* are all post-hard-boiled: the air in these regions was even too thin for old-time cynics like Chandler.)

Stylistics. There is not yet a study of the stylistics of film noir, and the task is certainly too large to be attempted here. Like all film movements film noir drew upon a reservoir of film techniques, and given the time one could correlate its techniques, themes and causal elements into a stylistic schema. For the present, however, I'd like to point out some of film noir's recurring techniques.

The majority of scenes are lit for night. Gangsters sit in the offices at midday with shades pulled and the lights off. Ceiling lights are hung low and floor lamps are seldom more than five feet high. One always has the suspicion that if the lights were all suddenly flipped on the characters would shriek and shrink from the scene like Count Dracula at sunrise.

As in German expressionism, oblique and vertical lines are preferred to horizontal. Obliquity adheres to the choreography of the city, and is in direct opposition to the horizontal American tradition of Griffith and Ford. Oblique lines tend to splinter a screen, making it restless and unstable. Light enters the dingy rooms of film noir in such odd shapes, jagged trapezoids, obtuse triangles, vertical slits, that one suspects the windows were cut out with a pen knife. No character can speak authoritatively from a space which is being continually cut into ribbons of light. The Anthony Mann/John Alton *T-Men* is the most dramatic but far from the only example of oblique noir choreography.

Schrader's three phases of film noir: left, "the first phase...studio sets and more talk than action," a tuxedoed and impeccably groomed Zachary Scott places a bet in a crowd of casino patrons in the elegantly titled *Mask of Dimitrios*. Below, phase two, a rough-hewn, ethnic and proletarian Richard Conte as trucker Nick Garcos, who stands off-center in a very different milieu and overhears negotiations between brokers Mike Figlia (Lee J. Cobb) and Midge (Hope Emerson) who regularly exploit those travelling along the *Thieves' Highway*.

The actors and setting are often given equal lighting emphasis. An actor is often hidden in the realistic tableau of the city at night, and, more obviously, his face is often blacked out by shadow as he speaks. These shadow effects are unlike the famous Warner Brothers lighting of the Thirties in which the central character was accentuated by a heavy shadow; in film noir, the central character is likely to be standing in the shadow. When the environment is given an equal or greater weight than the actor, it, of course, creates a fatalistic, hopeless mood. There is nothing the protagonist can do; the city will outlast and negate even his best efforts.

Compositional tension is preferred to physical action. A typical film noir would rather move the scene cinematographically around the actor than have the actor control the scene by physical action. The beating of Robert Ryan in *The Set-Up*, the gunning down of Farley Granger in *They Live by Night*, the execution of the taxi driver in *The Enforcer* and of Brian Donlevy in *The Big Combo* are all marked by measured pacing, restrained anger and oppressive compositions, and seem much closer to the film noir spirit than the rat-tat-tat and screeching tires of *Scarface* twenty years before or the violent, expressive actions of *Underworld U.S.A.* ten years later.

There seems to be an almost Freudian attachment to water. The empty noir streets are almost always glistening with fresh evening rain (even in Los Angeles), and the rainfall tends to increase in direct proportion to the drama. Docks and piers are second only to alleyways as the most popular rendezvous points.

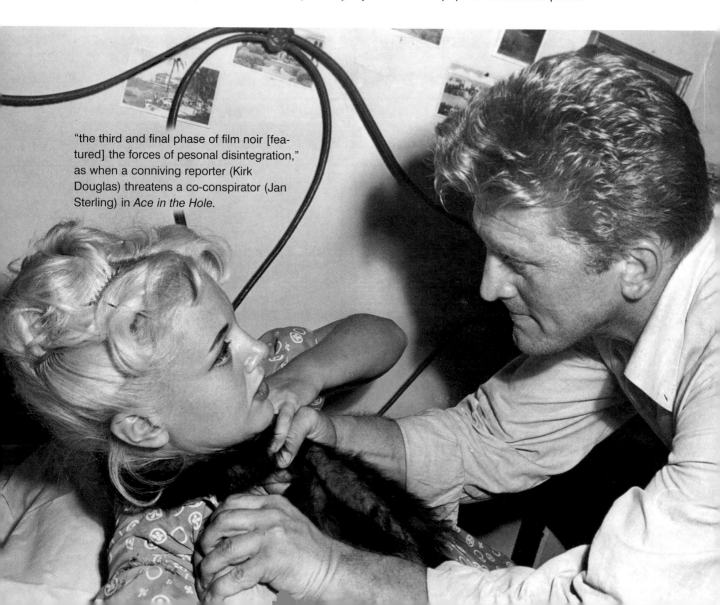

"the third and final phase of film noir [featured] the forces of pesonal disintegration," as when a conniving reporter (Kirk Douglas) threatens a co-conspirator (Jan Sterling) in *Ace in the Hole*.

There is a love of romantic narration. In such films as *The Postman Always Rings Twice, Laura, Double Indemnity, The Lady from Shanghai, Out of the Past* and *Sunset Boulevard* the narration creates a mood of *temps perdu*: an irretrievable past, a predetermined fate and an all-enveloping hopelessness. In *Out of the Past* Robert Mitchum relates his history with such pathetic relish that it is obvious there is no hope for any future: one can only take pleasure in reliving a doomed past.

A complex chronological order is frequently used to reinforce the feelings of hopelessness and lost time. Such films as *The Enforcer, The Killers, Mildred Pierce, The Dark Past, Chicago Deadline, Out of the Past* and *The Killing* use a convoluted time sequence to immerse the viewer in a time-disoriented but highly stylized world. The manipulation of time, whether slight or complex, is often used to reinforce a noir principle: the how is always more important than the what.

Themes. Raymond Durgnat has delineated the themes of film noir in an excellent article in the British *Cinema* magazine ("The Family Tree of Film noir," August, 1970), and it would be foolish for me to attempt to redo his thorough work in this short space. Durgnat divides film noir into eleven thematic categories, and although one might criticize some of his specific groupings, he does cover the whole gamut of noir production (thematically categorizing over 300 films).

In each of Durgnat's noir themes (whether Black Widow, killers-on-the-run, dopplegangers) one finds that the upwardly mobile forces of the Thirties have halted; frontierism has turned to paranoia and claustrophobia. The small-time gangster has now made it big and sits in the mayor's chair, the private eye has quit the police force in disgust, and the young heroine, sick of going along for the ride, is taking others for a ride.

Durgnat, however, does not touch upon what is perhaps the over-riding noir theme: a passion for the past and present, but also a fear of the future. The noir hero dreads to look ahead, but instead tries to survive by the day, and if unsuccessful at that, he retreats to the past. Thus film noir's techniques emphasize loss, nostalgia, lack of clear priorities, insecurity; then submerge these self-doubts in mannerism and style. In such a world style becomes paramount; it is all that separates one from meaninglessness. Chandler described this fundamental noir theme when he described his own fictional world: "It is not a very fragrant world, but it is the world you live in, and certain writers with tough minds and a cool spirit of detachment can make very interesting patterns out of it."

Film noir can be subdivided into three broad phases. The first, the wartime period, 1941-'46 approximately, was the phase of the private eye and the lone wolf, of Chandler, Hammett and Greene, of Bogart and Bacall, Ladd and Lake, classy directors like Curtiz and Garnett, studio sets, and, in general, more talk than action. The studio look of this period was reflected in such pictures as *The Maltese Falcon, Casablanca, Gaslight, This Gun for Hire, The Lodger, The Woman in the Window, Mildred Pierce, Spellbound, The Big Sleep, Laura, The Lost Weekend, The Strange Love of Martha Ivers, To Have and Have Not, Fallen Angel, Gilda, Murder My Sweet, The Postman Always Rings Twice, Dark Waters, Scarlet Street, So Dark the Night, The Glass Key, The Mask of Dimitrios,* and *The Dark Mirror*.

The Wilder/Chandler *Double Indemnity* provided a bridge to the post-war phase of film noir. The unflinching noir vision of *Double Indemnity* came as a shock in 1944, and the film was almost blocked by the combined efforts of Paramount, the Hays Office and star Fred MacMurray. Three years later, however, *Double Indemnity*s were dropping off the studio assembly line.

The second phase was the post-war realistic period from 1945-'49 (the dates overlap and so do the films; these are all approximate phases for which there are many exceptions). These films tended more toward the problems of crime in the streets, political corruption and police routine. Less romantic heroes like Richard Conte, Burt Lancaster and Charles McGraw were more suited to this period, as were proletarian directors like Hathaway, Dassin and Kazan. The realistic urban look of this phase is seen in such films as *The House on 92nd Street, The Killers, Raw Deal, Act of Violence, Union Station, Kiss of Death, Johnny O'Clock, Force of Evil, Dead Reckoning, Ride the Pink Horse, Dark Passage, Cry of the City, The Set-Up, T-Men, Call Northside 777, Brute Force, The Big Clock, Thieves' Highway, Ruthless, Pitfall, Boomerang!,* and *The Naked City*.

The third and final phase of film noir, from 1949-'53, was the period of psychotic action and suicidal impulse. The noir hero, seemingly under the weight of ten years of despair, started to go bananas. The psychotic killer, who in the first period had been a subject worthy of study (Olivia de Havilland in *The Dark Mirror*), in the second a fringe threat (Richard Widmark in *Kiss of Death*), now became the active protagonist (James Cagney in *Kiss Tomorrow Goodbye*). There were no excuses given for the psychopathy in *Gun Crazy*, it was just "crazy." James Cagney made a neurotic comeback and his instability was matched by that of younger actors like Robert Ryan and Lee Marvin. This was the phase of the "B" noir film, and of psychoanalytically-inclined directors like Ray and Walsh. The forces of personal disintegration are reflected in such films as *White Heat, Gun Crazy, D.O.A., Caught, They Live by Night, Where the Sidewalk Ends, Kiss Tomorrow Goodbye, Detective Story, In a Lonely Place, I the Jury, Ace in the Hole, Panic in the Streets, The Big Heat, On Dangerous Ground,* and *Sunset Boulevard.*

This third phase is the cream of the film noir period. Some critics may prefer the early "gray" melodramas, others the post-war "street" films, but film noir's final phase was the most aesthetically and sociologically piercing. After ten years of steadily shedding romantic conventions, the later noir films finally got down to the root causes of the period: the loss of public honor, heroic conventions, personal integrity, and, finally, psychic stability. The third-phase films were painfully self-aware; they seemed to know they stood at the end of a long tradition based on despair and disintegration and did not shy away from the fact. The best and characteristically noir films, *Gun Crazy, White Heat, Out of the Past, Kiss Tomorrow Goodbye, D.O.A., They Live by Night,* and *The Big Heat*, stand at the end of the period and are the results of self-awareness. The third phase is rife with end-of-the-line noir heroes: *The Big Heat* and *Where the Sidewalk Ends* are the last stops for the urban cop, *Ace in the Hole* for the newspaper man, the Victor Saville-produced Spillane series (*I, the Jury, The Long Wait, Kiss Me Deadly*) for the private eye, *Sunset Boulevard* for the Black Widow, *White Heat* and *Kiss Tomorrow Goodbye* for the gangster, *D.O.A.* for the John Doe American.

Appropriately, the masterpiece of film noir was a straggler, *Kiss Me Deadly*, produced in 1955. Its time delay gives it a sense of detachment and thoroughgoing seediness, it stands at the end of a long sleazy tradition. The private eye hero, Mike Hammer, undergoes the final stages of degradation. He is a small-time "bedroom dick," and makes no qualms about it because the world around him isn't much better. Ralph Meeker, in his best performance, plays Hammer, a midget among dwarfs. Robert Aldrich's teasing direction carries noir to its sleaziest and most perversely erotic. Hammer overturns the underworld in search of the "great whatsit," and when he finally finds it, it turns out to be, joke of jokes, an exploding atomic bomb. The inhumanity and meaningless of the hero are small matters in a world in which The Bomb has the final say.

By the middle Fifties film noir had ground to a halt. There were a few notable stragglers, *Kiss Me Deadly*, the Lewis/Alton *The Big Combo*, and film noir's epitaph, *Touch of Evil*, but for the most part a new style of crime film had become popular.

As the rise of McCarthy and Eisenhower demonstrated, Americans were eager to see a more bourgeois view of themselves. Crime had to move to the suburbs. The criminal put on a gray flannel suit and the footsore cop was replaced by the "mobile unit" careening down the expressway. Any attempt at social criticism had to be cloaked in ludicrous affirmations of the American way of life. Technically, television, with its demand for full lighting and close-ups, gradually undercut the German influence, and color cinematography was, of course, the final blow to the "noir" look.

New directors like Siegel, Fleischer, Karlson and Fuller, and TV shows like *Dragnet, M-Squad, Lineup* and *Highway Patrol* stepped in to create the new crime drama. This transition can be seen in Samuel Fuller's 1953 *Pickup on South Street,* a film which blends the black look with the red scare. The waterfront scenes with Richard Widmark and Jean Peters are in the best noir tradition, but a later, dynamic fight in the subway marks Fuller as a director who would be better suited to the crime school of the middle and late Fifties.

Film noir was an immensely creative period, probably the most creative in Hollywood's history, at least, if this creativity is measured not by its peaks but by its median level of artistry. Picked at random, a film noir is likely to be a better made film than a randomly selected silent comedy, musical, western and so on. (A Joseph H. Lewis "B" film noir is better than a Lewis "B" western, for example.) Taken as a whole period, film noir achieved an unusually high level of artistry.

"..there were a few notable stragglers" such as *The Big Combo* photographed by John Alton.

Film noir seemed to bring out the best in everyone: directors, cameramen, screenwriters, actors. Again and again, a film noir will make the high point on an artist's career graph. Some directors, for example, did their best work in film noir (Stuart Heisler, Robert Siodmak, Gordon Douglas, Edward Dmytryk, John Brahm, John Cromwell, Raoul Walsh, Henry Hathaway); other directors began in film noir and, it seems to me, never regained their original heights (Otto Preminger, Rudolph Maté, Nicholas Ray, Robert Wise, Jules Dassin, Richard Fleischer, John Huston, Andre de Toth, and Robert Aldrich); and other directors who made great films in other molds also made great film noir (Orson Welles, Max Ophuls, Fritz Lang, Elia Kazan, Howard Hawks, Robert Rossen, Anthony Mann, Joseph Losey, Alfred Hitchcock, and Stanley Kubrick). Whether or not one agrees with this particular schema, its message is irrefutable: film noir was good for practically every director's career. (Two interesting exceptions to prove the case are King Vidor and Jean Renoir.)

"...artistic solutions to sociological problems. And for those reasons film like...*Gun Crazy* can be works of art."

Film noir seems to have been a creative release for everyone involved. It gave artists a chance to work with previously forbidden themes, yet had conventions strong enough to protect the mediocre. Cinematographers were allowed to become highly mannered, and actors were sheltered by the cinematographers. It was not until years later that critics were able to distinguish between great directors and great noir directors.

Film noir's remarkable creativity makes its longtime neglect the more baffling. The French, of course, have been students of the period for some time (Borde and Chaumeton's *Panorama du Film Noir* was published in 1955), but American critics until recently have preferred the western, the musical or the gangster film to the film noir.

Some of the reasons for this neglect are superficial; others strike to the heart of the noir style. For a long time film noir, with its emphasis on corruption and despair, was considered an aberration of the American character. The western, with its moral primitivism, and the gangster film, with its Horatio Alger values, were considered more American than the film noir.

This prejudice was reinforced by the fact that film noir was ideally suited to the low budget "B" film, and many of the best noir films were "B" films. This odd sort of economic snobbery still lingers on in some critical circles: high-budget trash is considered more worthy of attention than low-budget trash, and to praise a "B" film is somehow to slight (often intentionally) an "A" film.

There has been a critical revival in the U.S. over the last ten years, but film noir lost out on that too. The revival was auteur (director) oriented, and film noir wasn't. Auteur criticism is interested in how directors are different; film noir criticism is concerned with what they have in common.

The fundamental reason for film noir's neglect, however, is the fact that it depends more on choreography than sociology, and American critics have always been slow on the uptake when it comes to visual style. Like its protagonists, film noir is more interested in style than theme, whereas American critics have been traditionally more interested in theme than style.

American film critics have always been sociologists first and scientists second: film is important as it relates to large masses, and if a film goes awry it is often because the theme has been somehow "violated" by the style. Film noir operates on opposite principles: the theme is hidden in the style, and bogus themes are often flaunted ("middle-class values are best") which contradict the style. Although, I believe, style determines the theme in every film, it was easier for sociological critics to discuss the themes of the western and gangster film apart from stylistic analysis than it was to do for film noir.

Not surprisingly it was the gangster film, not the film noir, which was canonized in *The Partisan Review* in 1948 by Robert Warshow's famous essay, "The Gangster as Tragic Hero." Although Warshow could be an aesthetic as well as a sociological critic, in this case he was interested in the western and gangster film as "popular" art rather than as style. This sociological orientation blinded Warshow, as it has many subsequent critics, to an aesthetically more important development in the gangster film, film noir.

The irony of this neglect is that in retrospect the gangster films Warshow wrote about are inferior to film noir. The Thirties gangster was primarily a reflection of what was happening in the country, and Warshow analyzed this. The film noir, although it was also a sociological reflection, went further than the gangster film. Toward the end film noir was engaged in a life-and-death struggle with the materials it reflected; it tried to make America accept a moral vision of life based on style. That very contradiction, promoting style in a culture which valued themes, forced film noir into artistically invigorating twists and turns. Film noir attacked and interpreted its sociological conditions, and, by the close of the noir period, created a new artistic world which went beyond a simple sociological reflection, a nightmarish world of American mannerism which was by far more a creation than a reflection.

Because film noir was first of all a style, because it worked out its conflicts visually rather than thematically, because it was aware of its own identity, it was able to create artistic solutions to sociological problems. And for these reason films like *Kiss Me Deadly, Kiss Tomorrow Goodbye* and *Gun Crazy* can be works of art in a way that gangster films like *Scarface, Public Enemy* and *Little Caesar* can never be.

Yvonne de Carlo and Burt Lancaster as the doomed couple in *Criss Cross*.

Three Faces of Film Noir

Tom Flinn (1972)

Rather than hazarding a definition of film noir, a thankless task which, hopefully, will be broached elsewhere in this magazine, this article contains a descriptive analysis of three films that the author paradoxically considers both typical and distinctive. Together they provide a sample of the noir output from the important years of 1940, 1944, and 1949. This in no way attempts to trace the limits of film noir since that style continued well into the Fifties and is still subject to periodic revivals. But film noir, like shoulder pads, wedgies, and zoot suits was an essential part of the Forties outlook, a cinematic style forged in the fires of war, exile, and disillusion, a melodramatic reflection for a world gone mad.

One of the earliest American examples of the film noir is *Stranger on the Third Floor,* an ambitious sixty-five minute "B" film made in 1940 at R.K.O. Although not entirely successful, it is extremely audacious in terms of what it seeks to say about American society, and particularly impressive in view of the way in which it predicts the conventions of the film noir. *Stranger on the Third Floor* was directed by Boris Ingster and scripted by Frank Partos, who deserves full credit for the thematic content of the film since he adapted it from his own story.

Like most noir films, *Stranger on the Third Floor* takes place in an urban milieu, in this case a studio-built New York of sleazy rooming houses and rundown restaurants, populated by hostile strangers and prying neighbors. The protagonist, Michael Ward, is a young journalist who discovers a murder at an all-night beanery. His exclusive story on the crime and the subsequent publicity get him the raise he needs to marry his girlfriend, but his testimony implicates a young ex-con (Elisha Cook Jr.) who is railroaded towards the chair by a conviction hungry D.A. The trial of the ex-con is a vicious rendering of the American legal system hard at work on an impoverished victim. The film displays a fine sense of caricature especially apparent in the figure of the judge, who when roused from a judicial stupor reprimands a sleeping juror. A realistic assessment of the gullibility of the average jury and a cynical appraisal of the sinister role of the police and prosecutors in obtaining confessions and convictions were hallmarks of the hard-boiled literature that paralleled and predicted what we call film noir. But even in Bay City, Raymond Chandler's outpost of corruption, trials were conducted with more decorum than is evidence in the legal proceedings in *Stranger on the Third Floor.* In the film the congenital cynicism of the genre is personified by Ward's elder colleague and mentor on the newspaper, the newspaper reporter being traditionally the most hardened of mortals (*Ace in the Hole*), who spends most of his time mixing wisecracks and whiskey at the press club bar.

Moved by the sincerity of the ex-con's courtroom outbursts, Ward begins to feel pangs of guilt, since it was his testimony that completed the web of circumstantial evidence responsible for the conviction. Back in his grimy room, he suddenly realizes that his obnoxious next-door neighbor, Mr. Meng (Charles Halton at his slimiest) is not snoring as usual. When banging on the wall does not bring an answer from the normally sensitive neighbor, Ward flashes back to several "run-ins" he had with Meng involving threats he had made on Meng's life. At this point Ward's paranoia reaches epic proportions and is expressed in a marvelously apt expressionistic dream sequence that is the psychological center of the film. Unlike the neat, modish Freudian dream montages of the fashionable Forties films of psychoanalysis (*Spellbound*), the dream in *Stranger on the Third Floor* is alive with subconscious desires, seething with repressions, awash with pent-up hatred, and constructed from the nightmarish circumstances of the character's real situation.

Ward's paranoia links him to other denizens of the urban jungles of Hollywood's nightmare films of the Forties, where the dividing line between dream and reality can be merely the whim of a director, as in Fritz

Lang's *Woman in the Window* (dream) and *Scarlet Street* (reality). In *Stranger on the Third Floor* Ward's paranoia fantasy works because the twin motivations of guilt (for participating in the sham trial) and fear (of being caught up in the system himself) are well established; while the climax of the dream in which the "victim," Meng, attends Ward's execution functions perfectly as dream logic expressing Ward's strong subconscious desire that Meng be alive.

The dream sequence itself is so completely expressionistic in style that it resembles an animation of one of Lynd Ward's woodcut novels (*God's Man, Madman's Drum*) with strong contrasts in lighting, angular shadow patterns, and distorted, emblematic architecture; in short, a kind of total stylization that manages to be both extremely evocative and somewhat theatrical. The use of a tilted camera destroys the normal play of horizontals and verticals, creating a forest of oblique angles recalling the unsettling effects of expressionist painting and cinema. This tilted camera was a favorite device of horror director James Whale (*Bride of Frankenstein*, 1935) and it later enjoyed a great vogue around 1950 (*The Third Man, Strangers on a Train*). In *Stranger on the Third Floor* the Germanic influence, so important in the creation of the film noir style, is quite obvious, and not confined to the dream sequence. Throughout the film the lighting by Nick Musuraca is very much in the baroque Forties manner with numerous shadow patterns on the walls.

Peter Lorre, who appears only briefly in Ward's dream, brings a full expressionistic approach to his brief role as an escaped lunatic, slithering through a door in a manner distinctly reminiscent of Conrad Veidt in *The Cabinet of Dr. Caligari*. In 1940 Lorre was quite thin and much more graceful than he had been in his debut as the pudgy child murderer in *M* made nine years earlier. Actually his role though even briefer than in *M* is quite similar, and in both films he manages to obtain the audience's sympathy in the final moments with just a few lines of dialogue.

Working in a more naturalistic style, Charles Halton portrays a particularly obnoxious specimen of hypocritical busybody, a vicious prude who is totally fascinated by sex; while Elisha Cook Jr. is suitably intense as the unjustly accused ex-con.

Unfortunately, John McGuire as Ward is stiff and reserved, though he does perform near the top of his limited range (compared with his disastrous role in John Ford's *Steamboat Round the Bend*). On the positive side McGuire handles a considerable amount of voice-story narration quite well, and his very vapidness is an aid to audience identification.

In comparison Margaret Tallichet (who later became Mrs. William Wyler) gives a remarkably honest and unaffected performance as Ward's fiancée. More sensitive than Ward, she is first to sense the disastrous effects

Below, the dawn of the noir style: cinematographer Nick Musuraca's dramatic lighting "is very much in the baroque Forties manner with numerous shadow patterns on the walls" as it captures Peter Lorre as the titled figure of *Stranger on the Third Floor* on a staircase, Left Elisha Cook, Jr. as the unjustly accused ex-convict.

Opposite, a posed still of John McGuire, Lorre, and Margaret Tallichet is lot for higher key.

of his involvement with the murder trial on their relationship. Later when Ward is being held for the murder of Meng, she searches for the man with a scarf (Lorre) who actually committed both murders. Thus in its last moments *Stranger on the Third Floor* becomes a girl-detective yarn. This segment of the film clearly prefigures *Phantom Lady* (1944) in which another working girl (both are secretaries) searches for the elusive witness that will save her man from the chair.

Thematically, *Phantom Lady*, based on a tepid thriller by Cornell Woolrich, is far less interesting than *Stranger on the Third Floor*; but Robert Siodmak's mise-en-scène is so exciting that other considerations pale in the face of his inventive direction. Like *Stranger on the Third Floor*, *Phantom Lady* concerns an innocent man convicted of murder, but Siodmak's work lacks the specific social criticism of the earlier film, though it retains the aura of menace in its portrait of the city, a quality that is absolutely de rigueur for any film noir. *Phantom Lady* was also filmed on studio sets, though in contrast to *Stranger on the Third Floor* the atmosphere of New York City sweltering in mid-summer heat is evoked with extreme veracity. With one or two exceptions the sets are near perfect in their simulation of reality, demonstrating a far greater interest in realism than is evident in pre-WW II films. The realistic atmosphere of the decor is aided by Siodmak's sparing use of background music, all the more remarkable in an era of "wall to wall" scoring. The suspense sequences, in particular, benefit from an adroit use of naturalistic sound.

Above, "Kansas (Ella Raines) and Inspector Burgess (Thomas Gomez) become, in effect, the new protagonists in the search to prove Henderson's innocence" in *Phantom Lady*.

Opposite, the suspenseful and noir-style sequence in which the Bartender (Andrew Toombes) follows Kansas down a wet urban street onto a "deserted railway platform...where the hunter becomes the hunted"

With *Phantom Lady*, Siodmak, who had served a tough apprenticeship in America (directing five "A" pictures followed by "vehicles" for two of Universal's biggest attractions, Lon Chaney Jr. and Maria Montez), established himself as one of the foremost stylists of film noir, creating a sombre world of wet streets, dingy offices, low-ceilinged bars, crowded lunch counters and deserted railway platforms, all unified by an atmosphere of heightened realism in which the expressive quality of the image is due entirely to lighting and composition. Siodmak arrived at this UFA-esque style naturally, since he directed in Germany from 1928-33. On *Phantom Lady* he enjoyed the services of legendary noir cameraman Elwood Bredell, who, according to George Amy, could "light a football stadium with a single match."

For a film of bravura visual style *Phantom Lady* opens rather unpromisingly on a closeup of Ann Terry (Fay Helm). Wearing one of those improbable creations that only Forties milliners could envisage, Miss Helm looks very much like a middle-aged neurotic left over from a Val Lewton film. Into Anselmo's Bar comes Scott Henderson, successful civil engineer on the brink of marital disaster. He suggests that they pool their loneliness ("no questions, no names") and take in a show, typically one of those Latin revues so popular in that era of Pan American solidarity. After the show he deposits his companion back at Anselmo's and returns to his wife's apartment. Here the nightmare begins. When he turns on the light he notices the room is already occupied by a formidable triumvirate of police officers (Thomas Gomez, Joseph Crehan, and Regis Toomey). Siodmak stages the confrontation with his usual flair; breaking the rules by deliberately crossing the axis during the interrogation to emphasize Henderson's isolation, framing him with a portrait of his murdered wife in the background, and tracking in slowly on the suspect (Henderson) while the cops deliver a snide, menacing third degree.

Like Ward in *Stranger on the Third Floor*, Scott Henderson is caught in an impenetrable web of circumstantial evidence, though his situation is further complicated, since a number of witnesses were bribed by the real murderer in an attempt to destroy Henderson's alibi (already very weak since he could not produce the "Phantom Lady" he took to the "Chica Boom Boom Revue").

In contrast to *Stranger on the Third Floor*, Siodmak handles Henderson's trial obliquely. The camera never

shows the accused, the judge, the jury, or any of the lawyers. Only the voice of the prosecutor (Milburn Stone) relates the proceedings as the camera dwells on the spectators, singling out Henderson's secretary, Kansas (Ella Raines) and Inspector Burgess (Thomas Gomez). The trial sequence serves as a transition.

Kansas, like Ward's fiancée in *Stranger on the Third Floor*, is a determined innocent who contrasts sharply with the corrupt society she must search. This juxtaposition was a favorite device in Forties films, reaching its climax in *The Seventh Victim* (Val Lewton/Mark Robson, 1945) in which schoolgirl Kim Hunter ferrets out a colony of Satanists in Greenwich Village. Kansas (the name reeks of Midwestern grit and determination) begins her quest by dogging the night bartender at Anselmo's (Andrew Toombes). Seated at the end of the bar she watches and waits [see illustration on page 283]. On the third night of her vigil she follows the bartender through the wet streets to a deserted El station where Siodmak emphasizes the vulnerability of his protagonist with a quick turnaround, in which the hunter becomes the hunted. Undaunted, Kansas follows the bartender downtown through narrow streets where, long after midnight, the residents are still lounging on their front stoops and the atmosphere is charged with latent violence.

The high point of her search (and of the film) is her encounter with Cliff Milburn (Elisha Cook Jr.), the trap drummer in the orchestra at the "Chica Boom Boom Revue." Seated in the front row, dressed in a black satin

Below, in a posed still, Franchot Tone reenacts his mannered performance as the sociopathic Jack Lombard and pointedly fixates on Ella Raines as Kansas. Just a few years after *Stranger on the Third Floor* and still early in the noir cycle, posed photographs more pointedly reflected the visual style of the movies.

sheath, and chewing at least three sticks of gum, Kansas is about as inconspicuous as Princess Grace on the Bowery. Naturally she has no trouble picking up the hapless musician and he takes her to a jam session which ranks as one of the most effective bits of cinema produced in the Forties. Siodmak gives full rein to his expressionistic propensities in a rhythmically cut riot of angles that "climaxes" in a drum solo that melds sex and music into a viable metaphor of tension and release.

Unfortunately, the last half of *Phantom Lady* is dominated by Jack Lombard (Franchot Tone), the real murderer, who is afflicted with delusions of grandeur, migraine headaches, and overly emphatic hand gestures. Van Gogh's "Self-portrait with a Bandaged Ear" on Lombard's studio wall neatly identifies him as the mad artist, but he comes off more like a re-fried Howard Roarke (*The Fountainhead*) than Van Gogh. Though he sounds vaguely Nietzschean, "When you've got my gifts you can't afford to let them get away," Lombard generated very little excitement.

Phantom Lady is primarily a work of style, created by the interaction of considerable intelligence (on the part of the director, producer, and cameraman) with very bland pulp writing (Woolrich's novel). Some of the dialogue is, as James Agee has pointed out, depressingly banal, but the film is redeemed by the originality of its mise-en-scène and by its all-pervading style which represents a considerable advance over the more overtly expressionistic *Stranger on the Third Floor*.

In the pessimistic post-war years, the noir influence grew like an orchid in General Sternwood's overheated greenhouse. Rare indeed was the Hollywood melodrama that did not include some noir element or theme. The influence of Italian neo-realism combined with already existing domestic tendencies toward location shooting to produce an expressive, increasingly veristic style tinged with violence and sadism. At the same time plots of bewildering complexity proliferated as Hollywood's affair with the flashback reached the height of absurdity during the period from *Passage to Marseille* (1944) to *The Locket* (1948). The newsreel reporter of *Citizen Kane* reappeared as the insurance investigator in Siodmak's *The Killers* (1946), while the comedies of Preston Sturges, such as *The Miracle at Morgan's Creek* (1944) and *Mad Wednesday* (1947) have intricate plots worthy of the author of "narratage."

Siodmak's *Criss Cross* (1949) combines complexity of narrative, a realism born of location shooting, and Siodmak's expressive stylizations. The opening aerial shot of Los Angeles sets the tone for what proves to be a fascinating chronicle of lower and middle class life in the western metropolis. Much of the action in *Criss Cross* takes place in the shadow of the funicular railway (Angel's Flight) in the Bunker Hill section of L.A. described most eloquently by Raymond Chandler (though none of the films made from his books or scripts can compare with *Criss Cross* in the evocation of this milieu):

"Bunker Hill is old town, lost town, shabby town, crook town. Once very long ago, it was the choice residential district of the city, and there are still standing a few of the jigsaw Gothic mansions with wide porches and walls covered with round-end shingles and full corner bay windows with spindle turrets. They are all rooming houses now, their parquetry floors are scratched and worn through the once glossy finish and the wide sweeping staircases are dark with time and with cheap varnish laid on over generations of dirt. In the tall rooms haggard landladies bicker with shifty tenants. On the wide cool front porches, reaching their cracked shoes into the sun, and staring at nothing, sit the old men with faces like lost battles..."

Criss Cross attains a kind of formal excellence, due to the tautness of its complex narrative structure, the uncompromising nature of its resolution, and the inexorable character of its Germanic fatalism. The film opens in medias res with Steve Thompson (Burt Lancaster) and Anna (Yvonne de Carlo) sharing a furtive kiss in the parking lot of the Rondo Club. The reason for their secrecy soon becomes obvious. Anna is married to Slim Dundee (Dan Duryea), a local tough guy who is giving himself a farewell party in a private room at the club. Gradually the audience becomes aware that Steve and Slim, obvious rivals, are connected in a robbery scheme. The action continues the next day as Steve, driving an armored truck, picks up a huge cash payroll at the bank. During the forty-minute run to the plant at San Raphelo, Steve reviews the intricate chain of circumstances that brought him into the robbery. By opening in the middle, the audience is forced to accept the

Another posed still uses a high-angle and character positioning to capture the sense of doom in the conclusion of *Criss Cross*: Dan Duryea's Slim Dundee brandished a revolver in front of the defenseless Anna and Steve Thompson..

central situation (the robbery) as reality, and the contrived circumstances leading up to it are given additional credence.

The success of *Criss Cross*'s fatalistic mood depends to a large extent on the complex relationship between Steve and Anna. Anna is a creature of dazzling insincerity, another in the seemingly endless succession of Forties femmes fatales. The archetype is, of course, Mary Astor hiding her Machiavellian designs behind a mask of gentility in *The Maltese Falcon* (1941). Barbara Stanwyck in *Double Indemnity* (1943) was of a tougher, less bourgeois breed, that reappeared with subtle variations in Siodmak's *The Killers* (1946) (Ava Gardner) and Tourneur's *Out of the Past* (1948) (Jane Greer). Anna definitely belongs to this second class of fatal women, although her essential coldness and grasping ambition are accompanied by immaturity, a general ineffectualness, and vulnerability. Her hold on her ex-husband Steve depends on his feeling sorry for her.

She is, in fact, persecuted by the police (at the instigation of Steve's mother), and tortured by Slim. But she finds it difficult to overcome the spectre of divorce, with its overtones of betrayal and failure, which divides her from Steve and reflects the film's central theme of treachery.

Anna is always seen from Steve's point of view for *Criss Cross*, like a Chandler novel, is set firmly in the first person. Steve narrates his flashbacks, supplying additional motivation and coloring events with his own fatalism. Siodmak complements the first person nature of the script (by Daniel Fuchs) with a number of subjective shots which make crucial thematic points. Steve's loneliness is expressed in a shot of his brother and future sister-in-law kissing in a corner of the dining room seen from Steve's point of view on the living room couch. A far more frightening example of the same technique occurs after the robbery goes haywire and Steve ends up in the hospital with his arm and shoulder in traction. Here Siodmak uses numerous subjective shots that force the audience to participate in Steve's nightmare situation. Lying helpless in the hospital bed he waits for Slim's vengeance, playing a cat and mouse game with a traveling salesman (Adam Williams), who turns out to be one of Slim's hirelings. The "salesman" snatches Steve from the hospital in a scene that can only be described as a paroxysm of pain. The ever-venal Williams is too easily bribed to take Steve to Anna instead of Slim, and the executioner is not far behind.

The role of Steve Thompson is so important to the film that those offended by Lancaster's mannerisms may not enjoy *Criss Cross*, in spite of a number of excellent character portrayals: Percy Helton, the rotund bartender with a voice like a wood rasp; Dan Duryea, with or without an icepick, the ideal pimp and smalltimer of the decade; Tom Pedi, Slim's henchman Vincent, who delivers his dialogue with a greedy verve ("That's the ticket"); John Doucette, another of the gang, with a dour voice to match his sombre personality; and Alan Napier, Finchley, the alcoholic mastermind of the big "heist."

The central importance of the robbery in *Criss Cross* demonstrates an increasing interest in criminal methods and mythology. *Criss Cross* is actually a "caper" film, a subgenre of the gangster film that can be traced back to *High Sierra* (1940) and further. The caper film concentrates all values and expectations on one last crime which, if successful, will put all the participants on easy street. The influence of *Criss Cross* can be seen in subsequent caper films including John Huston's *The Asphalt Jungle* (1950) where Sam Jaffe's Doc Riedenschneider resembles a Germanized Finchley, and Stanley Kubrick's *The Killing* (1956) which carries the temporal experimentation of *Criss Cross* to the point of absurdity.

Although *Criss Cross* has a more realistic, less decorative look than *Phantom Lady*, both films demonstrate similar photographic stylization. The sharp, fluid, high contrast photography and low key lighting in *Criss Cross* are the work of Franz Planer, another old UFA colleague of Siodmak's and another link between Weimar cinema and film noir. Siodmak himself never lost a taste for the "disguised" symbolism found in German silents. In one symbolic cut he juxtaposes his principals, appropriately clad in black and white, to form a visual pun on "criss cross".

As in *Phantom Lady*, Siodmak displays a real interest in American popular music, including a number by Esy Morales and his band which, unlike most Forties musical numbers, is an impressive musical performance, well integrated into the context of the film. Miklós Rózsa, who ranks as the chief composer for film noir (*Double Indemnity, The Killers*, ad infinitum) provided an effective score with garish harmonies that mirror the harsh conflicts of the narrative.

By 1949 the battle against that scourge of Hollywood known as the "happy ending" was largely won, and the essential pessimism of the film noir could be fulfilled. As a result, *Criss Cross* has a thematic completeness that *Stranger on the Third Floor* and *Phantom Lady* lack. Slim stalks into the doorway of the beachhouse hideout like an avenging angel, awakening memories of other destiny figures, Bernard Goetzke visiting the young couple in Lang's *Der müde Tod* (1921), or Hitu hounding the lovers in Murnau's *Tabu* (1931). With its thematic pessimism, realistic mise-en-scène, and aura of ambient fatalism, *Criss Cross* reflects something of the mood of a country about to discover the apocalyptic nature of the coming decade of nuclear stalemate.

Edmond O'Brien's shadow in *The Killers* suggests an alter ego, a darker self who cohabits that frame's space. This and the frame enlargement from *The Big Heat* on the opposite page of Gloria Grahame as Debbie are actually "two-shots" of only one character. The many mirror reflections of Debbie suggest her "other side" which is revealed during the course of the film [see also page 406].

Some Visual Motifs of Film Noir

Janey Place & Lowell Peterson (1974)

> A dark street in the early morning hours, splashed with a sudden downpour. Lamps form haloes in the murk. In a walk-up room, filled with the intermittent flashing of a neon sign from across the street, a man is waiting to murder or be murdered...shadow upon shadow upon shadow...every shot in glistening low-key, so that rain always glittered across windows or windscreens like quicksilver, furs shone with a faint halo, faces were barred deeply with those shadows that usually symbolized some imprisonment of body or soul.
>
> Joel Greenberg and Charles Higham, *Hollywood in the Forties*

Nearly every attempt to define film noir has agreed that visual style is the consistent thread that unites the very diverse films that together comprise this phenomenon. Indeed, no pat political or sociological explanations,"postwar disillusionment," "fear of the bomb," "modern alienation," can coalesce in a satisfactory way such disparate yet essential film noir as *Double Indemnity, Laura, In a Lonely Place, The Big Combo* and *Kiss Me Deadly*. The characteristic film noir moods of claustrophobia, paranoia, despair, and nihilism constitute a world view that is expressed not through the films' terse, elliptical dialogue, nor through their confusing, often insoluble plots, but ultimately through their remarkable style.

But how can we discuss style? Without the films before us it is difficult to isolate the elements of the noir visual style and examine how they operate. Furthermore, while film critics and students would like to speak of the shots and the images, we often lack a language for communicating these visual ideas. This article is an attempt to employ in a critical context the technical terminology commonly used for fifty years by Hollywood directors and cameramen, in the hope that it might be a good step toward the implementation of such a critical language. The article is not meant to be either exhaustive or exacting. It is merely a discussion, with actual frame enlargements from the films, of some of the visual motifs of the film noir style: why they are used, how they work, and what we can call them.

The "Noir" Photographic Style: Antitraditional Lighting and Camera

In order to photograph a character in a simple, basic lighting set-up, three different kinds of light, called by

some cinematographers the "key light," "fill light," and "back light," are required. The key light is the primary source of illumination, directed on the character. The key is generally a hard direct light that produces sharply defined shadows. The fill light, placed near the camera, is a soft, diffused or indirect light that "fills in" the shadows created by the key. Finally, the back light is a direct light shining on the actor from behind, which adds interesting highlights and which has the effect of giving him form by differentiating him from the background.

The dominant lighting technique which had evolved by the early Forties is "high-key lighting," in which the ratio of key light to fill light is small. Thus the intensity of the fill is great enough to soften the harsh shadows created by the key. This gives what was considered to be an impression of reality, in which the character's face is attractively modeled, but without exaggerated or unnatural areas of darkness. Noir lighting is "low-key." The ratio of key to fill light is great, creating areas of high contrast and rich, black shadows. Unlike the even illumination of high-key lighting which seeks to display attractively all areas of the frame, the low-key noir style opposes light and dark, hiding faces, rooms, urban landscapes, and, by extension, motivations and true character, in shadow and darkness which carry connotations of the mysterious and the unknown.

The harsh lighting of the low-key noir style was even employed in the photography of the lead actresses, whose close-ups are traditionally diffused (by placing either spun glass or other diffusion over the key light, or glass diffusion or gauze over the camera lens itself) in order to show the actress to her best advantage. Far removed from the feeling of softness and vulnerability created by these diffusion techniques, the noir heroines were shot in tough, unromantic close-ups of direct, undiffused light, which create a hard, statuesque surface beauty that seems more seductive but less attainable, at once alluring and impenetrable.

The common and most traditional placement of lights, then and now, is known as the "three-quarter lighting" set-up, in which the key light is positioned high and about forty-five degrees to one side in front of the actor, and the fill is low and close to the camera. Because the attractive, balanced, harmonious face thus produced would have been antithetical to the depiction of the typical noir moods of paranoia, delirium, and menace, the noir cinematographers placed their key, fill and back light in every conceivable variation to produce the most striking and offbeat schemes of light and dark. The elimination of the fill produces areas of total black. Strange highlights are introduced, often on the faces of the sinister or demented. The key light may be moved behind and to one side of the actor and is then called the "kick light." Or it can be moved below or high above the characters to create unnatural shadows and strange facial expressions. The actors may play a scene totally in shadow, or they may be silhouetted against an illuminated background.

Above all, it is the constant opposition of areas of light and dark that characterizes film noir cinematography. Small areas of light seem on the verge of being completely overwhelmed by the darkness that now threatens them from all sides. Thus faces are shot low-key, interior sets are always dark, with foreboding shadow patterns facing the walls, and exteriors are shot "night-for-night." Night scenes previous to film noir were most often shot "day-for-night"; that is, the scene is photographed in bright daylight, but filters placed over the camera lens, combined with a restriction of the amount of light entering the camera, create the illusion of night. Night-for-night, night scenes actually shot at night, required that artificial light sources be brought in to illuminate each area of light seen in the frame. The effect produced is one of the highest contrast, the sky rendered jet black, as opposed to the gray sky of day-for-night. Although night-for-night becomes quite a bit more costly and time-consuming to shoot than day-for-night, nearly every film noir, even of the cheapest "B" variety, used night-for-night extensively as an integral component of the noir look.

Another requirement of noir photography was greater "depth of field." It was essential in many close or medium shots that focus be carried into the background so that all objects and characters in the frame be in sharp focus, giving equal weight to each. The world of the film is thus made a closed universe, with each character seen as just another facet of an unheeding environment that will exist unchanged long after his death; and the interaction between man and the forces represented by that noir environment is always clearly visible. Because of the characteristics of the camera lens, there are two methods for increasing depth of field: increasing the amount of light entering the lens, or using a lens of wider focal length. Obviously, because of the low light levels involved in the shooting of low-key and night-for-night photography, wide-angle lenses were used in order to obtain the additional depth of field required.

Opposite, direct, undiffused lighting of Barbara Stanwyck in *Double Indemnity* creates a hard-edged, mask-like surface beauty. By comparison, "hard-boiled" Fred MacMurray is lit to seem soft and vulnerable.

On page 10, silhouetted figures standing in rigid position become abstracted Modern Man and Woman in the final sequence of *The Big Combo*. The back-lighting of heavy smoke and an ominously circling light visible in the background further abstracts the environment into a modern nether world.

Beside their effect on depth of field, wide-angle lenses have certain distorting characteristics which, as noir photography developed, began to be used expressively. As faces or objects come closer to the wide lens they tend to bulge outward. (The first shot of Quinlan in *Touch of Evil* is an extreme example.) This effect is often used in noir films on close-ups of porcine gangsters or politicians, or to intensify the look of terror on the hero's face as the forces of fate close in upon him. These lenses also create the converse of the well-known "endistancing effects" of the long, telephoto lenses: wide-angle has the effect of drawing the viewer into the picture, of including him in the world of the film and thus rendering emotional or dramatic events more immediate.

The "Noir" Directorial Style: Anti-traditional Mise-en-scène

Complementary to the noir photographic style among the better-directed films is a mise-en-scène designed to unsettle, jar, and disorient the viewer in correlation with the disorientation felt by the noir heroes. In particular, compositional balance within the frame is often disruptive and unnerving. Those traditionally harmonious triangular three-shots and balanced two-shots, which are borrowed from the compositional principles of Renaissance painting, are seldom seen in the better film noir. More common are bizarre, off-angle compositions of figures placed irregularly in the frame, which create a world that is never stable or safe, that is always threatening to change drastically and unexpectedly. Claustrophobic framing devices such as doors, windows,

stairways, metal bed frames, or simply shadows separate the character from other characters, from his world, or from his own emotions. And objects seem to push their way into the foreground of the frame to assume more power than the people.

Often, objects in the frame take on an assumed importance simply because they act to determine a stable composition. Framed portraits and mirror reflections, beyond their symbolic representations of fragmented ego or idealized image, sometimes assume ominous and foreboding qualities solely because they are so compositionally prominent. It is common for a character to form constant balanced two-shots of himself and his own mirror reflection or shadow. Such compositions, though superficially balanced, begin to lose their stability in the course of the film as the symbolic Doppelgänger either is shown to lack its apparent substantiality or else proves to be a dominant and destructive alter ego. Similarly, those omnipresent framed portraits of women seem to confine the safe, powerless aspects of feminine sexuality with which the noir heroes invariably fall in love. But in the course of the film, as the forces mirrored in the painting come closer to more sinister flesh and blood, the compositions that have depended on the rectangular portrait for balance topple into chaos, the silently omniscient framed face becoming a mocking reminder of the threat of the real women.

In the use of "screen size," too, the noir directors use unsettling variations on the traditional close-up, medium and long shots. Establishing long shots of a new locale are often withheld, providing the viewer with no means of spatial orientation. Choker close-ups, framing the head or chin, are obtrusive and disturbing. These are sometimes used on the menacing heavy, other times reserved to show the couple-on-the-run whose intimacy is threatened or invaded. The archetypal noir shot is probably the extreme high-angle long shot, an oppressive and fatalistic angle that looks down on its helpless victim to make it look like a rat in a maze. Noir cutting often opposes such extreme changes in angle and screen size to create jarring juxtapositions, as with the oft-used cut from huge close-up to high-angle long shot of a man being pursued through the dark city streets.

Camera movements are used sparingly in most noir films, perhaps because of the great expense necessary to mount an elaborate tracking or boom shot, or perhaps simply because the noir directors would rather cut for effect from a close-up to a long shot than bridge that distance smoothly and less immediately by booming. What moving shots that were made seem to have been carefully considered and often tied very directly to the emotions of the characters. Typical is the shot in which the camera tracks backward before a running man, at once involving the audience in the movement and excitement of the chase, recording the terror on the character's face, and looking over his shoulder at the forces, visible or not, which are pursuing him. The cameras of Lang, Ray, and Preminger often make short tracking movements which are hardly perceptible, yet which subtly undermine a stable composition, or which slightly emphasize a character to whom we then give greater notice.

The "dark mirror" of film noir creates a visually unstable environment in which no character has a firm moral base from which he can confidently operate. All attempts to find safety or security are undercut by the anti-traditional cinematography and mise-en-scène. Right and wrong become relative, subject to the same distortions and disruptions created in the lighting and camera work. Moral values, like identities that pass in and out of shadow, are constantly shifting and must be redefined at every turn. And in the most notable examples of film noir, as the narratives drift headlong into confusion and irrelevance, each character's precarious relationship to the world, the people who inhabit it, and to himself and his own emotions, becomes a function of visual style.

The Big Heat: opposite top left, high-key lighting is used to convey normalcy, the everyday, as Glenn Ford's detective character embraces his bourgeois wife (Jocelyn Brando).

Opposite top right, in contrast low-key lighting is used for a "dame" who inhabits the "other world." Shadow areas hint at the hidden, the unknown, the sinister.

Below, Bogart's "Mad Dog" Roy Earle finally realizes it is the bruised Marie (Ida Lupino) he loves in *High Sierra*. The low-placed key light creates a stark lighting in which interior feelings of the characters are finally exposed and laid bare.

Above left, hard direct lighting on an unmade-up face creates an unpretty close-up of a bitter and cynical Cathy O'Donnell as Keechie at the beginning of *They Live by Night*. Above right, the same actress in softer light shot through a heavy diffusion filter over the camera lens. The sense of intimacy is further conveyed through use of choker close-up.

Below left, Maddie and her prisoner husband in *They Live by Night*. The opposition of areas of light and darkness in the frame separates the two characters in space. Mattie will never get her husband back after turning informer to free him. Right, Barbara Stanwyck under the rich, black sky of a night-for-night shot in *Double Indemnity*. Each illuminated area in the shot required that an artificial light source be brought in.

Below left, a choker (extreme) close-up emphasizes the grotesque face of Howard da Silva in his last scene in *They Live by Night*.

Below right, at the beginning of that film, a high-angle shot of Bowie (Farley Granger) over the shoulder of Keechie (Cathy O'Donnell) that establishes her moral superiority over him.

On this page below, one of the very few traditionally balanced two-shots of these two characters in all of *In a Lonely Place*. Bogart and Grahame experience a rare moment of safety and security. Above left, they relax and smile. This shot cuts to this upsetting two-shot (at top right) when the policeman who has been trailing the couple walks into the bar. Two characters each in tight close-up convey intimacy being invaded.

Above, despite the flat lighting, the unsettled positions in an unbalanced frame, awkwardly posing at its edge, with glances slightly off-line and hands inelegantly intertwined, undercuts the "normalcy" of the engaged couple (Dana Andrews and Joan Fontaine) in *Beyond A Reasonable Doubt*.

Below, extreme framing devices: left, differences in lighting and screen size, and action played on different planes in depth separate a man and woman in *Night and the City*. Right: lonely characters isolated by framing devices in a composition of constricting vertical and horizontal lines manage to bridge the distance between them with a dramatic diagonal of exchanged glances from both *In a Lonely Place* and *Night and the City*.

Opposite page: *In a Lonely Place*: above top left, an extreme close-up of Bogart's eyes, framed by the isolating darkness of night and the city in the credits. Bottom left, a strange high-light under Bogart's eyes injects a sinister, demented quality into his mock description of his part in the murder. Right, top and bottom, A short track-in to close two-shot expresses the fear and claustrophobia felt by Grahame.

Opposite below, Dana Andrews as Det. McPherson framed behind a cabinet in *Laura*. The powerful foreground objects seem at once constricting and symbolic of a precarious situation which threatens at any moment to shatter to the floor.

with
GLORIA GRAHAME

Left, in *The Big Heat*: Glenn Ford and Gloria Grahame are linked by the area of shadow on the wall, which creates a dark bridge between their looks. Kick-lighting in the first shot of Lee Marvin watching Bannion in the bar immediately establishes him as a heavy threatening to erupt into violence. The restriction of depth of field and the turning of his head towards the camera give his figure power and control of the frame.

Opposite, top left, bold, architectural lines carried in sharp focus over the large depth of field of a wide-angle lens minimize Richard Widmark's compositional importance. Right, as the night-club owner makes the decision to "get Harry," this low, wide-angle close-up distorts his already grotesquely fat face. Strong cross-light from the right throws unusual shadows on the left side of his face, carrying connotations of the sinister and evil.

Opposite bottom left, a low-angle shot expresses the menace of Grahame's Lesbian masseuse in *In a Lonely Place*. Bottom right, isolated by labyrinthine staircases in an extreme high-angle long shot from *Kiss Me Deadly*.

An ominous portrait, emphasized by its dominant compositional function in making a balanced two-shot, stares out over the proceedings of *Woman in the Window*. The constant mirror reflections of Joan Bennett and the other characters subtly hint at their alter egos, revealed at the end of the film when the protagonist wakes up to discover it was all a dream.

Two policemen form a dark, vertical mass not counterbalanced by the smaller, lighter horizontal figure of the punk hoodlum upon whom they are about to administer the third degree in *On Dangerous Ground.* The cops' downward looks, the position of their bodies, and the line of the bed frame create a heavy top-left to bottom-right diagonal in a precarious and unbalanced composition.

Joan Crawford as the titled character in *Mildred Pierce*.

Violence and the Bitch Goddess

Stephen Farber (1974)

There are essentially two types of violent heroes in American films, those who perform the violence sanctioned by their society (soldiers, Western sheriffs, police detectives, business tycoons) and those who direct their violence against society (criminals, delinquents, rebels, and outsiders). Of course the two characters overlap; they share some of the same qualities. But I do think some interesting distinctions can be drawn.

The respectable heroes of American films often pursue their enemies with a fierceness and intolerance harsher than their duties require. Propagandistic Second World War movies ruthlessly stereotyped the Germans and especially the Japanese, celebrated American boys for cheerfully and pitilessly eliminating the Yellow Peril. The last image of *Bataan*, Robert Taylor turning his machine gun on the Japanese, and letting go in a near orgasmic fury of "righteous" slaughter, summarizes the hideous brutality that American war movies have exalted in the name of freedom and democracy.

In a movie like *Bataan*, since the aims of the American soldiers are defined as noble, their violence must be applauded. In Westerns, which provide a mythic idealization of violence in America, the "good" hero is allowed to use any means, including murder, to eradicate the "evil" in his society. We are told that the Westerner acts only defensively, never offensively (indeed, that is generally a justification for violence in American films), but this distinction blurs very easily. The hero's right to kill is rarely brought under question. Violence in these films reflects the moralistic complacency of the figures of authority, and grows from a tendency to dehumanize those who threaten the status quo.

The same kinds of complacency and intolerance are characteristic of policemen heroes of American films. Until very recently cops have generally been secondary characters in American movies. But the phenomenally successful *Dirty Harry* and *The French Connection* have spawned a couple of dozen police movies that are often implicitly fascist in their celebration of vigilante justice and their respect for the "order" provided by a billy club.

A more popular genre over the years has been the detective story, and although the private eye has often been presented as more independent and iconoclastic than his uniformed counterpart, many of these movies also have authoritarian overtones. A particularly ugly version of the American detective was created by Mickey Spillane in the early postwar years and became the hero of several American films of the middle Fifties, the only interesting one of which was Robert Aldrich's *Kiss Me Deadly*, because it subtly criticized its own hero. Spillane's Mike Hammer is the private eye as sadistic vigilante, on a personal crusade to save America from the scourge of Communists and degenerates. Hammer makes his own laws, carries out his own vendettas, all in the name of freedom and the American Way. Brutal, merciless, anti-intellectual, Hammer flourished during the McCarthy era and carried to an ugly extreme the deep-rooted American belief that the ends justify the means.

In these genre films violence is intuitively celebrated as being consistent with the highest American ideals; violence almost seems to be the most appropriate expression of American aspirations. The drive for success is by nature violent. America exalts the rugged individualist, the self-made man who wins a place in the sun on his own initiative, regardless of the means that he uses in his struggle to the top. We reward the ruthless businessman, the robber baron, the man with a gun.

Seen in one way, the gangster film is only a dark parody of a national myth. The gangster can be understood as a mutant variation on the American rugged individualist, living a perverted version of the American Dream; he acts out the wishes and values of the successful businessman, but with the high-sounding moral rationalizations stripped away. *Scarface* contains a burlesque of the traditional entrepreneur, and this Howard Hawks' film often plays as a weird black comedy. Tony seeks the same trappings of success that respectable Americans are taught to pursue. On the way to the top he acquires a fancy apartment, an elegant lounging robe, even a secretary, in imitation of the aristocratic gangster whom he admires; in one witty scene he shows off his bullet-proof shutters to his girlfriend as if he were demonstrating gold-lamé curtains. His credo is one that most Americans would respond to: "Do it first, do it yourself, and keep on doing it." The only difference is that Scarface does it with a machine gun.

In the late Forties, prizefight movies like *Champion* and *Body and Soul* were more self-conscious attempts to comment on the violence that the success drive stimulates. The heroes of those two movies become prizefighters because they have been rejected by American society, and they express their resentment by fighting in the ring. Yet in releasing their aggressiveness, the fighters, like the gangsters, are enacting a bizarre parody of the prototypical American success story. These movies take the form of poor boy making good, and they even include the standard Hollywood montage sequences for success stories (whether backstage musicals or prestige biographies or gangster films) in which brief shots of the hero's rise to fame are cut together in crescendo rhythm to create the sense of exhilaration that attends "making it" America-style. But for the prize-

fighter, as for the gangster, success leads finally to corruption and death, for the fighter has once again made the violence implicit in the American success story too explicit. In *Champion*, when Arthur Kennedy, the goody-goody brother of the heel-hero, Kirk Douglas, criticized him for his heartlessness after he fires his first manager, Douglas replies that the prizefight business is no different from any other business in America except that it brings the blood out into the open.

In *Body and Soul* too, the fight business seems to heighten the violence that is usually more subtly manifested in America. As the evil promoter Roberts says, "It's a free country. Everything's for sale." Friends are betrayed, good women left behind, honor smothered during the fighter's ascent, and he is eventually at the mercy of the syndicate to which he has sold himself. The brutality of the prizefight racket is intended as a metaphor for the corruption of the spirit in a belligerent capitalist society; Charlie's success as a fighter turns him into a "money machine." And it is interesting that in both of these films, when the hero finally decides to take a stand against the system that has victimized him, he does it by deciding to win that fight that he has been told to lose. The only alternative to his acquiescence in the ruthless spiral of success is another act of violence; he seems hopelessly trapped.[1]

Opposite, "*Kiss Me Deadly*...criticized its own hero...brutal, merciless, anti-intellectual, Hammer (Ralph Meeker, left, with Paul Stewart)

Below, *Body and Soul*: a betrayed Peg (Lilli Palmer) slaps Charlie Davis (John Garfield), "a poor boy making good."

Above, Sam Masterson (Van Heflin) is emotionally enmeshed and driven to violence by Martha (Barbara Stanwyck) and her "heroine's viciousness" reflected in her expression as she she watches his action in *The Strange Love of Martha Ivers*. Opposite, Lana Turner as the scheming heroine at the apex of a deadly triangle completed by John Garfield (left) and Cecil Kellaway in *The Postman Always Rings Twice*.

Norman Podhoretz has written about success in an autobiographical study of his own career, *Making It* (1967): "My second purpose in telling the story of my own career is to provide a concrete setting for a diagnosis of the curiously contradictory feelings our culture instills in us toward the ambition for success, and toward each of its various goals: money, power, fame, and social position . . . On the one hand, 'the exclusive worship of the bitch-goddess SUCCESS,' as William James put it in a famous remark, 'is our national disease'; on the other hand, a contempt for success is the consensus of the national literature for the past hundred years or more. On the one hand, our culture teaches us to shape our lives in accordance with the hunger for worldly things; on the other hand, it spitefully contrives to make us ashamed of the presence of those hungers in ourselves and to deprive us as far as possible of any pleasure in their satisfaction."

These comments about the ambivalence toward success in American culture generally are closely echoed in Robert J. Warshow's provocative remarks about the gangster film, in his famous essay on "The Gangster as Tragic Hero": "At bottom, the gangster is doomed because he is under the obligation to succeed, not because the means he employs are unlawful. In the deeper layers of the modern consciousness, all means are unlawful, every attempt to succeed is an act of aggression, leaving one alone and guilty and defenseless among enemies: one is punished for success. This is our intolerable dilemma: that failure is a kind of death and success is evil and dangerous, is, ultimately, impossible."

The dream of success is pursued fiercely, but it is also haunted by intense feelings of guilt and fear, and in the imaginations of the people who dramatize American success stories, these feelings of guilt and fear find expression in images of terror and violence. The success story is most often told as a story of destruction and betrayal. The crucial American drama of "Making It" slips again and again into dark, lurid melodrama.

During the Forties particularly, many success stories were also murder stories. One interesting genre was the woman's picture. During the war years and immediately afterward, strong women flourished in American films, and were often presented as monsters and harpies, hardened by greed and lust, completely without feeling for the suffering they caused. These films undoubtedly reflected the fantasies and fears of a wartime society, in which women had taken control of many of the positions customarily held by men. Fear of the violence that may attend success is a recurring anxiety in American films, but during the war years another psychological dimension was added to this anxiety, fear of the evil, overpowering woman with a shocking ability to humiliate and emasculate her men.[2]

The Postman Always Rings Twice, for example, concerns a woman who marries an older man for the money and security he can provide, and is eventually led to murder him because he is not ambitious enough to satisfy her greed. After she and her lover murder her husband, they fix up his roadside café as a stylish garden restaurant and turn it into a flourishing business enterprise.

The same type of scheming materialistic woman is the heroine of *The Strange Love of Martha Ivers*. As a child Martha has been perverted by her aunt's greed. In a moment of rebellion, she murders her aunt and then is trapped by the deed, and by her own irrepressible love of luxury, into living out the rest of her life in an ironic tribute to her aunt's values. She becomes a hard, ruthless businesswoman who controls her weakling husband by depriving him of sex; eventually she tries to convince an old childhood flame to murder her husband. In both of these movies money and the success drive are blamed for the heroine's viciousness. Violence is the inevitable result of the evil woman's ambition.

Billy Wilder's *Double Indemnity* (1944), remarkably similar in theme, chronicles a murder plot growing from a pervasive American fantasy of outsmarting the insurance company. Walter Neff (Fred MacMurray) is a cynical insurance agent who has always toyed with the idea of cheating his company with the perfect scheme. And Phyllis Dietrichson (Barbara Stanwyck), the married woman with whom he falls in love, plays on his vanity. She lets him feel that he is making the plans and triumphing over his corporation, while all the while she is manipulating him in her own scheme to win her elderly husband's money. Her avarice is completely cold-blooded, while Walter at least acts out of passion, admittedly of a sleazy variety, as well as greed. Phyllis shows no emotion at all after the murder of her husband; her mind is racing ahead to how she will get rid of Walter so that she can have the insurance money all to herself. The diabolical woman whose only lust is greed has rarely been more chillingly rendered.

A few years later, in Anatole Litvak's *Sorry Wrong Number* (1948), Barbara Stanwyck created another memorable portrait of the domineering American wife. Leona Stevenson meets her husband Henry (Burt Lancaster) at a college dance when she cuts in on a friend who is dancing with him; she then begins to chase him quite furiously, in a complete reversal of conventional courting procedures. Leona's father is a business tycoon, the head of a major drug company, and Leona dangles the prospect of success before the working-class Henry. When she first meets him at the dance, she asks him to come for a ride in her expensive European car, and

"When she says fiercely, 'I Leona take thee, Henry,' it is a declaration not of love but of brutal possession." Burt Lancaster's Henry is possessed by Barbara Stanwyck's Leona in *Sorry, Wong Number*.

offers him a cigarette from her gold case; she seals their courtship by offering him a lucrative job with her father's company. It is at this point that he grabs her for the first time and kisses her. The "love-match" seems indistinguishable from a business match; Leona has no qualms about buying love with her wealth and position. At the marriage ceremony she recites the wedding vow with implacable determination. When she says fiercely, "I Leona take thee, Henry," it is a declaration not of love but of brutal possession. Leona claims to love Henry, but her only way of showing it is by offering riches. The film draws an interesting connection between Leona's sexual aggressiveness and her materialism, a connection that most of the Forties 'black-widow' pictures imply consciously or unconsciously.

Once they are married, Leona asserts her domination over Henry with complete pitilessness. She refuses to let him leave her father's business or even her father's house (her Oedipal fixation is a fairly ludicrous example of the pop Freudianism so prevalent in Forties movies) and constantly reminds him of his dependence on her. When he tries to fight her, she develops a phony psychosomatic heart condition to keep him at her mercy. In some measure we understand and share her husband's frustration and resentment of her domination, and we feel she almost deserves the brutal murder that he plots for her at the end of the film. It is her own ruthless possessiveness that leads to her violent death.

At the same time, Henry's ambition makes him a willing victim. He is attracted to Leona for the very qualities that later stifle him, her success, her confidence, her toughness; he clearly loves her gilded life too much to give it up, even when his dignity is smothered by her power. Recalling his humble past, Henry tells Leona's father, "I couldn't go back to Grassville." He relishes his position in her father's business, as we can see in the brief scenes that show him ordering people around in his office and in the restaurant where he has lunch. Henry is just as ambitious and ruthless as Leona; his only complaint is that he wants to make it on his own, without having to depend on her patronizing favors. He wants more than what she gives him. Both Henry and Leona are familiar American characters, the ambitious businessman on the make, the heiress of the nouveaux riches, portrayed very harshly; their values contain the seeds of violence.

Mildred Pierce (Michael Curtiz, 1945) also concerns the terrible price a woman must pay for power, wealth, and success. In this film the domineering woman is split in two: the good Mildred Pierce (Joan Crawford), the bad daughter Veda (Ann Blyth). Mildred's ambition appears to be essentially generous, she only wants the good things in life for her two daughters. But all of the horror connected with ambition is projected onto Veda; she has absorbed the poison from her mother's success drive, and she grows up a greedy, heartless monster, who eventually becomes a remorseless killer. Mildred's values have nourished murder.

Mildred makes innumerable mistakes in her struggle to provide her daughters with the material possessions that she never had. When her husband Bert loses his job, she nags him incessantly about getting a high-paying job so that she can bring up her girls in style. She wants more than anything for the girls "to amount to something." So she buys expensive piano lessons for Veda, expensive ballet lessons for Kay. As she tells Bert coldly, "Those kids come first in this house. I'm determined to do the best I can for them."

Before long she loses Bert. To keep providing for her girls, she gets a job as a waitress, but she isn't doing well enough, and she arranges to buy property to open her own restaurant. Soon she is running a chain of restaurants and is a successful Los Angeles tycoon. And she has clearly been tainted by her success; in true Hollywood fashion, the change in her appearance defines her moral transformation. Her hair is now piled on top of her head, and her clothes become more severe and more mannish, her face haughtier and colder. In the opening scenes Mildred looks soft and womanly; at the height of her success, she has the harsh glint of a frigid career woman. She treats the decadent aristocrat Monte Barrigan (Zachary Scott), from whom she bought her first piece of land, with emasculating contemptuousness. Yet when her daughter pleads for the fancy life that Monte represents, Mildred humbles herself and goes to him to propose marriage, offering him a one-third share in the business as payment. As he bends to kiss her to seal the bargain, she mutters coldly, "Sold. One Barrigan." Mildred has sold everything, her husband, her feminine warmth, even her self-respect, to give her girls the rich material life that she thinks they must have. She is clearly an accomplice in Veda's growing corruption.

Above, *Mildred Pierce*: the titled heroine discovers the betrayal of her daugher Veda and Monte (Zachary Scott), all part of "the terrible price a woman must pay for power, wealth, and success" in film noir.

Mildred Pierce warns of the punishment that shadows success. At every turn Mildred suffers for her ambition. Her younger daughter Kay dies of pneumonia. And she loses her older daughter Veda, too, to the gas chamber. She complains, "I've worked long and hard, trying to give Veda the things I never had," and her only rewards are hatred, abandonment, death. When she buys Veda a dress, Veda scorns its cheap material. After her father leaves them, Veda begs her mother to marry his crude, lecherous partner so that she will have a new house, a maid, a limousine. On learning that Mildred is a waitress, Veda cries, "How could you degrade us, Mother?" Yet Mildred persists in making sacrifices for Veda. At the end she is even willing to be executed for her daughter's crime; but the irony is that she has never won Veda's love. Veda takes everything from Mildred, even, at the end, her mother's husband, and gives nothing. The film as a whole seems almost a vulgar, unconscious Americanization of *King Lear*, the story of a woman who buys her daughter everything imaginable, only to be repaid with a withering ingratitude.

There is a furtively ambivalent attitude toward success even in this film. The most evil character in the film, aside from Veda, is slimy Monte, and his greatest sin is that he has never worked for a living. Languorous, arrogant, devious, he embodies all of the American prejudices against the man of leisure. Mildred's robustness and energy are deliberately contrasted to his indolence. In the scene in which she belittles him for his dependence on her, the film's attitude is unclear. Mildred may look preemptory and cruel to us, yet the filmmakers cannot help preferring her sturdy, homely aggressiveness to Monte's ruffled-shirt decadence.

But in the characterization of Veda the filmmakers have considered the other side of the coin; she represents all their fears about success. Ambitious Americans often justify their avarice and their aggressiveness by saying that they are doing everything for their children; and they may well be trying to escape the humiliation of their own past by giving their children the luxuries that they had imagined for themselves while growing up in poverty. In the deepest sense, Mildred is selfish, living out her own dreams of material glory vicariously, through her pampered daughters. *Mildred Pierce* makes a shrill, melodramatic, but still pertinent criticism of this American compulsion by showing that the spoiled child is a moral monster, deadened by greed and unaffected by murder. What the film seems to say, with all its contrived plot machinations it's difficult to be sure, is that the obsessions of materialistic, success-oriented parents lead to violence and corruption; the fruit of ambition is murder.

The same themes are central to the more pretentious success stories of the next few years, movies like *All The King's Men* (Robert Rossen, 1949), and *A Place in the Sun* (George Stevens, 1951). In these movies violent resolutions attest to the same fears about ambition and success as in the black widow melodramas. In *All The King's Men* both the grassroots politician Willie Stark and the intellectual newspaperman Jack Burden start small and pure, but grow increasingly corrupt on their way to the top. As is usually the case in these success stories, the transformation in Willie is not really convincingly motivated. We simply have to accept the film's assumption that, as a person becomes more famous and more powerful, he also becomes more venal and more vicious; Willie's success involves such devious and macabre betrayals that it can only result in violence. He is murdered at the height of his success by a brother of the aristocratic girl who has soiled herself by becoming Willie's mistress.

The ambivalence of *All The King's Men* toward the American success ethic can be seen in the fact that, like *Mildred Pierce*, it condemns both the ambitious common man and the decadent aristocracy. Jack Burden's family is indifferent to social problems, lazy and complacent. And although his girlfriend's family is far nobler, they too are tainted by their detachment from the crude energy of working class America. Jack sells his soul to Willie Stark, his girlfriend sells her body, her father is disgraced, her brother becomes a murderer. The aristocrats who have never worked for a living are doomed to humiliation and death. (In this film, though, there is also a very confused current of admiration for the aristocracy.) Yet the working man who rises through his own initiative is also doomed. He becomes a ruthless egomaniac; he must be destroyed. The self-made man and the rich idler are both guilty, and the world crashes down around them in violence.

I would not suggest that all of these films can be reduced to one simple theme. Three of the films I have discussed, *Double Indemnity*, *Mildred Pierce*, *The Postman Always Rings Twice*, are based upon novels by James M. Cain, and their concern with destructive materialistic women cannot be explained simply in terms of a cultural obsession. Similarly, Robert Rossen directed three films about young men on the make whose ambition leads to murder and suicide, *Body and Soul, All The King's Men, The Hustler,* and it would be naive to ignore the qualities unique to Rossen in these films. Still, there are enough American films linking success and violence to suggest that the theme is an important one to our writers and directors.

Notes

1. The picture had changed by the middle of the optimistic Fifties, when *Somebody Up There Likes Me* celebrated Rocky Graziano as a true American hero; a juvenile delinquent, army deserter, and ex-convict, anti-social Rocky "makes good" when he becomes a champion. In this film, violence is seen as perfectly consistent with moral reformation and social accommodation. In fact, socially channeled violence seems necessary to Rocky's adjustment. The irony and bitterness of the Forties fight movies toward this same phenomenon have completely disappeared.

2. In their book *Movies: A Psychological Study*, Martha Wolfenstein and Nathan Leites discussed the dominating woman as one of the central obsessions of American films of the late Forties.

"I'm nobody's friend." Robert Montgomery as Gagin, "the man with no place," speaks with government agent Retz (Art Smith) in *Ride the Pink Horse.*

No Way Out: Existential Motifs in the Film Noir

Robert G. Porfirio (1976)

The film noir, a Hollywood staple of the 1940s and 1950s, has come into its own as a topic of critical investigation. By now both its foreign and domestic roots (German expressionism, French poetic realism; the gangster film and the hard-boiled novel) have been clearly established. The mordant sensibilities of the "Germanic" emigrés and their penchant for a visual style which emphasized mannered lighting and startling camera angles provided a rich resource for a film industry newly attuned to the commercial possibilities of that hard-boiled fiction so popular in the 1930s. It was a style and sensibility quite compatible with a literature dealing with private eyes and middle-class crime, one bent on taking a tough approach towards American life. Following the success of *Double Indemnity* and *Murder, My Sweet*, both made in 1944, this "Germanic" tradition was quickly assimilated by others and the era of film noir was in full bloom. The one major domestic contribution to the style, the post-war semi-documentary, moved the film noir out of the "studio" period into new directions. The police documentaries (*T-Men, Street with No Name*), the exposés (*Captive City, The Enforcer*) and the socially oriented thrillers (*Crossfire, The Sound of Fury*) in turn gave way to films which could no longer be placed within the noir tradition (*The Line-Up, Murder, Incorporated, On the Waterfront*). It is as if the film noir tradition fragmented as its initial energies dissipated along new lines, and all but disappeared in the 1950s when audiences dwindled and Hollywood resorted to new styles, subjects and techniques.

I have refrained for a number of reasons from referring to film noir as a genre. To treat it as a genre is certainly tempting, since it simplifies the way in which it can be handled, even though it may never place the film noir within a specific semantical locus. Yet we must ground the term in some sort of adequate working definition if it is to warrant serious consideration as an object of either film or cultural history. While it sidesteps the semantical problem, a genetic definition creates a host of new ones. For one thing, the film noir cuts across many of the traditional genres: the gangster film (*White Heat*), the Western (*Pursued*), the comedy (*Unfaithfully Yours*); and this means we must create a genre out of pre-existing categories.

Though the classic gangster film preceded the film noir, there remain gangster films of this period that are quite clearly noir (*The Gangster*, 1947) and others that are clearly not (*Dillinger,* 1945). The same could be said for the suspense thriller (*Strangers on a Train* is, while *I Confess* is not). And this is equally true for the private eye, mystery or crime film,some are and some aren't. As a matter of fact, if one looks at the descriptions of these films in the trade journals of the period or speaks with some of the people involved in their production, one discovers rather quickly that the term film noir was then unknown in America and that the closest equivalent was "psychological melodrama (or thriller)." And perhaps this is the appropriate English term, since there is a psychological dimension and at least some aspect of crime (real or imagined) in every film noir that I have seen.

In his article, "The Family Tree of Film Noir," Raymond Durgnat perceptively attacks generic definition by demonstrating that film noir, unlike other genres, "takes us into the realms of classification by motif and tone." Durgnat then hastily arranges the film noir into eleven thematic categories, including over 300 titles as diverse as *King Kong* and *2001: A Space Odyssey*. From the standpoint of critical justification, however, his conception resolves nothing and creates more problems than it answers. Paul Schrader, in his "Notes on Film Noir," provides a way out by suggesting that film noir be conceived of as a specific period or cycle of films, analogous to the French new wave or Italian neo-realism: "In general, film noir refers to those Hollywood films of the 40s and early 50s which portrayed the world of dark, slick city streets, crime and corruption. Film noir is an extremely unwieldy period. It harks back to many previous periods..."

It is a period which at most lasted no longer than twenty years: from 1940 (*Stranger on the Third Floor*) roughly to 1960 (*Odds Against Tomorrow*). It is an unwieldy period because it was less self-conscious and articulated than, say, Italian neo-realism and because of the lack of precision with which it has been treated. Its extreme commerciality, particularly in the 1940s before theatre audiences dried up, meant that the film noir included large numbers of "B" films, which most scholars have refused to take seriously.

Film Noir is by nature time-bound, and it is this that makes modern "revivals," whether done in period (*Chinatown*) or not (*The Long Goodbye*), something other than what they pretend to be. But to place these films within a specific time period is not enough. Schrader was right in insisting upon both visual style and mood as criteria. Their so-called "expressionistic" style was quite literally a combination of impressionistic (i.e. technical effects) and expressionistic (i.e. mise-en-scène) techniques, which can be traced back to the period of German Expressionism. The infusion of this style into Hollywood film-making was due partly to the talents of the European emigrés and partly to the growth of the classic gangster and horror genres of the 1930s which called for such a style. But the unique development of this style in the film noir was most immediately due to *Citizen Kane*. Welles' film not only invigorated a baroque visual style which was later to characterize the period, but also provided a new psychological dimension, a morally ambiguous hero, a convoluted time structure and the use of flashback and first person narration, all of which became film noir conventions. It is no surprise that Welles later made some classic films noirs (*The Stranger*, *Lady from Shanghai*, *Touch of Evil*) and some near misses (*Journey into Fear, Mr. Arkadin*) and provided a permanent blueprint for what might now be termed RKO noir. (Edward Dmytryk, who made *Murder, My Sweet*, has reaffirmed the influence of Welles on the RKO "look"; appropriately, both he and Welles have acknowledged a debt to Murnau.)

Visual style rescued many an otherwise pedestrian film from oblivion. But it was not everything; nor was the presence of crime, in some guise, the fundamental defining motif. The 1940s saw the production of many routine thrillers which contained the requisite visual style yet fail as film noir. What keeps the film noir alive for us today is something more than a spurious nostalgia. It is the underlying mood of pessimism which undercuts any attempted happy endings and prevents the films from being the typical Hollywood escapist fare many were originally intended to be. More than lighting or photography, it is this sensibility which makes the black film black for us.

As Alfred Appel has noted in his book *Nabokov's Dark Cinema*: "What unites the seemingly disparate kinds of films noirs, then, is their dark visual style and their black vision of despair, loneliness and dread, a vision that touches an audience most intimately because it assures that their suppressed impulses and fears are shared human responses." This "black vision" is nothing less than an existential attitude towards life, and as Appel has indicated it is what unifies films as diverse as *The Maltese Falcon* (private eye), *Detour* (crime), *The Lodger* (period piece), *Brute Force* (prison film), *Woman in the Window* (psychological melodrama) and *Pursued* (Western).

In attempting to discuss some of the existential motifs in American film noir, I do not wish to tie myself too closely to the specific philosophy which evolved through the writings of successive generations of thinkers. Indeed, existentialism as a philosophical movement was largely unknown in America until after World War II, when the French variety was popularized by the writings and personal fame of two of its greatest exponents, Jean-Paul Sartre and Albert Camus. William Barrett, in his excellent book *Irrational Man* (1962), argues that initially existentialism went against the positivist bias of Anglo-American culture: "The American has not yet assimilated psychologically the disappearance of his own geographical frontier, his spiritual horizon is still the limitless play of human possibilities, and as yet he has not lived through the crucial experience of human finitude." If existentialism did gain a foothold in post-war America, it was only after this optimism had been successively challenged by the Depression; the rise of totalitarianism; the fear of Communism; the loss of insular security; and, finally, the tarnishing of the ideal of individual initiative with the growth of the technocratic state. Even French existentialism, so closely tied to the underground Resistance and prison camps, represented an earlier response to many of the same challenges of the integrity of self.

Existentialism is another term which defies exact definition. As a philosophical school of thought it has included both Christian and atheist, conservative and Marxist. For our purposes, it is best to view it as an attitude characteristic of the modern spirit, a powerful and complex cultural movement erupting somewhere on the edges of the Romantic tradition, and therefore a result of some of the same cultural energies which led to surrealism, expressionism and literary naturalism. Existentialism is an outlook which begins with a disoriented individual facing a confused world that he cannot accept. It places its emphasis on man's contingency in a world where there are no transcendental values or moral absolutes, a world devoid of any meaning but the one man himself creates. Its more positive aspect is captured in such key phrases as "freedom," "authenticity," "responsibility" and "the leap into faith (or the absurd)." Its negative side, the side to which its literary exponents are most closely drawn, emphasizes life's meaninglessness and man's alienation; its catch-words include "nothingness," "sickness," "loneliness," "dread," "nausea." The special affinity of the film noir for this aspect of existentialism

Opposite, "The streets were dark with something more than night..." Edward G. Robinson in *Woman in the Window.*

Top right: Germanic angles and moods of film noir: Laird Cregar in John Brahm's *The Lodger* and Joan Crawford in *Possessed* (center).

Right, the prison as microcosm: Burt Lancaster in *Brute Force.*

is nowhere better evidenced than in a random sampling of some of its most suggestive titles: *Cornered, One Way Street, No Way Out, Caged, The Dark Corner, In a Lonely Place.*

In *The Myth of Sisyphus*, Camus recognized that the confrontation of life's emptiness made suicide a dangerous and tempting escape. To withstand this temptation, Camus and Sartre offered a few alternatives: a stubborn perseverance despite the absurdity of existence; a recognition of the community of men; an obsession with social justice; a commitment to Marxism. In an early film noir, *I Wake Up Screaming* (1941), the ostensible heavy, police Lieutenant Ed Cornell, demonstrates just this sort of perseverance. While interrogating the sister (Betty Grable) of the murdered girl he worshipped from afar, he responds to her question ("What's the use of living without hope?") with the telling reply, "It can be done." Sensitively portrayed by Laird Cregar, Cornell is no lout but a skilled detective, a man of some taste and intelligence. He becomes the ironic victim of the perfidy of a girl unworthy of his love (Carole Landis) and of the unyielding demand for professional perfection placed upon him by the police department. Unlike most of Camus' heroes, Cornell yields to the temptation of suicide, but remains a pathetic figure capable of engaging our sympathies.

It would be untenable to assert that the American film noir was directly affected by the writings of the European existentialists, although after the end of the war there were a few films like *Brute Force*, which in its use of a prison as microcosm and in the fascist nature of its major antagonist indicates a familiarity with French existential novels. In any case, such attempts on the part of Hollywood to borrow directly from that European tradition would have been rare indeed, particularly in the 1940s. It is more likely that this existential bias was drawn from a source much nearer at hand, the hard-boiled school of fiction without which quite possibly there would have been no film noir. Unfortunately, "hard-boiled" is but one more example of a popular term used rather ambiguously. It includes not only the writers of the Black Mask school, but also an extremely diverse group of major and minor talents: Hemingway, whom many consider to be the real father of the tradition; the pure "tough" writers like James M. Cain and Horace McCoy; and even the radical proletarian writers like B. Traven, Albert Maltz and Daniel Fuchs.[1] Scant critical attention has been paid to the literary tough guys, who have been forced to join the other "boys in the back room" (as Edmund Wilson once pejoratively termed some of them). Since they worked within narrow genres, set themselves limited goals and wrote fiction geared for a mass market, they lacked the elitist respectability of their famous Jazz Age predecessors. Although a few have recently come into their own, that they were taken seriously at all in the past was largely due to their association with the much brighter light of Hemingway's reputation and to the unique and almost symbiotic relationship which they had with the French existential writers. The very term film noir was coined in 1946 by the cinéaste Nino Frank from Marcel Duhamel's famous "Série Noire" book series.

Perhaps André Gide was not being completely candid when he surprised some American dignitaries at a party held during World War II by telling them that Dashiell Hammett was the one contemporary American novelist worthy of serious consideration, because he was the only one who kept his work free of the pollution of moral judgments. In any case, the virtue that Gide attributed to Hammett is present in his fiction, and the American intellectual community is no longer quite so willing to write off the adulation of their counterparts in France for such writers as some sort of foreign aberration.

It is not necessary to go further here in establishing connections between European existentialism and the hard-boiled literary tradition. If, as William Barrett suggests, existentialism is foreign to the generally optimistic and confident outlook of American society, then the vast popularity of the hard-boiled writers of the 1930s went far to "soften" this confidence and prepare audiences for a new sort of pessimistic film which would surface in the 1940s. Keeping in mind the debt to this literary tradition, here then are some of the major existential motifs of the film noir.

The Non-heroic Hero

The word "hero" never seems to fit the noir protagonist, for his world is devoid of the moral framework necessary to produce the traditional hero. He has been wrenched from familiar moorings, and is a hero only in the modern sense in which that word has been progressively redefined to fit the existential bias of contemporary

Above left, detachment: Bogart's Sam Spade sending Brigid (Mary Astor) "over" in *The Maltese Falcon*.
Right, "Some day fate can put the finger on you...": Tom Neal in *Detour*.

Below, "Everybody dies...": Burt Lancaster in *The Killers*.

Above left, Hemingway's tough guys: Charles McGraw and William Conrad in *The Killers*.

Right, passivity and neurosis: Robert Mitchum and Robert Ryan in *The Racket*.

Opposite, another "stoic stance" Alan Ladd's Raven impassively confronts his physically imposing employer in *This Gun for Hire*.

fiction. For the past fifty years we have groped for some term that would more aptly describe such a protago-nist: the Hemingway hero; the anti-hero; the rebel hero; the non-hero.

In one respect the Sam Spade of Huston's *The Maltese Falcon* (1941), as portrayed by Humphrey Bogart, is the least typical noir hero since he is the least vulnerable. Unlike Warner Brothers' first two attempts at the novel (1931 and 1936), this third is quite faithful to both the letter and the spirit of the Hammett original. The film's one unfortunate omission is the Flitcraft parable Spade tells Brigid O'Shaughnessy, for this is our only chance to peep into Spade's interior life. And what it reveals is that Spade is by nature an existentialist, with a strong conception of the randomness of existence. Robert Edenbaum sees Spade as representative of Hammett's "daemonic" tough guy: "...He is free of sentiment, of the fear of death, of the temptations of money and sex. He is what Albert Camus calls 'a man without memory,' free of the burden of the past. He is capable of any action, without regard to conventional morality, and thus is apparently as amoral...as his antagonists. His refusal to submit to the trammels which limit ordinary mortals results in a godlike immunity and independ-ence, beyond the power of his enemies...[but] the price he pays for his power is to be cut off behind his own self-imposed masks, in an isolation that no criminal, in a community of crime, has to face."[2]

If the film's conclusion mitigates a little the bleak isolation of Hammett's Spade, it maintains the "daemon-ic" qualities of his nature through the sinister aspect of Bogart's persona, so apparent in his final confrontation with Brigid (Mary Astor). In Huston's ending, Spade's ability to dismiss the falcon, the one object of "faith" in the story, as "the stuff that dreams are made of" shows him to be more detached than almost any Hemingway hero. This stoic stance would be emulated, but seldom equaled, by many of the actors who dominated the period: by Bogart himself (*Dead Reckoning, Dark Passage*), followed in rapid succession by Alan Ladd (*This Gun for Hire, The Glass Key*) and a veritable army of tough guys, Edmond O'Brien, Robert Mitchum, Robert Ryan, Richard Widmark, Burt Lancaster, Kirk Douglas. By their physical make-up, their vocal qualities and their dress, as well as by the dialogue given them, these actors defined the tough guy regardless of whether they played detective or criminal. They also suggested varying degrees of vulnerability.

Critics have reminded us that the Hemingway hero is a person "to whom something has been done"; that most central to this hero is the loss, and an awareness of it, of all the fixed ties that bind a man to a community. This is an apt description of the film noir hero as well, and a real strength of Hollywood's studio system was to cast to type. Vulnerability and a sense of loss were suggested in Humphrey Bogart's lined face and slightly bent posture; in Alan Ladd's short stature and a certain feminine quality about his face; in the passivity and the heavy-lidded eyes of Robert Mitchum; in the thinly veiled hysteria that lay behind many of Richard Widmark's performances; in Robert Ryan's nervous manner. But this vulnerability was perhaps best embodied in the early screen persona of Burt Lancaster, whose powerful physique ironically dominated the cinematic frame. Unlike the expansive and exaggerated characterizations of later years, the Lancaster of the film noir kept his energy levels under rigid control, rarely extending himself and then only to withdraw quickly like a hunted animal. Fittingly, his first screen role was in the Robert Siodmak version of *The Killers* (1946) as the Hemingway character Ole Anderson who passively awaits death at the hands of the hired assassins. Throughout the 1940s Lancaster was adept at capturing the pathos of a character victimized by society (*Brute Force; Kiss the Blood Off My Hands*) or by a woman (*The Killers; Sorry, Wrong Number; Criss Cross*).

As the period progressed, film noir heroes seemed to become increasingly vulnerable and subject to pres-

sures beyond their control. Bogart's roles moved from the lonely but impervious Sam Spade to the equally lonely but much less stable Dixon Steele of *In a Lonely Place*. The role of the detective shows the same sort of degeneration, and some succumbed to the corrupt world, becoming criminals themselves (Fred MacMurray in *Pushover*). This malaise is best seen in *The Dark Corner* (1946), whose detective Bradford Galt (Mark Stevens) strives to maintain personal integrity and hard-nosed style by mouthing the obligatory tough dialogue ("I'm as clean as a hard-boiled egg"). But it's not really enough, and Galt's angst is reflected in this cry: "I feel all dead inside...I'm backed up in a dark corner and I don't know who's hitting me!" Yet the typical noir protagonist wearily goes on living, seldom engaging in the kind of self-pity displayed by Dana Andrews' con man in *Fallen Angel* (1945) or his wayward cop in *Where the Sidewalk Ends* (1950).

The mise-en-scène of the film noir reinforced the vulnerability of its heroes. Although the habitat of the 1930s gangster was "the dark, sad city of the imagination," the gangster hero himself was generally well illuminated by a bright key-light, though his surroundings may have fallen off into darkness. Not so in the film noir. The hero moved in and out of shadows so dark as at times to obscure him completely; diagonal and horizontal lines "pierced" his body; small, enclosed spaces (a detective's office, a lonely apartment, a hoodlum's hotel bedroom), well modulated with some sort of "bar" motif (prison bars, shadows, bed posts and other furniture), visually echoed his entrapment. Small wonder that he found it hard to maintain any degree of rational control.

Alienation and Loneliness

The concept of alienation is crucial to most existentialists from Kierkegaard to Sartre. For them, man stands alone, alienated from any social or intellectual order, and is therefore totally self-dependent. We have seen how this alienation "works" for the private detective. By keeping emotional involvement to a minimum, the detective gains a degree of power over others but pays the price in terms of loneliness.

To a large degree, every noir hero is an alienated man. Even members of the police force or F.B.I. in the semi-documentary films are cut off from the camaraderie of their colleagues and forced to work undercover. The noir hero is most often "a stranger in a hostile world." In *Ride the Pink Horse*, the disillusioned veteran Gagin (Robert Montgomery) is referred to as "the man with no place," and he tells a local villager: "I'm nobody's friend." Even ostensibly happily married men (Edward G. Robinson in *Woman in the Window*, Dick Powell in *Pitfall*) become alienated from the comforts of home, usually for the sake of a beautiful woman. The homelessness of such characters as Harry Fabian (Richard Widmark) of *Night and the City* or Ole Anderson of *The Killers*, like that of an inhabitant of one of Robert Frost's bleakest winter landscapes, takes on almost cosmic dimensions. This estrangement is recapitulated in the mise-en-scène: bare rooms, dimly lit bars, dark, rain-soaked streets. In the shocking last sequence of *Scarlet Street*, the utter isolation of Chris Cross (Robinson) is underscored by means of an optical trick, all the people in the crowded street disappear from view, and we realise that for him they do not exist.

Sometimes the estrangement of the hero moves to even darker rhythms. Shubunka (Barry Sullivan), the title character of *The Gangster*, is reminiscent of Dostoevsky's "Underground Man" in his bitterness and the contempt he holds for his fellow men. In the prologue he tells the audience: "I knew everything I did was low and rotten. What did I care what people thought of me. I despised them." In the course of the film we find he despises himself almost as much; and at the end, betrayed by the one person he loved (Belita), he allows the syndicate figure who has wrested control of his rackets from him to shoot him down in the rain-soaked street. But before he dies, Shubunka delivers one of the most vitriolic speeches in the annals of film noir: "My sins are that I wasn't tough enough. I should have trusted no one; never loved a girl. I should have smashed [the others] first. That's the way the world is."

Even more misanthropic is Roy Martin (Richard Basehart), the elusive killer of *He Walked By Night*. A master of technology which rivals the police department's, Martin remains little more than a cipher and his motives for becoming a thief and a killer are unclear. Basehart's laconic performance contributed to this ambiguity (as, perhaps, do deficiencies of script and budget). Living alone in a darkened room in a typical Hollywood court, his only companion a small dog, he is literally the underground man, using the sewers as a means of travel and escape. Intelligent men like Shubunka and Martin are no mere victims of a slum environment; their criminality is rather the result of a conscious choice made sensible by the world they inhabit. For them, as for Sartre's characters in *No Exit*, "Hell is other people."

The major female protagonists of the film noir were no more socially inclined than the men. The "femme noire" was usually also a femme fatale, and a host of domineering women, castrating bitches, unfaithful wives and black widows seemed to personify the worst of male sexual fantasies. They were played with an aura of unreality by such actresses as Ava Gardner, Rita Hayworth or Gene Tierney, but perhaps most typically by Barbara Stanwyck and Claire Trevor. Even when the heroine was sweet and good (Ida Lupino in *On Dangerous Ground*, Joan Bennett in *The Reckless Moment*), she was for the most part a monad, unwilling or unable to avail herself of the benefits of society.

Existential Choice

The precipitous slide of existentialism toward nihilism is only halted by its heavy emphasis on man's freedom. In exchange for this benefit, the individual must be willing to cast aside the weight of outmoded beliefs in a tough recognition of the meaninglessness of existence. He must choose, in other words, between "being and nothingness," between the "authentic" and "inauthentic" life. The inauthentic life is the unquestioned one which derives its rationale from a facile acceptance of those values external to the self. To live authentically, one must reject these assurances and therein discover the ability to create one's own values; in so doing each individual assumes responsibility for his life through the act of choosing between

Top right, Mark Stevens in *The Dark Corner*: "...I'm backed up in a dark corner and I don't know who's hitting me."

Center, Edward G. Robinson in *Scarlet Street*: visual "echoes of entrapment" in the shadows and bars of the setting.

Right, a Man under Sentence of Death: Henry Fonda as the self-imprisoned killer in *The Long Night*.

two alternatives. And since man is his own arbiter, he literally creates good and evil.

For the most viable of the noir heroes this element of choice is readily apparent. The private eye exercises this choice in his willingness to face death, prompted only by a sense of duty towards rather dubious clients and a somewhat battered concept of integrity and professionalism. But what of the innocent victims, the fugitives from the law, and the criminals who often function as central protagonists? Existential freedom for them is much less apparent. Yet even the most victimized among them (like Edmond O'Brien in *D.O.A.* or Tom Neal in *Detour*) have some opportune moments to make choices which will affect their lives. With respect to the fugitives (John Dall and Peggy Cummins in *Gun Crazy*) and middle-class criminals (MacMurray in *Double Indemnity*), their choices appear more mundane than metaphysical and their acts less clearly rebellious against established conventions. Yet all are aware of these conventions, and their decision to disregard them indicates their willingness to live lives untrammelled by moral norms. They exist in a fluid world whose freedom is rather concretely embodied in sex, money, power and the promise of adventure. Thus, one may be motivated by the exhilaration of living dangerously (*Gun Crazy*), another by a desire to "beat the system" (*Double Indemnity*), others by a desire to break out of pedestrian daily routine and boredom (Robinson in *Woman in the Window*, Dick Powell in *Pitfall*, Van Heflin in *The Prowler*). Like Spade's Flitcraft, they can either fall back into the security of their former roles or make the leap into the absurd, take the gamble in which the stakes are their very lives.

Man Under Sentence of Death

Although many existentialists affirm that every act and attitude of man must be considered a choice, the existential attitude itself is not so much chosen as arrived at. Perhaps this is why the heroes of existential fiction are so perennially faced with the threat of imminent death; certainly such a threat forces the individual to re-examine his life. "The fable of the man under the sentence of death, writing to us from his prison cell or from the cell of his isolated self, is one of the great literary traditions." In a perceptive essay in *Tough Guy Writers of the 30s*, Joyce Carol Oates goes on to demonstrate the relevance of this undeniably existential situation to the fiction of James M. Cain, but its relevance to the film noir is equally apparent. Instead of writing his story, the hero tells it to us directly, and the combined techniques of first person narration and flashback enhance the aura of doom. It is almost as if the narrator takes a perverse pleasure in relating the events leading up to his current crisis, his romanticization of it heightened by his particular surroundings; a wounded man dictating in a darkened office (*Double Indemnity*); an ex-private detective in a dimly lit car telling his fiancée about his sordid past (Robert Mitchum in *Out of the Past*); a prisoner in a cell about to be executed (John Garfield in *The Postman Always Rings Twice*); an accountant dying from the irreversible effects of an exotic poison, trying to explain his "murder" and the vengeance he has exacted for it to a police captain (Edmond O'Brien in *D.O.A.*). One hero, Joe Gillis (William Holden) of *Sunset Boulevard*, is even able to look back upon a life that has been completed, like a character out of Sartre's *No Exit*, beginning his story as a corpse floating face-downwards in a swimming pool.

Like the Hemingway hero, most film noir protagonists fear death but are not themselves afraid to die; indeed a good deal of what dignity they possess is derived from the way they react to the threat of death. That the way one dies is important is seen in Philip Marlowe's special admiration for Harry Jones (Elisha Cook, Jr.), the frightened little crook who takes the poison offered him with grim laughter rather than betray his girl friend (*The Big Sleep*). It is seen in the manner in which Cody Jarrett (James Cagney) in *White Heat* spits out: "I made it, Ma. Top of the world!" just before he ignites the gasoline tank on which he is perched. It is seen in the way the Swede spends those last lonely moments in his hotel room after his refusal to run (*The Killers*). The boxer in *Body and Soul* (John Garfield) puts it best when he tells the racketeer he has just crossed: "So what are you going to do kill me? Everybody dies."

Meaninglessness, Purposelessness, the Absurd

The meaninglessness of man's existence flows naturally from existentialism's emphasis on individual consciousness and its key denial of any sort of cosmic design or moral purpose. For Camus it involved a recognition of the "benign indifference" of the world, and ultimately a reclamation of a measure of dignity through the sheer persistence of living on despite life's absurdity. This sense of meaninglessness is also present in film noir, but there it is not the result of any sort of discursive reasoning. Rather it is an attitude which is worked out through mise-en-scène and plotting. The characters confined to the hermetic world of the films move to a scenario whose driving force is not the result of the inexorable workings of tragic fate or powerful natural forces, but of a kind of pure, Heraclitean flux. Look at the plot of almost any film noir and you become aware of the significant role played by blind chance: a car parked on a manhole cover prevents the protagonist's escape and he is shot down by police in the sewers (*He Walked By Night*); an accountant notarizes a bill of sale and is poisoned for this innocent act (*D.O.A.*); a feckless youth is hypnotized into becoming the instrument of a murderer's devious plans simply because he accepted a cough drop in a crowded elevator (*Fear in the Night*, 1947; also *Nightmare*, 1956); a spinsterish psychology professor agrees to have dinner with one of her students and ends up killing him (*The Accused*). Such a list could go on endlessly, but these examples should indicate that such randomness is central to the noir world. The hero of *Detour* (Tom Neal) tells us: "Some day fate, or some mysterious force, can put the finger on you or me for no reason at all."

Chaos, Violence, Paranoia

The pre-existential world of the classical detective was ordered and meaningful; social aberrations were temporary and quickly righted through the detective's superior powers of deductive reasoning. A product of a rather smug Western society, such a world reflected a Victorian sense of order and a belief in the supremacy of science. The hard-boiled writers replaced this with a corrupt, chaotic world where the detective's greatest asset was the sheer ability to survive with a shred of dignity. Raymond Chandler described this world as a "wet emptiness" whose "streets were dark with something more than night." For most existentialists, the real world was equally inchoate and senseless. Sartre himself found the physical world, the world of "things-in-themselves,"[3] slightly disgusting and he associated it with images of softness, stickiness, viscosity, flabbiness. When, for example, Roquentin discovers existence in the experience of disgust in *Nausea,* it is a disgust engendered by the excessiveness of the physical world, represented by a chestnut tree with thick, tangled roots. For Sartre this world was disgusting precisely because it was too rich, too soft, too effusive; behind it lay the Jungian archetype of nature, the fertile female.

The film noir best expressed this effusiveness visually through a variety of techniques, the most important of which is the use of deep focus or depth-staging (here, perhaps, the primary influence of Orson Welles). As André Bazin pointed out, the use of this technique (as opposed to the shallow focus and "invisible" editing of Hollywood films of the 1930s) permitted the cinema more nearly to approximate the "real" world by allowing

"Hell is other people..." James Mason in Max Ophuls' *The Reckless Moment*, a film in which mise-en-scène characteristically creates environment.

the spectator to pick and choose from a wealth of stimuli. Deep focus was an important element of the noir visual style until changing conditions and production techniques in the 1950s brought the film noir period to a close. In conjunction with chiaroscuro and other expressionistic touches, deep focus helped to create a cinematic world which in its own way embodied those very qualities—decadence, corpulence, viscosity—that Sartre found so disgusting in the physical world. It was a cinematic world that was dark, oppressive, cluttered and corrupt; characterized by wet city streets, dingy apartments and over-furnished mansions, but above all by an atmosphere thick with the potential for violence. In *T-Men*, for example, an undercover agent (Dennis O'Keefe) shares a nondescript hotel room with a couple of thugs, their virtual prisoner. In one scene, deep focus allows us to keep in view the threatening, brutal figure of Moxy (Charles McGraw) in the background shaving, while the agent is in another room in the extreme foreground, trying to read unobserved a note warning him to flee for his life. In this one sequence, the whole unstable and menacing world of the film noir is brilliantly caught.

Camus said that "at any street corner the absurd may strike a man in the face." Given the special ambience of film noir, the absurd often takes the form of an undercurrent of violence which could literally strike a man at any moment: a trench-coated figure beneath a street lamp; a car parked on a dark side street; a shadow hiding behind a curtain. The atmosphere is one in which the familiar is fraught with danger and the existential tonalities of "fear" and "trembling" are not out of place; even less that sense of "dread" which is taken to mean a pervasive fear of something hauntingly indeterminate. And just as existentialism itself was partly a response to a war-torn Europe, so too was the disquietude of post-war America (the Communist threat, the Bomb) reflected in the films' fear-ridden atmosphere. Finally, if the Jungian archetype of the female lurks behind Sartre's conception of the natural world, she is equally present in the image of the city conveyed in these films, the city, that is, which Jung himself characterized as a "harlot." For the film noir protagonist the city is both mother and whore, and the stylized location photography of such semi-documentaries as *Cry of the City* or *The Naked City* adeptly captures its essential corruption and oppressiveness.

Sanctuary, Ritual and Order

Set down in a violent and incoherent world, the film noir hero tries to deal with it in the best way he can, attempting to create some order out of chaos, to make some sense of his world. For the detective, of course, this goes with the territory, but it is attempted with an equal sense of urgency by the amnesiac (*Somewhere in the Night*), the falsely accused (*The Blue Dahlia*), the innocent victim (*D.O.A.*), or the loyal wife or girl friend

Hemingway's "A Clean, Well-lighted Place." is epitomized in the offices of Philip Marlowe: Dick Powell as the investigator in *Murder, My Sweet* and Robert Montgomery in *Lady in the Lake*.

(*Woman on the Run, Phantom Lady*). Given the nature of the noir world, the attempt is seldom totally successful, and convoluted time structures, flashbacks and plots that emphasize action over rational development do nothing to help.

The Hemingway hero may withdraw to the sanctuary of the country or a café; or he may lean heavily on the ritualistic aspects of sport or art as a way of assuaging his pain and finding some order in his life. The noir hero does likewise, but he has far fewer resources to work with. There is no "country" left,[4] only the modern wasteland of such cities as New York, San Francisco and Los Angeles. And art is no longer redemptive: it is a measure of the decadence and avariciousness of the rich (*Laura, The Dark Corner*), or an affectation of refinement on the part of syndicate chiefs (*The Chase, The Big Heat*) or the criminally insane (*The Unsuspected, Crack Up*). In any case, its healing powers are lost to artist (*Phantom Lady, The Two Mrs. Carrolls*) and detective (*The Big Sleep, Kiss Me Deadly*) alike. There are still a few restorative rituals remaining to the film noir hero, in particular the private eye: sometimes they are little things like rolling a cigarette (Spade) or pouring and downing a drink (Marlowe); sometimes bigger, like taking a beating or facing death. And in the hands of actors endowed with a special grace (a Humphrey Bogart or Dick Powell), such ceremonies as smoking or drinking take on sacramental overtones.

The only sanctuary left for the hero is his Spartan office or apartment room, and he goes back there for spiritual renewal just as surely as Nick Adams goes back to the country. This is why Sam Spade almost loses control when the police confront him in his own living quarters. When doomed men like Walter Neff in *Double Indemnity* (Fred MacMurray) or Al Roberts in *Detour* (Tom Neal) withdraw to a darkened office or a small diner, they are reminiscent of the older waiter in Hemingway's "A Clean, Well-lighted Place." They can use the quiet and solitude to try to order their lives (and note that Roberts does not want to talk or listen to the juke box); they are like artists trying to carve an aesthetic order out of the diffuse materials of existence. And what they have created is quite temporary, no more than a "momentary stay against confusion."

Given a rather broad range of heroes and situations in the film noir, it is of course always dangerous to generalize. I have tried in this article to avoid the facile generalization, to take note of exceptions where they exist, and above all to remain faithful to the essence of the film noir. The period of the film noir was an extremely important one in American film history and had a profound effect on the later evolution of American cinema. It is of course impossible to do it justice in an article of this length. My rather narrow intention here has been to indicate the necessity of a critical reappraisal, following a lead established some years ago by Paul Schrader in the hope of opening up an approach to the subject which would free us of some of the semantical entanglements of the past.

Notes

1. Together with the "tough" writers, like Hammett, Chandler, McCoy and Cain, "proletarian" authors Fuchs, Bezzerides, Maltz and others were part of the literary exodus to Hollywood in the 1930s and 1940s. Many became friends or part of a radical colony there, but by and large the films noirs they were associated with exhibit more of an existential than a radical outlook (*Thieves' Highway* is a good example); a result no doubt of the political climate in America at the time.

2. "The Poetics of the Private Eyes," in *Tough Guy Writers of the Thirties*, edited by David Madden. (Carbondale, Illinois, 1968).

3. Sartre's particular dualistic system divides the world into two spheres: the objective, which exists quite apart from our minds, he termed "Being-in-itself"; the subjective, which is co-extensive with the realm of consciousness, he termed "Being-for-itself." It is the first that he found slightly repellent.

4. There are a few instances in which films noirs were not set in a city. But even here the setting does not prove to be any more redemptive: it is a swamp in *Gun Crazy*, a French province seething with repressed passions in *So Dark the Night*, unregenerate or oppressive Mexican towns in *Ride the Pink Horse* and *Touch of Evil*.

A proletarian fatal woman Anna (Yvonne de Carlo) watch-es Steve Thompson (Burt Lancaster) spread mayonnaise on his sandwich in director Robert Siodmak's *Criss Cross*.

Film Noir: A Modest Proposal

James Damico (1978)

Lamentably, the literature on film noir[1] is notable not only for its skimpiness, but for an absence of any truly rigorous or meaningful examination of its subject. Beyond sketchy and perfunctory assumptions concerning possible political and social causes, the bulk of the literature is taken up with a generally undisciplined cataloguing of what individual authors consider the thematic and stylistic consistencies of those films they term FN.

More disconcerting than the meagerness of volume, to be sure, is the lack of depth. There is as yet no book-length study of FN in English and, as far as I know, only in French.[2] The commentary that does exist, moreover, is composed primarily of oblique analyses and passing acknowledgments of FN in survey works which take either a film historical or popular socio-psycho-mythological point of view; cursory and often euphemistic references to FN in overviews of the work of individual directors; and lastly, writings which, largely through emphasis on director, actor, screenwriter or source author, intend in some fashion to deal with the classification itself.

Books written for a broad public, such as Michael Wood's *America at the Movies*[3] and Barbara Deming's *Running Away From Myself*[4] whose purpose is to examine film as a purveyor of popular myth and thus to suggest the cinema's social and psychological effect on and reflection of its audience, contain some pertinent notions about the social content of films in general and some perceptive insights into FN in particular, especially as to the cumulative meaning and effect of continuities of characters and situations from film to film. But they hardly take note of FN as a distinct entity and are obviously less interested in defining what distinguishes FN from other categories of film than in demonstrating how all films are alike.

Similarly, the popular film histories that recognize FN tend to accept extracinematic influences upon it as a given, or to treat the world as if it were merely a very large movie theater, as, for instance, Charles Higham and Joel Greenberg do in their sole attempt to situate FN in any context broader than other Hollywood films:

> A genre deeply rooted in the nineteenth century's vein of grim romanticism, developed through U.F.A. and the murky, fog-filled atmosphere of pre-war French movies, flowered in Hollywood as the great German or Austrian expatriates, Lang, Siodmak, Preminger, Wilder, arrived there and were allowed more and more freedom to unleash their fantasies on the captive audience.[5]

This is dubious history from many perspectives, but in principle it is indicative of a prevalent attitude towards the formation of FN evident in presumably more sophisticated works such as Colin McArthur's generic study of the gangster film, *Underworld USA*,[6] and Lawrence Alloway's *Violent America*[7] (which is primarily concerned with proposing American films as a formulaic and iconographic art). Both have intelligent and useful things to say about their central subjects and about elements of FN, Alloway on the violence that is integral to the category and McArthur on its recurrent structures. But Alloway, for example, is willing to assert, without the slightest attempt at demonstration, that "the vernacular existentialism that thrived in violent movies of the later 40s [derived] from the Resistance of Jean-Paul Sartre." (p. 25); while McArthur, equally unhindered by documentation, rehearses what has become a litany as the generating causes of FN:

> ...the great crash on Wall Street in 1929, the Depression and the rise of Fascism in Europe can be seen to have influenced the American cinema in general in its production...However, this obvious interest in the workings of society was accompanied, indeed stimulated, by a general mood of fear and insecurity, by the feeling that the formerly rigid laws of politics and economics were dissolving and that the

future involved only uncertainty. It seems reasonable to suggest the loneliness and angst and the lack of clarity about the characters' motives in the thriller. It seems reasonable, too, to suggest that its continuance into the post-war period was stimulated by the uncertainty of the Cold War, that its misogyny was connected with the heightened desirability and concomitant suspicion of women back home experienced by men at war, and its obvious cruelty was related to the mood of a society to whom the horrors of Auschwitz and Hiroshima and other atrocities of the Second World War had just been revealed." (pp. 66-67).

Reasonable as suggestions, perhaps, but, like most of his colleagues in the field, the author goes on to adopt these bare contentions innocent of any proofs as the basis of a comprehensive understanding of the root causes of what amounted to a significant social phenomenon. This is either to thumb one's nose at rational investigation or to risk making the most egregious errors of misapprehension.

The same order of breezy assumption seems to have afflicted FN criticism from its beginnings. In an apparent effort to provide historical, political and economic background on Hollywood film production, Borde and Chaumeton, who otherwise concentrate on impressionistic and often provocative readings of films and film groupings over a considerable time span, are given to periodic, casual declarations of such sweeping character as, in the case of films like *This Gun for Hire* and *Murder, My Sweet*, "for reasons that seem financial, cinema was under total submission to literature" (p. 19); or that because "from 1939 on, the names of many Hollywood producers were found on the subscription list of *The Psychoanalytical Review,*" the "cinema was not slow to profit from it" and to produce a cycle of films in which psychoanalysis figured in some manner (pp. 21-22). Though the subscription information is documented and thus at least constitutes solid data, it is hardly substantial enough to support the weight of the conclusion with which Borde and Chaumeton burden it.

The worst offender in this regard is Raymond Durgnat in his unfortunately influential article, "Paint It Black: The Family Tree of the Film Noir."[8] Certainly breezy and totally free of substantiation are such shot-from-the-lip, mentally convoluted Durgnat-isms as: "Late '40s Hollywood is blacker than '30s precisely because its audience, being more secure, no longer needed cheering up" (p. 73 above); "American weakness in [film] social realism stems from post-puritan optimistic individualism" (p. 75); and Senator Joseph "McCarthy's impact forced film noir themes to retreat to the Western" (p. 78). Durgnat's most baneful influence, however, has operated not in this area, but with regard to a process of aesthetic analysis which seems to me to require a higher priority in the examination of FN than even the critical matter of the category's socio-historical contexts.

Nearly all of the literature on FN, and especially that which addresses the classification directly, though often explicitly remarking on the inherent dangers, ignores and inevitable risks foundering on the Scylla and Charybdis of the dual question fundamental to a complete understanding of the category: whether FN can be considered a genre, and if not, on precisely what basis does its cohesiveness as a category rest. Among those authors who openly confront the question, it is all likelihood FN cannot be a genre (one of the few but frequently advanced arguments being that FN operates transgenerically, it therefore cannot itself constitute a genre; not unassailable logic, which by analogy would preclude an orange from remaining an orange because it is also part of a tangerine). In any event, these authors continue, though obviously of some eventual significance, the question may conveniently be set aside to take up whatever particular interests prompted them to their own investigation of FN.

Yet it would seem to be self-evident that the foremost task of any inquiry into the category ought to be the identification of exactly what it is that causes films intuitively classed as FN to appear to share affinities; that the imperatives which attend the examination of an aesthetic artifact require first of all the meticulous description of the object itself—much as they do with regard to archaeological artifacts—in order to delineate similarities and congruities, as well as indications of dissimilarities, between it and other objects of its class; so that by this process, through the correlation of the results of the examination with available knowledge of the society involved, one is enabled to make reasonable assumptions concerning the relationship of such objects to the society of which they are an expression.[9]

But, perhaps because it is a difficult and laborious task to disentangle the many social and artistic influences and, in particular, the knot of crossbred film genre and types present in FN, the literature on the category for the most part hedges or blinks this primary question or, worse, claims to answer it with unrefined generalities and self-assuming definitions, such as those quoted above, either unburdened by any system of procedure, or employing, as Durgnat does with such assured abandon, a completely spurious methodology.

A simple, straightforward methodology, however, was proposed by Borde and Chaumeton early in the discussion of FN:

> Thus, the method [of examining FN] asserts itself: from as technical, as objective a basis as possible, to study the most prevalent characteristics of the films that criticism has termed noir; then to compare their qualities, to search for a common denominator and to define the unique affective attitude that the works of the cycle tend to bring into play (p. 5).

Even if one has basic objections to this schema (and its last element is clearly a problem), one must recognize its viability as a first step. Yet it remains a method unapplied to FN in any systematic way. Unhappily and precedentially, the first not to apply it were Borde and Chaumeton themselves.

Though their chapter headings imply a developmental, inductive approach ("Towards a Definition of the Film Noir," "Sources of the Film Noir," "The War Years and the Formulation of a Style (1941-45)," "The Great Era [1946-48]," etc.), what the authors do in fact is to begin by simply deducing recurrent thematic elements in FN (crime, psychological emphasis, violence, oneirism), which are general enough to encompass large blocs of films and which of course tend to be inclusive rather than exclusive; and then having established an entirely open structure, they proceed to a recitation of impressions of various films (some of which, as I have indicated, are most provocative), weighting their views along the way with pseudo-scientific data, such as I

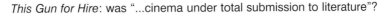

This Gun for Hire: was "...cinema under total submission to literature"?

have quoted. Beyond this, they make some important distinctions between FN and those films which they find to be merely influenced by the classification, especially singling out police and detective "documentaries" and period or Gothic thrillers. But they add another category, "the psychological crime film,"[10] a vague, catch-all grouping, and in stressing its alleged distinctions from FN only succeed in confusing and blurring distinctions already made.

As adapted and supercharged by Durgnat (whose article draws directly upon Borde and Chaumeton), these difficulties of unrigorous, deductive methodology and amorphous categorization are employed to construct a Babeling Tower of arbitrary, inapposite and ill-defined FN classifications, whose main divisions ("Blacks and Reds" and "Hostages to Fortune," for example) are indistinguishable in order and precision from such subdivisions as "The Sombre Cross-Section," and which are composed of literally hundreds of supposed FN titles, from *Easy Street* and *King Kong* to *Whatever Happened to Baby Jane?* and *2001*. Clearly this is categorrhea, and though probably the result of Durgnat being the first to bring the topic before a significant English audience, the scope and persistence of his impact on subsequent criticism are in the end incomprehensible. (As recently as December, 1974, *Film Comment* arranged most, but not all, of Durgnat's nominated divisions, subdivisions and film titles into a two-page "chart," which understandably rather than abetting its systemization, only exposed its absence.) Yet, whatever the cause and despite its manifest failings, the precedent approach established by Durgnat out of Borde and Chaumeton has been incontestably pervasive.[11]

In consequence, what is revealed most conspicuously by a survey of the literature of FN is the urgent need at this point for a complete restructuring of critical approach and methodology; in effect, a new attack on the subject which would be specific rather than general, inductive rather than deductive, and investigatory rather than conclusive; in short, an examination of FN which is interested in working from the objects of study outward rather than in imposing assumptions upon those which suit such assumptions.

II

It does little to deny the need for an inductive methodology to accept from the outset that FN obviously constituted a particular artistic response to a particular set of social, historical and cultural conditions in a wartime and postwar America undergoing profound social and psychological changes. To understand that, after all, is to do no more than acknowledge the phenomenon.

But it remains a matter for individual, detailed demonstration as to what degree and effect the conditions that contributed to FN may or may not have included popular and personal reactions to the cumulative tensions of the Depression, the rise of fascism and the coming of war; the problems attending the end of the war, including the presumed general post-conflict letdown following the nation's psychological sacrifices in an apocalyptic event which in reality seemed to have changed little; indications of imminent additional wars; the returning veterans' various difficulties in readjusting to civilian life; the burgeoning availability of consumer goods after a period of relative austerity; and other possible generating causes and associated phenomena, including some not usually suggested in the literature on FN, such as the lack of efficacious religious faith or a societal system of agreed-upon ethical and philosophical values to which the population could repair in a time of extensive psychological stress, and the broad shift in the society from an objective to a subjective point of view—that is, from at least a significant concern with group reactions to universal conditions such as economic depression and war, to a growing focus on entirely individual responses to social stimuli.

The important point I wish to extract from this observation, however, is the manifest historical nature of the formation of FN, a point which not only Durgnat, with his all-inclusive approach, has blurred or missed. Though it is my intuition that FN is not a category which can enlarged to include an appreciable number of films before 1940 or after 1955, it again seems to be evident FN must be investigated in its original context (this historical period roughly bounded by the dates just given) and defined within that context as to its constituent elements before any assertions may be made about its development as a film category with no significant time limitations.

This matter is directly related to what has been referred to as the fundamental question to be confronted in the study of FN: whether or not it constitutes a genre and, if not, of what does its cohesiveness as a category consist. Robert G. Porfirio has suggested that Paul Schrader's view of FN as a "specific period or cycle of films" offers "a way out" of the problem of genre (p. 133 above), his idea apparently being that a genre cannot be, as Porfirio puts it, "time-bound." Stanley J. Solomon not only subscribes to this idea, but claims it as a major reason he undertook to write a study of film genres admitting only those forms which span the full history of cinema.[12] Yet this concept ignores simple aesthetic record and traditional theory. Taking the drama as an example, one can point to countless time-limited genres, from those of longer duration, such Greek tragedy and English miracle and morality plays, to the relatively short-lived Jacobean tragedy, Restoration comedy and French *drame à these*, to name just a few. Additionally, developments within the last century, as Rene Wellek and Austin Warren observe in their *Theory of Literature*, have increased the number and curtailed the life span of genres:

> With the vast widening of the audience in the nineteenth century, there are more genres...they are short-er-lived or pass through more rapid transitions. 'Genre' in the nineteenth century and in our own time suffers from the same difficulty as 'period'; we are conscious of the quick changes in literary fashion, a new literary generation every ten years, rather than fifty...[13]

Quite clearly, a genre may be bound by time, and rather narrowly at that.

Long considered a fixed and unassailable concept, genre has during the past 25 years come under such intense scrutiny and reevaluation that its very definability has been called into question. Wellek and Warren review at length the inherent difficulties in establishing standards for the recognition of a genre and for distinguishing it from nominal subgenres (pp. 222-27); while Northrop Frye speaks for the modern understanding when he says that "the theory of genres [is] an undeveloped subject in criticism."[14] Yet like Wellek and Warren before him, he proceeds to sketch out how one phase of the theory ought ideally to operate (to underline my ensuing point, I have substituted in brackets cinematic terms for the literary ones, "poem," "literary" and "literature"):

> In the first place, [the film] is unique, a techne or artifact, with its own peculiar structure of imagery, to be examined by itself without immediate reference to other things like it...In the second place, the [film] is one of a class of forms...With this ideal of external relations of a [film] with other [films], two considerations...become important: convention and genre.

> The study of genres is based on analogies in form...and has to be founded on the study of convention. The criticism which can deal with such matters will have to be based on that aspect of symbolism which relates [films] to one another, and it will choose, as its main field of operations, the symbols that link [films] together."(pp. 95-96).

He goes on to explain that "symbol" as he uses it means a unit of communication...to which I give the name archetype: that is, a typical or recurring image. I mean by archetype a symbol which connects one [film] with another and thereby helps to unify and integrate our [cinematic] experience. And as the archetype is the communicable symbol, archetypal criticism is primarily concerned with [cinema] as a social fact and as a mode of communication. By the study of conventions and genres, it attempts to fit [films] into the body of [cinema] as a whole. (p. 99)

In effect, this outline drawn from Frye, amended by the incorporation of word substitutions, comprises an elaboration of Borde's and Chaumeton's schema which I have suggested might form the basis of a reasonable methodology for the study of FN. With appropriate word replacements, the following statement from Wellek and Warren also echoes this schema: "Modern genre theory...is interested...in finding the common denominator of a kind, its shared literary devices and literary purpose." (p. 225).

It is of course my intention by these correlations to postulate that a careful consideration of FN as a genre, modeled on a structure similar to Frye's which all but coincides with the inductive methodology previously set forth, would constitute not merely the most logical, but also the most expeditious and effective means of investigating FN at this time.

Though this directly opposes conventional wisdom in the area of FN scholarship, the objections raised in the literature to such a consideration have for the most part been based on an incomplete understanding of genre (e.g., Porfirio's misapprehension of its temporal limitations). As noted, one frequently cited impediment to FN being accepted as a genre is its transgeneric function; that is, its reputed participation in such amalgams as FN westerns, FN soap operas and FN gangster films. These dual forms may assuredly exist, we have Shakespeare's testimony that such mixing of genres is no modern development ("pastoral-comical, historical-pastoral, tragical-historical, tragical-comical-historical-pastoral"[15]), and we have present-day forms such as tragicomedies, comedy-horror films and satire-soap operas (as in *Mary Hartman*). All of these hybrids, ancient and recent, blend two or more genres with varying degrees of artistic success. But what is patent, and germane to the issue here, is that none of them in doing so automatically disqualifies one of its elements from consideration as a separate authentic genre.

Once having accepted that a genre approach to FN has theoretical and practical underpinnings, the specifics of proceeding present some difficulties; but Wellek and Warren offer a principle that is useful:

> Genre should be conceived, we think, as a group of...works based, theoretically, upon both outer form (specific meter or structure) and also upon inner form (attitude, tone, purpose, more crudely, subject and audience. (p. 221).

The authors later define "structure" as "e.g., a special sort of plot organization" (p. 223). And then adjudging

Woman in the Window: dreams with double reflections (portrayals. by Edward G. Robinson and Joan Bennett).

that the Gothic novel qualifies as a genre, they provide an analysis of it which has direct application to the question under consideration:

> ...there is not only a limited and continuous subject matter of thematics but there is a stock of devices (descriptive-accessory and narrative, e. g. ruined castles, Roman Catholic horrors, mysterious portraits, secret passageways reached through sliding panels, abductions, immurements, pursuits through lonely forests); there is, still further, a Knutswollen, an aesthetic intent, an intent to give the reader a special sort of pleasurable horror and thrill... (p. 223).

The typical FN projects precisely the same order of "limited and continuous subject matter or thematics" through a "stock of devices" both thematic and visual, and surely conveys an "aesthetic intent" to strike the audience with "a special sort of horror," if not exactly of pleasure, at the recognition of life's dark side. Further, as consistently as this inner form of "attitude, tone and purpose" may be traced from FN to FN, so even its outer form, a structure of a "special sort of plot organization" (though perhaps difficult to extrapolate into a generalized model of manageable size) may be delineated and expressed in as specific a form as Frye has done for one of the drama's oldest genres, Greek New Comedy (which he calls so conventionalized as to be a formula [p. 163]):

> Its main theme is the successful effort of a young man to outwit an opponent and possess the girl of his choice. The opponent is usually the father...[who] frequently wants the same girl, and is cheated out of her by the son...The girl is usually a slave or courtesan, and the plot turns on a...discovery of birth which makes her marriageable and marriage is the tonic chord on which [the play] ends.[16]

Such a model of FN plot structure and character type, which would affirm FN as an authentic genre, would of course have to be constructed and verified by a thoroughgoing inductive examination (the process to include, for example, in terms employed by Frye, Wellek and Warren, the detailed study of the "artifact" films individually, the identification of their "symbols" or "archetypes," and the search for "analogs" or "common denominators" among as many purported FN as possible). Though this process demands fare more time and study than I have as yet been able to devote to it, I believe I can suggest at least a rudimentary working prototype for such a model. It would run approximately as follows:

> PROPOSAL: Either he is fated to do so or by chance, or because he has been hired for a job specifically associated with her, a man whose experience of life has left him sanguine and often bitter meets a not-innocent woman of similar outlook to whom he is sexually and fatally attracted. Through this attraction, either because the woman induces him to it or because it is the natural result of their relationship, the man comes to cheat, attempt to murder, or actually murder a second man to whom the woman is unhappily or unwillingly attached (generally he is her husband or lover), an act which often leads to the woman's betrayal of the protagonist, but which in any event brings about the sometimes metaphoric, but usually literal destruction of the woman, the man to whom she is attached, and frequently the protagonist himself.

It should be emphasized that the purpose of such a model is not to describe a structure which exemplifies in precise detail every FN. There will naturally be many variations, substitutions, combinations, splinterings and reversals of constituents, depending upon psychological and aesthetic needs and audience acceptance. The aim is rather to describe a model which embodies the "truest" or "purest" example of the type. (Another of the many confusions about genre in FN literature is the lack of recognition that a genre has periods of birth, development, flowering, which presumably includes its purest examples, and even evolution into a new form of death. These periods in FN are clearly marked, as reflected in Borde's and Chaumeton's chapter divisions: birth around 1940; development and flowering from 1944 to 1948 or 1949; and transition from that point into an altered form which, depending upon one's understanding of FN, either ceases around 1955 or continues indefinitely evolving.)

What is significant about this suggested model is the number of films made in the period from 1944 to 1948 or 1949 and generally considered as FN that it does fit in detail: *Double Indemnity, The Woman in the Window, Scarlet Street, The Killers, The Lady from Shanghai, The Postman Always Rings Twice, Out of the Past, Pitfall,*

Criss Cross come to mind. There are dozens more which incorporate only slight variations. In *The Strange Love of Martha Ivers*, for example, the protagonist doesn't comply with the fatal woman's request to murder her husband, but the result is the same. The fatal woman in *The Blue Dahlia* is the returning vet's unfaithful wife, and though it is rather him than the other man that she wishes to get rid of, at the film's conclusion both she and the second man are dead. A similar development is manifested in *Murder, My Sweet*, in which the fatal woman's connection with the other man, while important (it is he who kills her) is splintered into her general treachery towards all men and especially the protagonist. This concept seems to be a holdover from an earlier period. In essentially the same situation, the protagonist of *The Maltese Falcon*, though he is greatly attracted, "won't play the sap" and save the fatal woman from punishment; so he "sends her over," metaphorically killing her (an act that becomes literal in *Double Indemnity, The Postman Always Rings Twice* and *Out of the Past*). In the post-1949 transitional, perhaps "degenerate" stage of the form, one can see apparent mutations and collapsing of elements. In *In a Lonely Place* the fatal woman has become completely trustworthy, but many of her former characteristics and those of the other man appear to have been incorporated into the now intensely neurotic protagonist.

There is of course a multitude of other correspondences to be evaluated which will perhaps delimit, broaden or even invalidate this provisional model. Largely, these are composed of the "themes" and "motif" observers have noted in FN and claimed as one of the two means of interrelating the films of this type, and which include among other elements the pervasive atmosphere of corruption, crime, psychopathology and evil; the constant resort to gratuitous violence; the omnipresence of the returning veteran; the importance of the oneiric in structure and substance; and recurrent visuals.[17]

Additionally, there are numerous putative FN which seem at first to resist any accommodation with the proposed model. Many of these, it may be seen, simply do not fit into the category, or (as Borde and Chaumeton conclude about police "documentaries") are merely influenced by FN. Other films may be encompassed into a general model by understanding how elements have been altered and condensed or expanded. Tommy Udo in *Kiss of Death*, as an instance, can be seen as combining the masculine and feminine qualities of the other man and the fatal woman of the model, which suggests that it is perhaps this kind of configuration in FN that produces the gratuitous violence which marks the category.

But what I wish to underline regarding this model and the approach it represents is the process it provides by which the constituents common to a majority of the films intuitively grouped as FN may be isolated, objectified and their examination facilitated, even if provisional particulars of the model are later to be discarded in favor of more useful ones or even to pursue another but related method. Eventually, and most importantly, it is this kind of study which will not only elucidate this intriguing category of film and intensify an understanding of its aesthetic qualities, but which may as well establish a basis for the specific determination of the social, political and psychological root causes which gave rise to the phenomenon.

Short of this high aim, however, there certainly seems to be substantial and abundant reason to assume that FN may constitute a genre and to encourage an orderly and scrupulous consideration of the assumption.

Notes

1. Hereafter the designation FN will be used to denote the terms film noir and films noirs.

2. I excerpt Amir Massoud Karimi's reproduced dissertation, *Toward a Definition of the American Film Noir (1941-1949)* (New York: Arno Press, 1976), which though helpful with certain antecedents, conceives of FN essentially as a branch of detective fiction. The French work is Raymond Borde and Étienne Chaumeton, *Panorama du film noir américain (1941-1953)* (Paris: Les Éditions de Minuit, 1955); translations from this volume are mine.

3. (New York: Basic Books, Inc., 1975).

4. (New York: Grossman Publishers, 1969).

5. *Hollywood in the Forties* (New York: A.S. Barnes and Co., 1968), pp. 19-20.

6. (New York: The Viking Press, 1972).

7. (New York: The Museum of Modern Art, 1971).

8. *Cinema*, Nos. 6 and 7 (August, 1970), pp. 48-56.

9. Auteurist and director-centered criticism has traditionally worked across the current of this kind of investigation, but this is less true of Alfred Appel, Jr., "The Director: Fritz Lang's American Nightmare," *Film Comment*, Vol. 10, No. 6 (November-December, 1974), pp. 12-17; and Peter Biskind, "'They Live by Night' By Daylight," *Sight and Sound*, Vol. 45, No. 4 (Autumn, 1976), pp. 218-22.

10. Approximately the term which Robert G. Porfirio endorses as the best English equivalent for film noir, in "No Way Out: Existential Motifs in the Film noir," *Sight and Sound*, Vol. 45, No. 4 (Autumn, 1976), pp. 212-17.

11. Even Paul Schrader's otherwise prudent "Notes on Film Noir," *Film Comment*, Vol. 8, No. 1 (Spring, 1972), pp. 8-13, lauds Durgnat's piece as "excellent," his work of classification as "thorough."

12. *Beyond Formula* (New York: Harcourt, Brace and Janovich, Inc., 1976).

13. (New York: Harcourt, Brace and Co., 1956), p. 222.

14. *Anatomy of Criticism: Four Essays* (Princeton, N.J.: Princeton University Press, 1971), p. 246.

15. "Hamlet," II. ii.

16. "The Argument of Comedy," in *Theories of Comedy*, ed. Paul Lauter (Garden City, N.Y.: Anchor Books, Doubleday and Co., Inc., 1964), p. 450.

17. The "visual style" so often reputed to FN (and the second means observers cite as correlating films classed in this category) is for me an extremely vexed question. I can see no conclusive evidence that anything as cohesive and determined as a visual style exists in FN. Assuredly, there is an emphasis on darkness and shadow, as there is in nearly all films of this period, but merely because an equal fashion for an emphatic brightness was manifested in a majority of Thirties films (whose subjects and outlook were similarly "bright"), a class of films blancs did not result. A visual style connotes a purposeful repetition from film to film of certain camera movements or angles: size of images; editing figures, devices or types; and/or a consistent movement of actors in relation to the camera. This is, after all, how we determine that Eisenstein's visual style differs from Welles'. No such patterns, however, are evident in FN. Its recurrent concentration on certain objects, types of faces, and perhaps settings, more nearly constitutes an iconography than a visual style.

The Blue Dahlia: "...objects, types of faces, and perhaps settings"—iconography or visual style?

"Just the facts, ma'am": L.A. police chief Bradley portrays himself in Eagle-Lion's B feature *He Walked by Night*, which may have "ironically" spawned "Dragnet" on television. (Jack Webb co-starred in the feature.)

Out of What Past? Notes on the B film noir

Paul Kerr (1979)

Ever since the publication of Borde and Chaumeton's pioneering *Panorama du Film Noir Américain* in 1955, there has been a continuing dispute about the genre's precise cultural sources and critical status.[1] In their attempts to provide film noir with a respectable pedigree, subsequent studies have cited not only cinematic but also sociological, psychological, philosophical, political, technological and aesthetic factors amongst its progenitors. What they have not done, however, is to relate these general and generally untheorized, notions of "influence" to the specific modes of production, both economic and ideological, upon which they were, presumably, exercised; in this case, those structures and strategies adopted by certain factions within the American film industry over a period of almost two decades. Instead, these archaeologists of the genre have excavated a wide range of "ancestors" for film noir, the influx of German emigrés and the influence of expressionism; the influx of French emigrés and the influence of existentialism; Ernest Hemingway and the "hard-boiled" school of writing; Edward Hopper and the "ash can" school of painting; pre-war photo-journalism, wartime newsreels and post-war neorealism; the creators of *Kane*, Citizens Mankiewicz, Toland and Welles; the Wall Street crash and the rise of populism; the Second World War and the rise of fascism; the Cold War and the rise of McCarthyism. Finally, several critics have pointed, in passing, to a number of even less specific sources, such as general American fears about bureaucracy, the bomb, and the big city, as well as one or two more substantial ones, including the industrialization of the female work-force during the war and the escalating corporatism of American capital throughout the 1940s.[2] However pertinent some of these suggestions, attempts to establish a "family tree" have usually revealed less about the formation of film noir in particular than about the poverty of film history in general. This article, therefore, is an attempt to refocus the debate on the specifically film-industrial determinants of the genre by concentrating on one important, industrially defined, fraction of it, the B film noir.

As I have indicated, most explanations have tended to credit either particular people (such as ex-employees of UFA and *Black Mask*) or events (the Depression and the war, for example) with the creation of, or, more accurately, a contribution to, film noir. Thus, in the first category, auteurists discuss the genre as if it were simply the chosen canvas of a few talented individuals, whether they were directors (Siodmak, Tourneur, Ulmer), writers (Chandler, Mainwaring, Paxton) or cinematographers (Alton, Musuraca, Toland). Similarly, genre critics generally consider film noir either in terms of its function as social myth or, more simply, as no more than a symptom of social malaise.[3] Borde and Chaumeton begin their chapter on sources with an account of film noir's literary and cinematic precursors, so endorsing an evolutionary model of film history, but they go on to propose a much more interesting industrial origin in Hollywood's "synthesis of three types of films which at that time had developed such an autonomy that each studio had its own specialties from among them; the brutal and colorful gangster film, whose style carried over to other productions at Warner Bros.; the horror film over which Universal acquired a near-monopoly; and the classic detective film of deduction which was shared by Fox and Metro-Goldwyn-Mayer."[4] Having gone this far, though, Borde and Chaumeton fail to ask why such a synthesis should ever have taken place, if indeed it did. There are, I think, only two other theories which have been seriously put forward vis-a-vis the relationship between film noir and the film industry, both of which are equally untenable. The first argues that the genre was the cinema's unmediated reflection of an all-pervading postwar gloom and the second, that it was the expression of a community finally freed from its Depression duties as a dream factory by an audience that no longer needed cheering up.[5] In spite of their diametrically opposing views of postwar American "morale," both theories employ a conception of Hollywood as monolith-ic, its products either determined by American ideology or entirely autonomous of it.

Clearly, if we want to go on using the notion of "determination" rather than relying on the dubious concept "derivation," it is necessary to approach the classic base/superstructure formulation with some caution. Indeed, Raymond Williams has remarked that

> ...each term of the proposition has to be revalued in a particular direction. We have to revalue "deter-mination" towards the setting of limits and the exertion of pressure and away from a predicted, prefig-ured and controlled content. We have to revalue "superstructure" towards a related range of cultural practices and away from a reflected, reproduced or specifically dependent content. And, crucially, we have revalued "the base" away from a notion of a fixed economic or technological abstraction, and towards the specific activities of men in real social and economic relationships, containing fundamen-tal contradictions and variations and therefore always in a state of dynamic process.[6]

This article, then, taking its cue from the oft-cited specificity of film noir as a genre, will attempt to relate it not to the general American social formation (as some species of "reflection"), nor to a monolithically conceived film industry, but rather to particular, relatively autonomous modes of film production, distribution and exhibi-tion in a particular conjuncture. What follows, therefore, is an exploratory rather than an exhaustive analysis of reciprocal relation which obtained between film noir's primary determinants, the economic and the ideological. (The third determinant, at least in Althusserian terms, is that of the political, the effectivity of which with respect to the film noir would have to include the production code, the antitrust suits and the Hollywood blacklist. The political instance, for reasons of brevity, has here been subsumed within the other two categories.) This analy-sis attends in particular to the relatively autonomous and uneven development of the B film noir, a category constituted, I will argue by a negotiated resistance to the realist aesthetic on the one hand and an accommo-dation to restricted expenditure on the other. Of course, none of these terms, relative autonomy, non-syn-chronicity, realism (not to mention film noir itself), is unproblematic; their employment here, however, is a nec-essary condition of any discussion which hopes to account for the existence of a genre at different times and in different places with a number of different inflections. The crucial theoretical formulation here is that of "deter-mination" itself, since the identity of the infamous "last instance" though classically considered to be the eco-nomic will actually fluctuate, at least in the short term. Thus, in the long term, Hollywood's ideological and eco-nomic aims are complementary; the reproduction of the conditions necessary for continued cinematic pro-duction and consumption, in other words, the perpetuation of the industry. In the short term, however, these determinants may be less compatible, and it is the shifting balance of relations between the two which accords Hollywood's "superstructure" its relative autonomy from its economic "base." Furthermore, the economic or ideological space opened up for the American cinema in this way is in direct proportion to the urgency with which ideological or economic priorities in the industry are negotiated.

To take an example, Antony Easthope has argued that "in the early Thirties Hollywood production was determined ideologically or even politically rather than economically"[7] but his argument, like so many others, hinges on a reading of American history in general and not that of the film industry. In fact, it seems equally plausible, if equally schematic, to suggest that Hollywood's product was dominantly determined economical-ly only in periods of economic crisis in the industry (like the early 1930s when several studios were actually bankrupted by a combination of reduced receipts and excessive capitalization), whilst in eras of relative eco-nomic stability but marked ideological and/or political unrest (like the mid-1940s, when receipts rose to a new high but both international and industrial relations were of crucial importance) that product would have tend-ed to be, primarily at least, ideologically determined. In modification of this latter formulation, however, it is nec-essary to add that low-budget and blockbuster film-making, neither of which was really established across the industry until the latter half of the 1930s, having their origins in precisely those economic conditions outlined above, might have been more vulnerable to economic imperatives ("masking" and "flaunting" their respective production values) than the admittedly slightly hypothetical "mid-budgeted" mainstream A products of the stu-dios at that time. This privileging of the economic imperative on the B film, in a period of film history which was otherwise primarily ideologically determinate (at least until about 1947), might begin to account for the presence of several aesthetically (and therefore ideologically) unorthodox practices within the B film noir.

Towards a definition

Before a discussion of such suggestions can legitimately begin, however, some kind of critical consensus about those "practices" and the period in which they were pursued is needed. The authors of the *Panorama* focus their own analysis on those films produced between 1941 and 1953 but more recent critics have broadened these bounds somewhat to include films made from the beginning of the 1940s (and sometimes even earlier) until the end of the following decade. If we employ the more elastic of these estimates and allow an additional, and admittedly arbitrary margin at the beginning of the period, we may be able to reconstruct at least some of the industrial determinants of the genre. Furthermore, several critics have tried to demonstrate that film noir comprises a number of distinct stages. Paul Schrader, for example, has outlined "three broad phases" for the genre: the first lasting until about 1946 and characterized by couples like Bogart and Bacall and "classy" studio directors like Curtiz; the second spanning the immediate postwar years, when shooting began to move out of the studios and into the streets; and the third and final phase in which both characters and conventions alike were subject to extraordinary permutations. Perhaps film history will ultimately explain the industrial underpinnings of such "sub-generic" shifts as well as the primary determinants and eventual demise of the wider genre itself.[8] Until then, whether the period of film noir production is relatively easily agreed upon or not, the volume of that production is decidedly more difficult to ascertain. This is due, to some degree at least, to the primacy of the economic and relative autonomy of the ideological instances of the film noir. Equally important is its controversial status as a genre at all, since it is usually defined in terms of its style rather than, as most genres are, in relation to content, character, setting, plot. Further difficulties derive from its relative inaccessibility as an object of study: retrospectives are all too rare and there are still no book-length analyses of the genre in English, even the *Panorama* remains untranslated. Film noir, therefore, has still not received its due in terms of either critical or archival attention.

Despite such difficulties, it still remains possible to offer at least an outline of the genre's defining characteristics.[9] Primarily, film noir has been associated with a propensity for low key lighting, a convention which was in direct opposition to the cinematographic orthodoxy of the previous decade. In the 1930s the dominant lighting style, known as high key, had been characterized by a contrast ratio of approximately 4:1 between the light value of the key lamp on the one hand and the filler on the other. Noir, with a considerable higher range to contrasts, is thus a chiaroscuro style, its low key effects often undiffused by either lens gauzes or lamp fresnels, as they certainly would have been in conventional high key style. Instead, noir sets are often only half or quarter lit, with the important exception of those brief sequences in the "blanc" (that is, "normal") world which are sometimes employed as a framing device at the beginning and end of the narrative. Otherwise, shooting tends to be either day-for-night or night-for-night and the main action has a habit of occurring in shadowy rooms, dingy offices, overlush apartments and rain-washed streets. In such settings both actors and decor are often partially obscured by the foregrounding of oblique objects, shutters and banisters, for instance, casting horizontal or vertical grids of light and dark across faces and furniture. Meanwhile, the arrangement of space within the frame is often equally irregular, both in regard to its occupation by actors and props as well as to the width and depth of focus. This can lead to a "discomposition" of the image (and consequent disorientation of the spectator) in terms of the neo-classical conventions of composition generally used and, indeed, reinforced by Hollywood. These kinds of disorientation can be accentuated by the use of "perversely" low and high camera angles (a perversity defined entirely in relation to contemporary realist criteria) and the virtual elimination of those other staples of realism, the establishing long shot and the personalizing close-up. In fact, the latter is often used ironically in the film noir in soft focus treatment of male villainy (signifying feminine decadence) whilst women, the conventional "objects" of such attention, are often photographed in harsh, unflattering and undiffused light with wide angle distorting lenses. Such an emphasis on unconventional camera angles and lighting set-ups, however, is often achieved at the (literal) expense of camera movement and classical editing.

A number of other realist conventions, including shot-reverse-shot alternation of points of view and the 180 degree rule, are also occasionally infringed by the film noir.[10] Finally there is a great deal of reliance on such fragmented narrative structures as the flashback, which adds an additional sense of inevitability to the plot and helplessness to characters. Hitherto, most definitions of the genre have more or less rested at this point, tending to ignore that plot and those characters. One recent critic, however, has assembled what he calls a "rudimentary working prototype" of characteristic content for film noir along the following lines:

> Either because he is fated to do so by chance, or because he has been hired for a job specifically associated with her, a man whose experience of life has left him sanguine and often bitter meets a not-innocent woman of similar outlook to who he is sexually and fatally attracted. Through this attraction, either because the woman induces him to it or because it is the natural result of their relationship, the man comes to cheat, attempt to murder or actually murder a second man to whom the woman is unhappily or unwillingly attached (generally he is her husband or lover), an act which brings about the sometimes metaphoric but usually literal destruction of the woman, the man to whom she is attached and frequently the protagonist himself.[11]

This schematic summary of film noir will have to suffice for purposes here, if only as a result of the extremely tentative account of the genre's determination outlined below.

The Coming of the B feature

The B film was launched as an attempt by a number of independent exhibitors to lure audiences back into their theatres at a time of acute economic crisis in the industry. Along with the double bill these independents had already, by the beginning of the 1930s, introduced lotteries, live acts, quizzes, free gifts and several other gimmicks in order to build up bigger audiences and, at the same time, keep those patrons they already had in their seats a little longer, so boosting box-office takings and confectionery sales whilst legitimizing admission prices. The double bill, however, had the additional, and, as it proved, crucial, advantage of enabling independent exhibitors to accommodate their program policies to the majors' monopolistic distribution practices (such as blind selling and block booking) and allowing them to exhibit more independent product at the same time. Of the 23,000 theatres operating in the United States in 1930, the five majors (MGM, RKO, Fox, Warners and Paramount) either owned or controlled some 3,000, most of that number being among the biggest and best situated of the first-run theatres; these 3,000 theatres, though comprising less than 14 per cent of the total number then in operation, accounted for nearly 70 per cent of the entire industry's box-office takings that year. This left the independents with some 20,000 theatres in which to screen what were either second-run or independent films. By the end of 1931 the double bill, which had originated in New England, had spread its influence on programme policy right across the country, establishing itself as at least a part of that policy in one-eighth of the theatres then in operation. In 1935, the last of the majors to adopt double bills in their theatres, MGM and RKO, announced their decision to screen two features in all but two of their theatres. By 1947, the fraction of cinemas advertising double bills had risen to nearly two-thirds. In normal circumstances, of course, any such increase in the volume of films in exhibition would have led to a similar increase in the volume of film production but this was not the case. Overproduction by the majors since the advent of sound had accumulated an enormous backlog of as yet unreleased material. It was not, therefore, until this reservoir of ready-made second features had been exhausted that it became necessary to set up an entirely new mode of film production, the B unit.

While those units within vertically integrated majors virtually monopolised the independent exhibition outlets a number of B studios established to meet the same demand were compelled to rely on the so-called States Rights system, whereby studios sold distribution rights to film franchises on a territorial basis. Lacking theatre chains of their own, several independent production companies were forced to farm out their product to a relatively unknown market. Monogram and Republic did eventually set up small exchanges of their own in a few cities and their main rival, PRC, even acquired some theatres of its own in the 1940s but the distinction between such venues and those owned by the majors should not be forgotten. Certainly, the producers of the B films themselves would have been acutely aware of the kind of cinemas in which the bulk of their products would have been seen and this may have been as influential a factor in B film production as the picture palaces were for the As. Mae D. Huettig,[12] for instance, has described how Los Angeles's eleven first-run theatres exhibited 405 films in the year 1939/40 of which only five were the product of independent companies, all but one of that five being shown at the bottom of a double bill. Wherever such double bills were programmed, however, few exhibitors could afford the rentals of two top quality (i.e. top price) products at the same time. The double bill, therefore, was a combination of one relatively expensive A film and one relatively inexpensive B, the former generally deriving from the major studios and costing, throughout the 1940s, upwards of $700,000 and the later being produced by low budget units at the same studios as well as by several B studios, at anything less than about $400,000.[13] In general, the A feature's rental was based on a percentage of box-office takings whilst the Bs played for a fixed or flat rental and were thus not so reliant on audience attendance figures at all, at least, not in the short term. In the long term, however, these B units would be compelled to carve out identifiable and distinctive styles for themselves in order to differentiate their product, within generic constraints, for the benefit of audiences in general and exhibitors in particular.

In most cases the B film noir would have been produced, like all Bs, on a fixed budget which would itself have been calculated in relation to fixed rentals. In illustrating the effects such economies exercised on these Bs I have restricted reference, as far as possible, to one large integrated company, RKO, and one small independent company, PRC.[14] At the beginning of the decade the budgets of RKO's most important production unit in the B sector were approximately $150,000 per picture; at PRC, several years later, most units were working with less than two-thirds of that amount. To take two examples: Val Lewton's films at RKO had tight, twenty-one-day schedules whilst Edgar G. Ulmer's at PRC were often brought in after only six days and nights. (To achieve this remarkable shooting speed night work was almost inevitable and Ulmer's unit used to mount as many as eighty different camera set-ups a day.) Props, sets and costumes were kept to a minimum except on those occasions when they could be borrowed from more expensive productions, as Lewton borrowed a staircase from *The Magnificent Ambersons* for his first feature, *The Cat People*. Nick Grinde, a veteran of B units in the 1940s, has described how a producer would resist charges of plagiarism on the grounds that "the way he will shoot it no one will recognize it for the same set. He'll have his director pick new angles and redress the foreground...[and]...will even agree to shoot at night..."[15]

Night shooting, of course, was an obvious and often unavoidable strategy for getting films in on short schedules as well as fully exploiting fixed assets and economizing on rentals. (It also suited those employers who sought to avoid IATSE overtime bans.) Mark Robson, an editor and later director in Lewton's unit, has recalled that "the streets we had in *The Seventh Victim*, for instance, were studio streets and the less light we put on them the better they looked."[16] Similarly, expensive special effects and spectacular action sequences were generally avoided unless stock footage could be borrowed from other films. This "borrowing" became known as "montage" and involved the use of a "series of quick cuts of film," as Grinde has explained:

Fanny Minafer (Agnes Moorhead) and her brother George (Tim Holt) on the staircase in *The Magnificent Ambersons*.

You can't shoot a first-rate crime wave on short dough, so you borrow or buy about twenty pieces of thrilling moments from twenty forgotten pictures. A fleeing limousine skids into a street-car, a pedestrian is socked over the head in an alley, a newspaper office is wrecked by hoodlums, a woman screams, a couple of mugs are slapping a little merchant into seeing their way. And so on until we end up on a really big explosion.[17]

Not all such "thrilling moments" were "borrowed" from "forgotten pictures," however. Fritz Lang, for example, has noted that footage from *You Only Live Once* (UA 1937), including a classic bank robbery sequence, found its way into *Dillinger* (Monogram 1945).[18]

The exploitation of borrowed footage and furniture was only really possible as long as films were being shot inside the studios. Until the middle of the 1940s location shooting was extremely rare and even independents like Monogram and PRC had their own studio facilities. As fixed and variable costs began to escalate at the end of the war, however, production units were encouraged to go out on location and this practice was extended by the prolonged studio strikes of 1945-47. In 1946, the abolition of block booking encouraged the appearance of a number of small studio-less independent production companies and these also contributed to the "street" rather than "studio" look in the latter half of the decade. Constraints at both the production and distri-

Stranger on the Third Floor: in the title role Peter Lorre, whom RKO used (and paid) for just 2 days, menaces Jane (Margaret Tallichet),

bution ends of the industry meant that the running length of Bs fluctuated between about fifty-five and seventy-five minutes; raw footage was expensive, audiences had only limited amounts of time and, of course, exhibitors were keen to screen their double bills as many times a day as possible. In 1943 the government reduced basic allotments of raw film stock to the studios by 25 per cent and once again it was the B units which were hardest hit. Consequently "montages" became even more common. Cast and crews on contract to B units were kept at a manageable minimum by prohibiting plots with long cast lists, crowd scenes and complicated camera or lighting set-ups. Similarly, overworked script departments often produced unpolished and occasionally incoherent scripts. (Film titles were pre-tested with audiences before stories or scripts were even considered.) Despite such drawbacks, however, the B units, throughout the 1940s and as late as the mid-1950s, employed the same basic equipment as their big budget rivals, including Mitchell or Bell and Howell cameras, Mole Richardson lighting units, Moviola editing gear and RCA or Western Electric sound systems. Such economics as B units practiced, therefore, were not related to fixed assets like rents and salaries but to variable costs like sets, scripts, footage, casual labour and, crucially, power.

RKO's production of noir B's seems to have been inaugurated in 1940 with the release of Boris Ingster's extraordinary *Stranger on the Third Floor*. The studio had emerged from receivership at end of the previous decade, a period of some prosperity for the other majors, to make only minimal profits of $18,604 in 1938 and $228,608 in 1939. In 1940 the studio lost almost half a million dollars and began to augment its low budget policy with B series like *The Saint* and *The Falcon*. It was not until 1942, however, when RKO plunged more than two million dollars into debt that the trend towards the B film noir became really evident. In that year, George Schaefer was fired as president and replaced by his deputy, Ned Depinet, who immediately appointed Charles M. Koerner, from RKO Theatres Inc., as vice-president in charge of production. It was at this point that Val Lewton was brought to the studio to set up his own B unit. Within the limitations I have outlined, as well as the generic constraints of having to work in the "horror" category, Lewton's unit, and others like it, were accorded a degree of autonomy which would never have been sanctioned for more expensive studio productions.[19] At PRC the situation was rather different. The company had been formed in March 1940 by the creditors of its predecessor, the Producers' Distributing Corporation, and with the cooperation of the Pathé Laboratories. The new Producers' Releasing Corporation had five separate production units and the Fine Arts Studio (formerly Grand National). At first the emphasis was on comedy and westerns; PRC produced forty-four films, mostly in these genres, in the 1941/42 season. By 1942, however, PRC had acquired twenty-three film exchanges and with the replacement of George Batchelor by Leon Fromkess as production head, there was an increased diversification of product. While most units concentrated on comedies and musicals, others began to turn out cut-rate westerns and crime thrillers. It was also in 1942 that Edgar G. Ulmer began work for the studio. Allowed only about 15,000 feet per picture, Ulmer's unit, like Lewton's, economized with stock footage (as in *Girls in Chains* PRC 1943) and minimal casts and sets (as in *Detour* PRC 1946).

Artistic ingenuity in the face of economic intransigence is one critical commonplace about the B film noir (and about people like Lewton and Ulmer in particular). Against this, I have suggested that a number of noir characteristics can at least be associated with, if not directly attributed to, economic and therefore technological constraints. The paucity of "production values" (sets, stars and so forth) may even have encouraged low budget production units to compensate with complicated plots and convoluted atmosphere. Realist denotation would have thus been de-emphasized in favor of expressionist connotation (in *The Cat People*, RKO 1942, for example). This connotative quality might also owe something to the influence of the Hays Office, which meant that "unspeakable" subjects could only be suggested, *Under Age* (Columbia 1941), although concerned with the criminal exploitation of young girls, could never actually illustrate that exploitation. Similarly, compressed shooting schedules, overworked script editors and general cost cutting procedures could well have contributed to what we now call film noir. Nevertheless, an analysis of film noir as nothing more than an attempt to make a stylistic virtue of economic necessity, the equation, at its crudest, of low budgets with low key lighting, is inadequate: budgetary constraints and the relative autonomy of many B units in comparison with As were a necessary but by no means sufficient condition for its formation. It was, I have suggested, constituted not only by accommodation to restricted expenditure but also by resistance to the realist aesthetic, like the B film generally, it was determined not only economically but also ideologically. For instance, the double bill was not simply the result of combining any two films, one A and one B, but often depended on a number of quite complex contrasts. *The Saint in New York*, for example, was billed with *Gold Diggers in Paris*, *Blind Alibi* with *Holiday*. According to Frank Ricketson Jr., the tendency of both distributors and exhibitors to ensure that

> Heavy drama is blended with sparkling comedy. A virile action picture is mated with a sophisticated society play. An all-star production is matched with a light situation comedy of no-star value. An adventure story is contrasted with a musical production.[20]

Initially, of course, B films had been little more than low budget versions of profitable A releases but as the industry was rationalized after the Depression this imitative trend was partially replaced by another differentiation. Thus, while early Bs had tended to remain in the least expensive of successful genres, westerns, situation comedies, melodramas, thrillers and horror films, the exhibitors themselves began to exert a moderating influence (by means of intercompany promotions like Koerner's within the integrated companies; by means of advertisements in the trade papers among the independents). By the end of the 1930s, therefore, double bills were beginning to contrast the staple A genres of that decade, gangster films, biopics, screwball comedies, mysteries and westerns, with a number of Poverty Row hybrids, mixtures of melodrama and mystery, gangster and private eye, screwball comedy and thriller (and later, "documentary" and drama). In part, of course, this hybrid quality is explicable in terms of studio insecurities about marketing their B products; nevertheless, the curiously cross-generic quality of film noir is perhaps a vestige of its origins as a kind of "oppositional" cinematic mode. Low key lighting styles, for example, were not only more economic than their high key alternatives, they were also dramatically and radically distinct from them.

Stylistic Generation

In considering the concept of stylistic differentiation it is useful, at this point, to introduce the work of the Birmingham Centre for Contemporary Cultural Studies on "the process of stylistic generation."[21] Although specifically addressed to the "styles" adopted by such subcultural groups as Teds, punks and Rastas, this work seems to me to be applicable, with some reservations, to the style of the B film noir. Whether or not one can legitimately describe Poverty Row as a subculture is clearly a matter for serious debate but, until we have some kind of social history of Hollywood, a final decision on the matter is premature. Lacking such knowledge, it remains striking how appropriate some of the Birmingham conclusions are for the present study. In their analysis the authors make admittedly eclectic use of Levi-Strauss's concept of bricolage; but whereas Levi-Strauss is concerned with situations and cultures where a single myth is dominant, John Clarke concentrates on the "genesis of 'unofficial' styles, where the stylistic core (if there is one) can be located in the expression of a partly negotiated opposition to the values of a wider society."[22] (I will return to the notion of "negotiated opposition" later). Clarke proposes a two-tiered theory of stylistic generation, the first axiom of which states that the generation of subcultural styles involves differential selection from within the matrix of the existent and the second, that one of the main functions of a distinctive subcultural style is to define the boundaries of group membership as against other groups. I hope that the pertinence of these two axioms (the first "economic," the second "ideological") to the group which has designated the B film noir will become apparent. Clarke even goes on to discuss the process whereby such subcultural styles are assimilated into/recuperated by the dominant culture; a process which Raymond Williams refers to as "incorporation." The defusion and dilution of the B film noir's unorthodox visual style within the aesthetic of the A film clearly fits this kind of pattern, with the most economically secure studios at that time, MGM, Fox and Paramount, tending to produce not only fewer films in the genre than their competitors but also more lavish ones like *The Postman Always Rings Twice*, *Laura*, and *Double Indemnity*. Furthermore, it was Fox who was to launch and lead the breakaway police procedural strand at the end of the 1940s, a strand which emanated from and to a certain extent replaced that studio's location-based *March of Time* series.[23]

Meanwhile, the monopoly structure of the industry, which had been initially, if indirectly, responsible for the

B phenomenon, was being challenged. In May 1935 the Supreme Court voted to revoke Roosevelt's National Industrial Recovery Act (under which A Code of Fair Competition for the Motion Picture Industry had more or less condoned the industry's monopoly practices) on the grounds that it was unconstitutional. Opposition to motion picture monopolies was mounting, not only among the independent companies but also in the courts and even in Congress itself. Finally, in July 1938, the Department of Justice filed an Anti-Trust suit against the majors, United States versus Paramount Pictures Inc. et al., so launching a case which was to reach the Supreme Court a decade later. In the suit the majors were accused of separate infringements of Anti-Trust legislation but, in November 1940, the case was apparently abandoned; in fact it was merely being adjourned for the duration of hostilities, the government being unwilling to provoke Hollywood at a time when the communications media were of such crucial importance. The suit was settled out of court with the signing of a modest Consent Decree, the provisions of which included an agreement by the majors to "modify" their use of block booking, to eliminate blind selling and to refrain from "unnecessary" theatrical expansion. Most important of all the Decree's requirements, however, was the majors' agreement to withdraw from the package selling procedures which had compelled independent exhibitors to screen shorts, re-issues, serial westerns and newsreels with their main features. The last provision expanded the market for low budget production almost overnight. Whereas at the end of the 1930s there had been very few independent companies, by 1946 (the year in which block booking was finally abolished) there were more than forty. The Anti-Trust Commission never entirely dropped their case against Hollywood, however, and finally, in 1948, the five fully integrated companies were instructed to divest themselves of their theatrical holdings. Paramount was the first to obey this ruling, divorcing its exhibition arm from the production/distribution end of its business in late 1949. RKO followed in 1950, 20th Century-Fox in 1952, Warner Bros. in 1953 and MGM in 1959. Rather ironically, the divorce meant the demise of many independent studios which had thrived on providing films for the bottom half of the bill; quite simply, low budget productions could no longer be guaranteed fixed rentals in exhibition. Consequently, one of the first casualties of divorcement was the double bill. The majors cancelled their B productions and the independents were forced to choose between closure and absorption. In 1949 PRC was absorbed by Rank and transformed into Eagle Lion; the following year it ceased production altogether and merged with United Artists. In 1953 Monogram became Allied Artists Pictures Corporation and began to operate an increasingly important television subsidiary. Republic, whose staple product had always been westerns and serials, was finally sold to CBS in 1959 and became that network's Television City studio.

It was thus between the first filing of the Anti-Trust suit in 1938 and the final act of divorcement in 1959 that the B film noir flourished. Obviously, however, the trend towards media conglomerates and away from simple monopolies was by no means the only "political" determinant on cinematic modes in that period, a period which witnessed American entry into the war, the rise of McCarthyism and a series of jurisdictional disputes in the labor unions.[24] During the Second World War the international market for American films shrank drastically and the domestic market expanded to take its place. By 1941, the cinemas of continental Europe, where the majors had earned more than a quarter of their entire box office in 1936, were no longer open to American distributors. Even in Britain, where most cinemas remained open throughout the war and where attendance actually rose from a weekly average of nineteen million in 1939 to more than thirty million in 1945, the Hollywood majors were unable to maintain even prewar profits. The introduction of currency restrictions severely limited the amount that American distributors could remove from the country; thus, only half their former revenues, some $17,500,000,were withdrawn in 1940 and only $12,900,000 in 1941. Meanwhile, however, American domestic rentals soared from $193,000,000 in 1939 to $332,000,000 in 1946. By the end of the war, average weekly attendance in the US was back at about 90,000,000, its pre-war peak. As the majors' profits rose, the volume of their production actually fell: having released some 400 films in 1939 the big eight companies released only 250 in 1946, the balance being made up by a flush of new B companies. This geographically, but not economically, reduced constituency may have afforded Hollywood the opportunity to take a closer look at contemporary and specifically American phenomena without relying on the "comfortable" distance provided by classic genres like the western or the musical. That "closer look" (at, for instance, urban crime, the family and the rise of corporations) could, furthermore, because of the national specificity of its audience and as a result of the "dialectic" of its consumption (within the double bill) employ a less orthodox aesthetic than would previously have been likely.

The aesthetic orthodoxy of the American cinema in the 1940s and 1950s was realism and so it is necessary to relate cinematic realism to the film noir. Colin MacCabe has suggested its two primary conditions:

(1) The classic realist text cannot deal with the real as contradictory.

(2) In a reciprocal movement of the classic realist text ensures the position of the subject in a relation of dominant specularity.

These two conditions, the repression of contradiction and the construction of spectatorial omniscience, are negotiated through a hierarchy of narrative discourses:

> Through the knowledge we gain from the narrative we can split the discourses of the various characters from their situation and compare what is said in these discourses with what has been revealed to us through narration. The camera shows us what happens, it tells the truth against which we can measure the discourses.[25]

Elsewhere MacCabe has restated this notion quite clearly: "classical realism...involves the homogenization of different discourses by their relation to one dominant discourse, assured of its domination by the security and transparency of its image."[26]

It is this very "transparency" which film noir refuses; indeed, Sylvia Harvey has noted that "One way of looking at the plot of the typical film noir is to see it as a struggle between different voices for control over the telling of the story." From that perspective, film noir represents a fissure in the aesthetic and ideological fabric of realism. Thus,

> Despite the presence of most of the conventions of the dominant methods of filmmaking and storytelling, the impetus towards the resolution of the plot, the diffusion of tension, the circularity of a narrative that resolves all the problems it encounters, the successful completion of the individual's quest, these methods do not, in the end, create the most significant contours of the cultural map of film noir. The defining contours of this group of films are the product of that which is abnormal and dissonant.[27]

Gill Davies, on the other hand, has suggested that such "dissonance" can quite comfortably be contained by the "weight" of generic convention.

> The disturbing effect of mystery or suspense is balanced by confidence in the inevitability of the genre. Character types, stock settings and the repetition of familiar plot devices assure the reader that a harmonious resolution will take place. This narrative pattern pretends to challenge the reader, creates superficial disorientation, while maintaining total narrative control. Our knowledge of the genre (supported in the cinema with the reappearance of certain actors and actresses in familiar roles) takes us through a baffling narrative with the confidence that all problems will ultimately be solved.[28]

In terms of film noir, however, I would argue that the "surplus" of realist devices catalogued by Harvey and Davies indicates an attempt to hold in balance traditional generic elements with unorthodox aesthetic practices that constantly undermine them. Film noir can thus be seen as the negotiation of an "oppositional space" within and against realist cinematic practice; this trend could only be effectively disarmed by the introduction of a number of stock devices derived from other genres (such as melodrama or the detective story). It is not an object of this article, though, to gauge the degree to which that resistance was or was not successful. Rather, its task is to begin to establish those historically contemporaneous strands of realism, Technicolor, television and the A film, against which any such resistance would necessarily have defined itself.

Television and Technicolor

In 1947 there were only 14,000 television receivers in the United States; two years later that number had risen to a million. By 1950 there were four million and by 1954 thirty-two million. In the face of such swiftly escalating opposition and as a consequence of the impending demise of the double bill (in the aftermath of the Anti-

Trust decision), several of the smaller studios began renting theatrical films for television exhibition and even producing tele-films of their own. Thus, in 1949, Columbia formed a subsidiary, Screen Gems, to produce new films for and release old films to the new medium. In 1955, the first of the five majors, Warner Bros., was persuaded to produce a weekly ABC-TV series, to be called Warner Brothers Presents, based on three of that studio's successful 1940s features: *King's Row* (1941), *Casablanca* (1942) and *Cheyenne* (1947). It is perhaps worth pointing out that Cheyenne was the only one which lacked elements of the "noir" style and also the only one to enjoy a mass audience; indeed, it was ultimately "spun off" into a seven-year series of its own while the other two-thirds of the slot were quietly discontinued. In December of 1955 RKO withdrew from film production altogether and sold its film library to a television programming syndicate; two years later, the old RKO studio itself was in the hands of Desilu, an independent television production company owned by ex-RKO contract player Lucille Ball and her husband Desi Arnaz. In fact, Lucille Ball's comedy series *I Love Lucy* had been the first "filmed" (as opposed to live) series on American television; it was only dislodged from its place at the top of the ratings by another filmed series, *Dragnet*. The latter, characterized by high key lighting, sparse shadowless sets and procedural plots, was to provide a model for television crime fiction for more than two decades. It is particularly ironic, therefore, to note that *Dragnet* derived from a 1948 B film noir produced by Eagle Lion, *He Walked by Night*, a film which contains what is perhaps the most dramatically chiaroscuro scene ever shot in Hollywood. In 1954 Warner Bros. released a cinematic spin-off from the series, again called *Dragnet*, but this time without a trace of the stylistic virtuosity which had characterized its cinematic grandparent. (The fact that this film proved unsuccessful at the box office, far from invalidating my thesis about the relationship between television and the film noir, actually corroborates my account of the different "spaces" occupied by the discourse of realism in television and the cinema.) Very simply, the low contrast range of television receivers meant that any high contrast cinematic features (like films noirs) were inherently unsuitable for telecine reproduction.

If film noir was determined to any degree by an initial desire to differentiate B cinematic product from that of television (as A product was differentiated by color, production values, 3D, wide screens and epic or "adult" themes), as, too, its ultimate demise relates to capitulation to the requirements of tele-cine, that "difference" can also be seen as a response to the advent of color. The first full-length Technicolor feature, *Becky Sharp*, was released in 1935 (by RKO), and its director, Rouben Mamoulian, one of the few professionals in favor of color at that time, has described in some detail the aesthetic consensus into which the new process was inserted:

> For more than twenty years, cinematographers have varied the key of lighting in photographing black-and-white pictures to make the visual impression enhance the emotional mood of the action. We have become accustomed to a definite language of lighting: low key effects, with sombre, heavy shadows express a somberly dramatic mood; high key effect, with brilliant lighting and sparkling definition, suggest a lighter mood; harsh contrasts with velvety shadows and strong highlights strike a melodramatic note. Today we have color, a new medium, basically different in many ways from any dramatic medium previously known...Is it not logical, therefore, to feel that it is incumbent upon all of us, as film craftsmen, to seek to evolve a photodramatic language of color analogous with the language of light with which we are all so familiar.[29]

Mamoulian's implicit appeal to a "logic of the form" might well have impressed some of the "creative" workers associated with A film productions but it is unlikely to have been heard sympathetically among employees of the Bs. Indeed, the advent of color actually exacerbated the situation he had outlined: the Technicolor process demanded "high key effects, with brilliant lighting and sparkling definition" as a very condition of its existence. It is, therefore, hardly surprising that a cinema of "low key effects, with somber, heavy shadows" flourished in counterpart to it. Furthermore, the films actually employing Technicolor were often characterized by exotic locations, lavish sets, elaborate costumes and spectacular action sequences (generally of the musical or swashbuckling variety) and so fell into an expanding group of "color-specific" genres, Westerns, musicals, epics, historical dramas, et cetera, leaving melodramas, thrillers, and horror to the lower budgets of black and white. Finally, in 1939 the really decisive blow for the industrial endorsement of color was struck by unprecedented success of *Gone with the Wind*. However, wartime economic and technological restraint frustrated much further movement to color for several years, as it also postponed the rise of television, and perhaps the very "dormancy" of the Technicolor phenomenon in those years encouraged those engaged in and/or committed to black and white to continue to experiment. If the war years saw no great increase in Technicolor features (from eighteen in 1939 to twenty-nine in 1945), the postwar period witnessed a rapid acceleration of color production; in 1949 *Variety* confidently predicted that 30 per cent of all forthcoming features would be in color and 15 July 1952 *Film Daily* announced that well over 75 per cent of features in production were shooting in color.

At the other end of the color quality spectrum, but perhaps equally influential on the film noir, was the development of a number of low budget, two-color processes. In 1939, the first of these, Cinecolor, became available and the following year the first full-length Cinecolor feature, Monogram's *The Gentleman from Arizona*, was released. Costing only 25 per cent more than black and white stock and considerably less than Technicolor and with the additional advantage of overnight rushes, Cinecolor (and other "primitive" chromatic processes like it, Vitacolor, Anscocolor, Trucolor) naturally appealed to and was rapidly adopted by certain genres at the low budget end of the industry. By 1959, Allied Artists, Columbia, Eagle Lion, Film Classics, MGM, Monogram, Paramount, 20th Century-Fox, United Artists and Universal had all made some use of these processes. Meanwhile, on the A front, Technicolor did have its disadvantages. For instance, because of the prism block between the back element of the lens and the film gates, neither wide-angle lenses nor those with very long focal lengths could be accommodated by the new three strip cameras. Indeed, even the introduction of faster (black and white and color) negative stock in 1938 was unable to produce any depth of focus without wide angle lenses and, for Technicolor, faster film necessitated stronger floodlighting throughout the late 1930s, the 1940s and into the 1950s; floodlighting which in turn made for a flatter image and a marked lack of contrast. For black and white, on the other hand, the introduction of faster film stock allowed a decrease in lighting levels and aperture openings commensurate with previously impractical chiaroscuro effects. Single source lighting became steadily more feasible and was attractively economic, cheap on both power and labor. Similarly, night for night shooting, which generally involved the payment of prohibitive overtime rates, was particularly applicable to B units which paid set rates for all hours worked.

Apart from color, perhaps the most important technological development in the late 1930s was the introduction of a new range of Fresnel lenses which, for the first time, made it possible to place large diameter lenses close to a powerful light source without loss of focus. Consequently, spotlights began to replace key light functions. While color stock still needed diffused high key lighting, the new fast black and white stock opened the way for smaller lighting units, such as Babys or Krieg Lilliputs, which permitted lower lighting levels. In 1940, small spotlights with Fresnel lenses and 150- or 300-watt tungsten incandescent bulbs began to outmode heavier, less mobile Carbon Arc lamps. The combination of swinging keys, lightweight spots and mobile military cameras made unorthodox angles possible but involved the erection of previously unnecessary set ceilings. It was for precisely this reason that Sid Hickox, Howard Hawks' cameraman on *To Have and Have Not* (1944),

> ...had a problem with his set ceilings: in wanting to hang the incandescent light low, he had to remove most of the ceilings, but the camera shooting from the floor would reveal the lights themselves. So he set up ready-made three quarter ceilings of butter muslin, just sufficiently dark to conceal the incandescents massed behind them, with the other incandescents only a fraction beyond the range of vision.[30]

There were also important developments in camera production in this period. The Mitchell BNC, produced in 1934 but not used in Hollywood until 1938, enabled synch-sound shooting with lenses of 25mm widths for the first time. The only new 35mm camera introduced in the 1940s in any quantity was the Cunningham Combat Camera, a lightweight (13 lb.) affair which allowed cinematographers to move more easily whilst filming and to set up in what would previously have been inaccessible positions. Even more appropriate for hand-held and high or low angle shooting, however, was the Arriflex, which was captured from German military cameramen. (The subjective camera opening sequence in Delmer Daves' *Dark Passage* in 1947, inspired by the previous year's *Lady in the Lake*, was shot with a hand-held Arriflex.[31]) In 1940 the first practical anti-reflective coatings became available, coming into general cinematic currency after their use in *Citizen Kane*. These micro-thin coatings, known as Vard Opticoats, together with twin-arc broadside lamps which were developed for Technicolor, minimized light loss at the surface of the lens (through reflection or refraction) and at the same time accelerated shutter speeds and facilitated the use of good wide-angle lenses, though once again only with black and white. So-called Tolandesque deep focus was therefore only technologically possible from 1938 when the new fast 1232 Super XX Panchromatic Stock could be combined with Duarc light, 25mm wide-angle lenses and considerably reduced apertures. Wide-angle lenses were extensively used thereafter until they were somewhat anachronized by the advent of wide screens in 1953 and the accommodation to television standards later in that decade. In the same way, the use of deep focus photography continued until it was necessarily abated by Hollywood's brief romance with 3D which lasted from 1952 until 1954. The first CinemaScope murder mystery, Nunnally Johnson's *Black Widow* (1954), suffered from its screen size just as much as those 3D thrillers released around the same time, *I, the Jury* (1953) and *Dial M for Murder* (1954), all of which illustrate precisely how such processes militated against projects which might, only a few months earlier, have been films noir.[32]

This line of argument should not, however, be mistaken for a covert reintroduction of the tenets of technological determinism.[33] Indeed, these various "innovations" were all either side effects of the (profoundly ideological) desire for ever-increasing degrees of verisimilitude (Technicolor, Deep Focus) or were determined by a negotiated differentiation from and resistance to that realism (exemplified by the A film, by television and by Technicolor itself) in accordance with economic restraints. I would like, finally, to suggest that it was, specifically, the absorption of a color aesthetic within realism which generated the space which film noir was to occupy. Indeed, just as the advent of radio in 1924 had provoked a cinematic trend away from realism until it was reversed in 1927 with the coming of sound to the cinema, so while color originally signified "fantasy" and was first appropriated by "fantastic" genres, it was too soon recuperated within the realist aesthetic. Compare, for instance, the realist status of black and white sequences in *The Wizard of Oz* (1939) and *If* (1969). The period of this transition, the period in which the equation between black and white on the one hand and realism on the other was at its most fragile, was thus the period from the late 1930s, when television, Technicolor and the double bill were first operating, to the late 1950s, when television and color had established themselves, both economically and ideologically, as powerful lobbies in the industry, and the double bill had virtually disappeared. That period, of something less than twenty years, saw the conjunction of a primarily economically determined mode of production, known as B film-making, with what were primarily ideologically defined modes of "difference," known as the film noir. Specific conjunctures such as this, of economic constraints, institutional structures, technological developments, political, legal and labor relations, are central to any history of film; they represent the industrial conditions in which certain representational modes, certain generic codes come into existence. This is not to argue that cinema is somehow innocent of extra-industrial determinants but simply to insist that Hollywood has a (so far unspecified) relative autonomy within the wider American social formation, however theoretically unsatisfactory that "relativity" remains. The point of this article, therefore, has been to map out an influential fraction of that Hollywood terrain and, as part of that process, to challenge the conceptual catch-all of "mediation" with the concrete specificities of industrial history.

Notes

1. Raymond Borde and Étienne Chaumeton, *Panorama du Film noir Américain* (Paris: Les Éditions de Minuit, 1955). I use the term "genre" in this article where others have opted for "subgenre," "series," "cycle," "style," "period," "movement," etc. For a recent discussion of critical notions of (and approaches to) film noir, see James Damico "Film noir: a modest proposal" in *Film Reader* no. 3, 1978.

2. In an article on "Woman's place: the absent family of film noir" (in E. Ann Kaplan, *Women in Film noir* (London:

British Film Institute, 1978, p. 26), Sylvia Harvey has described how "the increasing size of corporations, the growth of monopolies and the accelerated elimination of small businesses" all contributed to an atmosphere in which it was "increasingly hard for even the petit bourgeoisie to continue to believe in certain dominant myths. Foremost among these was the dream of equality of opportunity in business and of the God-given right of every man to be his own boss. Increasingly, the petit bourgeoisie were forced into selling their labor and working for the big companies, instead of running their own businesses and working for themselves." Other genres have been analyzed in this way: for example, Will Wright's *Sixguns and Society* (Berkeley: University of California Press, 1975) treats the development of the Western as a (generically coded) reflection of the development of American capital.

3. This is not to deny the possible efficacy of such approaches, but rather to insist on their being predicated on the sort of industrial analysis attempted here.

4. Borde and Chaumeton's chapter on "The sources of film noir," translated in *Film Reader* no. 3, p. 63.

5. An example of the first is Paul Schrader, "notes on film noir" in *Film Comment*, vol. 8, no. 1, Spring 1972, p. 11; of the second, Raymond Durgnat, "Paint it black: the family tree of film noir" in *Cinema*, nos. 6-7, August 1970.

6. Raymond Williams, "Base and superstructure in Marxist cultural theory," in *New Left Review*, no. 82, November-December 1973.

7. Antony Easthope, "Todorov, genre theory and TV detectives," mimeo, 1978, p. 4.

8. The poverty of film history already referred to is less material than conceptual. For a useful contribution to the historical debate see Edward Buscombe's "A new approach to film history," published with other papers from the Purdue University Conference in the 1977 Film Studies Annual.

9. Much of the stylistic detail in this outline is indebted to J.A. Place and L.S. Peterson, "Some visual motifs of film noir" in *Film Comment*, vol. 10, no. 1, January-February 1974.

10. For further examples of such infringements see Stuart Marshall, "*Lady in the Lake*: identification and the drives," in *Film Forum*, vol. 1, nos. 1-2, 1977; Stephen Heath, "Film and system: terms of analysis," in *Screen*, vol. 16, nos. 1-2, Spring/Summer 1975; Kristin Thompson, "The duplicitous text: an analysis of *Stage Fright*," in *Film Reader*, no. 2, 1977; and idem, "Closure within a dream: point-of-view in *Laura*," in *Film Reader*, no. 3, 1978.

11. Damico, "Film noir: a modest proposal."

12. Mae D. Heuttig, *Economic Control of the Motion Picture Industry* (Philadelphia: University of Pennsylvania Press, 1944).

13. These figures are, of course, approximate,several of the smallest B companies actually produced films on budgets of less than $100,000, but they do at least indicate the degree of economic difference between the various "modes."

14. Producers' Releasing Corporation: for information on this see Todd McCarthy and Charles Flynn (eds.), *Kings of the Bs* (New York: Dutton, 1975); Don Miller, *B Movies* (New York: Curtis Books, 1973); idem, "Eagle-Lion: the violent years, " in *Focus on Film*, no. 31, November 1978.

15. Nick Grinde, "Pictures for peanuts," in *The Penguin Film Review*, no. 1, August 1946 (reprinted London: Scolar Press, 1977, pp. 46-7).

16. Mark Robson, interviewed in *The Velvet Light Trap*, no. 10, Fall 1973.

17. Grinde, "Pictures for peanuts," p. 44.

18. Peter Bogdanovich, *Fritz Lang in America* (London: Studio Vista, 1967).

19. For information on the Lewton unit see Joel Siegel, *Val Lewton, the Reality of Terror* (London: Secker and Warburg/BFI, 1972). For further detail on RKO see the special issue (no. 10) of *The Velvet Light Trap*. On production in general see Gene Fernett, *Poverty Row* (Satellite Beach, Florida: Coral Reef, 1973).

20. Frank Rickerson Jr., *The Management of Motion Picture Theatres* (New York: McGraw-Hill, 1938), pp. 82-3.

21. Stuart Hall and Tony Jefferson (eds.), *Resistance Through Rituals: Cultural Studies,* nos. 7-8, Summer 1975; reprinted London: Hutchinson, 1976.

22. John Clarke, "Style," in ibid., pp. 175-92.

23. Fox's *March of Time* series lasted from 1934 until 1953 and its photojournalistic aesthetic carried over into that studio's "documentary" fictions in the late 1940s. Similarly, MGM's series of shorts, *Crime Does Not Pay,* which ran from 1935 until 1948, also complemented Metro's own output in that genre.

24. For one account of the effect of these pressures on the cinema see Keith Kelly and Clay Steinman, "Crossfire: a dialectical attack," in *Film Reader* no. 3.

25. Colin MacCabe, "Realism and the cinema: notes on some Brechtian theses," *Screen*, vol. 15, no. 2, Summer 1974, pp. 10-12.

26. Colin MacCabe, "Theory and film: principles of realism and pleasure," *Screen*, vol. 17, no. 3, Autumn 1976, p. 12.

27. Sylvia Harvey, "Woman's place," p. 22.

28. Gill Davies, "Teaching about narrative," *Screen Education*, no. 29, Winter 1978/79, p. 62.

29. Rouben Mamoulian, "Controlling color for dramatic effect," in *The American Cinematographers,* June 1941, collected in Richard Kozarski (ed.), *Hollywood Directors 1941-1976* (New York: Oxford University Press, 1976) p. 15.

30. Charles Higham, *Warner Brothers* (New York: Charles Scribner's Sons, 1975) p. 157.

31. Editor's Note: released in the same year, shot at different studios (Warners and MGM) in just a few months apart, the contexts for subjective camera were quite different: visual emulation of novelist Raymond Chandler's first-person prose in *Lady in the Lake* versus the concealed facial features of escaped convict Vincent Parry before plastic surgery turns him into Humphrey Bogart. Moreover, *Lady in the Lake* was photographed almost entirely on sound stages with a BNC on a dolly while the opening sequence of *Dark Passage* was shot partially on a practical location with both Arriflex and BNC. Later interior sequences are shot on stage sets with a BNC.

On location for *Dark Passage*, Director Delmer Daves (smoking at right) watches the fight between Baker (Clifton Young) and Vincent Parry (Humphrey Bogart) being shot with a Mitchell BNC.

32. The major sources of technological history drawn on here are Barry Salt, "Film style and technology in the thirties," in *Film Quarterly*, vol. 30, no. 1, Fall 1976 and "Film style and technology in the forties," in *Film Quarterly*, vol. 31, no. 1, Fall 1977; and James Limbacher, *Four Aspects of the Film* (New York: Brussel & Brussel, 1968).

33. See, in this respect, Patrick Ogle, "Technological and aesthetic influence upon the development of deep focus cinematography in the United States" and Christopher Williams' critique of that article's elision of notions of ideology and economy. Both are anthologized in *Screen Reader*, 1 (London: SEFT, 1977).

Kathie Moffett (Jane Greer) and Jeff Bailey (Robert Mitchum) in *Out of the Past.*

The Filmic Transaction: On the Openings of Film Noirs

Marc Vernet (1983)

To begin this interrogation, we might ask why the genre of films often called noirs begins with an air of quietude. Why multiply, in the very first minutes, the signs of tranquility? Ordinarily, film noirs are characterized by their singular brutality and surfeit of violence. What paradoxical necessity, then, requires that their opening moves should take place so quietly? Without doubt, this air of safety is more or less relative since one may identify the distinctive traits of the film noir in its very first images. However, when these traits appear they are often nestled within a reassuring tableau. Nothing in these first scenes can compare with those which will soon follow. How could the spectator comprehend the sound and the fury which will soon engulf this initial quiescence?

This structure of sudden contrasts reflects more than an interest in dramatic forms. Something else is taking place here which may shed some light on the problem of suspense and the place of the spectator in the narrative film.

1. *The Set-Up* [Mise en place]: "Everything in its place..."

Here we will consider six films[1]: *The Maltese Falcon* (John Huston, 1941); *Double Indemnity* (Billy Wilder, 1944); *The Big Sleep* (Howard Hawks, 1946); *The Lady from Shanghai* (Orson Welles, 1947); *Out of the Past* (Jacques Tourneur, 1947); and *The Enforcer* (Raoul Walsh, 1950).[2]

The opening movements of each one will display a network of signs denoting tranquility and thus constitute by degrees a tableau which is comforting to the spectator and coherent from the point of view of the narration. In *The Maltese Falcon*, for example, Sam Spade is rolling a cigarette when in walks Miss Wonderly, an attractive and apparently proper young woman whose parents are travelling in Hawaii. In *The Lady from Shanghai*, O'Hara is taking a leisurely stroll when he meets a mysterious young woman riding in a horse-drawn carriage. On a beautiful, summer afternoon, Neff knocks at the door of a luxurious villa, interrupting the sun bath of the young Mrs. Dietrichson (*Double Indemnity*). In a little country town, the hero of *Out of the Past* abandons his gas station for a pastoral meeting with his fiancée. The venerable General Sternwood (*The Big Sleep*) assures a pampered and sheltered existence for his two young daughters. The beginning of *The Enforcer* is not quite identical to those above. However, the action does unfold inside police headquarters, confirming that the initial dramatic movement will take place on the side of law and order.

On this pleasant foundation, the initial relations between characters will be woven and the elements necessary for beginning the intrigue will appear. This schema, which is not really new and permits many variations, resembles a situation described by Vladimir Propp in his analyses of Russian folk tales.[3] It is the establishment of a contract in which someone requests the aid of the hero and promises him repayment for his efforts.

According to Propp, the primary function of the contract is to describe precisely the responsibilities of each of the characters and to regulate the relations which bind them together. In much the same manner, the opening scenes of many film noirs designate and clarify the roles and attributions of each character. The vulnerability of the victim and of the dispatcher [destinateur] is thus emphasized through factors of age, sexual difference, dress, and irresponsibility. General Sternwood, for example, is powerless: one of his daughters seems without any sense of discretion and the other spends her time combating boredom with alcohol. With her superficial elegance and air of discomfort, Miss Wonderly appears lost in San Francisco where she has come to rescue her sister from the clutches of a sinister individual. The young woman in *The Lady from Shanghai*

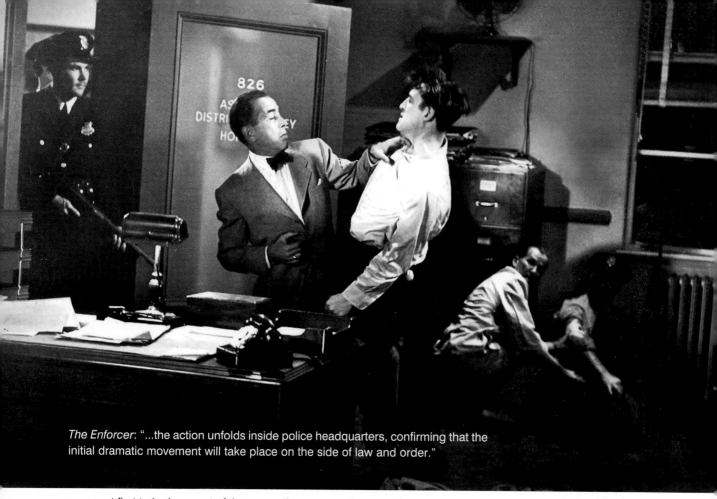

The Enforcer: "...the action unfolds inside police headquarters, confirming that the initial dramatic movement will take place on the side of law and order."

seems at first to be innocent of the gang who menaces her and the surprised Mrs. Dietrichson has trouble hiding her exposed body. And in *The Enforcer*, even though Rico is distraught with fear, it is represented as being an unreasonable and unwarranted fear.

On the other hand, the strength and appearance of the heroes inspires no doubts in their abilities. With past experience in the police force, Marlowe (*The Big Sleep*) is able to handle dangerous affairs without difficulty. The blasé Spade sees Miss Wonderly's problems as little more than routine. O'Hara has travelled the world over. He knows how to use his fists, and when necessary, a gun. The experience of the police inspector in *The Enforcer* finds itself redoubled by the efficacity of the organization which supports him.

But beyond delimiting these positions, the encounters between heroes and victims inaugurate a precise series of exchanges. First, the heroes deplore their initial idleness: Neff and Spade are happy to escape the grey walls of their offices, Marlowe is looking for work, and O'Hara a new form of distraction. The inspector in *The Enforcer* becomes impatient when he sees the investigation brought to a premature conclusion, and it is not at all certain that the hero of *Out of the Past* will be satisfied with the life of petty bourgeois domesticity which awaits him. For their part, the victims only wish to gain their lost tranquility as rapidly as possible. Miss Wonderly wishes the reestablishment of order before her parents arrive home, General Sternwood wants to rid himself of a petty blackmailer, and Rico seeks some form of secure shelter. At the beginning of these films, heroes and victims are both idlers but in different ways: the former wish to leave their idleness behind, the latter to regain it. The heroes restore peace to the victims in order to gain excitement for themselves.

A second form of exchange involves money: the heroes have little, the victims are wealthy, Mrs. Dietrichson and Mrs. Bannister (*Double Indemnity* and *The Lady from Shanghai*) both have very rich spouses, and in *The Maltese Falcon* and *The Big Sleep*, the comfort of the daughters is guaranteed by the wealth of the parents. The heroes have small salaries and less hope of enriching themselves; thus the opportunities afforded by the victims are initially welcomed.

A third variety of exchange is suggested by the idleness of the female characters, the fact that they are single or that their husbands are absent, which affords the possibility of a romantic liaison with the lonely heroes. (Three films do not have a feminine victim or dispatcher: *The Big Sleep, Out of the Past* and *The Enforcer*. However, all three place the virility of the victims in question: General Sternwood because of his age, the old boss of the mechanic because a woman has cheated and left him, Rico because of his debilitating fear.)

In its opening scenes, the film noir thus begins by distributing a restricted set of corresponding elements which, in their turn, regulate a series of multiple exchanges between the victim/dispatchers, on the one hand, and the heroes on the other:

	Victims/Dispatchers	Heroes
Strength/Experience	-	+
Trouble	+	-
Money	+	-
Gender	feminine	masculine
Sexual Availability	+	+

The contract also determines the task which the heroes must accomplish. At first these tasks seem inconsequential when compared to the usual work of the film detective: locate and return home a man or a woman (*Out of the Past, The Maltese Falcon, The Big Sleep*), silence a petty blackmailer (*The Big Sleep*), chase off some hoods (*The Lady from Shanghai*), or guard a prisoner until morning (*The Enforcer*). Moreover, these tasks appear to be somewhat beneath the training and ability of the heroes. They have all the qualities required to accomplish the work before them, and even if they are not always able to complete their mission, as in *The*

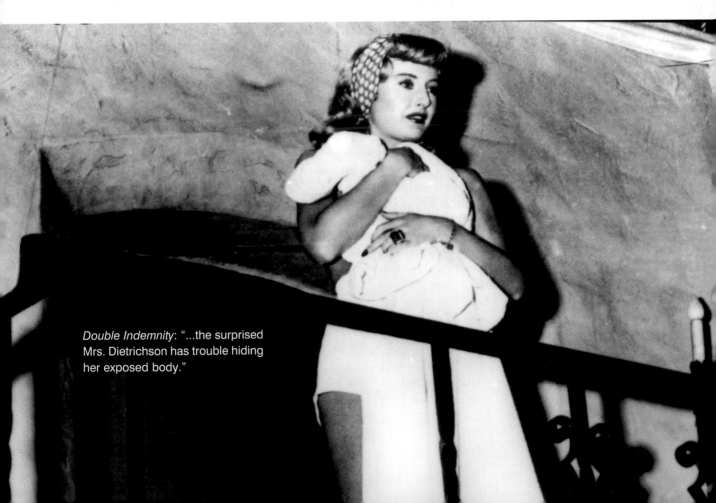

Double Indemnity: "...the surprised Mrs. Dietrichson has trouble hiding her exposed body."

Lady from Shanghai, they have knowledge of the necessary clues such as the names, addresses, and activities of the malefactors. Therefore, what takes form in the accomplishment of the task appears to be more a rapid restoration of normality than the beginning of a long and dangerous adventure. The "contract" is a guarantee, then, insurance that things will not get out of hand. The impossible is not considered therein. The detective or his like have one job to do. Its requirements are precise and remuneration has been fixed beforehand. In itself, this reinforces the sense of calm, order, and propriety which marks the beginning of the film noir. Spade acts paternally with Miss Wonderly, O'Hara and Mrs. Bannister exchange plesantries, Marlowe and General Sternwood tell stories, Neff and Mrs. Dietrichson flirt without really exceeding the bounds of decency. So far, society is peaceful and orderly.

Finally, this contract appears to be short-term, both for the heroes and the spectator. According to certain conditions, it is going to "make something happen." It frames and directs the events to come, channeling the fiction, giving it sense and signification. The text must lead without fail to a truth, the terms of which are already (or nearly) constituted. From the very beginning, the film noir insists on the transparency of the disguise: it will suffice to merely uncover the mystery. In the opening sequence of *The Enforcer*, for example, the culprit is already under lock and key. The police arrive in the middle of the night to place an indispensable witness under protective custody and only a few hours separate us from the beginning of the trial.

Both the titles and opening credits of film noirs seem to participate in the structuring of this type of fiction. They offer, in effect, a foretaste of what will be the truth: the final pleasure, the solution of the intrigue. The two abandoned cigarettes, side by side, at the end of the credits to *The Big Sleep* suggest that the hands and lips of the couple are otherwise occupied. The credits of *The Maltese Falcon* present a "historical" discourse ("1539, Charles V..." etc.) at the same time as the "actual" image of the fabulous statue, thus confirming its existence. The very title of *The Enforcer* places the hero in a position where he is required to protect the letter of the law no matter what the cost. Finally, the slow but inexorable advance of the man on crutches, which illustrates the title sequence of *Double Indemnity*, recalls the determinedness of *The Enforcer* and provides a preview of the character who will avenge himself without pity.

Titles and credits thus consolidate an a priori impression in which the final sequence prevails over the first: the story will advance in a rectilinear fashion. They establish what Freud would call a "purposive idea," working beneath the development of the fiction as a structuring absence.[5] And even though the enigma will detail this force and dispatch it from the scenic space, when uncovered, it stands revealed as the fundamental interest of the fiction. Although it may be diverted and slowed down, like the central characters of the films, nothing will prevent it from finally attaining its ends. There is another aspect of the film noir which supports this idea: the flashbacks which often organize the global structure of the narrative. Here the final truth preexists the actual telling of the story; the hero will evidently survive his adventure without too much damage.

When the film noir takes off, and when the intrigue begins to take form, everything seems destined to go well. This is the "set-up" [mise en place]: where the setting into play of the narrative seems to correspond to a satisfactory arrangement of the elements of the fiction. It is also a time of stability and certainty in which the spectator persuades himself that knowledge of what is important, and pleasurable, is at hand: adventure, love, wealth, and easy living, along with the resolution of the intrigue, as eventualities which no one doubts. The first movement of the film noir sets in motion a narrative machine whose every part is well-oiled and in gear: the characters are fully drawn and their functions clearly established (hero/victim/aggressor); a problem has been carefully and completely laid out with the conditions of its solution clearly stated (this task to accomplish, these actions foreseen).

Although the set-up is logically speaking the first step in the development of the narrative, chronologically speaking it does not have to be the first sequence of the film. In *Double Indemnity*, for example, the set-up takes place in the second sequence while the first sequence functions as what I will identify as the usual second movement of the film noir. Here it is a question of the inversion of a model which is typical of the other films, but whose final result is, as we shall see, identical to them. In addition, the set-up does not necessarily take place within the confines of an autonomous segment. Its constituent elements may be distributed across several scenes in conjunction with other elements which cannot be integrated into the systematic functioning of the movement [mise en place] such as an especially strong menace or a character whose role is ambiguous. This is the case in *Double Indemnity*, but it is also true for *The Enforcer* and for *The Big Sleep*, whose intrigue is much more complicated.

2. The Enigma [Pot au noir]: The "black hole"[6]

Perhaps you are waiting for romance, but in the film noir, it's revolvers that count. The nearly perfect accord of the first movement now falls into chaos. Having barely taken the second step, you are already on a collision course with violence. The smile on the face of the spectator vanishes as brusquely as Archer's when the barrel of a gun rises into the frame. One shot: Archer and Geiger are dead (*The Maltese Falcon*, *The Big Sleep*). Rico misses a step and falls to his death on the concrete below (*The Enforcer*). Two surly types shadow Rita Hayworth in *The Lady from Shanghai*; a killer orders the young fiancée to follow him in *Out of the Past*. Only moments ago foreknowledge of the truth was certain, but now the expected disappears from the film with a brutal and unpredictable force.

The principal function and effect of this second movement in the film noir is to detail the fiction, to slow down and divert its development. Murder eliminates the first witnesses and thus the first indices of the truth. Only Rico can testify against Mendoza, only Archer can identify his murderer, and only Geiger can explain the nature of the affairs he was involved in. The narrative thread is broken: the hero, and the spectator, are suddenly engulfed by a black hole [le pot au noir]. The truth which seemed so close dissolves and scatters to the

The Big Sleep: "Perhaps you are waiting for romance, but in the film noir, it's revolvers [Editor's note: or "automatics" like the one in his hand] that count."

four winds. The intrigue has hardly been unmasked when a flashback carries us back either to the first move-ment or into a time where all certainty fades.

In the film noir, there are several possibilities for linking the first and second movements in order to main-tain the progression of the fiction: unexpected murder, murderer unknown (*The Maltese Falcon*, *The Big Sleep*); death (whether expected or unexpected) already accomplished, murderer known, flashback (*The Enforcer*,[7] *Double Indemnity*). Neither *The Lady from Shanghai* nor *Out of the Past* assumes these routes, but even so, one may note that in the former the film opens with a flashback sketched in by the voice-off narration of the hero, and in the latter, even if it is not a question of a return to the past, there is a return of the past as Bailey is forced to resume his criminal activities. In addition, death's brutal intervention is signified in *The Lady from Shanghai* by Rita Hayworth's gun, the theme of her conversation with O'Hara, and by the two hoods lurk-ing in the shadows. In *Out of the Past*, it is marked by the sudden appearance of the killer. In fact, these last two films belong to an intermediate category which borrows elements from the two, more general categories.

These three varieties of linkage respond to the same necessity: they interrupt and disconnect the narrative, hollowing out the fiction and shooting it full of holes. The second movement of the film noir is a black hole. As a generalized inversion of signs, it demonstrates the structure of an enigma, a lacuna in which all certainty sud-

The Lady from Shanghai: until the movie's ending, the worldly O'Hara misperceives the true nature of Elsa Bannister.

denly fails, as well as a force which turns the space of the fiction inside out with an unexpected violence. He who must talk is silenced (*The Maltese Falcon, The Big Sleep, The Enforcer*), an honest man is discovered to be a former criminal (*Out of the Past*), an insurance agent is revealed as a murderer (*Double Indemnity*), an innocent young woman, apparently without protection, is found to be a liar, married, and never without the protection of a pistol and two bodyguards (*The Lady from Shanghai*). In *The Big Sleep* and *The Lady from Shanghai*, the victim turns out to be a consenting one, and in *The Maltese Falcon* and *The Big Sleep*, the dispatcher, whose good faith was never in doubt, is found to be lying, or at the very least, not telling the whole truth. The confident and experienced detective commits a gross error overturning the investigation (*The Big Sleep, The Maltese Falcon, The Enforcer*); the sailor who has known every danger is led onto a boat by a woman (*The Lady from Shanghai*).

This generalized inversion of signs may take several other forms: passage from day to night, or night to day (*The Maltese Falcon, Double Indemnity, The Lady from Shanghai, The Big Sleep, Out of the Past*); from interior space to exterior space (*The Maltese Falcon, Double Indemnity, The Big Sleep*), or from exterior to interior (*Out of the Past, The Lady from Shanghai*); from country to city (*Out of the Past, The Lady from Shanghai*), or from city to gardened suburbs (*Double Indemnity, The Big Sleep*); and from sunshine to storm (*The Big Sleep*) or vice versa (*Double Indemnity*). In certain films, these shifting oppositions can be extremely vigorous and forceful. In Welles's film, for example, O'Hara makes off with the mystery woman in an open carriage, continuing his journey through the park. Consider then, this ensemble of signs: nature, horse-drawn carriage, darkness, male driver, a woman pedestrian is given a lift, confidence. A few moments later, after the mystery of Mrs. Bannister is revealed, all this is left behind in the interior of a parking lot. O'Hara is chilled, then: concrete, automobile, light, a woman driver, a male pedestrian left behind, caution. During the scene of Archer's murder in *The Maltese Falcon*, it is the spatial axes themselves which are turned around and subverted. Archer looks off-screen high and to the right while lunging toward the right hand side of the frame. From below, a revolver is raised into the frame along its right side, held to the right hand of the assassin, one must then conclude that the camera is situated in the place of the murderer. But it is not there that Archer glances; it is rather more to the right as if the assassin were left handed. Nothing is in its proper place. What is expected from above comes from below, and what must come from the left seems to come from the right. All sense of continuity is lost.

This sense of disorder and reversal, however, is in every case relative. What the spectator witnesses is incontrovertible: there is never a moment where he doubts what he sees. The sense of the action may be difficult to comprehend, but the representation of the event is always produced as a clear and coherent picture. Even if it shrouds the scene in mystery, the black hole never places in doubt the reality of the event it portrays. It requires for itself a minimum of coherence even if it raised more questions than it answered.

3. Disjunction and Contiguity

The oppositions internal to the first movements [mise en place] of film noirs are complementary, and in fact, they cancel out one another within their own system of exchange. The lacunae of the second movements [pot au noir] do not prevent the comprehension of the represented actions. However, the oppositions which take place between the first and second movement are mutually exclusive, setting up a system of irresolvable antinomies: the hero cannot be both strong and vulnerable, the woman good and evil, the dispatcher frank and deceitful. For the spectator, each term and each element is not necessarily less "true" than its contrary, for each functions perfectly within the context of its own system. It is not their existence which the subsequent interrogation must support and explain (separating truth from falsehood, the judgment of one condemning the other), but rather the fact of their coexistence.

The spectator can only try to accept and understand the distance which separates the two ensembles, for this disjunction is the result of powerful oppositions which threaten the collapse of the narrative. The fiction passes from a minor familial squabble to an unexpected slaughterhouse, from pastoral romance to cataclysm, or from a commonplace inquiry to an inexplicable mystery. The gap between the two movements is an asyndeton: a rupture in the chain of significations where the spectator feels as if he has somehow skipped a necessary logical step. The bridge between the two movements has escaped him; the second [pot au noir] does not appear to be logically derived from the first [mise en place]. There is instead a disconnection, a gap, where the spectator feels the absence of a necessary structural relation. Without this, the film would lapse into prattle without value or meaning; it would no longer be a classical narrative. Only the restitution of a logic not yet apprehended can maintain this structural relation and evade a collapse of the fiction. In this, the openings of film noirs reprise an essential feature of the dream-work as described by Freud who explains that if two contiguous images appear without any apparent logical relation between them, their simple succession will nevertheless indicate that a causal relation exists between them.[8] The very fact that the "black hole" immediately follows the "set-up" suggests that even if the rapport between them is not yet visible, it is nonetheless necessary.

Although generally felt as unpleasurable (sudden death, sinister decors, confusion) the black hole will manifest the force of its relation with the set-up by revealing the gaps and marking out the absences contained within its own movement (who is the killer? what is the connection? what is going to happen now?). In other words, the possibility of this enigma [pot au noir] must be conditioned by a relation which precedes it in the set-up [mise en place]. The logic of this relation is missing, of course, but the spectator believes in it all the same, betting on its existence in order to maintain the film's "sanity." To appear realistic, the second movement must somehow anchor itself, or derive a portion of itself, from the interior relations of the first movement. Thus considered, the first movement is placed into doubt as having decoyed and deceived the spectator. The fiction it proposed now seems flawed, corroded, blown apart, the pleasures it promised are now impossible. Having stopped dead in its tracks, the well-oiled machine which produced such an agreeable, straightforward, and seamless story, has now fallen into pieces. Its discretion and meaning have been suddenly exhausted through its collision with the black hole.

Now, the first function which we can attribute to the openings of film noirs in the form "set-up/black hole" would be to create and delimit a certain kind of fictional space. Thus, in uncovering a gap, we have already begun to fill it in, and in destroying one line of logic, we have already begun to construct another. It is a question, then, of bridging the two movements, reducing and explaining the distance which separates them, and filling in the holes which the enigma has bored into the text.

What can be made of this situation? We know that Levi-Strauss has defined the enigma as a question without an answer or an answer without a question; or more precisely, for him it is the impossibility of each answer connecting up with its question and vice versa.[9] The ensemble "set-up/black hole" seems to contain these two models within itself. The first movement proposes an answer which suddenly fades away and the abrupt appearance of the second movement seems to provide the answer to a question which has not yet been asked. The mystery of the film noir is particularly intense when the set-up and the black hole cross paths without appearing to have met one another. In this manner, the first movement projects onto the second an answer which it cannot find and the second movement reverts back on the first as a question which it cannot ask.

Question II <------------------------------> (Answer I)

(Question II) <-------- --------------------> Answer II

It is only with the resolution of the intrigue at the film's conclusion that the answer will finally rejoin its question.

Levi-Strauss also notes that in the myth of Oedipus it is not surprising that the resolution of the riddle of the Sphinx precedes the act of incest. For him the two are equivalencies: the impossible intercourse supposed by the form "question/answer" is homologous with that of "mother/son." In like manner, the structure of the film noir seems to join together that which is impossible; to cancel the distance which forbids the union of its two movements. As the spectator wishes to see the film re-composed by transgressing the barriers which have been thrown up before him, he appears to participate in the incestuous wish which is the impossible conjunction of the set-up and the black hole.

But does this explain why the openings of film noirs should place two disjunct movements side by side in apparent continuity? The two movements contradict and exclude one another from the point of view of both expression and content. However, they are presented together, and for the spectator who believes equally in both, it is not a question of understanding the first or the second movement, but rather set-up and black hole. This abusive relation between two contradictory movements is also a form of "incest": an impossible intercourse which is nevertheless realized.

In sum, the film noir functions according to an incestuous exchange: the first act ("set-up/black-hole") is exchanged for the final act ("question/answer").[10] The former unravels itself as the latter is accomplished. The two beginning movements are continuous when question and answer are discontinuous (see schema above). At the end of the story, this continuity will be broken down when question and answer will finally rejoin one another:

$$Q\ I\ <\text{-------- --------------------}> A\ I$$
$$Q\ II\ <\text{-------- --------------------}> A\ II$$

In effect, the final solution presents the victory of one form over the other: the heroes reestablish, for themselves or for others, the initial situation by defeating the antagonists. In this sense, the solution of the intrigue is a re-placing of the first movement which reestablishes a belief in the power of the heroes and the truth of the fiction. The unravelling of the film thus permits a mediation of the first and second movements which explains the reasons and motivations underpinning their relationship. This mediation is itself a disjunction, though, in that it reestablishes the oppositions by eliminating the "and" of the logical connections and by reinstating the function of difference: one term or the other. The endings of *Double Indemnity, The Lady from Shanghai*, and particularly *The Maltese Falcon* are exemplary in this respect. Here the woman is condemned, which is to say rendered evil and pushed aside, for having confused the difference between good and evil or between love and the desire for power; in short, for having transgressed the categories of the heroes' personal code.[11] And here we can note that the "incest form" which we examined does not exhaust the forms of exchange in the film noir. The "triangle" has often been pointed out as a principal form of relation among the characters: the young hero desires and conquers a rich woman who is quite often tied to an older man or some other representative

The Maltese Falcon: "...the woman is condemned, which is to say rendered evil and pushed aside, for having confused the difference between good and evil or between love and the desire for power; in short, for having transgressed the categories of the heroes' personal code."

of patriarchal authority (*Double Indemnity, The Lady from Shanghai, Out of the Past, The Big Sleep, The Maltese Falcon*).[12] However, in most of these films the woman is made guilty and despite her protestations she is either abandoned or killed by the hero. In this manner, the resolution of the intrigue is guaranteed by the annulment of the incestuous relations. The only film which does not conform to this trajectory (*The Big Sleep*, where the hero and the woman are happily united even though only minutes before she was believed complicit with the gangsters) is one where the intrigue is so confused that its resolution is not clearly apparent to the spectator.[13]

To commit or not to commit incest: this is the fundamental problem of the film noir. It is important that at least for a moment, this question was possible before becoming impossible, and that even though it was forbidden on one level, it was realized on another. The film noir thus accomplishes what Freud recognized as the primary function of the art work: to overturn and reinforce defensive structures at one and the same time. We might call this operation a filmic transaction: "I know that incest is impossible, but even so, I see it accomplished." In the same way, the filmic transaction resembles the structure of fetishism, permitting us to maintain a pleasant and comforting belief against the contradictions of reality.[14]

The first movement of the film noir guarantees this function by assuring, in its own right, a comforting belief: the heroes dominate a situation where all the elements of the ensemble work together without gaps or discord to form a stable and balanced fiction. This belief is only a happy illusion, however. It is overturned by the eruption of the enigma [pot au noir] which, on the one hand, uncovers an anomaly (the black hole: that which one has expected has not come to be), and on the other exposes the illusion of the set-up, destroying the belief which it permits. The black hole thus threatens to destroy the possibility of pleasure promised by the set-up. From this point of view, the element of suspense promised by the intrigue (that is, the knowledge that something is wrong or that some fact is missing) does not seem to rely on the spectator not knowing what will happen. The set-up has previewed for him the pleasures which the text promises, but the black hole has confirmed the risk of un-pleasure in the continuation of the narrative. In this structure of suspense, the spectator only knows what cannot happen. There are only two possible solutions to the intrigue, he thinks, the good and the bad. But what he believes is the disappointment of his first pleasure, that is, the eruption of evil in place of good. In the film noir, suspense is always a balanced mixture of belief and hope, but this belief is only possible because a disturbance has brutally and unexpectedly disrupted the text: the black hole which consumes the sense of narrative. However, the structure of suspense may not maintain any indecisiveness which will threaten its already established trajectory: a satisfactory solution corresponding to the situation of the set-up. For the fiction, all solutions are happy ones provided that they are believable. A resolution is disappointing only when the spectator has foreseen another one, that is, when he has invested his belief in another end to the story.

Even if they are not in themselves suspenseful, the beginnings of film noirs are of necessity a time of suspense in that they condition the possible positions of the spectator with respect to the text: quiet expectation or unpleasant surprise. The desire of the spectator is always to recover what has been lost, to find once again his initial, happy belief.

Hoping to maintain a first impression, afraid of having recognized what is missing in place of what one desired to see: in the structure of suspense which typifies the film noir, it is possible to recognize a configuration characteristic of the fear of castration and its fetishistic elision. The air of suspense. Doesn't this celebrated apprehension of the spectator in the film noir correspond to the fetishist's stare, fixed on a shoe or a piece of feminine lingerie, which marks the last moments of his belief in the phallic woman and the problem of castration she poses? The black hole thus comprises a movement where the hero is deprived of his strength and his power; hereafter, the film must work to restore his stature. It is this initial belief in the hero which is first in the film and first as well in the cinema where, in the best fictions, good must overcome evil. The film noir acts out the destruction of this fiction, this collapse of the narrative-representational cinema. In this it constitutes a passage to the limit where the cinematic signifier would no longer be weak because it could welcome any signified, where this signifier could no longer lure the spectator since its contrary would have equal force, and where its value would be diluted in an infinite play of signification. But this fictional destruction is only momentary. The film noir hastens to reestablish its structuring oppositions, to straighten out its situations, to reinstate, as it were, the cinematic institution which it threatens.

Translated from the French by David Rodowick

Notes

1. This choice has not only been determined by membership in the subgenre of film noir, but also by the frequency with which these films are shown and by the pleasure which they give me. Each film is representative of this subgenre, I think, so I will designate them globally, according to my hypothesis, as "film noirs."

2. The title credits Bretaigne Windust but it is generally known that Raoul Walsh is the actual director of the film.

3. *The Morphology of the Folktale*, tr. Laurence Scott (Austin and London: Univ. of Texas Press, 1968). [Tr. note: Although Vernet footnotes Propp at this point, in his discussion of the function of the contract, he is undoubtedly referring to subsequent interpretations of Propp by Claude Bremond, Roland Barthes, and others. See for example Barthes' discussion in "Introduction to the Structural Analysis of Narratives," pp. 101-4.]

4. [Tr. note: These terms are used in Propp's sense to designate functions which are attributable to, and shared by, individual characters. A "dispatcher" is a character who sends the hero on his or her quest, often promising remuneration in exchange for aid. A "victim" suffers injury as the result of the actions of the villain. Heroes, dispatchers, and other characters may thus function alternately as victims.]

5. Tr. note: ct. Sigmund Freud's *The Interpretation of Dreams*, tr. James Strachey (New York: Avon Books, 1965), pp. 567-70.

6. Tr. note: In the original, pot au noir, a French expression whose only near English equivalent is "pitch-pot," that is, a mysterious fog bank which legendarily lures and entraps vessels.

7. This is taking into consideration that Rico is himself his own killer.

8. Tr. note: See for example, the section of *The Interpretation of Dreams* entitled "The Means of Representation," p. 349 et. passim.

9. Cf. "The Scope of Anthropology" in *Structural Anthropology*, Vol. 2, tr. M. Layton (New York: Basic Books, 1971), p. 22.

10. When I speak of "incestuous forms," it should be clear that I am using Levi-Strauss' sense where the relation between incest and the solution of the enigma is a homology ("The Scope of Anthropology," op. cit., pp. 23-24). This formula should then be understood in the context of remarks made by Roland Barthes ("As, fiction, Oedipus was at least good for something: to make good novels, to tell good stories..." *Pleasure of the Text*, tr. Richard Miller (New York: Hill and Wang, 1975), p. 47), by Christian Metz (cf. "The Imaginary Signifier," tr. Ben Brewster, *Screen*, 16, No. 2 (Summer 1975), pp. 14-76), and by Raymond Bellour (cf. "Alternation, Segmentation, Hypnosis," *Camera Obscura*, Nos. 3-4 (Summer 1979), pp. 71-101). There is no question of referring to the notion of incest, or of Oedipal relations, as "objects" in the film. Rather, they are understood to inform the structure of the text through a homologous relation.

11. On the function of ambivalence in the figure of Woman as double, see Julia Kristeva's "The Bounded Text" in *Desire in Language*, tr. Thomas Gora, Alice Jardine, and Leon S. Roudiez (New York: Columbia Univ. Press, 1980), pp. 36-63.

12. Note here that wealth functions as a sign which establishes an opposition with the hero, since the factor of age does not.

13. Raymond Bellour suggests to me that even if this resolution is not clearly understood, it is readily comprehended because the film privileges the constitution of a mythic couple (Bogart and Bacall) which overshadows the problems of the narrative.

14. Cf. Victor N. Smirnoff's "La transaction fetichique," *Nouvelle Revue de psychanlyse*, No. 2 (Fall 1970), pp. 41-63. [Tr. note: The relation between fetishism and belief in the spectatorial relations offered by film has been argued by Christian Metz, among others. See his "The Imaginary Signifier."]

Despite this posed shot of Marlowe pitching woo to Mrs. Grayle, "*Films in Review* [determined that] *Murder, My Sweet* was a film that 'supported positive values.'"

Film Noir: Style and Content

Dale E. Ewing, Jr. (1988)

The idea of an American film noir affords the analyst of ideology and culture an interesting definitional problem. The term itself is the invention of movie critics who hold the opinion that style is the sole vicinity in which meaning can be found in the cinema. And although these critics have done well in defining a consistent "film noir spirit," their work has been less than satisfactory in identifying precisely which movies this spirit fits. It is the argument of this study that the term film noir has been applied too loosely to give us an accurate definition of the subject. In the first section, an attempt will be made to prove this contention by reviewing the style-is-content literature on noir and then undertaking a metacritique of it. In the second section, a new interpretive method for looking at film noir will be proposed that uses style and content as interrelated principles that work in the films to create a totality of meaning. In this sense, a particular film cannot be defined as a film noir because it reflects one aspect or several aspects of the film noir spirit; it has to reflect every aspect of the film noir spirit or it is something other than noir.

The viewpoint projected here is that, although films noirs were supposed to be more nihilistic than the usual Hollywood films, they were still Hollywood films. In other words, a film noir cannot be defined adequately until the movie in question is evaluated as a complete work in which the themes develop from a plot that has the conventional beginning, middle, and end characteristic of Hollywood movies during the noir period.

Film noir means "black film," and it was a French appellation given to an unusually despairing group of Hollywood crime thrillers that began showing in France after World War II. These films had a dark style of visual presentation that combined gothic chiaroscuro lighting effects with an ambiguous and dislocated sense of space borrowed from the technical achievements of German Expressionism. Although the subject matter of film noir varied—it seemed to overlap into several previously established crime genres—the French saw in it strong affinities with a literary genre popular in their country called "série noire."[1] Série noire literature included French translations of Gothic novels and what in America are called "hardboiled" mystery novels. The world projected in film noir corresponded most closely to these latter works.

The American hardboiled mystery was an attempt to create a grittily realistic world of criminals and detectives, but its chief emphasis was on urban sordidness and melodrama. The hardboiled mystery novel fell into two categories. The stories of Dashiell Hammett and Raymond Chandler were about tough, outspoken private detectives. Heroes such as Phillip Marlowe and Sam Spade were interesting figures primarily because their creators gave them a sense of social justice and a certain amount of stoic virtue underneath their cynicism. The other category of hardboiled fiction—exemplified by the novels of James M. Cain and Cornell Woolrich—depended on a more faux naif approach in which the writers delighted in showing ordinary people becoming embroiled in crime due to some unlucky accident or character fault. In Cain's *Double Indemnity*, for example, an insurance salesman, Walter Neff, falls in love with one of his clients, an attractive housewife. The housewife, it turns out, is thoroughly despicable. She persuades Neff to kill her husband so they can cash in on his life insurance policy. In Woolrich's *The Window*, a small boy who lives in a tenement sees his neighbors rob and murder a sailor. The boy has a reputation for lying, and no one believes his story except the killers themselves. Even after they make an attempt on his life, no one believes him. The killers are eventually caught, but it is by accident rather than human design.

In his 1970 article, "The Family Tree of Film Noir," Raymond Durgnat suggests that an American film noir was usually preceded by a French version—*La Chienne* became *Scarlet Street*, *La Bête Humaine* became

Human Desire.[2] But one of the earliest critics to write about film noir, Jean-Pierre Chartier, viewed the American strain as far more nihilistic:

> One speaks of a French school of black films, but at least *Le Quai des brumes* or *Hotel du Nord* had touches of revolt, love entered in the mirage of a better world. In these films, there was hope and even if characters were in despair they solicited our pity or sympathy. But here they are monsters, criminals, or sick people without excuse, who act as they do because of the fatality of evil within them.[3]

Chartier does not, however, attempt to account for the pessimism of American film noir. The first critics to analyse motive in these productions were Raymond Borde and Étienne Chaumeton. When their book-length study *Panorama du Film Noir Américain* appeared in 1955, the authors argued that film noir was a synthesis of three of Hollywood's most popular genres, the gangster movie, horror films—such as Val Lewton's style-conscious *Cat People*—and the private detective film. Borde and Chaumeton explained that these earlier genres contained the seeds of alienation and revolt that film noir was to later more sharply define. From the detective movie, film noir got its powers of observation and atmospheric detachment. From horror films, such as *I Walked with a Zombie* and *Cat People*, film noir gained a mise-en-scène of repulsion and dread. The gangster film bequeathed to film noir its rebellious, gun-toting antiheroes. Borde and Chaumeton concluded that film noir, in its eclectic borrowing of generic influences, developed into a distinctive genre of social commentary. Film noir, according to Borde and Chaumeton, was expressing deeply pessimistic themes that were related to the aftershock of the Depression and the 1930s gangster era, America's involvement in World War II, and the social upheaval caused by the post-war readjustment to civilian life. The authors also suggested that the arrival in Hollywood of a large number of German directors—among them Fritz Lang, Robert Siodmak, Curtis Bernhardt—all of whom were refugees from Hitler, were the dominating force behind its gloomy expressionistic style.[4]

At this point, it should be pointed out that French film analysts were of the school of thought that "style is content" in the movies. This approach was not accepted in America in the 1950s—which makes American and French ways of reading films diametrically opposite during this period. For example, when the French critic Chartier saw *Murder, My Sweet*, he saw the private detective hero, Marlowe—as he searches for the missing girlfriend of the gangster Moose Malloy—getting repeatedly drugged and beaten against a dark, stylistic background of corrupt police and seemingly honest citizens deceiving one another.[5] At the same time, in the United States, the American critic Clayton Henry, Jr., went to a screening of *Murder, My Sweet*, and, although he saw the same negative qualities Chartier saw, he realized that the plot tied together all these loose ends when Marlower saved the day and married the pretty heroine, Ann. Such factors led Henry to write, in the American publication *Film in Review,* that *Murder, My Sweet* was a film that "supported positive values."[6]

By the late 1960s, however, American film analysts had begun to come over to the French style method. It is beyond the scope of this study to account for this change, but the critics Charles Higham and Joel Greenburg laid the foundations for the American version of the style argument in their 1968 book *Hollywood in the Forties*. In their chapter "Black Cinema," concentrating on film noir's most provocative visual components, they provided a melodramatic description of its basic intention: to create a world without "a single trace of pity or love."[7] For Higham and Greenberg, this pessimistic world view was defined by sensational visual imagery:

> A dark street in the early morning hours, splashed with a sudden downpour. Lamps form haloes in the murk. In the walk-up room, filled with intermittent flashing of a neon sign from across the street, a man is waiting to murder or be murdered....[8]

These kinds of images, Higham and Greenberg explain, are what gives film noir its "specific ambience." In a remarkably colorful passage, they describe some of the ways film noir develops this ambience through the use of trains speeding through the night:

> These trains, transporting their passengers on sinister errands, clank and sway through storm-swept darkness, their arrival at remote stations signalled by the presence of mysterious raincoated figures,

while in the narrow corridors, the antiseptic, cramped compartments, assignations are made, and more often than not, a murder is planned.[9]

The authors suggest that such images have no other purpose than to employ romantic pessimism as a kind of slap in the face of American naivete and innocence. Higham and Greenberg state that film noir shows viewers "a world waiting to pounce in at the gates of the respectable, the jungle is already thrusting upwards."[10]

It might be argued that American film critics were adding to their analysis of the film noir their own impressions of living through the calamitous 1960s and early 1970s. They were casting a cynical look back on the middle-class innocence of their post-World War II generation. The stylistic gloom of film noir afforded an appealing paradigm of disorder. At the surface of life, America reflected an innocent appearance, but this was only repression, which is a breeding ground for all sorts of irrationalities and fears. Higham and Greenberg's metaphor of a "jungle thrusting upward" corresponds to Jung's idea that when a man represses his evil side, it causes a shadow to be cast on his unconscious. If the individual fails to acknowledge his evil side, his repressive mechanisms cause the "shadow" to grow to the point where it will burst out into his conscious mind and overwhelm him.[11]

After 1970, all film noir criticism seemed to spring from this central idea. In an influential article written in 1972, the critic and screenwriter Paul Schrader suggested that the style of film noir consistently undermined traditional plot resolutions in which the hero triumphs over the forces of evil:

American film critics have always been sociologists first and scientists second: film is important as it relates to large masses, and if a film goes awry it is often because the theme has been somehow "violated" by the style. Film noir operates on opposite principles: the theme is hidden in the style, and bogus themes are often flaunted ("middle class values are best") which contradict the style.[12]

Schrader believed that the film noir style was representative of a struggle for freedom within an otherwise repressive film form. Hollywood films had a classical or "Aristotelian" approach to art that attempted to imitate nature in such a way as to convince spectators that their religious and secular institutions corresponded to a universal order. In the final analysis, this universal order was regulated by principles of cosmic harmony—forcing the classical drama into a position where it was necessary for it to illustrate this concept by following a prosaic chain of causation from beginning, middle, to end.[13] In *Romeo and Juliet*, for example, the plot unfolds in a step-by-step fashion, like a series of carefully choreographed ballet routines designed to illustrate disorder and eventual reconciliation. For Schrader, the film noir style radically deconstructed the idealism of this formula by adding to it an underlying mood of tension and cynicism.

In their cumulative reference guide, *Film Noir: An Encyclopedic Reference to the American Style*, Alain Silver and Elizabeth Ward agree wholeheartedly with Schrader:

[These films] reflect a common ethos: they consistently evoke the dark side of the American persona. The central figures in these films, caught in their double binds, filled with existential bitterness, drowning outside the social mainstream, are America's stylized vision of itself, a true cultural reflection of the mental dysfunction of a nation in uncertain transition.[14]

The "existential bitterness" Silver and Ward refer to has been described by Robert Porfirio as "undercutting any attempted happy endings and prevents the films from being the typical Hollywood escapist fare."[15] From Porfirio's point of view, film noir epitomizes a black vision of American life in which the only shared responses are fears and repressed impulses:

What keeps film noir alive for us today is something more than a spurious nostalgia. It is the underlying mood of pessimism.... This...is nothing less than an existential attitude towards life. It places its emphasis on man's contingency in a world where there are no transcendental values or moral absolutes.[16]

By now, it should be clear that the spirit of film noir—as identified in the literature discussed above—was one of relentless pessimism and alienation. In an excellent series of articles that developed out of the British Film Institute Summer School in 1975—which was published in a short book, *Women in Film Noir*, edited by E. Ann

Kaplan—this textual pessimism and alienation was viewed as a purveyor of dominant and repressed ideologies concerning the place of women in society:

> Film noir is particularly notable for its specific treatment of women. In the films of another genre, the Western, women, in their fixed roles as wives, mothers, daughters, lovers, mistresses, whores, simply provide the background for the ideological work of the film which is carried out through men. Since the placement of women in this way is so necessary to patriarchy as we know it, it follows that the displacement of women would disturb the patriarchal system, and provide a challenge to the world view. The film noir world is one in which women are central to the intrigue of the films and are furthermore usually not placed safely in any of the familiar roles mentioned above. Defined by their sexuality, which is presented as desirable but dangerous to men, the women function as the obstacle to the male quest. It is largely because of this interplay of the notion of independent women vis-a-vis patriarchy that these films are of interest to feminist film theory.[17]

The authors in *Women in Film Noir* talk more about story than analysts such as Silver and Porfirio. However, their discussions are necessarily subordinated to the question of domination and emancipation from the male gaze. The male gaze denotes a specific style of visual presentation in which the male is the subject and the women is the object.[18] All of the authors in the study agree that the noir world is defined in male terms. Women in film noir are viewed through the eyes of men who measure their worth according to sexist and oppressive standards. The contradiction rests in threatening women's roles that victimize the male heroes and undermine the patriarchal order. The extent to which the hero becomes disenchanted with these roles and attempts to combat them illustrates the dialectical relationship between the oppression and empowerment of women as a group.

In respect to defining a general spirit of textual alienation and oppression, the style-is-content literature reflects a remarkable consistency. But how is this spirit applied to specific films and how does it operate? This question raises a fundamental problem with the style-is-content literature. None of the analysts mentioned—from Higham and Greenberg to Sylvia Harvey—ever explain in their studies how a particular film that supposedly reflects the noir spirit does so in terms of overall closure. At this point, some perspective is needed on what the critics have said and whether or not it affords an adequate definition of the subject. To be fair, their assessment of film noir is not altogether inaccurate. However, their tendency to construct generalizations based on the style of the films has caused them to overlook the way content is expressed. The critics, for example, never pinpoint specific points of view in the films. They never examine one film and then elaborate on the implications of its actual conclusion. This is because literal conclusions are wholly suspect in modern film criticism. They usually represent "bogus themes" that contradict the spontaneous purity of the style.

When critics make such artistic preferences, it is generally with good intentions: they desire to broaden the horizons of art. But problems develop when a certain perference becomes a mono-causal theory of reality. Its terms become "reified," to use Max Weber's expression; the theory seems to acquire a life of its own, and many people will follow its lead without questioning it. Because style has become something of a mono-causal theory in film noir criticism, it seems important to analyze the value of its approach.

The style-is-content argument in film noir studies touches upon the problem of values clarification in art criticism and scholarship. In America especially, movies were not considered an object of serious study until the late 1960s, when film courses began to be taught in community and four-year colleges. The teaching method in these courses was primarily descriptive. How was a film made? What distinguished the cinema from other representational art forms such as painting and theatre? What were a film's textures, structures, and symbols? On campuses, key movements in film were discussed such as Nouvelle Vague, and individual movies were dissected—as if under a microscope—then relegated to the latest genre or subgenre the critics and analysts had discovered.

This emphasis on formal achievements was not as cold and reductionist as it might sound. It had an antecedent in the longing for freedom expressed in modern art theory in the 1930s and 1940s. Believing that fascism and Stalinist Realism were debasing art and culture, critics such as Alfred Barr and Clement Greenberg came to view style as the principal liberating factor in art. Content was dismissed because it implied a certain amount of reflection upon already existing norms, values, and beliefs. The purpose of art was not to reproduce old values—political, religious, ethical—because these values had become trivialized by mass culture. The fundamental purpose of art was to produce new forms in acts of spontaneous creation.[19]

During the same period that Barr and Greenburg were writing, Alexander Astruc was developing, in France, a similar line of reasoning that he applied to film: his important theory of camera-stylo (camera-pen). This approach argues that the theme of a movie is implicit in its visual style and that visual composition is more important than the meanings found in spoken dialogue. In the past, filmmaking had imitated literature and the play; this had been one of its biggest mistakes. Astruc stated that "the cinema will gradually break free from the tyranny of what is visual, the image for its own sake, from the immediate and concrete demands of the narrative, to become a means of writing just as flexible and subtle as written language."[20]

According to Astruc, the cinema was just as much an art as writing or painting, and one of its central aims was liberation from content. By the 1960s, Susan Sontag, in her essay "On Style," was calling for the limitation of the human content in art. One of the central purposes of art, she explained, was to "fend off tired ideologies like humanism or socialist realism which put art in the service of some moral or social idea."[21] Sontag went on to formulate a philosophy of art as "dehumanized representation":

> All works of art are founded on a certain distance from the lived reality which is represented. This "distance" is, by definition, inhuman or impersonal to a certain degree; for in order to appear to us as art, the work must restrict sentimental intervention and emotional participation, which are functions of "closeness." It is the degree and manipulating of this distance...which constitute the style of the work. In the final analysis, "style" is art. And art is nothing more or less than various modes of stylized, dehumanized representation.[22]

Sontag concluded that this act of distancing encompassed a language of possibility and liberation because it represented "movement...not just away from but toward the world."[23] This point is restated in somewhat clearer fashion by Ernst Fischer in his 1967 book *Art Against Ideology*:

> Art is now obliged to reveal the real world behind the apparent one, to drive men who are escaping into irresponsibility back into reality.... The fetishes of our time are objects of external life: mechanisms, institutions, clichés, "facts," phrases. To get rid of fetishes means to break through this substitute reality of connivance and to reveal the latent reality. But the fetish formations in a highly developed industrial society are so dense and strong that without the help of shock the imagination can scarcely hope to break through them into reality. How can art, using old methods, challenge if not defeat the barbarism which is establishing itself in the midst of our civilization? If art is determined to fight against the fetishes, it must adapt itself to the conditions of that struggle and risk breaking with the old categories of aesthetics.[24]

Critics such as Barr and Greenburg, Sontag and Fischer, were using style as the basis for a heuristic theory of art in which the artist was supposed to make a clean break with traditional values. In 1970, in his book *Expanded Cinema*, Gene Youngblood explained how this metacritical conception of art could be applied to film. According to Youngblood, the purpose of film is to broaden our spiritual horizons by extending the technical and aesthetic possibilities of the medium into new, exciting frontiers. But Youngblood insists that before this can happen, the cinema must first do away with the traditional idea of the film as escapist entertainment:

> Commercial entertainment works against art, exploits the alienation and boredom of the public, by perpetuating a system of conditioned response to formulas. Commercial entertainment not only isn't creative, it actually destroys the audience's ability to appreciate and participate in the creative process. To satisfy the profit motive, the commercial entertainer must give the audience what it expects, which is conditional on what it has been getting which is conditional on what it previously received, ad infinitum.[25]

Art and film theorists such as Greenburg, Barr, and Youngblood, in their conviction that representational art created a trivialized and debased mass culture, came to regard style as the aesthetic platform upon which to uplift society by making a break with popular forms of artistic expression and creating new ones. But as Stanley Aronowitz has observed, in *The Crisis in Historical Materialism*, their ideals backfired and created an elitist art criticism that "served to legitimate the production of an academic canon of high culture."[26] This would have been less of a problem had the modernist and realist categories remained mutually exclusive. However, inevitably, modernist standards of value descended into critical interpretations of so-called popular art as well. All of this discussion of movies as art and art as a tremendous liberating force had a definite impact on film and cultural analysts who came across the French work on film noir. When these analysts began to "discover" film noir, they were delighted that its modernist style seemed to propose a counter-cinema within the traditional narratives to which it was applied. Unfortunately, their use of an interpretive values model that worked independently from the specific historical contexts and values contexts, which made up the overall narration of film noir, made their assessments only half true.

At this point in our study, it is necessary to propose a new interpretation of the use of style and content in film noir. Where modern style-is-content analysts have been concerned with the cataloging of paranoid figurations, lighting techniques, and camera angles, they have used the elliptical language of style to support a normative criticism. If merely silent and disjointed sound fragments of the films existed, the logic behind drawing historical observations from incomplete evidence would be understandable enough. But film noir is not like a series of hieroglyphs in which only a few symbols have been translated. The films themselves are intelligible, complete works, that contain elements of plot, theme, and the conventional beginning, middle, end, common to traditional American films, novels, plays, and short stories. In believing they have discovered a Rosetta stone in the film noir style, modern critics have become stuck on form and neglected content. The Hungarian critic, Georg Lukács, sees an inherent fallacy in this—a kind of theoretical imbalance:

> Content determines form.... The distinctions that concern us are not those between stylistic "techniques" in the formalistic sense. It is the view of the world, the ideology of weltanschauug...that counts. It is the...attempt to reproduce this view of the world which constitutes "intention" and is the formative principle underlying the style.... Looked at in this way, style ceases to be a formalistic category. Rather, it is rooted in content; it is the specific form of a specific content.[27]

Lukács' argument offers extremely important insights into the nature of film noir. The fact that analysts have made generalizations about film noir from its stylistic qualities does not necessarily invalidate their conclusions; it only forces them to take into account basic objections to their method. Bill Nichols, in his article "Style, Grammar, and the Movies," suggests that it is not as important to value content over style as it is to fuse them both into an integrated critical theory.[28]

If style and content are viewed as working together in film noir as a kind of monad, it becomes possible to use this perspective as a way of qualifying some of the generalizations made by the style-is-content analysts. For these analysts, the idea of an American film noir is the idea that certain Hollywood films reflect a spirit of alienation, nihilism, despair, loneliness, and dread. But these negative terms have been applied so loosely as to have lost all meaning. If we are to inquire into the precise nature of these terms, we must begin our inquiry with the film story itself. If the principal characters in a given film are unhappy and alienated, what are their reasons? If the protagonist is despairing and nihilistic, what does he do about it? If we follow the style-and-content approach, the "story" will tell us what he does. If the hero is able to reconcile these negative terms—learn something positive from his alienation and despair—then we are not dealing with a black film. If the hero suffers continually and never learns anything, then we are looking at a genuine film noir in the light of what James Agee called "the cruel radiance of what is."

NOTES

1. Alain Silver and Elizabeth Ward, eds., *Film Noir: An Encyclopedic Reference to the American Style* (Woodstock, NY: Overlook Press, 1979), p. 1.

2. Raymond Durgnat, "The Family Tree of Film Noir," *Cinema* (UK), 6/7 (1970), p. 49.

3. Jean-Pierre Chartier, "Les Am,ricains aussi font des films 'noirs'." *Revue du Cinéma*, No. 2 (1946), p. 70. (Translation mine).

4. Raymond Borde and Etienne Chaumeton, *Panorama du Film Noir Américain* (Paris: Les Éditions de Minuit, 1955), pp. 29-37.

5. Chartier, "Films 'noirs'," p. 68.

6. Clayton Henry, Jr., "Crime Films and Social Criticism," *Films in Review*, 2, No. 5 (1951), p. 33.

7. Charles Higham and Joel Greenberg, *Hollywood in the Forties* (Cranbury, NJ: A. S. Barnes, 1968), p. 21.

8. Higham and Greenberg, p. 33.

9. Higham and Greenberg, p. 34.

10. Higham and Greenberg, p. 36.

11. Jeffrey Burton Russell, *The Devil: Perceptions of Evil from Antiquity to Early Christianity* (Ithaca, NY: Cornell University Press, 1979), p. 31.

12. Paul Schrader, "Notes on the Film Noir," *Film Comment*, 8, No. 1 (1972), p. 13.

13. William Charles Siska, *Modernism in the Narrative Cinema: The Art Film as Genre* (New York: Arno Press, 1980), pp. 23-24.

14. Silver and Ward, Film Noir, p. 6.

15. Robert G. Porfirio, "No Way Out: Existential Motifs in the Film Noir," *Sight and Sound*, 45, No. 4 (1976), p. 213.

16. Porfirio, p. 213.

17. E. Ann Kaplan, ed., *Women in Film Noir* (London: BFI Publishing, 1980), pp. 2-3.

18. Christine Gledhill, in Kaplan, *Women in Film Noir*, p. 11; cf., Sylvia Harvey, in Kaplan, *Women in Film Noir*, p. 33.

19. See Alfred Barr, *Cubism and Abstract Art* (New York: Museum of Modern Art, 1936); and Clement Greenburg, *Art and Culture* (New York: Beacon, 1961).

20. Alexander Astruc, quoted in David Thomson, *Overexposures: The Crisis in American Filmmaking* (New York: Oxford University Press, 1981), p. 70.

21. Susan Sontag, *Against Interpretation* (New York: Farrar, Straus & Giroux, 1967), p. 31.

22. Sontag, p. 30.

23. Sontag, p. 31.

24. Ernst Fischer, *Art Against Ideology* (New York: Braziller, 1969), pp. 168-169.

25. Gene Youngblood, "Art, Entertainment, Entropy," in Gerald Mast and Marshall Cohen, eds., *Film Theory and Criticism* (New York: Oxford University Press, 1979) pp. 754-760.

26. Stanley Aronowitz, *The Crisis in Historical Materialism* (South Hadley, MA: Praeger, 1981), p. 275.

27. Georg Lukács, *The Meaning of Contemporary Realism*, trs. John and Necke Mander (London: Merlin Press, 1979), p. 19.

28. Bill Nichols, "Style, Grammar, and the Movies," *Film Quarterly*, 28, No. 3 (Spring 1975), pp. 34, 44.

Manhunter: William Petersen as FBI profiler Will Graham.

Kill Me Again: Movement Becomes Genre

Todd Erickson (1990)

Film noir was just a term, which French cinéaste Nino Frank reputedly invented it in 1946, when the movie houses of post-World War II Paris were deluged with a wave of hard-edged American crime pictures. After their first viewing of movies such as *Double Indemnity, Laura, Phantom Lady*, and *Murder, My Sweet*, other French critics picked up and fostered the use of the term in their writings, most notably Raymond Borde and Étienne Chaumeton in their groundbreaking study *Panorama du Film Noir Américain* (1941-1953) published in 1955. Remarkably, as Part One of this volume confirms, thirteen years passed before an English-language book, *Hollywood in the Forties* by Charles Higham and Joel Greenberg, used the term and formally recognized film noir as a distinct body of films. And, while there have been scores of English language articles and books dedicated to the subject since then, until recently, film noir was a term rarely encountered outside of film schools, cinema books, and motion picture retrospectives.

In 1995 thanks to the contemporary cinema's flourishing cycle of self-conscious noir, the term is rapidly being absorbed into everyday American life. The ubiquitous medium of modern television pays homage to film noir through period recreations such as Showtime Network's cable series *Fallen Angels*, and millions of viewers have been introduced to the stylistic decorum of the noir milieu through primetime programming like Fox Network's *X-Files*. Even journalists use fusion phrases such as "cable noir," "TV noir," "pop noir," and "cyber noir," to help them describe creations influenced by the somber mood and visual style of film noir.

The increased awareness of the term, film noir, can also be attributed to haphazard movie critics, who, seemingly anxious to show-off their cinematic IQs, assign the term to virtually any contemporary motion picture favoring dark, wet streets and/or a central character in jeopardy. In turn, the studios and mainstream independent distributors, none of which had ever promoted a theatrical release as a "film noir" prior to Orion Pictures' *The Hot Spot* in 1990,[1] have increasingly begun to rely on noir-descriptive quotes from critical reviews to market their pictures.

This evolution toward the acceptance and casual use of the term and its many variations has energized the long-standing argument over how film noir should be classified within the scope of cinema history and criticism. Is it a genre or a movement? A style? A mood? Was film noir time-bound, or does it still exist in the American cinema?

Fortunately, the passage of time, the accumulation of critical data, and most important, the contemporary cinema's new cycle of noir-influenced crime films, have given us a perspective on film noir not previously accessible. From this more favorable vantage point, we can understand film noir not only as a movement, but also as a genre, which developed within, and emerged from, the movement itself.

As a movement, the film noir incorporated a specific attitude; a cynical, existentially bitter attitude derived from the hard-boiled school of fiction, as well as the attendant socio-cultural influences of the day, which were visually expressed through lighting, design and camerawork assimilated from the German Expressionist cinema via the gangster and horror genres of the thirties.

Robert Porfirio cites *Citizen Kane* (1941) as the prototype of a visual style and narrative perspective from which the movement's tendencies were adopted.[2] The stylistic and narrative devices that Welles utilized in *Citizen Kane*, such as Gregg Toland's deep focus photography, extreme camera angles, optical effects, flashbacks, and voice-over narration became representative cinematic components of the overall film noir movement, a movement that darkened the mood, or tone, in virtually all of the cinematic product of Hollywood from that era.

Although noir found its best avenues of expression in the detective and the gangster genres, as a movement it cut across all generic lines. That's why social dramas (*It's a Wonderful Life*, 1946) and other genre films, such as the Western (*Pursued,* 1947) and Science Fiction (*The Day the Earth Stood Still*, 1951) were affected and transformed by the stylistic elements and thematic concerns of noir. Of course, these genre films were not film noir. To use a hybrid expression, they were "noired."

It was not until the noir genre had successfully emerged in the eighties (from its embryonic state in the sixties and seventies) that we could understand film noir on two distinct planes. First, as an overall cinematic movement which, to some extent, modified most of Hollywood's product during the forties and fifties, and secondly, as a (new) genre that emerged from the overall movement, utilizing the subject matter that was at the very core of its existence: the presence, or portent, of crime.

The detective and gangster genres were ripe for evolution within the context of the early forties American cinema, and the force of the noir movement made such an evolution possible. In theory, Robert Porfirio explained how this occurred:

> The film noir acted as something of a conduit, drawing from many of the major commercial genres of the thirties and transforming them (via its mood, style, etc.) into the more modern forms of the 1960s. To carry this metaphor a bit further, if the film noir served as a nexus or channel for the established genres to traverse, it was one whose function was short-lived, for as 'older' genres became 'newer' ones, the film noir itself died out, dissipating its energies among certain of the genres that displaced it."

Because of the peculiar qualities that film noir brought to these existing genres, they were altered and re-codified so that they gradually built up their own specific generic expectations for the viewer. "The more a genre develops," observed Marc Vernet, "which is to say the more films it contains, the more the codes tend to play the role of a guarantee to the spectator."[4]

What made the noir films of the forties such as *Double Indemnity* (1944), *The Killers* (1946) and *Out of the Past* (1947) so revolutionary in their day was that they distorted the viewer's psychological reference points by establishing a new set of generic codes. This new set of generic codes incorporated iconography from the detective and gangster genres, the distinctive narrative voice (or attitude) of the hard-boiled writers, and the first-person sensibility of the expressionistic subjective camera, through which the underworld could be experienced vicariously by the viewer.

Using Raymond Chandler's character of Philip Marlowe as an example, J.P. Telotte explained how the narrative voice of the hard-boiled writers was significant in constructing the noir film:

> Thanks to Chandler's first-person narration, all that we see in the Marlowe novels is what the detective himself sees; his experiences, and his thoughts, are ours. This outer-directedness ultimately proves just as important as Marlowe's moral stance (style an equivalent of theme), since it equally defines our relationship to the world he inhabits. Through Marlowe we become different from, and in many ways stronger than, that world. We perceive its truth, understand its ways, and avoid its pitfalls as no one else in the novels can. What this singular experience produces, in effect, is a new vantage on the relation of the psyche and surface, as how we perceive becomes our one sure proof against what waits on those "mean streets.[5]

Fritz Lang, one of the great directors of the German Expressionist movement and later the film noir, explained the vicarious experience his films provided through the subjective camera:

> You show the protagonist so that the audience can put themselves under the skin of the man. First of all, I use my camera in such a way as to show things, wherever possible, from the viewpoint of the protagonist; in that way my audience identifies itself with the character on the screen and thinks with him...in *The Big Heat* Glenn Ford sits and plays with his child; the wife goes out to put the car in the garage. Explosion. By not showing it, you first have the shock. "What was that?" Ford runs out. He can-

not even open the car. He sees only catastrophe. <u>Immediately (because they see it through his eyes), the audience feels with him</u>. [emphasis added][6]

By the mid-fifties, filmmakers as well as movie-goers had come to rely on these new codes that were peculiar to a particular type of crime film, which endowed the viewer with visual and psychological, via the protagonist's first-person perspective, to the nightmarish underworld of dead-end America. By the time films such as *Kiss Me Deadly* (1955) and *Touch of Evil* (1958) were produced near the end of the movement, it was evident a new genre had been created, based on the stylistic and narrative conventions filmmakers had self-consciously absorbed from the overall noir movement. "This process of evolutionary development seems to be an almost natural feature in the history of any form, whether that of a single genre or of Hollywood cinema as a whole," reasons Thomas Schatz. "As a form is varied and refined, it is bound to become more stylized, more conscious of its own rules of construction and expression."[7]

Even though American critics and filmgoers were unfamiliar with the term, at that time, film noir's generic codes had become embedded in the filmmaker's cinematic vocabulary. However, this familiarity induced a new set of generic expectations which the genre was not ready, or capable, of fulfilling. These new expectations could not be realized, in part, because they came at a time when filming with black-and-white film in the Academy aperture was rapidly being phased out.

American filmmakers were unable and unwilling to spontaneously translate the cinematic vocabulary of the film noir to the widescreen, color format that was becoming the norm in American cinema's competition with television for the viewing audience. "Television, with its demand for full lighting and close-ups, gradually undercut the German influence," stresses Paul Schrader in "Notes on Film Noir," "and color cinematography was, of course, the final blow to the 'noir' look."[8]

"...in *The Big Heat* Glenn Ford sits and plays with his child; the wife goes out to put the car in the garage. Explosion."

In addition, the overall mood of the nation was in a vibrant upswing, drastically reducing the scope of the noir canvas on which society's problems could be painted. The House Un-American Activities Committee investigations were winding down, the Korean conflict had ended, industry and labor were setting records, and reported crimes were at an all-time low in the nation, a sharp contrast from the 1952 FBI report that Borde and Chaumeton cited, when crime had reached record proportions.

In retrospect, the unique combination of elements fueling the noir movement, and the noir genre it spawned, had dissipated (with the exception of the Cold War) to such an extent that by the early 1960s the noir sensibility was barely decipherable in the American cinema.

Although the noir movement had exhausted its energies, as Porfirio suggests, by transforming several older genres into the new forms of the sixties, the noir sensibility never completely died. It remained dormant in the American cinema for nearly two decades, being kept alive through television series that paid homage to it, such as *The Fugitive, Dragnet, Lineup*, and *Peter Gunn*.[9] The seventies brought motion picture retrospectives, cable television, premium movie channels, and home video, all stimulating more demand for programming and greater interest in the original movement among film critics, historians, and filmmakers.

Don Johnson and Virginia Madsen in *The Hot Spot.*

The American cinema's ongoing quest for greater realism was assisted by the Motion Picture Association of America's institution of a rating system in 1966, which permitted more explicit acts of sex and violence to be depicted on the screen. Occasionally, a noir film would surface, as evidenced by *Point Blank* (1967), *Hickey & Boggs* (1972), *The Friends of Eddie Coyle* (1973), *The Outfit* (1974), *Night Moves* (1975), and *Taxi Driver* (1976), giving validity to the idea that noir was capable of existing in the contemporary American cinema.

More often than not, the noir attempts of the late sixties and seventies paralleled the wave of critical noir literature at the time, kindled by a nostalgic curiosity which saw *Murder, My Sweet* (1944) remade as *Farewell, My Lovely* (1975), *They Live By Night* (1949) as *Thieves Like Us* (1974), and *The Big Sleep* (1946) remade with the same title in 1978. Among the remakes of this transitional/nostalgic period, only *Farewell, My Lovely* was "more atmospherically faithful to the ethos" of the original version.[10]

On the other hand, in spite of its

faithfulness to the late thirties' Los Angeles setting, *Chinatown* (1974) is the only "period noir" which manages to maintain an air of timelessness in its presentation. Even its sequel, *The Two Jakes* (1990), and other period attempts such as *The Public Eye* (1992) are wildly distracting in their period perspectives, and ultimately fail to maintain the slightest notion of the true noir spirit.

Summing up the wave of nostalgia that was sweeping through the American cinema during that period, Richard T. Jameson contemplated the difference between the films of the original noir cycle and the remakes of the transitional period in a 1974 article titled "Son of Noir":

> If the films noir (or the noir descendants) of today are any sort of response, it must be of a markedly different kind. Of nostalgia-tripping, recreating the artifacts of the past for the sake of doing so...it is a decadent process, and if anything is illuminated thereby, it's the calculated self-interest of people who want to sell what the public is buying. That in itself is a cynical response to a cynical era hungry for optimism, an almost precise reversal of the climate in which noir was born.[11]

A few years later, Foster Hirsch echoed Jameson's observation, noting that "In the sixties and seventies the genre was clearly a self-consciously resurrected form. Thrillers made in the noir style became a nostalgic exercise, touched with that note of condescension which often results when one generation reconstructs artifacts of an earlier era's popular culture."[12]

However, near the close of the seventies, there were many socio-cultural factors present, ranging from post-Vietnam War disillusionment to the Feminist movement, and an alarming wave of international terrorism, which mirrored many of the factors present in post-World War II America. Added to that, the eighties ushered in the era of the leveraged buyout on Wall Street, described by Bryan Burrough as "a time when virtually everything, old standards, morals, sometimes even the truth, was sacrificed in the almighty hunt for The Big Deal."[13] According to Fred Steeper, whose firm polled public opinion during the 1988 U.S. presidential campaign, "The upcoming '90s have been prefaced by economic uncertainty due to budget deficits, fear of the hazards of environmental pollution, and sexual doubt fueled by the AIDS crisis. Such evolving dangers tend to make people think that not everything should be tolerated. There's a sense that the moral fabric of society has been pulled asunder."[14]

When asked if he saw any parallels between the socio-cultural environment of post-World War II America and that of contemporary society, Lawrence Kasdan, the writer/director of *Body Heat* (1981), said he felt the women's liberation movement was "a comparable type of event" in America where "it created an atmosphere during the seventies where there was this same type of distrust of women that the guys returning from World War II had when they wondered where their women had been at night while they were away fighting the war."[15] Virginia Madsen, an actress who has portrayed a femme fatale in several theatrical features and pay-television movies including *Slam Dance* (1987), *The Hot Spot* (1990), *Gotham* (1988), and *Third Degree Burn* (1989) observed, "It's amazing, the leading men seem to be getting weaker, while the leading women are getting stronger, character wise. I think inevitably stories about women are fascinating to an audience, our society is fascinated by women. Men and women are both confused by females and why they do the things they do."[16]

Alan Waxenberg, publisher of the popular magazine *Good Housekeeping*, believes that a cycle that began in the early fifties with the infancy boom created a societal pressure that forced women to be nothing more than homemakers. "The sixties and seventies were years of experimentation, taking women away from the home. The materialism of the early eighties then set for a reactive re-emphasis on domesticity as a matter of choice."[17] Leslie Shelton, an advertising executive, added that "the pressure to achieve in a lot of areas within a relatively short period of time, which is new to women, has created unsettling feelings, which are evidenced in guilt and insecurity."[18]

In addition to these various socio-cultural influences, there are three principal factors which have stimulated the resurgence of noir in the contemporary American cinema: (1) Technical advancements made with color film stock; (2) the pervasiveness of crime and the public's fascination with sensational crime stories; and, most importantly, (3) a definitive noir sensibility among contemporary filmmakers.

1. Technical advancements made with color film stock.

The noir movement was heavily influenced by German Expressionism's quest to reveal the "deeper reality" (psychological motivations) of its characters through the intense interplay of light and shadow. Many of noir's finest cinematographers came from the German Expressionist cinema, and the precedent of their black-and-white film sensibility dictated its use on the American screen. Black-and-white film was also a guarantee of realism for audiences of that period; it provided superior exposure latitude; and, the economics of filmmaking in the forties simply made color film noir, such as *Leave Her to Heaven* (1945), the striking exception.

Unlike the color film stock used in the sixties and seventies, modern high-speed color negative films provide filmmakers exceptional low-end latitude, and render true blacks. This means that the shadowy, high contrast images familiar to film noir can now be realized with color film.

By the mid-sixties, motion pictures filmed in color were standard in the industry, which meant that color film had gradually supplanted black-and-white film as a guarantee of realism to movie audiences. The rapid advancements made with color film stock contributed not only to an expanded ability to create realism on the screen, but also an increasing reliance on natural light, and ultimately, faster shot set-ups. Referring to the Kodak 5293 high speed film that was first available in 1982, Ric Waite, the cinematographer of *48 Hours*, said:

"It allowed us to shoot with minimum lighting in our night exteriors and almost nothing but natural lighting and maybe a few 60-watt bulbs, for the interiors. I started to light a scene one night and I decided to believe that if I could see it in the lens, then I would be able to see it in the rushes the next day. That was taking a real chance. We did in four nights a complicated chase scene that covered four to six blocks, and it was a scene we'd have needed at least twelve days to light and set up had it not been for this new stock."[19]

Five years later, Kodak introduced a superior color stock rated at 400 ASA, the 5295. "The '95 is very fine grained and holds the shadowy blacks extremely well," said Jack Green, the director of photography for *Bird* (1988), a dark, brooding bio-pic on the late jazz great, Charlie "Bird" Parker. Continuing, Green said that Clint Eastwood, the director, wanted a stylized look with *Bird*:

He told me to work with the idea that this was a black-and-white film which we just happened to be shooting with color stock.... Black is by far the hardest of all visual tones to keep. The blue sensitivity of the '95 is what helps keep the black dense.[20]

Yet again, in 1989, Kodak introduced an even faster film stock, the 5296 500 ASA (which Fuji Film Co. matched with its own 500 ASA film). Cinematographer Marc Reshovsky explained the benefits of the 5296 stock:

> It has great sharpness of image and extreme low graininess.... The only thing you have to be careful of is not over lighting and bringing the fill up too much, because the stock's so sensitive. We filmed in this huge hangar, and there was a shadowy area on the set that I thought was too dark. But when I saw the dailies, it was brighter than it was to the eye at shoot time, which is pretty amazing.[21]

In photographing the remake of *D.O.A.* (1949), Yuri Neyman, the cinematographer for *DOA* (1988) shot the beginning and end of the remake in black-and-white, in a style he called "an homage to the naive, subjective camera of the forties." The rest of the film was shot in color because, as Neyman says, "we wanted to create a film noir in color. That suggested a very muted palette."[22] While the black-and-white sequences parenthesize the color portion of the *DOA* remake from a critical perspective, the juxtapositioning of the two film stocks illustrates that color cinematography can provide the exposure latitude necessary to achieve the expressionistic lighting effects that noir depends on for heightened suspense and psychological insight.

Undoubtedly, the technical advancements made with color film during the past decade has greatly contributed to the distinct ambience of modern noir, as well as boosting the confidence of filmmakers desiring to project their noir sensibilities on the screen. The quality and range of modern high-speed color film stock means that virtually all lighting in contemporary filmmaking can now be effected for artistic purposes rather than for exposure.[23]

Opposite, Dennis Quaid in the 1988 remake, *DOA*. Below, lighting a neo-noir night exterior: a gang of bike-riding *yakuza* menace Andy Garcia in *Black Rain*.

2. The pervasiveness of crime and the public's fascination with sensational crime stories.

Crime stories abound in modern America, with newspaper headlines shouting Cocaine Worth $20 Billion Seized in Biggest Bust Ever,[24] Crooked Cop Tapes Wrenching Tale,[25] and Contract Killings in Suburbia.[26] Magazines have echoed the spread of crime with headlines such as Victims of Crime,[27] The Cotton Club Murder: Cocaine and Hit Men in Hollywood, A 1980s Film Noir,[28] and Fear in the City: Darkness Descends on the City of Angels.[29]

As for television, America's most popular news medium, there were at least nineteen network or nationally syndicated tabloid programs on the air in 1989,[30] two of which aired interviews with the infamous mass murderer Ted Bundy just hours before he was executed for his crimes by the Florida State Correctional System. In 1995, CNN News' ratings skyrocketed as millions of viewers tuned in daily during the court proceedings of Hall of Fame football hero/celebrity product endorser, O.J. Simpson, on trial for the double-murder slayings of his ex-wife and her friend. "Crime is the dark shadow spreading across TV," warns Howard Rosenberg, television critic for the *Los Angeles Times*. "The small screen is now the nation's rap sheet, offering tragedy as entertainment via tabloid programs and lurid dramas that mindlessly regurgitate or distort front-page stories."[31]

Echoing a 1989 survey of 690 city officials from across the United States, which indicated that two of the three worst problems facing American cities were drugs and crime,[32] Mike Shumacher, Chief Probation Officer for Orange County, California, admitted that "kids are more criminally sophisticated now. They seem to be more violence-prone and more drug-prone."[33]

Of course, it stands to reason that with crime's headline status and its social implications in daily American life, Hollywood would be anxious to cash in. Many former law enforcement officers, crime victims, and even criminals, have written books and sold the movie rights to their personal stories, spawning embittered legislative battles over the rights of criminals to profit from their crimes.

Referring to the allure of television crime shows in the book, *TV Genres*, Brooks Robard points out that "A little like voyeurs, the audience gets to ride in the back seat of the squad car and experience firsthand the seamy side of life. Implicit in such vicarious adventure is the audience's secret wish to explore its own darker impulses."[34] Much of film noir's appeal is that it allows us to encounter characters and situations that we would never experience in our normal lives. We want to witness the nightmare, so to speak, but we want to do it from a safe perspective.

Motion pictures are not the only artistic medium reflecting and profiting from crime in modern America. Art, literature and music all demonstrate, in some way or another, crime's influence in their creative efforts. For example, the art world of the eighties experienced a revival of interest in expressionistic art. One of the most widely publicized, exhibited and collected artists of the decade, Robert Longo, "deals almost exclusively in social paranoia, Apocalyptic Pop."[35] The modern versions of the expressionistic movement are known as "neo-expressionism" and "agit-pop," both styles known for their ability to "restore our moral vision, and help us see the hell behind the headlines," according to Michael Kurcfeld in an article titled, "Dark Art for a Dark Age."[36]

Hard-boiled fiction also witnessed a significant growth in its appeal to mainstream audiences. Besides the increased interest in the original hard-boiled writers such as Cain, Chandler and Woolrich, several of fifties pulp novelist Jim Thompson's works were reprinted, optioned for film development, and eventually made into films. Contemporary crime novelists, such as James Ellroy, Gerald Petievich, Joseph Wambaugh, and Walter Walker have brought an even greater realism to the sex, violence and underworld milieu typical of the hard-boiled tradition. And, some of these writers readily admit the influence of film noir in their work, as James Ellroy relates:

There's a scene from the movie *Out of the Past* where Robert Mitchum has been sent down to Mexico to pick up Bad Girl Jane Greer, who shot Kirk Douglas and stole 40 grand from him. Mitchum has seen her in a bar, and you take one look at him as he sees this woman, and you know he's going to flush his f---ing life down the toilet for this woman. In the chaste manner of '40s melodramas, they meet a couple of times for a drink, speak elliptically, and they end up on the beach one night and the waves are breaking, and they're holding each other and she says to him, You don't want me. You don't need me. I'm no good, I shot Kirk Douglas, I stole 40 grand from him, I'm bad, I'm evil, you don't want me, you don't need me; and Mitchum draws the woman to him and says, Baby, I don't care. And that's it, essentially, for me. I'm too ambitious and circumspect to flush my life down the toilet for a woman, and I'm happily married to a woman who's eminently good and strong and sane; but I love the romantic notion of it, and can also see through it in a hot f-ing flash. One of the things I've tried to do with obsession in my books is feel the sensuality that's personally incomprehensible to me. I want the reader to be sucked into the vortex of that sensuality, into the perspective of demonic and obsessed heroes and psychotic killers.[37]

Even contemporary music, with its ability to convey lyrical messages rapidly, emits a restlessness used to underscore various moods in film. In the case of *To Live and Die in L.A.* (1985) the title lyrics by the rock group, Wang Chung, emphasize the entrapment and existential repercussions of the city.

3. A definitive noir sensibility among contemporary filmmakers.

Referring to the key distinction between film noir of the classic period and contemporary noir films, Alain Silver noted that "if there is a significant difference between then and now, it is in what motivates the creation of the

A fence (Michael Chong, left) is robbed by corrupt federal agents Vukovich (John Pankow, center) and Chance (William Petersen) in *To Live and Die in L.A.*

<u>films.</u>" [emphasis added][39] Undoubtedly, the primary motivating factor in the creation of noir films today is the peculiar attraction and high level of self-consciousness contemporary filmmakers have for the stylistic and narrative conventions of the classic film noir. Why the peculiar attraction? "Noir has a timeless appeal," explains Eugenio Zaretti, art director of *Slam Dance* (1987). "Because a noir hero has no exit, no options, and is constrained to do what destiny bids. People respond to noir because it is an element of daily life. We are all constrained, because of conditioning, to do things we'd prefer not to do."[40]

Modern filmmakers are clearly unabashed in their affinity for noir, and the function of self-consciousness in their work. Regarding his motivation for making *Johnny Handsome* (1989), Walter Hill said, "...This seemed to be a film noir. I could see this movie being made in 1948 with John Garfield."[41] When asked about his attraction to film noir, director John Flynn (*The Outfit*, 1974; *Rolling Thunder* 1977; *Best Seller*, 1987) said:

"Whenever anybody asks me that, I go back to Louie Calhern's line in *The Asphalt Jungle* when his wife, remember she is bedridden, and he stops before he went out to his retreat to meet Marilyn Monroe, and he was playing with her (his wife), and she said, "Why do you deal with all those terrible people?" And he said, "Crime is simply a left-handed form of human endeavor." It's just another way of looking at things. It's kind of fascinating. Hemingway said about war, not that he liked war, but that the pressures of war were so great that it stripped people of their veneers and you saw what was really in their hearts. I suppose that most crime stories happen in such desperate and dangerous circumstances, that the same rule would apply, you might have an aspect of someone's character revealed to you that you would not get in a more mainstream story."[42]

Bob Swaim, director of *Masquerade* (1988), spoke of the dichotomy between sex and love, and the role crime plays in his pictures:

It's not that I think crime is an aphrodisiac, I just like putting ordinary people in extreme situations, and crime is a convenient circumstance. I am fascinated by the dark side of sex, and how love is its redeeming element.... What I tried to do with *Masquerade* was create a classic film noir without imitating the great films of the genre. I tried replacing the forties' style of long shadows with the wholesome look of a Bruce Weber ad for Ralph Lauren and hired adolescents to play grownups.... What I like about film noir is that it's desire rather than action that is the motivation. Love is the element you can never plan out. It changes everything."[43]

Michael Mann, director of *Thief* (1981) and *Manhunter* (1985), and creator of the television series *Miami Vice*, explained his interest in the thematic concerns of noir:

The darkness in working at night and the romance of wet, shiny streets is appealing to me for the same reason it was appealing in the forties and fifties. Most importantly, the questions about our society that cause the thematic ideas behind both pictures [*Thief* and *Manhunter*] are the same thematic ideas that were prevalent in the forties and fifties (more the forties, pre-McCarthyism) and channel one into the same cinematic tools and formal devices to tell these stories: man, man's condition, living a contradiction. These are modernist problems and have their roots in themes apropos to the forties and early fifties and to Weimar Germany in the 1920s.[44]

In an article for *Film Comment* magazine, Joel and Ethan Coen, the brothers who produced and directed *Blood Simple*, acknowledged their sensibility, and affinity for noir's antecedents:

When people call *Blood Simple* a film noir, they're correct to the extent that we like the same kind of stories that the people who made those movies liked. We tried to emulate the source that those movies came from rather than the movies themselves. *Blood Simple* utilizes movie conventions to tell the story. In that sense it's about other movies, but no more so than any other film that uses the medium in a way that's aware that there's a history of movies behind it.[45]

Perhaps David Mamet, the writer/director of *House of Games* (1987), put it most succinctly:

I am very well acquainted with the genre, both in print and on film, and I love it. I tried to be true.[46]

Because of their familiarity with the original noir films, filmmakers working from a contemporary noir point of view readily refer to titles from the noir index as influential reference points. Nestor Almendros, the cinematographer for Robert Benton's *Still of the Night* (1982), said that to achieve the look that they wanted for their film they sought inspiration from Edward Hopper's paintings and certain classic films noir:

> We looked at a lot of Fritz Lang movies, *Secret Beyond the Door*, *The Woman in the Window*, *Scarlet Street*. We also saw *The Criminal Life of Archibaldo de la Cruz,* by Luis Buñuel, another wonderful thriller. We watched all of these movies before we started working. So, *Still of the Night* is like a film that eats other films.[47]

Contemporary film noir is a new genre of film. As such, it must carry the distinction of another name; a name that is cognizant of its rich noir heritage, yet one that distinguishes its influences and motivations from those of a bygone era. The term for this new body of films should be "neo-noir," because these films still are noir films; yet a new type of noir film, one which effectively incorporates and projects the narrative and stylistic conventions of its progenitor onto a contemporary cinematic canvas. Neo-noir is, quite simply, a contemporary rendering of the film noir sensibility.

To illuminate the relationship between film noir and neo-noir more precisely, consider the following excerpt from John Belton's essay, "Cinemascope in Historical Methodology," with my word substitutions in brackets:

> [Neo-noir], then, is not an old wine in a new bottle. It must be understood not as a product of the period in which it was invented, but as a product of the period in which it was finally innovated. The form it takes is determined by the forces that prompted its (re)creation in the [seventies and eighties]. The [neo-noir] could not have existed during the [classic film noir period]. Neither the technology nor the conditions under which it was ultimately developed were the same. As the protomaterialist Heraclitus once observed, "you cannot step twice into the same river, for other waters are continually flowing on.[48]

It would be impossible to recreate the noir film of the forties and fifties within the context of the contemporary American cinema because our perspective of that era is one that is shaped by the burden of experience and

Attaglia (Tom Signorelli, left) is menaced by Frank (James Caan) in Michael Mann's *Thief*.

hindsight. The "period" remakes of the seventies as well as *Chinatown* illustrate this point, for even if they succeed in capturing the authentic narrative voice, or sensibility of the archetypal film noir, (which regrettably few manage to do), they are not, and never can be, the same.

A film could be shot today with black-and-white film stock in the Academy aperture and it could be designed to look like the urban milieu of the forties; the buildings, the automobiles, the clothing, etc.; yet, you could not recreate the awareness and sensitivity to that era's popular culture that a filmmaker living and experiencing life in that era did.

Even if Billy Wilder or Fritz Lang or Robert Siodmak were to attempt to make a noir film with a perfectly recreated period setting, their final product would not be the same as what they produced during the original cycle because they would not be able to divorce themselves from the reservoir of their own personal experiences and the modern sensibility with which they are necessarily burdened. Perhaps their modern noir vision would be even more compelling and disturbing than their contributions to the original cycle, but all the same, it would be different, it would be neo-noir. This applies not only to the director, but also the writer, the cinematographer, in short, anyone creatively involved with the film.

It is interesting to note that contemporary filmmakers believe that in working from the noir perspective, they are actually working with the conventions of a "genre." But the noir films of the contemporary American cinema are different from the films noir of the forties and fifties, for the noir movement was a phenomenal occurrence in cinematic history that will never be duplicated. Film noir, at its inception was an innocent, unconscious cinematic reaction to the popular culture of its time. The contemporary film noir is self-conscious, and well aware of its heritage. As Stephen Schiff wrote in reference to film noir in his article entitled "The Repeatable Experience," "It's a matter of ontology. When a being is aware of itself, it becomes a different being."[49]

Since 1971, over 300 noir-influenced pictures have been released as theatrical features by the major studios or independents. Another 400-plus noir attempts were distributed directly into ancillary markets such as home video, pay cable, foreign, and in some instances, syndicated or network television.[50] The fact that such

Below, more cynical portrayals of contemporary officials: a corrupt lawyer (William Hurt, right) in *Body Heat* and a corrupt cop (Richard Gere) in *Internal Affairs*. Opposite, the doomed couple (Peter Gallegher and Alison Elliott) in *The Underneath*: Steven Soderbergh's stylish remake of *Criss Cross*.

a large number of contemporary films have attempted to achieve the noir ambience clearly indicates the extent of self-consciousness at play in the modern cinema.

But, despite the breadth of noir-consciousness among filmmakers in the American cinema, relatively few pictures, perhaps one in five, actually succeed as authentic noir. Why so few? Because there's a virtual checklist of elements that have to coalesce on any given production for a film to achieve noirvana.

As with any film, it all starts with the script. Is the story "voiced" properly? Are the characters and dialogue believable? Does it have a plausible plot that enhances the suspension of disbelief? Are traditional noir stylistics such as the subjective camera, first-person sound effects, and extreme visual perspectives utilized properly? Is noir iconography appropriately utilized? Is the casting plausible? Does the music score appropriately highlight character nuances, emotions, plot points and overall mood shifts? If all of these elements come together in a single production, there's a good chance the picture will provide the viewer with a vicarious experience of the nightmarish world of noir. While it is not feasible within the scope of this observation to discuss every contemporary noir attempt released, a brief overview can help provide an overall perspective of the breadth of the noir influence in the contemporary American cinema.

Which films of the contemporary cycle actually succeed as authentic neo-noir? The following chronologically listed titles, while not inclusive, provide a good reference point to begin with: *Who'll Stop the Rain?* (1978), *Thief* (1981), *Body Heat* (1981), *Breathless* (1983), *Blood Simple* (1984), *To Live and Die in L.A.* (1985), *Witness* (1985), *Manhunter* (1986), *Blue Velvet* (1987), *Best Seller* (1987), *House of Games* (1987), *Cop* (1988), *The Grifters* (1990), *Kill Me Again* (1990), *Internal Affairs* (1990), *Presumed Innocent* (1990), *Delusion* (1991), *Reservoir Dogs* (1992), *Red Rock West* (1992), *Pulp Fiction* (1994), *The Last Seduction* (1994), *The Usual Suspects* (1995), and *The Underneath* (1995).

The Underneath, a remake of *Criss Cross* (1949) is a product of the current trend to mine ideas from Hollywood's classic period. Remakes of films noir have steadily increased from the seventies to the present, with mixed success, critically, and at the box office. One of the more successful remakes (in terms of gross box office dollars) was *No Way Out* (1987), a political/espionage thriller loosely based on *The Big Clock* (1947).

The Postman Always Rings Twice (1946) was remade under the same title with the Depression era setting of the Cain novel in 1981. *Out of the Past* (1947) was heavily diluted in 1984 as *Against All Odds*, *The Blue Gardenia* (1953) became *The Morning After* (1986), and *D.O.A.* (1949), *The Narrow Margin* (1951), *Detour* (1945), and *Kiss of Death* (1947) were modernized with the same titles in 1988, 1993, and 1995 respectively.

Unfortunately, noir remakes, such as those cited, rarely manage to achieve the soul-piercing anxiety that authentic noir successfully invokes in its audience. Nevertheless, it appears the trend of remaking the classic films noir from the forties and fifties will continue well into the cinematic future, as several more remakes are being readied for release, including *Brute Force* (1947) and *Kiss Me Deadly* (1955).

The high-tech revolution and sci-fi imaginations converged during the eighties to influence futuristic noir visions such as *Blade Runner* (1983), *Terminator* (1985), and *RoboCop* (1987). Often referred to as "tech noir," from the name of a nightclub in James Cameron's *Terminator*, these films are distinctively recognizable by their use of robotic characters and apocalyptic cityscapes. Comic book noir like *Batman* (1989), which Andrew Sarris said captured "both the dynamic expressionism of Fritz Lang's *Metropolis* and the morbid futurism of Ridley Scott's *Blade Runner*,"[51] falls on the fringe of the tech noir category, with exceptional technical achievements providing an atmosphere that overshadows its ineffectual story line and cardboard characters.

Buddy-cop films such as *Lethal Weapon* (1987) that spawned two sequels; *Stakeout* (1987); *Colors* (1988); *Tango & Cash* (1989); and *Bad Boys* (1995) have been popular during the last few years, as well as variations which paired a cop and a criminal in *48 Hours* (1982), and a cop and a public defender in *Shakedown* (1988).

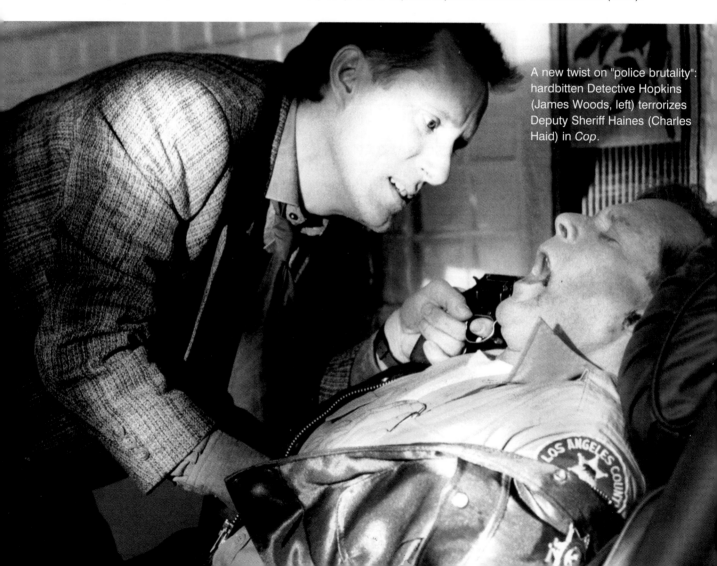

A new twist on "police brutality": hardbitten Detective Hopkins (James Woods, left) terrorizes Deputy Sheriff Haines (Charles Haid) in *Cop*.

While all of these pictures attempt to maintain a noir look with their night-for-night photography, wet pavement, and mannered, low-key lighting, with the exception of *Colors*, the noir atmosphere is substantially undercut by an over-emphasis on the humorous aspects of the relationships. There is room for humor, albeit black humor, in a noir picture, as *Blood Simple* (1984), *Cop* (1988), and *Pulp Fiction* (1994) aptly demonstrate.

Pictures like *52 Pick-Up* (1986), *At Close Range* (1986), *Someone to Watch Over Me* (1987), and *Fatal Attraction* (1987) are valid attempts, but fall short of tapping into the noir spirit because they fail to maintain the tense narrative/visual perspective that can be realized through identifying intimately with a particular character. For instance, in *Fatal Attraction*, the audience is forced to digest the unfolding events through the eyes of not only Dan Gallagher, but also his wife, Beth, and the antagonist, Alex Forrest. The result is that we "watch" the protagonist (Gallagher) struggle through his crisis rather than experiencing it vicariously along with him.

While there are several other films that effectively inhabit neo-noir terrain such as *Suspect* (1987), *True Believer* (1987), *Mortal Thoughts* (1991), and *Guilty as Sin* (1993), the majority of contemporary noir attempts fail to render the heightened level of co-experience authentic noir provides. As Alain Silver notes in reference to modern noir attempts, "Whether from a position of ignorance or knowledge, the interaction of the protagonist and viewer seems much more seldom to reveal the instability, the dark undercurrent that served as a thematic constant of the noir cycle."[52]

Since neo-noir has become firmly established in the American cinema, it is reasonable to assume that audiences will continue to be fascinated with the genre because the noir film communicates to us about our fears and desires more realistically than any other film formula. Alfred J. Appel wrote that the noir vision "touches an audience most intimately because it assures them that their suppressed impulses and fears are shared responses."[53] J.P. Telotte noted that we are always seeking patterns of order and continuity in both our individual and cultural experience, because they offer us a defense against the contradictions of the problem-free lives we want to lead. By confronting (in cinematic terms) the very issues we seek to avoid in real life, Telotte suggested, we engage in a psychoanalytic practice often referred to as a "talking cure." Continuing this line of reasoning, he said, "In trying to articulate our personal and cultural anxieties, the film noir similarly works out such a cure, offering a better sense of ourselves, or at least a clearer notion of who we are individually and socially."[54]

Film noir and its contemporary descendent, neo-noir, offer some of the most fascinating insights the cinema has provided on topics such as ambition, corruption, redemption, greed, lust, and loyalty. The best of the noir films work on a poetic level; with their conscientious interplay of light and shadows, duplicitous imagery, deceptive plots, elliptical dialogue, and multiple forced perspectives, adding layers of connotative meaning to their film-texts. Most important, however, is the heightened level of co-experience with which the truly authentic noir grips its audience.

As we emerge from the darkness of the cinema (and the nightmarish darkness of the noir film) into the light of the theatre lobby, we breathe a sigh of relief, and contemplate our tense encounter with the flip side of the American Dream. By vicariously confronting the noir world on the screen, whether through the film noir, or its modern offshoot, neo-noir, we are able to validate the patterns of order and continuity we seek to establish in our lives. More precisely yet, "by means of the night...we see the light of day."[55]

Notes

1. Dennis Hopper, personal interview, 18 March 1993. Hopper wrote the copy and designed the one-sheets that were utilized in Orion's marketing campaign for *The Hot Spot*.

2. Robert G. Porfirio, *The Dark Age of American Film: A Study of the American Film Noir* (diss., Yale University, 1979), pp. 112-116.

3. Porfirio, p. 11.

4. Marc Vernet, "Genre" in *Film Reader* (Evanston: Northwestern University, February 1978), p. 16.

5. J.P. Telotte, *Voices in the Dark: The Narrative Patterns of Film Noir* (U. of Illinois Press, 1989), p. 22.

6. Peter Bogdanovich, *Fritz Lang in America* (New York: Praeger, 1967), pp. 86-87.

7. Thomas Schatz, *Hollywood Genres: Formulas, Filmmaking, and the Studio Syst*em (Philadelphia: Temple University Press, 1981), 149.

8. Paul Schrader, "Notes on Film Noir," *Film Comment* (Spring, 1972), p. 12.

9. Brian G. Rose, ed., *TV Genres* (Westport, CT: Greenwood Press, 1986), p. 34.

10. Alain Silver and Elizabeth Ward, eds., *Film Noir: An Encyclopedic Reference to the American Style* (Woodstock, NY: Overlook Press, 2nd Edition, 1987), p. 101.

11. Richard T. Jameson, "Son of Noir," *Film Comment* (November, 1974), pp. 31-32.

12. Foster Hirsch, *The Dark Side of the Screen: Film Noir* (San Diego: A.S. Barnes, 1981), pp. 202-203.

13. Bryan Burrough, "Top Deal Maker Leaves a Trail of Deception in Wall Street Rise," *The Wall Street Journal* (22 Jan., 1990), p. 1.

14. Ron Gales, "As the '80s Wane, a New View of the Good Life Emerges," *Adweek* (13 Feb., 1989), p. 34.

15. Lawrence Kasdan, personal interview, 10 November 1989.

16. Paula Parisi, "Virginia Madsen: This Versatile Femme Fatale Keeps Hollywood Guessing," *The Hollywood Reporter* (26 May, 1989), p. 18.

17. Gales, p. 38.

18. Ibid., p. 34.

19. Samir Hachem, "48 Hours," *Millimeter* (December, 1982), p. 191.

20. Ric Gentry, "Bird: DP Jack Green Creates a Black-and-White Style Film on Color Stock," *Film & Video* (September, 1988), p. 10.

21. Iain Blair, "Look at New Methods for Lighting Music Videos," *Film & Video* (January, 1990), p. 50.

22. Laurie Halpern Smith, "Yuri Neyman's Compelling Vision," *Movieline* (April, 1988), p. 27.

23. Stephen Gersor, "Expressionism in Film," *Crimmers: the Harvard Journal of Pictorial Fiction* (Winter, 1975), p. 49. For those apprehensive about color cinematography's compatibility with the modern noir vision, consider a remark by Wassily Kadinsky, leader of the "Blue Rider" German Expressionist group: "Color directly influences the soul; color is the keyboard, the eyes are the hammer, the soul is the piano with many strings. The artist is the hand that plays, to create vibrations in the soul."

24. Stephen Loeper, *Los Angeles Herald Examiner* (1 Oct., 1989), p. 1.

25. Ralph Blumenthal, *Los Angeles Herald Examiner* (18 Sept., 1989), p. 4.

26. Stephen Braun, *Los Angeles Times* (10 Feb., 1995), p. 1.

27. Ted Gest, *U.S. News & World Report* (31 July, 1989), p. 16-19.

28. Jeanie Kasindorf, *New York* (24 July, 1989), p. 24-33.

29. Harlan Ellison, *Los Angeles* (September, 1988), p. 103-107.

30. Howard Rosenberg, "It's a Crime What They Offer to TV," *Los Angeles Times* (27 Jan., 1989), p. F1.

31. Howard Rosenberg, *Los Angeles Times* (23 Sept., 1989), p. F1.

32. Paul Leavitt, "Drugs Top Cities' Fears," *USA Today* (13 Jan., 1989), p. 3.

33. *Los Angeles Times* (26 Feb., 1989), p. A56.

34. Rose, p. 12.

35. William Wilson, "Art from the Dark Side," *Los Angeles Times*, Calendar (1 Oct., 1989), p. 8.

36. Michael Kurcfeld, *L.A. Weekly* (16 Sept., 1988), p. 19.

37. Steve Erickson, "James Ellroy: Crime Fiction Beyond Noir," *L.A. Weekly* (21 July, 1989), p. 19-20.

38. Wang Chung, "To Live and Die in L.A.," (Geffen/Warner Bros. Records, M5G 24081), p. 1985.

39. Silver and Ward, p. 370.

40. Kristine McKenna, "L.A. Noir: 'Slam Dance', The Look of a Lonely Paradise," *Los Angeles Times*, Calendar (27 Sept., 1987), p. 44.

41. Jeff Schwager, "Walter Hill: The Good, the Bad, and the Handsome," *Village View* (6 Oct., 1989), p. 7.

42. John Flynn, personal interview, 22 August, 1989.

43. Hal Rubenstein, "Crazy Love," *Vogue* (April, 1988), p. 82.

44. Michael Mann, written interview, 22 November, 1989.

45. David Mamet, response to questionnaire, 20 February, 1989.

46. Hal Hinson, "Bloodlines," *Film Comment* (February, 1986), p. 18.

47. John A. Gallagher, "Nestor Almendros: The Master Eye," *Millimeter* (February, 1983), p. 118-122.

48. John Belton, *Cinema Journal* 28:1 (Fall, 1988), p. 29-30.

49. Stephen Schiff, *Film Comment* (March/April, 1982), p. 35.

50. Sources include *Daily Variety's* annual anniversary issues, American Film Market and Cannes Film Festival issues of *The Hollywood Reporter*, *Exhibitor Relations Company*, NATO News, *Boxoffice*, and *The Comprehensive Guide to Home Video* (1995 edition).

51. Andrew Sarris, *Video Review* (January, 1990), p. 54.

52. Silver and Ward, p. 372.

53. Alfred Appel, "Dark Cinema and Lolita," *Film Comment* (September, 1974), p. 26.

54. Telotte, p. 222.

55. Jon Tuska, *Dark Cinema: American Film Noir in Cultural Perspective* (Westport, CT: Greenwood Press, 1984), p. xvi.

A neo-noir perspective, looking up at a betraying femme fatale (Joanne Whalley-Kilmer, left) and her menacing accomplice (Michael Madsen) in *Kill Me Again*.

Drew Barrymore as Anita and James Legros as Howard, a juvenile fugitive couple in *Guncrazy*,

Son of Noir: Neo-Film Noir and the Neo-B Picture

Alain Silver (1992)

The "Classic" period of American Film Noir encompasses several hundred motion pictures from *The Maltese Falcon* (1941) to *Touch of Evil* (1958) produced by scores of different filmmakers between roughly 1940 and 1960. While that noir cycle of production never formally concluded, the attempts to sustain its viewpoint were few in the 1960s and 1970s. Particularly near its end, however, the decade of the 1980s brought a significant resurgence of interest in the themes and protagonists that typified classic film noir. The 1990s so far have added scores more to the titles of the preceding decade. If there is a most significant difference between then and now, it is in what motivates the creation of the films.

At the height of the movement individual noir films transcended personal and generic outlook to reflect cultural preoccupations. From the late 1970s to present, in a "Neo-Noir" period, many of the productions that recreate the noir mood, whether in remakes or new narratives, have been undertaken by filmmakers cognizant of a heritage and intent on placing their own interpretation on it. As writer/director David Mamet told Todd Erickson [on page 203 above]: "I am very well acquainted with the genre, both in print and on film, and I love it. I tried to be true."

Guncrazy (1992) is not a remake, but a mixture of fugitive couple and "kid noir" concepts. The film does echo classic period titles, particularly the visual imagery of Joseph H. Lewis' 1950 original *Gun Crazy* in scenes of the couple locked in a parody of embrace while they shoot at cans and bottles. The ingenuous dialogue is more in the manner of Nicholas Ray's *They Live by Night* (1947). Because the characters themselves, Howard and Anita, are much more like Ray's Bowie and Keechie than those in Robert Altman's aimless, direct remake, *Thieves Like Us* (1974), they naively romanticize their sordid dilemma, epitomized when they break into a house and dress up for a candle-lit dinner.

Guncrazy, like its namesake and many recent productions, is also a low-budget picture. In the classic period, film noir may have been disproportionately involved with productions done on limited means. The original *Gun Crazy* as well as *Kiss Me Deadly* (1955), *D.O.A.* (1950), *Detour* (1945) and scores of others were all made on limited budgets and shooting schedules, which seemed to mesh well with the spare, ill-lit locales that typified the noir underworld. In many ways, the resurgence of interest in the noir style by low-budget filmmakers represents a return to the roots of the cycle. The "B-film" or "programmer," the less costly productions of the 40s and 50s from the major studios, such as *Thieves' Highway* (Fox, 1949), *Scene of the Crime* (MGM, 1949), or *Black Angel* (Universal, 1946), whose second-tier actors, writers, and directors were featured on the bottom-half of double bills, has transformed itself into the limited release and made-for-video efforts of the 80s and 90s. The low-budget feature, made at a cost ranging from less than $500,000 to $3 or 4 million cannot be financed based on U.S. theatrical prospects alone but must follow the dictates of the foreign, video, and cable markets. Not only do those markets still prize the "action" picture or "thriller," whose spare narratives translate more easily for non-English speaking audiences, but the violence and compulsive sexual behavior that has always been part of film noir are more "saleable" than ever. Since many productions of the classic period were criticized at the time for their violence and unsavory themes, this is just another aspect of neo-noir's return to its roots.

Many films like the three 1990 adaptations of Jim Thompson's novels have been made on limited, non-studio budgets. At the higher end are *The Grifters* and *After Dark, My Sweet*, which were both released in 1990. While *The Grifters* did well in terms of box office (grossing in excess of its budget, while *After Dark, My Sweet* grossed less than half of its cost). Both of these downbeat neo-noirs were relative successes. Still when com-

The Kill-Off: staging action on a very limited neo-B budget.

pared to the 5-to-1 box office to budget ratio of a classic period A-picture such as *Double Indemnity*. While no neo-B has broken through, the low risk and high upside-potential sustains independent productions such as the ultra-low budget *The Kill-Off*, which evokes both Thompson and the noir tradition at a fraction of the cost.

In fact, in the worst of neo-noir, the failing is seldom because of monetary restrictions. *Hit List* and *Relentless* (both 1989) are two low-budget examples by the same director, William Lustig. What imbalances the former picture are the performances, with Rip Torn, Lance Henriksen, and Leo Rossi acting at one level and Jan-Michael Vincent and Charles Napier at another. While *Hit List* turns on the concept of the wrong address, the modus operandi in *Relentless*, where the killer chooses his victims by opening a page at random from the telephone directory, is even more arbitrary. Although Judd Nelson's portrayal of the psychopath brought the picture much opprobrium, his manic interpretation works within the context much as did Richard Basehart's performance in the classic *He Walked by Night* (1948). The ironies of the displaced cop (Leo Rossi) trying to prove himself and the old veteran (Robert Loggia) dying because of his carelessness are reinforced by the iconographic context of prior work, particularly Loggia's in *Jagged Edge*. In this sense, *Relentless* maximizes the impact of its limited means. While the flashbacks to the killer's abused childhood at the hands of his police officer-father may seem an "antique" device, it economically fulfills a necessary narrative function. Both films use actors with big-budget credits both to mask their limited means and to exploit the audience awareness of screen personas.

Sean Young's androgynous, "hysterical" performance in *Love Crimes* (1992) is part of this same low-budget tactic. In pop-critical jargon, director Lizzie Borden takes a cinematic ax and gives her audience forty whacks. The net effect, however, is a more direct statement about social patriarchy and prejudice against women in law enforcement than in similarly themed pictures with bigger budgets such as *Blue Steel* and *Impulse* (both 1990).

Not only is such economy the key in "neo-B," it helps generate a higher percentage of films that are rooted in the noir tradition without overwhelming it, like such self-conscious, high-budget efforts as *Shattered*

(1991) or *Final Analysis* (1992). In copying *Fatal Attraction* (1987), *Body Chemistry* (1990) must circumvent the obstacles of short schedule and less celebrated actors; and it certainly had no budget to re-shoot endings after test screenings. Despite that, the result is both stark and affecting. Without the clutter of freight elevators or operatic arias, *Body Chemistry* focuses relentlessly on the central premise; and when its "hero" is gunned down it arrives literally and figuratively at a very different conclusion. *Mortal Passions* (1990) takes types from the hard-boiled mold of James L. Cain. Its plot turns fraternal loyalty into betrayal, literally buries bodies in the back yard, and has a would-be femme fatale fall in love with a prospective victim. In its final sequence it recalls more than anything Cain's ending to *Double Indemnity*, the novella.

Cain is not credited here, of course, nor even in *Kiss Me A Killer* (1991), which is an "unauthorized" Latino version of *The Postman Always Rings Twice*. The high-budget 1981 remake with Jack Nicholson and Jessica Lange in the John Garfield/Lana Turner roles restored the impulsive sexuality but little of the determinism of Cain's original or the 1947 adaptation. *Kiss Me A Killer* borrows sub-plots liberally from other classic films, from Siegel's *Crime In the Streets* (1956) to Hitchcock's *I, Confess* (1953) but centers on the Mexican-American wife of a white bar owner and a guitar-playing drifter named Tony who helps transform the place into a salsa hot spot. Like Visconti's 1942 *Ossessione*, this unsanctioned adaptation of the novel emphasizes the loutish qualities of the husband to build empathy with the killers and captures Cain's obsessive and fateful mood better than its costlier counterparts.

The $1 million-budgeted *The Killing Time* (1987) and *Jezebel's Kiss* (1990) both feature youthful revenge seekers. Both use "name" actors such as Beau Bridges, Malcolm MacDowell, Wayne Rogers, and Meredith Baxter-Birney to mask their fiscal origins. The key to both stories is revealed in flashback: they have returned to obtain reprisal for the death of a parent which they witnessed as children. As it happens both films are situated in small California coastal communities, and the deaths are tied to land swindles. For both films, locations

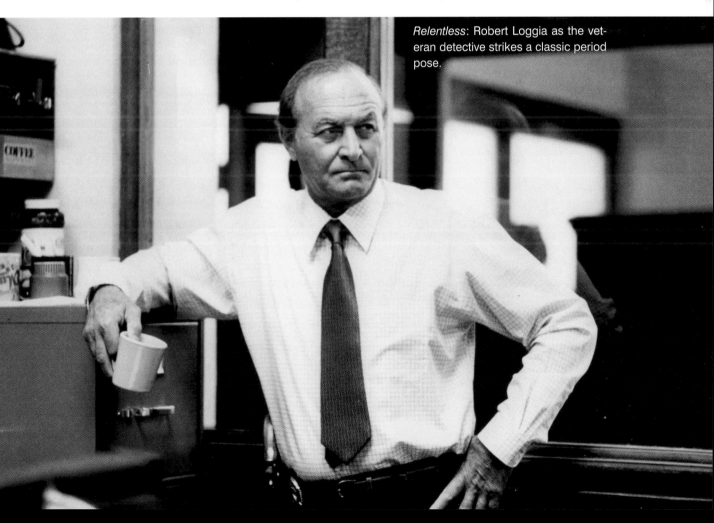

Relentless: Robert Loggia as the veteran detective strikes a classic period pose.

sand the limited cast allow production values to be maximized. The protagonist of *The Killing Time* murders and takes the place of the small town's new deputy sheriff and features a performance by Kiefer Sutherland that evokes Jim Thompson's Deputy Lou Ford. *Jezebel's Kiss* has a title character who rides into town on a Harley, and a lead performance that is best left undescribed.

More recent, modestly-budgeted pictures, which consider the issue of criminal "professionalism," *Diary of a Hitman* and *Reservoir Dogs* (both 1992), use stylized performances to create a noir ambience. Dekker, the title character of *Diary of a Hitman*, is a throwback and the film's narrative style follows suit. The story unfolds as a flashback, a message which Dekker is leaving on his "booking agent's" answering machine, and his voiceover narration is used heavily throughout. Forest Whitaker's portrayal of Dekker, who early on confesses to being troubled by his work and maintaining the illusion that "it's not personal," recalls Mark Stevens in The *Dark Corner* (1946) or *Cry Vengeance* (1954) in the best "B" manner.

Dekker's key comment is "I was a pro. A pro is a pro, right?" The answer from "Mr. Pink" in *Reservoir Dogs* is "a psychopath ain't a professional." From the perspective of the classic noir style and narrative, *Reservoir Dogs* is pointedly aware of a relationship to those conventions. The sociopathic "Mr. Blonde" might well be alluding to *Point Blank* when he confesses to being "a big Lee Marvin fan." The plot of *Reservoir Dogs* derives from the caper film. An organizer brings a group of otherwise unrelated criminals together for one job and keeps their true identities from each other with "colorful" names. The botched robbery itself is never seen, only its aftermath as the survivors come to the rendezvous point and argue over what happened and what to do now. Flashbacks within flashbacks economically create narrative layers that are both "traditionally" noir and endistance the modern viewer from identification with the criminal protagonists. Equally endistancing are slow motion optical effects and moments of grisly humor. While it shares the multiple points of view of writer/director Quentin Tarantino's later, more expensive, and much more celebrated *Pulp Fiction* (1994), *Reservoir Dogs* is a more tightly constructed and ultimately much darker film.

In *Genuine Risk* (1990), *Delusion* (1991), and even *Femme Fatale* (1991), the titles are completely unambiguous and the budgets even lower. Equally remarkable is how well these pictures succeed in the noir tradition. *Femme Fatale* is the most complicated, recalling elements of *The Locket* (1947) and *Chicago Deadline*

Forest Whitaker in *Diary of a Hitman.*

Neo-noir femme fatales: Katherine Barrese (left) as the revenge-seeking, motorcycle-riding, and possibly amnesiac title character in *Jezebel's Kiss*. Right, Jennifer Rubin as the opportunistic Patti, who sings "These Boots Are Made for Walkin'," at the close of *Delusion*.

(1949), in which a man marries a woman who turn outs to be someone else or, more accurately, someone suffering from a multiple personality disorder. Like the reporter in *Chicago Deadline*, her husband pieces her other lives together through a succession of leads, while dodging some street hoodlums whom another of her personalities swindled. In the end the protagonists survive only because of the whim of these hoodlums.

The plot of *Delusion* owes even more to Al Robert's "mysterious force" in the classic *Detour* or to the chance events in Ida Lupino's *The Hitch-hiker* (1953). Embittered over his longtime employer's sale of the company, George O'Brien has embezzled a million dollars and is driving to Las Vegas with the cash in his trunk. He stops to help a young couple, Patti and Chevy, in a car that has swerved off the road, and they abduct him. O'Brien does not realize that the young tough has not been planning to kill him and does not know about the money, until Chevy kills someone else. Now O'Brien is a witness; and they dump him in the desert. He survives; but by the time he tracks them down, Patti has found the money and is preparing to go off on her own.

Stylistically both of these films benefit from the isolated or seedy locales, which permit a spare and stark visualization in the manner of *Border Incident* (1949) or *On Dangerous Ground* (1952). As in *After Dark, My Sweet* or *Kill Me Again* (1990), the desert locations in *Delusion* permit an arrangement of figures in a landscape that create a sense of otherworldliness or mirage (the film's original title), of acting out a bad dream without having recourse to optical effects or mood lighting. At the victim's trailer site or in a rundown motel at the aptly named Death Valley Junction, the isolated environment underscores the narrative tension in the classic noir manner. The last shot literally drives off from O'Brien as he stands looking at the wounded Chevy lying in the dusty driveway, and it continues moving away down the road as the end credits roll, figuratively abandoning the protagonist to his fate.

Genuine Risk may be the most self-conscious neo-noir and neo-B of these three films, as locations, lighting style, and art direction constantly underscore the sordidness of the milieu. The script is outrageous and features lines like "A racetrack is like a woman...a man weathers so much banality in pursuit of the occasional orgasmic moment." What distinguishes *Genuine Risk* is the offhandedness of its violence, where people are beaten or die painfully, abruptly and without reason in stagings that capture the disturbing tone of videotapes of real events from surveillance cameras. It also has some wryness and novelty in its plot and casting, most notably Terence Stamp as a 60s British pop-star turned petty mobster. Although deceived by this mobster's wife, the "hero," a hapless petty criminal and compulsive gambler named Henry, survives. And while just about everyone else perishes, he goes back to the track for another play.

The plots of these pictures, all budgeted at under a million dollars, take only what they can afford from the classic tradition; but that is a considerable amount. All have enough money for a femme fatale, a hired killer or two, a confused and entrapped hero, an employer ripped-off, a shakedown. Two have flashbacks, two have gang bosses, and one a psychiatrist. The locations vary from Los Angeles to Las Vegas, from Death Valley to

Tom Berenger (left) as the amnesiac real estate developer in *Shattered* with Corbin Bernson as his partner.

Big Bear Lake, but two have mansions, two cheap motels, and two isolated rural locales where killers take their proposed victims. Like its antecedent, neo-noir and neo-B in particular makes few if any extravagant demands in terms of production value.

From television to comic books, film noir has exerted and continues to exert its narrative and stylistic influence. It has been a while since *Dragnet, Naked City, Johnny Staccato, The Fugitive, Run for Your Life,* and *Harry-O* were on network; but movies-of-the-week and cable originals frequently explore the noir terrain on a limited budget. While both were given after-market theatrical releases, such recent and extremely self-conscious neo-noir projects as John Dahl's *Red Rock West* (1992) and *The Last Seduction* (1994) originated as made-for-cable movies. After the short-lived, animated cop series *Fish Police*, can it be too long before an angst-ridden Bart Simpson puts on a fedora and skateboards down his own mean streets?

The resurgence of interest in the themes and styles of film noir in recent years has benefited filmmakers at all budget levels. If film noir is no longer the American style, certainly no other movement has emerged to replace it. Unless and until filmmakers discover another mirror to hold up to American society, none ever will.

Sean Young is the androgynous, "hysterical" D.A. in *Love Crimes*, held captive by Patrick Bergin.

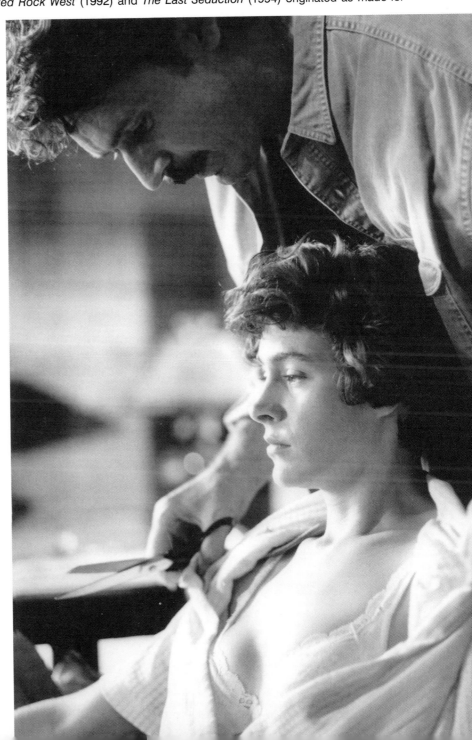

On Dangerous Ground: Robert Ryan as troubled homicide Det. Jim Wilson, who finds sanctuary and solace in the rustic home of the blind anti-femme fatale Mary Malden (Ida Lupino).

Lounge Time: Postwar Crises and the Chronotope of Film Noir

Vivian Sobchack (1998)

[A] definite and absolutely concrete locality serves as the starting point for the creative imagination. But this is not an abstract landscape.... No, this is a piece of human history, historical time condensed in space.

M. M. Bakhtin

"Have you ever noticed if for some reason you want to feel completely out of step with the rest of the world, the only thing to do is sit around a cocktail lounge in the afternoon?"

Lizabeth Scott to Dick Powell in *Pitfall*

My aim in this essay is to locate and ground that heterogeneous and ambiguous cinematic grouping called film noir in its contemporaneous social context.[1] This may, at first, seem a redundant project, given the extremely large body of scholarly work that has been published on noir, nearly all of it, in one way or another, attempting to relate the films to changes in American culture during the second World War and its aftermath.[2] As Joan Copjec points out in the introduction to her recent revisionist anthology, *Shades of Noir:*

> Film noir criticism correlates filmic elements with historical "sources": World War Two, an increase in crime, mounting paranoia regarding the working woman's place in society, and so on—thinking that it has thereby located the "generative principle" of the films. But this reference to external sources in no way resolves the question of the internal logic of the films.[3]

I would argue, then, that my project here is less redundant than it is radical. That is, I want literally—not metaphorically or allegorically—to locate film noir in its historical and cultural context. I want to look at the films' concrete and visible premises—premises that, in existing concretely and visibly in both the films and the culture, materially ground both the internal logic of the films and the external logic of the culture and allow each to be intelligible in terms of the other.

Thus, in speaking of grounds and premises, I am speaking radically, concretely, materially of the prereflective phenomenological conditions for the intuitive reading of film noir as "about" its historical and cultural moment—a reading we've done all along and yet whose logic still eludes us. These radical grounds and material premises figured concretely before us and to which we should pay heed are the cocktail lounge, the nightclub, the bar, the hotel room, the boardinghouse, the diner, the dance hall, the roadside cafe, the bus and train station, and the wayside motel. These are the recurrent and determinate premises of film noir and they emerge from common places in wartime and postwar American culture that, transported to the screen, gain hyperbolized presence and overdetermined meaning. In sum, to locate the historical and cultural intelligibility of film noir, I want not to allegorize or resort to metaphor, but "to return to the things themselves."[4]

To begin, it seems important to rehearse a certain amount of "canonical" knowledge about both noir and its context—if only to highlight how right our intuitions feel about the relationship between the two and yet how difficult it is to explicate the grounds of this perceived connection, this phenomeno-logic.

1

Let us start with the context. It is now a commonplace to regard film noir during the peak years of its production as a pessimistic cinematic response to volatile social and economic conditions of the decade immediately following World War II. Whether considered a genre or a style, the films circumscribed as noir are seen as

"...the cocktail lounge, the nightclub, the bar...": drinks and cigarettes in *Woman in the Window* and, above, *Murder, My Sweet*.

playing out negative dramas of postwar masculine trauma and gender anxiety brought on by wartime desta-bilization of the culture's domestic economy and a consequent "deregulation" of the institutionalized and patri-archally informed relationship between men and women. The social context in which noir emerged is marked as "transitional," and its overarching themes are the recovery of a lost patriarchal order and the need for the country to literally and metaphorically "settle down." The national scenario and its cast of characters are by now familiar: returning veterans trying to reinsert themselves both into the workplace and family life after a long absence; working women who had realized themselves as economically independent during the war being remanded, not always willingly, to the hearth and motherhood; official rhetoric establishing the family unit and the suburban home as the domestic matrix of democracy even as divorce rates and personal debt escalated; economic and social ambivalence about the future deepening as the home front was reconfigured from a wartime economy that promoted the social unity of production and self-sacrifice to a peacetime economy emphasizing the privatized pleasures of consumption. All of these elements were entailed in a newly-troubled domestic economy that had previously determined American domestic life by separating the public and pri-vate sectors across gender lines into the workplace and the home. Furthermore, grounding this postwar domestic melodrama were first implicit and then explicit anxieties and imperatives brought on by that novel form of international political enmity called the Cold War—an enmity that motivated the further coalescence of the military-industrial complex and gave rise, as a substitute for a phenomenological sense of personal and national security, to the paranoid structures and nationalist sensibilities of the security state.

Thus, between 1945 and 1955, the years generally (if problematically) acknowledged to bracket film noir's most significant period of production and reception, themes such as the impossible return to a highly mythol-ogized "home front," attempts to "settle down," and the desire for "stability," "security" and "loyalty" (rather than mere loyalty oaths) resonate and mark to an extraordinary degree the lived sense of insecurity, instabili-ty, and social incoherence Americans experienced during the transitional period that began after the war and Roosevelt's death in 1945, lasted through the Truman years (1945–1952), and declined as the Eisenhower years (1952–1960) drew to a prosperous close. By Eisenhower's second term, the country had learned to love the security state and the Bomb and had, indeed, settled down—into what David Reid and Jayne L. Walker describe as "a cold torpor" that now, for some, "passes in national mythology as the United State's golden age."[5]

However, the early postwar period, identified with film noir's "classic phase," was marked not by torpor but by domestic anxiety and political purpose. Domestic anxiety was informed not only by the constantly rising prices of food, clothing, and other necessities (blamed by manufacturers on labor's successful bid for wage increases), but also by increasing rents and a nationwide housing shortage. Indeed, in 1947, President Truman publicly focused on the housing crisis as "the foremost of the many problems facing the nation."[6] As Dana Polan has noted in *Power and Paranoia: History, Narrative, and the American Cinema, 1940–1950*:

During the war 50 percent of the American population is renting and frequently doing so in habitations far below needs and expectations. There is a dramatic housing crisis (lack of available sites, the absence during most of the war of any sort of rent control) that is frequently represented in narratives of the time (*Since You Went Away* [1944], *Twin Beds* [1942], *The More the Merrier* [1943]). The housing problem continues on into the post-war period when a new suburbia will suddenly be offered as the necessary solution.[7]

The political aim of the administration in the early post-war period was to consolidate America's hold on the European and world imagination and to secure a preponderance of power, but—against the ground of domes-tic problems—official rhetoric did not necessarily translate into a sense of social security. As Reid and Walker point out:

Despite bravado in the Truman White House, the public mood by any measure (Gallup or even novel-istic) was fearful and apprehensive: fearful of a renewed Great Depression (at least up to 1947); fearful afterwards of international communism (the Attorney General's list of "subversive organizations" was drawn up in 1947)....The temper of the times was jittery and skittish. Respectable opinion was pursued by a host of phantasms.[8]

It is within this context of postwar fear and present apprehension of the future that the wartime past becomes secured in national memory as itself safe and secure. Reid and Walker note how quickly the war and the home front became the objects of national nostalgia—the former "sentimentalized into 'the good war'" and the latter characterized as having achieved a "chain-mail solidarity" in the social sphere:

> How swiftly forgotten were the thousands of work stoppages, including hate strikes, racial strife...John L. Lewis's duel with Roosevelt, the congressional attack on the New Deal, and the bitter and morose 1944 presidential election (now remembered only for FDR's "Fala" speech). Paradoxically, it was precisely the success of "wartime nationalism" and its subsequent deflection into the...crusade against communism and the national security state that dissolved these memories.[9]

Thus it is that, in the decade that follows World War II and gives us the Korean War and an ongoing Cold War, both wartime and the home front together come to form a re-membered idyllic national time-space of phenomenological integrity and plenitude. A mythological construction, this chronotope (a concept developed by Soviet literary theorist Mikhail Bakhtin to which I return later) emerges in postwar culture itself and becomes the lost time and place of national purpose, cohesion, and fulfillment.[10] Indeed, the chronotope of the idyllic wartime home front stands as this country's lost object of desire until Camelot—that other mythological spatiotemporal construction about loss (though not of a past but a future)—replaces it in the national mythology after John F. Kennedy's assassination in the early 1960s.

Within the context of the postwar period's national (and personal) insecurity about the future and its longing for the purposefulness, unity, and plenitude of a mythologized national past, film noir provided—or so film historians, critics, and anecdotal experience have told us—the cinematic time-space in which contemporaneous cultural anxieties found vernacular expression. Dark in tone (if not always chiaroscuro in lighting), twisted in vision (if not always in framing), urban in sensibility (if not always in location), impotently angry and disillusioned in spirit (if not always in execution), noir circumscribed a world of existential, epistemological, and axiological uncertainty—and inscribed a cinema that film critics and scholars saw as an allegorical dramatization of the economic and social crises of a postwar period they located roughly between 1945 and 1958.

In *Film Noir: The Dark Side of the Screen*, Foster Hirsch gives us a litany of selected titles that locate us in terms of place and mood and, as he puts it, "conjure up a dark, urban world of neurotic entrapment leading to delirium": *Murder My Sweet* (1944), *Scarlet Street* (1945), *Detour* (1945), *The Woman in the Window* (1945), *The Dark Mirror* (1946), *The Dark Corner* (1946), *The Black Angel* (1946), *The Big Sleep* (1946), *Kiss of Death* (1947), *Possessed* (1947), *Ruthless* (1948), *They Live by Night* (1948), *The Naked City* (1948), *Cry of the City* (1948), *Street with No Name* (1948), *The Window* (1949), *Caught* (1949), *The Dark Past* (1949), *D.O.A.* (1950), *Panic in the Streets* (1950), *Night and the City* (1950), *Edge of Doom* (1950), *No Way Out* (1950), *The Narrow Margin* (1952), *Jeopardy* (1953), *Killer's Kiss* (1955), *The Killing* (1956).[11] In the same vein we could add *Double Indemnity* (1944), *Cornered* (1945), *Out of the Past* (1947), *Pitfall* (1948), *The Night Has a Thousand Eyes* (1948), *The Set-Up* (1949), *On Dangerous Ground* (1951), *The Big Heat* (1953), *Nightmare* (1955), *Touch of Evil* (1958) and, of course, those titles that evoke noir's femmes fatales: *Phantom Lady* (1944), *The Blue Dahlia* (1946), *Fallen Angel* (1946), *Gilda* (1946), *The Lady from Shanghai* (1948), *The File on Thelma Jordan* (1950), *Angel Face* (1952). There are, of course, many more—along with corollary discussions about the criteria for their inclusion and exclusion as noir.

Making the extremely apt point that it is "tricky" to "read *noir* ...as a series of social notations either in sympathetic response to or in reaction against a national frame of mind...because it is not primarily a social form, in the way that the stories of gangsters in the thirties were," Hirsch nonetheless—like the rest of us—cannot refrain from doing so.[12] Rehearsing the national scenario during the noir years and pointing to the "disoriented," "disconnected," "amnesiac and somnambulist" veteran as the only noir character "connected directly to the period, without any symbolic exaggeration," he tells us nevertheless:

> Specific social traumas and upheavals remain outside the frame. *Noir* never insisted on its "extracurricular" meanings or its social relevance. But beneath its repeated stories of double and triple crosses,

its private passions erupting into heinous crimes, the sleazy, compromised morality of many of its characters, can be glimpsed the political paranoia and brutality of the period. In its pervasive aura of defeat and despair, its images of entrapment, the escalating derangement of its leading characters, *noir* registers, in a general way, the country's sour postwar mood. This darkest, most downbeat of American film genres traces a series of *metaphors* for a decade of anxiety, a contemporary apocalypse bounded on the one hand by Nazi brutality and on the other by the awful knowledge of nuclear power.[13]

2

Recent revisionist scholarship has called into question both the historical periodization of noir as well as the historical and stylistic specificity of those textual features that circumscribe the films as an object of study and, as Fred Pfeil notes, are "conceded to be...constitutive...even by critics who otherwise disagree over where it belongs and what it means."[14] In the first instance, in an extraordinary essay in the previously mentioned *Shades of Noir* , Marc Vernet persuasively "undoes" film noir as a historical and stylistic coherence and interrogates the logic that underlies its "postwar" periodization and the critical linkage of noir texts to their historical context. He notes how the various bracketings of noir are variously "stretched back a bit (to 1941 for the father, *The Maltese Falcon* , or even 1940 if *Stranger on the Third Floor* is recalled) and forward a bit (to 1958 if *Touch of Evil* is to be included)."[15] And here, in support of Vernet's critique of the historical elasticity that marks noir criticism and has interpretive consequences, we might consider that Raymond Borde and Etienne Chaumeton's seminal *Panorama du Film Noir Américain* locates noir between 1941 and 1953, Amir Karimi's *Toward a Definition of the American Film Noir* more narrowly between 1941 and 1949, and Robert Ottoson's *A Reference Guide to the American Film Noir* most expansively between 1940 and 1958. One way around the dilemma such elasticity poses in terms of linking noir specifically to postwar culture has been to further segment it and speak of its "classic period"—most often the decade between 1945 and 1955. However, as Vernet suggests:

> this way of breaking up time has no real validity whatsoever. 1945 marks the end of World War Two, which is not a cinematographic event, and 1955 marks either the appearance of the book by Borde and Chaumeton or the year that RKO studio sold its stock of films to television, events that are totally incommensurable with the historical weight of the first date.[16]

In the second instance, Vernet also challenges the specificity of those stylistic and narrative features that are critically agreed upon as constitutive of noir and catalogued by Pfeil in his contribution to Copjec's revisionist volume:

> ...iconographically they stretch from the dark city streets and lurid jazzy bars to the privatized, alienated space of the car and the modern urban apartment, and down to the close-up level of the cigarette, drink, swanky dress, trenchcoat and slouch hat; stylistically, from the use of voice-over and flashback to expressionistic lighting and decentred and unstable compositions, often in deep space; narratively, they include a new emphasis on deviant psychological motivation, the deviousness and frustrating confusion of the male protagonist's project or quest, and the outright hostility, suspicion and sexual attraction between the often confused and weary male protagonist and the duplicitous, powerful femme fatale (with a good asexual wife-mother figure optionally dead or waiting in the wings); and thematically, they consist above all in the "absurd" existential choice of moral behaviour according to one's own individual ethical code, in a hopelessly dark universe in which more consensual authorities are ineffectual, irrelevant, or corrupt.[17]

Vernet calls the basic historical and generic specificity of this circumscription into question. His strategy is to track those stylistic and narrative noir elements taken as constitutive and canonical (expressionist lighting and framing supposedly derived from German cinema; convoluted emplotment, characterization, and moral universe supposedly derived from hard-boiled American detective fiction) back to silent cinema and across generic lines. Breaking down the historical coherence of style and narrative topoi, he further interrogates the logic that has linked noir's supposed textual coherence to its historical context. Though he concedes that American films made after the war are different from those made before, these differences are so broadly located that they cannot be seen as constitutive features of a generic coherence. Postwar films are marked by "a more serious tone, a shrinking of the frame, a change of style in the physical appearance of the actors and décor, and finally the weakening of censorship."[18] Thus, Vernet—who has earlier reminded us that *film noir* is a French term coined by French *cinéastes* within the historical specificity of a particular moment of French social and political relations with America and American culture—diffuses noir's always already tenuous coherence.

Indeed, his overarching argument is that "*film noir* has no clothes": invented by French critics and elaborated by American scholars, it is a "cinephilic ready-made."[19] His iconoclastic conclusion is that as "an object or corpus of films, *film noir* does not belong to the history of cinema; it belongs as a notion to the history of film criticism," and his evaluation of that criticism is harsh:

> *Film noir* presents a fine example of cinema history and aesthetic reflection that is founded on distribution (in France at a certain point in time) and critical discourse, and not on production (in the United States during several decades), in a complete ignorance of the larger cultural context. This is not only because the history of the cinema that already exists works with very short periods..., but also because no one has sufficiently reflected on the ideological conditions that could have presided over the advent of a kind of fiction. The result is a sort of imaginary enclosure in which what appeared to be evident to spectators becomes a venerable concept for feminists and historians, and in which the resulting critical work ends up occulting the films themselves and their production.[20]

And yet if film noir is shown to have no clothes, its body remains—even for Vernet. There are, after all, "the films themselves"—and, even for Vernet, the perception of at least a minimally sufficient historical coalescence (if not coherence) to suggest that there is, indeed, a "there" there. Criticizing the "complacent repetition" of the inherited topoi of noir, even Vernet admits: "Doubtless there is something true there, but what that truth relates to remains a question."[21]

3

What is the "there" there of film noir? And what is its "truth"—or, more precisely, the force and charge of its phenomenological presence to us as meaningful and relevant to human lives lived off the screen and outside the theater? Noir's substantial "there" and its cultural truth are grounded and come together, I would argue, in its material premises. As Dean MacCannell points out, "*Film noir* established democracy's dark side, not as an articulated message but as a critically constructed mise-en-scène."[22] Thus, the phenomeno-logic of noir and its experienced truth are to be found concretely in the visible "heres" that are brought together there on the screen and "co-here" in what is perceived as a comprehensible and particular world. This coherence cannot be completely subsumed under the more overarching and therefore somewhat more abstract thematic of "the city" so significant to noir criticism. What "co-heres" are more particular places, and they exist both in the city and the small town where they concretize an existential world in which (if I may offer a serious double entendre) "there is no place like home."

Robert Siodmak's *The Killers* (1946) is exemplary in this regard. It is telling that not a single scene in the film occurs in what could be considered a normal (that is, culturally normative) domestic space. The film begins in an inhospitable small-town diner (where much of what is on the menu is unavailable). It moves to an anonymous room in a boardinghouse where "the Swede" waits to be murdered. Then, in flashbacks, its characters occupy a variety of self-similar, nearly denuded hotel rooms, cocktail lounges and cafes, and yet more hotel rooms relieved only by a pool hall, a prison cell, a hospital room, and office space. If one stretches it a bit, we do enter the empty vestibule of the Colfax mansion to watch its owner die on the stairs at the film's end. And there is a scene earlier when Reardon, the insurance investigator cum noir detective, talks to Lt. Lubinsky, a former friend of the Swede, that takes place outdoors on Lubinsky's Philadelphia apartment rooftop where, in a supposedly domestic off-hour, he is painting kitchen chairs.

In a moment so startling as to be uncanny, emerging from a space that has no place in this film, Lubinsky's wife steps out of a door holding a pitcher of lemonade that seems to have come from another dimension.

The Killers: "...not a single scene in the film occurs in what could be considered a normal...domestic space."

Indeed, that pitcher of lemonade functions much like Barthes's photographic "punctum," compelling and disturbing us with its evocation of an idyllic time and domestic space that doesn't belong and can gain no admittance to such a world as the one in which *The Killers* takes place. The lemonade comes from a coherent space and time that must stay forever off-screen here, behind a door, always out of visibility and beyond reach of characters such as the double-crossed Swede, femme fatale Kitty Collins, and even Reardon, the insurance investigator who travels from place to place seeking answers and cannot be imagined sitting at rest on a porch somewhere else than here. Evoking the pastoral, the familial, the generational, the secure and stable world of an idyllic time-space that we will—in the historical context of noir—(re)call the "home front," that pitcher of lemonade slakes no ironic thirst for something slightly sour but rather serves an unquenchable nostalgia for the sweetness of an America forever lost from view. This is lemonade from *Mrs. Miniver* (1942), *Meet Me in St. Louis* (1944), or *Centennial Summer* (1946). Indeed, the uncanny wrongness of the offer of lemonade from another time and place in *The Killers* is matched only by the unutterably sad rightness of the fact that the beneficiary of the Swede's tiny life insurance policy is someone who turns out to be a hotel chambermaid.

In *Power and Paranoia* , Dana Polan underscores a "negative existentialism" in American films of the 1940s that is constituted, in part, as a relation to environment: "one in which environments...don't reflect back to a character his/her personality or values—that is, his/her freedom to shape externality according to individual desire—but, quite the contrary, rather demonstrate the radical externality and even resistance of environment to the imprinting of a self upon environment."[23] That "radical externality," and "resistance" are nowhere made so concrete and visible as in the Swede's denuded boardinghouse bedroom—the only markers of human presence are the Swede himself, awaiting his death on the bed, and Kitty Collins's silk scarf. Such radical externality and resistance can also be found in the cocktail lounges, hotel bars, diners, roadhouses, and motels that spatialize film noir—those rented rooms or tables or counter stools that resist individual particularity and are made for transients and transience, those quasi places that substitute perversely for the hospitable and felicitous places and domesticity of a "proper" home in which such necessary quotidian functions as sleeping and eating and drinking are secured and transfigured into intimate social communion.

In terms of Polan's description, it is clear that although there are occasional houses in film noir, there are hardly, any homes. As he points out, "the imperatives of war invest themselves in a particular representation of home."

> At the extreme, the forties home is not simply a haven against the outside world but a separate world of its own, a vast act of the imagination....Home becomes a self-enclosed environment...with its own rules, its own language games, its own memory...and its own rituals....Home here works rigorously to close out the world of ambiguous interaction, of ambivalent meanings. It is the mark of a certain surety and security.[24]

Thus, in noir, homes are given to us only in glimpses—as something lost or something fragile and threatened. (Here, 1949's *Reckless Moment* comes to mind). Indeed, the few homes that do appear seem anachronistic, evoking the retrospectively idyllic and mythic time-space of the war years and the home front. Unlike the noir house, the rare noir home is furnished and lit in the overstuffed and chintzy manner of *Mrs. Miniver* and *The Best Years of Our Lives* (1946). In this regard, it is telling to remember a pre- and protonoir moment in *Since You Went Away* (1944) in which such a wartime home visibly diminishes, its private domesticity fragmented and depersonalized into a mere house. Claudette Colbert's housewife not only leaves home to take a job as a welder but also breaks up and transforms the spatial and emotional integrity of the family's home by taking in a paying boarder. This economic purchase, disintegration, and depersonalization of the domestic space and function of the home is heightened in wartime and postwar culture as much as it is in the period's films, and it exists as the concrete ground for the retroactive fantasy of the home front. The housing shortage is phenomenologically informed by a sense of the larger, irrevocable loss of home that runs throughout the war and postwar years, however different its specific material causes in each period. Thus we can understand the hysterical edge to various wartime and postwar comedies of mishap surrounding housing—the most exemplary, perhaps, *Mr. Blandings Builds His Dream House* (1948).

Both the culture and noir's retroactive fantasy of home in this historical period constitutes, as Gaston Bachelard might put it, a "felicitous space," a "eulogized space," a space "that may be grasped, that may be defended against adverse forces, the space we love."[25] Evoking the poetic and felicitous image of the house (what we identify here as the *home*), Bachelard phenomenologically describes a particular form of topophilia. The image of the house puts us "in possession of a veritable principle of psychological integration" and provides us a "topography of Intimate being."[26] As he elaborates in an extraordinary passage that resonates in the context of the culture's lost home front and the absence of hospitable spaces of "intimate being" in film noir:

> ...there is a ground for taking the house as a *tool for analysis* of the human soul. With the help of this tool, can we not find within ourselves, while dreaming in our own modest homes, the consolations of the cave? Are the towers of our souls razed for all time? Are we to remain, to quote Gérard de Nerval's famous line, beings whose "towers have been destroyed"? Not only our memories, but the things we have forgotten are "housed." Our soul is an abode. And by remembering "houses" and "rooms," we learn to "abide" within ourselves. Now everything becomes clear, the house images move in both directions: they are in us as much as we are in them.[27]

In this context, wartime and postwar American culture's loss of home and the spatial and psychological integration it imaginatively and mythically provided is historically—and cinematically—poignant. Thus, as Dean MacCannell points out: "To better understand the opposition *noir* /homeless, it is necessary to sustain examination of the unusual moment in film noir, its glimpses into the interior of allegedly normal homes and communities."[28] In this regard, he suggests Hitchcock's *Shadow of a Doubt* (1943) as exemplary. Linked regularly by scholars to noir (however problematic such linkage is in terms of periodization, thematics, and iconography), *Shadow of a Doubt* visibly contrasts the impersonal, radical externality of Uncle Charlie's urban hotel room [see page 62 above] with the emotional intimacy of his namesake niece's small-town home and bedroom [below]. Compared to young Charlie, Uncle Charlie's soul has no abode, is not "housed"; it lives in exis-

Shadow of a Doubt: Uncle Charlie has no home telephone.

tential—and life-denying—negativity. Following MacCannell, we might look also to the "unusual moment" in films of the wartime and postwar period not usually linked to noir in which the loss of home and the ability to "abide" in one's soul is literalized and suddenly transforms the mise-en-scène into the concretely particular premises that ground the noir world. Here, *It's a Wonderful Life* (1946) is exemplary. In the sequence in which George Bailey, presumably ruined and contemplating suicide, is taken by his guardian angel, Clarence, to look upon a Bedford Falls from which George's existence and his existential acts have been erased, we see not only the concretization of Polan's "existential negativity," but also the literal transformation of Bedford Falls from the quintessential fantasy site of home and home front to a nightmarish and radically external site of domestic and social fragmentation. In the film's most "unusual" and powerful moment, Bedford Falls is grounded in the mise-en-scène of noir: there are sleazy bars, shoddy boardinghouses, cheap music, and disconnected and homeless people. For a brief but punctal moment, the "towers" of Bedford Falls' souls have been "razed for all time." *It's a Wonderful Life* is hardly a noir film in its final recuperation of home, intimacy, and abiding souls. Nonetheless, in making visible for a brief, conditional moment a world in which there is no place like home, it condenses and concretizes the impersonal and incoherent premises of noir with such unveiled hysteria that it is unsurprising (if still quite startling) that Bedford Falls and the Baileys provide the dark center for David Thomson's extraordinary noir novel, *Suspects* (described by the *Los Angeles Times* as both "a movie fan's delight" and "a mordant commentary on the loss of national innocence"[29]).

Polan's discussion of the "negative existentialism" of forties cinema considers the other—the less felicitous—side of Bachelard's phenomenological poetics of space. He tells us:

> ...if the *project* (to use the existentialists' term) is a narrative activity through which human beings work to come to terms with an environment and make it their own, forties narrative can serve as the site of a kind of reversibility of meaning—what we might call a *symbolics* of narrative space—in which environment ceases to be a reflection or object of human projects and turns instead into a potential disruption, subversion, dispersion of projects....Such a symbolics is...the measure of a gap between intention and realization.[30]

Thus, the Swede's boardinghouse room with its sparse furnishings and the myriad hotel rooms, cocktail lounges, bars, roadside diners, and even the cold interiors of the houses of the rich and corrupt that constitute the environment of *The Killers* particularly and film noir's environment generally all refuse individual subjectivity and intimacy (as they encourage individual isolation and secrecy). As Polan points out, this is not an expressionist mise-en-scène:

> Where a number of critics have argued the influence on forties film (and especially on *noir*) of an expressionist aesthetic, it is important to emphasize that the expressionism here is most often not the triumph of a subjectivity in which environment somehow reflects back to a character his/her own internal nature but, quite the contrary, an expressionism that demonstrates the radical externality and alterity of environment to personality.[31]

In noir, then, a house is almost never a home. Indeed, the loss of home becomes a structuring absence in film noir. It is particularly telling to think here of the ironic "domesticity" that runs through *Double Indemnity* (1944) or *Mildred Pierce* (1945)—films that are linked irrevocably to noir but pose problems to its particular urban iconography. The suburban house into which Phyllis Dietrichson invites insurance agent Walter Neff is merely a house: its furniture plain, its decorations sparse and impersonal, motel-like. It doesn't look lived in. Indeed, its interior decoration is best described in a line of dialogue offered by a character about a house in a later film noir, *The Big Heat* (1953): "Hey, I like this. Early nothing." And, even in her domestic beginnings, Mildred's home is also figured as merely a house: drab, plain, unmarked by the people who live there and supposedly constitute a family. The kitchen in which Mildred bakes her pies has none of the warmth and coziness of Norman Rockwell's kitchens and is hardly a felicitous space. And this lack of felicity is echoed in the bitterness of her voice-over narration that accompanies a flashback: "I was always in the kitchen. I felt as though I'd been born in a kitchen and lived there all my life except for the few hours it took to get married."

The irrevocable loss of the home in noir is also figured in the "radical externality" and cold glitter of the houses of the rich, where money buys interior decoration and fine art but no warmth, no nurturance. As Bachelard puts it, quoting Baudelaire, "in a palace, 'there is no place for intimacy.'"[32] Thus, there is a wonderful irony in the absolute precision of Waldo Lydecker's comment about his house to detective Mark McPherson in the protonoir *Laura* (1944): "It's lavish, but I call it home." Although we can trace the negative imagery of the empty and emotionally hollow houses of the rich and successful back to certain women's melodramas of the 1930s such as *Craig's Wife* (1936) where the wife's obsessive and hostile perfectionism constructs her husband as an unwelcome intruder in the house, the impersonal homes of the rich figure frequently in noir as signs of empty acquisition. (It is more than coincidental, then, that *Craig's Wife* is remade in 1948 as *Harriet Craig* , starring the post-*Mildred Pierce* Joan Crawford.) After her marriage to Monte, Mildred Pierce's house is bigger and more furnished than the cold little parody of a home in which she lived her first marriage to Bert, but its size existentially echoes the hollowness of a space that is not inhabited emotionally, that is lived in display or deceit rather than in intimacy or authenticity. It is apposite that, in *The Killers*, all we see of the Colfax mansion is a huge empty vestibule marked by a cold and geometrically tiled floor. "Inhabited space transcends geometrical space," Bachelard tells us. "A house that has been experienced is not an inert box."[33] In his phenomenological topo-analysis, he concedes the house as "first and foremost a geometrical object" that, if analyzed rationally, "ought to resist metaphors that welcome the human body and the human soul." Nonetheless, he continues, "transposition to the human plane takes place immediately whenever a house is considered as space for cheer and intimacy, space that is supposed to condense and defend intimacy."[34]

Cheer and intimacy, however, are hardly the stuff of noir houses, of noir hotel and motel rooms. This is made as explicit in the dialogue as it is in the mise-en-scène. The sentiments expressed by Dana Andrews in *Fallen Angel* (1946)—" What a dump!"—echo throughout the films. *The Little Black and White Book of Film Noir* provides us the oddity (unique in American film) of a genre in which both male and female characters explicitly and regularly comment (usually with sarcasm) on the decor.

—You call this dump a hotel?

—That's what the sign says. Fresh sheets every day, they tell me.

—How often do they change the fleas?

Alan Ladd and desk clerk, The Blue Dahlia

—Well, the place looks lived in.

—Yeah, but by what?

Richard Erdman and Dick Powell, Cry Danger

—What a place. I can feel the rats in the wall.

Franchot Tone to Elisha Cook Jr., Phantom Lady

—Quite the hacienda.

John Maxwell to Van Heflin, The Prowler

—I hear you're living in the same old dump.

—*House* is what it's called.

Robert Ryan and Robert Mitchum, The Racket

—A neglected house gets an unhappy look. This one had it in spades.

William Holden, Sunset Boulevard

—Tell me, you think I'm going to like this rat trap we're going to?

—The Antlers? You bet'cha. It's a swell place. It's got a dining room, plenty of class, everything, and besides that, it's the only hotel in town.

Ida Lupino and bit player, Road House

—But I like goldfish. I'm gonna get a couple for the room—you know, dress it up a little bit. It adds class to the joint, makes it a little homey.

Tom D'Andrea to Humphrey Bogart, Dark Passage[35]

In sum, the intimacy and security of home and the integrity and solidity of the home front are lost to wartime and postwar America and to those films we associate at both the core and periphery of that cinematic grouping we circumscribe as noir. Both during and after the war, the phenomenological coherence of the domestic life of family and home was shattered, dispersed, and concretely remembered elsewhere: in hotels and boardinghouse rooms and motels, in diners, in bars, in swanky and seedy cocktail lounges and nightclubs, all places for transients, all fragmented, rented social spaces rather than coherently generated places of social communion, all substitutes for the intimate and integral domestic space of home. Polan quotes a telling line of dialogue from a non-noir, wartime film, *All Through the Night* (1942), in which a nightclub owner cynically remarks: "If my customers start thinking about home and mother, I'm a dead duck." Polan goes on to point out: "much of forties cinema stages the impossibility of...spiritual redemption through the forces of domesticity—through the imposition of a domestic space" that has become "unavailable in an America for whom innocence is becoming a mark of a vanished past."[36] Thus home in the postwar period exists only through reminiscence and in the nostalgic imaginary of *A Tree Grows in Brooklyn* (1945) or *I Remember Mama* (1948).

This perception of the loss of home—this new American homelessness of a kind historically different from its counterpart in the present day—does not find its expression as mere metaphor. It is not simply the hyperbolic trope of filmmakers and film critics (and, here, definitely not of French critics for whom the American notion of home is unimportant and, perhaps, unintelligible). The wartime and postwar period's myth of home

No goldfish are in evidence as
Tom D'Andrea gets the drop on
fugitive Humphrey Bogart in a cheap hotel room in *Dark Passage.*
Below, more dark domesticity in *Phantom Lady* where the Franchot
Tone (right) remarks to Elisha Cook, Jr.: "What a place. I can feel the
rats in the wall."

—Listen, I know a little place.

—I'm sure you do.

Edmond O'Brien to Ella Raines, *The Web* (above)

fifties, however, these actual spaces were not historically lost and their virtual presence on the screen did not stand in direct contradiction to the space outside the theater. These spaces were not the objects of nostalgia as were the home and the home front—nor were they merely metaphors. Rather, these were actual spaces charged with particular temporal meaning for the culture's life-world, and their representations on screen foregrounded a phenomenological expression of that life-world's insecurity and unsettledness, its transitional and hence transient status.

I should like to suggest that film noir's relation to its historical and social context can be best described not as metaphoric but as synecdochic and hyperbolic.[38] That is, actual spaces and places in American culture are not sublimated on the screen through the substitutions of metaphor (although they may lead to metaphorical thinking), but neither are they quite articulated according to the prevailing conventions of realism, exemplified by a film such as *The Best Years of Our Lives*.

Rather, noir represents concrete parts of the whole landscape of American wartime and postwar culture—but its synecdochic selectivity and partiality result in a hyperbolic textual exaggeration of aspects of that context's actual life-world. This is to argue that the baroque qualities of noir's visual style, the particularities of its narrative thematics and structure, emerge as an intensified form of selection, foregrounding, and consequent exaggeration of actual cultural spaces charged with contingent temporal experience.

Film noir's concrete spatiotemporal articulations are concretely found (if in less exaggerated form) in the extratextual life-world. Transported to the screen, attended to with an intensity that borders on hysterical fixation, they tell us not only about the limits placed on noir's narrative possibilities, but also about their significance in the cultural world from which they were selected and against which they are turned from ground to figure in a peculiar and revealing reversal. The hotel or boardinghouse room, the cocktail lounge, the nightclub, the diner or roadside cafe, the bar and roadhouse, the cheap motel—these are the recurrent and ubiquitous spaces of film noir that, unlike the mythic sites of home and home front, are actual common-places in wartime and postwar American culture. Cinematically concretized and foregrounded, they both constitute and circumscribe the temporal possibilities and life-world of the characters who are constrained by them—and they provide the grounding premises for that cinematic grouping we have come to recognize as noir.

4

At this point, as a way to comprehend how the concrete premises of noir ground its narrative possibilities, I turn to Mikhail Bakhtin's elaboration of a concept he called "the chronotope." Simply put (by Michael Montgomery, one of very few scholars to have used the concept for film analysis), the chronotope "may be defined generally as any topological pattern in the artistic work that possesses the characteristics of a semantic field or grid."[39] At the least, chronotopes "constitute a set of template schemata that invest a causal chain with 'real' social contexts."[40] At the most, however, the chronotope—a term derived from physics—is meant to emphasize not only the absolute interdependence of time and space in the constitution of narrative and its significance but also the human "relativity" of their "ratio"—or, if you will, their historical rationality. As Bakhtin puts it, the chronotope is the "organizing center" of "fundamental narrative events," the "place where the knots of narrative are tied and untied." For him, "without qualification," to the chronotope "belongs the meaning that shapes narrative."[41]

First outlined during 1937–1938 and subsequently developed in two major essays—"Forms of Time and Chronotope in the Novel" and "The *Bildungsroman* and Its Significance in the History of Realism (Toward a Historical Typology of the Novel)"—the chronotope, as Michael Holmquist glosses it, is literally, "time-space." A unit of analysis for studying texts according to the ratio and nature of the temporal and spatial categories represented. The distinctiveness of this concept as opposed to most other uses of time and space in literary analysis lies in the fact that neither category is privileged; they are utterly interdependent. The chronotope is an optic for reading texts as x-rays of the forces at work in the culture system from which they spring.[42]

Charged by Bakhtin with a variety of connotations and functions, the chronotope is a tool for synthetic analysis, not only for identifying and reasserting the force and information of concrete space on the temporal structure of the novel but also for comprehending historically the phenomenological relation between text and context in a way richer than that afforded by traditional generic analyses. As Montgomery notes, "One of Bakhtin's express purposes in developing the chronotope in the first place is to work past conceptions of genres he perceives as being too limiting to explore the more fundamental discursive patterns from which artistic works take their shape and which permit them to be understood and analyzed as cultural artifacts."[43] Although Bakhtin clearly distinguishes "a sharp and categorical boundary line between the actual world as a source of representation and the world represented in the work," he sees the chronotope as a spatiotemporal structure of meaning that links both worlds, and he tells us: "Out of the actual chronotopes of our world (which serve as the source of representation) emerge the reflected and created chronotopes of the world represented in the work."[44] The power of the chronotope is that it "references real-life situations with everyday associations for audiences, helping to create a sense of shared place. Through longstanding artistic usage, chronotopes also become associated with 'fixed expressions' and metaphorical patterns of thinking....addressing the relationship of the represented locale to the community site."[45] Thus, the categorical boundary line between text and context is "not something absolute and impermeable." Text and context, the represented and the real world, "are indissolubly tied up with each other and find themselves in continual mutual interaction" in a continual process of "uninterrupted exchange."[46] Chronotopes serve as the spatiotemporal currency between two different orders of existence and discourse, between the historicity of the lived world and the literary world (here, the world of cinema).

In regard to the chronotope's structure and function as inherently specific and historical, it is worthwhile quoting some fairly lengthy passages from Bakhtin's *Bildungsroman* essay on Goethe:

...everything is intensive in Goethe's world; it contains no inanimate, immobile, petrified places, no immutable background that does not participate in action and emergence (in events), no decorations or sets....time, in all its essential aspects, is localized in concrete space, imprinted on it. In Goethe's world there are no events, plots, or temporal motifs that are not related in an essential way to the particular spatial place of their occurrence, that could occur anywhere or nowhere ("eternal" plots and motifs). Everything in this world is a *time-space*, a true *chronotope*....

Time and space merge here into an inseparable unity, both in the plot itself and in its individual images. In the majority of cases, a definite and absolutely concrete locality serves as the starting point for the creative imagination. But this is not an abstract landscape, imbued with mood of the contemplator—no, this is a piece of human history, historical time condensed in space. Therefore, the plot (the sum of depicted events) and the characters do not enter it from the outside, are not invented to fit the landscape, but are unfolded in it as though they were present from the very beginning. They are like those creative forces that formulated and humanized this landscape, made it a speaking vestige of the movement of history (historical time), and, to a certain degree, predetermined its subsequent course as well, or like those creative forces a given locality needs in order to organize and continue the historical processes embodied in it.

Such an approach to locality and to history, their inseparable unity and interpenetrability, became possible only because the locality ceased to be a part of abstract nature, a part of an indefinite, interrupted, and only symbolically rounded out (supplemented) world, and the event ceased to be a segment of the same indefinite time that was always equal to itself, reversible, and symbolically embodied. The locality became an irreplaceable part of the geographically and historically determined world, of *that* completely real and essentially visible world of human history, and the event became an essential and non-transferable moment in the time of this particular human history that occurred in this, and only in this, geographically determined human world. The world and history did not become poorer or smaller as a result of this process of mutual concretization and interpenetration. On the contrary, they were condensed, compacted, and filled with the creative possibilities of subsequent *real* emergence and development.

And it is this new sense of space and time that has led to an essential change in the orientation of the artistic image: that image felt an irresistible attraction to a particular place and to a particular time in this world that had become definite and real.[47]

What Bakhtin emphasizes here about the concretion of time and space in the charged chronotopicity of the artistic image resonates in relation to my earlier evocation of Bachelard's phenomenological "poetics of space." And Bakhtin's insistence that time is realized—and read—in space, that the two interpenetrate and allow for the "emergence" of meaning, recalls Erwin Panofsky's delineation of the uniqueness of cinema as its correlative and correspondent "dynamization of space" and "spatialization of time."[48] We may think, too, of Polan's discussion of narrative and the meaningful (negative) correlation of existence and environment. However, what is unique about Bakhtin's chronotopic phenomenology is—as indicated in the passage above—its structural provision of historical specificity, relativity, and dynamism. As Holmquist points out, Bakhtin "thought of himself less as a literary critic than as a 'philosophical anthropologist,' for the questions he seeks to answer...are less those that occupy historians of literature than questions about the nature of human consciousness under particular cultural and historical conditions."[49]

For Bakhtin, then, chronotopes are much more than topological patterns. Never merely the spatiotemporal backdrop for narrative events, they provide the literal and concrete ground from which narrative and character emerge as the temporalization of human action, significant in its diacritical marking of both cultural and narrative space. It is in this diacritical valuation of concrete space and its circumscription of temporal activity that chronotopes are not merely descriptive but rather constitutive of what we apprehend as genre. As Gary Morson and Caryl Emerson suggest: "It is as if each genre possesses a specific field that determines the parameters of events even though the field does not uniquely specify particular events."[50] Thus, certain chronotopes come to be associated with specific genres, although it is also possible for several chronotopes in complementary and contrary relation to combine in a single generic structure.

For Bakhtin, an exemplary—albeit minor—chronotope is the road, a spatiotemporal structure that has much resonance in film studies but that, like film noir, poses certain problems to the circumscriptions of traditional generic analysis. (The road picture is often—and uncomfortably—considered a subgenre of the adventure film, itself broad and ill-defined, or it is dealt with as a discrete category, discussion of which tends to elide issues of its generic status.) The chronotope of the road concretely structures and limits the nature and process of narrative events that temporally figure against the ground of its spatialization.[51] It radically inscribes time as passage and journey and thus tends to exclude (or especially privilege by virtue of their exceptionality and contrast) those temporal structures that emerge from a cultural space oppositionally articulated as self-contained and self-sustaining—like, for example, the "home." Only certain kinds of characters find their way onto the road or can be met along its way stations and resting places—and the road's particular spatialization will circumscribe temporal interactions among those characters, the nature and depth of their encounters and social relations. The road is, of course, a single and deceptively simple example of the many novelistic chronotopes Bakhtin identifies and explores. Furthermore, in part because of his extended focus on more general chronotopic structures such as folkloric time and adventure time, the chronotope of the road remains underelaborated and underhistoricized. There are consequential differences between the road of the picaresque and the road of the Winnebago, between a meandering country road and a tollroad or urban freeway. And, as Michael Montgomery asks, "What study of the 1960s road film, for instance, could afford to neglect Western landscapes, California, Zen, biker films, rock and roll tours, or psychedelic trips?"[52] Nonetheless, because it speaks to us so immediately of comprehended possibilities and limitations, of a phenomeno-logic of both personal and cinematic narrative, Bakhtin's chronotope of the road is extremely suggestive of how concrete spatiotemporal articulations generate narrative structures, figures, characters, and tropes.

Carnivals and Commonplaces, Montgomery's singularly sustained effort to relate Bakhtin's concept of the chronotope to film genre, explicates a number of Bakhtinian chronotopes and does an illuminating chronotopic analysis of a variety of films. However, Montgomery also criticizes the generality of many of Bakhtin's "master chronotopes" and suggests that any application of chronotopic analysis "must strive to give Bakhtin's chronotopes the cultural specificity they lack." In sum, "classical forms" of such chronotopes as adventure time or folkloric or idyllic time need "a great deal of fleshing out if we are to speak confidently of the semantic associations they continue to engender for audiences."[53] Furthermore, he suggests the investigation of "new chronotopes as they emerge throughout distinct periods of filmmaking to determine whether they possess their own peculiar 'narratibility.'"[54]

What, then, can be said of the select and hyperbolically articulated chronotopes of film noir and their less isolated and therefore less exaggerated sources in wartime and postwar American culture? What novel form of temporal existence do the cocktail lounge and nightclub (both tony and seedy), the anonymous hotel or motel room, or the cheap roadside cafe, spatially generate and concretize for character and culture alike in the 1940s?

If we look at films of the 1930s (whether comedies or gangster films), cocktail lounges and nightclubs and hotels are generally figured as celebrated and glamorous spaces—the places where sophisticated and affluent people display their wit, strut their stuff upon a polished dance floor that reflects the grace of Fred and Ginger, amuse themselves with all the fluff and romance of a feather boa, and gamble with money and hearts they can afford to lose. As Lewis Erenberg points out in an essay on the "legitimization of nightlife" after the repeal of Prohibition, "actual nightclubs continued to exist, and in some cases expanded during the Depression."[55] *Life Magazine* ran features on various nightclubs like the Stork Club throughout the 1930s.

During the Depression, syndicated stories, gossip columns and [motion] pictures showed couples at play in a world of case and fun, spending money and enjoying life at a more intense level. The vision of consumption, personal freedom and fulfillment, though hedged in by many consoling messages that money was not everything, kept alive the dreams of nightclubs as the epitome of smart city living.[56]

Featured in film comedies such as *My Man Godfrey* (1936), *The Awful Truth* (1937), or *Bringing Up Baby* (1938), the "moderne" art deco nightclub exists as an idyllic capitalist chronotope. Most middle- and upperclass people don't work at night, and so labor is elided and time becomes spatialized as a place of "leisure"— dynamized, narrativized in a concrete and "clubby" space of socially lavish and lavishly social display. This chronotope is not belied by the nightclub in the gangster film but rather, focusing on the "night work" of those staging the scene, figured from its other side.

Erenberg notes that the mediated but very real legitimization of the nightclub, which started in the 1930s after Repeal, culminated during the war years: "The prosperity brought by defense spending and the rootlessness of a nation at war, made World War II the biggest era for the nightclubs."[57] Through reference to the Coconut Grove fire in 1942, he also notes the expanded range of classes, professions, and ages that then constituted the nightclub clientele. He summarizes:

> Clearly, by 1942, the nightclub had become part of the promise of American life. Perhaps this is what the large number of service men in attendance represented. These young men were celebrating inductions or furloughs, and they were part of a national trend during the War. Uprooted from their homes with money to spend, ordinary soldiers from around the country for the first time had the chance to patronize nightclubs. Fueled by wartime expenditures, the nightclub achieved the height of its prosperity.[58]

In some ways, the nightclubs and cocktail lounges as they are figured in various representations of the period as lavish places of social leisure, romantic encounter, and public display bear a strong resemblance to Bakhtin's "salon," a chronotope he discusses briefly as a fundamentally new time-space that finds its full significance in the novels of Stendhal and Balzac but is drawn from the real historical "parlors and salons of the Restoration and July Monarchy."[59] Pointing to the mix of social types—from politicians and businessmen to "courtesan-singers"—who mingle in the salon, Bakhtin notes that it is here that "webs of intrigue are spun, denouements occur" and "dialogues happen" that reveal the "ideas" and "passions" of the characters.[60] And he continues:

> here in their full array [that is, brought together in one place at one time] are all the gradations of the new social hierarchy; and here, finally, there unfold forms that are concrete and visible, the supreme power of life's new, king—money.

Most important in all this is the weaving of historical and socio-public events together with the secrets of the boudoir; the interweaving of petty, private intrigues with political and financial intrigues, the interpenetration of state with boudoir secrets, of historical sequences with the everyday, and biographical sequences. Here the graphically visible markers of historical time as well as of biographical and everyday time are concentrated and condensed; at the same time they are intertwined with each other in the tightest possible fashion, fused into unitary markers of the epoch.[61]

Thus, the salon bears resemblance to the nightclub and cocktail lounge as they are figured in film genres of the 1930s and 1940s, from gangster films and comedies in the earlier decade to the darker intrigues and boudoir secrets of noir in the later. Indeed, as Montgomery notes, the "unstable blends of public and private spheres of influence" that characterize the salon also evoke the tight intertwining of "petty, private intrigues with political and financial intrigues" in Rick's Café Americain of the prewar *Casablanca* (1943) and the restaurant and cocktail lounges of the postwar *Mildred Pierce* (1946).[62] It is historically apposite that, in *This Gun for Hire* (1942), a nightclub singer (noir actress Veronica Lake) wants to settle down and get married but continues her "club spectacle in order to seduce a possible traitor and discover his secrets"[63] —or that, in *Casablanca* , the denouement of the political question concerning America's isolationism or involvement in

World War II is not only tightly intertwined with a private romantic triangle, but that its temporalization is generated and resolved through the chronotope of the nightclub where the "ideas" and "passions" of the characters are revealed in the "dialogue" the salon allows. Indeed, as Erenberg points out, "That such a question could be posed in terms of a nightclub and its quixotic 'New Yorker' owner is a measure of how much a part of American culture the nightclub had become."[64]

In the salon spaces—nightclubs, cocktail lounges, and bars—of the postwar period, private, domestic intrigue and the "secrets of the boudoir" are more often intertwined with financial intrigue than with patriotism or political intrigue (except when the latter is characterized through the former in the fairly frequent person of a corrupt and greedy politician). Indeed, from the postwar period onward into the 1950s, in the salon spaces of films like *Mildred Pierce* or *Gilda* or *The Blue Dahlia* (all 1946) or *The Big Heat* (1953), the corruption of political life is not so much temporalized as is the financially based corruption of domestic life. It is pertinent here that in the non-noir *The Best Years of Our Lives* (also 1946), the one irresolvable postwar relationship in the film is that between the veteran pilot and his restless wife—figured as a nightclub singer.

Corollary to the nightclub and the cocktail lounge and their confusions of public and private spheres of influence, of business and personal intimacy, of financial and boudoir secrets, are those other remembered places that fragment and substitute for domestic space much as Mildred's restaurant replaces her kitchen—namely: hotels, motels, and even cheaper boardinghouse rooms. Though not precisely salon space like the nightclubs and lounges and bars that share some of their qualities, in noir and in the culture of the period with its rented housing and housing shortages, the rooms of hotels and motels and boardinghouses figure as spaces of social dislocation, isolation, and existential alienation.

More salon space in *Mildred Pierce*.

They also function in noir and in the culture as spaces where financial intrigue and boudoir secrets come to rest—albeit, if we think of the Swede, lying on his bed holding Kitty Collins's scarf and awaiting his murder, never in peace. Noting the character of the essentially urban space of the hotel and its extension into the countryside in the form of the motel (and, we might add, into the provincial town in the form of the boardinghouse), Polan writes:

> If Gyorg[y] Lukács (in the... preface to *History and Class Consciousness*) saw the hotel as a perfect image of an old Europe's fall into chaos and despair, the motel seems an appropriate image for a later moment where the elegant decadence of an aristocracy has given way to a mass-life run through with petty crimes, petty intrigues. The motel is the figure of furtiveness and a life dominated by the endless but transitory interaction of people all with something to hide. Significantly, the years from the thirties on witness a discourse on the motel not as adventure or romance spot, but as the place of festering, wasteland rot.[65]

(And here it is impossible not to think of the resolution of this social degradation of space and personal relations in the Bates motel in 1960's *Psycho*.)

Thus the petty crimes and the petty intrigues of the salon, where public and private business intertwine and constitute deals and dangerous liaisons as the ground of narrative action, move from city to country, from glamorous thirties' hotels and nightclubs and restaurants to "Mildred's" and then to shabbier hotels, seedy motels, and boardinghouses, to roadside diners (see *The Postman Always Rings Twice*, 1946), bars, and cafes (see *Roadhouse*, 1948). Salon space is reconstituted and fragmented in the historical period that begins during the war and lasts into the 1950s. Rather than bend out of shape the time-space of a chronotope whose own novelty is historically linked to "the Restoration and July Monarchy" and to the novels of Stendahl and Balzac to fit the cultural and imaginary spaces of America in the 1940s, a new and historically intelligible chronotope is called for.

What I suggest is a larger chronotopic structure, akin to Bakhtin's major and more general ones, that includes the privileged spaces of wartime and postwar American culture transported and hyperbolized on the screen in film noir. Specifically, I designate the life-world (both cultural and narrative) spatialized from nightclubs, cocktail lounges, bars, anonymous hotel or motel rooms, boardinghouses, cheap roadhouses, and diners as constituting the temporalization of what I call *lounge time*. The spatiotemporal structures and smaller chronotopic units (or motifs) like the cocktail lounge or the hotel room that constitute lounge time emerge in their historical coherence as threats to the traditional function, continuity, contiguity, and security of domestic space and time. They substitute for and fragment into "broken" status the nurturant functions of another and more felicitous chronotope discussed earlier: the home. They transport spatially contiguous and intimate familial activity (eating, drinking, sleeping, and recreating) from private and personalized to public and anonymous domain. They substitute impersonal, incoherent, discontinuous, and rented space for personal, intelligible, unified, and generated space. They spatially rend and break up the home—and, correlatively, family contiguity and generational continuity.

Children do not normally—or normatively—find their way into these spaces. (It is telling that the psychotic babysitter in the hotel in *Don't Bother to Knock* [1952] attempts to kill her charge in order to keep a date in the hotel bar.) Women at home in these spaces are rarely mothers (although they may yearn to be like Veronica Lake's character in *This Gun for Hire*), nor are men fathers. (Only after the homicide detective sells his house and sends his daughter away after his wife has been killed by a bomb meant for him is the world of *The Big Heat* transformed to noir.) The cycles and rituals of family continuity and generation have no place, and therefore no temporal articulation, in cocktail lounges and hotel rooms.[66] No weddings, no births, no natural deaths (although plenty of unnatural ones), no familial intimacy and connection can be eventful in lounge time. Here, women have no anchor in domesticity and men no clearly defined work. Women do not make babies and bread (although, like Mildred, they may perversely create a business empire making pies), and their sexuality remains undisciplined. Men have no fertile fields to sow and reap, no occupation to sustain both family and patriarchal kingdom and mark their masculinity in signs of labor and amassed capital, no private retreat from

The Postman Always Rings Twice:
Cora (Lana Turner) and Frank (John Garfield)
in the roadside diner.

the public sphere in which to relax and recreate and enjoy the fruits of socially sanctioned labor. The "traditional" divisions of the prewar domestic economy—remembered and mythified as the idyllic patriarchal kingdom—are impossible in such places.

Correlative to the fragmentation of the coherence of domestic space and its temporalization in idyllic narratives, the cultural space-time isolated and intensified in the lounge time of film noir also radically transforms recreational time, making leisure more a condition to be suffered than pleasurably embraced. Indeed, leisure, as lounge time in the mise-en-scène of noir, is temporalized not as idyllic and regenerational activity (nor even the frivolous expenditure of energy figured in the nightclubs of the 1930s). Rather, it is temporalized negatively as idle restlessness, as a lack of occupation, as a disturbing, ambiguous, and public display of unemployment. Very few men (or women) can be said to labor in film noir. Most of them wait, hang on and hang around, making plans that go up in the smoke of a torch song or too many stubbed-out cigarettes. The men and women who inhabit the urban lounges, hotels, and isolated roadside cafes and diners of noir are restless, are transients. (Hence, in terms of chronotopic motifs, lounge time could well include bus and train stations and their waiting rooms.) Without real roots and occupation, they meet by chance, act impulsively, have no strong social curbs on their passions and fears. In sum, they embody and narrativize the very quality of the spaces in which they spend aimless time: they are centers for emotional activity without social commitment, are fractured by random appeals to their basic drives and desires. Both their life-world and their characters do not cohere. Indeed, like the bars, hotel rooms, and roadside cafes they frequent, they are literally and semiotically incoherent—a threat to the very language of patriarchal and capitalist culture (even as they are its perverse production). In sum, dispossessed, displaced from the culture's "traditional" signifiers of social place and function, their actions are temporalized as socially problematic, ambiguous, and dangerous (and, of course, often for those very qualities, extremely attractive).

The threat that lounge time poses to the traditional domestic economy dictates that its spatiotemporal boundaries limit and contain its "loose" women and "idle" men in what can only be described as a hermetically sealed—quarantined—social space. The dramas temporalized within it and determined by it are not allowed integration with the culture's traditional—by this time, retrospectively mythified—spaces of domesticity and labor. At most, events generated by and in lounge time briefly contaminate the spatiotemporal coherence of what is perceived to be and figured as the traditional and idyllic life-world of the (prewar) culture. Hardly seen at all, that idyllic life-world of domestic peace and harmony, of proper occupation for both sexes, is a structuring absence that contributes to the closed off yet unstable spatiotemporal nature of lounge time. That world previously described in the chronotopes of the supposedly stable prewar home and the retroactive and nostalgic postwar fantasy of the unified wartime home front are constructed on convention and its maintenance, on clearly defined and hierarchically valued sexual identities correlated with a specific division, valuation, and reward of domestic labor along gender lines, and on the contiguous relation of family and community that promises—through spatial and temporal integration—cultural regeneration and continuity.

In "Forms of Time and Chronotope in the Novel," Bakhtin devotes substantial discussion to a master chronotope that he identifies with folkloric time: the idyllic chronotope. His gloss on the positive and "special relation time has to space in the idyll" is particularly relevant both to the felicitous chronotopes of home and the wartime home front that provide the structuring absences of film noir and to the negative and infelicitous master chronotope of noir that I describe as *lounge time*. The idyllic chronotope includes a variety of pure and mixed types that focus on "love, labor, or family." No matter what the types and their variants, however, Bakhtin sees them as having "several features in common, all determined by their general relationship to the immanent unity of folkloric time" (which undoes historical time by focusing on basic life processes and temporal cycles rather than on the transience and variety of cultural forms).[67]

Idyllic chronotopes, then, are characterized by "an organic fastening-down, a grafting of life and its events to a place, to a familiar territory,...and one's own home." The events generated within the life-world of the idyll emerge from the secured familiarity of its spaces and the hermetic and integral wholeness of its temporality. As Bakhtin describes it:

> This little spatial world is limited and sufficient unto itself, not linked in any intrinsic way with other places, with the rest of the world. But in this little spatially limited world a sequence of generations is localized that is potentially without limit....[The] blurring of all the temporal boundaries made possible by a unity of place also contributes in an essential way to the creation of the cyclic rhythmicalness of time so characteristic of the idyll. (225)

Whereas the idyllic chronotope has relevance to the familiarity, stability, and rootedness of home and the familial and generational and even national solidarity of the wartime home front, the noir chronotope of lounge time evokes the life-world and space-time of a parallel, yet anti-nomic, universe. Though it constitutes a hermetic whole, its internal constituents and potential contiguities are fragmented and unfastened down. Furthermore, its spaces are visibly unfamilial, unfamiliar, and anonymous. Yet, isomorphic with the structures of the idyllic world, lounge time is also limited spatially, also self-sufficient, also sealed off from contact with the rest of the world. (Here it is worth recalling the line of dialogue from *Pitfall* [1948] used as an epigram at the beginning of this essay): "Have you ever noticed if for some reason you want to feel completely out of step with the rest of the world, the only thing to do is sit around a cocktail lounge in the afternoon?") The sequence of events as they occur and take on significance in lounge time also becomes cyclical—but instead of generating and continuing kinship relations, lounge time generates their denial and betrayal. (Here, one might remember Mildred Pierce and her treacherous daughter Veda as exemplary.) Undoing generational time in repetitive patterns in which the past and future collapse, lounge time de-generates.

In terms of narrative events and their repetitious temporal nature, Bakhtin further elaborates the idyllic chronotope as "severely limited to only a few of life's basic realities. Love, birth, death, marriage, labor, food and drink, stages of growth." And he goes on to say:

> Strictly speaking, the idyll does not know the trivial details of everyday life. Anything that has the appearance of common everyday life, when compared with the central unrepeatable events of biography and history, here begins to look precisely like the most important things in life. But all these basic life-realities are present in the idyll not in their naked realistic aspect...but in a softened and to a certain extent sublimated form. (226)

Such a description evokes the idyllic, homey, cyclical and softened space-time of family meals and holidays and stages of growth characteristic of, for example, *Meet Me in St. Louis*. It does not evoke Phyllis Dietrichson in *Double Indemnity*, pushing a shopping cart up and down the aisles of a supermarket, wearing dark glasses and planning the murder of her husband with Walter Neff over canned goods. And yet this extraordinarily ironized scene of domesticity sits in a highly structured—if perverse—relation to the idyllic chronotope described by Bakhtin.

Lounge time creates a parallel emphasis on basic life-realities, but these are antinomous to those of the idyllic chronotope. Bakhtin identifies the love idyll and sees its richest "conjunction with the family idyll...and with the agricultural idyll." Here—and this is particularly poignant set against the unemployment, the lack of occupation, of so many of the characters in noir—Bakhtin notes:

> The labor aspect...is of special importance...; it is the agricultural-labor element that creates a *real* link and common bond between the phenomena of nature and the events of human life....Moreover—and this is especially important—agricultural labor transforms all the events of everyday lift, stripping them of that private petty character obtaining when man is nothing but consumer; what happens is that they are turned into essential life *events*. (226-27)

Hence we see the association of the idyllic with the pastoral—an association that reverberates both in the offer of lemonade in *The Killers* and in noir's primarily urban mise-en-scène. Furthermore, alienated from a connection to the kind of work that elevates the quotidian into eventfulness, figured only as petty consumer, characters in lounge time avoid labor—seeking the fast buck and easy money, talking about the deal and the plan and the big fix or score.

Bakhtin also points to the idyll's elevation of basic realities such as eating and drinking because of their connection to nature and labor and family:

> Wine is likewise immersed in...its cultivation and production, and drinking it is inseparable from the holidays that are in turn linked to agricultural cycles. Food and drink in the idyll partake of a nature that is social or, more often, family, all *generations* and *age-groups* come together around the table. For the idyll the association of *food* and *children* is characteristic. (227)

Not only are children underage and not generally allowed in the spaces of lounge time, but the characters who sit around the tables in nightclubs, cocktail lounges, and roadside cafes hardly know each other. And although the spaces of lounge time are spaces in which food and drink are foregrounded, hardly anyone actually eats (although almost everyone drinks), no one is nourished, no "natural" thirst is slaked. Indeed, in *Clash by Night* (1952), one character ironically asks another: "Do you think beer has food value, Miss Doyle?"

Furthermore, "in the idyll, children often function as a sublimation of the sexual act and of conception; they frequently figure in connection with growth, the renewal of life, death" (227). Focus in lounge time and noir is on passion, libido, hate, vengeance, and boredom rather than on love and the sublimation of sexuality in family. Childlessness, whether from selfish choice, barrenness or sterility, abortion, or a child's death, reverses the idyll's happy concern with birth and regeneration. In *Mildred Pierce*, one of Mildred's two children dies from illness, and she is despised and betrayed by the other. Her best (and unmarried) friend tells her: "Personally, I'm convinced that alligators have the right idea. They eat their young." Death, of course, is never natural in lounge time, but murder is. Hence, we have noir's ironic emphasis on life "insurance." Marriages are institutions not to be nurtured and revered, but to be gotten out of—through infidelity, separation, divorce, or murder. There are also no stages of growth in lounge time—not only because there are no children in its spaces, but also because behavior is compulsive and repetitive and thus becomes cyclical even as it seems initiated by chance and in impulse.

Bakhtin notes that in the idyll all these basic life-realities are "softened," take a certain "sublimated form," and are represented in "nonliteral" fashion. Like their appealing counterparts in the idyll, the perverse basic life-realities that provide the focal events of lounge time and noir are also represented in nonliteral fashion. However, rather than being "softened" and "sublimated," they are intensified and hyperbolized through baroque visual style and convoluted narrative structure. Thus, a certain mode of hysteria and overwroughtness becomes the norm of lounge time and noir's everyday life.

Though all these elements of lounge time seem structured in direct opposition to the pastoral idyllic chronotope, there are ways in which lounge time parallels the idyll. Given our particular interest here in the historical relation of lounge time and noir to its specific context in wartime and postwar America, most significant, perhaps, is the idyll's relation to history. Bakhtin describes the idyll as structured in folkloric time. That is, the specificity of history is subordinated to and disavowed by regeneration and repetition, cyclical activity. Lounge time also focuses on repetition (however obsessive or compulsive), on cyclical activity (however unagricultural) like sitting around hotel rooms planning heists or in cocktail lounges listening to torch songs. And one of the primary narrative enterprises of noir is to subordinate and disavow the "central, unrepeatable events of biography and history" that rarely find their articulation or make their mark in the anonymity of a hotel room or a nightclub or a diner. However, unlike in the idyll, the hermetic spaces and cyclical temporality of lounge time and noir are threatened by a return of the repressed that—because of the hermetic spaces and repetitive temporality—has no other place to go. Characters keep attempting to escape their specific biography or the particulars of history, and they live in fear of the revelation of shady individual pasts to those in their amorphous present. Earlier crimes, betrayals, failures, and infidelities are desperately hidden and generate new crimes, betrayals, failures, and infidelities, but return nonetheless from *Out of the Past*. Indeed, the space-time configuration of lounge time generates the flashbacks characteristic of noir as a perverse formal manifestation of the repetition and cyclicity of a folkloric time that ultimately overcomes and undoes history—and the possibility of change. Thus, its characters are forever fixed, paradoxically, in a transitional moment. If lounge time and noir undo historical time, they are, nevertheless, informed by it, and it is most particular.

Bakhtin tells us that the idyll "assumed great significance in the eighteenth century when the problem of time in literature was posed with particular intensity, a period when precisely a new feeling for time was beginning to awake." He points to the development of special forms of the idyll in which the "real organic time of idyllic life is opposed to the frivolous, fragmented time of city life or even to historical time." And he mentions the appearance of the idyllic "elegy." For Bakhtin, the significance of the idyll to the development of the novel is enormous, and he decries the fact that "its importance as an underlying image has not been understood and appreciated..., and in consequence all perspectives on the history of the novel have been distorted" (228). Its influences can be seen across a range of novelistic types from the provincial novel to the idyll-destroying *Bildungsroman*, from the sentimental novel to the family novel and the novel of generations. In the latter, he notes, the "idyllic element undergoes a radical reworking":

> Of folkloric time and the ancient matrices only those elements remain that can be reinterpreted and survive on the soil of the bourgeois family and family-as-genealogy. Nevertheless the connection between the family novel and the idyll is manifested in a whole series of significant aspects, and that connection is precisely, what determines the basic—family—nucleus of this type of novel. (231)

Bakhtin goes on to discuss the "destruction of the idyll," which "becomes one of the fundamental themes of literature toward the end of the eighteenth century and in the first half of the nineteenth" (233). The hermetic nature and organicity of the idyllic world is still valued, but its "narrowness" and "isolation" are emphasized:

> Opposed to this little world, a world fated to perish, there is a great but abstract world, where people are out of contact with each other, egoistically scaled-off from each other, greedily practical, where labor is differentiated and mechanized, where objects are alienated from the labor that produced them. It is necessary to constitute this great world on a new basis, to render it familiar, to humanize it. (234)

Furthermore, the *Bildungsroman* shows up the idyllic world and its psychology as "inadequate to the new capitalist world." In this new novelistic form, we see:

> the disintegration of all previous human relationships (under the influence of money), love, the family, friendship, the deforming of the scholar's and the artist's creative work and so forth—all of these are emphasized. The positive hero of the idyllic world becomes ridiculous, pitiful and unnecessary; he either perishes or is re-educated and becomes an egoistic predator. (234–35)

If different in its phenomenological inflection and, thus, its inscription, time was also felt in some new way and represented with great intensity in the 1940s as the United States first debated its entry into the war and then went off to fight the good fight and to come home after it to a troubled capitalist domestic economy. It is during this period that the idyllic chronotopes of home and the wartime home front take on particular significance, that special forms of the idyll emerge in which the "real organic time of idyllic life is opposed to the frivolous, fragmented time of city life or even to historical time." As Montgomery points out, "In the two years following the War, as Americans readjusted to peace, they reverted to the small town ideal. In mainstream Hollywood, a similar reactionary movement took place, with war themes suddenly out and several new film versions of 'timeless' literary classics in the works."[68] There also appears during this period specific forms of the idyllic "elegy"—here, again, we can look to the likes of *Centennial Summer* or *Meet Me in St. Louis* or *I Remember Mama*.

As Dana Polan suggests, "the imperatives of war invest themselves in a particular representation of home." This investment is in the chronotopic structure that informs the idyll, in precisely the ahistorical quality of folkloric time. Using as example *The Big Clock* (1948), a film whose very title represents an intensified awareness of time, he discusses home as "a self-enclosed environment...with its own rules, its own language games, its own memory...and its own rituals." It closes out ambiguity and ambivalence and closes in security. Polan goes on, however, to expand this notion of home as an existential phenomenon: "as a sign, 'home' is something not necessarily limited to a specific locale, a specific building. It is an attitude—a way of perceiving environment....Home's values can extend outward—through the stability of a job, the camaraderie of friends, through places invested with the succoring warmth of the home."[69]

Given the labor disputes, given the economic instability experienced both in terms of the basic life-realities like food, clothing, and housing and the destabilization of the gender lines that had staked out the domestic economy in its proper place, given actual unemployment and the fragmentation of families and the dispersal of friends, if home was as much a way of "perceiving the environment" as it was a concrete place, then—in the world of the 1940s both during the war and after—many Americans were homeless.

And yet they couldn't move on. Where, in the Cold War and paranoid security-state culture, could they go? What were the motivations that spoke to the temporalizing of a concrete future and its anticipation? Like the characters of noir, much of America was fixed, paradoxically, in a transitional moment—looking back toward a retrospectively idyllic world that could not be historically recuperated (even if it could be represented), looking forward, like the Swede, with a certain inertial apprehension of a probable dead end. Indeed, as Bakhtin describes the economic and existential question posed by a capitalist economy to the "positive hero of the idyllic world," the Swede stands as the putative hero of a *Bildungsroman* frustrated—he must exist as "ridiculous, pitiful and unnecessary" or he "either perishes or is re-educated and becomes an egoistic predator." The Swede is indeed reeducated both by Kitty and by Colfax, but his new knowledge—capitalist to the core and all about love for money—is unbearable. He finally opts for death.

The boundaries of lounge time stand, then, as more than the four walls of the Swede's hotel room—or of the nightclubs and cocktail lounges and bars that he and Kitty and Colfax and all the characters of film noir so often frequent. They are the concretion of a historical, existential situation. As Montgomery points out: "The chronotopic analysis of film locales may illustrate the 'boundaries' of an audience's world as they were perceived to exist, the society's attitudes toward 'change,' or the exclusionary practices that denied certain members full participation in their community's plans for the future."[70] Thus, although its motifs can be traced backward into the 1930s and forward to the present renaissance and radical reworking of noir, lounge time is one of the dominant—or master—chronotopes of the historical period that begins in the early 1940s with the rumblings of war and declines in the 1950s as the "security state" becomes a generally accepted way of life. As such, it provides us the concrete ground, the premises, that frame and create a "global viewpoint" from which the period's films may be "judged" and "set against the world outside the text."[71]

Emerging out of actually lived cultural spaces, the represented space of lounge time is a perverse and dark response, on the one hand, to the loss of home and a felicitous, carefree, ahistoricity and, on the other, to an inability to imagine being at home in history, in capitalist democracy, *at this time*. It is no wonder that in noir so many people need a drink or try to get lost in a bottle. A master chronotope that grounds both the period's texts and contexts and makes them intelligible each to the other, lounge time represents the nether side of Bakhtin's idyll. It represents both the historical necessity and the historical failure to constitute the "world on a new basis, to render it familiar, to humanize it." Thus, noir's characters are forever fixed in a transitional moment—stabilized negatively in space and time, double-crossed by history.

The noir world of bars, diners, and seedy hotels, of clandestine yet public meetings in which domesticity and kinship relations are subverted, denied, and undone, a world of little labor and less love, of threatened men and sexually and economically predatory women—this world (concretely part of wartime and postwar American culture) realizes a frightening reversal and perversion of home and the coherent, stable, idealized, and idyllic past of prewar American patriarchy and patriotism. In short, lounge time is the perverse "idyll of the idle"—the spatial and temporal phenomeno-logic that, in the 1940s, grounds the meaning of the world for the uprooted, the unemployed, the loose, the existentially paralyzed. Lounge time concretely spatializes and temporalizes into narrative an idle moment in our cultural history—a moment that is not working but, precisely because of this fact, is highly charged. Evoking George Bailey at the moment he looks not only at the conditional loss of all the safety and security that was Bedford Falls but also at the loss of his own identity, noir historicizes in the most concrete manner the moment when the idyllic and "timeless" identity and security of the patriarchal American "home" was held hostage to a domestic future beyond its imagination.

Notes

1. For the source notes citations, see M. M. Bakhtin, "The *Bildungsroman* and Its Significance in the History of Realism (Toward a Historical Typology of the Novel)," in *Speech Genres and Other Late Essays,* trans. Vern W. McGee (Austin: University of Texas Press, 1986), 49; and *Pitfall,* dir. André de Toth, screenplay Karl Kamb (United Artists, 1948). This essay is a major revision and elaboration of a much shorter essay delivered at the annual meeting of the Society for Cinema Studies in 1984 and circulated among colleagues in the following years. Portions of it have been cited prior to publication in Robert Stam, *Subversive Pleasures: Bakhtin, Cultural Criticism, and Film* (Baltimore: Johns Hopkins University Press, 1989), 12; Robert Stam, Robert Burgoyne and Sandy Flitterman-Lewis, *New Vocabularies in Film Semiotics: Structuralism, Post-Structuralism, and Beyond* (London: Routledge, 1992), 217-18; and Fred Pfeil, "Home Fires Burning: Family Noir in *Blue Velvet* and *Terminator 2,"* in *Shades of Noir: A Reader,* ed. Joan Copjec (London: Verso, '994), 229-31.

2. By now, not only is the literature on noir too extensive to be exhaustively listed here, but it also overlaps with a good deal of writing on the crime and detective film as well as with feminist work on melodrama. The seminal French texts that elaborated noir after the term was first coined by Nino Frank in *Ecran français* 6 (28 August 1946) are Jean-Pierre Chartier, "Les Américains aussi font des films noirs," *La Revue de cinéma* 2 (November1946): 66-70, and Raymond Borde and Etienne Chaumeton, *Panorama du Film Noir Américain (1941-1953)* (Paris: Editions de Minuit, *1955).* Key early works in English on noir published in the 1970s include Cohn McArthur, *Underworld US.A* (New York: Viking Press, 1972); Paul Schrader, "Notes on *Film Noir,"* *Film Comment* 8, no. 1 (spring 1972): 8-13; Raymond Durgnat, "The Family Tree of Film Noir," *Film Comment* 10,110. 6 (1974): 6-7—as well as several other pieces in that issue; J. A. Place and L. S. Peterson, "Some Visual Motifs of Film Noir," *Film Comment* no. 1 (January-February 1974): 30-35; Robert Porflrio, "No Way Out: Existential Motifs in the Film Noir," *Sight and Sound* 45, no. 4 (1976): 212-17; J. S. Whitney, "A Filmography of *Film Noir,"* *Journal of Popular Film,* no. 3-4 (1976): 321-71; Amir M. Karimi, *Toward a Definition of the American Film Noir, 1941-1949* (New York: Arno Press, 1976); James Damico, "Film Noir: A Modest Proposal," *Film Reader 3* (February 1978): *48-57;* E. Ann Kaplan, ed., *Women in Film Noir* (London: BFI, 1978); Alain Silver and Elizabeth Ward, *Film Noir, An Encyclopedic Reference to the American Style* (Woodstock: Overlook Press, 1979); Jack Shadoian, *Dreams and Dead-Ends: The American Gangster/Crime Film* (Cambridge: MIT Press, 1979); and Paul Kerr, "Out of What Past? Notes on the B Film Noir," *Screen Education* 32-33 (1979/80): *45-65.* These have been followed by several book-length works: Foster Hirsch, *The Dark Side of the Screen: Film Noir* (San Diego: A. S. Barnes, 1981); Robert Ottoson, *A Reference Guide to the American Film Noir* (Metuchen: Scarecrow Press, 1981); Jon Tuska, *Dark Cinema: American Film Noir in Cultural Perspective* (Westport: Greenwood Press, 1984); Dana Polan, *Power and Paranoia: History, Narrative, and the American Cinema, 1940 -1950* (New York: Columbia University Press, 1986); J. P. Telotte, *Voices in the Dark: The Narrative Patterns of Film Noir* (Chicago: University of Illinois Press, 1989); Frank Krutnik, *In a Lonely Street: Film Noir, Genre, Masculinity* (London: Routledge, 1991); and most recently Ian Cameron, *The Book of Film Noir* (New York: Continuum, 1993), and Copjec, *Shades of Noir.*

3. Copjec, introduction to *Shades of Noir,* xi-xii.

4. Edmund Husserl, *Cartesian Meditations,* trans. Dorion Cairns (The Hague: Martinus Nijhoff, 1960), 12-13. (The phrase in German is *zu den Sachen selbst.)*

5. David Reid and Jayne L. Walker, "Strange Pursuit: Cornell Woolrich and the Abandoned City of the Forties," in Copjec, *Shades of Noir,* 88.

6. Truman quoted in Gorton Carruth, *The Encyclopedia of American Facts and Data,* 8th ed. (New York: Harper and Row, 1987), 5. For more on housing in the period covered in this essay, the reader is directed to *Call It Home: The House That Private Enterprise Built* (New York: Voyager, 1992); this videodisc covers the history of privately built housing in America from the 1920s to the 1960s through archival materials that address both real and imaginary relations to house and home.

7. Polan, *Power and Paranoia,* 254.

8. Reid and Walker, "Strange Pursuit," 88, 90.

9. Ibid., 90.

10. M. M. Bakhtin, "Forms of Time and Chronotope in the Novel: Notes toward a Historical Poetics," in *The Dialogic Imagination: Four Essays by M. M. Bakhtin,* ed. Michael Holquist, trans. Caryl Emerson and Michael Hoiquist (Austin: University of Texas Press, 1981), *84-258.*

11. Hirsch, *Film Noir,* 10.

12. Ibid., 17.

13. Ibid., 21. (Emphasis mine.)

14. Pfeil, "Home Fires Burning," 229.

15. Vernet, *"Film Noir* on the Edge of Doom," in Copjec, *Shades of Noir,* 4.

16. Ibid., 4.

17. Pfeil, "Home Fires Burning," 229.

18. Vernet, *"Film Noir* on the Edge of Doom," 20.

19. Ibid., 2.

20. Ibid., 25-26.

21. Ibid., 2.

22. Dean MacCanneil, "Democracy's Turn: On Homeless *Noir,"* in Copjec, *Shades of Noir,* 288.

23. Polan, *Power and Paranoia,* 208.

24. Ibid., 253.

25. Gaston Bachelard, *The Poetics of Space,* trans. Maria Jolas (Boston: Beacon Press, 1964), xxxi. In regard to the "eulogized space" of the home in this period, see also Stephanie Coontz, *The Way We Never Were: The American Family and the Nostalgia Trap* (New York: Basic Books, 1992).

26. Ibid., xxxii.

27. Ibid., xxxiii.

28. MacCannel, "Democracy's Turn," 297 n. 12.

29. David Thomson, *Suspects* (New York: Vintage Books, 1985). *Los Angeles Times* commentary is taken from the back cover of the first Vintage Books Edition, 1986. (It is also worth noting in the context of the present discussion that the novel has a sole illustration used as a frontispiece: a photograph by Wright Morris titled "Reflection in Oval Mirror, Home Place, Nebraska, 1947." In the mirror we see the interior of a room, a closed door, and a small table covered with photographs; given its presentation, the space of the intimate is transformed by the photographer into "radical exteriority.")

30. Polan, *Power and Paranoia,* 209.

31. Ibid., 210.

32. Bachelard, *The Poetics of Space,* 29.

33. Ibid., 47.

34. Ibid., 48.

35. Peg Thompson and Saeko Usukawa, ed., *The Little Black and White Book of Film Noir: Quotations from Films of the 40s and 50s* (Vancouver, BC: Arsenal Pulp Press, 1992), 10-12, *35.*

36. Polan, *Power and Paranoia,* 249. On this topic, see also Elaine Tyler May, *Homeward Bound: American Families in the Cold War Era* (New York: Basic Books, 1988).

37. MacCannel, "Democracy's Turn," 281-82.

38. Here, I would direct the reader to Harold Bloom, *A Map of Misreading* (New York: Oxford University Press, *1975),* 83—loS, in which the author links various figural devices such as synecdoche and metaphor to specific psychic structures.

39. Michael V. Montgomery, *Carnivals and Commonplaces: Bakhtin's Chronotope, Cultural Studies, and Film* (New

York: Peter Lang, 1993), 5-6.

40. Ibid., 84-.

41. Bakhtin, *The Dialogic Imagination, 250.*

42. Michael Holmquist, glossary to Bakthtin, *The Dialogic Imagination,* 425-26.

43. Montgomery, *Carnivals and Commonplaces,* 125 n.2.

44. Bakhtin, *The Dialogic Imagination,* 253.

45. Montgomery, *Carnivals and Commonplaces, 6.*

46. Bakhtin, *The Dialogic Imagination,* 254.

47. Bakhtin, "The *Bildungsroman*," 42, 49-50.

48. Erwin Panofsky, "Style and Medium in the Motion Pictures," in *Film Theory and Criticism: Introductory Readings, Second Edition,* ed. Gerald Mast and Marshall Cohen (New York: Oxford University Press, i~79), 246.

49. Michael Holmquist, introduction to Bakhtin, *Speech Genres and Other Late Essays,* xiv.

50. Gary Saul Morson and Caryl Emerson, *Mikhail Bakhtin: Creation of a Prosaics* (Stanford: Stanford University Press, 1990), 370.

51. Bakhtin, *The Dialogic Imagination,* 243-45.

52. Montgomery, *Carnivals and Commonplaces,* 84.

53. Ibid.

54. Ibid., 8f. (Here it should be mentioned that Montgomery's last chapter is in response to this issue of "new" chronotopes; it focuses on the chronotope of the shopping mall in films of the 1980s.)

55. Lewis A. Erenberg, "From New York to Middletown: Repeal and the Legitimization of Nightlife in the Great Depression," *American Quarterly* 38, no. 5 (winter 1986): 761.

56. Ibid., 773.

57. Ibid., 774.

58. Ibid., 774.

59. Bakhtin, *The Dialogic Imagination,* 246-47.

60. Ibid., 246.

61. Ibid., 247.

62. Montgomery, *Carnivals and Commonplaces,* 20. (Montgomery discusses the nightclub, bar, and hotel as salon space in relation to *Written on the Wind [1956].* See pp. 67-72.)

63. Polan, *Power and Paranoia,* 80.

64. Erenberg, "From New York to Middletown," 775.

65. Polan, *Power and Paranoia,* 232-33. For historical discussion of the extension of the hotel—via the motel—into nonurban America, see also John A. Jable, "Motels by the Roadside: America's Room for the Night ," *Journal of Cultural Geography 1,* no. 1 (fall-winter 1980): 34-49.

66. For a discussion of the "structuring absence" of the family in film noir, see Sylvia Harvey, "Woman's Place: The Absent Family of Film Noir," in Kaplan, *Women in Film Noir,* 22-34. In relation to more contemporary articulations of the family and its relation to noir, see also Pfeil, "Home Fires Burning," an essay that draws upon an earlier version of this present one.

67. Bakhtin, *The Dialogic Imagination,* 224-25; page numbers hereafter cited parenthetically.

68. Montgomery, *Carnivals and Commonplaces,* 23.

69. Polan, *Power and Paranoia, 253.*

70. Montgomery, *Carnivals and Commonplaces,* 121-22.

71. Ibid., 81.

Jane Greer in *Out of the Past.*

"Lounge Time" Reconsidered: Spatial Discontinuity and Temporal Contingency in *Out of the Past* (1947)

R. Barton Palmer (2004)

The chief taxonomic difficulty that haunts film genre study is its dependence on circular reasoning. Discussions of genre, as Robert Stam suggests, are inevitably characterized by a "tautological quality."[1] *Stagecoach* and films that seem similar to it are westerns because they share certain conventions of setting, theme, and visual style; and these are the features we have determined westerns must have. So *Stagecoach* is a western because it is said to be one. This unavoidable circularity is a reflex of the fact that generic categories are cultural (or, perhaps better, discursive). Being stipulative, genres can hardly be made the object of either a logical or scientific analysis. A film is a western not because it possesses some essential qualities that necessitate that it be grouped with other films that can then be known collectively as "westerns."

In the absence of any unchallengeable procedures for definition, then, arbitrariness of a sort must determine what films we select as "authentic" members of a generic class and what films we exclude because they lack what we maintain are the requisite features. In fact, arbitrariness (of different degrees) figures in what genres we decide to recognize in the first place. Thus any search to determine or fix the supposedly *sine qua non* features of a genre (or a series or any grouping characterized by shared features) is bound to end in failure. But such formulations as we may devise are useful as heuristics. We may employ them as provisional frameworks to guide our mapping of intertextual relations, even as we recognize that these relations are always much too complex to reduce to some menu of unarguable propositions.

In film noir studies, the question of definition has provoked an inordinate amount of discussion because film noir is, in its classic phase at least, a post facto category. This fact lays bare the discursiveness of generic analysis. The films precede the term by which they will subsequently become known, which is thus exposed as a way of talking about artifacts that already exist. While what are now known as films noirs were being turned out by the postwar American film industry, no one in Hollywood was apparently aware that such a descriptive term existed. John Ford knew he was making westerns and had, presumably, some idea of this genre in mind during his career, but neither Robert Siodmak nor Billy Wilder knew they were making what would come to be called films noirs. If not a category of production, the term "film noir," imported from France along with the *politique des auteurs*, was, instead, and quite obviously from the very outset, a category of taste. It was introduced in American film culture as a strategy for "saving" what could thereby be claimed as the more distinguished products of Hollywood. The average American film, perhaps a largely forgettable foray into popular entertainment, was thought by some to deserve critical disdain. In contrast, the term film noir marked out an area of artistic production that could be justly valued. Hence the term style (with its connotations of an individual approach to artistic creation) was from the outset mobilized to describe this body of Hollywood films.

For many early Anglophone theorists, defining film noir thus became an issue most often approached not through some kind of empirical analysis, but through a tendentious form of evaluation. Mise-en-scène and visual stylization broadly conceived (the areas of production over which directors had most control) were declared more important than narrative materials or cultural themes, for scripts seemed the dubious products of hack screenwriters and pulp novelists that had been imposed on directors by philistine producers. But this emphasis on the visual was not universally accepted. There were those who regarded film noir as yet another genre to be defined, at least in the first instance, by shared storytelling traditions. And so was raised a central critical question, which has been variously answered during the last four decades. Is film noir a style or a genre? Or, to rephrase in terms of the cultural politics I have here sketched out, can the series be most appropriately considered the product of a group auteurism in some sense or is it, instead, essentially the transference to the screen, with a subsequent broadening, of several pre-existing literary genres?[2]

We hardly need reminding that this kind of debate has not raged around the other Hollywood genres (musicals, biopics, melodramas, etc.), and the reason is that these other forms have never been co-opted into a *politique des genres* whose purpose is to distinguish between dross and artistic gold. Aiming at the discovery of some workable essentialist formula, much of the otherwise valuable critical work done on film noir has neglected that there is, as Pierre Bourdieu puts it, "an economy of cultural goods," whose "specific logic" must be approached through a description of "the different ways of appropriating such of these objects as are regarded at a particular moment as works of art, and the social conditions of the constitution of the mode of appropriation that is considered legitimate."[3] The visual style/genre debate, we may observe, following the sociological perspective Bourdieu advocates, seems properly a matter of warring critical protocols rather than a disagreement about what the films in question could be established on some inarguable grounds "to be." Naturally, we cannot debate the truth or falsity of a "mode of appropriation," only its relative value or interest within a set of "social conditions." The reader should consider this a prefatory warning to what here follows.

Going over this well-trodden ground is worthwhile because it sharpens our appreciation for a provocatively original attempt to resolve the style/genre debate, published as part of Nick Browne's more general project of "reconfiguring" the study of American film genres: Vivian Sobchack's "Lounge Time: Postwar Crises and the Chronotope of Film Noir." An implicit goal of her analysis is to render irrelevant the question that has vexed

Jeff Bailey (Robert Mitchum), dazed and confused by the seductive gaze of Kathie Moffett (Jane Greer), lingers too long in their Mexican idyll.

work on film noir for many years by emphasizing the mutual indispensability (or, perhaps better, inseparability) of form (style) and content (narrative patterns and themes). To do so, Sobchack has recourse to a historical commentary that attempts to "locate and ground that heterogeneous and ambiguous cinematic grouping called film noir in its contemporaneous social context."[4] This is an ambitious goal, and it is hardly surprising that her view of film noir is not without its problems. What I hope to do here is to identify these in the spirit of broadening the usefulness of her approach, focusing on Jacques Tourneur's *Out of the Past*, which has been acknowledged as one of the "key works of film noir."[5] Any understanding of a genre, it hardly needs emphasizing, must be able to explain key works, and Sobchack's view, as we will see, must be modified considerably in order to accommodate Tourneur's film.

An obvious virtue of Sobchack's approach is that it eschews the simplicities of reflection theory in exploring the connection of film noir to its historical moment. She is certainly correct in not expecting to locate untransformed in the films the prominent social themes of postwar America, such as the anxieties experienced by returning veterans, the sudden flourishing of a violent misogyny in popular culture, the political uncertainties alarmingly widespread in a post-atomic age, and, most important perhaps, a pervasive sense of rootlessness and anomie that finds varied expression, from an incredible growth in church membership to the burgeoning popularity of existentialist thought among American intellectuals.[6]

Instead, Sobchack uses the chronotope, a formal concept not hitherto often employed in film studies, whose explanatory power is that it permits the *rapprochement* of "the internal logic of the films and the external logic of the culture," causing "each to be intelligible in terms of the other" (130). In other words, once we identify the chronotope of film noir, which she christens "lounge time," we can analyze the formal ways in which cultural themes find their characteristic representational form within the films themselves. The chronotope is a unique coinage, borrowed from the Russian theorist Mikhail Bakhtin, who uses it to account for the essential differences between broadly different literary forms such as the chivalric romance and the pastoral, each of which, he argues, are characterized by a particular (and unique) chronotope.

By way of preliminary comment, which will need considerable nuancing below, the following can be said about this kind of approach. Developing an overarching scheme of different literary (or cinematic) forms at least promotes (if it does not require) a now largely discredited essentialism. Divergent genres by definition are each understood by reference to the same irreducible, determinant element. In addition, the membership of any particular text in a given genre is thus to be decided by the presence/absence of that element. Using the chronotope, in other words, certainly does not obviously avoid the taxonomic circle that haunts traditional approaches to genre description. If we accept Sobchack's argument, then film noir is to be defined by a particular chronotope, and only films with that feature can be considered truly noir.

But we can certainly agree with Sobchack that the chronotope approach is of great usefulness in pointing to a feature that seems (at least in part) to have led critics to identify the body of films now known as noir. The chronotope (a melding of the Greek words for "time" and "space"), validates, as Bakhtin puts it, the "intrinsic connectedness of temporal and spatial relationships that are artistically expressed in literature" and therefore serves to define "genre and generic distinctions, for in literature the primary category in the chronotope is time."[7] What Bakhtin means here is that the particular way time is organized in any kind of fictional representation determines other conventions, including, and especially, that of setting. Thus in the medieval chivalric romance, "the entire world is subject to 'suddenly,'" meaning that "the unexpected, and only the unexpected, is what is expected." As a result, the chivalric romance displays a "corresponding subjective playing with space, in which elementary spatial relationships and perspectives are violated" (152, 155). In the chivalric romance, space thus becomes a miraculous landscape where the customary laws of human experience may at any moment be suspended, generating both events and even forms of being that are, from the perspective of everyday experience, "impossible." But the laws that rule everyday life sometimes do apply. Knights are wounded and killed, ladies worry about defending their castles against enemies, and kings can be betrayed by their most trusted subordinates. But the limitations of human nature may be spectacularly transcended (and then as suddenly re-imposed) at any given moment. This raising of unexpectedness to a first principle shapes a world of infinite plasticity and variety in which handsome knights rightly concerned about their own mortality and green ogres who can ride off carrying their own severed heads share the same narrative space.

Departing from Bakhtin's insistence on the primacy of temporal organization, Sobchack, however, first identifies what she calls "the films' concrete and visual premises," or, roughly speaking, the story world and its manner of representation:

These radical grounds and material premises figured concretely before us and to which we should pay heed are the cocktail lounge, the nightclub, the bar, the hotel room, the boardinghouse, the diner, the dance hall, the roadside café, the bus and train station, and the wayside motel. These are the recurrent and determinate premises of film noir and they emerge from common places in wartime and post-war American culture that, transported to the screen, gain hyperbolized presence and overdetermined meaning (130).

These "premises" are said to belong to a culture in transition between the collective, public experience of a world war that required the widest marshalling of all the nation's resources and the desired return to "the family unit and the suburban home as the domestic matrix of democracy" (131). They are the publicly accessible (if hardly socially approved) spaces of entertainment, dining, travel, and lodging, whose function is to provide for those literally, and also metaphorically, in transit. The bar and the cheap hotel, of course, substitute for what cannot be obtained in a world where nothing, we might say, is "settled." The characters who inhabit or frequent

Mobster Whit Sterling (Kirk Douglas) explains to Kathie (Jane Greer) why she should stick with him.

these (usually quite unwelcoming) fictional spaces feel the deprivation of the safety, security, and comfort of the bourgeois home, site of nurturing family relationships. Film noir is thus theorized as a specific response to the social conditions imposed by wartime and its aftermath: "In sum, the intimacy and security of home and the integrity and solidity of the home front are lost to wartime and postwar America and to those films we associate at both the core and periphery of that cinematic grouping we circumscribe as noir" (146). In Sobchack's view, noir films broaden their emotional and intellectual appeal by metaphorizing these settings, which are thus turned into the visual and thematic expression of a "world of existential, epistemological, and axiological uncertainty" (133).

This description of film noir is persuasive, even though, I would suggest, it theorizes the "determinate premises" of noir films at the wrong level of specificity. What I mean is that Sobchack's analysis is too closely tied to the particular premises she anatomizes. As Bakhtin's discussion of the chivalric romance should suggest, a chronotope requires a general category of setting (a miraculous world) rather than something rather specific (say, a castle and the surrounding forest). Arguing for the usefulness of chronotopic analysis for film study, Michael V. Montgomery has made the point that Bakhtin's categories are often formulated at too general a level.[8] Point well taken, but we must be circumspect about such re-formulations as we indulge in to adapt Bakhtin's concept for use in a different medium with narrative traditions often quite distinct from those in literature. The problem with Sobchack's anatomy of noir premises, to state it simply, is that in too many noir films the main settings are not cocktail lounges, cheap bars, bus stations, and roadside diners.

In fact, many noir films (John Stahl's *Leave Her to Heaven* and Vincent Minnelli's *Undercurrent* immediately come to mind) even avoid altogether the "dark city" where such accommodations for those "in transit" are normally to be found. Both these films are set mainly in homes of the wealthy. At the same time, no viewer of 1940s Hollywood film could fail to notice the contrast between, on the one hand, the inhospitable, dangerously permeable and anonymous spaces where the dark narratives of film noir most often (and at least in part) unfold and, on the other, the single family house that is a conventional element of film melodrama, its rooms full of family and its walls resisting any intrusion from the uninvited. And Sobchack's perception that the noir story world reflects a deep sense of both contingency and anxiety is, I believe, indisputable.

There is, however, another and larger problem with her view: it is incomplete. The unique usefulness of Bakhtin's concept of the chronotope lies not in its hardly innovative theorization of the way in which fictional settings are both drawn from the real and are then, suitably transformed, made a part of a generic story world. The chronotope is a richer analytical tool and is designed to account for the particular movement of narrative in both its senses—that is, in terms of story and storytelling time—within a given fictional genre, showing how a characteristic form of setting becomes its reflex. As Bakhtin puts it more poetically, "time becomes, in effect, palpable and visible; the chronotope makes narrative events concrete, makes them take on flesh, causes blood to flow in their veins" (250). Although she terms the noir chronotope "lounge time," Sobchack never comments on how time is structured in film noir. We gain no sense therefore of how the represented world she describes takes shape, how time becomes "palpable and visible." Her essay briefly alludes to, but offers little comment on, the different forms of narrative time carefully anatomized by Bakhtin, and these certainly merit a closer look. But, first, some consideration of Tourneur's film is in order.

Out of the Past, so aptly re-titled from its novelistic source (Daniel Mainwaring's *Build My Gallows High*), exemplifies not only a cultural theme, but a principle of narrative structure in the body of films known as noir. Thematically speaking, noir films characteristically focus on their protagonists' "dark pasts", which are frequently explored in some form of backward turning that is motivated by a present crisis. In film noir, someone (or something) is always coming "out of the past." This backward turning may be found in the discursive arrangement of story events, whose forward movement is interrupted by the filling in of some bypassed gap; or it may figure as an element of characterization, with an intradiegetic narrator relating what has gone before and thereby demonstrating the presence of the past within his own thoughts. These two methods reflect the classical rhetorical theory of *in medias res* construction, as in, for example, Virgil's *Aeneid*. A third possibility is that the present admits the return of characters who were thought to belong to the past and who, it seemed, had been bypassed as the protagonist embarked on a "fresh start."

As *Out of the Past* demonstrates, these three forms of backward movement may be found in the same text: the film's narrative loops back to examine the protagonist's involvement in a murder, even as he narrates the events in question, explaining his innocence to the woman he now intends he marry; and this movement brings into the unfolding present the beautiful *femme fatale* with whom he had once in love, as well as the powerful man from whom he had taken her away. The manipulative schemes and betrayals of this unholy couple are repeated as the story goes forward, but this time with even more deadly results. The past, in short, cannot be escaped and, worse yet, must find renewed expression in the present, which is often doomed, as in *Out of the Past*, simply to repeat it.

Thus the crisis the typical noir story develops can be resolved (or at least understood) only by a return in some sense to the past and to the postponed, unresolved difficulties it insistently bequeaths to the present. And so the present is always already contingent, its apparent solidity subject to a sudden, often thoroughgoing disruption that is connected somehow to what has been left behind but is not, as the story begins, in any sense "over." Such a sense of time was undoubtedly widespread in the culture, forming part of the dominant structure of feeling of the era. As historian William Graebner observes of the "culture of contingency" that was America in the 1940s, "the past was the repository of the most frightening memories—of desperate joblessness and totalitarianism, of separation and death in war" (52). If to many the present seemed marked by precariousness, this was a feeling that "flowed from being drafted and shot at, from witnessing the murder of the Jews, and from subjecting others—the populations of Dresden and Hiroshima to start with—to the possibility of sudden, undeserved death" (19).

This sense of contingency, of existential brittleness, certainly marks the experience of the characters in *Out of the Past*. In fact, "frightening memories" of what has gone before yet cannot be laid to rest provide the energy for the forward motion of the narrative after a false start marks out a quite different road not taken. A car arrives in the sleepy town of Bridgeport, California, high in the Sierras and far from the Los Angeles indicated on a road sign in one of the film's several establishing shots of mountains, sky, and empty vistas. Joe Stefanos (Paul Valentine), to all appearances an arrogant big city hood, has come for a former business "associate," Jeff Markham (Robert Mitchum), who has changed his name to Bailey and moved to the country in an attempt to escape his past. Jeff now owns and operates a service station, and he has made a new life, befriending a deaf mute Jimmy (Dickie Moore) and romancing the beautiful Ann (Virginia Huston), who has thrown over her suitor of many years, Jim (Richard Webb), even though Jim still nurtures hope of winning her away from the stranger. Despite his hard work and quiet life, Jeff has not yet attained to respectability in the closed society of this isolated small town, but he is quite obviously trying to make a life for himself despite the fact that there are those, including Ann's parents, who trust to neither his virtue nor his reliability.

On the day Stefanos arrives, Jeff and Ann are trout fishing in the mountains, enjoying a romantic interlude. Like others in Bridgeport, Ann is intrigued but worried by Jeff's exoticness. He lacks the deep knowability that others have in this small community. Jeff has no past by which those in Bridgeport can measure him; he exists for them only in the present moment of his law-abiding self-sufficiency. Now quite obviously in love with him, Ann, however, needs to know more. She must be assured that the man Jeff Bailey appears to be is the man he truly is. She asks how many places has he been. "One too many," he answers. But now, it seems, his days of dangerous wandering are over. Pointing to the lake shore, Jeff says he likes "this one right here." And that one place, far from the others he has been, is the centerpiece of a vision Jeff has for the rest of his life:

> You see that cove over there. Well, I'd like to build a house right there. Marry you. Live in it. And never go anywhere else.

Ann shares his vision of rootedness and commitment, but her acceptance of this proposal (if that is what Jeff is making) is tinged with doubt. "I wish you would," she says, putting his offer and all it entails into the suspended state of the subjunctive. Her questioning becomes more insistent. Was he ever married? "Not that I remember," Jeff answers. This seems to put Ann on more solid ground. But before the couple can go any further in making plans, Jimmy arrives from the garage to announce that Stefanos has come looking for Jeff.

What makes possible Jeff's dream of a life with Ann is the solidity of his new identity, of the name he gives himself and the life he is making for himself. That life depends on hard work, on becoming a respected and contributing member of the community, on establishing meaningful relationships with others. Jeff's rivalry with Jim for Ann's affection, and the reluctance her parents later show about endorsing her romance with a "stranger," would provide themes for a melodrama that could suitably be set in the single setting of Bridgeport and whose point would be to establish the unified, domestic identity of its protagonist. As he himself suggests, Jeff would be defined by that house he would build in the cove and by the one woman he would allow to share his life there with him. All other places, all other times (and, of course, all other women) would have no part in the life, unmarked by disruptions other than the natural ones time should bring, that Ann and Jeff would live there.

But such singularity of place and continuity of time do not define the noir protagonist. Jeff's projection of a conventionally domestic future, and his inhabiting of a morally unexceptional present, are both disrupted by the arrival of Stefanos, one of many agents in the film who come "out of the past" to admonish others that they cannot refashion themselves or entertain any thoughts of a fresh start. Stefanos not only reminds Jeff who he used to be, a private eye named Markham who once got mixed up in the personal affairs of big-time gambler Whit Sterling (Kirk Douglas). He also insists that Joe must become that person again, reminding him that, now identified, he cannot escape the reach of Sterling; further attempts at evasion are useless.

On one level, then, the arrival of this even stranger stranger in Bridgeport merely externalizes what is in Markham's character, his inability to become something other than he once was. Just as Jeff is contemplating

The soft-spoken thug Joe (Paul Valentine) watches over
the perennially elusive femme fatale Kathie (Jane Greer) .

a future, the past asserts its prior claims. We sense this inner limitation in the tentativeness of his proposal to Ann, as well as in her own evident uncertainty that he can live out the vision of domestic bliss he sketches for her. On another level, however, this sudden, unexpected confrontation represents the deadly workings of contingency. Stefanos, who does Sterling's strong arm work, was not looking for Markham when he found him. He was simply making his way by chance through Bridgeport some time back and happened to spot Markham working at a gas station. And now Sterling wants Jeff to drive over to his house on Lake Tahoe, and Sterling's wish is obviously a command that Jeff cannot (or perhaps will not) ignore. Jeff arranges for Ann to take him there in her car and, on the way, tells her who he used to be, but (or so he thinks) no longer is. His protestations are belied by a telling change of costume. Waiting outside Ann's house (tellingly, this is a domestic space he chooses not to enter), Jeff has abandoned the open-necked shirt and poplin jacket suited to life in the country for a trenchcoat and fedora, the uniform of the hard-boiled urban detective. He wooed Ann during a sunny afternoon by the lake, but she drives him to Tahoe at night, whose shadows better suit the darker persona he is in the midst of reassuming.

The flashback narrated by Jeff distributes his true identity over a series of places, none of which is his home: from New York, where Markham, but not Fisher (Steve Brodie), his partner, is hired to track down Kathie Moffett (Jane Greer), Sterling's erstwhile girlfriend who has stolen $40,000 and shot him in the process; to Acapulco, where Jeff finds Kathie and falls in love with her, reneging on his promise to return the woman and the stolen money to Whit; to Los Angeles, which provides them refuge until they are discovered by Fisher at a racetrack; to a cabin in the Sierras where Fisher, attempting to blackmail his former partner, is shot dead by Kathie, who flees leaving her lover to bury the body; and, finally, to Bridgeport, the place Jeff seeks out as a refuge against the crime he did not commit, the woman he still feels drawn toward, and the employer whom he had betrayed.

Some of these "premises" belong to the noir chronotope as Sobchack defines it: Sterling's "office" in New York: the "Negro" night club where Jeff gets vital information from Kathie's maid; the café in Acapulco where he hangs out in hopes of running into her and which quickly becomes "their place"; the racetrack where Fisher just happens on Jeff placing a bet ("There's wasn't one chance in a million we'd bump into our past," as Jeff says). But others do not: Kathie's Mexican bungalow; the beach where Jeff first makes love to her; and, most tellingly, the cabin in the woods where the fugitive couple lives for some time before Fisher tracks them down.

All these exceptions to Sobchack's anatomy of "premises," it might be pointed out, are domestic or, at least, proto-domestic in the sense that they serve as the reflex of Jeff's desire to transform Kathie from Whit's plaything (a homicidal gold digger with robbery on her mind who has no moral qualms about her "attachment" to the rich gambler) to a monogamous woman now satisfied to live on love and no longer in the rich style to which Whit's generosity had accustomed her. But that Kathie and Jeff can become a couple and truly inhabit any domestic space is an illusion from the outset. Both have betrayed the powerful Whit, and a fear of his vengeance drives them into a hiding from which they can emerge only to their peril. Their rejection of the criminal underworld Whit represents is thus necessarily incomplete. The life they lead is not for themselves, but in opposition to the powerful male who has a claim on each of them.

The places where they share a life are thus a form of disguise. Because it must be defined by transitoriness and deception, no home they establish could become the center of a properly middle-class existence. As Sobchack observes, referring to films such as *Double Indemnity* and *Mildred Pierce*, "the loss of home becomes a structuring absence in film noir" (144). It is not surprising, then, that *Out of the Past* contains, in a distanced and ironic form, the vision of domestic time and space it otherwise excludes. And it denies that sense of natural time (man in his "seven ages") and singular space (the concept of "home") by devising narratives that deprive its protagonists not only of rootedness, as Sobchack observes, but of any prospect for a future that, beyond the reach of contingency, will unfold unretarded by the morally ambiguous past.

These two different visions of life figure in the exchange that takes place between Ann and Jeff, his confessional flashback now at an end. Ann has listened to things that have hurt her, but she affirms that "it's all past." Eager for her acceptance, Jeff nevertheless must admit that "maybe it isn't." This conversation takes place between characters who belong, in a sense, to different chronotopes. In melodrama, the innocent but misguided can reform their ways and accept monogamy in that single space that, as Jeff points, out, looking at the cove, is transformed into a home by the embrace of marriage and the duty of earning a living.

Melodrama thus constructs time as significant in the sense that both character and space may change in the course of its unfolding. Contingency and its reflex, spatial discontinuity, characterize this form of story, but only in part. For the melodramatic notion of time centers on a moment of turning (thematically, the crisis of development that leads to growth and maturity). This turning finds its reflex in the singularity of space and character it projects for the protagonist, who, literally and metaphorically, "settles down" to a predictable and monogamous existence. The melodrama ends in an unfolding present whose uniformity can be disrupted only by the tragedies actuarial tables can measure; it is a form given to projected closure and the notion of "happily ever after."

In the film noir, by way of contrast, the innocent but misguided or obsessed man cannot escape the fatal entanglements he has, after all, chosen and which, in the end, answer better to his nature, with its impulses toward restlessness and duplicity. Lacking a moment of reformative turning, the film noir juxtaposes the false promise of a future with the reality of a present that, instead, turns back to the past, trapping the protagonist "between times" and in a multiplicity of irreconcilable spaces. As does Jeff Markham, such protagonists ordinarily come to their end "in transit," attempting to escape what they never can, which is themselves.

In the case of *Out of the Past*, what gives the story its forward movement is the possibility that Ann may be right that the past can be laid to rest, expunged from the present as the man who protests his love for her promises his relinquishing of a past self. And yet Jeff leaves her with a contradictory admission of resignation and resolve: "I'm tired of running. I've got to clean this up some way." But that, of course, proves to be impossible. At Whit's huge lake house in Tahoe, Jeff discovers that Kathie has returned to Whit, who now holds evidence (Kathie's murder of Fisher, which can be "pinned" on Jeff) that delivers Jeff back into his power. Whit dispatches him on a fool's errand to San Francisco, where he is to be made the fall guy for the murder by Stefanos of Whit's accountant, Eels (Ken Niles), who may go to the police with evidence of tax fraud that will send Whit to jail.

In the threatening city, Jeff manages to defeat this scheme and, in the process, obtain the tax records. He moves easily and readily through a series of dangerous spaces in nighttime San Francisco, even assuming for a time yet another false identity. Jeff's intention is to free himself from Whit's control by keeping the records now in his possession. Fingered for the murder to the police by Whit, however, he finds that his innocence is at present impossible to establish and returns to hide out in the woods near Bridgeport. Stefanos is dispatched to kill him there and climbs a rise from which to take a fatal shot, but Jimmy, in one of those bizarre killings that characterize film noir, hooks him with a fishing line and pulls him down to his death on the rocks below. Reassured by Ann that she still loves him, Jeff goes to Whit at Tahoe once again, and the two men, both betrayed by Kathie, decide to deliver her to the police to stand trial for Fisher's murder. As before, however, she manages to reassert her power over them, first by shooting Whit (this time fatally) and then by blackmailing Jeff to accompany her on yet another flight (her third) from a shooting. His plan to escape from Kathie's power now a failure (for only with Whit's help could he establish that she murdered Fisher), Jeff knows that his only hope for deliverance is the police, whom he secretly phones. As they speed away down the mountain, Kathie spots the roadblock ahead, realizes Jeff's betrayal, and shoots him dead before she is herself gunned down by the police.

If the film ends with a sense of projected closure, it is because Jim, with Jeff now dead, resumes his relationship with Ann. Unlike her dead lover, Ann finds she can leave the past behind. Her moment of reformatory turning comes when, questioning Jimmy about Jeff's last moments, she is answered with a saving lie. Jimmy tells her that Jeff had chosen to leave with Kathie. As not in the noir world, the past, once identified as a false start, can be left behind. In the film's closing shot, Jimmy waves goodbye to the sign over Jeff's garage, acknowledging his affection for and loyalty to a man whom he had known in his better (if hardly entirely authentic) self. The world of melodrama, we might say, reasserts its control. It is, after all, the default fictional universe

A fatalistic Jeff (Robert Mitchum) looks his future in the eye as a determined Kathie (Jane Greer) leads him to his doom.

purveyed by the Hollywood system with its reaffirmation of consensus values, including a distribution of outcomes for its characters based on their moral worthiness. The noir narrative is strangely framed by a melodramatic movement, whose goal is possession of Ann and the singularity of character that is suitably contained by a single fictional space. As the film opens, Jeff is the protagonist in that drama, but, as it ends, his place has been usurped by Jim. Destroyed by a past from which he cannot escape, Jeff becomes a past that the other characters can easily transcend.

Sobchack does not find a close parallel to this kind of story among the chronotopes identified by Bakhtin. But one of these is what he terms the "adventure novel of everyday life," in which the adventure time of pure romance (an unfolding of moments, not causally linked, which effect no changes in the characters who experience them), but "depicts only the exceptional, utterly unusual moments of a man's life…that are very short compared to the whole length of a human life….[but] shape the definitive image of man, his essence, as well as the nature of his subsequent life." (116) That this is a time of adventure is established by the fact that this is a "time of exceptional and unusual events, events determined by chance." Such a conception of story time results in a multiplicity of settings, drawn from real life, and a human image that is "private and isolated." (119) Correspondingly, then, time is represented as a series of separate moments, "chopped up into separate segments…deprived of its unity and wholeness." (128) With human time carefully distinguished from natural time, "the individual changes and undergoes metamorphosis completely independent of the world." (119) It is moreover "always the case that the hero cannot, by his very nature, be a part of everyday life; he passes through such life as would a man from another world." (121) In fact, the primary image of this protagonist's world is "the road." He is a character perpetually in transit, fixed in a sense of time and space that is particularly suited to "portraying events governed by chance." (244) This particular chronotope, I suggest, would be especially appealing to a culture obsessed by contingency and rootlessness, experiencing life, both personal and political, as a series of chance encounters and disconnections that do not admit of "settling down" in any meaningful sense. As Sobchack observes, film noir offers a conception of representational time/space that contrasts with the chronotope of the idyll, discussed at length by Bakhtin, which, as she points out, has "relevance to the familiarity, stability, and rootedness of home." (160) But the chronotope that structures film noir is also, I believe, connected to one of the larger categories identified by Bakhtin.

This might not, in the end at least, be a terribly important point. The noir protagonist might well resemble his predecessors in picaresque fiction of earlier eras. Like them, he is ever in transit through a series of disconnected moments as he finds himself incapable of entering into the quite different temporality of everyday life. To put this another way, the home, source of wholeness and connection, is a "structuring absence" in the story of his self-realization; it is a place that Jeff Bailey can refer to only as wish, perhaps barely as intention. And yet, to follow the line of reason pioneered by Vivian Sobchack, his experience of time is also culturally specific, without antecedent in the general types of narrative anatomized by Bakhtin. The road on which he meets with adventure leads not forward into some ever receding future, but, instead, turns back upon itself. The path he treads is ever the same path. Like Sisyphus, he is condemned to relive what has been, in an illusion of movement that is actually a form of cruel stasis. As does Jeff Markham/Bailey in *Out of the Past*, he can only live out the division of his self between what is and what has been, glimpsing (but only glimpsing) the possibilities of rootedness and singularity, of the wholeness of everyday time, that deceptively seem within his imagination and reach.

NOTES

1. *Film Theory: An Introduction*, Oxford: Blackwell, 2000, p. 202. In *Reconfiguring American Film Genres* (Los Angeles: University of California Press, 1998), Nick Browne observes that in cinema studies older taxonomic approaches have been losing their appeal: "The implicit, ideal order of the structuralist system of genre has dissolved…The structuralist project of the 1970s carried forward and defined this tendency [to assume an internal genetic finality] by identifying genres with distinctive patterns of narrative order and visual iconography." In place of this now largely abandoned approached, Browne advocates a view of genres as "specific assemblances of local coherencies—discrete, heterotopic instances of a complex cultural politics" (xi). Browne's statement fairly characterizes the approach taken in this essay, which is opposed to any postulating of "an internal genetic finality" for the film noir phenomenon.

2. These issues are explored in more depth in my "The Sociological Turn of Adaptation Studies: The Example of Film Noir," in Robert Stam and Alessanda Raengo, eds., *Companion to Film and Literature* (Oxford: Blackwell, 2004).

3. *Distinction: A Social Critique of the Judgment of Taste*, trans. by Richard Nice, Cambridge, MA: Harvard University Press, 1984, p. 1.

4. In Browne, p. 129. Further references noted in the text.

5. Alain Silver and Elizabeth Ward*, Film Noir: An Encyclopedia Reference to the American Style*, Third Edition, Woodstock, NY: Overlook Press, 1992, p. 218.

6. As William Graebner observes, "the seminal events of the forties seemed to confirm that humanity had, indeed, been set adrift from its ethical moorings. Like life itself, values seemed to come and go, without pattern or reason," *The Age of Doubt: American Thought and Culture in the 1940s* (Boston: Twayne, 1991), pp. 19-20. Further references noted in the text.

7. From "Forms of Time and of the Chronotope in the Novel," in *The Dialogic Imagination: Four Essays*, trans. by Michael Holquist (Austin: University of Texas Press, 1981), 84-5. Further references noted in the text.

8. *Carnivals and Commonplaces: Bakhtin's Chronotope, Cultural Studies, and Film*, New York: Peter Lang, 1993, see esp. pp. 5-6.

This modern-day Pandora (Gaby Rodgers) opens the "great whatsit" box and unleashes radioactive demons upon the corrupt world of Mike Hammer in *Kiss Me Deadly*.

Voices from the Deep: Film Noir as Psychodrama

J. P. Telotte (2004)

My ambitions in this article are fairly simple. First, I want to suggest a trope that could be useful for thinking about the film noir. Second, I want to approach this form in what might seem a rather "spacey" way; that is, I want to talk about depth: the depth of noir's subjects, the deep recesses of the mind it commonly explored, the depth of field that was one of its stylistic hallmarks. Rather than just using this vantage to survey the form, though, I want to suggest how these varied dimensions overlap and help constitute its distinctive voice. I offer this "deep" vantage to help place noir's generic stories of crime, murder, mystery, and detection within the context of postwar American film and to model another way we might consider approaching our cinema in that era.

Certainly, the film noir of that period was fascinated with exploring the deep recesses of American culture, with the dark realms of gangsters and organized crime, as well as with the petty and even accidental criminal, with everything that seemed to threaten both the individual and social status quo. At the same time, it found new narrative material in subjects that had been repressed or, for various reasons, conveniently pushed to a cultural background in the war years—topics like juvenile delinquency (*City Across the River* [1949]), corruption in office (*Boomerang* [1947], *The Phenix City Story* [1955]), racism (*Crossfire* [1947]), and rapacious big business (*All My Sons*, *The Big Clock* [both 1948]). Taken together, these various cultural concerns clearly point to what David Bordwell describes as noir's "challenge to dominant values" (75).

With these explorations of crime, corruption, violence, and varied social failings the film noir moved into the dark recesses of American culture in a way that we had not seen since the social problem films of the Depression era. And these explorations were all the more troubling given the lack of those cultural scars—bombed-out cities, devastated landscapes, hordes of displaced people, etc.—that the rest of the world sported at the time. But noir in its own way compensates for that lack, borrowing heavily from certain cultural images of the war that our films, especially the newsreels and documentaries, had offered up and left as a disturbing legacy—images, as Jon Tuska says, "that could and did haunt the minds of Americans" (155) and left them to consider what could be in our world. Thus, to correspond to those depths, film noir repeatedly offered its own surface icons: dismal cityscapes, decaying if not bombed-out buildings, and individuals aimlessly wandering the night streets—all of which had to leave viewers hoping, like the protagonist of Maxwell Shane's *Nightmare* (1956), that these images were all just part of "some crazy dream."

Yet a recurring noir motif is the *insistence* of these dark elements, the upwelling of what 1930s crime films defined as a criminal underworld into our normal world, the connection between those icons and something deeper, perhaps outside the movies and the otherwise comforting situation of the movie theater. Noir films emphasized that those stark images were part of our own, not some distant, foreign culture, and repressing them, returning them to the depths where we might have preferred they remain, or simply containing them within the bounds of conventional generic narrative would be more difficult than vanquishing some foreign enemy, despite the efforts of a film like *The Big Heat* (1953) to suggest we think of and deal with them in the same way.

While exploring these cultural chasms, noir, as we know, proved equally adept at plumbing the individual depths of the troubled mind. Of course, the noir predilection for voice-over, flashback narratives,[I] films whose style typically implies a psyche dredging up prior events and trying to make some sense of them, already points in this direction; as do the various films in which psychiatrists and psychological inquiry play prominent roles, or in which psychotic figures are central, as in *The Dark Past* (1948), *He Walked by Night* (1949) or *In a Lonely Place* (1950). In fact, as Laurence Miller notes, approximately 260 different forms of psychopathology have been identified, all of them surfacing at various points in the noir canon (Miller). Here too we find an effort to create an iconicity that might correspond to and encode these depths: dutch angles, extended subjective shots, wide-angle distortions, and most obviously the surrealist-inspired imagery of films like *Spellbound* (1945) and *The Dark Past*.

We might also note how very near are those noir films whose subject is the traumatized psyche to the era's popular psychodramas, such as *The Snake Pit* (1948), *The Rack* (1956), or *The Three Faces of Eve* (1957). Both types of films seem intent on locating and mapping the source of trauma, although the noir works emphasize its particular face: the psychotic crimes, desires, and violence that are the surface symptoms of these deep impulses. Yet all of these films are, in a sense, stories about depth. They explore the mystery of ourselves, plumb the surface of self that we show the world, penetrate our human depths. They do so not simply to dredge up what is there, but to make some sense of what is in those depths and to help accommodate us to the repressed dimensions in our personal or cultural psyches. In effect, they remind us how those human depths connect—and at times fail to connect—with the surface or face we show to the world, to the unity we, as well as our movies, usually try to construct. In fact, we might do well to think of the noir film as always a kind of psychodrama, for this approach provides a useful metaphor for linking its cultural and individual explorations. Yet Paul Schrader and others assert that we should think of noir as "first of all a style" (63) of an unusu-

The Snake Pit: Virginia Cunningham (Olivia de Havilland) ponders her psychodrama as her pipe-smoking shrink (Leo Genn) and Freud himself (picture on wall) look over her shoulder.

al, even strained sort. To include this vantage on noir, I want to stretch my initial trope a bit further. By thinking of the film noir as a sort of psychodrama, or more broadly as an effort to link depths and surfaces, we might be able to retain a sense of that style as we accommodate the larger noir perspective.

A film like *Nightmare* can start us in this direction. Its protagonist is musician Stan Grayson, a performer, someone who must present a pleasing front to his audience, although that front belies his depths. For his bandmates term him "too modern" and reject his arrangements as "too progressive," and he is haunted by a recurring dream. Stan's story begins with a face rising to the surface of a dark pool as he recounts this terrifying dream in which, in "a queer, mirrored room," he kills a stranger. When he tries to escape through one of the mirrored doors there, he plummets into darkness. On awakening, Stan finds bruises, as if from a struggle; he notes blood on his hands; and on his bureau are various objects from the dream. Thanks to these tangible signs, the dream refuses to go away, despite his brother-in-law Rene's clumsy psychoanalytic effort at trying to "talk" him out of it. Like some postwar trauma—which indeed it seems to metaphorize—it haunts Stan's every moment, seemingly marking him as a murderer, burdening him with guilt, and compelling him to explore its dark depths.

His initial effort at resolving this trauma, though, is to separate surface and depth, culture and self. He feels that "out there," in the world around him, "everything was status quo"; only "in here," in the self, is there a problem. When that disconnection brings no relief, he tries to reconnect the "out there" and "in here." He wanders the streets of New Orleans, looking for someone to help put the pieces of his dream—and his life—together.

Police psychologist Andrew Collins (Lee J. Cobb, foregound) ponders his psychodrama: held hostage by the armed escaped killer—who is now his patient—Al Collins (William Holden) and his moll Betty (Nina Foch) in *The Dark Past*.

Thus, he asks his friends to identify a strange, perhaps "progressive" piece of music he recalls from the dream. A montage of day and night street scenes, many shot in dutch angle and with a mobile camera, externalizes his trauma as a disturbing image field. Seeking distraction, Stan and Rene drive deep into bayou country, an area neither knows, and when a storm comes up, turn onto an unmarked road—a recurring motif in films of this period—which leads to a large, empty house where Stan finds his mirrored room, the scene of the dream murder. There, behind a series of locked and mirrored doors—surfaces that open onto dark secrets—he uncovers more of his dream's elements, including bloodstains, and finds that a murder did occur. Eventually, with Rene's help, he learns that the neighbor in his hotel had hypnotized him and used him in a plot to kill the neighbor's wife and her lover. With that solution—and the death of the murderous neighbor—Stan returns to his regular life, his girlfriend, and the stage with his band.

It is a pat ending for an otherwise rather unsettling disclosure—that we are easily manipulated by forces beyond our consciousness, control, or understanding, forces at work behind our neighbor's door and intent on frustrating our desire for unity or wholeness. It reminds us how easily we can be plunged into depths from which we might never recover. And it never recuperates Stan's "progressive" character or the fact that he did kill someone. Even that strange music he heard and that we link to his "progressive" nature is revealed to be no more than a record played at the wrong speed. But then no resolution—save for the *Dallas*-type retreat in which everything proves to be a dream—could really work here. The deaths, like those millions in the war, cannot be erased, and like our cultural psyche, the individual one, here opened up and its vulnerable nature briefly explored, could hardly be filled in like some pothole. Knowing of his manipulation, moving through those mirrored doors, seeing a link between the "out there" and the "in here" has to suffice.

Perhaps part of the problem is that *Nightmare* seems like a post-war film come ten years too late. It is, in fact, a remake of the 1947 production *Fear in the Night*, a work that does seem to direct its narrative at some sort of post-war trauma, as a way of coping with our national guilt over the massive deaths of the war and a kind of loss of cultural identity and purpose that followed. But by 1956 *Nightmare* could not make those same connections, draw very effectively on that earlier cultural climate. Consequently, its metaphoric potential never quite connects, and we are left with a trope that floats unmoored through this narrative, with what we might think of as a signifier strangely cut off from its signified.

We might note a similar problem of balance or correspondence in the film's rather un-neat style, one that involves more than just the expressionist hallmarks we expect in film noir. *Nightmare*'s already disturbing visual scheme is fitted to a narrative that moves by fits and starts: shifting into and out of flashback, offering sequences that seem like narrative blind alleys (such as Stan's meeting a blond who recalls the girl in his dream), and begging the question of causality (why Stan was targeted for this plot). The film itself, with its surfaces and depths[2] and maze-like plot, does seem almost like "some crazy dream," like the very stuff its narrative tries to repress or explain away, and that its protagonist cannot escape.

But let me emphasize that visual scheme for a moment. Its various components are ones we know well—low-key lighting, distorting close-ups, unbalanced compositions, an emphasis on oblique lines and reflective surfaces (pools of water, mirrors)—all of which conspire to make this world look strange, to distort its surface. Yet that stylized imagery shares time with starkly realistic location photography and an emphasis on depth of field–elements usually catalogued as hallmarks of film realism. In their key essay on noir style, Place and Peterson hold that one of noir's "requirements" is a "greater 'depth of field'" (31) than normal in American cinema. This emphasis on deep focus and a composition in depth, remains fairly consistent in both noir's earlier entries and its later, more neorealist examples. *Nightmare* works this combination to intriguing effect, especially in its murder room scene that plays off of the tension between deceptive mirrored surfaces and the dark depths those doors conceal. But then, as Schrader also notes, another of noir's striking traits was its ability "to weld" such "seemingly contradictory elements into a uniform style" (56). The general success of that "welding" prompts Bordwell's assertion that noir is quite conventional in its own way, that it "no more subverts the classical film than crime fiction undercuts the orthodox novel" (77). Despite its flimsy effort at closing its dreamy narrative, at shutting its mirrored doors on its disturbing glimpses of a deeper, darker world, at satisfactorily

Nightmare: disturbed jazzman Stan Grayson (Kevin McCarthy) confronts his literal multiple personalities reflected in mirrors.

balancing surface and depth, though, *Nightmare* cannot quite pass for a classical Hollywood film, and the very clash of styles it illustrates suggests something of the hidden, the repressed in this form, as well as in the larger body of American cinema.

In this almost "contradictory" character we might begin to make out another sort of depth analysis that surfaces to varying degrees in the film noir. For these films often seem to flaunt their style, in various ways to foreground—that is, to draw up near the surface—their markedly inflected nature. Obvious examples are the frequent prologues that note how the ensuing story will unfold. For example, the subjective narrative *Lady in the Lake* (1947) begins with Philip Marlowe talking to us, warning that "You'll see it just as I saw it. You'll meet the people; you'll find the clues." [see page 144] The docudrama *Boomerang* (1947) opens with a 360-degree pan of a small town square, as a voice-of-god narrator notes that "the basic facts of our story actually occurred in a Connecticut community much like this one." And *Nightmare*'s dream-investigation begins with that head appearing in a dark pool, while a voice, bespeaking our own experience, recalls how "At first, all I could see was this face. . . floating toward me." Since this is what we too "first. . . see," the narration quickly points up how the film looks, how its story will unfold, and how easily we might be drawn into it. The larger effect of such openings, such initial signs, is to make us more aware, in a manner classical Hollywood films usually avoided, of narrative style itself.

What such a self-consciousness begins to suggest is an extra level of dredging up and working out, another sort of psychodrama ongoing in American postwar/cold-war films. For just as they located new subjects in what had been culturally or individually repressed, so does the film noir seem intrigued with the traditional and unremarked voice in which the American cinema spoke and with inspecting its typical inflections. In fact, in this period, we might see it as the film industry's own psychodrama, exploring the given language of the movies and holding, along with the givens of culture and self, elements of classical narrative up for examination, in the process letting us glimpse the discontinuities and gaps within the imaginary realm of wholeness and completeness classical cinema had traditionally sought to offer.

On one, very broad level, as I have elsewhere traced out (Telotte, *Voices in the Dark*), this impulse generates a kind of reflexive turn through a focus on the various ways in which modern media wield their nearly invisible, even hypnotic powers over us. In fact, several of the best noirs analyze the inner workings of the film industry, notably *In a Lonely Place* and *The Big Knife* (1955), while others do a kind of depth analysis on elements of the larger communication industry: newspapers (*The Big Carnival* [1951], *Beyond a Reasonable Doubt* [1956]), radio (*Nightmare Alley* [1947]), television (*Trial without Jury* [1950], *The Glass Web* [1953]), and even the stage (*A Double Life* [1948], *The Sweet Smell of Success* [1957]). A film like *The Harder They Fall* (1956) is particularly exemplary, as it shows how the combination of newsreels, television, radio, and newspapers effectively create a persona—as a skilled press agent manipulates the media to turn a lumbering, unskilled Argentine giant into a supposed heavyweight boxing contender—and hints as well of how those same forces might shape or misshape our own identities, just as Humphrey Bogart's agent figure is nearly corrupted by the forces he tries to control. But probably the most famous example of this impulse is Billy Wilder's *Sunset Boulevard* (1950), which explores the shaping hold film has on us, how its seeming depths link up only with a false surface and can deprive us of any real experience of depth.

On another, less obvious level, this impulse surfaces in that strange, at times contradictory style we have described—one that constantly seems to shift between the sort of conventionally constructed reality we expect in film narrative and a rather bizarre mode of vision that cannot help but remind us how contrived film realism actually is, how much the depths it does depict are themselves but a surface construct. This problematic styling shows up most clearly in films like *Nightmare*, *The Dark Past*, and *Blackout* (1954), works whose use of realistic mise-en-scène, often shot on location, are filled with a dream-like imagery that reflects a character's strained, psychotic state. But the prime example is Robert Aldrich's *Kiss Me Deadly* (1955), a film that moves far afield from the Mickey Spillane novel it adapts to investigate the nature of both the popular detective and film narrative itself.

II.

Sunset Boulevard's place in this context may be all too obvious. It is, after all, about the film industry and what it can do to those who surrender to its seductive power. As such, it may have helped inspire the similar focus of *In a Lonely Place*, which appeared the following year,[3] and also suggested the viability of Aldrich's jaundiced look at the industry's destructive effects on its workers, *The Big Knife* (1955). Yet the way *Sunset Boulevard* talks about the film industry seems especially noteworthy alongside a film like *Kiss Me Deadly*, its combination of subject and style a milepost for the later film. It begins with an in-depth tracking shot, as a car moves down a Hollywood street, and it ends with death and madness—the end results of its penetration into Hollywood's depths—brought into close-up. Speaking from the point of his death—delving back into his life, as if trying to gauge the depths that led to this end—murdered screenwriter Joe Gillis describes a series of wrong turns he took as he moved deeper into this world. From a start as a promising young writer, he turned to producing simple formula stories "that would sell." When those formula pieces fail, creditors hound him, and so one day he accidentally turns into faded film queen Norma Desmond's driveway and hides his car in her garage. From that literal turning point, Joe finds himself, almost unwittingly, moving deeper into her world: working in her cavernous living room, moving into the room above her garage, shifting to the "husband's room" adjoining Norma's suite, and eventually, we gather, sharing her bed. When he tries to leave, Joe is shot and falls into Norma's pool, where he lies floating until the police fish him out. And Norma, thinking she is again before Cecil B. DeMille's cameras, walks into the foreground, blurring the image as she announces, "I'm ready for my close-up."

Norma Desmond (Gloria Swanson) is ready for her "final close-up" as her faithful servant (Erich von Stroheim) directs in *Sunset Boulevard*.

The narrative of this steady movement ever deeper into a dangerous cinematic world and its subsequent move out, ending on Norma's blurred close-up, rather literalizes the activity of a psychodrama. It also has a resonance in the film's visual style. For the opening tracking camera anticipates the fluid tracking and panning shots that constantly draw us into Norma's cluttered home, emphasizing its cavernous rooms, the jumble of her Hollywood career, and, ominously, the door to her room. That fluid movement suggests an intriguing depth to this world and mimics Joe's curious exploration of it. It suggests too the film's structure around the examination of these depths. Yet the doors, mirrors, pictures and portraits of Norma, even the movie screen on which the camera several times comes to rest—and perhaps the surface of the pool in which Joe's body floats—hint of something else: a lack of real depth or substance in this homage to self and cinema Norma Desmond has built.

Another element of that realist style, the film's emphasis on layered images, further underscores the troubled—and troubling—sense of depth being explored here. For as Joe moves through Norma's house or sits working on her filmscript, he seems buried in her world's clutter, as tables, lamps, and pictures fill the foreground, constrict the frame, and swallow him up in the background. The same elements that help construct a sense of depth thus also work to turn it into something else, to reconstruct this world not as alluring and realistic image, but as trap, prison, burial chamber, or in an anticipatory postmodern turn, even as collage. Joe here seems placed in a far more elaborate box, but essentially of the same sort as Norma orders for her dear dead pet monkey. Even the entry to Norma's house works in much the same way; it is constructed in depth, a barred door opening onto a solid, interior one, the combination suggesting both restricted entry and entrapment, depth and depthlessness. Thus we several times see Joe framed behind the barred door in a composi-

Sunset Boulevard: Betty (Nancy Olson) tells Joe Gillis (William Holden), "Look at this street. All cardboard, all hollow, all phoney, all done with mirrors. You know, I like it better than any street in the world."

tion that points up his entrapment here.

What the depth of *Sunset Boulevard*'s mise-en-scène ultimately reveals, then, is a world that has lost any real depth—a cinematic world that too easily renders its inhabitants similarly dimensionless, flat, leaves them, in perhaps a nice metaphor for the movie star, floating on a sheer surface. This point is made, almost ironically, by a character who seems immune to this lure. Joe's co-writer Betty Schaefer takes him down the Paramount back lot and notes, "Look at this street—all cardboard, all hollow, all phoney, all done with mirrors. You know, I like it better than any street in the world." She then fleshes out this confession of her love affair with the movies by revealing how she had once rendered herself like that phoney, constructed street: doing all she could, including getting her nose fixed, to try to get before the camera—only to be rejected because she could not act.

This scene emphasizes not only how illusory the cinematic world's depth is, but also how it invites us to become like it, to construct a facade of self. In effect, it warns against investing unwarily and too heavily in the film world, lest we wind up like the principal characters at the close of *Sunset Boulevard*. Joe, shot by Norma, lies floating in her pool. Max still attends to Norma, helping sustain the fantasy that she is a movie queen beloved by her fans, while maintaining his own tangential link to the film world. And Norma walks into the foreground, into the camera at film's end, her image blurring—and in the process mocking the deep focus that has suggested this world's depths. It is, finally, just a world of movies, of film, of surfaces that, like Norma herself, have lost contact with the real depths of this world, and its tragedy is that, for all their awareness of its falseness, its facades, its hollowness, the people here almost without exception embrace it, opt to float on that shimmering surface.

Cecil B. DeMille plays himself as he comforts the delusional Norma (Gloria Swanson) in *Sunset Boulevard*.

III.

While *Sunset Boulevard* emphasizes subject in its psychodrama of the movie industry, *Kiss Me Deadly* more emphatically foregrounds style. It does, in a marked shift from Spillane's novel which is set in New York, place detective Mike Hammer's investigations in a Hollywood setting, thereby hinting of some connection between the film industry and the criminal underworld. But its concern is more with the nature of his movements, with the style of the detective and the detective film, through which it can better comment on films of its own type.

Like the other films discussed here, it too begins with a testimony to depth, to the realistic imperative it seemingly implies, and to the sort of activity we expect in such films, the drawing out of some deeply buried knowledge. The character Christina runs diagonally down a highway and then directly towards the camera. She seems to flee from something in the dark as she moves toward the lights of the approaching cars. As we later learn, she carries some special knowledge which, she feels, must be brought to the surface; as she tells Mike Hammer, "when people are in trouble, they need to talk." His investigation of her subsequent murder largely follows from this start, as he probes those depths from which she has come, tries to find out "why" she was in such trouble. In the manner of classical detective films, *Kiss Me Deadly* seems intent on digging up these hidden facts and bringing criminals to justice.

But the opening's style also prepares us for a swerve in a different direction—just as Hammer's car,

Kiss Me Deadly: the trompe-l'oeil scene as Hammer (Ralph Meeker) interrupts Velda (Maxine Cooper) mid-workout [see also frame 21 on page 313 below].

strangely enough, takes Christina back in the direction from which she was fleeing. For the shots of Christina running are pointedly mismatched—and repeatedly so. At first she is running down the center of the highway; then we note she is running alongside the road. This shot sequence recurs several times and, in the process, serves notice—like the credits which then scroll in reverse—that something peculiar is going on here. The cinematic construction of space, which usually depends on the matching of such cuts-on-action, self-destructs, so that our experience of depth here becomes unanchored, intrudes annoyingly into our field of investigation.

That investigation includes the characters of *Kiss Me Deadly*, especially Hammer, who clearly have little human depth. As Edwin Arnold and Eugene Miller note, Ralph Meeker plays the detective in a way that shows "the emptiness inside," "his dead soul" (41). He is a private eye with all of the type's worst traits exaggerated; he is thuggish, sadistic, unfeeling, interested in fast cars, a quick payoff, and, as Christina surmises, himself. His recurring line is, fittingly, "What's in it for me?"—perhaps because there seems so little "in" him. In fact, he seems minimally suited for plumbing this world's depths, for digging up the secret behind Christina's murder and his own near death precisely because he has so little real depth or understanding. Thus he typically uses others to do his work—his secretary Velda, his friend Nick, the gangster Carl Evello's sister Friday—while his own bumbling injures and even kills those he uses.

In this way *Kiss Me Deadly* offers a rather different take on both the style and subject of the conventional detective film—a take that enables it to explore film's own depths in this period. As Aldrich described his project, "In terms of style, in terms of the way we tried to make it, it provided a . . . showcase to display my own ideas of movie-making" (Arnold 42). And they prove to be rather unconventional ideas about film and the film detective. As we have noted, one of the pillars of classical narrative, continuity editing, often disappears—or to be more precise, repeatedly fails, as in a later work like *Breathless* (1960), so that we see the seams in the narrative, the manipulations of our point of view, the mismatched fragments of the story constructed for us. Similarly, Hammer often seems a rather disjointed construct: knowledgeable and dumb, cocky yet vulnerable, and in an improbability born of many other generic efforts, brought back several times, as his friend Nick puts it, "as if from the dead" to continue his fumbling efforts.

But then the world in which Hammer and the other characters move seems to have little real depth or dimension either, despite its location shooting, save for what is transparently constructed by the cinematic apparatus. In fact, *Kiss Me Deadly* repeatedly emphasizes just how artificial or deceptive the appearance of depth here is—in both the world and its characters. Consider, for example, the trompe l'oeil effect when Mike goes to Velda's apartment and watches her exercise. Slowly, a pan of the camera reveals that we have been looking not deep into her apartment, but at a near wall covered in mirrors that reflect Velda and the apartment's interior. As other examples, we might think of the various times when a reverse angle shot puts us in a spatially illogical position, at an impossible depth, as when a car falls onto Nick and we watch from the car's point of view as it crosses an incredibly long distance. Similarly, when Mike enters Gabrielle's apartment, we see him inexplicably through the bars of her bed—a bed that, reverse shots reveal, is shoved against a back wall. When Mike slaps around William Mist, we watch the entire action from a point of view located within Mist's medicine cabinet. And when Mike finally discovers the object of his quest, "the great whatsit," we see first from Mike's vantage, as he peers into a small locker at the Hollywood Athletic Club, and then from within, behind the "whatsit" that, a reverse angle shows, fills the locker's base.

Admittedly, this last scene, offering its impossible low, reverse-angle shot four times, serves a conventional narrative function. It shows Hammer in an awkward, low- angle close-up which, with the wide-angle lens, distorts his face, emphasizes his near-manic look, and reminds us of his sadistic glee in torturing the morgue doctor and slapping around the club attendant to get access to the locker. As in the visual distortions found in many other noirs, this shot series externalizes a distortion within the central character, like the similar wide-angle close-ups of the mobster Carl Evello and his henchmen, and so stylistically links the detective and his enemies.

Yet far more important is the pattern of camera placement in such scenes that brings us up short by bringing the illusion of depth itself up short, making us aware of this world's illusory nature. Conventionally, classical narrative asks us to do a kind of "cognitive mapping" (Bordwell 59) of the world it visualizes, to imaginatively construct the larger dimensions of a supposedly coherent world that we never see in its entirety. But here, the construction frequently fails. Thus, when Hammer dispatches a thug who is following him, we cut from a high-angle shot as Hammer knocks him down a long flight of stairs to a far low-angle shot, done with a wide-angle lens. While the cut maps us in depth, the lens dissolves it by distorting and enlarging the foreground while making the background recede from view. As a result, Hammer nearly disappears from sight, while the thug appears to fall *up* the stairs. Similarly, in Gabrielle's apartment building, a series of reverse-angle shots of the stairs creates Escher-like images that flatten out the illusion of depth and leave us unsure whether we are looking up or down. Appropriately, given its name, the Hollywood Athletic Club scene underscores this constructed depth. As Hammer enters, he walks from the camera into the background, momentarily blurring the image, and when he leaves, he walks directly into the camera, again blurring the focus before the scene dissolves in but another of the film's repeated and unconventional strikes at the traditional reality illusion of Hollywood film.

Still, we can describe Hammer's investigation, perhaps with a bit of ironic justification, as a kind of in-depth exploration. As Velda describes his usual process, "First you find a little thread, the thread leads you to a piece of string, the string leads to a rope, and from the rope you hang by the neck." In the labyrinthine quality this remark suggests, *Kiss Me Deadly* recalls many other detective-type noirs, as Hammer goes from one lead to another. The frequent shots of him carefully checking the hallways of his apartment building or Christina's former rooms, walking the streets of Los Angeles, and looking through seedy buildings for Lily Carver and Carmen Trivago emphasize his efforts to thread this labyrinth in the fashion of so many of his cinematic predecessors. But much of this movement, like Stan's in *Nightmare*, seems nearly pointless, a stylized rendering of the work of detection, depth exploration as convention. The real key to his investigation is a far different in-depth movement—literally looking inside Christina's body to locate a key she swallowed. This grotesque "internal" investigation, this ultimate movement within, counterpoints Hammer's physical movement and suggests the sort of "dead" end, the morbid satisfactions to which the detective's conventional moves often lead.

That sense of our generic desires and satisfactions may be best imaged, though, in the "great whatsit," the long sought-after box that Hammer finally locates. Just what is the "great whatsit"? Aldrich never lets us see; the box's contents remain something of a mystery—and a problem for anyone who has to explain to all-too-literal-minded students what sort of unstable atomic matter it holds. All we do see when first Mike and then Gabrielle open it is a brilliant and painful light. Yet this light seems a fitting image for a film that tries to penetrate the depths of our films and our culture, for it suggests at once the blinding power of those cultural images we hide away and the potential light of the cinema, as it tries to illuminate the depths of our world. No simple depiction of fissionable matter, the "great whatsit" evokes both the corrosive norm and explosive possibility of our cinema. This surprising box of light serves up just what we desire—or deserve—or at least what Aldrich thinks we need to see.

Kiss Me Deadly closes with an appropriately in-depth image, that of a beach in the foreground and Dr. Soberin's house in the background, silhouetted against a dark sky as it explodes. The composition fits with what we generically expect and what the film's send-up of cinematic language offers. A wounded Mike rescues Velda from a locked room as the house burns, and a subsequent long shot of the house exploding seems coded to satisfy our conventional desires, to tell the usual story of background and foreground: it would establish the hero and his girl escaping, leaving the deadly house in the background, and running to the sanctuary of the beach in the foreground. But no couple enters the foreground; no one is saved; no neat resolution implausibly follows; no satisfactory coda attaches to these terrible events. We simply end with a series of long shots that show total destruction and, fittingly, a "The End" title which, in place of the expected hero and heroine, itself moves to close-up and definitively shuts the door on the sort of exploration of depth classical films usually offer.[4] In probing the depths of the mystery he stumbles upon, in trying to fathom the implications of the "great whatsit," Mike Hammer accomplishes little, partly because he is, as Arnold and Miller note, "such an obvious fraud" (40), not much of a detective.

In its efforts to investigate our modern condition, to probe our human depths, this film locates an equally unavailing and fraudulent dimension in our movies, especially our typical genre works. For they too at times get caught up with surfaces: with generic conventions and characters, with predictable plot moves, with classical patterns of reality construction. But with its own reflexive turn, *Kiss Me Deadly* manages something more, something which the film noir was moving toward. It finds its own depths to probe in the constructed space of the cinema and of generic storytelling that it has excavated for our inspection.

IV

In bringing together this congery of cultural, psychic, and aesthetic depths that mark the film noir, I cover much ground that is probably fairly familiar. Perhaps I also prove Jean Baudrillard's accusation that "In America. . . space. . . is the very form of thought" (16). But my "spaciness"—recounting the familiar and thinking not so much in typical ideological terms but in terms of depth—might be helpful. For in this way we might better see what is paradoxically on the surface and yet, thanks to its nearness, at times seemingly deeply buried and unaccounted for, a way in which, even in their familiar generic moves, noir films have managed to challenge mainstream cinema. Or perhaps it might be better to think of them as a kind of primal assault on various sorts of security we have come to expect in our films: a cultural security, a psychological security, and an aesthetic security, lodged in our notions of genre and classical narrative. For while these films seem to work at the traditional task of linking the "out there" with the "in here," depth with showy surface, deep concerns with a satisfying, unifying coda, they do so in a way that interrogates the linkage, and that thus leaves us, as it were, still caught within their own depths. And if the challenging nature of these films is not quite new, the manner in which they manage this challenge deserves more exploration.

Kiss Me Deadly: A haughty Lily Carver (Gaby Rodgers) stands by as Doc Kennedy (Percy Helton) puts his hand out for a pay-off, as an annoyed Mike Hammer (Ralph Meeker) realizes that he's not the only one asking, "What's in it for me?"

Paul Virilio has described what he terms a "crisis in the conceptualization of 'narrative'" in our time, a "crisis" that is "the other side of the crisis of the conceptualization of 'dimension' as geometrical narrative, the discourse of measurement of a reality visibly offered to all" (24). What I have done here is simply follow Virilio backwards, read his notion retrospectively—and a bit playfully. His point, I gather, is that in recent times, thanks to the increasing sense of speed of all events, our sense of space, of dimension has become distorted and problematic, and with it all that we conceptually model on that previously "sure" foundation has revealed its equally insecure footing. Architecture, the graphic arts, even narrative itself—everything that draws on a kind of spatial conceit, that we conceive of in terms of extension, dimension, and *depth* reflects this ongoing change in our sense of reality—and an increasing anxiety that attends it. That anxiety follows from a variety of uncertainties about our world and ourselves, the sort of uncertainties that have always been noir's stylistic and thematic stock-in-trade.

While Virilio's remark aims at a postmodern rather than postwar culture, the film noir, when read in this context, seems prescient. In the 1940s and 1950s it not only spoke symptomatically of postwar disenchantment and alienation, but also sensed other sorts of cultural "crisis" that still lay largely beneath the surface. Obviously, the America that emerged from the war was but distantly related to prewar society, and that of the Korean War even less so. And our ability to address that world adequately through our cinema would increasingly be called into question. That dubiousness had to do not simply with our subjects of public discourse, as we noted, but with a deep uncertainty about whether we even had a language to address these anxieties adequately, a way of measuring, articulating, or depicting them. And behind that anxiety lay yet a larger problem we would increasingly confront, the problem film always has to face, that of reality itself, its slippery and even evanescent nature, its tendency to disappear even as it seems constructed for us in such depth and affirmed by all the conventions of dimensionality.

The classical film noir responds to those cultural, personal, and aesthetic anxieties of the era, while it also points to this larger confrontation with the real that seems to power the recent resurgence of this form. In various ways, it draws much of the pattern of film narrative near the surface, thereby making us more conscious of how it works. Film's conventional armory of invisibility—cuts on action, glance-object shifts, eyeline matches, subjective shot identification, etc., all designed to help the narrative seem natural and self-revealing rather than manipulated and manipulating—begins to call attention to itself. Similarly, its conventionalized subjects and stories, like the ever so clever and resilient private eye and his beautiful girl Friday, or the mystery that is never too deep or unavailing to be unraveled or explained away, start to seem affected and calculated. In effect, a deep pattern, a cinematic repressed, if you will, rises from its depths to be seen in a new light.

While the works examined here hardly capture the full range of film noir, they do reflect a growing awareness of something that had gone repressed and that needed to be drawn up from the depths and, like Mike's "great whatsit," opened up and reassessed. That is the way in which the cinema itself had become a kind of unexamined psychic mechanism, a dark pool of dreams of the sort that *Nightmare* so effectively visualizes in its opening scene: one that defined our desires, fashioned a language through which we vaguely understood our world, and constructed us as consumers of what it had to offer. In the post-war era, we seemed to be awakening to—or from—these depths. And with the film noir, thanks to its penchant for looking into the dark, for plumbing our world's depths, for employing great depth of field, for drawing up close the very language of cinema, we had a tool that could help in such a reassessment—in a psychodrama of cinema itself.

WORKS CITED

Edward T. Arnold and Eugene L. Miller, *The Films and Career of Robert Aldrich*, Knoxville: University of Tennessee Press, 1986.

Jean Baudrillard, *America*, Translated by Chris Turner, London: Verso, 1988.

David Bordwell, Janet Staiger, and Kristin Thompson, *The Classical Hollywood Cinema: Film Style and Mode of Production to 1960*, New York: Columbia University Press, 1985.

Laurence Miller, "The Central Role of Insanity in Film noir," paper presented at the 19th Annual Florida State University Conference on Literature and Film, Jan. 27, 1994, Tallahassee, FL.

Janey L. Place, and Lowell S. Peterson, "Some Visual Motifs of Film noir" (1974), reprinted in *Film Noir Reader*, editors Alain Silver, James Ursini, New York: Limelight, 1996, pp. 64-75.

Paul Schrader, "notes on film noir" (1972), reprinted in *Film Noir Reader*, pp. 52-63.

J.P. Telotte, *Voices in the Dark: The Narrative Patterns of Film Noir*, Urbana: University of Illinois Press, 1989.

Jon Tuska, *Dark Cinema: American Film Noir in Cultural Perspective*, Westport: Greenwood Press, 1984.

Paull Virilio, *Lost Dimension*, translator Daniel Moshenberg, New York: Semiotext(e), 1991.

NOTES

1. As one of the key components of a noir "stylistics," Paul Schrader describes the "love of romantic narration" that seems to characterize a number of the most important films of this type [see page 95 above]. Working from his assessment, many critics seem to assume that the voice-over, flashback style is the typical method of noir narration and have come to include it in any catalogue of noir's "generic" traits, even though it occurs in only a small portion of those films we typically label "noir."

2. We should note the complementary imagery of the conscious and unconscious mind that attends this narrative play of surface and depth. Rene, who deals in logic and rational explanations, builds a boat in his spare time. Stan, who is nearly swallowed up by his traumatized psyche, is almost drowned by the hypnotist who has been manipulating him.

3. As is also the case with *Kiss Me Deadly*, *In a Lonely Place*'s dissection of the film industry represents a major shift in emphasis from the Dorothy B. Hughes novel on which it is based.

4. There has always been much debate about the ending to *Kiss Me Deadly*, an ending that for many, steeped in the conventions of classical detective films, never seemed quite satisfactory or "right." The recent release of a new version of the film with a different ending restored—one showing Mike and Velda still alive in the surf—confirms that a more conventionally "correct" ending was shot, although it remains one that seems ill-paired with the rest of the narrative. And of course even that "happy" ending simply leaves unexplored the eventual fate of these characters who have "escaped" to but a few yards away from what seems a nuclear explosion.

Hammer sneers at both Friday (Marian Carr) and Charlie Max (Jack Elam).

Rita Hayworth in her iconic pose as *Gilda*.

Manufacturing Heroines: Gothic Victims and Working Women in Classic Noir Films

Sheri Chinen Biesen (2004)

While much has been made about the sexual "femme fatale" temptress in classic noir films, female images in many of these pictures also included "good girl" victims (or "redeemers') and "working girls" or career women. In these film noirs of the classical Hollywood studio era, images of female stars were often, in fact, "manufactured" by creative and executive men who held positions of power within the motion picture production system. The screen personas of women in 1940s noir films evolved from the proto-noir gothic redeemer and the hard-boiled femme fatale, to a more multifaceted working career woman as America entered World War II. As the war progressed, these images eventually coincided with a number of women gaining greater power in creative and executive positions in Hollywood—and in many classic film noir productions.

An interesting case in point is Joan Fontaine, a female star very much "manufactured" by men, who embodied the gothic heroine in Alfred Hitchcock's proto-noir *Rebecca* (1940) and *Suspicion* (1941). Fontaine epitomized the noir redeemer "woman as victim" and Hitchcock's psychological thrillers *Rebecca* and *Suspicion* initiated the female gothic film cycle (which continued with *Shadow of a Doubt*, *Spellbound* and *Notorious*—an interestingly dark hybrid of the female gothic and wartime espionage thriller) that is linked to film noir. Like hard-boiled "serie noir," the term "film noir" was also derived from "roman noir," or "black novel," which 18th and 19th century French critics called the British gothic novel. As in film noir, gender distress, psychic trauma (or insanity) and misogyny were intrinsic to gothic thrillers. The gender distress of film noir and gothic thrillers crystallized amid the cultural disruption of World War II. Female hysteria and crimes of passion

"..."an interesting case in point,"
Joan Fontaine in *Rebecca*.

were hallmarks of the gothic roman noir. Both *Rebecca* and *Suspicion* cleverly used psychology and high-lighted the female point-of-view of the heroine's psyche to gain endorsement from Hollywood's Production Code censors and critical Academy Award acclaim, despite a gothic premise portraying husbands committing crime—in *Rebecca* "accidentally" murdering, or in *Suspicion* "appearing" to intentionally poison, their wives.[1]

By 1941, Hitchcock and Fontaine (as well as actresses Ingrid Bergman and Vivian Leigh) were under contract to independent film producer David O. Selznick, a powerful Hollywood "talent broker" who profitably loaned his director and female stars to various Hollywood studios. After Fontaine's success as naive gothic ingenue in *Rebecca*, RKO borrowed Hitchcock and Fontaine for *Suspicion*, then paid Selznick a lucrative $116,750 for the actress. (Selznick loaned out his contract female star and paid her a mere $17,833 salary, then noted: "I don't care...so much about how much she makes as I do about making sure we keep her in line."[2]—Selznick's nearly $100,000 profit from loaning Fontaine to RKO indicates he cared about both power and money.) Fontaine had lobbied Hitchcock for the role with a personal handwritten card to "Dear, darling Hitch." The actress pleaded, "I must do that picture...I am even willing to play the part for no salary, if necessary."[3] Selznick retaliated to Fontaine in a nine page letter in August 1940 to a "very dear, very young Joan...After all...I have gone through to get you out of the frustrated bitplayer-and-second-lead-in-Republic-Westerns status in which you had found yourself" which regrettably most studios felt was her "maximum due. Too many people in Hollywood...know of your work before 'Rebecca,'" and the "unprecedented and expensive steps which I took." Selznick substantiated his "expensive investment" in Fontaine, as star commodity "developed as a result of a risk and a gamble that I took...against the unanimous opinion of everyone inside and outside our company, including Hitch"[4]—implying this opposition to her was held by all of Hollywood.

Here, male executive authority and the gender dynamics of the production process underscored the narrative gender distress central to the proto-noir female gothic thriller. Men had power, made decisions, and determined how women were represented on screen. In fact, a *Ladies Home Journal* article, "Star Factory,"

Fontaine is again a gothic victim for producer David O. Selznick, with Cary Grant in *Suspicion*.

traced the "manufacturing process" of female stars with photos of Fontaine being trained, groomed and refined by RKO studio as a "finished product, a masterpiece created and sold by Hollywood's master craftsmen."[5] Fontaine's depiction as feminine commodity illustrates how Hollywood studios groomed contract acting personnel to enhance performance, via a process to create "talent," produce and "construct" star persona, and promote female actresses into starlets while male actors were publicized as being "natural" and simply "playing themselves." Male studio executive authority sculpted female stars. Fontaine (as raw starlet material) was "developed" and "made" into a star by Selznick, and her persona was constructed and "molded" by both Selznick and Hitchcock. During *Rebecca*, Fontaine's first production for the independent producer, Selznick wrote: "For months now I have been trying to tell everybody connected with 'REBECCA' that what I wanted in the girl, especially in the first part, was an <u>un</u>glamorous creature, but one sufficiently pretty and appealing, in a simple girlish way, to understand why Maxim would marry her...<u>not</u> glamorous."[6]

There were even turf disputes over who could rightly claim credit for discovering and developing Fontaine. Selznick explicitly warned in a September 1940 memo that Hitchcock "had better not make himself look ridiculous" by claiming to have "developed" Fontaine. Another dispute arose when RKO got wind of *Suspicion*'s potential success. In a November 1941 memo Selznick complained, "RKO has been sending out some annoying stories that would indicate that Fontaine is an RKO discovery and player and that 'SUSPICION' is the climax of her career with them. Just to make matters worse, they talk about her "free lancing," and infer that she was purchased by them as a free lance artist." The very thought of Fontaine's autonomy as a star, or any independence from his development apparatus, posed a threat to Selznick's authority as talent broker. Despite the handsome profit he made off of loaning Fontaine to RKO, Selznick took issue with the studio's attempt to cash in and take credit for the "manufacturing" efforts of his contract star. "I suggest you advise their publicity department that if they don't behave we will have to publicize how RKO threw her out as worthless before I signed her for 'REBECCA.'"[7] *Suspicion* screenwriter Sam Raphaelson also had opinions about Fontaine. "She must carry the whole finish. I think she should rise to an ecstasy unprecedented in the acting career of Miss Fontaine at the second beat when she realizes Johnny didn't kill [his best friend] Beaky." Raphaelson then conceived of her performing a "lyric dance of solemn happiness" at the film's conclusion.[8] (No subtlety here, but quite an imaginative variation on Hitchcock's trademark psychological ambiguity and star performance restraint.)

By the end of *Suspicion*, former comedy star Cary Grant's "dark side" and unpredictably dangerous masculine charisma typifies a mysterious, potentially malignant gothic male other, culminating in the actor's strikingly noir ascent up a shrouded spiral staircase with a deadly glass of poisoned milk to murder his young wife. *Suspicion*'s bleak climax shows an ominous Grant climbing the stairs in a pitch-black room, bringing the lethal drink (lit from inside the glass so it glows in the dark) to Fontaine's bedside. The darkness shadows Grant's face, almost in complete silhouette, lit from below in extremely low-angle "low-key" horror style to demonize his features. Most prewar 1940s American film viewers were not ready for a menacing proto-noir lover-turned-murderer in Grant. Based on preview audience survey cards from 1941, filmgoer reception was decidedly downbeat toward *Suspicion* portraying the actor in a sinister role. "Why ruin Cary Grant on such a long drawn out picture as this? Please put him in more comedies with Irene Dunne." Another viewer actually complained, "the house maid is around the scene entirely too much for her minor position in the story" and argued, "Anyone who has seen some number of moving pictures tends to anticipate her having an affair with Cary Grant." Other viewers protested: "Up to the last scene everyone thought Cary Grant was the murderer so why confuse the entire audience by changing the impression. He should admit to trying to murder her, then after confessing, attempt to murder her."[9]

Although Fontaine's distraught ingenue does not correspond to the classic hard-boiled gender roles of lethal femme fatale—where in a full blown noir narrative an erotic woman would be a sexual predator killing off her male counterpart—her gothic victim can be seen as a psychological prototype for the more passive noir "good girl" redeemer.[10] While many were at a "loss to conceive any possible ending short of an asylum for the heroine," several viewers thought Fontaine should have a stronger role: "she should...kill him in self-defense or escape and be killed during the pursuit." Another called her an "immature, driveling sentimentalist with no conception of real love—just a sex-starved intellectualist grabbing the first man who showed any interest in her," willingly drinking the "supposed poison her husband offers, proclaiming love for her would-be murderer. What sane woman would act that way?" Others complained, "It was a great mistake to put two such actors in a picture that was ridiculous from start to finish...difficult to understand...especially after Joan Fontaine drinks what she thinks is death potion. And how the audience laughed! Did you think Cary Grant's promise to reform at all convincing? I don't think it fooled anyone but the wishy-washy Joan Fontaine." They added, "She should pull a gun out" when she goes to the cliffs at the film's finale "for the purpose of killing him."[11]

Brandishing a weapon certainly suggests crime and combat. Stronger screen images of women would soon coincide with "Rosie the Riveter" and working females in America's wartime homefront. Fontaine would eventually win a Best Actress Oscar for her gothic noir heroine. Released within months of Pearl Harbor, Hitchcock's film was a dark segue of sorts, as Depression-era screwball comedies declined in the early 1940s and hard-hitting crime narratives increased, capturing the gender distress and changing roles of women during this time, and culminating in bleaker films noir by the end of World War II. The increasing film noir style seen in Hollywood's female gothic cycle accelerated over the course of the duration as seen in Hitchcock's noir espionage thriller *Notorious* (1946). How gender (and masculinity) played out on Hollywood screens was significant. The tough, conflicted spirit, narrative corruption and hard-bitten psyche so characteristic of film noir proliferated amid the bleak paranoia and harsher realities of the wartime filmmaking climate in America's increasingly hard-boiled homefront, and—as censorship shifted—the rough and tumble world of pulp fiction detectives that Hollywood could finally adapt with a darker nuanced style during the 1940s.

Images of the hard-boiled femme fatale crystallized in such classic noir films as Billy Wilder's *Double Indemnity* (1944), Tay Garnett's *The Postman Always Rings Twice* (1945-46), Edgar Ulmer's *Detour* (1945), Fritz

Notorious: "...how gender and masculinity play out" in the Hitchcock/Selznick spy narrative where two men vie a woman with a shady past: lovers Cary Grant and Ingrid Bergman confront cuckolded husband and Nazi collaborator Claude Raines.

Lang's *Scarlet Street* (1945) and Howard Hawks' *The Big Sleep* (1945-46). Embodying the evil, alluring "spider woman', Barbara Stanwyck's deadly cool Phyllis Dietrichson calls the shots, disposes of her husband's first wife then the husband himself, manipulates and kills her lover, and generally raises the bar on female badness in *Double Indemnity*. Stanwyck's character in *Double Indemnity*, as well as Lana Turner's lethal Cora in James M. Cain's other "sordid" and censorable novel, *The Postman Always Rings Twice*, was based on a real life femme fatale, Ruth Snyder, who conspired with her lover to brutally murder her husband for insurance money in one of the most sensational tabloid stories of the roaring twenties as her unforgettable image in the electric chair splashed across the front page of *The New York Daily News*.[12] In low-budget cult classic noir, *Detour*, shot in six days at "poverty row" minor studio PRC, Ann Savage's Vera is a no-frills, lowdown venomous shrew and downright "unruly" woman. Joan Bennett's unabashedly irreverent, double-crossing Kitty in *Scarlet Street* is the ultimate duplicitous temptress. These images of women were often created and developed by men.

Joan Bennett as "ultimate duplicitous temptress" Kitty with Dan Duryea as Johnny in *Scarlet Street*.

In *The Big Sleep*, producer-director Howard Hawks "manufactures" and glamorizes Martha Vickers' dangerous and petulant femme Carmen Sternwood to such wonderful perfection that she almost outshines her more well-behaved sister Vivian, played by sultry co-star Lauren Bacall. Hawks was, of course, key in discovering Bacall, hiring the former cover girl as a contract female star commodity for his independent production company, then grooming and manufacturing "The Look" as a husky noir siren opposite Humphrey Bogart in *To Have and Have Not* (1944). Hawks also signed another beautiful young ingenue, Ella Raines, as the major asset of his other independent production company. Like Selznick, Hawks purchased, "owned', developed and refined new feminine star talent, then sold his actresses' contract to various Hollywood studios and made a profit. Hawks sold Raines to Universal for the noir picture *Phantom Lady* (1944), then sold Bacall to Warner Bros. after her success in *To Have and Have Not*, while filming *The Big Sleep*. However, Bennett's strikingly bold femme fatale in *Scarlet Street* is not only a feminine persona and product "manufactured" by men (such as filmmaker Lang and producer Walter Wanger, Bennett's husband). The female star, in fact, enjoyed greater creative and executive influence as a business partner in the independent production company that produced *Scarlet Street*.[13]

Images of noir women also become more multifaceted. As early as 1940, Boris Ingster's modest B film *Stranger on the Third Floor* presents a noir heroine (Margaret Tallichet as Jane) who is not a sexual temptress, but rather a respectable working girl who even functions as a female detective solving the murderous crime in finding—and nearly becoming victim to—Peter Lorre's psychopathic throat-slashing murderer who turns out to be an insane asylum escapee. Even the women in Hawks' *The Big Sleep*, co-scripted by female screenwriter Leigh Brackett, are more nuanced as the noir picture showcases a variety of working girls—from taxi drivers to rare book clerks (including Dorothy Malone's film debut) to Bacall (Vivian) singing in gambler Eddie Mars' casino cabaret. In fact, in Robert Siodmak's *Phantom Lady*, Raines' working noir heroine, Kansas, epitomizes the female detective who not only tracks down criminals, but also takes time off her job to disguise herself and play the role of a more sexual "loose" femme fatale to solve the case and clear her boss from the chair for allegedly murdering his wife. This active female character coincided with a homefront audience of working wartime women, and was also the product of Hitchcock protege, writer-producer Joan Harrison, who co-scripted Hitchcock's roman noir gothic films *Rebecca* and *Suspicion*.[14]

Another example of a working noir heroine is Gene Tierney's "good girl" turned advertising executive in Otto Preminger's classic, *Laura* (1944). As a successful career woman, Laura Hunt is a fascinating character that is complex, elusive, yet almost ethereal, like a ghost or supernatural spirit that seemingly haunts the narrative and whom no one in the film really understands. The film begins as Laura is perceived to be brutally murdered in her own apartment and a detective proceeds to piece together various stories to solve the crime. She turns out to be alive, but remains mysterious and absent from the first half of the film despite the fact that she appears in her painted portrait, in flashback memories and in fantasies of the male characters' imagination of her. Ultimately, we are introduced to the character Laura through her image as it is constructed in the minds of the men around her. She becomes an object that many different male characters (from a wide variety of social backgrounds and classes) aspire to, seek to attain and even kill for.

However, while Laura is ephemeral, there are appealing facets to her noir heroine; Tierney captures the human "every woman" quality of Laura's character, tapping in to homefront working women, while simultaneously appearing otherworldly. Yet, in many ways, she is not fully formed. As the story unfolds this absentee career girl becomes an ambiguous figure whose very nature is suspect. While Laura is characterized by those around her as a sweet, warm and earnest "all-American" girl-next-door, she demonstrates that she is secretive and is also capable of duplicitous behavior. It is not exactly clear as the film progresses whether she is a femme fatale who commits murder and lies to detectives (and whose motives are called into question), or whether she is an innocent victim with good intentions who serves as a "redeemer" for the crooked men in her life. In fact, as the film *Laura* fuses a gothic thriller narrative with a hard-boiled detective story, Tierney's noir heroine becomes all of these things: bad girl, good girl, working woman and male fantasy.

Opposite, top, *Phantom Lady*: Ella Raines goes under cover as Kansas. Below, *Laura*: Gene Tierney (left) as the title character and Clifton Webb as Waldo Lydecker.

Laura's reappearance "from the dead" in the doorway of her dark apartment transpires like a dream. Dana Andrews' detective (Mark) is lost in the fragile beauty of her portrait and has drifted into unconsciousness to ponder her deceased visage. At that point, it is not even clear to Mark (or viewers) whether he is awake or in a trance, or whether the female figure before him is real or just a figment of his imagination. When it becomes clear that she is Laura "in the flesh'—very much alive and not a masculine fantasy—we realize there may be a disparity between her image, in mind and on canvas, and the real woman. Laura becomes a kind of mythic noir heroine who contradicts her mystique (while ironically adding to it) with her sudden mysterious appearance. Yet, we don't really know who she is, and neither does Andrews' detective Mark. Her entry calls every crime-solving fact (and our understanding of her character and the film's story) into question as she uproots the detective's methodical piecing together of the case. Moreover, in creating a new dilemma of mistaken identity, Laura's belated arrival implicates her for the murder of another woman (with her fiancé) in her own apartment.

Ultimately, Preminger's film is as much about deciphering who Laura is as it is about solving a murder crime. The "myth" and mystery of Laura, and of her ever-present image in the painting, reinforce the disparity between a projected female persona and the unraveling layers of who she is. Laura's character is, in fact, "manufactured" not only by the men in the narrative, but also by the male production executives involved in

Below, moments before Det. Mark McPherson (Dana Andrews) awakens [see also moments later on page 29], Gene Tierney's Laura appears in the flesh to fulfill her status as a mythic noir heroine.

making the film. Twentieth Century-Fox studio chief Darryl Zanuck had very distinct and different ideas about the nature of her female gothic crime heroine than did the film's producer-director Otto Preminger. Zanuck was influential in developing *Laura* more fully and in removing Tierney's voice-over narration by her character that was originally in Vera Caspary's 1943 novel and in early versions of the studio's film adaptation. Zanuck urged Preminger to expand *Laura*'s noir heroine beyond a naive gothic ingenue victim, yet maintain enough fresh innocence where she does not realize how much trouble she is in, but to avoid making her a cheap tramp or loose femme fatale.[15] Preminger considered Laura a more sexual woman of the night. The creative tension between Zanuck and Preminger added more depth and intrigue to Tierney's screen character. Laura's evolution from career woman to dream girl fantasy to deceitful femme and finally a more multifaceted variation of the gothic victim by the end of the film—almost killed but ultimately redeemed by Waldo's (Clifton Webb) murderous attempt on her life (proving her innocence)—is fascinating. Laura emerges as a contradictory noir heroine with flaws, virtues and dimensions that do not fit the classical mold of hard-boiled femme fatale, and whose feminine presence permeates the film.

Like *Laura*, *Phantom Lady* and *Gilda* (1946), *Mildred Pierce* (1945) is a film noir that employs conventions of "roman noir" gothic melodrama in its central "working" redeemer character. Such noir films as *Laura*, *Gilda* and *Mildred Pierce* revolve around a female protagonist whose presence is so intrinsic to the film that she not only structures the story, but also becomes the namesake of the entire picture. The character of Mildred Pierce, an unhappy housewife and mother of two daughters, embodies the noir redeemer and gradually evolves into a Rosie-the-Riveter style career woman when her husband leaves her and she builds her own business to support her family. The active female lead role was an ideal comeback vehicle for former-diva, Joan Crawford. A woman also contributed to the film's production. Screenwriter Catherine Turney was involved in adapting James M. Cain's novel, yet male Hollywood executives such as Warner Bros. producer Jerry Wald masculinized the story to turn it into a detective crime film.[16] Like *Laura*, the picture becomes a "who done it', where the noir heroine is implicated. Mildred's character is, in fact, suspected of murder through the entire picture as the film literally opens with a bang and the crumbling man who has been shot in the dark calls out "Mildred" before he falls and dies.

Mildred is presented as an amalgam of noir redeemer, working woman and a mysterious, possibly guilty, femme fatale who carries on with other (shady) men, remarries a con artist, spoils one daughter (who becomes a monster) and neglects the other (who dies). Mildred even seemingly admits her guilt when she almost attempts suicide shortly after the murder before she is interrogated by police detectives. *Mildred Pierce* combines female melodrama with a hard-boiled detective narrative to create a noir heroine that, like Laura Hunt, defies conventional notions of a gothic redeemer or femme fatale. Yet, Crawford, who won a Best Actress Oscar for the role, portrays Mildred as a humane, compassionate character who is ultimately victimized not only by the dubious men who betray her for money once she achieves success in her career, but also by her spoiled, ruthless and greedy daughter who, after running off to pursue a cabaret career and stealing her husband, turns out to be the actual lethal femme murderess (for whom Mildred is willing to take the blame).

Gilda is yet another classic noir film which is a variation of a female gothic melodrama and a more hard-boiled gangster detective crime narrative. Rita Hayworth's bold performance as wild sex siren is an exceedingly memorable character whose presence lives on well beyond the film as one of the all-time great classic femme fatales. Gilda was, in fact, a woman with much bravado accentuating her smoldering sensuality, who was also terribly vulnerable and treated sadistically. Hayworth's charismatic heroine was an erotic role that was "manufactured" and emphasized by a powerful creative executive woman involved in the production of the film, producer (and former writer) Virginia Van Upp who was also head of production at Columbia studio in 1945 (through 1947).[17] As Hayworth's real life marriage to Orson Welles unraveled during the making of the film, Van Upp had a close relationship with female lead Hayworth, mentored the star and supervised the writing of the project (by screenwriter Marion Parsonnet) while producing the picture. When compared to earlier gothic heroines ('manufactured" and refined by more male-dominated filmmaking personnel such as Selznick and Hitchcock with Fontaine) women more actively involved in such creative or executive positions as writing

A furred, bejeweled, and pensive Joan Crawford as the title character in *Mildred Pierce*, "...an amalgam of noir redeemer, working woman and a mysterious, possibly guilty, femme fatale."

or producing noir films—whether writer Brackett on *The Big Sleep*, Turney on *Mildred Pierce*, Harrison producing *Phantom Lady* or Van Upp producing *Gilda*—contributed to more fully-developed and unpredictable noir heroines who were more complex and assertive (often non-traditional "working" career women) variations on the conventional femme fatale.

Although just as Tierney's Laura is surrounded by men who find her sexually attractive and consorts with many of them, on another level *Mildred Pierce* and *Gilda* are female-centered noir stories that become sex melodramas. Mildred is having affairs with men—although they (Mildred's opportunistic suitors) are the sexual aggressors, while Mildred is reluctant and far more interested in material success for the purpose of indulging and impressing her irresponsible daughter. Gilda, on the other hand, appears to be more brazen. She is far more openly defiant and cognizant of her own sexuality, and irreverent in her active pursuit of her independence. As a dangerous femme, Gilda is deviant in using the power of her erotic female image to arouse and manipulate men for her own pleasure. Hayworth's character Gilda strives to be a "working girl" pursuing a career singing, dancing and performing strip tease in a cabaret of wildly ecstatic male patrons. Despite her transgressive behavior, however, like the female gothic ingenue, Gilda is not evil or malicious, but instead a victim of the misogynistic, violent men around her as she becomes involved in a series of bizarre, dysfunctional relationships that accentuate her gender distress. She marries a mysterious crime boss who owns a gambling casino, taunts and tantalizes her ex-lover who manages her husband's illegal business affairs, then eventually weds her ex-flame when the kingpin is suspected dead. Marital bliss is rather a wedded nightmare for Gilda as she becomes a virtual prisoner of her twisted heterosexual relations in these domestic unions. Like Laura Hunt and Mildred Pierce, Hayworth's character Gilda transcends her diva sexuality and image as a femme who men desire to evolve into a sympathetic, multidimensional noir heroine. She is human, has flaws and even exhibits self-destructive behavior.

In *Gilda*, Van Upp and Hayworth create a complex noir female protagonist who simultaneously embodies an independent woman, a victim, a redeemer, an active "working" girl pursuing a career of sorts (albeit interrupted), and a sexual femme fatale wreaking havoc in men's lives (as they battle their own demons). However, in ultimately defying lethal femme stereotypes, this dangerous classic noir woman has a heart. Like the other "manufactured" noir heroines of *Suspicion*, *Stranger on the Third Floor*, *Laura*, *The Big Sleep*, *Phantom Lady*, and *Mildred Pierce*, Gilda's provocative and alluring image as quintessential 1940s femme fatale—like Hayworth's famous wartime pin-up poster—is ultimately all for show, an act, a masquerade to save her pride (and no doubt appease censors). Her sexual exploits are allegedly not for real, just meant to emotionally hurt her tormented beau (Glenn Ford) with whom she has a history. In the end, Gilda actually turns out to be a "good girl" (despite her "bad girl" image) who is less naive than other gothic redeemers (such as Fontaine in *Suspicion*), and more comfortable with her own sexuality, but who ultimately tames her "unruly" independence, makes amends and gets together with her man—in a noir finale where the Hollywood couple disappears into the dark.

NOTES

1. "Last night I dreamt I went to Manderley again." These words, conjuring an eerie recollection of a heroine's past, opened Daphne du Maurier's gothic novel *Rebecca*, providing a prelude to the voice-over narration found in film noir. Du Maurier's story—a masterwork of infidelity, dysfunctional sexual relationships, and domestic murder—drew fire from chief censor Joseph Breen in Hollywood's Production Code office when Selznick purchased the screen rights to produce it. Disquietly embedded in these gothic thriller films was, as Thomas Elsaesser explains, an "oblique intimation of female frigidity producing strange fantasies of persecution, rape and death—masochistic reveries and nightmares, which cast the husband into the role of sadistic murderer." The female gothic film cycle developed dark stylistics and revolved around what Thomas Schatz calls "gender difference, sexual identity, and the 'gender distress' which accompanied the social and cultural disruption of the war and postwar eras." Like hard-boiled detective narratives, the gothic centered on an "essentially good though flawed and vulnerable protagonist at odds with a mysterious and menacing sexual other." In the gothic, a young innocent female meets,

Above, as in *Notorious,* two men (Glenn Ford and George Macready, foreground) one older, one younger, vie for the affections of Rita Hayword as *Gilda*, "a complex noir female protagonist who simultaneously embodies an independent woman, a victim, a redeemer, an active 'working' girl pursuing a career of sorts."

has an affair and marries a suave enigmatic stranger. Her charming but mysterious older lover or husband, with a dubious past and with secrets to conceal, becomes an alluring but potentially predatorial sexual presence. Thomas Schatz, *Boom and Bust: American Cinema in the 1940s*, (History of American Cinema, Volume 6: 1940-1949), Scribners, 1997, pp. 233-236. Grant's menacing performance in *Suspicion* personified a masculine sexual predator. (And off-screen, as an independent freelance star with his choice of roles at different studios, Grant enjoyed significantly more control over his career than did Fontaine.) Misogynism and a masochistic self-destruc-tive protagonist's point-of-view magnified gender and sexual distress in gothic thrillers. These psychological impulses and a subjective point-of-view extended into film noir, structuring and framing increasingly hard-boiled crime narratives on screen. Hitchcock's gothics *Rebecca* and *Suspicion* even embedded misogynism into the filmmaking process. Hitchcock put Fontaine through his "finishing school" on the set of *Rebecca*, yet she received an icy reception from the rest of the cast. Hitchcock and Selznick used intimidation tactics to make it clear that actor Lawrence Olivier wanted Vivien Leigh (soon to be his wife) in the lead female role. The verisimilitude of Fontaine's shy, naive—progressively emotive—ingenue performance on- and off-camera contributes to the gothic melodrama's narrative excess and patriarchally-coded "hysteria." In *Rebecca*, Fontaine is a mousy (albeit working) female companion who quits her job to marry a charming wife-murderer and costumes herself in flouncy ball gowns by the end of the film. Her character in *Suspicion* is initially a more bookish (even comparatively androgynous) intellectual at the opening of the narrative who becomes increasingly hysterical (like her role in *Rebecca*); Fontaine is gradually glamorized as the film progresses, eventually feminized in frilly diaphanous negligees by the time Grant brings "poisoned" milk to her bedside in what she imagines is an attempt to murder her.

2. David O. Selznick Archive, HRC 8-40. Drawing on 1930s horror cycles, Hitchcock's gothic *Suspicion* invoked progressively bleak film noir style. Featuring an ominous image of Cary Grant, "charming enough to make any woman love him...desperate enough to ruin the life of the woman he loved," publicity noted the *"terror"* Grant, "at his dramatic best," inspired in heroine Joan Fontaine.

3. Alfred Hitchcock Collection, MHL (undated).

4. Selznick, 8-40. Selznick indeed launched Fontaine's career; yet, the discourse he activated to keep his star in line was startling in its severity.

5. Eric Ergenbright and Jack Smalley, "Star Factory," *Ladies Home Journal*, 1937. See also Cynthia Baron, "Manufacturing Starlets But Teaching Actors the Tricks of the Trade: A Look at Popular Discourse in the Classical Hollywood Era," University of Southern California, Los Angeles, 1996.

6. Selznick, pp. 10-39.

7. Selznick, pp. 11-41. He added, "If they don't behave, any future deals with RKO will include a clause that we will get the same credit in publicity and advertising that we have on the screen."

8. Raphaelson in Hitchcock, pp. 6-41.

9. Hitchcock, pp. 6-41.

10. See Janey Place, "Women in film noir," in E. Ann Kaplan, ed., *Women in Film Noir* (London: BFI, 1980).

11. Hitchcock, pp. 6-41.

12. Sheri Chinen Biesen, "Censorship, Film Noir and *Double Indemnity*," *Film and History,* 25:1-2, 1995; Sheri Chinen Biesen, "Raising Cain with the Censors Again: The Postman Always Rings Twice," *Literature/Film Quarterly*, 28:1, 2000.

13. Thomas Schatz, *The Genius of the System*, (NY: Simon and Schuster, 1988); Sheri Chinen Biesen, "Bogart, Bacall, Howard Hawks and Wartime Film Noir at Warner Bros.: To Have and Have Not and The Big Sleep," *Popular Culture Review*, 13.1, 2002.

14. Lizzie Francke, *Script Girls* (London: BFI 1994); Sheri Chinen Biesen, "Joan Harrison, Virginia Van Upp and Women Behind-the-Scenes in Wartime Hollywood Film Noir," *Quarterly Review of Film and Video*, 20.2, 2003.

15. Darryl Zanuck, Twentieth Century-Fox Collection, USC 11-43.

16. Warner Bros. Archive.

17. See Biesen, Francke.

"Alfred Hitchcock has confessed his familiarity with the German films of Murnau and Lang..." as is evident in one of his "first entries in the noir series, *Suspicion*."

The Strange Case of Film Noir

Robert G. Porfirio (2012)

When I first began teaching a college course in film noir and researching it for my doctoral dissertation in the early seventies there was little on the subject in English and only one book-length study, Borde and Chaumeton's yet-to-be translated monograph. Now, over thirty years later, there are numerous courses on the subject and a voluminous amount of written material in English, French, and many other languages. While I find the acclaim presently given film noir at both academic and popular levels a bit surprising, what is even more surprising to me is that film noir is still a contestable topic. Back then I would have thought that by now all ontological and epistemological controversies would be settled, yet the debate rages on, among scholars and fans alike. It is indeed tempting to simply give up the chase and agree with Peter Wollen who quipped that film noir is whatever Borde and Chaumeton say it is. But if there is no consensus it's certainly not due to any lack of effort on the part of Alain Silver, who, from the publication of the groundbreaking first edition of *Film Noir An Encyclopedic Reference to the American Style* in 1979 through subsequent editions and revisions and a series of *Film Noir Readers,* has attempted, at the very least, to provide us with a sense of film noir if not a precise definition thereof,[1] And while that sense seems to favor film noir as a film movement, no extended case for such has found its way to publication, though it was been touched upon by others, myself included.[2]

In arguing for such a conception I am, understandably, restricting our attention to what of late has been termed the "classic period" of American film noir as opposed to that group of films now called neo-noir—a term coined by Todd Erickson who distinguishes them from classic film noir primarily by virtue of their use of new cinematic techniques and a self-consciousness generated by the awareness of contemporary filmmakers that they are working within an established "noir" convention.

Erickson (correctly in my estimation) makes the case that because of this self-consciousness classic film noir has generated an offspring, neo-noir, which today takes on all the auspices of a genre.[3] How could it be otherwise? For once the defining "marks" of a particular cultural practice are recognized and deemed marketable there is the inevitable rush to popularize and peddle as practice becomes product, and art movements are certainly no exception (surrealism being a prime example). Indeed, it was in the 1930s that the major commercial film genres (western, romance, comedy, gangster, horror, detective/mystery, swashbuckler, etc.) were established, as "Hollywood" became a global system and sought to capture and hold domestic and international markets alike through the use of formulaic practices.[4] If anything, classic film noir represents an attempt to break with those formulaic practices as Borde and Chaumeton and other French cinéastes pointed out so early on. Yet by virtue of its own transgressive nature the noir cycle was doomed. For as the transgressive aspects of film noir became conventionalized, as the beleaguered Production Code finally gave way to the rating system, and as newer production techniques replaced the old, classic film noir disappeared until its rebirth as neo-noir in the late 1960s. Ironically, for a term that was virtually unknown in America during the classic period even among the filmmakers themselves (Robert Aldrich being the exception), in the postmodern era film noir is the driving force behind what James Naremore has termed the "noir mediascape,"[5] just as the terms "noir" and "noired" have become popularized.

The problems inherent in trying to pin down film noir as a specific genre or style of filmmaking have been discussed at some length by Alain Silver and other critics over the years, and there is no need here to cover that ground again.[6] Since film historians of a sociological persuasion have given us the notion of film movements—a class of phenomena typically more restricted to a given social context and period—why should we not investigate film noir along those lines, especially if it is less problematic than other approaches? Film movements, of course, bear some resemblance to the more universalized aesthetic notion of art movements. Film sociologists, however, point out that film movements tend to be more tied to a specific time and culture and so they prefer to conceive of them in terms of Anthony F.C. Wallace's notion of "revitalization movements" ("deliberate and self-conscious attempt to provide a more satisfying culture").[7] So far four such phenomena have been identified: German expressionism, Soviet "expressive realism,"[8] Italian neo-realism, and the French New Wave. As a film movement, then film noir can be conceived along the lines of a pervasive effect (rather than a restrictive genre) and located within a specific sociocultural context and temporal scheme, with the traditional stages of ascent (1940-1945), peak (1946-1950), and slow decline (1951-1960).

While there are problems inherent in treating film noir as a film movement (not the least of which is that the term itself was a post facto classification), they can, I believe, be overcome, and the advantages of such a conceptual model far outweigh the disadvantages. For one thing it allows us to isolate classic film noir as a distinct body or cluster of films where certain formal standards can be brought to bear (e.g, closed composition, disjunctive editing, etc.), much like genre criticism. At the same time, the notion of a film movement guarantees that those formal changes associated with it be grounded in a real, material context. This grounding in turn opens us up to the subtle interplay between the micro-social level ("Hollywood" as product, praxis, and subculture) and the macro-social context. whose complex interaction with film culture can then be elaborated upon. We can then engage the "world" of film noir in an ongoing dialectic with its historical matrix, explicating every sort of cultural code (e.g. themes, iconography, or even larger patterns of meaning) to explore the complex process of mediation between a film culture and the material world.[9]

If we rethink film noir in terms of a film movement we may also be able to avoid some of the controversies that have haunted critical film theory for the last thirty or so years (e.g. auteurist vs. structuralist). For although most approaches to film noir tend to suppress stylistic differences to demonstrate the manner in which a group of films are similar, those differences which distinguish a Hitchcock-directed film noir from, say, a Lang-directed one can be handled quite nicely as personal idiolect, while those qualities which draw our attention to a rather heterogeneous group of films as noir (mood, disjunctive editing, chiaroscuro visuals, etc.) can then be identified as movement-idiolect, a term typically associated with art movements. Traditionally, art movements come into being when the quite restrictive idiolect[10] of the individual creator (e.g. the language of *The Sound end the Fury)* is elaborated through the body of works of a given individual (as corpus idiolect, e.g. all of Faulkner's fiction) and further elaborated through a specific art movement. We are speaking here of the process through which innovation becomes aesthetic convention, the unconscious becomes coded and individual practice becomes social praxis. But as so many postmodem critics are quick to point out, no author is in complete control of his text since aesthetic texts are built from larger aesthetic "worlds" and from the materials of the real world as well. Fortunately, these larger aesthetic worlds, often identified as intertext or context, have been given a good deal of recent critical attention.[11] And in so far as an aesthetic movement becomes distinguished by a specific aesthetic world, idiolect becomes identified with sociolect (the language of a social group, class, or subculture), a key nexus between a restrictive aesthetic world and the more accessible social one. If anything, the proliferation of the film noir world into virtually every media and its internationalization since the late 1990s is indicative of the manner in which a movement-idiolect becomes the sociolect of a distinct subculture.[12] It is also a good example of how the cutting edge of an art movement is quickly blunted as its devices are conventionalized and disseminated, or, as Fredric Jarneson would have it, culture becomes commodified.[13]

It would seem that if we are to consider the noir cycle in terms of Wallace's revitalization movements we run into trouble right away in attempting to demonstrate that it was "deliberate and self-conscious." Less problematic is the second half of the equation—"The attempt to provide a more satisfying culture." Virtually every filmmaker interviewed back in the 1970s (whether writer, director, photographer, or composer) was by degrees chafed by the studio system of the 1930s, at times rankled by the ways it repressed personal creativity, and rather consistently anxious to push the boundaries—the Production Code being a particular bête noire among writers and directors.[14] It seems to me that the degree to which these films noir involve audiences of all ages today, or seem more modern than their predecessors, or even play into our notions of postmodernism, is a good measure of the success of their creators, Yet there are critics who still decry the fact that those involved in the production of these films noir lacked a sense of identification with some larger phenomenon—but such lack of identification is often the case with art movements, the early impressionists being a prime example. More telling perhaps are those theorists who subsume film noir into such larger cultural movements as modernism or postmodernism or view it as little more than an American extension of French poetic realism or German expressionism—a confusion, it seems to me, of text with context or intertext.[15]

More problematic is the first half of the equation since "deliberate" and "self-conscious" are attributes we normally associate with the creators of the neo-noir films of today. But if we are the least bit supple in applying these terms to the filmmakers of the classic period I believe we will find a degree of cohesiveness between the two groups of newcomers to the Hollywood system throughout the 1930s and 1940s whose talents were a prerequisite to the growth of film noir. The first group, the Germanic emigrés, came to Hollywood from Europe during this period. And while there was a degree of rivalry among them, there was also a good deal of camaraderie based on common experiences (most were of Jewish background, many fled to America through France via a virtual "underground railroad" initiated by Robert Siodmak in the 1930s). While not all were members of an American Popular Front, they understandably shared an antipathy towards fascism and likely a sensibility that was quite sensitive to the creation of the dangerous and threatening world of film noir. Unlike their fellow emigrés of the Frankfurt School, they were not hostile towards American popular culture, and most were quite responsive to it. Yet for all of their involvement in American culture and social customs they were still outsiders harboring a sense of detachment matched by that found in the hard-boiled "school" of fiction and the stance of many of its protagonists. Perhaps the Germanic predisposition toward Lorelei figures matches as well the misogynistic bias of much tough guy literature.

In addition to these Europeans there was also a group of incipient filmmakers—mostly writers but directors and actors as well—who migrated from the east coast, whom I have termed the "domestic émigres,"[16] and who were, for the most part, variously involved in the American Popular Front. The majority came to Hollywood in the late 1930s and early 1940s and most were "lefties" (to use a term popularized by Clifford Odets), veterans of one form or another of the radical theater that flourished on the east coast in the 1930s. There are too many to list here but a representative sampling would indicate their importance to film noir: Jules Dassin, Cy Endfield, John Garfield, Elia Kazan, Joseph Losey, Ben Maddow, Albert Maltz, John Paxton, Abraham Polonsky, Nicholas Ray, Robert Rossen, and Orson Welles. Together with writers such as Daniel Mainwaring, A.I. Bezzerides, and Dalton Trumbo, and emerging talents like Edward Dmytryk and Adrian Scott, the more politically inclined among them developed an authentic esprit de corps, which of course was shattered with the advent of the Red Scare and the Hollywood blacklist.[17] On the micro-social level, the combined effects of the Red Scare, the consent decree (divorcing the studios from their ownership of theaters in 1948), the advent of television, changes in the disposition of film audiences, and, finally, the rise of independent productions changed Hollywood forever. Yet these eastern "mavericks" helped nudge film noir in the direction of the social commentary/exposé with such entries as *Crossfire* (1947), *The Prowler* (1951), and *Underworld Story* (1950). Even though their ranks were broken and decimated by the House Un-American Acitivities Committee (HUAC) and the blacklist, the ones who remained to work in Hollywood moved it in the direction of more topical genres that would appeal to a new generation of filmgoers with films such as *The Wild One* (1954), *On the Waterfront* (1954), and *Rebel Without a Cause* (1955). Finally, it was noir icons Burt Lancaster and Kirk Douglas who led the fight to wrest control of the production of Hollywood films from the major studios with their own independent production companies (Hecht-Lancaster and Bryna respectively).

If Hollywood's political "awakening" in the late 1930s made it fashionable for members of the colony to "go left" as one social analyst asserts,[18] it is also true that the domestic émigrés, especially the more radical among them, devoted much of their energy to advancing the cause of trade unionism and forging a Popular Front within the film industry. They were particularly influential in securing industry recognition of the Screen Writers

Guild as a bargaining agent in 1940, and the Marxist domination of this organization continued throughout much of the decade. Yet Hollywood's Popular Front was always a heterogeneous political amalgam, including Republicans and New Deal Democrats as well as radicals, but it was the anti-fascist spirit that provided a key nexus between the Germanic and domestic émigrés. However, it is not at all surprising that the Europeans trod more quietly than their American counterparts since their status as immigrants put them in a more precarious position. Very few were inclined to beat a hasty retreat to their native lands, as Berthold Brecht and Hanns Eisler were forced to do, though the fact that even a filmmaker with the prodigious reputation of a Fritz Lang was touched by the blacklist was sufficient cause for discretion on their part.[19] And while the films noir with which they were involved are often cited as critical of American social mores, most the Germanic émigrés had a peculiar fondness for American culture despite their critical eyes[20]—a provocative synthesis that left them perfectly attuned to that hard-boiled tradition which provided the noir cycle with much of its content. Today we recognize that none of those who were then newcomers to Hollywood were revolutionaries. A greater irony lies in the fact that of all the émigrés, especially those whose careers touched upon the radical theater, the one who was arguably the least radical was the one most skilled at synthesizing a variety of avant-garde aesthetics, and it was Orson Wells who proved to be the greatest influence on the Hollywood cinema of the 1940s. Having established the degree to which kinship promotes a sense of self-consciousness, we can now begin to define film noir in terms of the three broad criteria which determine a film movement.

A "Radical Aesthetic Break"

Given the repressive structure of the Hollywood film industry in the 1930s, one would not expect as radical an aesthetic break as might be found in other art movements. Yet there was a definite break with the traditional studio film of the 1930s (Hollywood's version of the classic narrative text) which valorized the smooth unfolding of the story (or in today's critical parlance, favored story over discourse) and used every device at its disposal to place the spectator in a position of coherence: continuity cutting (i.e. decoupage classique); optical effects such as wipes and dissolves; balanced lighting; the star system; shallow focus, etc. [21] When "The End" title appeared audiences expected and typically got closure, if not always a happy ending. So story was king and producers such as Irving Thalberg, David O. Selznick, and Darryl F. Zanuck based their reputation (and their power) on their ability to ferret out a compelling story, thereby making the producer the most important cog in the creation of the studio film. Occasionally a writer like Preston Sturges began to experiment with this structure (e.g. *The Power and the Glory* [1933]), and when Sturges began to direct his own films in 1940 he paved the way for the emergence of other writer-directors, who in turn began to displace the producer in importance. Among the most important of these as far as the noir cycle is concerned were John Huston, Billy Wilder, and especially Orson Welles. Welles was a major contributor to the film noir but it is his role in the production of *Citizen Kane* that is significant here. A unique film standing outside the noir cycle, *Citizen Kane* remains the key proto-noir in so far as it signaled a break with the classic studio film which opened the way for the film noir. In the interest of brevity I will simply list here those aspects of *Citizen Kane* which constitute an important part of the film noir's distinctive idiolect:

Depth staging

The sequence shot

Subjective camera positions to suggest psychological states

Anti-traditional mise-en-scene

Expressive montage instead of decoupage classique

A baroque visual style characterized by mannered lighting and photography

Formative use of sound: for example, overlapping dialogue, aural bridges, modulations in the amplification of sound effects

The displacement of "wall-to-wall" romantic scores with expressive and interpretative music

The use of documentary conventions with the structure of a narrative film

A convoluted temporal structure involving the use of first person voice-over narration

Psychological or Freudian overtones

Use of an investigator who attempts to order an inherently incoherent and ambiguous world

A morally ambiguous protagonist

Welles had more latitude than virtually any other filmmaker within the studio system—a latitude not seen again until the rise of independent productions in the 1950s. The result was *Citizen Kane,* which at its release tested the expectations of its audiences and which, more importantly for us, provided a virtual palimpsest of film noir's intertext. From his background in radical theater, Welles brought with him a taste for experimentation, a penchant for dealing with social issues, and a troupe of actors new to Hollywood. From radio he brought to Hollywood Bernard Herrmann, who signaled the break with the romantic scores of the past; a penchant for innovative and formative uses of sound including the authoritative connotation of a stentorian narrator; and the use of actors to restage actual events.[22] Finally, despite his insistence that he learned most about the cinema from viewing the films of John Ford, Welles was a great admirer of F.W. Murnau and spent a good deal of time viewing the German classics, especially those kammerspiele films associated with the second phase of German expressionist film.[23]

Indeed it was this second (or "compromised") phase of German expressionism that was truly the forerunner of film noir, not the classic earlier phase whose extreme visuals and acting styles found a more conducive vehicle in the horror film *(Son of Frankenstein* [1939] is the exemplar here). It was during this second stage that the fluid visual style of Fritz Wagner and Karl Freund displaced the static, fixed camera of pure expressionism, that the expressive potential of editing was tapped by directors like Pabst and Murnau, that more subtle shades of lighting made possible the greater range of *stimmung* associated with the kammerspiele film, that the popular "Thriller" was given respectability by Fritz Lang, and that the artificial quality of studio sets began to give way to the sociological interest of the so-called street films. *Stimmung* (or mood, or "inner vibration" if you will) was put to the service of "psychological realism in the *kammerspiele* film, and this in turn has its analog in the noir cycle where virtually every entry has a psychological dimension and where a variety of devices (visual and aural) were put to use to portray 'inner states.'"[24]

If we look at but three of the major contributors to film noir, the influence of the *kammerspiele* films becomes readily apparent. Orson Welles we have already mentioned. A less obvious figure, Alfred Hitchcock, has confessed his familiarity with the German films of Murnau and Lang and stated that the first picture he would claim as stylistically his own is *The Lodger* (1927), a film with strong roots in the "Germanic" tradition. His first entries in the noir series, *Suspicion* (1941, whose imposed "happy ending" unfortunately blunted the original novel, *Before the Fact,* on which it was based), and Shadow *of a Doubt* (1943) reverberate with elements of the *kammerspiele* film. The third key figure is Fritz Lang, himself a major force in the development of this second phase of German expressionism. Of his many entries in the noir cycle, those in which he was most invested (often as one of the producers) display the greatest kinship to that earlier tradition: *Woman in* the *Window* (1944), *Scarlet Street* (1945). *Secret Beyond the Door* (1948), and *House by the River* (1950). Yet these are only three among scores of other Europeans with a background in this tradition who enriched the Hollywood film industry generally while contributing to that aesthetic break which defines the film noir.[25] At this point then, let us now turn our attention to the second of the three determinants of a film movement.

A Distinct Cluster of Films

Upon first consideration this criterion would seem less problematic to demonstrate than some of our earlier assertions, since we are here only dealing with classic film noir. Today most film theorists seem relatively comfortable placing the cycle within the parameters 1940 and 1960. In more theoretical terms, film noir was a movement which bridged the classic text (the story-bound studio film of the 1930s) with the postmodern one (including neo-noirs to the present). Yet for whatever consensus there is as to the noir period, the question "What constitutes a film noir?" remains; and here controversy perennially rears its ugly head. The best English-language equivalent in American journals of that era would probably be the term psychological crime film, and this is accurate enough since there is certainly a psychological dimension (i.e. as opposed to the environmental determinism of the crime and social problem films of the 1930s) and some sort of crime (real, imagined, or dreamt) in every film noir I have seen. It is also comprehensive—indeed so comprehensive and all-inclusive that it loses its validity as a critical criterion. This is why I believe some formal standards must be brought to bear so that film noir can be measured against those films which preceded it and those which succeeded it—with the added proviso that we do not become too doctrinaire in imposing a rigid visual style (or styles) or narrative structure(s) in assessing each candidate's inclusion. It also seems to me that those standards (visual, aural, or narrative) can only be understood in contradistinction to the classic studio film, that is, in so far as they transgressed the standards (including the Production Code) that Hollywood established in the l930s as requisite to a good story-line.

The noir visual style is nothing less than a shrewd combination of techniques which traditional film theory has polarized as either *expressionistic* (unusual camera angles, formative editing, mannered lighting. etc.) or *realistic* (the sequence shot, depth staging, location photography, etc.). Its narrative structure is not a set of typologies but something akin to the postmodern text by virtue of the way it disrupts a cohesive story via chronological and/or (primarily) causal disorders. This is what differentiates a noir western dealing with a family "feud," like *Pursued* (Raoul Walsh, 1947), from a contemporaneous black-and-white western also dealing with a feud, like *My Darling Clementine,* (John Ford, 1946). It is also why early attempts to "fit" hard-boiled fiction into studio styles and formulae failed until the advent of the noir cycle with entries such as *The Maltese Falcon* (John Huston, 1941), *The Glass Key* (Stuart Heisler, 1942), and *Murder, My Sweet* (Edward Dmytryk, 1944).

While it is nicely symmetrical to place the noir cycle within the parameters of 1940 and 1960, its initiating date is not simply arbitrary. For it was in 1940 that *Stranger on the Third Floor,* arguably the first true film noir, was released. More importantly, the film was produced at RKO, the studio where *Citizen Kane* was to be filmed shortly after and whose flairs, most critics in this field agree, were the most definitive of the noir style. *Stranger on the Third Floor* combined the talents of photographer Nicholas Musuraca, composer Roy Webb and art director Albert D'Agostino who formed the "core" of the RKO noir style. Perhaps most relevant to this style was D'Agostino who had already been exposed to the "Germanic" style when working at Universal, where the art department included Charles Hall and Herman Rosse—key figures in the development of the definitive look of the Universal horror film, beginning with *Frankenstein* (1931). Unlike earlier noir pretenders, *Stranger on the Third Floor* is sufficiently unique in the way it combines elements from a variety of classic film genres—gangster/crime, detective, horror, even social problem—to usher in the noir era, though it is a far cry from *Citizen Kane* in terms of quality and originality. While Frank Partos's story betrays its pulp sources in its illogic and incongruities, it is indebted to them as well in its depiction of an oppressive, fear-ridden world, one that we would come to associate with the fiction of Woolrich. And if we look back further, it is also beholden to the *kammerspiele* film*,* as is quite evident in the expressionistic bias of Latvian-born Boris Ingster's direction (one contemporary critic noted that he was better at directing shadows than actors) and Peter Lorre's performance as the pathetic, crazed killer—reminiscent of his role in *M* (1931).

It is probably no mere coincidence that film noir found its beginnings and its most definitive style at RKO; for of all the major studios RKO was the most beset with the type of "crises mentality" that opened the door for innovation, due in no small part to the rather rapid shifts in ownership (Rockefeller—Floyd Odium—Howard Hughes—General Tire) and production chiefs (George Schaefer—Charles Koerner—Dore Schary—William Dozier) that characterized it from the late 1930s till its virtual demise in 1957. If George Schaefer's emphasis on quality allowed for the production of *Citizen Kane* then Charles Koerner's insistence on mass appeal painted in the direction of the B film where Val Lewton's "horror" unit and the Scott/Dmytryk "thriller" units flourished. Though limited by budget and genre constraints, Lewton's unit, employing several of the veterans of the old Mercury unit, was cohesive enough to imbue each film with a consistent "atmosphere," and indeed some of its entries come closer to film noir than to the horror genre (especially *The Seventh Victim* and *The Leopard*

Man (both 1943)). Two of Lewton's directorial proteges, Robert Wise and Jacques Toumeur, went on to make important contributions to the noir cycle as well. Edward Dmytryk, Adrian Scott, and their leftist associates at RKO were, if not the most numerous contingent of Marxists in 1940s' Hollywood, certainly the most visible. Working with screenwriter John Paxton, Dmytryk and Scott released a version of Chandler's *Farewell, My Lovely (Murder, My* Sweet. 1943) that turned Hollywood in the direction of the hard-boiled private eye more assuredly than Huston's earlier version of *The Maltese Falcon,* while their version of Richard Brooks' *The Brick Foxhole (Crossfire, 1947)* put the social problem film well within the boundaries of film noir.[26] It would seem that the lower budget B film allowed filmmakers greater latitude in terms of filmic techniques as well as narrative content.[27]

With the acquisition of RKO by Howard Hughes in 1948 and HUAC's renewed interest in Hollywood, political winds at the studio turned severely to the Right and those films with a "liberal" social message began to disappear. Dore Schary managed to exit gracefully but many others there were caught in the political crossfire. While the Red Scare forced several key producers, directors, and writers to exit RKO, the studio maintained a number of essential personnel, especially at the technical level, so that the RKO noir series continued through the mid-1950s, aided by the arrival there of directors such as Nicholas Ray and Fritz Lang. Undercapitalized, RKO was unable to compete with the so-called "Big-Five" majors (in terms of implementing new technology such as wide screen, color, and bigger budgets), and so it fell victim to changing audience tastes and the competition of television in the 1950s (in many respects television dramas replaced the B film). In a sense, its demise paralleled that of the noir cycle and did so for some of the same reasons.

Though released through United Artists (RKO was no longer functioning as a production company), *Odds Against Tomorrow* (1959) has much of the style and texture of an RKO noir and not surprisingly since it was produced and directed by Robert Wise and has Robert Ryan in a lead role. Forward-looking though it is in its use of a cool jazz score and 1.85:1 aperture, it looks backward as well, its brilliant black-and-white photography enhancing its interiors with classic noir style (Venetian blinds, shadows, lowered ceilings, etc.) and its use of deep focus on exteriors, contrasting daytime and nighttime locales. Add a narrative structure built around a heist gone wrong which intercuts the lives of its two principals (Robert Ryan and Harry Belafonte) and which plays upon the psychological and sociological implications of their tenuous relationship before they die atop a flaming oil storage tank and you have all the ingredients of a classic film noir. By my reckoning *Odds Against Tomorrow* was one of the last entries in the cycle and a fitting epitaph.

Sociocultural Trauma

This third and final criterion of film movements appears to be the most obvious. Film historians are quick to point out that because the Depression, World War II, and the Red Scare paralleled the rise and fall of film noir in chronological order they must have had a good deal to do with its ascent and descent. Yet one must be wary of such a facile explanation. For one thing, the majority of the Depression took place in the 1930s, the decade in which "Hollywood" became a global system, the major commercial genres were established, and Americans flocked to the picture palaces as a means of escape from the harsh realities of life. As discussed, the 1930s was the era during which the classic studio film reigned supreme, and if we are correct in defining the film noir in opposition to that classic text then the Depression did little to stimulate the growth of the noir cycle. But as students of American culture know, the Depression provided fertile ground for the growth of popular culture in the United States (in the form of pulps, comic books and strips, radio shows, magazines, parlor games, etc.), and it is precisely here that the Depression influenced the noir cycle—by providing the intertext which Hollywood would (at times) be forced to assimilate in succeeding decades. Certainly hard-boiled and proletarian fiction was popular enough in the 1930s, but Hollywood's response to these writers was to bowdlerize them and force their fictions to fit pro-existing commercial genres (e.g. the best Hollywood could do with Hammett in the 1930s was *The Thin Man* series, which was more domestic comedy than hard-boiled detective story). In a more oblique way, however, the Depression did contribute to noir insofar as it furthered the dominant position of Hollywood, which became a magnet for all those struggling artists and writers that we have dubbed the domestic émigrés. Nor can we discount the effects of the Depression in Europe, which advanced the cause of fascism and the outbreak of war theme. The Germanic émigrés who departed from Europe as a result of these events not only enriched the Hollywood film industry but were an essential ingredient in the development of film noir.

As far as the effects of America's entry into World War II on film noir are concerned, critics and historians seem to take one of two approaches. The French cinéastes emphasize Hollywood's response in terms of the production of war-orientated propaganda films and the need to reinforce American values (thus, films begin to depict gangsters fighting the Nazis and other fifth-column types as opposed to the apolitical stance of Raven in *This Gun For Hire* (1942)). This they view as an impediment to the production of films noir, almost truncating the movement just as it was starting. American critics, on the other hand, while not opposed to this view, tend to focus on the effect of the war on the tastes and sensibilities of the American audience and on the presentation of certain themes within the noir cycle. Thus the wartime brutalities of the weekly newsreels seasoned audiences for the heightened violence of the film noir, just as the sadistic practices of the "enemy" in the propaganda films prepared them for its analog in the noir cycle. The displacement of men by women in the workforce and the fears of returning veterans over the fidelity of their wives (or girlfriends) are used in turn to "explain" the characteristic femme fatale of film noir (rather than the intertext, as mentioned above).

At the most mundane level, World War II drew away some of Hollywood's key personnel (particularly actors and directors), thereby opening the door to new talent. At the same time, the experience of many filmmakers "in the field" during the war helped to encourage the use of authentic locales in the post-war period.[28] But perhaps the most compelling force behind the growth of the noir cycle in the 1940s was the changing marketplace. For one thing, the war cut Hollywood off from an international market that had accounted for up to 40 percent of its profits at the height of the 1930s. The film industry attempted to increase domestic attendance (weekly attendance figures reached their peak in 1946) through a variety of tactics, most of them successful, at least for a while: Saturday morning and afternoon matinees and all-cartoon shows to attract the kids; door-prizes and various give-a-ways to attract the adults; longer exhibition hours; and, most importantly for our purposes, increased use of the "double feature" at most theaters other than the prestige first-run houses in major markets. Double features of course meant increased production, especially of B films, and for studios like Monogram or PRC this was virtually their entire output. And the B film, the true domain of the film noir, allowed, as we have seen, for a greater degree of "experimentation." Hollywood also attempted to attract larger numbers of adult males, less a staple of weekly attendance figures during the 1930s but an increasingly important market segment as the war veterans began to return home. And this last, perhaps, was the most compelling force leading Hollywood to assimilate the hard-boiled intertext left virtually untouched in the 1930s since males were the major consumers of pulps and tough fictions.

Of course, sociocultural trauma can as easily end a film movement as initiate it, and this seems to have been the case with film noir. If I were to pick a specific year as the start of the demise of the noir cycle it would be 1948, the year in which both the consent degree and the blacklist began to have a major effect on the film industry.[29] This was about the time the social problem films of the cycle began to be displaced by the semi-documentaries, and these in turn began to be formulaic as the police procedurals became dominant. Even the procedurals began to focus more on the heroics of the government agents rather than on their entrapment with the criminal demimonde as in *T-Men* (1948) or on the activities of fugitive criminals as in *He Walked by Night* (1949) before they finally succumbed to anti-Communist hysteria as America turned Right: *Walk a Crooked Mile* (1948), *I Was a Communist for the FBI* (1951), *The Whip Hand* (1951). By the early 1950s, this type of film noir was hardly transgressive. If anything, it tended to reinforce conservative American values and, not surprisingly, its format was easily assimilated by television (*Treasury Men in Action* (1950), *Dragnet* (1951), *Racket Squad* (1951), *The Lineup* (1954), *Naked City* (1958)). Television also started to draw the adult male audience away from theaters with such "attractions" as sports and crime shows. Understandably, the major studios turned away from B movies toward A films whose budgets allowed them to deploy a variety of "new" techniques (including improved color, wide and wider screens, stereophonic sound, and briefly 3-D) which were corrosive of the visual style of film noir (by emphasizing the film plane over the depth plane, balanced lighting over chiaroscuro, "star" over "icon") and which once again began to valorize story over technique. The number of theater screens in the United States began to dwindle (until replaced by the multiplex theaters starting in the 1960s), and the double feature became a thing of the past.

If film noir became less transgressive in its declining years, by 1968 there was little to transgress (at least as far as the Production Code was concerned) as Hollywood's older moral establishment threw in the towel and the Code was abandoned in favor of the rating system. In one sense this change represented a victory for film noir (however pyrrhic), although the commercial potential of this "moral" liberalization was not lost on the film producers who hoped to lure viewers away from their television sets and from the burgeoning art houses where foreign films were far less concerned with moral standards. Actually, by 1968 "Hollywood" no longer existed as a distinct colony and subculture: the major studios, which had been replaced by the independent production companies that followed in the wake of Hecht-Lancaster, no longer produced films: instead, they rented their facilities to others and functioned essentially as they do today, as a major vehicle for the distribution of films worldwide. And, as the American film industry attempted to maintain world dominance, budgets, and film stocks grew larger and effects more "spectacular."

By a strange twist of fate, it was the French new wave—whose homage to American B films generally and to the film noir specifically was no secret—that helped to move American films away from bloated projects like *Cleopatra* (1963) towards smaller, more innovative films like *Bonnie and Clyde* (1967, directed by Arthur Penn, though Jean-Luc Godard was originally considered for the position). Penn's previous film, *Mickey One* (1965), was itself an homage to the new wave, so self-reflexive that the protagonist (played by Warren Beatty) speaks directly to the audience (as the putative night club audience becomes the film audience). In any case, by the mid-1960s film noir was a known entry in the United States.[30] Filmmakers were quite aware that they were working with a tradition. In *Harper* (1966), for example, Paul Newman (as Lew Harper née Archer) looks at the audience incredulously when one of his sarcastic jibes goes completely over the head of the Pamela Tiffin character and, in an even more nuanced action, allows the killer, his friend Graves (Aruthur Hill), to go unpunished.[31] *Kiss Me Deadly* (Aldrich, 1955), arguably the most self-reflexive film noir of the cycle, concludes with the two protagonists momentarily surviving a nuclear blast. *Point Blank* (Boorman, 1967), arguably the breakout neo-noir film, opens with its protagonist, "Walker" (Lee Marvin), being shot at point blank range in a cell on a deserted Alcatraz island. He "miraculously" survives to extract revenge from those who crossed him but ends up once again in the shadows on Alcatraz—suggesting that Walker may in fact have been dead from the beginning of the film. Here Marvin's persona—silver-white hair and impassive features belying a penchant for instantaneous violence—matches perfectly the cold steel and glass of contemporary Los Angeles. He is a protagonist who fits well Camus' pejorative description of the "denatured hero" of tough fiction and who is an adequate foe of the fashionable denizens of a corporate (and rather legitimatized) underworld. As Borde and Chaumenton observed in updating their classic study to include neo-nor films: "color confers on the urban setting of steel and glass, which has been visually transformed over the years, a preponderant place, as if the actor were no more than the emanation of this. And this victory of color values…suggests a new kind of morbid toughness."[32] In such a world, a more traditional existential "anti-hero" such as James Caan's Frank in *Thief* (Michael Mann, 1981) seems woefully out of place and appropriately disappears into the night at the end, having cut all ties with the world.[33] It is as if film noir has lost its innocence as filmmakers seek to mine the tradition for nuance (and for popular appeal) and as movement becomes genre, film becomes product, and text becomes metatext.

Notes

1. Especially, Alain Silver and Elizabeth Ward (eds) *Film Noir: An Encyclopedic Reference to the American Style* (Woodstock: Overlook Press, 1992), pp. 1-6. Alain Silver and James Ursini (eds), *Film Noir Reader* (New York: Limelight Editions, 1996), pp. 3-15; and Alain Silver, Elizabeth Ward, James Ursini, and Robert Porfirio (eds), *Film Noir: The Encyclopedia* (New York: Overlook Duckworth, 2010), pp. 15-22 and 349-350.

2. See, for example, Todd Erickson's "Kill Me Again: Movement becomes Genre," in Silver and Ursini (eds), *Film Noir Reader*, pp. 307-329; my "No Way Out: Existential Motifs in the Film Noir," also in Silver and Ursini (eds) *Film Noir Reader*, pp. 77-93; and my introduction to Robert Porfirio, Alain Silver, and James Ursini (eds), *Film Noir Reader 3* (New York: Limelight Editions, 2001), especially pp. 2-3. I have, however, covered this topic extensively in my unpublished dissertation, "The Dark Age of American Film: A Study of the American Film Noir," Vols 1 and 2, (Ann Arbor, MI.: University Microfilms, 1980).

3. See Erickson, "Kill Me Again."

4. In a sense film noir provided a gateway for more contemporary commercial genres to emerge as many of its talents—those in particular who were not drummed out of Hollywood by the blacklist—turned to more topical material. Elia Kazan and Nicholas Ray are exemplar here.

5. See James Naremore, *More Than Night: Film Noir in its Contexts* (Berkeley: University of California Press, 2008).

6. The evasive nature of film noir in terms of consistent iconography or narrative patterns has fueled a good deal of the debate. For a concise but lucid overview, see Appendix C in Silver and Ward (eds), *Film Noir*, 3rd edition, pp. 372-385. To its credit, the transgeneric nature of film noir has made it a staple of contemporary film criticism since many see there the seeds of the postmodern metatext.

7. A.F.C. Wallace, "Revitalization Movements," in *American Anthropologist* 58 (1956). Terry Lovell's article, "Sociology and the Cinema," *Screen* 12 (1) (Spring, 1971); 15-26, a seminal application of this concept to film, indicates its usefulness in defining French New Wave.

8. I'm not fond of the term "expressive realism" but use it here because George Huaco labels it thus in his seminal study of the first three movements, *The Sociology of Film Art* (New York, Basic Books, 1965). Huaco's study relies on a rather crude base-superstructure model and lacks the methodological sophistication of Terry Lovell or Andrew Tudor's important discussion of film movements in *Image and Influence* (New York, Viking, 1974), to which I am indebted. For a more contemporary sociological approach (though one lacking in a discussion of film movements) see Graeme Turner, *Film as Social Practice* (London: Routledge, 4th edition, 2006).

9. James Naremore comes close to just such an analysis in *More than Night*.

10. For the conception of the personal idiolect as a "species" of the unconscious I am indebted to Bill Nichols's "Style, Grammar and the Movies," in Nichols (ed.) *Movies and Methods* (Berkeley: University of California Press, 1976), pp. 607-628 and to Gregory Bateson, to whom I was directed by Nichols's article.

11. See, for example, Gene Phillips, *Creatures of Darkness: Raymond Chandler, Detective Fiction and Film Noir* (Lexington: The University of Kentucky Press, 2000); Stephen Faison, *Existentialism, Film Noir, and Hard-Boiled Fiction* (Amherst: Cambria Press, 2008); Alistair Rolls and Deborah Walker, *French and American Noir: Dark Crossings* (Basingstoke: Palgrave Macmillan, 2009); Paula Rabinowitz, *Black and White and Noir: America's Pulp Modernism* (New York: Columbia University Press, 2002) and James Naremore, *More Than Night*.

12. Since 2005 there has been a "[Film] Noir of the Week" website featuring a review/synopsis of a different classic film noir each week with its own blog link and touting "The Film Noir Foundation" for donations towards preservation of classic films noir. Regarding the influence of film noir on comic books and strips, when I interviewed Will Eisner, creator of *The Spirit*, in 1972 he told me that among the influences on his visual style were films such as *Citizen Kane* and those "crime thrillers" of the 1940s that we now term classic film noir.

13. Frederic Jameson, *Postmodernism, or, the Cultural Logic of Late Capitalism* (Durham, NC: Duke University Press, 1991).

14. Many of these interviews are contained in Porfirio, Silver and Ursini (eds), *Film Noir Reader 3*. This spirit of rebelliousness extended even to producers like Dore Schary, who was proud of "smaller" black and white films, especially those that dealt with social issues, and had no qualms about clashing with owners such as Louis Mayer and Howard Hughes.

15. Yet commentators like Jean-Pierre Chartier even in 1946 recognized the difference between the French films noir of the 1930s and the American films noir which eliminated the romantic sensibility of the French films and often

replaced romance with the allure of the femme fatale. See "Americans Also Make Noir Films," in Alain Silver and James Ursini (eds), *Film Noir Reader 2* (New York: Limelight Editions, 1999), pp. 21-23.

16. Porfirio, *Dark Age of American Film*, chapter 4.

17. In a series of interviews I had with Edward Dmytryk in 1976 he described the camaraderie among Hollywood's "lefties." He felt the dearth of intellectuality in the Hollywood of the 1930s was mitigated by the arrival of the European and domestic émigrés—giving the edge in that domain to the Marxists. He was quick to point out that most studio chiefs were apolitical and he demonstrated a certain disdain for liberals like Dore Schary.

18. Leo C. Rosten, *Hollywood: The Movie Colony, the Movie Makers* (New York: Harcourt, 1941).

19. See Lang's interview in Porfirio, Silver and Ursini (eds) *Film Noir Reader 3*, especially pp. 58-60.

20. As Curtis Bernhardt put it, "Foreign directors who came to this country...have a clearer snapshot of the culture than the native who has been immersed in it all his life," in Porfirio, Silver and Ursini (eds), *Film Noir Reader 3,* p. 230.

21. For a more comprehensive discussion of the ways film noir broke with the conventions of the classic studio film, see Porfirio, "Dark Age of American Film," especially chapters 5 and 6.

22. From Welles's experience with radio's *March of Time*, which, together with the film series of the same name, proved to be the major source of the semi-documentaries of the noir cycle.

23. I was told this by David Bradley (director of the noir *Talk About a Stranger*, 1952), who knew Welles from their association with the Todd School, which they both attended.

24. I read scores of film reviews of putative films noir in the trade papers of the era. Since the term film noir was unknown in the United States at the time, the most typical appellation was "psychological thriller."

25. For a book-length study of the influence of the Germanic émigrés (among others) on Hollywood film see Larry Langman, *Destination Hollywood: The Influence of Europeans on American Filmmaking* (Jefferson, NC: McFarland, 2000).

26. During a conversation, Dmytyrk told me that his visual style, particularly at RKO, was influenced primarily by Welles and Murnau.

27. At least according to Dore Schary. See Porfirio, Silver and Ursini, *Film Noir Reader 3*, especially pp. 180-181.

28. See, for example, the interviews of Joseph Lewis and Sam Fuller in Porfirio, Silver and Ursini (eds), *Film Noir Reader 3*.

29. Most "lists" of films noir, though they may vary in terms of titles, are rather consistent in affirming 1947 as the peak of production of films noir (see, for example, the lists of films noir by year in Silver, Ward, Ursini, and Porfirio (eds), *Film Noir: The Encyclopedia*, pp. 343-345, and a comparison of such lists in Andrew Spicer, *Film Noir* (Harlow: Longmans/Pearson Education Limited, 2002), p. 28.

30. Higham and Greenberg's *Hollywood in the Forties* was published in 1968. L.A. Filmex's "Salute to Film Noir" (the original source of Paul Schrader's seminal "Notes..." which were handed out to attendees some two years before they were published in *Film Comment*) took place in 1970.

31. At the film's finale neither character can, and as Harper echoes Graves's "Ah, hell," the film underscores this stasis by closing on a freeze frame of Newman, an affirmation, perhaps, of Borde and Chaumeton's final comment on neo-noir films in their 1979 postface to their seminal study: "Deriving from the world of the novel, from the gratifying frisson of fear, and from a certain qualitative notion of pleasure, the noir series has, over the years, linked up with the anguish of a society that no longer knows where it is headed."

32. Borde and Chaumenton, *Panorama*, p. 158.

33. In Jameson, *Postmodernism,* Fredric Jameson has observed that the older existential antiheroes have disappeared along with existentialism itself.

Hammer (Ralph Meeker) and Velda (Maxine Cooper) in

DEADLY"

"KISS ME

Kiss Me Deadly: Evidence of a Style

Alain Silver

At the core of *Kiss Me Deadly* are speed and violence. Moving Mickey Spillane's Mike Hammer from New York to Los Angeles situates him in a landscape of somber streets and decaying houses even less inviting than those stalked by Spade and Marlowe in the preceding decades of Depression and War years. Much like Hammer's fast cars, the movie swerves frenziedly through a series of disconnected and cataclysmic scenes. As such, it typifies the frenetic, post-Bomb L.A. with all its malignant undercurrents. It records the degenerative half life of an unstable universe as it moves towards critical mass. When it reaches the fission point, the graphic threat of machine-gun bullets traced in the door of a house on Laurel Canyon in *The Big Sleep* in the 40s is explosively superseded in the 50s as a beach cottage in Malibu becomes ground zero.

From the beginning, *Kiss Me Deadly* is a true sensory explosion. In the pre-credit sequence, a woman stumbles out of the pitch darkness, while her breathing fills the soundtrack with amplified, staccato gasps. Blurred metallic shapes flash by without stopping. She positions herself in the center of the roadway until oncoming headlights blind her with the harsh glare of their high beams. Brakes grab, tires scream across the asphalt, and a Jaguar spins off the highway in a swirl of dust. A close shot reveals Hammer behind the wheel: over the sounds of her panting and a jazz piano on the car radio, the ignition grinds repeatedly as he tries to restart the engine. Finally, he snarls at the woman, "You almost wrecked my car! Well? Get in!"

As in Aldrich's earlier *World For Ransom*, the shot selection and lighting provide immediate keys to the style, to film noir. But in *Kiss Me Deadly*, the opening dialogue between Hammer and Christina in the car is the significant component in establishing another sort of hero: one that is sneering, sarcastic, and not really a hero at all.

                         HAMMER
    Can I have my hand back now?
         (Pause.)
    So, you're a fugitive from the laughing house.

                         CHRISTINA
    They forced me to go there. They took away my clothes to make
    me stay.

                         HAMMER
    Who?

                         CHRISTINA
    I wish I could tell you that. I have to tell someone. When peo-
    ple are in trouble, they need to talk. But you know the old
    saying.

                         HAMMER
    "What I don't know can't hurt me"?

                         CHRISTINA
    You're angry with me aren't you? Sorry I nearly wrecked your
    pretty little car. I was just thinking how much you can tell
    about a person from such simple things. Your car, for instance.

                              HAMMER
Now what kind of message does it send you?

                            CHRISTINA
You have only one real lasting love.

                              HAMMER
Now who could that be?

                            CHRISTINA
You. You're one of those self-indulgent males who thinks about
nothing but his clothes, his car, himself. Bet you do push-ups
every morning just to keep your belly hard.

                              HAMMER
You against good health or something?

                            CHRISTINA
I could tolerate flabby muscles in a man, if it'd make him more
friendly. You're the kind of person who never gives in a relationship, who only takes. (sardonically) Ah, woman, the incomplete sex. And what does she need to complete her? (mockingly
dreamy) One man, wonderful man!

                              HAMMER
All right, all right. Let it go

What kind of man is Mike Hammer? *Kiss Me Deadly*'s opening dialogue types him quickly. Christina's direct accusation of narcissism merely confirms what the icons suggest about "how much you can tell about the person from such simple things": the sports car, the trench coat, the curled lip, the jazz on the radio. Aldrich and writer A.I. Bezzerides use the character of Christina to explain and reinforce what the images have already suggested, that this is not a modest or admirable man.

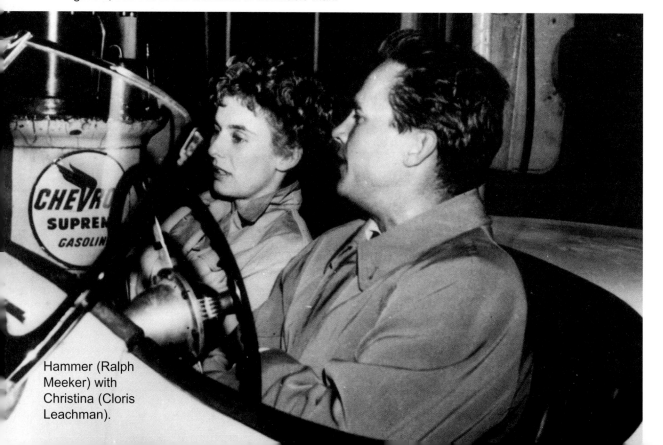

Hammer (Ralph Meeker) with Christina (Cloris Leachman).

Hammer follows the old mover (Silvio Minciotti) to the doorway of 325 Bunker Hill, where Mr. and Mrs "Super" (James McCallian, Jesslyn Fax) look on.

The dialogue also reveals that Hammer knows exactly who he is and the image he presents: "What kind of message does it send you?" It sends the one Hammer wants to send, a message which Christina, the "fugitive from the laughing house," can discuss directly. This is a first hint of what will be something of a role reversal in the way men and women speak. The older male characters, the Italian house mover and Dr. Soberin, will use figurative images and make mythical allusions, rather than speak directly about people and objects. The younger women, Christina, Velda, and even Carver, usually say what is on their minds.

The dark highway of the opening is a kind of narrative limbo: the elements of the plot have not yet been brought into line, let alone focused. Certainly, contemporary viewers brought with them expectations about character and plot both from the underlying novel and from the conventions of film noir. The opening selectively underscores aspects of those expectations while withholding detail. Visually, the discussion of the "laughing house" and Hammer's materialism is shot entirely in a medium two shot of Christina and Hammer, either from the front or rear, in the cockpit of his car. The viewer is not distracted from the character interaction, in which Hammer "loses" the verbal sparring: he is effectively "put down" by Christina until he must tell her to "let it go." *Kiss Me Deadly* has no clearly defined landscape at this point to use as a textural reinforcement. The countryside and the rural gas station are all unidentified settings. They are open, shadowy, and, even within the fringes of the station's neon lights, menacing. Generically this last trait primes the viewer for Christina's murder under torture and Hammer's near death.

In terms of subject/object tension, the Aldrich/Bezzerides conception of Hammer is both more objective and "anti-Spillane." Spillane's use of first-person prose is certainly in the hard-boiled tradition.

All I saw was the dame standing there in the glare of the headlights waving her arms like a huge puppet and the curse I spit out filled the car and my own ears. I wrenched the car over, felt the rear end start to slide, brought it out with a splash of power and almost ran up the side of the cliff as the car fishtailed. The brakes bit in, gouging a furrow in the shoulder, then jumped to the pavement and held. Somehow I had managed a sweeping curve around the babe.

This offhanded objectification of women is in play from the novel's first paragraph. This attitude along with Spillane's lurid sadomasochism and his rabid anti-Communism in the shadow of McCarthy are legendary. From the opening Aldrich and Bezzerides take the events and little else. Spillane's recurring protagonist, Hammer, provides the predetermined viewpoint of the narratives. Hammer's deprecations and wisecracks in the novel are not detached or objective descriptions of people and events and are part of his "color." Aldrich and Bezzerides abandon most of this also or rather, in Aldrich's preferred method, they "stand it on its head."

Of the opening dialogue only one line, "They forced me...to make me stay," is from the novel. But much more is changed than just the words. In terms of plot, elements such as the Rossetti poem or the radioactive "great whatsit" are inventions of the filmmakers. Among the characters, Nick the mechanic is wholly original. In terms of attitude, Hammer becomes a grinning predator, the antithesis of Chandler's urban knight and with survival instincts sharper even than Sam Spade's. Even Spillane's Hammer has some glimmer of sympathy for a "damn-fool crazy Viking dame with holes in her head" and follows the trail of those who tried to kill him, out of simpleminded outrage at their misdeeds: "I wouldn't need to look at their faces to know I was killing the right ones. The bastards, the dirty, lousy bastards!" The film Hammer is incorporated into a more sophisticated system that combines the undertone of film noir with Aldrich's moral determinism. While Hammer wants to know "what's in it for me," all around him crime breeds counter-crime, while thieves and murderers fashion the implements of their own destruction.

For Spillane, Hammer's very name revealed all: a hard, heavy, unrelenting object pounding away mindlessly at social outcasts like two penny nails. The filmmakers refine this archetype slightly: Hammer does think, mostly about how to turn a buck. Christina is arguably the most conventionally "sensitive" of the picture's characters. She reads poetry and, although mockingly, lyricizes her own predicament. It is not without irony that she is the "loony," the one institutionalized by society, yet quickest to penetrate Hammer's tough-guy pose. In that first scene, she helps to reveal that the hero of the film in *Kiss Me Deadly* is closer to other characters in Aldrich's work than to Spillane's. He inherits the cynical greed of Joe Erin in *Vera Cruz* and anticipates the transcendent egomania of Zarkan in *The Legend of Lylah Clare*. As Ralph Meeker's interpretation propels Hammer beyond the smugness and self-satisfaction of the novel into a blacker, more sardonic disdain for the world in general, the character becomes a cipher for all the unsavory denizens of the noir underworld.

The informal inquiry into Christina's death by the unidentified government agents expositionally establishes that Hammer's professional as well as personal conduct is unscrupulously self-seeking: "Who do you sic on the wives, Mr. Hammer?" Throughout much of the scene, Hammer is framed in the shot's foreground, sullenly staring at a blank wall off camera, ignoring the baiting remarks. His snide retort, "All right. You've got me convinced: I'm a real stinker," is effectively true. Because the committee members have made more than a few gibes about Hammer, his response does not yet alienate the viewer. But a dichotomy between audience and the "hero's" viewpoint is building, is creating a subject/object spilt which runs counter to the first person elements of the novel. Hammer first asks, "What's in it for me?" as he speaks to Pat Murphy in the corridor after the inquiry. That utterance completes the character composite: Hammer is certainly not like Callahan in *World for Ransom*, not another selfless "Galahad" as he begins a quest for "something big," for the private eye's gra▨▨▨

Hammer is a quester. He is not an outsider in the noir underworld or any equivalent of a mythic "other world." If this is a foreign or alien milieu, Hammer is at home there. For Hammer, the dark streets and ramshackle buildings are a questing ground which is conspicuously detached from the commonplace material world. Deception is the key to this world. Deception not detection is Hammer's trade. His livelihood depends on the divorce frame-up and the generally shady deal. Deception is Lily Carver's game also, from the false name she assumes to the vulnerable pitch of her voice to the pathetic way she brings her hand up against her face like a wing of Christina's dead canary. Failure to deceive is what costs Christina and others their lives.

This deception and uncertainty, as in most noir films, lay the groundwork for *Kiss Me Deadly*'s melodramatic tension. The plot-line has all the stability of one of Nick's "Va-va-voom's," so inversion becomes a constant; and subsurface values become central concerns. In this milieu, the first "torpedo" set to go off when a car key is turned necessarily posits a second rigged to explode at a higher speed. From the viewer's objective vantage, the shift from one level of appearances to another is occasionally discernible. An early example is the transformation of the sensual Carver, first framed behind a bed post and swinging a hip up to expose more of her leg through the fold of the terry cloth robe, then becoming shrill and waif-like for Hammer's benefit. Usually, though, the viewer is also deceived.

For those on a quest in the noir underworld, instability is the overriding factor and disjunction is the rule. The sensational elements in *Kiss Me Deadly* follow this rule. The craning down and the hiss of the hydraulic jack as the screaming Nick is crushed under the weight of a car; the pillar of fire that consumes Lily Carver; the eerie growl of the black box; even a simple "Pretty pow!" as Nick jams a fist into his open palm, these random acts have no organizing principles. They transcend context to deliver a shock that is purely sensory. Still they fit homogeneously into the generic fabric and the subversive whole of the narrative.

Cast somewhat against type Dan Duryea is Joe Callahan, who is warned not to "play Galahad" in *World for Ransom*, but whose emotions compel him to assist Marian Carr as Frenessey.

Most of *Kiss Me Deadly*'s visual devices are derivations from the generic styles of Aldrich's prior work in *World For Ransom* or *Vera Cruz*: high and low angles, depth of field, constriction of the frame through foreground clutter. The long take or sequence shot, however, is used more extensively and more specifically than before. There are four examples of it in *Kiss Me Deadly*, all of which might be classed as interrogation scenes: Pat Murphy's first visit to Hammer's apartment, and Hammer's questionings of Harvey Wallace, Carmen Trivago, and Eddie Yeager. The specifics of the shots vary, from the slow traveling into close shot during the brief discussion with the truck driver, Wallace, to the elaborate tracking and panning in Hammer's apartment, shifting characters front to back and left to right in an uneasy search for equilibrium. In no sequence shot does Hammer get answers to everything he asks; yet each takes him to the brink of some discovery.

More than anything else these shots serve as a sort of punctuation in the narrative line. In the scenes with Trivago and Yeager especially, the sustained camera seems to externalize a reflective pause. Hammer only half listens in these scenes, wandering about and sampling Trivago's wine and spaghetti or, with Yeager, glancing over at the sparring match. They also create visual pauses at odd intervals. While they diminish tension on the one hand by preserving a level of stasis or consistency, barring the cut and the extreme angle, they reinforce it on the other, playing first with the viewer's expectancy of the cut and then with the interior movements of the camera. As the possibility of a change in angle is removed only for a set period that cannot exceed the length of the sequence, so the pause is a baited one, barely allowing Hammer and/or the audience time to "catch their breath."

As in *World for Ransom*, the trap is a part of *Kiss Me Deadly*'s figurative scheme. Again, its constructs are primarily visual. But the elaborate "capture" of Callahan in the earlier picture is distilled down to single shots in *Kiss Me Deadly*. For example, in the high angle long shot of Hammer outside Lily Carver's room, the dark foreground of stairway and balustrades are arrayed concentrically about Hammer's figure and seem to enclose him. Usages such as this contribute to *Kiss Me Deadly*'s figurative continuity of instability or inversion and the lurking menace, all set up in the opening sequences.

What most distinguishes *Kiss Me Deadly*'s figurative usage from that of earlier and many later Aldrich films is the added dimension of an explicit, aural fabric of allusions and metaphor. The Christina Rossetti poem, "Remember Me," is a recurrent example. Other background sounds are keyed to character. The Caruso recording with which Carmen Trivago sings is the Flotow opera, *Martha*. Another classical piece plays on the radio in Christina's room as the manager remarks, "She was always listening to that station." A prize fight is being broadcast in the background when Evello and Sugar Smallhouse are killed.

While these sounds may not be as fully incorporated into the narrative structure as the poem is, all provide immediate textural contrast if not subsidiary meaning. The sibilant tone of Evello's gasp as he is killed echoes the hiss of the car jack in Nick's murder. As tropes both recall in turn the equation of vitality with a "deep breath" made by the old mover. The play of sounds and meaning can create other anomalies. For instance, at one point Velda approaches Mike asking, "But under any other name, would you be as sweet?" and he, not paying attention to her, says, "Kowalski." On one level, all these can be appreciated as textural noise or non sequiturs. On another, they are conscious metaphors and puns.

As with Callahan, "chance" is a factor. As Hammer says, "If she hadn't gotten in my way, I wouldn't have stopped." Velda's statements about the "great whatsit" and "the nameless ones who kill people" reinforce the sense that the vagaries of chance or destiny, a word which the mythically-minded Dr. Soberin would likely have preferred, are an underlying constant. Soberin himself is one of the most consciously allusive characters in Aldrich's films. He brings up the notion of rising from the dead after Christina expires: "Do you know what that would be? That would be resurrection." He mentions Lazarus again during a conversation with Hammer. The old moving man also speaks of "the house of my body" that can only be left once. These concepts run parallel to Hammer's own search for meaning in the cryptic pentameter of the Rossetti poem: "But when the darkness and corruption leave/A vestige of the thoughts that once we had."

Myth becomes a surface value entirely in the case of the "great whatsit." What Pat Murphy utters, a "few, harmless words...just a bunch of letters scrambled together, but their meaning is very important.... Manhattan project. Los Alamos. Trinity," are as much words to conjure with as Soberin's pedantic analogies. Soberin's references to Lot's wife and "cerberus barking with all his heads" are too archaic and unfrightening to keep Gabrielle/Lily Carver from opening her own Pandora's box. In the final analysis, the "great whatsit" contains pure phlogiston. The quest for it becomes the quest for the cleansing, combustible element, for the spark of the purifying fire that reduces the nether world of *Kiss Me Deadly* to radioactive ash.

As modern myth, as anti-myth (discussed in more detail in the Addendum), and/or as film noir, *Kiss Me Deadly*'s narrative outlook is equally somber. "A savage lyricism hurls us into a world in full decomposition, ruled by the dissolute and the cruel," wrote Borde and Chaumeton in *Panorama du Film Noir Américain*, then "to these savage and corrupted intrigues, Aldrich brings the most radical of solutions: nuclear apocalypse."[1] *Kiss Me Deadly* is also a key to the development of Aldrich's visual style. In this "apocalyptic" context, the choices of angle, framing, staging, lighting, and all the other elements which constitute a visual style are all in play in a particularly expressive way.

Mike Hammer's interaction with the character portrayed by Marian Carr in *Kiss Me Deadly* is considerably less chivalrous than in *World for Ransom.* Not one to respect personal space, Hammer introduces himself and is shortly thereafter manhandling her.

Nine Elements of Style in *Kiss Me Deadly*

1. Angle. A low angle point-of-view shot, such as that of the feet of Hammer's captors (see Frame 1, below left), also functions to withhold critical information, the faces of the men, and to have the viewer co-experience Hammer's mental note-taking of his only clue: the style of Soberin's shoes. Framing works with the choice of angle in that, objectively, both the fact of the viewer empathy with Christina, who the dialogue reveals has just been tortured to death, and the position of her white, lifeless legs in the center of the frame draw attention away from the aspect of the dark shoes in the surrounding foreground.

This low angle is "motivated," that is, the camera is placed on the floor to simulate Hammer's semiconscious sprawl. In contrast, the ground level medium shot when Sugar interrupts Hammer's examination of the shoes in Evello's bathhouse (2) represents a director's and not a character's point-of-view. That angle similarly restricts the visual information which the viewer receives (how Hammer renders Sugar unconscious remains an off-screen mystery), while the tilt upward combines with a shorter focal length lens to distort perspective and exaggerate the magnitude of Sugar's fall.

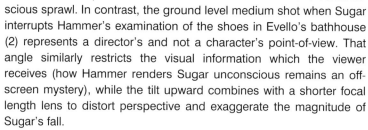

The tilted angles in the hospital room (3, 4) alternate between directorial and character point of view. As a disembodied voice calls Mike's name, the sequence begins with an optical device used over a shot of Velda and the nurse. A rippling effect through an image from what is ostensibly—see more particulars in "opticals" on page 316—the character's point of view is a convention for awakening from a dream or returning to consciousness. The tilting off from horizontal approximates the imbalance which Hammer experiences as he comes to; but that tilting is carried over into a shot which includes Hammer (3). The shift between "first person" and "third person"—the scene ends in the former mode (4)—serves to objectify the unusual angle. As first-person usage and its conventions are undercut, the split between Hammer's viewpoint and that of the narrative is accentuated.

The use of an extreme high angle or overhead, as in Hammer's first visit to Carver's apartment (5), even more significantly restricts the reading or denotation of a shot. Because it shifts away from connotations of either dominant force or point of view, which may be present in a low or eye-level setup, such a shot moves towards an omniscient perspective. By association and by interaction with the shot's material content, this shift can cause the viewer to sense, subconsciously at least, that he or she is looking down on the scene from a deific or deterministic vantage.

The most frequent use of other than eye-level camera placement in *Kiss Me Deadly* is the slight high and low angles which clarify interpersonal relationships. In certain medium close two shots, the camera aiming down at Nick (6) or later at the morgue attendant over

Hammer's shoulder implies that he intimidates or controls them to some degree. When Velda comes to Mike's apartment, the more extreme angle over him down at her (7) is appropriate to the degree in which he dominates her. Even as he looks away from Velda in her own bedroom (8), Hammer still dominates. Conversely, the very similar shots aimed upwards at Carver (9) or Pat Murphy (11) or over Carver at Hammer (10) all reverse that effect to suggest a weaker position on his part. Angle combines with framing and/or cutting for enhanced effect.

2. Framing. The recurrent use of objects and faces in the foreground of various shots, either as indeterminate shapes or held in focus by depth of field, creates a visual tension. These elements both conceal a portion of the rear ground and compete with more "significant" content for viewer attention, as with Christina's legs, mentioned above (1). Conversely, the severe cropping in a close shot of a battered Ray Diker (12) at his front door or a medium shot of Carver aflame in the beach house (13) concentrate viewer attention by forming a kind of natural iris. The first shot of Hammer (24) framed off center against the night sky anticipates more severe manipulations.

On a connotative level, the foreground clutter of the stairs, banisters, and corridors present in high angle long shots of both Hammer alone (5) and later with Carver (14) occupies a larger portion of the frame relative to the smaller human figures. Rather than forming simple black wedges, they have a textural presence made up of highlights and a confusion of angular shapes. The characters at frame center thus appear caught in a tangible vortex or enclosed in a trap.

The shot of Hammer at Soberin's feet (15) is a telling transliteration of the novel which relies on framing, decor, mise-en-scene, and the association of sound and image for its full effect. Spillane wrote. "They had left me on the floor.... Something moved and a pair of shoes shuffled into sight so I knew I wasn't alone." In the film, Hammer is unconscious and in the shot, so that it cannot be subjective. Instead of being on the floor he lies on a bare set of bed springs suggestive of a cold, metallic decay. The shoes are below. While Soberin's stentorian voice drones on about resurrection, the springs cast a maze of shadows enmeshing his feet and Hammer's face in the same tangled web.

3. Mise-en-scène. The staging of the elements in a shot or the mise-en-scene combines with framing and depth of field to further define Hammer's relationship to his environment and other characters. He has a tendency to stare off towards a point outside the frame. Instances vary from the three shot in the morgue to the interview by

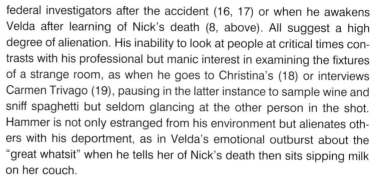

federal investigators after the accident (16, 17) or when he awakens Velda after learning of Nick's death (8, above). All suggest a high degree of alienation. His inability to look at people at critical times contrasts with his professional but manic interest in examining the fixtures of a strange room, as when he goes to Christina's (18) or interviews Carmen Trivago (19), pausing in the latter instance to sample wine and sniff spaghetti but seldom glancing at the other person in the shot. Hammer is not only estranged from his environment but alienates others with his deportment, as in Velda's emotional outburst about the "great whatsit" when he tells her of Nick's death then sits sipping milk on her couch.

The choice of setting and the use of real locations reinforce this sense of alienation. The general decay of the city coupled with specific usages such as the flashing street lights and isolated gas station (20) create, as mentioned earlier, an overtone of lingering menace. The pan up from the street lights is to Ray Diker's decrepit Victorian house perched on a dark hill. The departure from the gas station leads to death for Christina.

Other usages comment metaphorically on the confusion of identities. The mirrors and panning movement when Hammer visits Velda in her exercise room create a complex of confusing doppelgängers. As the shot opens, the viewer sees two sets of figures as Hammer steps into the room. The pan reveals that neither set was "real" and displaces them with the actual people reflected in still another mirror (21). Even as Velda elaborates figuratively on the possible consequences of his investigation and speaks of a "thread" leading to a "rope" by which he might well "hang," she spins around on the pole. The mise-en-scene, her action and the setting, actively undercuts the surrounding reality.

At least one identity-transfer, that of Hammer and Christina, which is suggested narratively by their interaction in the first scenes, is elaborated upon by the staging. Specifically, the X-shaped pose which Christina assumes as she flags down Hammer's car (22) is recalled in the painted figure seen on the wall of her room when Hammer examines it (center top of 18). That figure, bisected by the lamplight, is reflected in turn in the later image of Hammer tied to bed at Soberin's beach house (25).

Hammer's answering machine, which was a very unusual device in 1955, is part of his dissembling lifestyle. When he first listens to playback from the wall-mounted, reel-to-reel tape recorder, Hammer stands leaning against the living room wall (26). He and the machine are on the right and left of a medium shot with his shadow between

them. The machine becomes a second shadow, another self, an embodiment of the mechanistic, emotionless aspect of Hammer's psyche. The framing and mise-en-scene reinforce this relationship. In a later scene, when Murphy comes to Hammer's apartment, Hammer is in the left background in front of the machine. (27). With his coat off, the gray tone of Hammer's shirt and the device behind him blend, so that it appears perched on his shoulder or even growing out of it.

On a less symbolic level, much of the mise-en-scene simply adds a layer of distracting action behind that in the foreground. The use of depth of field to keep the sparring and shadow boxing in the background in relative focus as Hammer interviews Eddie Yeager (28) injects a constant, unsettling motion into the shot which could reflect the inner disturbance of both men, just as the sudden droop of Yeager's cigar conveys his dismay at the mention of Evello's name. When Hammer walks over to the side of the gym to make a call, the shadow of a large bag swaying on a rear wall in the center of the shot (29) perpetuates the distraction.

4. Lighting. All the shadows, whether in the gym, more obviously in the shot of Soberin's shoes, or more subtly in the shadow cast over Hammer's face when he stops at the roadblock (31), are stylistic corroborations of Velda's sense of impending danger. Other elements of lighting function similarly. The low light on Hammer and Christina conform to a convention of visual expression which associates shadows cast upward of the face (32) with the unnatural and ominous, the ritual opposite of sunlight. The low light when Carver opens the box of radioactive material (33) is, most appropriately at that moment in the film, hellish. Her demonic aspect as she screams anticipates her immolation by Soberin's "brimstone."

Side light is used conventionally to reflect character ambivalence. For example, in the low angle medium close shot of Hammer looking down at Nick's body (34). Framed against a night sky, Hammer is both literally and figuratively isolated in surrounding darkness. The half of his face cast in shadow is emblematic of an impulse to abandon the search generated by the sudden death of his friend, an impulse which accounts for the sense of loss and indecision that he manifests in the remainder of the film.

Lighting combines with framing to create the constricting wedges and trap-like arrays of foreground material mentioned above. In the hard shadow line which cuts across the top of the frame and obscures Hammer's face in his first visit to Carver's apartment (35), it functions independently of framing to instill a sense of peril and comment on the interaction of characters and objects. The lamps which form a

dark triangle behind Carver, as she bends to open the "great whatsit" (36), define visual geometry that is deterministic in implication: i.e., her head is "directed" to align itself with the apex of the triangle.

5. Depth of Field. The presence of depth in the medium close two shot of Hammer and Yeager permits a distracting rear ground which draws attention away or externalizes character emotion. A more "active" use of depth is found in the close two shot of Christina and the gas station attendant (37). Because his profile is present in the left foreground, he is not only more noticeable than the boxers in the gym but he severely restricts the amount of the frame in which she can move. As such he externalizes, even as he exchanges pleasant words with her, the pervasive sense of constriction which she experiences as a fugitive.

The depth of field in Hammer's first call on Carver situates him by the door while she reclines in the near ground holding a gun on him (35; compare a posed reverse angle on page 48 above with the actual angle adjacent). Despite the potential for violence expressed by the gun, the angle (low) and the deep focus define a large field in which Hammer can move back and forth. Unlike other objects or clutter in the foreground, Carver's head and the three

bars in the bed frame work against each other. The center bar separates her both from Hammer and from her gun, which she holds awkwardly. The left bar cuts into her head. The right bar completes a rectangle in which Hammer, posed comfortably with his hands in his pockets, is alone with the gun but not threatened by it. Lacking constriction, he can come forward out of the shadows to smile at Carver from the edge of the bed and establish his dominance over the scene.

Initially, there is staging in depth when Hammer is followed by an unidentified man and stops at a newsstand. With the dark figure in the center rear, Hammer's face is entrapped by the foreground clutter of hanging papers and a bare light bulb (38). Moments later the depth is removed as usage shifts to a long focal length lens tighter on Hammer (39). This lack of depth intensifies the sense of isolation and real danger implicit in the lonely street at night. Detached from the rear ground, which is both out of focus optically and blurred by the panning movement following him down the sidewalk, Hammer cannot flee into the surrounding decor but is held in the shallow plane of the lens and must turn to face his assailant who is photographed in that same plane. When Hammer turns to sneer (40), a long lens frames him left. A clock

face, blurred by the shallow depth, at right, adds possible figurative layers ("distorted time,""hour of reckoning" or ?).

Depth of field and focus shift are used almost immediately in the movie in the pre-credit opening. Although the first shots of Christina running are on her legs (A below) and torso (B) and dolly back with her, the third set up—which is repeated several times—is static as she hurries from background to a tight foreground low angle and lights from a passing car flash across her face. Each reiteration is shorter that the previous one; but the follow focus consistently stays sharp as a small figure (C) skurries forward and ends in a medium close shot (F). This usage of movement within the frame, with shifts in focus and lighting at the end, dynamically underscores the chaotic emotional state of the still-unnamed woman in a trench coat (C-F below).

6. Opticals. The most unusual optical device in *Kiss Me Deadly* is the title sequence. Over a shot of Hammer and Christina in his car, the main title ("DEADLY/KISS ME"), cast names, and technical credits all appear and move across the screen from top to bottom, stacked to be

read bottom line first, like signs painted on the roadway (41 and also the inset onpage 302). This inversion of conventional titles is gimmicky but also appropriate and evocative of the skewed events which will follow.

The standard optical rippling effect (at right) used when Hammer comes to in the hospital—that combines with aural distortion of Velda saying, "Mike"—is not really a visual POV of regaining consiousness, because as the next shot reveals, Hammer's eyes are closed. The angle of that shot is objective, that is, not from the POV of Velda, whose presence leaning in over the bed has already been established, so that the implicit eyeline toward something down low, the "Mike" towards which her gaze is directed, is crossed by the camera, which is counter to fundamental visual conventions. When Hammer does open his eyes, he does not focus on the source of the voice but on a ceiling light. Repeatedly subtle inversions undercut what seems to be normal usage and normality.

The final explosion is accomplished by optically enhancing the flashing lights and special effects smoke used at the actual beach house (42) with more optical enhancement of the pyrotechnic destruction of a realistic miniature (43). [Note: the fact that the lens size and angle used for the real house and miniature are different is masked by incutting shots of Hammer and Velda escaping. Without those shots, In the altered version discussed in the Addenda, a jump cut from real to miniature house made the size and angle shift quite apparent.] While not a literal optical, one of the few process shots in the movie is used to merge the characters and the exploding house (55). This follows a location shot of Hammer and Velda at the actual house (56). (The shots of Hammer and Velda stumbling away in darkness, intermittently illuminated by the explosions behind them could have been created optically but the use of a lightning shutter on a powerful light accomplishes that faster and cheaper [58]). The moving overlay of the end credit subtly reinforces the disequilibrium of the figures in the surf trying to keep their footing while being struck by waves (57).

Most of the transitions in *Kiss Me Deadly* are accomplished by fades or direct cuts. The dissolve from Hammer looking out the win-

dow of his apartment to him kissing Velda in the center of the room is unusual for two reasons: it overlays two shots taken from the same camera position, outside the window (44) which Hammer's POV reveals is on an upper floor; and it represents a kind of projection/wish fulfillment in which a character imagines or anticipates an event and the dissolve reveals what he was anticipating.

7. Camera Movement. Camera movement, both traveling and panning, figures in many of the sequences already discussed, such as the mirror shot of Hammer and Velda or the attack on Hammer in the street. Occasionally, the camera will move sideways "under" an establishing shot to introduce objects into the foreground and restrict the open area of the frame, for example, the bed post in Carver's room. At other times, as with the sequence shot of Hammer's interview with the truck driver, Wallace, the camera moves slowly inwards, reducing the dimensions of the frame around the characters and intensifying its "closure" or constriction (45) even as the duration of the shot adds tension. An even more dynamic usage is the boom down towards Nick as he is crushed, in which the viewer becomes an active participant in his murder, by literally being in the position of the car as it kills him.

8. Duration of Shot. Various aspects of the three sequence-shot interviews with Wallace, Eddie Yeager, and Carmen Trivago have already been mentioned. As discussed earlier, the withholding of a cut in each sequence introduces a tension between the viewer's expectation of a "normally" occurring cut and its absence, so that when the withheld cut finally arrives subconscious tension is released. Even shorter shots, as when Carver shoots Hammer and he slowly twists and falls (46), can be slightly "abnormal" as Aldrich holds the angle for a few extra beats.

In the scene with Trivago, sequence-shot tension is accentuated both by the literal violence of the events when Hammer breaks his record to extort information and the frenetic motion of the continuous

traveling back and forth in his long, shallow room. Even while the shot is held, the image changes as characters reposition themselves; and clutter such as Trivago's clothes on a line (19) impinges and recedes in the foreground. In the scene with Yeager, the sequence shot binds together a number of "individual" shots (30, 28, 29) linked by traveling and panning and each affected by its respective framing, lighting, depth, etc.

9. Montage. As with duration of shot, montage is primarily a binding mechanism in *Kiss Me Deadly*, joining or opposing other elements of stylistic expression for a compound effect. A simple example that epitomizes the most basic power of montage as posited by Kuleshov is found in two shots from Hammer's questioning of the morgue attendant. As the man reaches down to put the key he found in Christina's body back into a desk, Hammer slams the drawer shut on his hand (48). The shot is powerfully violent in itself, even though neither man's head or shoulders is visible. Aldrich cuts to a close-up of Hammer grinning (47), and in a single shot captures all the sadistic impulses of Spillane's character. To the silent evocation of abstract meaning which Kuleshov defined, Aldrich adds the additional dimension of sound, so that Hammer grins not just at the sight of the morgue attendant's crushed hand but at his screams and whimpers as well. Later Aldrich combines an insert (49) and a sound effect to transform the "great whatsit" into a living, growling beast.

While angle creates the basic meaning in the shot of Carver aimed upwards over Hammer's shoulder (9), montage intensifies it when it is intercut with a shot of Hammer aimed down over Carver's shoulder (10). As in his interview with the federal men (16, 17); his discussion with Velda (8); and the other instances already described, in this latter shot Hammer looks away distractedly. This reverse not only reveals his expression but elaborates the force of Carver's dominance or direction of Hammer at that point in the film, a force which links the two separate shots. As an overlay (50) reveals, the shot of Pat Murphy over Hammer (11) is composed identically to that of Carver over Hammer. It defines a similarly dominant moment and is complemented by and intercut with another angled shot of Hammer over Murphy's shoulder.

There are many "normal" reverse shots in *Kiss Me Deadly*, such as the cut from Christina facing the oncoming headlights (1) to behind her (2), where the context is highly charged. At other times a shift of angle from high to low may merely accompany a simple change in camera position as with Hammer's interrogation (16, 17). Even more severe shifts in angle occur in the intercuts as Hammer discovers the "great whatsit" in a locker (51, 52) and as he and Carver hurry away from her building (53, 54). These extreme high/low shifts compel the

viewer to reread the shot and create a visual undercurrent of rupture and instability.

As many of these examples demonstrate, the interaction of montage and angle, framing and staging, lighting and depth of field create a multiplicity of stylistic expressions. In the sequence shot in the gym, eight of the nine elements of style contribute towards the totality of literal and figurative meaning:

1. Angle: The pivotal gym-sequence shot opens with an eye-level view of a man punching a bag, follows a figure who crosses the shot to a stairway, and then tilts down to a high medium shot of Hammer coming up. It levels off again as Hammer reaches the top of the stairs and remains at eye-level for the remainder of the shot (30). The angle shifts at the beginning to disorient the viewer, which in turn subtly connotes, even in broad daylight and in a large room full of other people, the instability and menace all around.

2. Framing: The framing adjusts to follow Hammer in the beginning, then is balanced in the two shot with Yeager (28). Hammer is on the left when he places a call later (29), so that the shadow of the bag can occupy the center of the shot. Hammer is the narrative center and mostly the visual center. But other people and objects distract from that and reduce his implicit control over past, present, and future events.

3. Mise-en-scene: Yeager begins the interview with a smile on his face and his cigar pointed upwards. His expression sours and the cigar drops down when Hammer mentions Evello's name. The presence of numerous others in the background raises the noise level and distracts visually from the principals who are static in the foreground (28). The subtle chaos again bespeaks an underlying instability and loss of control.

4. Lighting: Full light is used throughout the section with Yeager, but many dark areas and a bright spot formed by the street door below accompany the high angle of Hammer on the stairs (30). The full-lit background combines with mise-en-scene and depth of field to permit the distraction in the two shot (28). A separate key light casts the shadow on the wall during Hammer's phone call.

5. Depth of Field: There are three instances: in the high angle of Hammer (30) allowing him to be recognized while still near the bottom of the stairs; in the two shot (28) keeping the rear ground fairly well-defined; and in the phone conversation picking out sharp shadows on the wall behind.

6. Opticals: The fade which concludes the sequence shot is followed by a shot of Evello's pool, revealed when a woman in a black bathing suit walks away from the front of the camera.

7. Camera Movement: Tilting, panning, and traveling are used as Hammer moves up the stairs and into the gym. The shot remains static for some time as he speaks with Yeager, then a dolly move to the side follows him to the phone.

8. Duration of Shot: The gym-sequence shot serves to concentrate and reinforce the tension and character interaction created by the other elements. This is particularly true given the amount of movement and re-framing and refocusing in the shot, all of which add to the difficulty of using one take for the entire sequence. Each element of movement works with the lack of a cut to enhance the tension.

9. Montage: None in this sequence shot, opened and closed by a fade.

Addendum (1996)

Since this article first appeared in 1975, *Kiss Me Deadly* continues to be one of the classic period's most discussed films. In the "Postface" of a new printing of their text, a decade after Paul Schrader called it "the masterpiece of film noir,"[2] Borde and Chaumeton wrote: "1955, the end of an epoch. Film Noir has fulfilled its role by creating a particular disquiet and providing a vehicle for social criticism in the United States. Robert Aldrich gives this happening a fascinating and shadowy conclusion, *Kiss Me Deadly*. It is the despairing opposite of the film which, fourteen years earlier, opened the noir cycle, *The Maltese Falcon*."[3]

One of the most discussed aspects of *Kiss Me Deadly* is its ending, which the filmmakers themselves referred to as "Let's go fission."[4] Borde and Chaumeton were a bit more effusive when they spoke of "savage lyricism" and "nuclear apocalypse." Before going further, it should be noted that the long-missing ending was finally restored in a second edition VHS and the various DVD releases of the movie, including the latest Criterion version with commentary by James Ursini and me. Unfortunately both the 16mm prints and early video version of *Kiss Me Deadly* were missing scenes no. 305 and 307.[5] As I mentioned in the third edition of *Film Noir: An Encyclopedic Reference to the American Style*, some commentators most notably Jack Shadoian in *Dreams and Dead Ends* and J.P. Telotte in *Voices in the Dark*, questioned whether Mike and Velda stumble into the surf. Shadoian even suggested that since many of Raymond Durgnat's recollections are wrong, so is his version of the ending.[6] Telotte did not know "whether such accounts indicate the existence of an alternate ending for the film or simply represent the kind of creative recollection, prodded by wish fulfillment, that often marks film commentary."[7] One might wonder why any commentator would "wish" for Velda and Hammer to survive. Certainly audience expectations might be for that survival; but in terms of narrative irony, it would seem most apt for Hammer to witness the apocalypse which he and others have wrought [see Aldrich's remarks below].

Even critics who accept the existence of this ending further compounded the problem by such assertions as "the studio added a final shot still there in some prints showing Hammer and Velda standing amid the waves."[8] In his article "Creativy and Evaluation: Two Film Noirs of the Fifties" [reprinted below pages 406-415] that compares *Kiss Me Deadly* with Fritz Lang's *The Big Heat*, Robin Wood suggests that Aldrich did not want these two cuts in the finished picture. In a more recent piece Edward Gallafent asserts that a "gesture to the benign couple remains in some prints."[9]

These shots should have always been in all the prints, and Aldrich never regarded them as any sort of gesture. While they had never seen a complete print, Edward Arnold and Eugene Miller asked Aldrich about the ending, and he replied, "I have never seen a print without, repeat, without Hammer and Velda stumbling in the surf. That's the way it was shot, that's the way it was released; the idea being that Mike was left alive long enough to see what havoc he had caused, though certainly he and Velda were both seriously contaminated."[10] Viewers of the laser disc of *Kiss Me Deadly* can catch a glimpse in the theatrical trailer included at the end of the disc of one shot of Mike and Velda in the surf as the house explodes. Fortunately in 1996 thanks to the efforts of our colleague Glenn Erickson and MGM/UA archivist John Kirk, whom I referred to Aldrich's personal print that had been bequeathed to the Directors Guild of America, the restoration process began.[11]

Wood remarks that "the sledgehammer sensibility that is both the strength and weakness of *Kiss Me Deadly* prohibits any nuance."[12] Even Andrew Sarris' early assessment suggests an uncontrolled atmosphere: "Aldrich's direction of his players generally creates a subtle frenzy on the screen, and his visual style suggests an unstable world full of awkward angles and harsh transitions."[13] Wood's critique may reflect the same ambivalence towards Aldrich's authorial consciousness and/or political correctness as Raymond Borde had when he questioned Aldrich's beliefs in 1956: "We've been discouraged so often that we are wary of American liberals. Like most left of center Americans, Aldrich can evidently deceive us from one day to the next."[14] Borde's concern about being deceived did not diminish his enthusiasm for *Kiss Me Deadly* as expressed in *Panorama du Film Noir Américain*. In 1968 Sarris also believed that *Kiss Me Deadly* was a "most perplexing and revealing work...a testament to Aldrich's anarchic spirit."[15]

The posed photograph of Ralph Meeker and Maxine Cooper in the Pacific surf, which was for decades the most tangible proof that Aldrich's ending had been altered.

Whether Aldrich or A.I. Bezzerides were leftists, anarchists, or any other type of "ist" outside of the context of the films themselves seems less of a concern for more recent commentators. Perhaps this is because *Kiss Me Deadly* typifies those rare films that transcend critical modalities. Borde and Chaumeton, Schrader, Durgnat, Sarris, Wood, and scores of other critical writers all agree on the merits of the film. Structuralist, formalist, feminist, auteurist, and Marxist critics alike have all found something to admire in it. A quarter of century apart, Borde and Wood both remark on how Aldrich transformed Spillane's solipsistic and reactionary novel into something remarkable. Whether or not *Kiss Me Deadly* does anticipate the freeform narratives of the New Wave or, it could be argued, the self-conscious stylistic de-constructions of later Godard, or the neo-noir explorations of downtown Los Angeles, it is undeniably multi-faceted and complex in attitude.

For many observers the mixture of film noir, McCarthyism, and "va-va-voom" has, to use Sarris' celebrated analogy from *The American Cinema*, caused a confusion between the forest and the trees. Borde sensed it when he wrote that "on the extreme right, certain imbeciles have identified this thriller as the quest for the Grail."[16] Shadouin may not have been aware of Borde's assertion but was reacting to my comment [see p. 306 above] when he wrote that "Hammer is the inheritor of a superfluous culture and a superfluous role, a modern, ironic Galahad whose quest leads him to a fire-breathing atomic box."[17] Telotte takes up this issue and ultimately concludes that "like Perceval, Mike fails as a quester."

As I suggested in my original article, *Kiss Me Deadly* obviously is a quest for a noir grail. Whether or not Hammer "fails" as a quester is less important than the quest itself. From his name to his survival of the assault to his ability to overcome Evello's thugs, Hammer clearly has, as Shadouin notes, mythic qualities; but in myth some protagonists succeed and others fail. Aside from the question of "Subject/Object split and First Person Usage" (which was a sub-head in the *Film Comment* version) my other context in originally writing that Hammer is not another Galahad but is a quester was Aldrich's *World for Ransom*.[18] In that film Julian March, the principal antagonist, actually says to the white-suited hero Mike Callahan: "You shouldn't play Galahad. You're way out of character." Ignorant of more distant past behaviors to which March may be referring, the viewer has only seen Calahan shelter a woman who betrayed his love and risk his life for the good of society. The irony in Marsh's comment is that for Calahan "playing Galahad" is not "way out of character." Superficially, that same irony does not apply to Hammer and his "what's in it for me?" attitude in *Kiss Me Deadly*. What is actually in play in *Kiss Me Deadly* is not a standard archetype but a part of process that social historian Mike Davis describes as "that great anti-myth usually known as noir."[19] Hammer is indeed an "anti-Galahad" in search of his "great whatsit," a perfect colloquialism to stand in for and parody the fabled concept of a Grail. Wood calls Christina's perception of Hammer's narcissism at the beginning of *Kiss Me Deadly* "abrupt and rhetorical." But in an anti-mythic structure, a classic invocation of the epic hero, like Virgil's "Of arms and the man I sing" must be transformed into an antiheroic equivalent, something like: "You're the kind of person that has only one true love: you." This tension between myth and anti-myth, between hero and antihero, is one key to *Kiss Me Deadly* and the root of the complexity that Wood finds lacking. Hammer is a radically different character than many who preceded him in film noir and in Aldrich's work as well. For Aldrich, who often spoke of turning concepts on their heads, Hammer is the consummate anti-idealist.

Most recent commentaries beginning with Telotte have refocused on narrative issues. R. Barton Palmer have several comments, such as calling Hammer a "knight" because "he proves vulnerable to the desperation of ladies in distress" or saying "real locations...do not seem nightmarish,"[20] that run counter to most readings. Palmer does call Aldrich "perhaps the most political of noir directors."[21] This runs counter to Gallafent's assertions about Aldrich's intentions. Gallafent explores the history of Spillane's prose and the evolution of Aldrich's assessment of his work through interviews; but he never cites Aldrich's most direct statement on the film's "sex and violence."[22] Gallafent characterizes "the release of massive physical violence"[23] in the scene where Hammer beats up a pursuer as an expression of Hammer's sexual frustration. In fact, complete with obscure allusions to the work of Douglas Sirk, Gallefent tries to make the entire narrative revolve around sexual frustration. One hesitates to think what unprecedented orgasmic connotations Gallafent might derive from the final explosion.

Still other commentators have taken analysis of the components of sex and violence much further than Gallafent. For one critic Hammer's violent beating of that same pursuer is an example of his repressed homosexuality in a world full of masculinized women and phallic symbols that is ultimately "homophobic as well as misogynistic."[24] Carol Flinn searches not for a great whatsit but for "feminine sexuality which displays itself so lavishly across this and other examples of film noir."[25] In considering "aural signifiers" Flinn raises several points. For instance, her mention of Christina's labored breaths at the film's beginning being "closer than they ought to be" and creating "a break in cinematic verisimilitude"[26] suggests an aural equivalent to the unusual visual elements in *Kiss Me Deadly*. Other subtle effects, such as a dog barking outside Christina's house that seems to foreshadow Soberin's reference to "Cerberus barking with all his heads," understandably go unnoticed; but many obviously odd sound elements, like the character Mist's loud snoring or Evello's literal expiration or even the growl of the box itself, are inexplicably overlooked amid discussions of dialogue and music.

Despite these wide-ranging critical excursions, one never gets the sense that the depths of *Kiss Me Deadly* have been fully probed. Certainly *Kiss Me Deadly* ranks with the most important examples of film noir by any director. It has the menace of *Night and the City*, the grim determinism of *Out of the Past*, the cynicism of *Double Indemnity*, the reckless energy of *Gun Crazy*, and the visual flourish of *Touch of Evil*. Its focus on the underlying sense of nuclear peril that haunted the end of the noir period could not have been more apt. If *Kiss Me Deadly* also reflects such contemporary issues as McCarthyism and moral decline, those, too, are part of the fabric of film noir.

As it happens, Aldrich's early career as assistant director and director coincides with the beginning and end of the classic period of film noir; and he would revisit many of the noir cycle's themes, sometimes accompanied by A.I. Bezzerides, in later films. But as a symbol of what film noir epitomized or of the powerful, malevolent forces lurking in the Aldrich/Bezzerides vision of the modern world, nothing would ever loom larger than a mushroom cloud over Malibu.

Addendum (2016)

> "This is the West, sir. When the legend becomes fact, print the legend."

In the fall of 1997, in conjunction with the premiere of the restored print at the Los Angeles County Art Museum, I opined to a writer for the *Los Angeles Times*:

> "Somebody mishandled the negative," Silver suggests. "Nobody took the ending out on purpose. You can tell someone broke the negative. The print quality worsens, there are awkward jump cuts, the music is chopped off. The most obvious thing is that whoever did it made a new optical title to cover himself."[27]

After making these comments, I thought to myself, "Finally! Literally and figuratively, this is the end of the story." What I failed to consider, apologies to John Ford and his scenarists on *Liberty Valance*, is that "This is film noir. When the legend is more interesting, print the legend." The accidental, "other" version that was never meant to exist simply will not die.

Ironically by including the "altered ending" in their 2011 DVD and Blu-ray release, The Criterion Collection has kept the phony controversy alive. Even before its release, one reviewer had misread their intention: "...what Criterion has dubbed a 'Controversial <u>alternate</u> [emphasis mine] ending,' which cuts about a minute's worth of footage that dramatically changes the fate of some of the film's characters."[28] Another reviewer cited an "even bleaker alternate ending."[29] If, as I presume, the abridgement happened long ago when some negative handler in the depths of UA's film vault pulled the master out for new prints to be made, inadvertently mangled the celluloid and sloppily used a wet splicer to cover his or her tracks, it was pure mischance—not censorship, re-release changes, instructions from Aldrich or anything other than simple fate putting the finger on it—that changed the ending of the movie. Then for decades, lack of awareness kept it that way. Even after the fanfare (albeit a small one) that accompanied the restoration, the misbegotten "alternate" will not go away. It just dances around like Hammer and Velda in the surf. Since the restoration, a new generation of academic writers are now printing the legend: "*Kiss Me Deadly* was first screened with the end title superimposed over the fiery bungalow, not, as in the Aldrich version (restored in the Criterion release), Mike Hammer and his secretary-lover Velda retreating into the dark Pacific surf."[30] It was not "first screened" that way; and, hopefully it never will be screened that way again.

Notes

1. Raymond Borde and Étienne Chaumeton, *Panorama du Film Noir Américain* (Paris: Les Éditions de Minuit, 1983), p. 277.

2. See "notes" reprinted above, p. 96.

3. Borde and Chaumeton, p. 277.

4. Robert Justman, *Kiss Me Deadly* Shooting Schedule, November 23, 1954, p. 5.

5. A.I. Bezzerides, *Kiss Me Deadly* screenplay, p. 130. Bezzerides wrote:

   ```
   305 BEACH - VELDA AND MIKE
   Velda helps Mike and they run through the darkness which is stabbed by sharp
   flickers of light. Now, as they COME CLOSER TO CAMERA, there is a tremendous
   explosion. Light gushes fiercely upon them. and they stop, turn.

   306 ON BEACH COTTAGE
   It is a boiling ball of fire.

   307 ON BEACH - VELDA AND MIKE
   As he holds her, to protect her from the sight. Debris from the shattered
   house falls hissing into the sea behind them.

                                                          FADE OUT:
                         T H E   E N D
   ```

   1st A.D. Robert Justman refers to these two scenes as "Der Tag." In the final (and official) print of the film, through an optical effect the title, "The End," emerges and is brought forward out of the bright white flames engulfing the house (scene 306) and remains superimposed over Velda and Mike in the final shot (scene 307).

6. Jack Shadouin, *Dreams and Dead Ends, The American Gangster/Crime Film* (Cambridge, Massachusetts: MIT Press, 1977), pp. 349-350.

7. J.P. Telotte, *Voices in the Dark, The Narrative Patterns of Film Noir* (Chicago: University of Illinois Press, 1989), p. 213.

8. Robin Wood, "Creativity and Evaluation: Two Film Noirs of the Fifties," *CineAction!*, No. 20/21 (November, 1990), p. 20.

9. Edward Gallefent, "Kiss Me Deadly" in *The Book of Film Noir* (New York: Continuum, 1993), p. 246.

10. Edwin T. Arnold and Eugene L Miller, *The Films and Career of Robert Aldrich* (Knoxville, Tennessee: University of Tennessee Press, 1986), p. 246.

11. Glenn Erickson's most recent online article about the process is at http://www.noiroftheweek.com/2007/07/restoration-of-kiss-me-deadly-1955.html.

12. Wood, p. 19.

13. Andrew Sarris, *The American Cinema* (New York: E.P. Dutton, 1968), p. 85.

14. Raymond Borde, "Un Cinéaste Non-conformiste: Robert Aldrich." *Le Temps Moderne* (May, 1956), p. 1684.

15. Sarris, p. 84.

16. Borde, p. 1688.

17. Shadouin, p. 273 and in Note 13, p. 350.

18. In fact, the outline of nine elements of style originally produced with Janey Place was designed around examples found in *World for Ransom*. *Kiss Me Deadly* was substituted at the request of *Film Comment*.

19. Mike Davis, *City of Quartz* (New York: Vintage, 1992), p. 37.

20. R. Barton Palmer, *Hollywood's Dark Cinema, The American Film Noir* (New York: Twayne, 1994), p. 95/p. 96.

21. Ibid., p. 104.

22. Aldrich's reply to attacks by the Legion of Decency and other appeared as "Sex and Violence Justified" in *America*, No. 92 (May, 1955).

23. Gallafent, p. 242.

24. Robert Lang, "Looking for the 'Great Whatzit': [sic] Kiss Me Deadly and Film Noir" *Cinema Journal*, Vol. 27, No. 3 (Spring, 1988), p. 33.

25. Carol Flinn, "Sound, Woman, and the Bomb," *Wide Angle*, Vol. 8, Nos. 3/4, 1986, p. 116.

26. Ibid., p. 122.

27. Bill Desowitz, "Cult Classic Mystery," *Los Angeles Times*, July 12, 1997, page F10.

28. Brad Brevet, "Blu-ray review: 'Kiss Me Deadly' (Criterion Collection)," June 21, 2011, www.coming soon.net/movies/news /553809-blu-ray-review- kiss-deadly-criterion- collection.

29, Nathan Rabin, "Kiss Me Deadly, July 6, 2011, www.avclub.com/ review/kiss-me-deadly-58491.

30. Robert Kleyn, "Kiss Me Deadly," *Framework*, Vol 54.1 (spring 2013).

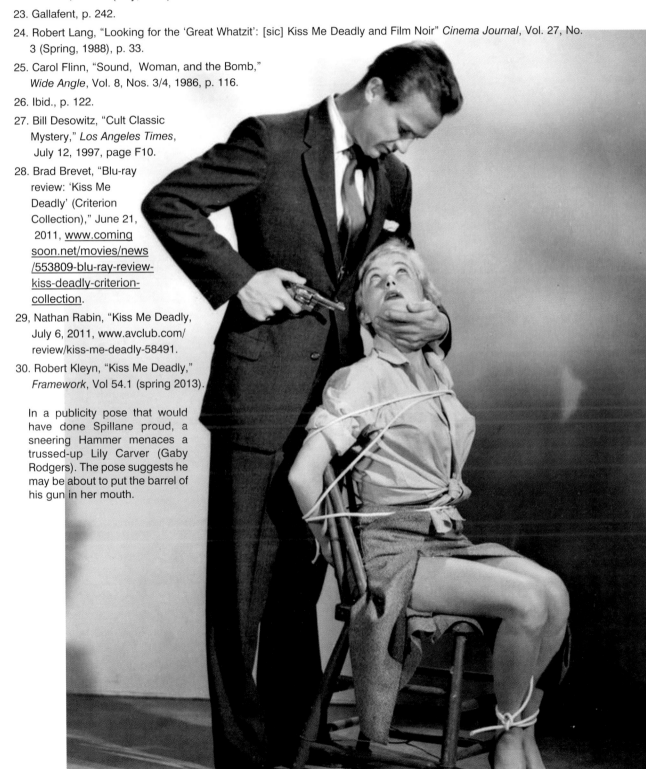

In a publicity pose that would have done Spillane proud, a sneering Hammer menaces a trussed-up Lily Carver (Gaby Rodgers). The pose suggests he may be about to put the barrel of his gun in her mouth.

Diane (Jean Simmons) and Frank (Robert Mitchum) in *Angel Face.*

At the Margins of Film Noir: Preminger's *Angel Face*

Richard Lippe

I have greatly admired *Angel Face* for a long time and had often considered writing on the film but when it came to doing so, I realized that I couldn't account for various aspects of it which seemed relevant to its over-all conception. It has been only recently that I have begun to think that I could produce an interpretation of the film that did justice to its complexity. In this paper, I am not attempting to offer a reading of the film that pretends to explain what the film is about in any sort of all-encompassing manner. Aside from my concern with Preminger's critical reputation, my intention is to discuss certain thematic and stylistic aspects of *Angel Face* that I think are of particular importance to my perception of the film.

Otto Preminger was proclaimed an auteur by the *Cahiers du Cinéma* critics in the 1950s and promoted as such in the early 60s by the original *Movie* critics. By the mid-1960s, the popular press had adopted the notion of the director as auteur/artist although it tended to disregard the underpinnings of the auteur theory. While there was a superficial acceptance of the theory, journalistic critics continued to concentrate on the film's subject, they never grasped the principle that what gives the auteur's film distinction isn't the subject matter itself but how the director regards it. This was particularly evident in their responses to Preminger's films. In the early to mid-60's Preminger undertook several "big" subject projects based on best-selling novels and the resulting films were, for the most part, judged largely on the literary status of their source materials. That Preminger's mise-en-scène often produced complex attitudes toward his material was ignored; instead, the films were criticized for their commercialism which was taken as an indication of Preminger's vulgar sensibility. On his part, Preminger refused to make apologies and, as a result, the reviews became increasingly hostile. And, eventually, Preminger himself was under attack; like Hitchcock, he had created a somewhat outrageous media persona to promote his films, but whereas the press delighted in Hitchcock's various self-promotional strategies, Preminger was accused of using tactics to gain the public's attention. Gradually, Preminger lost his battle with the critics and lost his public as well. Driven by the press from the blockbuster novel, he took refuge in eccentric treatments of already idiosyncratic subject matter (*Skidoo; Tell Me That You Love Me, Junie Moon*).

Preminger's critical reputation, at least outside France, has always stood on the superficially more modest (i.e., low budget) black/white films of the 1940s and early 50s. As a result of the present backlash, even these have largely fallen into neglect. The rehabilitation of Preminger's obviously more problematic late work has yet to be undertaken and seems to be not so impossible a task as is generally assumed. Meanwhile I want to examine one of the most remarkable of the earlier films, *Angel Face*, which, in fact, I feel to be no less ambitious, scarcely less eccentric in relation to the norms and no more understood than the late films.

Angel Face (1952) is the last film Preminger made before establishing himself as an independent producer-director; the film also marks the end of his association with the film noir which began with *Laura* and includes *Fallen Angel, Where the Sidewalk Ends* and *The Thirteenth Letter*. But with the exception of *Laura*, there has been almost nothing written on these films although they are often cited, *Angel Face* in particular, in discussions of the film noir cycle. For that matter, critics writing on Preminger, many of whom consider *Angel Face* one of his most provocative and enigmatic films, have been reluctant to deal with it in detail and attempt to define what the film actually does by falling back on what became the clichés of early Preminger criticism: "objectivity" and "neutrality." I want to argue that what has been mistaken for neutrality is in fact an unusually sophisticated complexity of attitude. But before elaborating, I want to consider the early auteurist position on Preminger and the film.

Jacques Rivette, in his article "The Essential,"[1] a typically esoteric and mystifying piece of *Cahiers du Cinéma* criticism, acknowledges that the film related to a Preminger thematic but evades the implied promise of pursuing this in favor of using the film as a pretext for pursuing the mirage of the cinematic "essential," a favorite project of the early auteurist critics but extremely dubious in relation to the impure nature of an art form that derives from other art forms. In Rivette's estimation, *Angel Face* is an "...utterly enigmatic film..." and, as such, characteristic of Preminger's cinema of which he says, "In the midst of a dramatic space created by human encounters he would instead exploit to its limit the cinema's ability to capture the fortuitous (but a fortuity that is willed), to record the accidental (but the accidental that is created) through the closeness and sharpness of the look; the relationships of the characters create a closed circuit of exchanges, where nothing makes an appeal to the viewer" (p. 134). Rivette's description of Preminger's approach to his subject is highly perceptive but what is perhaps most intriguing is that the observation could have been just as easily made about an early 50s Rossellini film like *Voyage to Italy*. There are, of course, many points at which these two filmmakers don't intersect; what connects Preminger and Rossellini, it seems to me, is that both are employing formal strategies which counter certain rules of the classical cinema. In Rossellini's work, these challenges are direct and radical; Preminger, on the other hand, produces these strategies while remaining within the bounds of classical style, continually pushing against those bounds, emphasizing certain of the devices it makes available while virtually eliminating others. The neglect of Preminger by the semiotic school may be accountable for by that school's preoccupation with the typical and the representative and its tendency to reduce classical cinema to a more or less constant set of narrative patterns and stylistic devices. Preminger's cinema, in its stylistic and thematic idiosyncrasy, resists reduction to the "typical."

"...the relationships of the characters create a closed circuit of exchanges, where nothing makes an appeal to the viewer": the fated couple in *Angel Face*, Robert Mitchum and Jean Simmons.

In "From *Laura* to *Angel Face*,"[2] Paul Mayersberg begins by noting that in Preminger's contract films there is a "...preoccupation with the personality of women...." Although there are numerous later Preminger films that are centrally concerned with women's identity and experience (e.g. *Bonjour Tristesse, Exodus, Bunny Lake Is Missing,* etc.),[3] Mayersberg primarily restricts himself to the early films because his concern is to illustrate that, while these were studio assignments, they display stylistic and thematic consistency. And it is for this reason that Mayersberg is interested in the films' female characters, whom he reads as the means by which Preminger imposes his thematic concerns on the material. Hence, for Mayersberg, *Angel Face* is Preminger's most fully realized study of the obsessive personality. But, in Mayersberg's schema, it doesn't really matter whether or not the character who embodies the thematic is female or male. Nevertheless, Mayersberg's article is of interest, aside from his tracing of Preminger's thematic concerns, in that it perhaps inadvertently acknowledges the extent to which Preminger's cinema is woman-centred. Aside from Molly Haskell, who, in *From Reverence to Rape*,[4] includes Preminger along with Ophuls, Sirk and Lubitsch as directors whose achievements are often underrated because the critics don't take the work of a "woman's director" seriously, there seems to have been no critical investigation of Preminger's work in relation to the melodrama and/or the woman's film. While such films as *Laura, Fallen Angel* and *Angel Face* have the necessary characteristics to be identified as belonging to the noir genre, these films also are, through a combination of subject and treatment, a complex genre mixture. *Fallen Angel*, for instance, has a hero who is positioned between two women who represent, respectively, the active/sexual and the passive/non-sexual. This pattern is found in numerous noir films, but in *Fallen Angel*, its relation to the melodrama is explicit.[5] *Fallen Angel* is, in its triangular relationship which pivots on the hero's choice, a male-centred melodrama in the tradition of a film like *Sunrise* to which it bears comparison. Although both films employ male and female archetypes, in *Fallen Angel* these images are neither aligned with nor reduced to elemental forces within nature. Instead, the identities of the film's central protagonists are shown to be the result of a social system that encourages patterns of domination and/or exploitation between the sexes. In the film, it isn't evil but economic forces that have made Linda Darnell greedy and Dana Andrews desperate. And, although Alice Faye, as the "good" woman, functions as Andrews' salvation, the film also suggests that her motives include freeing herself from the repressive social and sexual conditions of her small town existence. *Angel Face*, on the other hand, has strong affinities to the woman's film; more specifically, as the film's central female protagonist is obsessed, it belongs to what has become, since the early 1940s and the introduction of psychoanalysis into popular culture, a sub-genre of the woman's film. The film links a woman's destructive behavior to madness, but unlike such films as *The Dark Mirror*, *The Locket* and *Possessed*, *Angel Face* doesn't deal with psychiatry or provide an explicit psychoanalytic explanation to account for its heroine's illness. In this respect and others, i.e., the heroine's strong attachment to her father, the film has parallels to *Leave Her to Heaven*, which is another film, like those mentioned above, that belongs to both the noir and the woman's film genres; but, although *Leave Her to Heaven* is of considerable interest in that Stahl's direction and Gene Tierney's persona work to undercut the film's ideological project of making the Tierney character and her demands monstrous, the film lacks *Angel Face*'s systematic analysis of gender and class relations.

In discussing the way in which Preminger's films work, Mayersberg says that Preminger "...detaches the spectator to a degree and allows him to judge the characters for himself." In part, this claim is based on the fact that Preminger is a mise-en-scène filmmaker who tends to avoid using montage to construct "meaning" for the viewer through cutting to a specific object, gesture, detail, etc. But the claim is also based on the assumption that Preminger himself has an "objective" attitude toward his material. Mayersberg implies this when, after analyzing a sequence from *Daisy Kenyon* to illustrate Preminger's approach and how it functions, he says: "It is, in effect, part of Preminger's detachment, because as a style it does not force an attitude or an emotional experience on the spectator. The spectator, like the camera, arrives at the experience. Then the camera moves on and the experience is modified and enriched: the moments become functions in a total development" (p. 16). As with Rivette, Mayersberg's project is to argue that Preminger's sensibility, which is expressed through his mise-en-scène, is highly attuned to the medium and its potential to record, in the Bazinian sense, the more intangible aspects of human behaviour and interaction. For these critics, Preminger's supposed "detachment" affords him the means to comment on the "human condition." But, on the contrary, while Preminger uses mise-en-scène to produce a critical distance from his subject, he doesn't exist outside of or transcend the concerns of his films: he is deeply implicated in the films' thematic. Similarly, Preminger's films often contain characters who are ambiguous in their behavior but the films don't express an impartial attitude to the characters and their situations.

Although cultural politics shaped auteur criticism to a degree, this criticism, which has been invaluable to the development of a critical/theoretical rethinking of the cinema, was, for the most part, as the introduction of the concept of ideology into film criticism has shown, non-political. Despite the various arguments put forth against authorship, it remains, I think, a significant element in critical discipline. To recognize that specific cultural, social and historical factors contribute to the construction of an individual, the work s/he produces and its reception is crucial; but it is also important to recognize that human intelligence and creativity exist.

Angel Face,[6] unlike Preminger's other contract films, wasn't a Twentieth Century-Fox production; the film was made at RKO which, at the time, was owned by Howard Hughes who requested Preminger's services because he wanted a director who could work quickly under pressure. In his autobiography,[7] Preminger says that Hughes' primary reason for making the film was to pique Jean Simmons, with whom he was having conflicts. Simmons had 18 working days left to her contract and Hughes was determined to get another film out of her. To obtain his commitment, Hughes agreed to Preminger's demands, which included a new script by writers of his choice and with whom Preminger worked. In effect, Hughes gave Preminger almost total freedom to do as he wanted with the project.

While there seems to be a more or less agreed critical consensus about film noir conventions, critical emphasis tends to vary as to what constitutes a noir film: iconography, visual style, narrative structure, protagonists, thematic concerns, the historical moment are, among others, variables in how these films are to be

"To both Diane and Frank, control is a major concern."

read. In narrative structure, *Angel Face*, for instance, doesn't employ such "typical" noir conventions as voice-over narration or the flashback which are predominantly associated with the central male protagonist; and the film isn't centered on a male's investigation of a woman to ascertain her guilt or innocence. On the other hand, the film is typical in having a transgressive woman and, thematically, deals with obsessive behavior and alienation. By the time *Angel Face* was made, Robert Mitchum had become one of film noir's leading icons; but the casting of Jean Simmons, who had been recently imported from England where she specialized in playing innocent but victimized heroines, is equally important to the film. Simmons' Diane, despite having certain features in common with the typical femme fatale, is far removed from this model. Preminger was, as Robin Wood has pointed out,[8] the first director to provide her with a characterization that fully utilized the innocent/sexual tension underlying Simmons' persona. In this respect, it is instructive to compare *Angel Face* to *Where Danger Lives*, another Hughes-produced film noir of the early 50s, in which Mitchum is also attracted to and becomes involved with an unstable woman who, it is gradually revealed, is homicidal. In John Farrow's film, Faith Domergue primarily exists to endorse the film's misogyny and complacent cynicism toward heterosexual relations which is what, in effect, the typical film noir is in great part about. *Where Danger Lives* is representative of the worst aspects of the tradition; in contrast, *Angel Face* is an example of a progressive usage of its conventions and thematics.

Gender and Power

As I said, Diane has features that relate her to the archetypal femme fatale of the film noir, she manipulates and eventually murders to get what she wants. But Diane differs in that her concern isn't gaining the power money accords, she already has access to this kind of power, and there is no ambiguity about her commitment to Frank [Robert Mitchum], as she, before and after the trial, wants to testify to his innocence. On the narrative level, what motivates her behavior in an obsessive attachment to her father and a pathological hatred of her step-mother. The latter Diane justifies through her perception that Catherine [Barbara O'Neil] has destroyed her father's initiative to pursue his career as a writer. In effect, Diane is maintaining that Catherine has emasculated her father; but, as the film reveals, Charles [Herbert Marshall] is more or less contentedly indulging his cultural interests while living off his wife's money. If he harbors any resentment toward Catherine, it seems to be the product of his disdain for her middle-class sensibility. In contrast to her father's passive character, Diane's is active. Although she is ultra-feminine in appearance and works to reinforce gender roles (in her relations with her father, Diane is both an ideal daughter/child and comforting mother figure), Diane displays, in various ways, an identification with and understanding of the masculine identity. For instance, Diane's sports car associates her with risk-taking and adventure, and, to Frank, both Diane and her car are equally attractive. But, more tellingly, in her handling of Frank and Mary [Mona Freeman], whom she perceives as a rival, not unlike Catherine, whom she must eliminate, Diane knowingly plays on Frank's fears of being entrapped within domesticity. In the initial café scene, after Frank has telephoned Mary, Diane questions whether he's reporting in to his wife. Having spent the evening with Frank, Diane, the following day, meets with Mary, using the pretext that she wants to help the two financially, to undermine Mary's confidence in Frank. Later, when Diane and Frank again meet at the café, she implies that Mary's possessiveness prevented her from being receptive to the offer. To Frank's "Look, I'm a free agent," Diane replies, "...but you know what girls are." Clearly, Diane isn't speaking as a representative member of her own sex here but is, instead, alluding to her and Frank's mutual understanding of "what girls are" like. While giving Frank the impression that he is taking control of the situation, it is, in fact, Diane who is in control.

To both Diane and Frank, control is a major concern, for Diane it is linked to the possession of an individual, but for Frank it is a guarantee of his masculine identity. While there are numerous films noirs in which the lead male protagonist acknowledges his loss of control, which is often attributed to Fate, Frank, crucially, never fully perceives the possibility of this happening to him. The reason he doesn't, as the film makes clear, is bound up to a belief in male superiority. This is most evident in his treatment of Mary; although he quickly abandons her, he expects Mary to take him back when he's through with Diane. With Diane, Frank is more tentative in his actions, in part, because he knows there is more at stake. Then, too, Diane alternates in presenting herself as an innocent child seeking paternal approval and a sexually adult woman who wants him as her lover.

In *Angel Face*, there is an intimate relation between control or the loss of control and entrapment and, although the film doesn't make this perception gender-specific, it does suggest that it is an issue of particular importance to the male's identity. For instance, when Frank enters the Tremayne household as a chauffeur, he is already aware that Catherine, through her money, controls Charles but he is also confronted by the Japanese servant complaining that his wife, having become influenced by American habits, is trying to dominate him. Later, as Preminger indicates, Frank begins to sense Diane's control; he cross-cuts scenes of Diane with her father in the main house and scenes in which Frank, in his quarters, anxiously watches from the window and, then, with the realization that Diane isn't going to come, makes an attempt to telephone Mary to assert himself.

The film's central metaphor for the control/entrapment opposition is the car. As I mentioned, on the one hand, Diane's sports car associates her with masculinity; but, on the other, Frank sees Diane and the car as a means to fully regain his masculine self-image. (He was a professional racer before World War II.) To Frank, the car represents an image of phallic potency but, within the film's context, it increasingly becomes identified with his entrapment. Although Frank has been aware that Diane wants Catherine dead, it isn't until the murder (and, significantly, the murder weapon is Catherine's car) that he senses the possible threat she poses to his masculinity. (In *Angel Face*, in contrast to a typical film noir pattern, e.g., *The Postman Always Rings Twice, Double Indemnity,* the woman doesn't need the man to help her commit the murder.) It is at this point that Frank attempts to disengage himself from Diane but the murder, in fact, leads to their marrying. After the trial, Diane gives Frank a potential access to the car when she bets it against Mary's taking him back; Mary, in refusing to do so, rejects his notions of masculine privilege. In the film's climactic sequence, the car becomes the site of Diane's control and Frank's entrapment. Diane, in offering to drive Frank to the bus station, seems to think that there is still a chance that she can convince him to stay. It isn't until Frank's shout, as he's opening the champagne, of "Watch it," as Diane steps on the gas, that Diane makes the decision to kill Frank and herself. The enraged look on Diane's face on hearing his command is similar to her look after Frank slapped her in their initial meeting. In that encounter, Diane returned the slap. Here, her instantaneous decision to kill them is her intuitive reaction to his assumption of a masculine prerogative that excludes any sense of her autonomy or individual identity.

Undoubtedly, *Angel Face* has one of the most devastating endings in the entire history of cinema. In part, the ending's impact is attributable, as it has been previously in the Catherine/Charles car scene, to the horrific manner in which the characters meet their death; but the impact also stems from the unexpectedness of Diane's action, arguably, the viewer, not unlike Frank, hasn't contemplated the possibility. (Although the viewer is provided with indications of how and when Catherine and Charles will be killed, the action, in its abruptness, is equally startling.) There are other films noirs, i.e., *Double Indemnity, Out of the Past*, in which, by the film's conclusion, the central couple is dead. But, in these films, although the victim-hero is fatally shot by the woman and he, in turn, precipitates her death, in *Angel Face* Frank isn't given this final assertion of his control over the woman. Also, Frank lacks the pessimistic romanticism often associated with the noir victim-hero who, through his death, achieves, as in *Out of the Past*, a degree of tragic nobility. In fact, when compared to the typical film noir male, Frank has nothing that connotes a "glamorous" identity: he isn't, for instance, in an ambiguous position to the criminal world and the law nor is he, for that matter, guilty of committing a crime of any sort. (Diane's attorney, Fred Barrett [Leon Ames], comes closest to being a male criminal figure in the film.)[9] Then, too, it isn't Fate, which is never a factor in Preminger's films, that leads Frank to his death but, as I said, the conviction that his masculine identity secures him a controlling position in gender relations. On the other hand, Frank, more characteristic of the typical film noir male, tends to project his distrust of the feminine and a woman's wants onto the women herself. Pointedly, in respect to this, when Diane, who has given him no reason to doubt her love, says, "Do you love me at all? I must know," he responds with "I suppose it's a kind of love...but, with a girl like you, how can a man be sure?"

Women and Film Noir

Although each of the three female protagonists of *Angel Face* relates to images of women associated with the film noir, Preminger doesn't provide these characters with the conventional identities that these types suggest, in each case subtly qualifying and undermining the spectator's expectations.

1. Diane identifies Catherine as a domineering, mean-minded woman who takes pleasure in humiliating her father and denying her wants; but Catherine, as she's presented, doesn't fulfill the bitch image Diane has assigned her. If Catherine denies Diane, as she does in deciding against financing Frank's sports car garage project, it is because she's trying to contain Charles' indulgence of her: in the scene which immediately follows Catherine's interviewing Frank about his plan, she, after attempting to telephone her lawyer about the project, is confronted by Charles who offers a perfunctory expression of his affection and then informs her that she's getting a $300 bill for a dress he thought Diane should have. The scene, in addition to foregrounding Charles' cynical attitude towards his financial dependency, suggests that Catherine has cause to reprimand him. The scene also suggests, as does an earlier, intimate scene between Charles and Diane in which they jokingly dismiss the seriousness of Catherine's near asphyxiation, that Charles tends to promote a sex and class (Catherine's bourgeois identity vs. the "aristocratic" refinement Diane is seen as sharing with her father) barrier between the two women. As Catherine isn't the monstrous woman Diane claims, her death is neither deserved nor gratifying. It isn't until she's killed her that Diane comes to this realization and recognizes that Catherine, too, loved Charles.

2. In its Diane/Mary opposition, *Angel Face* employs the archetypes of the "bad" and the "good" woman; in the film noir cycle, the opposition occurs perhaps most notably in Jacques Tourneur's *Out of the Past* in which the sexual Kathie/Jane Greer is contrasted to the innocent Ann/Virginia Huston who unconditionally commits herself to the film's hero, Jeff/Robert Mitchum, providing understanding, support and love. In

"I suppose it's a kind of love...but, with a girl like you, how can a man be sure?"

Preminger's film, Mary, in various ways, contradicts the Ann stereotype. Unlike Ann, for instance, Mary is, as the film implicitly conveys, when she, in her slip, is unperturbed by Frank's unexpected arrival at her apartment, a sexualized woman. Clearly Mary isn't in the tradition of the chaste virginal type most classically exemplified by Janet Gaynor in *Sunrise*. And, as is made explicit, in her rejecting of Frank, she refuses to passively accept his unwillingness to make a commitment. When he attempts to return, Mary, after informing Bill [Kenneth Tobey] that she wants to speak for herself, says: "...I want a marriage and not a competition. I want a husband and not a trophy that I have to defend over and over again." In a sense, Mary, in this scene, voices what Diane comes to feel about Frank's assumption of his independence. Although Mary and Bill can be taken as the film's "good" couple, *Angel Face*, doesn't, in actuality, construct the conventional polarization of the two couples.

3. As I have indicated, Diane has certain characteristics which type her as a femme fatale; but, when compared to the archetypal transgressive woman of the film noir, Diane appears highly unconventional. Briefly to recapitulate: although she manipulates Frank, her motive isn't that he provides a means to her gaining power. What Diane wants is Frank's love; as with her father, Diane has made a total commitment to Frank, and at no point in the film does she betray him. Diane doesn't implicate Frank in her plans to kill Catherine and, after the deaths, she twice tries (in the second instance, Diane thinks that she may have already lost Frank) to testify that she alone was responsible for the killings. Uncharacteristically, in *Angel Face* it is Diane and not Frank who is the more vulnerable of the couple. Although Preminger makes Diane's vulnerability apparent in several scenes between her and Frank before the deaths of Catherine and Charles, it is after the trial sequence that he fully develops this aspect of her identity. Having returned to the Tremayne house, Diane, after telling Frank that she regrets what she's done, tries to explain herself and why she had wanted Catherine dead. While Diane's explanation doesn't adequately justify her actions, it is a genuine attempt on her part to make Frank understand her present and past feelings. To Diane's plea that he grant her a degree of forgiveness, Frank responds with indifference. But Diane's vulnerability is most strikingly depicted in the scenes in which she, after Frank has left her for Mary, wanders through the house entering Charles' room, then Frank's (I discuss these sequences in more detail later). In terms of the film's plot, these sequences aren't necessary, but they are crucial to Preminger's conception and sympathetic portrayal of Diane. Although Preminger doesn't employ technical devices to produce a viewer identification with Diane (in the above-mentioned scenes, there are, for instance, no POV shots of the objects Diane associates with the presence of the two men). Preminger con-

Below, Diane and Frank take their final car ride.

structs, through narrative and characterization, a woman-centered film noir that sustains (unlike *Leave Her to Heaven,* in which Tierney's suicide is followed by a lengthy amount of footage devoted to the restoration of the "good" couple) its commitment to the woman who, ostensibly, is the film's femme fatale figure.

In Preminger's film, a reason why Mary and Bill don't become the alternative "good" couple is that Diane and Frank aren't the typical "bad" couple of the film noir. In their first meeting, Frank slaps Diane because she's hysterical; seemingly, what impressed Diane about Frank and prompts her to follow him, is his ease in taking control, his masculine display of authority. On the other hand, Frank's attraction to Diane is more obvious: her aggressiveness is a challenge, she's beautiful and rich. While Frank, at one point, tells Diane that they don't belong together because of their different social positions, Diane, for Frank, holds a fascination because of her class privilege. Although Diane is associated with aggressive sexuality and crime she isn't so much corrupt as spoiled and, consequently, she isn't even capable of corrupting Frank; she knowingly uses her access to money to keep Frank's interest, but he is no less guilty, fully realizing the financial potentials she offers him.[10] The union of Mary and Bill can be read easily enough as the film's restoration of "normality," but in this case normality is defined as the absence of desires beyond the most commonplace and material; and, significantly, after the deaths of Diane and Frank, the film does not re-introduce Mary and Bill. Instead, the film's final shot is the arrival of the taxi-cab to pick up Frank, the driver blowing his horn to summon his fare from an empty house whose occupants are all dead. The shot symmetrically echoes the opening (the ambulance, driven by Frank, arriving at the house at night): one of the bleakest and least reassuring instances of closure and the "restoration of normality" in the entire Hollywood cinema.

Preminger and mise-en-scène

Given that *Angel Face* is a film noir the viewer would be led to assume that the film's identification figure is to be the lead male protagonist. (This is reinforced in the casting of Robert Mitchum who has top-billing in the film's opening credits.) As the initial scenes of *Angel Face* are centered on Frank's experiences, it seems that we are being encouraged to take him as our identification source; and, with Frank, the viewer is placed in relation to a disorientating situation in entering the Tremayne house. After leaving Catherine's bedroom, Frank and Bill are seen in a medium long shot walking down the stairs; as Bill exits the frame screen right, Frank's attention is drawn screen left towards an off-screen space in which someone is playing a piano. As Frank continues to look screen left and gradually walks in that direction the camera begins to pan left keeping him in the frame. Frank and the camera keep moving until Diane, sitting at the piano, is also in the frame. What is important here is that Preminger doesn't cut to Diane which would have suggested a POV shot from Frank's perspective; instead, by constructing the two-shot through camera movement to introduce Diane he discourages viewer identification with Frank and, simultaneously, her objectification.

I am not suggesting that the above-mentioned two-shot in itself prevents any further possible viewer identification with Frank. But it does initiate a detachment from Frank which is crucial to the film's concerns. In fact, up until Diane's killing of Catherine and Charles, Frank remains the more accessible of the two lead protagonists. To an extent, we are sharing his orientation towards Diane; this occurs because Preminger doesn't give us full access to either the intentions behind her actions or her machinations: perhaps the most extreme example of the latter is that Preminger withholds the information that Diane has tampered with Catherine's car to transform it into a murder weapon. On the other hand, Preminger, through his close-ups of Diane, when she's playing the piano, produces a certain intimacy between her and the viewer which has no equivalent elsewhere in the film; although, paradoxically, with these close-ups, Diane is arguably at her most impenetrable. Prior to her killing of Catherine and Charles, Preminger allows for an ambiguous attitude on the viewer's part towards Diane but, in its aftermath, she becomes, although now a murderess, the emotional center of the film. Diane and her situation become increasingly poignant while Frank, in his response to her, becomes increasingly unpleasant. The sequences in which Diane wanders the house are exemplary here: there are no POV shots, and Preminger keeps her in long shot throughout until the final track-in to medium shot. The sequence described below is preceded by Diane's wandering from Catherine's room to Charles' which she enters pausing at his chess board and picking up one of the pieces. Diane then proceeds to Frank's quarters initiating a two shot sequence: the first shot begins with Diane entering the quarters and glancing around; she then lifts up the cover of a suitcase to see if it's empty, goes into an adjoining room and fondles a shirt on the bureau, returning to pick up Frank's sports jacket which she caresses; she then moves towards a window bench at which she and Frank had previously sat, pauses and exits the frame as the image fades indicating a time lapse. With a fade-in, the camera moves right from the window and tracks in towards Diane who is sitting in an armchair with Frank's jacket wrapped around her. She stares into space until she hears the sound of a car arriving at which point she gets up and exits the frame. *Angel Face*, among other things, illustrates that the viewer identification process is much more complicated than it is often assumed to be.

Throughout the film, Preminger's highly complex mise-en-scène is everywhere evident: for instance, the film's control/loss of control motif is visualized in his handling of the first murder sequence which is prefaced with a shot of Diane dropping an empty cigarette packet off the cliff on which the Tremayne house stands. The sequence itself begins with a shot of Diane at her bedroom window looking down at the pavement area and garage below; in addition to alluding to the height indication of the previous shot, it suggests that Diane presumes that she has control over what is about to happen. Preminger also introduces viewing height through a camera movement which begins as a tracking shot of Catherine and Charles as they move toward and then get into the car; as Charles closes Catherine's car door and exits the frame to get to his door the shot continues and the camera cranes up and tracks forward to frame in close-up the shift lever which Catherine has just placed in the drive position. While Diane thinks she has complete control, she doesn't know that her father will also be in the car. In the shot immediately preceding the murder scene, Diane sits down at her piano and begins to play; after the long shots of the car plunging down the cliff, Preminger dissolves back to Diane who, still playing the piano, maintains her illusion of control.

In *Angel Face*, there are more than 30 dissolves, the amount being, I think, as uncharacteristic of a Preminger film as it is of the typical classical Hollywood film. What these dissolves impart to the film is a degree of lyricism which is taken up in the piano music associated with Diane; like Diane's music, the dissolves function as counterpoint to the film's eruptions of violence which are particularly abrupt and brutal.

Conclusion

With *Angel Face*, the viewer is confronted by an extremely complex tangle in which class and gender concerns are pointedly raised: on the one hand, there is Diane's class privilege and, on the other, Frank's gender privilege. Contrary to Mayersberg's contention, Preminger isn't neutral either in his attitude towards his material or in his presentation of it. What his distanciation provides the viewer with is the opportunity to reflect on the concerns he is dealing with. This is altogether different from claiming that Preminger is objective in treating his subject. Mayersberg, in the *Movie* of 1962, presented this alleged "objectivity" on the level of the individual; its function was to leave the spectator free to judge the motivations and actions of the characters. But Preminger's attitude to his characters is, as I have tried to show, neither neutral nor undefinable (however complex); the function of the distance upon which his mise-en-scène insists is to allow us to pass beyond personal motivation to the awareness of the web of class and gender positions within which they struggle.

Notes

1. Jacques Rivette. "The Essential," *Cahiers du Cinéma*, *The 1950s Vol. 1*, Ed. Jim Hillier. (Routledge Kegan Paul, 1985): pp. 132-135.

2. Paul Mayersberg. "From Laura to Angel Face," *Movie*, No. 2 (September 1962): pp. 14-16.

3. *Bonjour Tristesse* is a fascinating companion piece to *Angel Face*. In *The Films in My Life* (Simon and Schuster, 1975), François Truffaut backhandedly suggests that Françoise Sagan used *Angel Face* as her inspiration for her celebrated novel.

4. Molly Haskell. *From Reverence to Rape*. (Penguin Books Inc. 1974): p. 159.

5. Contrary to those critics who claim that the film noir and the melodrama are polar opposites, I see them as complementary genres as both are centrally concerned with gender relations and particularly the entrapment thematic.

6. Set in Beverly Hills, the film begins with ambulance drivers, Frank/Robert Mitchum and Bill/Kenneth Tobey, answering a call from a hill-top mansion where Catherine Tremayne/Barbara O'Neil has almost been asphyxiated by gas in her bedroom. Mrs. Tremayne thinks someone tried to murder her but her husband, Charles/Herbert Marshall, discounts the possibility, insisting it was an accident. About to leave the house, Frank finds Diane Tremayne/Jean Simmons in the living room playing the piano; when he tells her that Mrs. Tremayne, her stepmother, will survive, she becomes hysterical. Frank and Bill return to the hospital and Diane follows in her sports car. At a nearby cafe, where Frank is attempting to call his girlfriend Mary/Mona Freeman, Frank and Diane meet again. Frank cancels his date with Mary and takes Diane out. Diane tells Frank that she and her father are very close, much to the annoyance of her stepmother. Later, she offers Frank a live-in job as the family chauffeur suggesting that Mrs. Tremayne might help finance his plans to start a sports car garage. When Mrs. Tremayne withdraws her support, Diane says she did so to spite her. Soon after, Diane claims that Mrs. Tremayne tried to asphyxiate her but Frank finds the story highly suspect. Diane, sensing that Frank is becoming uncomfortable with his situation and intends to leave, convinces him to stay until she can sell her jewels which will give them the money to buy a garage business and start a new life together. In actuality, Diane has decided to make another attempt at murdering her stepmother: when backed out of the family garage, Mrs. Tremayne's car is positioned near the edge of a steep drop-off; Diane removes a mechanism from the car so that it remains in reverse when Mrs. Tremayne puts the car shift into the drive position and steps on the gas. Although Diane's plan succeeds, she inadvertently also kills her father who was a passenger in the car. An insurance investigation leads to the conclusion that the car was tampered with. As Frank is a mechanic and Diane's suitcase was found in his room, they are charged with murdering the Tremaynes to get Mrs. Tremayne's money. After recovering from the shock of her father's death, Diane tells her attorney, Fred Barrett/Leon Ames, that she alone was responsible for the deaths. Barrett, thinking that the admission will raise issues about Diane's mental state and, more importantly, tie up the estate which she inherits, argues that a confession at this point would be taken as an attempt on her part to protect Frank. Intending to exploit the jury's sentimental notions regarding young lovers, Barrett has Frank marry Diane before the trial. Through a combination of insufficient evidence and Barrett's manipulation, Frank and Diane are acquitted. After a return to the Tremayne house, Diane tells Frank that she regrets what she's done; she also says that her love for her father blinded her to the fact that Catherine also loved him. But Frank offers her no compassion; he informs Diane that he wants a divorce and intends to return to Mary. Telling Frank that Mary, unlike herself, couldn't love a man who might have murdered, Diane bets her sports car against Mary's taking him back. Since Frank's rejection, Mary has become involved with Bill and, when Frank confronts her with his return, she rejects him on the grounds that she no longer wants to compete for his affections. Diane, thinking that she may have lost Frank, goes to Barrett to make an official statement wanting both to clear Frank's name and appease her guilt. Barrett says that her confession is now pointless and advises that, if she persists, her sanity will be questioned. When Frank returns Diane's car, he tells her that he's going to Mexico. She offers to drive him to the bus station. With both in the car, Diane throws the car shift into reverse and backs it off the drop-off, killing Frank and herself.

7. Otto Preminger. *Preminger: An Autobiography* (Doubleday & Company, Inc. 1977): pp. 123-126.

8. Robin Wood. *The International Dictionary of Films and Filmmakers: Volume III Actors and Actresses.* (St. James Press, 1986): pp. 576-577.

9. Barrett is also associated with the control/loss of control motif in his threatening Diane that she will wind up in a mental institution if she persists in wanting to confess to the killings.

10. In this respect, the Catherine/Charles and Diane/Frank relationships reflect each other.

Burt Lancaster as Ole "The Swede" Andersen in *The Killers*.

The Killers: Expressiveness of Sound and Image in Film Noir

Robert G. Porfirio

In cinema I find the best way of approaching the crime film is to let your audience in on the secret. Not to ask them who did it, but rather to let them follow the story line from one character's point of view.

Robert Siodmak[1]

As an illustration of some definitive aspects of film noir's visual style and their relationship to narrative structure *The Killers* (1946) is altogether fitting. First, this film drew its inspiration from a short story by Ernest Hemingway, the acknowledged "father" of the "hard-boiled school" of fiction which provided film noir with its most notable literary antecedent. Second, the film's director, Robert Siodmak, was a major contributor to the noir cycle (with at least ten entries by my reckoning) and was one of a group of Germanic emigrés who came to America and infused Hollywood with expressionistic proclivities. Despite an ostensible antagonism between the "realistic" impetus of the hard-boiled tradition and the "formative" tendencies of expressionism, Siodmak was exemplary in the way he worked within the Hollywood system to synthesize such contradictory strands into a fabric which could be perceived as homogenous. For the noir cycle, this would lead to the rise of the semi-documentary film policier beginning with *T-Men* and culminating, outside the cycle, with the highly popular TV series *Dragnet*. Siodmak's own *Cry of the City* (1948) provides an important line between the "closed" form of the early studio-bound noir films and the "open" form of the later police thrillers shot on location (cf. my entry in *Film Noir: An Encyclopedic Reference to the American Style*.)

Siodmak's noir films can provide us with numerous instances of the expressive use of sound and images, perhaps none more telling than those which eliminate the use of diegetic dialogue. Of course, the "jam session" from *Phantom Lady* (1944) comes quickly to mind since it stands out as a startling visual expression of Cornell Woolrich's own fear-ridden vision. Yet the two sequences from *The Killers* discussed below are perhaps more worthy of our attention because they owe less to the "influence" of their literary author and are less extrusive to the narrative body of the film: the robbery at the Prentiss Hat Co. looks forward to the motifs of the "caper" film just as the attempt of the two killers to execute Riordan at the Green Cat nightclub looks backward to the *Phantom Lady* "jam session" in its concatenation of jazz, sexuality, and the threat of violence. Although the emotional impact of each varies somewhat, both reflect the formative desire of the implied author, in this case Siodmak, to affect an audience through a variety of stratagems. These include the sequence shot, i.e., an entire sequence photographed in one unbroken shot; montage; and a heterogeneity of visual conventions.

The Sequence Shot: Spatial and Temporal Articulations

Contrary to critics who assert that the film noir eschewed the "realism" of the long take and highly mobile camera in favor of an editorial formativeness, both were well within the cycle's repertory. Of course, when the long take entailed intricate trucking movements (as opposed to depth-staging only), the time and expense involved therein forced many more modestly budgeted (or "talented") productions to "get by" with the formative effects of noir lighting and editing. Yet, post-war Hollywood had an impressive arsenal of new equipment at its disposal and an array of styles as varied as Welles' and Minnelli's from which to draw, so a consistent if conservative deployment of these techniques was to be expected, at least until the advent of wide-screen created new demands. The film noir was as sensitive to these techniques as any genre,[2] although one is hard pressed to detect there the "liberating" camera of the Hollywood musical or the "inquiring" one of neo-realism. As it had with deep focus, the film noir assimilated the moving camera and the long take into its own closed form, con-

trolling diegetic space in an architectonic manner (like any of the planned and edited sequences of Hitchcock) that ideally provides the viewer with a metonymic "lock" on its hermetic world. Simply put, the expressive components of the moving camera and long take draw the audience into a pre-determined reading of the scene.

I have chosen to illustrate this effect with the robbery sequence from *The Killers* (1946). There are a number of cogent reasons for selecting this example. Critics have often cited this film for its dark fatalism and closed form, qualities usually attributed to the compelling influence of director Robert Siodmak and his cinematographer Elwood Bredell. Of course, the producer, Mark Hellinger, and the studio, Universal, were familiar with Siodmak's "Germanic" sensibilities through his past work. Since a fluid camera was never Siodmak's "signature," it is not surprising that critics have chosen to describe the film's "brooding fatalism" in terms of its constrained visuals and fixed camera. Thus, *The Killers* offers a fairer test of the impact of the certain visual expressions than the work of directors such as Welles or Ophuls, whose careers have always been associated with more conspicuous technique including long takes and elaborate camera moves. And while the robbery sequence is not the only instance of elaborate camera movement in *The Killers*, it is an exceptional example in that it involves not merely a long take but a sequence shot, the two-minute length of which rivals those of Welles. Indeed this instance maintains precisely those unities of time and space that have caused the sequence shot to be extolled as a "realist" technique par excellence, but here those unities camouflage a highly contrived camera movement that controls the off-screen space with a closed form and that substitutes a formative manipulation of mise-en-scène for the temporal plasticity of traditional editing. Finally, this sequence has seldom been acknowledged as the effective "germ" of a subsequent type of caper film, one which used the plein air setting of a studio exterior to achieve the "look" of the semi-documentary. As such, it is a telling example of the noir cycle's unique synthesis of "realism" and expressionism.

The reader should remember also that the robbery itself is part of an overall narrative structure that estranges the viewer from its actions. The script of *The Killers* develops through flashbacks to a remote diegetic past. This particular flashback begins after the viewer witnesses the assassination of its most sympathetic participant, Ole Anderson (Burt Lancaster), at the film's beginning. This mode of enunciation is made even more alienating through the monotonous narration of an unenthusiastic insurance executive named Kenyon (Donald McBride), who is forced to read an old newspaper account of the affair although he has scant interest in reopening the case. Since all of the "normal" diegetic sounds that might be associated with the robbery have been eliminated in favor of McBride's voice and Miklós Rózsa's subdued background score, the scene is articulated through some of the conventions of the documentary, which audiences associate with "detachment." This detachment is enhanced by the objective persuasion of the crane-mounted camera which sweeps down from its initial imperious position (Figure 1) to bring the participants into close visual range. This position is held very briefly (2) before withdrawing for the action of the robbery itself (3 through 8). Such codes of expression combine to dissipate much of the tension implicit in the immediacy of the spatio-temporal order of the sequence shot.

Initially the camera does no more than to reaffirm the narration establishing the site of the robbery as the Prentiss Hat Co. (1) before descending in a rightward arc to reveal the gang entering the factory disguised as workers (2), a ploy which the narrator has already informed the audience was woefully easy for them to effect. However, after the camera moves back up and over the fence to pick up each member of the gang as he enters the industrial area (3), it begins to anticipate the action, tracking towards the paymaster's building even before the four robbers make their own move towards it (4). On the other hand, the narrator, droning on about the details of the robbers' plan and its execution, occasionally falls behind the visual revelations of those events.

The calculated nature of the visuals is quite apparent once the men enter the building (4), for the camera swings in a leftward arc up the side wall and positions itself outside the windows of a second floor office. Once there, it simply waits for the gang to arrive upstairs and come within view. The whole robbery is presented from this vantage point (5), while the voice of the narrator provides the audience with unseen details. After this short interval, the camera again "beats" the men back down to ground level and pauses until they have time to catch up as a slow-moving vehicle arrives to cover their getaway (6). The camera then trucks backward and begins to ascend, as the gang hurries to the cars parked outside in the street (7). The camera continues to rise, finally reaching a much higher and wider angle for the sequence's conclusion. This final vista permits the viewer a privileged position, somewhat removed from the violent action of the climax. At the same time, it provides the necessary space for a rigidly controlled mise-en-scène to simulate the aleatory: as the gang leader's dark coupe, pursued by a guard on foot, makes its escape in one direction (8, right foreground), the other two cars proceed in the opposite direction; and the first, a light coupe in the left background, is barely able to maneuver around a truck which is pulling out into the street. The second car, a dark sedan (middle of 8), is forced to turn around and go the other way. As the guard redirects his attention towards it, he is shot in the ensuing exchange of gunfire.

All of this action is presented from an "omniscient" perspective, looking down from the camera's final position above the action. This position perfectly reinforces the clinical detachment of the narrator as he describes the confrontation, first identifying the guard by name, even giving his address, and then offhandedly remarking

that "he fell to the ground with a bullet in the groin... and is now in the Hackensack hospital where doctors say he will probably recover." Such a detached attitude towards violence is typical of noir; and the clipped tone of McBride's comments anticipate the perfunctory epilogues of television shows like *Dragnet*, where the fates of the police and criminals alike receive the same impersonal descriptions.

The formative and architectonic nature of this sequence shot, as part of a film noir, reinforces the underlying concept of a chaotic universe, prone to unexpected and deadly eruptions of violence. The chance nature of who is harmed and who escapes unscathed creates a narrative tension which the dynamic of the sequence shot sustains and enhances. Perhaps the simplest way to isolate the noir implication of such a staging in *The Killers* is to compare it with the "robbery" in De Sica's *Bicycle Thief* or one of the riot scenes in *Medium Cool*. In those instances, a very different manipulation of the diegetic space creates a very different attitude towards the aleatory.

Intra-sequence Editing: Formative Functions of Sound and Image

The gunfight sequence in the Green Cat night club not only mixes diverse visual techniques but synthesizes these with a complex number of aural elements, both motivated and unmotivated.

This sequence is part of a larger segment set in the Green Cat during which Kitty Collins (Ava Gardner), seated at a table with insurance investigator Riordan (Edmond O'Brien), reveals to him in a flashback "all she knows" about the hat company robbery and her part in it. As the film's femme fatale, Kitty is its principal locus of moral ambiguity; and the Green Cat, as an obvious metaphorical extension of Kitty (who is of Irish origin and has a feline name), is invested with an aura of eroticism and danger. This places it at the center of other narrative ambiguities, which the gunfight underscores but does not resolve. In an earlier scene, under pressure from Riordan over the telephone, Kitty had suggested the Green Cat as a rendezvous point. Riordan had wisely declined in favor of a more neutral and public location. Yet after meeting her and escorting her into a cab, Riordan curiously decides to go with her to the Green Cat. The cutaways explicitly suggest that they are being tailed by a short, sinister man (Ernie Adams, whose frequent casting in such parts makes him something of an icon for the audience). He, in turn, is followed by Al (Charles McGraw) and Max (William Conrad), the two killers from the opening segment.

The association of the Green Cat with Kitty's sexual power is reinforced by a long dissolve which moves from a romantic flashback between her and Ole back to the nightclub. Further links to this romantic moment are created metaphorically by the burning candle on the table between Kitty and Riordan and the motivated romantic melody being performed by the club's piano player. Riordan's remark about her tale of infidelity is "I would have liked to have known the old Kitty Collins." After this line, a cut to Kitty's approximate POV reveals the presence of the short man at the bar. In an "orthodox" dialogue sequence, the cut back to Kitty reveals a change in demeanor, as if she were reacting to noticing the man. She asks to leave and suggests that Riordan take her to his hotel room. But the shot from Kitty's point of view is not a traditional one. Kitty is seated and the last part of her conversation with Riordan is shot in slightly low angle medium close-ups. The shot of the bar is from a slightly high angle. Moreover, the camera is angled towards the street-side wall of the nightclub, against which Kitty is seated, and photographs the bar with a statue of a green cat (or at least, one presumes it is that color, from the establishment's name if not from the black-and-white image) in the foreground. Such an angle could hardly be Kitty's literal point of view. Kitty never actually turns her head towards the bar but only shifts her eyes in that direction. In addition, the cat statue suggests her figurative presence in her own POV, somehow impelling the sinister man's actions.

The narrative information easily combines with this mysterious behavior by Kitty to sustain her identification as the femme fatale for the viewer. This paradigm is further extended as, exactly on Riordan's line to Kitty, "Too bad it had to catch up with you now," the nightclub pianist segues into a "boogie" jazz riff. Its insistent rhythm has associations of disquietude and sexual energy. A low angle shot of Kitty standing next to Riordan as she suggestively asks him to "wait here for me" while she goes to "powder her nose" is the last "normal" moment before the killers go into action.

The sequence of their attack begins with a cut to a wider shot, taken from behind the bar (Figure 9). The camera dollies to the left, then pans left with Kitty and pauses as she goes into the ladies' room before continuing in a leftward arc ending on the entryway to the club. During this pan, the slightly dissonant jazz riff picks up tempo and volume, as it blends with the cacophony of environmental sounds, people talking and laughing, etc. Another subtle revelation, hard to pick out in the camera move, is that the sinister man is no longer at the bar. At this point, the soundtrack is the perfect cue for the viewer's disquietude with its ambivalent connotations: the sexual innuendo of the jazz confirms Riordan's attraction to Kitty, while the dissonance reaffirms her negative attributes, and the ironic (that is, unknown to Riordan) element of danger in the sinister man. What is more, as the killers now appear in the entryway, an extra-diegetic element is added. The non-motivated underscore swells with Miklós Rózsa's "Killers' Motif"[3] (which later became essentially the first four bars of the theme from the television series *Dragnet*), the meaning of which has been palpably inscribed on the audience in the film's opening segment. The slow, steady repetition of this motif in counterpoint with the jazz riff begins to mask the sounds of the nightclub. An anticipatory tension is generated by the overdetermined status of the sound track throughout this sequence; and this is matched by a diversity of visual techniques which so alternate point of view and so control diegetic space that the heterogeneous signifiers are given the semblance of "wholeness."

To begin, when Al enters the club followed by Max (Figure 10), the camera is stationary. This permits Al to escape the visual field and exit frame right. Subsequently, however, the camera pans to the right to follow Max, reversing itself along the same arc used to follow Kitty. In so doing it recovers lost space and terminates in a position which recaptures Al and "fixes" him to the bar (11). At this point, the controlled objectivity of the camera motivates a cut to a subjective shot, taken from the approximate point of view not of Al (in the foreground of 11) but of Max (in the mid-ground of 11) and revealing Riordan alone at the table (12). The denotative effect of this virtual shot/countershot is to indicate that Max is aware of Riordan but not vice versa, as Riordan is glancing down at the table-top. Although the next shot of Max is head on, from a position in front of the bar (13), it is too close to Max to suggest Riordan's POV. Riordan is therefore outside the frame but still perilously within Max's visual field. The premeditated, objective stance of the camera is reaffirmed a moment later when a waiter comes around the bar and the camera is pushed back and pans slightly left as he walks down the bar, turns to pick up a drink, and then exits the frame. The waiter's natural actions have shifted the perspective of the frame so that other patrons along the bar are now visible; and as the waiter leans back, he opens a space for one of these patrons to turn

towards camera. This man is Sam Lubinsky (Sam Levene), a retired policeman who is assisting Riordan's investigation. Lubinsky's expression reveals little; but his gaze is directed to a point which suggests a congruence with Max's look. This carries the strong connotation that Lubinsky is aware of Riordan's exposed posture, perhaps even part of some plan to protect him. His immediate gesture, placing his hand beneath his coat for an instant, is to check for his gun. In an earlier scene, Lubinsky had kidded Riordan when the latter "lost" his gun. When Lubinsky now glances towards the opposite end of the bar (14), the camera pans off to the right and reframes on a medium long shot of the killers. Camera movement here transforms diegetic space by changing an objective shot to a semi-point of view, as the movement off Lubinsky's look onto the other two men implies that he is aware of the two killers. This is in spite of the fact that the narrative has not made it clear that either Lubinsky or Riordan "objectively" know who these men are. These shifting perspectives which combine to focus on both meaningful (Max, Riordan, and Lubinsky) and non-meaningful (the waiter) characters require the viewer carefully to read each shot and camera move and create a tension between objective and subjective information. This tension is also articulated in the intensity of the frenetic jazz piece and the legato of its musical counterpoint. As these subsume the realistic background noise, the "objective" reality of the associated images is further compromised.

The frequency and volume of the "Killers' Motif" increase again with the next cut, a long shot of Al and Max maneuvering at the bar from an "impossible" angle over Riordan's left shoulder, physically impossible because he is seated directly in front of some wooden wall paneling and a mirror (Figure 15, compare with Figure 12). The mirror had been particularly noticeable behind Riordan as he talked with Kitty before her flashback. Its slight tilt forward created an oddly distorted background behind his close-ups which literally "mirrored" but were different from the action behind her. Although they faced each other as they spoke, Kitty herself was not visible in that mirror. Now the camera is suddenly positioned on the other side of that mirror; and the rimlit seated figure of Riordan in the foreground has no depth, so that the low angle of his silhouette appears unnaturally high and graphically detached from the action. At the top of the frame a ceiling piece almost makes it seem as if Riordan is watching the killers prepare to attack though a window or a two-way mirror.

Manipulated in this manner, the traditional semi-subjective purview of the intended victim and the heightened music serve to increase viewer agitation, regardless of whether one "identifies" with Riordan or not. This tension is finally relieved by the gunfight itself. It begins with a slight downward tilt of the camera; then as the shot is held stationary the killers draw their guns. Riordan overturns the table and ducks for cover; in fact, he literally disappears from the frame. As the killers open fire, the music is so dominant that the gunshots and screams of the patrons can hardly be heard. There are more shots than visible muzzle blasts and Max winces in pain. Only at this point does a cutaway show Lubinsky firing away at the two men from the side. The cut back to the master reveals Al doubling over from a wound; he falls as Lubinsky enters this shot and moves up to him. Then in a semi-reverse, gun in hand, Riordan suddenly leaps up from behind the table. While the viewer may wonder if Riordan got off any shots, he moves quickly to the ladies room to discover that Kitty has gone out the window.

The visual confusion of the gunfight is accompanied by an interplay of diegetic and non-diegetic aural effects. At the first gunshot, the jazz riff terminates. In the motivated context, a flurry of gunshots, the club pianist might well be likely to stop playing. But the brass and strings play chords on the underscore which onomatopoeically mimic the muted sounds of the shots and the onlookers' screams. When the shooting subsides, the score briefly restates the "Killers' Motif" then segues to a "chase" theme as Riordan rushes to the ladies' room. Riordan is nonplused to discover that Kitty is missing, which perpetuates the implicit narrative "gaps" or confusion of the previous scene. Was Lubinsky's presence at the Green Cat part of a plan and were the identities of the killers known beforehand? Is this why Riordan surprised Kitty by deciding to take her there? If so, then why did he let her have a chance to escape? Was he disarmed by her fatal charm? Did Kitty signal or receive a signal from the sinister man, who in turn slipped out to cue the killers? The conclusion of the film, in which the remainder of the original robbery gang is killed off and Kitty is presumably arrested, does not resolve these ambiguities. Rather it expressively overcomes them through the structure of false homogeneity. This structure positions the viewer carefully within its chain of signifiers and by manipulation of sound and image, as Borde and Chaumeton first suggested, "make the viewer co-experience the anguish and insecurity which are the true emotions of contemporary film noir."[4]

Notes

1. Robert Siodmak, "HOODLUMS: the Myth...," *Films and Filming*, Vol. 5, no. 9 (June, 1959), p. 10.

2. As I suggested in my essay on "Existential Motifs in the Film Noir," it may be misleading to refer to film noir as a genre. Since part of what this brief piece is meant to illustrate is the influence of style in defining specific meaning in an individual film and in defining groups of film that share a common style, such as film noir, I use the term genre here in its broadest sense of a "sort" or specie of film, not in the common and more restricted usage implying a group of films defined outside of style by narrative structures, icons, etc.

3. Editor's Note: Rózsa's name for the cue was "Danger Ahead" and in 1953 his publisher's sued *Dragnet* composer Walter Schumann and won a cash settlement plus co-credit (and half royalties) for Rózsa from that point on.

4. See above, "Towards a Definition of Film Noir," p. 59.

The Swede faces the Killers.

Both *Gun Crazy* and its alternate title *Deadly is the Female* are epitomized in this scene (with John Dall as Bart Tare and Peggy Cummins as Annie Laurie Starr).

What Is This Thing Called Noir?

Alain Silver and Linda Brookover

> Of course, I'm not talking about commonplace affairs, planned out and prudent, but of an all-consuming passion that feeds on itself and is blind to everything else: of Mad Love. This love isolates the lovers, makes them ignore normal social obligations, ruptures ordinary family ties, and ultimately brings them to destruction. This love frightens society, shocks it profoundly. And society uses all its means to separate these lovers as it would two dogs in the street.[1]

In motion pictures the epitome of amour fou or "mad love" has most been associated with couples on the run. These fugitive couples were outcasts and outlaws, hunted and hopeless, and usually dead or dying at the film's end. As a sub-genre, the "fugitive couple" film has a long history from D.W. Griffith's *Scarlet Days* in 1919 to 1994's *Natural Born Killers* or *True Romance*. But even admitting such modern variants as *Thelma and Louise*, there are still only a score or two of pictures that fit this type. Many if not most of these were made as part of the classic era of film noir, in a fifteen year span from *You Only Live Once* (1937) to *Where Danger Lives* (1952). Both the obsessive character of amour fou and the alienated posture of the fugitives in relation to society as a whole are prototypical of the themes of film noir.

In his survey of noir, "Paint It Black," Raymond Durgnat gives a thumbnail sketch of the fugitive couples under the heading "On the Run": "Here the criminals, or the framed innocents are essentially passive and fugitive, and, even if tragically or despicably guilty, sufficiently sympathetic for the audience to be caught between, on the one hand, pity, identification and regret, and, on the other, moral condemnation and conformist fatalism."[2] As usual, Durgnat's prose is so densely packed that it masks the shortcomings of his analysis. What permits, even compels, viewer pity or identification with the innocent and guilty is the nature of most fugitive couples' love: obsessive, erotically charged, far beyond simple Romanticism.

I. The Innocent

"Teach me how to kiss."

Since film noir is as much a style as it is a genre, the manner in which the wild passion of the fugitives is portrayed is more significant than the plot points which keep them on the run. Some of these lovers are little more than children, like Bowie and Keechie in Nicholas Ray's *They Live by Night* (1947) or the high school girl and her simple-minded, ex-convict pen pal in the recent *Guncrazy* (1992). In their naiveté, typified by Keechie's request to Bowie to teach her how to kiss, both films recall Fritz Lang's seminal couple in *You Only Live Once*.

Lang's narrative focus in *You Only Live Once* is typical of his deterministic world view and, like his earlier *Fury* (1936), is as concerned with the outrage of the unjustly punished as with the fugitive couple. The director's naturalistic staging relies on the conventions of casting and the innate audience sympathy for stars Henry Fonda and Sylvia Sidney to maintain identification with a fugitive couple irrevocably at odds with the forces of law and order. As Eddie Taylor is released from his third term in prison, he is greeted at the gate by his fiancée, Jo Graham. Eddie promises her that he is through with crime; and he marries her, settles down, and takes a job as a truck driver. Yet after a local bank is robbed and an employee killed, Eddie becomes a prime suspect. Although innocent, he is arrested, convicted on circumstantial evidence, and, in view of his past record, sentenced to death. Not only is Eddie Taylor thus rapidly overwhelmed by the fateful forces of the film's narrative, but Lang accents his harsh determinism in *You Only Live Once* with an accumulation of chance encounters and telling images, culminating when the truck used in the robbery, evidence which could prove Taylor's innocence, slips silently beneath the surface of a pool of quicksand. That image becomes a metaphor for the luck-less Taylor, slowly and helplessly drowning under the weight of circumstantial events. Ultimately, because Lang is, in Andrew Sarris' words, "obsessed with the structure of the trap,"[3] the fateful turn of events is more important than the reasons for Eddie and Jo's devotion to one another.

Henry Fonda's interpretation of Taylor contains residues of hope and idealism which are almost incongru-ous in a man thrice-imprisoned by society for his past criminal acts. Nonetheless this outlook would become prototypical of later characters in the same predicament as Eddie. Whereas Lang's *Fury* concentrated on the question of mob psychology and recruited such stereotypes as the gruffly authoritarian sheriff, the politically motivated governor, and even the righteously liberal district attorney to probe that psychology, Lang does not elect to dramatize many of the possible parallel events in *You Only Live Once*.

As the title suggests, the individual protagonists, Eddie and Jo, and their one life are the major concern. On the date set for his execution, Eddie is sent a message that a gun has been hidden for him in the prison hospital. By the act of slitting his wrists, he has himself admitted to the hospital, finds the gun, and, holding the prison doctor as a hostage, demands his release. Both Eddie and the warden are unaware that the actual rob-ber has been captured and that a pardon is being prepared for Eddie. When this word arrives and the warden announces it to him, Eddie assumes that it is merely a ruse. He refuses to give up and impulsively shoots the chaplain who bars his way.

As *You Only Live Once* is more subjective than other of Lang's films, so is its direction keyed to the emo-tions of Eddie and Jo. In the opening sequences, a series of elegiac details establish Eddie and Jo's romantic dependence on each other, culminating as they stand in the evening by the frog pond of a small motel where Eddie explains to Jo that the frogs mate for life and always die together. Even as they feel secure in themselves, the motel manager is inside searching through his collection of pulp detective magazines under the harsh glare

Henry Fonda as proto-noir fugitive Eddie Taylor, ex-con but innocent of a murder charge.

of his desk lamp. When he finds several photos and a story on Eddie's criminal past, Lang underscores the irony first with a shot of a frog jumping into the pond and diffracting Eddie's reflection in the water. Then comes a view of a dark, vaporous swamp where the truck that could prove Eddie innocent of a crime of which he is not yet aware sinks into the quicksand. Although the frog pond scene could have either ridiculed the naiveté of Lang's characters or awkwardly stressed their lowly social status, Lang's staging and cutting makes it a simple, evocative metaphor for the entire narrative. As with Fonda's optimism, this elegiac moment is also a stylistic prototype for the treatment of a young and innocent couple on the run that endured throughout the film noir cycle.

When Jo, now pregnant, joins Eddie after his escape, the audience must expect that, for this couple as it would be for numerous later fugitives in film noir, the only way to freedom is through death. After their baby is born and entrusted to Jo's sister, they drive toward the border to escape. At a roadblock a flurry of gunfire forces them to abandon the car and flee on foot. A few yards from freedom, both are shot, Eddie falling last while he carries the already mortally wounded Jo in his arms. Despite the non-realistic, quasi-religious conceit—reworked from Lang's *Der Müde Tod* (1921)—of having the dead chaplain cry out "Open the Gates" in voice-over, the final shot of this couple through the cross hairs of a police sniper's gun scope is an image that is both characteristically noir and surprisingly modern. Thirty years later, Arthur Penn went a little further when he staged a realistic ending to *Bonnie and Clyde* (1967) by having them and their car perforated by scores of bullets. Of course, Penn's film purported to be the saga of the real Bonnie and Clyde. Lang's fugitive couple was merely inspired by those actual killers on the run.

They Live by Night shares an elegiac aspect with *You Only Live Once* in its contrast of the lovers' feelings with the insensitivity of the world around. In a way, Nicholas Ray's film is something of a fable. Its characters with their odd-sounding names, Bowie, Keechie, T-Dub, Chicamaw, exist in a world of grubby garages and cheap motels, cut off from the mainstream, from the ordinary, in an aura of myth. As its fugitive lovers are little more than children, the noir ironies of *They Live by Night* are reinforced even more strongly than in You Only Live Once by the very youth and innocence of its "outlaw" protagonists.

As the brief prologue explains, Bowie and Keechie are not just "thieves like us." That is not why society isolates them. As an early writer on Ray's work suggested "by their very simplicity and their desire for happiness, they are isolated, exposed to the hatred of a culture which would destroy that which it no longer possesses: purity in its desires."[4] That may seem an oversimplification; but Bowie, at least, really is too naive to survive. It is not merely that he is just a "kid" (the nickname which the press gives him to add color to their depiction of his flight) playing at being a man. It is because his lack of sophistication permits real criminals like T-Dub and Chicamaw to take advantage of him. How else but through his naiveté could they persuade Bowie that the only way to clear himself of an old criminal charge is to get money for a lawyer; and how else to get money for a lawyer than by helping his friends to rob a bank! Even Keechie's common sense cannot save Bowie from his own ingenuousness. She may help by removing him from the influence of T-Dub and Chicamaw; but the couple cannot remove themselves from the constraining influences of society itself. It surrounds them. Like the doorbell of the wedding broker that plays an off-key wedding march, while he hawks a "deluxe ceremony including a snapshot of the happy couple," the real world touches them with its cheapness and insensitivity. It entices them with the hope of escape like the bungalow of a backwoods motel where they find temporary refuge.

In the end, Bowie is guilty and he must die. But unlike Eddie Taylor, in Ray's hands, Bowie's fate seems less a question of implacable destiny than simple mischance. The fact that Keechie survives creates an alternate prototype for the ending of a fugitive couple drama. The Christmas tree and the small presents they leave behind when they must flee their bungalow are icons of hope and kindness that help sustain Bowie and Keechie in their brief time together.

It could be argued that the poignancy of the relationships in both *You Only Live Once* and *They Live by Night*, linked to life-mates in the animal world or wedding chapels and Christmas trees, may seem more romantic than noir. What is darkest about these movies, particularly in the context of mainstream Hollywood, is that

Young fugitives, Bowie (Farley Grainger) and Keechie (Cathy O'Donnell) tie the knot while on the run in *They Live by Night*.

Opposite, parole officer Griff Marat (Cornel Wilde) interviews a fetching new charge, Jenny Marsh (Patricia Knight) in *Shockproof*.

one or both halves of each couple perish. Obviously one of the motivating factors is the straightforward concept of moral retribution, of the need that is both abstractly dramatic and backed by the dictates of the Hollywood production code for the guilty to die. It is by emphasizing the innocence of their protagonists, literally for Eddie who is not guilty of the crime for which he is condemned and emotionally for Bowie who is ensnared by the older, duplicitous criminals, that filmmakers such as Lang and Ray make these films even darker and firmly imbed them into the noir cycle

More "upbeat" examples of the fugitive couple plot in film noir could be the Douglas Sirk/Sam Fuller *Shockproof* (1949) or *Tomorrow Is Another Day* (1951, directed by Felix Feist the scenarist/director of the manic *The Devil Thumbs A Ride* four years earlier). Both of these couples survive, but the noir sensibility of these pictures is sustained through amour fou. Like *You Only Live Once*, both feature protagonists who have already been convicted of a crime when the narrative opens. *Shockproof* adds the element of the "rogue cop" in the parole officer whose obsessive love drives him to flee with a women parolee accused of murder. *Tomorrow Is Another Day* goes even farther. The prospective couple are a bizarre admixture of innocence and depravity. The man, Bill (Steve Cochran), has grown up in prison convicted for a murder committed under the influence of an uncontrollable temper while still a youth. Paroled as an adult, he is sexually inexperienced. As portrayed by Cochran, better known for such supporting roles as the gangster who cuckolds Cagney's Cody Jarrett in *White Heat*, Bill has a physical maturity which belies his stunted emotional growth. The woman, Catherine (Ruth Roman), who becomes the object of Bill's obsessive love is a taxi dancer/prostitute. Again the element of the rogue cop is introduced, this time when a detective, who is himself in love with the woman, sexually assaults her and is killed. Like most of Hollywood's fugitive couples, including Eddie and Jo and Bowie and Keechie, the lovers of *Tomorrow Is Another Day* are proletarian. As with the couple in *Shockproof*, who find work in an oil field, Bill and Catherine seek refuge in the anonymity of migrant farming.

In the end, the subtlest irony of both *Shockproof* and *Tomorrow Is Another Day* is that neither of these couples take charge of their own destiny and create their own salvation. Rather they survive because they are both exonerated by their victims. For many fugitive couples, particularly in the context of film noir, the emotional sustenance which may be derived from any hope of escape or the kindness of strangers is secondary to their own obsessive love. When amour four is, as Buñuel suggesteda an all-consuming passion, every action, hiding out, stealing money, killing interlopers, is a desperate attempt to stay free where that passion may be sustained.

In the car and on the run in, clockwise from top left: *Tomorrow is Another Day*, *You Only Live Once*, *Shockproof*, and *They Live by Night*.

II. The Guilty

"We go together. I don't know how. Maybe like guns and ammunition go together."

Although it was made just two years later, *Gun Crazy* and its couple are far-removed from the innocence of *They Live by Night*. When Clyde first shows Bonnie his gun in Arthur Penn's film, she casually fondles the barrel. As a sexual metaphor such a staging pales in comparison to the meeting of the lovers in director Joseph H. Lewis' *Gun Crazy*. The first shot of Annie Laurie Starr, the sideshow sharpshooter of *Gun Crazy* (originally released as *Deadly is the Female*), is from a low angle as she strides into the frame firing two pistols above her head. Bart Tare accepts her open challenge to a shoot-off with anyone in the audience; and soon he and Laurie are firing at crowns of matches on each other's head. The sequence ends with an exchange of glances between the two. Laurie, the loser, smiles seductively. Bart, the victor with his potency established, grins from ear to ear.

This is merely the first meeting. Bart gets a job with the carnival, and from then on, Laurie wears her beret at an angle, her sweaters tight, and her lipstick thick. When a jealous sideshow manager fires them both, Laurie tries to convince Bart that there is more money to be had by staging shooting exhibitions in banks rather than tents. When he hesitates, she sits on the edge of a bed, demurely slips on her stockings, and issues her ultimatum: take it or leave me. Bart capitulates.

The aura of eroticism which Lewis builds so intensely into the first part of *Gun Crazy* is, albeit 1950 vintage, anything but subtle.

Below, before (right) and after changing looks and fleeing the police, Steve Cochran as Bill and Ruth Roman as Catherine, the proletarian fugitive couple in *Tomorrow Is Another Day*.

Opposite, sex, guns and money: a bathrobed Annie Laurie Starr (Peggy Cummins) smokes and pouts as Bart Tare (John Dall) cleans their weapons.

As Borde and Chaumeton enthusiastically noted back in 1955, "*Gun Crazy*, we dare say, brought an exceptionally attractive but murderous couple to the screen."[5] The physical aspect of the lovers does much to influence the viewer's perception; and the performance of the actors can sustain or counteract the visual impression, often assisted by the physical details of costuming and make-up. Catherine in *Tomorrow Is Another Day*, for instance, appears, in all senses of the word, "guiltier" with blonde hair, heavier make-up, and the gaudier clothes of her profession. As a plainly dressed brunette, her image is entirely different. Fred MacMurray's sneer as Walter Neff and Barbara Stanwyck's brazen, square-shouldered sexuality are keys to their outlook in *Double Indemnity*. Their underlying emotional estrangement is reinforced by the mise-en-scène. Two typical moments are found in the often reproduced scene stills of the couple side-by-side in a market but not facing each other (page 374 below) or her hiding behind his apartment door (page 113 above). How would the audience have perceived them if they had displayed emotions towards each other as they did in the publicity still reproduced in the thumbnail on page 359?

Because they are an "attractive couple," because, as Bart puts it, they go together explosively like guns and ammunition, the intensity of the budding amour fou of the couple in *Gun Crazy*, is immediate and overt. His companions on the carnival outing cannot help but sense it, as does the sideshow manager, who hires Bart nonetheless. While Laurie's passion is less obvious at first, she not only marries Bart, but pins her hopes on him. At that point, the full madness of amour fou is ready to erupt.

As *Gun Crazy* progresses, the lovers' continued physical attraction is keyed, for Laurie at least, to the excitement of their crime spree. Laurie tells Bart that she gets afraid and that is why she almost shoots down innocent people. Her real feelings are most clear in the celebrated long take during a small-town bank robbery. With the camera in the back of a stolen Cadillac for the entire sequence, Bart and Laurie drive in dressed in Western costumes, ostensibly to be part of the town's festival. The suggestion, of course, is that they are throwbacks to another era, desperadoes of an ilk closer to Jesse James or Belle Starr than Bonnie and Clyde. While

Bart is inside the bank, Laurie uses her charms to distract and knock out a policeman who happens by. The encounter has agitated and thrilled her. As they race off, she looks back, her hands around Bart's neck as if to embrace him. In that sustained, breathless glance, backwards towards the camera, her smile is unmistakably sexual.

By more contemporary standards, the mere innuendo of sexual pleasure from a criminal act may seem rather tame. But the staging of the scene in *Gun Crazy*, the tightly controlled perspective from the back of the car and the entire sequence shot without a cut, creates a tension for the viewer that is subtly analogous to the couple's. The release of the tension as the sequence ends is keyed to Laurie's expression. What is building, to use more contemporary terminology, is an addiction. Laurie's addiction to violence, initially motivated by the desire for "money and all the things it will buy," is now the need for an adrenaline rush. In feeding her habit, Bart is a typical co-dependent. Unlike earlier fugitive couples, who flee to save themselves from unjust accusations, Bart and Laurie choose to become criminals. As they come to depend more and more on each other, the process of *They Live by Night* is reversed. Rather than being innocents whose total, platonic interdependence becomes a sexual relationship, Bart and Laurie's purely physical attraction becomes emotional.

Appropriately then, the emotional climax of the picture follows immediately after their last job together. Laurie had planned for them to separate and rejoin later to throw off any pursuers. They drive to where a second car is waiting and start off in opposite directions. Abruptly and at the same moment, they veer around and rejoin each other. Like Buñuel's archetypes, Lewis' couple stand embracing each other in the street and figuratively serve notice on society that they will not be separated. After this declaration of amour fou, that they will perish is a given. They die together, he shooting her in a last, perverse act of love.

Bart and Laurie will not separate in *Gun Crazy*. Opposite, sex and money are literally mxed: Steve McQueen and Ali Macgraw as the McCoys in 1972's *The Getaway*.

III. The Ones Who Got Away

"You'd do the same for me, Doc, wouldn't you? I mean if I got caught, wouldn't you?"

Both film versions of *The Getaway* (1972 and 1994) star actors who are real-life married couples with established screen personas. Jim Thompson's laconic bank robber, Doc McCoy, is portrayed by Steve McQueen and Alec Baldwin, actors who share strong teeth and gritty expressions, and usually evoke expectations of heroic actions in the viewer. Both versions are adapted from Thompson's novel by Walter Hill, whose other neo-noir work, such as *Hickey & Boggs* and *The Driver*, also features hard-bitten professionals living on the fringes of society in the noir underworld. As directed by Sam Peckinpah, the earlier version with McQueen has a harder edge. The supporting players are nasty, garrulous, and otherwise unattractive in line with Peckinpah's naturalist bent and, of course, given to offhanded and extreme violence. The Baldwin Doc is on the one hand beefier and sports flashier dental work, but on the other hand has a more romantic regard for his lifestyle and his wife. In the hands of various adapters, the novelist's usual assumptions about the sordidness of crime and its corrupting influence on the criminal's will, became instead a story of betrayal and redemption, of self-righteous violence and paranoiac romance. Still as a narrative of amour fou and the fugitive couple, the two versions of *The Getaway* provide an expressive link to the films of the classic period of film noir. In a sense, just as *You Only Live Once* anticipated much of what would befall the fugitive couples of the 1940s and 50s, *The Getaway* films put a 70s and 90s spin on the plot with the most obvious difference being, as the title indicates, that these couples are the guilty ones who get away.

One of the supporting heavies in *The Getaway* (1994) remarks to Doc: "You got a smart little woman there... you taught her real well. She figures we do most of the work and you get most of the cash." One of the consistent aspects of both versions, which is certainly retrograde given the societal conditions of the 1990s despite being co-scripted by a woman, is that Carol's position as the film opens is subservient to Doc. Obviously couples portrayed in the classic period of film noir reflected the patriarchal prejudices of American society. Still, from *You Only Live Once* to *Tomorrow Is Another Day*, the outlook and fictional experiences of the couples injected a more egalitarian tone. In both versions of *The Getaway*, the Carols use their sexuality to control their husbands' fates. Ironically, the liberating power of the women's sexuality, which literally gets Doc out of jail, is psychologically imprisoning for Doc. His reaction when he learns of Carol's infidelity is understandable in a patriarchal context and certainly in terms of amour fou.

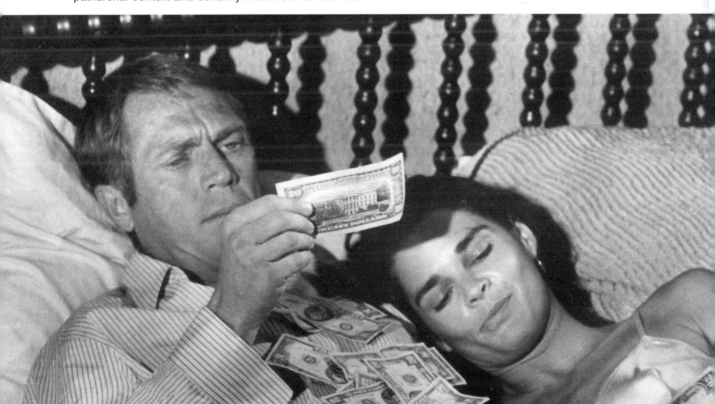

As with the male actors, the screen personas of the respective Carols, Ali MacGraw in 1972 and Kim Bassinger in 1994, "glamorize" the character. The title sequence of the latter version exemplifies this. Compared to the introduction of the MacGraw Carol as she visits Doc/McQueen in prison, the Bassinger Carol is first seen at target practice. A slow motion, extreme close-up of a finger pulling a trigger injects a note of genre awareness that verges on parody. The actors' names are superimposed as the frame widens via a zoom back to reveal the muzzle flash and recoil of the shots and a cutaway reveals tin cans jumping as they are hit. Doc and Carol are first seen in a two shot. She wears a sleeveless turtle neck under a black halter top, the lines of which mirror his shoulder holster. The first shot of her alone is as she fires a smaller caliber handgun. She wants the .45, but a smiling Doc asserts that "It's mine." Her answer, "but I want it," effectively summarizes the dynamics of their relationship. The associations of gunplay and sexplay develop naturally from the staging and statements ("We go together...like guns and ammunition...") of more than forty years earlier in *Gun Crazy*. Not only does the 90s Doc have the big gun that Carol wants, but he struts around displaying it tucked into his waistband.

In contrast, the opening of the 1972 version focuses on Doc already in prison. Carol is first seen in the form of two snapshots taped to the wall of his cell. Moreover Peckinpah unabashedly puts forth his typical naturalistic metaphors. The first shot is of a kneeling doe, followed by a stag. From this, there is a pan up to reveal a prison watch tower. Finally a long shot of sheep zooms back to reveal rows of cell blocks. Over this noise from the prison textile mill fades in. The isolated male and female animals prefigure Doc's overwhelming sense of sexual repression. The machine noise; Doc upsetting chess pieces and his opponent's remark, "Oh, man, it's just a game"; the destruction of the match stick bridge—all this overt symbolism establishes a deterministic undertow; and even though the machine noise stops with marked abruptness when Doc is released, this undertow will grip Peckinpah's fugitive couple unrelentingly. Throughout the film, other elements from Lucien Ballard's flat lighting scheme to the clipped dialogue delivery reinforce the realism. In the escape from the bank robbery, a crossing guard stops Doc and Carol's car. The red, hand-held "Stop" sign which she holds up for them to see is a typical expression of noir fatalism always threatening to capsize a scheme that goes back to the grind of the starter motor in *Double Indemnity*. For Wilder and Chandler adapting Cain, the engine finally starts. For Peckinpah and Hill interpreting Thompson, the delay creates a moment of chaos and violence which the characters must stoically endure.

While the narrative events of both *The Getaway*s are closely aligned, the tone of Peckinpah's violence is markedly different. His car chases are full of odd angles and cut points. The sound effects complement the lighting, they are muted and hollow. For Peckinpah, violent action is a transcendent activity. The slow motion and other stylistic manipulations create a distorted perspective for the viewer that is meant to be roughly equivalent to the temporal and sensory distortions which real violence imposes on its participants. Roger

Alec Balwin and Kim Basinger as the McCoys in 1994 *The Getaway*.

Donaldson, the director of the 1994 The Getaway, stages and edits the same action sequence in a more standard way, which, although the viewer/camera rides in the careening vehicles with the fugitive couple, has a depersonalizing effect.

Both films have the parallel plot line of the two-timing accomplice, Rudy, who kidnaps a veterinarian and his wife to help him track the couple. Rudy's seduction of the wife and the cuckolded vet's suicide also provide an ironic counterpoint to Doc's sense of betrayal because Carol bought his freedom with sexual favors. The 1994 Carol is slightly more emphatic when she asks "You'd do the same for me, wouldn't you, Doc? You'd humiliate yourself for me?" As a "90's woman," Bassinger's Carol not only wants the biggest gun, she wants to control her own destiny. MacGraw's Carol winces when she shoots people; but she does shoot them. When Bassinger expertly plays the dumb decoy or runs interference for her husband's scam from the driver's seat, it belies her ability to drive, shoot, and even throw a punch like a man. In this sense, she is closer to Annie Laurie Starr.

Outside the darker context of the classic period, both The Getaways offer a detached perspective on the questions of the fugitive couple, amour fou, and what is this thing called noir. If the moral issues at stake—trust, fidelity, family values, and self-esteem—are subsumed within the action, then why are the McCoys the ones who get away? Perhaps it is precisely because moral values are at stake. In the 50s, neither the deadliness of the female, which the original title of *Gun Crazy* proclaimed, nor the overpowering impulse of amour fou could permit Bart and Annie to run off together without pointedly getting married. Unlike most of the fugitive couples of the classic period, the McCoys are already married and already criminals when the films begin. No matter that they rob and kill, the film McCoys are faithful to each other in the truest sense. The Carols "expiate" their infidelity by killing Benyon. Doc accepts the overriding loyalty betokened by her "betrayal" and finally realizes that he would do the same for her. The graphically overt sex scenes, iconically reinforced in both versions because the viewer knows that the actors are actually married to each other, make the McCoys more real and less noir.

Is it still that same amour fou which so discomfits society? In the films' last sequences, the couples ride off to safety in Mexico in a dilapidated pick-up truck with an old geezer/guru of morality. In the 1972 version, that figure sums it up as, "Thats the trouble with this Goddamned world, no morals! Kids figure if they ain't living together, they ain't living." 1994's old philosopher is a widower but he knows that if his wife were alive today he would be going "nowhere but home. It's a tough haul sometimes, but well worth it. I think the most important thing in life is something you've got to give to each other." In the 90s, that's amour fou and the pop version is the end-title song lyric: "Now and Forever, I will be your man."

Even if it were not in the aftermath of *Wild at Heart* and *True Romance* or in the same year as *Natural Born Killers*, this sentiment might seem old-fashioned; and, to the extent that the noir outlook and/or mad love are the conceits of past times, it is old-fashioned. The emotions of the fugitive couples may be extreme, perhaps even unreasonable, but not irrational. They understand the perils of obsessive love, but cling to each other anyway. Some might say they are too violent in their amour fou, too imbalanced. Others might agree with Buñuel that "the real monsters are those men and women incapable of loving too much."[6]

Notes

1. Luis Buñuel quoted in Giuseppe Lo Duca, *L'Érotisme au Cinéma* (supplement), Montreuil: Edilu, 1968, p. 44.

2. Reprinted above, p. 80.

3. Andrew Sarris, "The American Cinema," Film Culture, No. 28 (Spring, 1963), p. 14.

4. François Truchaud, Nicholas Ray, Paris: Editions Universitaires, 1965, p. 17.

5. Reprinted above, p. 55much."[6]

Right, Neff and Phyllis.

Phantom Lady: Ella Raines as Kansas in the studio of Franchot Tone's migraine-plagued, mad artist, Jack Marlow.

Phantom Lady, Cornell Woolrich, and the Masochistic Aesthetic

Tony Williams

Despite the conclusions of the Wisconsin-Madison neo-formalist school,[1] film noir still remains to be reckoned with as an important movement in Hollywood narrative both in terms of its stylistic innovations and subversion of patriarchal gender norms.[2] It is in the latter connection that the work of Gaylyn Studlar promises significant gains in its applications to film noir.[3] The aim of this paper is to apply Studlar's thesis to the writer Cornell Woolrich and Robert Siodmak's Phantom Lady (1944) noting both its relevance and the oppositions which the film text counters to a complete supremacy of the masochistic aesthetic's operations.[4]

Studlar's work questions the Freudian-Lacanian-Metzian theoretical hegemony of cinema spectatorship and "woman's place." In Freud's scenario the child renounces pre-Oedipal bisexuality and the mother as "love object" in order to submit to patriarchal Law and castration. However, Studlar emphasizes Gilles Deleuze's work on masochism, challenging basic Freudian tenets of sado-masochistic duality, to reveal a hitherto neglected "masochistic aesthetic" in the field of psychoanalysis. In contrast to sadism's elevation of the father, masochism promotes the mother in a particular textual fashion. A work such as Sacher-Masoch's Venus in Furs contains a world that is "mythical, persuasive, aesthetically oriented, and centered around the idealizing, mystical exaltation of love for the punishing woman. In her ideal form, as representative of the powerful oral mother, the female in the masochistic scenario is not sadistic, but must inflict cruelty in love to fulfill her role in the mutually agreed upon masochistic scheme."[5]

This psychoanalytic model naturally challenges Laura Mulvey's visual pleasure argument which asserts that "male scopic desires must centre around control, never identification with or submission to the female."[6] Cinema spectatorship also becomes less of a predominantly masculine activity with its emphasis upon the sadistic male gaze. In Studlar's view, the spectator (male or female) regressed to the infantile pre-Oedipal phase, submitting to (and identifying with) the overpowering presence of the screen and the woman on it. Spectatorship and identification thus become a more complex process than in Mulvey's original formulation, having a bisexual component which has associations with the early phases of pre-Oedipal developments.

"Through the mobility of multiple, fluid identifications, the cinematic apparatus allows the spectator to experience the pleasure of satisfying 'the drive to be both sexes' that is repressed in everyday life dominated by the secondary process. The cinema provides an enunciative apparatus that acts as a protective guise like fantasy or dream to permit the temporary fulfillment of what Kubie describes as 'one of the deepest tendencies in human nature'; but like the wish and counterwish to fuse with or separate from the mother, the wish to change gender identity is also an ambivalent desire."[7]

Fulfillment of desire may also involve destruction, a fact true not just of films such as The Devil is a Woman but also of Cornell Woolrich novels such as Waltz into Darkness.

It is important to understand the masochistic phenomenon historically and not regard it in the same universal a-historic manner as Freud's original formulation of the Oedipus complex. Recent research has shown that masochism increased dramatically in the early modern period of Western culture that coincided with "increased emphasis on individuality."[8] Viewing several case histories Baumeister argues that "masochism is essentially an attempt to escape from self, in the sense of achieving a loss of high-level self-awareness."[9] Although he notes evidence of desires to escape sex roles,[10] enacting "fantasies that are radically divorced from normal reality,"[11] among predominantly upper socioeconomic white males, his findings have further implications. The masochistic scenario may illustrate a tendency of artist (as well as audience) to escape oppressive gender roles that western capitalist society has defined as "normal" in prescribing arbitrary definitions of "self." In the light of these important theories both the place of Cornell Woolrich and a 1944 film adaptation of one of his works merit close attention.

Author of *Phantom Lady* (under the pseudonym "William Irish") Cornell Woolrich (1904-68) is now recognized as an important force in the literary background of film noir, offering a significant alternative to the "hardboiled" school of Hammett, Cain and Chandler with their emphasis on phallic pleasures of control and mastery.[12] In terms of recent critical investigations of "male hysteria" and gender construction Woolrich's work offers fertile territory. Recognizing the male hysteric tradition in both literature and film, Jonathan Rosenbaum comments that Woolrich "can give it a sexual undertone without ever making its meaning strictly gender-based as it is frequently in Poe and Hemingway, Sternberg and Peckinpah. His heroines tend to be phallic while his heroes often verge on being sissies and fear becomes the universal democratic place on which they can meet as equals."[13] Woolrich's fervent emotional style, his powerful heroines (such as Julie Killeen of *The Bride Wore Black* [1940] who reduces her male victims to states of pre-Oedipal passivity) and the frenzied amnesiac of *The Black Curtain* (1942) who has lost masculine control of his destiny, are dynamic figures in Woolrich's world but have not been depicted in American movies. Hollywood investment in patriarchal norms of gender construction may be a significant reason for this although, as we shall see, it cannot entirely suppress this alternative as in the case of *Phantom Lady*. In a recent article on Robert Siodmak, J.P. Telotte notes that "Siodmak's films appear almost classic texts for illustrating gender tensions that were surfacing in post-World War II

"Pretty tie, expensive. I wish I could afford it." Inspector Burgess (Thomas Gomez) mockingly questions a passive Scott Henderson (Alan Curtis) in front of two Detectives about his wife's death.

America."[14] Although the film *Phantom Lady* came out in 1944, it is an anticipation of those subversive gender tensions which would emerge in *Out of the Past, Gilda, Criss Cross* and *Night and the City*. They are key texts in illustrating the insecurity of male control when attempts were made to reintroduce the pre-war patriarchal status quo. Writing of Siodmak's work (but in terms also applicable to *Phantom Lady*) Telotte notes of the director's male characters that "What finally makes Siodmak's world so disturbing though, is that his male characters, too, seem fluid, potentially phantoms, as if they, too, were infected by a contagious evaporation of the self."[15] This influence may be attributed to the work of Cornell Woolrich and the dominance in his writings of the masochistic aesthetic.

Studlar's description of masochism as an obsessive recreation of the movement between "revelation and concealment, appearance and disappearance, rejection and seduction" accurately resembles Woolrich's classic novels, especially *The Bride Wore Black* (1940) and *Black Angel* (1942), which contain worlds of "a sensual heterocosm in which the female is mystically idealized as the loving inflictor of punishment."[16] Both Woolrich and Edward Hopper were influenced by cinema in their respective artistic mediums.[17] There are many parallels between Studlar's research and the work of Woolrich which demand further investigation.

If the male spectator identified with the masochistic male character, he is aligned with a position usually assigned to the female. If he rejects identification with this position, one alternative is to identify with the position of power: the female who inflicts pain. In either case, the male spectator assumes a position associated with the female. In the former, he identified with the culturally assigned feminine characteristics exhibited by the male within the masochistic scenario; in the latter he identifies with the powerful female who represents the mother of pre-Oedipal life and the primary identification.[18]

Woolrich has much in common with this scenario. Biographical research has revealed his mother fixation, bisexual tendencies and inability to follow the Oedipal trajectory of "normal" human development. His first, F. Scott Fitzgerald-influenced novel, *Cover Charge* (1927), introduced the passive male hero, often at the mercy of the powerful female, who would frequently appear in his later work. But his most powerful fiction appeared in the decade of film noir, the '40s, often in the "Black" series of novels. Most of his work was filmed within a year or so of its initial appearance either under his own name or his pseudonyms, William Irish and George Hopley.[19] Woolrich was often displeased with the film versions of his work.[20] One of his major works remains to be filmed while two appeared as films some 20 years after their initial appearance as novels.

	Cornell Woolrich	William Irish	George Hopley
1940.	*The Bride Wore Black*		
1941.	*The Black Curtain*		
1942.	*Black Alibi*	*Phantom Lady*	
1943.	*The Black Angel*		
1944.	*The Black Path of Fear*	*Deadline at Dawn*	
1945.			*The Night Has A Thousand Eyes*
1947.		*Waltz into Darkness*	
1948.	*Rendezvous In Black*	*I Married a Dead Man*	

The late appearance of *The Bride Wore Black* and *Waltz into Darkness* (Truffaut's *La Sirène du Mississippi*) as films is mysterious.[21] However, one reason may be the fact that the heroines of these works were such powerful threats to patriarchal ideology that they could not be successfully incorporated into the 1940s norms of Hollywood gender representations. The only comparison is *Detour*'s (1945) heroine (the appropriately named actress Ann Savage). Although we are familiar with the femmes fatales of *Murder, My Sweet* (1944), *Double Indemnity* (1945), and *Out of the Past* (1948), all these pale into insignificance when compared to Julie Killeen and Bonnie. Both women are far too powerful to gain access even into the contemporary cracks within the dominant Hollywood ideology that made film noir possible.

Julie Killeen is a powerful avenging figure, able to disguise herself by embodying male romantic fantasies of the "ideal female" and eventually killing her victims after reducing them to positions of helpless dependency. Julie wreaks so much damage upon patriarchal order that even the traditionally imposed Hays Code ending of "punishment for her sins" would have appeared ludicrous. Bonnie in *Waltz into Darkness* is more of a castrating threat to male power than Julie.

Rendezvous in Black has never been filmed to date. Although it is a male re-working of *The Bride Wore Black*, its assault on patriarchal gender construction makes it too threatening. The avenging hero murders the wives and girlfriends of his victims in revenge for the death of his sweetheart. The novel makes clear his excessive over-idealization of his lost love and his collapse into male hysteria. Thus his ambivalent sexual nature, hysterical actions and passivity before death reveal him as another Woolrich male who does not operate according to the masculine action dynamics of the Law of the Father. The hero of *The Black Curtain* exhibits hysteria when he discovers that his amnesia has caused loss of masculine control in society. This dilemma was excellently acted by Cary Grant in the half-hour radio version.[22] In *The Black Angel*, a quiet housewife becomes an avenging female to save her husband. In one case her actions indirectly cause the death of one of Woolrich's recurrent male victims on the altar of romanticism. Like Julie, the heroine "becomes an idealized, powerful figure, both dangerous and comforting,"[23] a role which Carol Richmond of *Phantom Lady* plays, causing the death of two male victims. While Scott Henderson becomes passive and impotent on death row, Carol is active on his behalf, thus reversing the typical male-female trajectory. She turns from sweet secretary to threatening pre-Oedipal mother and sexually active femme fatale. Although *Deadline at Dawn* substitutes the symbolic function of the city expressing capitalist alienation for the powerful female as a main narrative device, the novel's heroine still has actively to urge her passive boyfriend to save himself from the accusation of murder. *Black Alibi* is a notable exception to Woolrich's other work but this may be due to the novelist's experimenting with the "sadistic" aesthetic in crime fiction. Another explanation may lie in the fact that the original short story revealed the hero as the perpetrator of the crime.[24] Although the novel made him innocent this initial narrative device may explain the virtual absence of the masochistic motif.

Woolrich may have influenced other films. Based on Steve Fisher's novel, *I Wake Up Screaming* (1941) modelled the psychotic cop Cornell on Woolrich. In what was possibly an inside reference to the real-life author, the film cast Laird Cregar as Cornell. Although his resemblance to Woolrich was non-existent (unlike the novel's description), the industry knew of Cregar's unhappy existence as a bi-sexual at the time.[25] Burt Lancaster's roles in Siodmak's *The Killers* (1946) and *Criss Cross* (1948) are undeniable echoes of Woolrich's doomed male victims of romanticism, especially in their respective manipulation by femme fatales Ava Gardner and Yvonne DeCarlo. Another example is Richard Widmark's performance in Dassin's *Night and the City* (1950). Before his death he collapses into the arms of Gene Tierney like a little boy before his mother.

Although modifying Woolrich's short story, Hitchcock's *Rear Window* (1954) preserved the hero's important role as well as developing the cinematic apparatus motif.[26] This also occupied an important element in *The Window* (1950) where a little boy observes a murder committed by two dark mirror image parental figures, watching a window as if viewing a cinema screen. The dark parents are the alter egos of his economically oppressed father and mother (Arthur Kennedy and Barbara Hale) turning to robbery, murder and prostitution to survive inside capitalism. It is not without significance that the biggest threat to the boy comes from the dark mother (Ruth Roman).

Woolrich's "fervent emotionalism,"[27] male passivity before either avenging female or dark universal malevolent powers, and the role of suspense (usually presented as a race against time as in *Phantom Lady, Deadline at Dawn* and *The Night Has A Thousand Eyes*)[28] are all integral components of the masochistic aesthetic. Louis Bernard's tortuous romanticism and passivity in *Waltz into Darkness* represents the imaginative masochistic desire for reunion with the mother. It is finally realized in that "kiss of farewell" when Bonnie changes from hostile oral mother into the good maternal spirit:

Their very souls seemed to flow together. *To try to blend forever into one*. [Italics mine] Then, despairing, failed and were separated, and one slipped down into darkness and one remained in the light.[29]

Bonnie thus represents that "dialectical unity between liberation and death, the bonding of Eros with Thanatos that places the former in the service of the latter."[30] She is the idealized mother to Louis's pre-Oedipal child.[31]

Like *Deadline at Dawn* and *Three O'Clock*,[32] *Phantom Lady* contains Woolrich's hysteric suspense formula of the race against time. It resembles a compulsive Freudian Fort/da game in which death (and return to the womb) is the dominant motif. Deleuze's observations concerning the masochistic's suspension of the ultimate gratification of death, the obsessive return to the continuously re-enacted moment of separation from the oral mother, are all relevant to understanding Woolrich's technique in novels such as *The Black Path of Fear*.

Studlar's investigation of the masochistic aesthetic has certainly great relevance to the novels of Cornell Woolrich and the Dietrich/von Sternberg cycle of films.[33] But when we examine the film *Phantom Lady*, we find that the masochistic scenario is more in the nature of a crack within the dominant patriarchal ideology rather than an overpowering element in the filmic text. We must remember that every film is a complex of intersecting elements in potential competition with each other. Also it may be under the influence of social and historical factors that govern what may be adapted at any particular time. According to Frederic Jameson, a set of circumstances may circumscribe an area beyond which any text can not stray. Any given historical moment may foreground some generic possibilities and make others unlikely.[34] In the case of *Phantom Lady*, both the novel and film are lacking in comparison to *The Bride Wore Black, Waltz into Darkness,* and *Rendezvous in Black* where the masochistic aesthetic is more fully realized. As well as the reasons listed above for the imperfect realization of Woolrich's subversive gender depictions on screen, we must remember the dominance of the Oedipal trajectory of classical Hollywood cinema in which the female becomes subjected to male control either by death or marriage.[35] At the climax of the film Carol is confined to the office and the offer of monogamy. However, enough remains of the masochistic model in the film to argue that the aesthetic, if not dominant, is there as a fissure, a gap in the ideology which permits the partial expression of the female voice. It exists as an alternative operation against patriarchal control of the text. Even if subdued at the climax, it is still there, attempting to strain against narrative bounds.

In both novel and film Carol Richmond fulfills the role of the oral mother threatening two males in her quest to save Scott Henderson from the electric chair. She intimidates the barman from the Anselmo by usurping the prerogative that Mulvey associates with male-dominated cinema, the sadistic power of the gaze. She pursues him and causes his death in a manner reminiscent of Deleuze's description of the "bad" pre-Oedipal mother:

"She appealed to them, self-possessedly but loudly enough to be heard, and the calm clarity of her voice stopped them all short. 'Don't. Let him alone. Let him go about his business.'

But there was no warmth nor compassion about it, just a terrible steely impartiality. As if to say: Leave him to me. He's mine."[36]

In visually dominating the drummer, Cliff, by acting out the sexually powerful femme fatale role Carol assumes the uterine mother's function with its associations of prostitution.[37] This is excellently realized in that "jam session" sequence in the cellar lit in the German expressionist manner in which Carol lords it over drugged musicians. As in the Dietrich/von Sternberg films "the femme fatale does not steal her 'controlling gaze' from the male, but exercises the authority of the pre-Oedipal mother whose gaze forms the child's first experience of love and power."[38]

But the narrative cannot allow Carol's total dominance. In the last 10 minutes she is reduced to the helpless position of the threatened, screaming female before her last-minute rescue by Inspector Burgess, representative of the Law of the Father. Also, the male victims are figures whom the masculine audience can easily reject. They are not Robert Mitchum of *Out of the Past* nor Glenn Ford in *Gilda*. The audience is removed from them.

This explains Siodmak's transformation of Woolrich's "normal" murderous engineer, Lombard, into Franchot Tone's stereotyped Mad Artist, "complete with delusions of grandeur, symbolic migraine headaches, and overdone hand gestures."[39] He appears to owe more to Siodmak's German expressionist interests rather than the hard-boiled world of '40s noir. However, this change is easily understandable when we remember tra-

ditional concepts of masculine depiction in Hollywood cinema and its tendency to project unmasculine features of lack of control, impotence and emotionalism on to figures such as Elisha Cook, Jr. with whom the audience would find it impossible to identify.[40] Lombard's original engineer function is too closely associated with
male control. The film thus seeks to make him different. However, in the novel he is one of Woolrich's doomed
victims on the altar of romanticism. He exhibits qualities usually associated with stereotypical notions of the
female and becomes a plaything for the whims of unseen, oral mother, Marcella Henderson:

> He'd spent most of his life around oil-fields in God forsaken parts of the world; and he hadn't had much
> experience with women. He didn't have any sense of humor about things like that. He took her seri-
> ously. And of course she liked that part of it all the better, that made the game more real.... After all,
> when a guy's that age, and not a kid any more, he takes it hard when you kick his heart around like
> that.[41]

Franchot Tone's Marlow is a Nietzshean mad artist. He is associated with modern art artifacts as well as a Van
Gogh self-portrait. The film uses these tactics to remove him as a threat to typical definitions of the masculine.

Carol "Kansas" Richmond (Ella
Raines), standing at frame center,
smoking, with her suit and hair
empahsized by a kick light,
strikes a masculine and dominating pose over her jailed and passive boss (Alan Curtis).

A mad modernist artist is less of a threat to gender stereotypes than a mad, masculine engineer.[42]

But although the masochistic aesthetic is not completely dominant either in novel or film, enough traces remain of its presence as a subversive influence. Examination of both works reveals underlying tensions which are not completely recuperated despite attempts to do so.

The novel begins and ends with the male perspective. It opens with Scott Henderson. Three pages describe his attitudes before he notices the mysterious female. The novel ends with Inspector Burgess's final moral to the reunited couple, Scott and Carol: "If you've got to have a moral, I give you this: don't ever take strangers to the theatre unless you've got a good memory for faces."[43]

This resembles the classic detective fiction discourse in which everything is satisfactorily resolved by a controlling agent in the type of fiction associated with Conan Doyle, Agatha Christie and the "hard-boiled" school. It is an unsatisfactory climax to a novel which exhibits so many of Woolrich's better concepts Scott's passivity before his fate, Carol's active control in trying to save his life by taking on female roles that are merely the construction of male fantasies,[44] and the bi-sexual implications of such role transferences. Carol is instrumental in trapping Lombard in the novel,"The best man of us all." as Inspector Burgess describes her.

The film's opening scenes differ. From the close-up of her hat as the camera tracks out before Scott enters the bar, Anne Terry's control over the male narrative (and Scott) receives emphasis. Anne refuses to give her name, thus rejecting male control of her identity. Scott's inability to learn her name is later ridiculed by the voice of the unseen District Attorney (Milburn Stone) at his trial.

Scott's return home further reveals his impotence before the dominant female presence. As he enters his apartment calling his wife, a cop (Regis Toomey) switches on the light. Inspector Burgess stands beneath Marcella's portrait with an accusing look on his face. The camera pans left in the next shot when Scott discovers Marcella's dead body. Acting as if malevolent agents of the dead Marcella, the cops stand cynically watching.

Marcella's portrait appears predominantly throughout the following interrogation. She dominates Scott in death as she did in life.[45] His masculine world of "Engineer" is undermined by Marcella's image controlling the frame. The camera pans right as he speaks of his marital difficulties whilst walking away from the picture. It pans left as Scott returns to his original position beneath Marcella surrounded by the two cops. As he begins to relate his evening's humiliation, "She just sat there and laughed. She kept laughing at me," Marcella's portrait appears at a canted angle leftwards. Toomey is to the right of the portrait. He acts as chorus of the

Henderson strikes up a conversation with the "Phantom Lady" in the large hat, later discovered to be Ann Terry (Fay Helm).

patriarchal world view,"Nothing makes a man madder than that!" The portrait also dominates the frame in the next shot when Scott tells of Marcella's refusing a divorce. Another cop makes the sardonic comment, "Making a patsy of you, eh?"

Thus the visuals explicitly associate the cops as Marcella's functionaries in reducing Scott into helpless masochistic passivity. The casting of Alan Curtis as Scott, an actor not particularly noted for predominantly masculine roles, reinforces this interpretation.[46] He breaks down like the traditional "hysterical female" after seeing Marcella's body carried out by uncaring medics.

The cops surround Scott on either side. A slow tracking shot begins until he becomes isolated in close-up. As the camera moves in it emphasizes Scott's passivity. The envious class-conscious cops make hostile comments about his clothes in a manner usually associated with male comments about female costume: "A very neat dresser, Mr. Henderson." "Yeah, everything goes together." "Pretty tie, expensive. I wish I could afford it." Finally, the scene (with its visual associations of rape) ends with Burgess noticing that Scott's tie does not match his suit. The appropriate tie is round his wife's neck.

In the next sequence we meet Scott's secretary, Carol, played by Ella Raines. If Alan Curtis was not sufficiently "masculine" to be a successful Hollywood hero, Ella Raines was conversely not sufficiently "feminine," so her career was relatively brief.[47] *Phantom Lady* was her most significant film. Carol is efficient enough to run Scott's office on her own. But she is under the dominance of patriarchal ideology. Scott's voice over the dictaphone giving her daily orders limits any possibility she may have of independent control in the masculine world of Scott Henderson Incorporated.

"Franchot Tone's Marlow is a Nietzshean mad atist." One of his pieces reflects his obsession with his own hands. The French release title was, in fact, *The Hands that Kill.*

However, when Scott receives the death sentence Carol becomes an avenging female, pursuing the barman and drummer Cliff Milburn with the power of the gaze to gain information, thus usurping a traditional male prerogative. In the car Carol is transformed by harsh noir lighting into both a Woolrich avenging fury and hostile oral mother figure. Changing into her "hooker" role she entices Cliff by manipulating his look for the purposes of her own control.

But the filmic text can only allow Carol so much latitude before two male forces of patriarchy intervene. The first is Inspector Burgess (Thomas Gomez) who offers his support. Thus, the power of the Law will eventually dominate the narrative until it rescues Carol after she has relinquished the power of the avenging female by collapsing into hysteria.

The second figure is Marlow who represents the dark forces of male chaos, an opposing figure to patriarchy-prescribed gender roles. Entering Cliff's room after Carol has fled, his speech not only reiterates the "mad artist" discourse by which the narrative can make him an "other" but also reveals his female perception. "She was magnificent. She loathed you but she went with you. She would have humiliated herself to make you talk."

As portrayed by Franchot Tone, Lombard/Marlow is clearly a victim of socially restrictive gender definitions of male and female roles. Although the narrative attempts to depict him as a mad artist, an "other," it is clear that his insecurities in bearing an oppressive male role in capitalist society have overpowered him. Rejected by Marcella, he has psychotically erupted against an imagined threat to his socially constructed ego. Yet, Tone's performance contains a mixture of sympathy and pathos that clearly marks him as victim rather than monster. His act was the ultimate expression of male hysteria when his everyday "masculine" role became as impotent as that of Scott's before the cops. Like Scott he has clearly repressed "feminine" qualities which explode in murderous expression.

Up to Marlow's appearance Carol has occupied the role of the avenging Woolrich female. But the film's patriarchal narrative form can bear the strain no longer. A progressive subordination of her role begins until she is no longer the "threat" but "the threatened." She must lose all trace of her previous pre-Oedipal status by now occupying a subordinate position within the "sadistic" portion of the narrative in which she is threatened by Marlow until Inspector Burgess can successfully intervene.

When Carol eventually finds Anne Terry, the film clearly reveals that females are also victims of patriarchal ideology. After the death of her fiancé, Anne has collapsed into a nervous breakdown. She is as much a victim of romantic love ideology as is Lombard/Marlow. When Carol discovers her, Anne is living in her grandmother's house where she "had lived all her life." Dominated by the dead hand of the past, Anne tells Carol about her grandmother. "She was very happy here. She married the man she loved. I'll never marry." However, recognizing Carol's similar love (or entrapment) she gives her the hat needed for evidence before therapeutically breaking down in recognizing the death of her love.

After Inspector Burgess's rescue Carol once more occupies the subordinate secretarial role after Scott has seemingly resumed the boss demeanor. But although the film attempts to impose a "happy" ending by means of the classical Hollywood marriage motif,[48] the climax can be read in a much more subversive manner. Despite the film's ideological project of undermining Carol's dominant role by attempting to assert male control at the climax, both the opening and closing shots significantly operate against this. A tension is created in the overall structure impossible to recuperate successfully.

We remember that the film began with a close-up of Anne's hat. The enigmatic female, not the male (as in Woolrich's original), begins the narrative. At the climax Inspector Burgess and Scott await Carol. Both men leave as if nothing has happened. Scott tells Carol of the dictaphone messages awaiting her. Rescued from the electric chair he appears to show no gratitude to her. The formal boss-secretary relationship appears to resume as Carol presses the vocal instrument of male control.

Listlessly listening she hears Scott's marriage proposal. "You're having dinner with me tonight, and tomorrow night, and every night." The camera tracks in to a close-up as the message plays. It stops as the dictaphone needle sticks in the groove endlessly repeating "every night." An enigmatic look of pleasure emerges on her face in the final image.

Two interpretations are possible here. First, the climax represents the successful Oedipal project of subordinating the female to the male. As victim Carol takes pleasure in her own future oppression as both wife and secretary. But a second interpretation is also more likely. A contradiction certainly exists in the combination of needle sticking and a triumphant look on Carol's face. The dictaphone is symbolic of male control, a control that the film reveals as being non-existent in the cases of Scott, Marlow, the barman, and Cliff. Even Inspector Burgess admits his error about Scott's guilt to Carol mid-way in the film. We remember the powerful femme fatale role which she occupied in her pursuit of the guilty males. It is hard to believe that she will ever successfully settle down into the passive role of wife/secretary. The needle sticks on the words, "every night," the time in which Carol was at her most powerful. Carol's triumphant look may assert the latent presence of the "masochistic aesthetic" still awaiting another re-emergence in opposition to patriarchal power. The needle sticking opposes the male control triumph of the female outside the confines of the text. This scene anticipates those future victories of her sister "phantom ladies" in a later generation.

Notes

1. See David Bordwell, Janet Staiger and Kristin Thompson, *The Classical Hollywood Cinema: Film Style and Mode of Production to 1960* (New York: Columbia University Press 1985): pp. 74-77; Edward Branigan, *Point of View*.

2. For a relevant selection of work in this field see Raymond Borde and Étienne Chaumeton, *Panorama du film noir Américain* (Paris: Éditions d'aujourd'hui 1953; 1976 reprint); Raymond Durgnat, "The Family Tree of film noir,"

"Kansas" is dismayed to learn of Ann Terry's descent into madness from Dr. Chase (Virginia Brissac). From his expression, Marlow's thoughts about the insane "Phantom Lady" could be "welcome to the club."

Cinema (Britain) 6/7 (August 1970): pp. 48-56; Paul Schrader, "Notes on Film Noir," *Film Comment*, 10.1 (January-February 1974): pp. 30-35; E. Ann Kaplan, ed., *Women in Film Noir* (London: British Film Institute 1978); Alain Silver and Elizabeth Ward, *Film Noir: An Encyclopedic Reference to the American Style* (Woodstock, New York: The Overlook Press 1979); Jon Tuska, *Dark Cinema: American Film Noir in Cultural Perspective* (Westport, CT: Greenwood Press 1964).

3. Studlar's doctoral thesis (to be published this year [Editor's Note: 1988] by the University of Illinois Press) in its application to cinema deals exclusively with the Paramount Dietrich/von Sternberg films. For an outline of her position see Gaylyn Studlar, "Masochism and the Perverse Pleasures of the Cinema," *Quarterly Review of Film Studies*, 9.4 (January-February 1985): pp. 267-82; and "Visual Pleasures and the Masochistic Aesthetic," *Journal of Film and Video* 37.2 (Spring 1985): pp. 5-26. However, the findings are equally applicable to other areas of cinema such as film noir, horror and the musical. I am grateful to Professor Studlar for her suggestions in correspondence dated June 24th, 1987 and November 1st, 1987. See also Linda Bundtzen, "Monstrous Mothers: Medusa, Grendel and Now Alien," *Film Quarterly* 50.3 (Spring 1987): pp. 11-17; and Linda Mizejewski, "Women, Monsters and the Masochistic Aesthetic in Fosse's Cabaret," *Journal of Film and Video* 39.4 (Fall 1987): pp. 5-17.

4. This article is abased upon a paper delivered at the Mid-West Popular Culture Association Conference on October 16, 1987 at the Meramec campus of St. Louis Community College. I am grateful to the *CineAction!* editorial group for suggested revisions.

5. Studlar, Masochism, p. 267; see also Gilles Deleuze, *Masochism: An Interpretation of Coldness and Cruelty* (New York: George Braziller 1971).

6. Laura Mulvey, "Visual Pleasure and Narrative Cinema," *Screen* 16.1 (Autumn 1975): pp. 6-18. See also the criticism by D.N. Rodowick, "The Difficulty of Difference," *Wide Angle* 5.1 (1982): pp. 7-9.

7. Studlar, "Visual Pleasure and the Masochistic Aesthetic," p. 13.

8. See Roy F. Baumeister, "Masochism as Escape from Self," *The Journal of Sex Research*, 25.1 (February 1988): pp. 28-59, especially 51.

9. Baumeister, pp. 28-29.

10. Baumeister, p. 41.

11. Baumeister, p. 45.

12. On Woolrich as the real literary inspiration of film noir see Stephen Jenkins, "Dashiell Hammett and Noir: Out of the Vase?" in *Monthly Film Bulletin* 49, No. 586 (November 1982): p. 276. See also John Baxter, "Something more than night," *The Film Journal* 2.4 (1975): p. 9, who cites a passage from Woolrich's *The Black Path of Fear* (1944) as contributing towards noir lighting effects. This is also mentioned by Bordwell 77 who cites 1940s comic strips and German expressionist lighting techniques.

13. Jonathan Rosenbaum, "Black Window: Cornell Woolrich," *Film Comment* 20.5 (September-October 1984): pp. 36-38.

14. J.P. Telotte, "Siodmak's Phantom Women and Noir Narrative," *Film Criticism* 11.3 (Spring 1987): p. 2.

15. Telotte, p. 9.

16. Studlar, p. 8.

17. Woolrich briefly worked as a Hollywood screenwriter, taking the pseudonym of scenarist "William Irish" for four of his novels. See Francis M. Nevins Jr. "Introduction," Cornell Woolrich writing as William Irish, *Phantom Lady* (New York: Ballantine 1982): pp. ix-xiii. For one example of cinema in Woolrich see *The Black Angel* (New York: Ballantine 1982): p. 131. On Hopper's use of cinema see Erika L. Doss, "Edward Hopper, Nighthawks and Film Noir," *Postscript* 2.2 (Winter 1983): pp. 14-36.

18. Studlar, p. 14.

19. Hopley was Woolrich's maternal middle name. See Francis M. Nevins Jr. "Introduction," Cornell Woolrich writing as George Hopley, *The Night Has a Thousand Eyes* (New York: Ballantine 1982): p. xiv.

20. See the February 2, 1947 letter of Woolrich to Mark Van Doren concerning the filming of *Black Angel*. This was kindly reproduced for me by Mike Nevins.

21. For a description of the films and their flaws see Francis M. Nevins Jr. "Fade to Black," *The Armchair Detective* 20.1 (1987): pp. 39-51; "Fade to Black, Part Two," *The Armchair Detective* 20.2 (1987): pp. 160-175.

22. On the significance of Cary Grant in terms of bi-sexuality see Andrew Britton, "Cary Grant: Comedy and Male Desire," *CineAction!* 7 (December 1986): pp. 36-52.

23. Studlar, Masochism, p. 268.

24. See Francis M. Nevins Jr., "Introduction," Cornell Woolrich, *Black Alibi* (New York: Ballantine 1982): p. xi.

25. See Joel Greenberg, "Writing for the Movies: Barry Lyndon," *Focus on Film* 21 (Summer 1975): p. 48.

26. See Roberta Pearson and Robert Stamm, "Hitchcock's Rear Window: Reflexivity and the Critique of Voyeurism," *Enclitic* 7.1 (Spring 1983): pp. 136-45.

27. See Francis M. Nevins Jr. "Introduction," Cornell Woolrich, *Nightwebs* (New York: Harper & Row 1971).

28. Phantom Lady's chapters are all headed by the number of days or hours preceding Scott Henderson's execution.

29. Cornell Woolrich writing as William Irish, *Waltz into Darkness* (New York: Ballantine 1983): p. 319.

30. Studlar, p. 280.

31. See Studlar, p. 271 for an illuminating parallel to this scene in terms of the masochistic aesthetic.

32. See William Irish, *I Wouldn't Be in Your Shoes* (Philadelphia & New York: Lippincott 1943).

33. For some pertinent observations on the role of the masochistic aesthetic in the Paramount cycle see Florence Jacobowitz, "Power and the Masquerade: The Devil is a Woman," *CineAction!* 8 (March 1987): p.34.

34. Frederic Jameson, *The Political Unconscious* (Ithaca: Cornell University Press 1981): pp. 145-48.

35. The work of Raymond Bellour on classical Hollywood narrative is relevant here. For some qualifications to Studlar's work in terms of arguing for a sado-masochistic dialectic within the viewing subject see Tania Modleski, *The Women Who Knew Too Much* (New York: Methuen 1988): pp. 9-13.

36. *Phantom Lady*, p. 110.

37. Studlar, *Visual Pleasure*, p. 24, n. 13.

38. Studlar, p. 23.

39. Nevins, "Introduction," *Phantom Lady*, p. xiii.

40. For a significant article on this actor's function in *The Big Sleep* (1946) see Christopher Orr, "The Trouble With Harry: On the Hawks Version of The Big Sleep," *Wide Angle* 5.2 (1982): pp. 66-71.

41. *Phantom Lady*, p. 219.

42. On the cultural significance of this transformation in terms of contemporary attacks of modernism see Diane Waldman, "The Childish, the Insane and the Ugly: The Representation of Modern Art in Popular Films and Fiction of the Forties," *Wide Angel* 5.2 (1982): pp. 52-65.

43. *Phantom Lady*, p. 240.

44. The heroine's observations about Marty in *Black Angel* deserve quoting:

"Out of all the thousands and thousands of fine constructive women in this world, what evil star made him pick her out? What got him about her? Couldn't he see, couldn't he tell? And the answer, of course, was self-evident. What gets any of us about any of them; what gets any of them about any of us? The image in our minds. Not the reality that others see; the image in the mind. Therefore, how could he see, how could he tell, how could he free himself, when the image in his mind all along, and even now, was that of a lovely creature, all sunshine, roses, and honey, a beatific haloed being, a jewel of womankind? Who would even strive to free himself from such a one? Watch out for the image in your mind." [p. 66]

Woolrich's ability to identify himself with both male and female positions receives classic exemplification here.

45. The role of the portrait is a special icon in film noirs such as *The Woman in the Window* (1944) and *Laura* (1945). For some relevant observations on this motif see Janey Place, "Women in Film Noir," E. Ann Kaplan, ed. *Women in Film Noir*, pp. 47-50. One recalls Keene's fascination with the portrait of the imprisoned Mrs. Paradine in *The Paradine Case* (1947) and the power exerted over Cregar's Cornell by Carole Landis's portrait in *I Wake Up Screaming*. For an interesting discussion of the former film in terms of male impotence and female ambiguity see Michael Anderegg, "Hitchcock's *The Paradine Case* and Filmic Unpleasure." *Cinema Journal* 26.4 (Summer 1987): pp. 49-59.

46. According to Ephraim Katz, *The International Film Encyclopedia* (London: Macmillan 1979, p. 293), he was originally a male model before entering films in 1936.

47. She was a joint discovery of Charles Boyer and Howard Hawks (Katz, p. 944).

48. See Janet Bergstrom, "Alternation, Segmentation, Hypnosis: Interview with Raymond Bellour," *Camera Obscura* 3/4 (1979): p. 88.

From his intent stare (not to mention the ominous lighting on the artist's face), Inspector Burgess is clearly tuned in to Marlow's egomaniacal sociopathy.

Double Indemnity, hint: insurance agent Walter Neff (Fred MacMurray) and black widow Phyllis Dietrichson (Barbara Stanwyck) are not talking about ration coupons or green stamps.

Noir 101

Philip Gaines

Back when I normally taught production classes to students whose interest in the "history" of movies ranged from slim to none, on several occasions I forced some reluctant observers to endure an entire term of film noir. And while these dark retrospectives were initially met with the kind of enthusiasm usually reserved for a dead mackerel, within a few class sessions all of these reluctant film historians, whose incoming attitudes were either down on Hollywood or apathetic about any films but their own, were hooked on noir. When the Editors of this book originally approached me about quickly synthesizing my course approach (apparently they lost the rights to another piece) and presenting my outline for a sort of Film Noir 101, I wasn't sure how well my free-form approach would work when experienced purely on paper. You'll have to judge that for yourself.

I've found that many of the overview books on film noir (and I lost count of how many when it got to be more than a couple of dozen of them) are pretty useless. Of course, if I had to pick my ideal point of view, it would have to be one that tackles the noir phenomenon like most of its heroes tackled their travails, making it up as they went along. Since that's a hard method to sustain over an entire academic term, the "text" I previously used was just a selection of photocopied essays. Then I discovered that almost all of them were reproduced in *Film Noir Reader* now transformed in *Film Noir Compendium*, which should be everyone's new basic text. Of course, I had appended the original *Film Noir Reader* within *Reader 2*, where this piece first appeared, but now have it all in the single volume *Compendium*.

One advantage that has exploded in the 21st century is the ready availability of screenable copies of the key movies, whether on Blu-ray, standard DVD (with or without the de rigeuer commentaries, of which the editors of this book seem to have made a cottage industry), and digital download. It's like being with Neff and Phyllis strolling down the grocery-store aisle in *Double Indemnity* and pondering their choices, literally and figuratively, 24/7.

I won't bother to take a position in the style versus content, movement versus genre debate. I have one, but flogging it in a lecture is usually counter-instructive for students who would rather hear the crisp report of a gat in a dark alley than dogma. Besides Noir 101 is about gats going off in dark alleys first and about postwar angst, the residues of German Expressionism, and the dialectic between patriarchal structures and Leibniz's monads second, sixth, and three hundred and forty-third respectively.

Possible Introductory Essays (all reprinted in *Film Noir Compendium*)

Borde and Chaumeton, "Towards a Definition of Film Noir"

Raymond Durgnat, "Paint it Black"

Paul Schrader, "Notes on Film Noir"

Janey Place and Lowell Peterson, "Some Visual Motifs of Film Noir"

Robert Porfirio, "No Way Out: Existential Motifs in the Film Noir"

1. Opening with a Bang: *Double Indemnity*

I'd certainly get more laughs with *Detour* (someday fate points that finger at you) and definitely put more people to sleep if I opened with *The Postman Always Rings Twice* (tried it. Once). I've also used *Laura* as the introductory movie, but *Double Indemnity* is a lot funnier and a lot grimmer. It also exemplifies more aspects of noir than just about any other film. It was based on a hard-boiled novel (by James M. Cain), co-scripted by a major hardboiled guy as well (Raymond Chandler), directed by a refugee not from German Expressionism but German Fascism (Billy Wilder), and shot and scored by preeminent noir craftsmen, John Seitz and Miklós Rózsa, at a major studio (Paramount). So in delivering introductory comments on film noir, one can touch on the source literature, earlier film movements, the political context in the world (war in Europe) and in Hollywood (the first film noir nominated for an Academy Award), or visual and aural styles and have examples right at hand. In terms of the narrative, which is the aspect of film noir that is readily accessible to most students, *Double Indemnity* really packs a wallop: femme fatale (in spades); flashback; first person narration (heavily ironic to boot); ace investigator; more greed than Von Stroheim could throw at you; hetero- and a soupçon of homo-eroticism; and, even without the cut scene of Keyes watching Neff entering the gas chamber, some pretty harsh shuffling off this mortal coil by assorted characters. It's even got pompous company owners, proletarian figures who go bowling, statistics, and a sweet young thing, whom the hapless hero discovers too late.

An excellent alternate title is *Out of the Past* for most of the same reasons as those above.

Possible Additional Reading

Cain's original novella (it's short and Cain gives up nothing to Woolrich or even Jim Thompson in evoking thoroughly twisted people with spare prose)

Willian Bendix and the aptly named Buzz, driven well past distraction by the sound of "jungle music" in *The Blue Dahlia*.

Richard Schickel, BFI Monograph on *Double Indemnity*

Claire Johnston's essay in *Women in Film Noir*

Maurice Zolotow's description of Wilder/Chandler set-tos in *Billy Wilder in Hollywood* (also recapped in Ward/Silver, *Raymond Chandler's Los Angeles*)

2. Pre-noir

There are few images from early cinema more striking than the faces of Griffith's *Musketeers of Pig Alley* and a short film such as this quickly demonstrates the depth of noir's roots. It's simple to explain that the style and content of pre-noir ranges from the tilted chiaroscuro of German Expressionism to E.G. Robinson's mouthing "Mother of Mercy, can this be the end of Rico" in *Little Caesar*. When one actually considers the key films of German Expressionsm, from *Caligari* to *The Last Laugh*, it's clear that American gangster films are the best bet. If one insists on opening with something German, the choice is *M*. Von Sternberg's *Underworld* captures qualities of both antecedents, but I usually show *Scarface* and refer to Universal horror films, *I Was A Fugitive from a Chain Gang*, and a list ranging from *King Kong* to *Citizen Kane* for further research.

Possible Additional Reading

The texts on pre-noir include the introductory comments from Schrader's "Notes" and Carlos Clarens' book *Crime Movies*

3. The Classic Period: *The Maltese Falcon*

Schrader's "Notes" first proposed and Silver/Ward et al in their subsequent books have established a consensus on what they call the "classic period" of film noir: it begins with *The Maltese Falcon* and it ends with *Touch of Evil*. Not long really, less than two decades; and nobody agrees on all the pictures in between. Even if one opts for the suggestion of Porfirio and a couple of others that *Stranger on the Third Floor* is the first noir film, *The Maltese Falcon* is a much more appropriate and compelling introduction to classic noir. Bogart's still got it, and while I don't require the Hammett book be read, I recommend it and/or one of the first four Chandler novels. The context is the development of noir inside and outside the hard-boiled tradition. Hammett, Graham Greene, Raymond Chandler, and Cornell Woolrich provide a wide choice of literary sources, so alternate film selections are *This Gun for Hire*, *Murder, My Sweet* and *Phantom Lady* all of which feature heavy-handed visuals but the latter two may draw some snickers for their graphic excesses.

Possible Additional Reading

Carl Richardson, "Film Noir in the Studio: the Maltese Falcon" in *Autopsy: an Element of Realism in Film Noir*

More off-the-wall (and in cheek), *The Maltese Touch of Evil*

4. Post-war angst: *Nobody Lives Forever*

The clichéd assumption about post-World War II noir is that it dramatized the post-traumatic stress syndrome (masquerading under some less enlightened name such as "battle fatigue") of the the combat veteran. In fact, noir had plenty of alienation going for it before World War II came along. There are some memorably disturbed veterans, for instance, William Bendix as the manic Buzz Wanchek who loses control whenever he hears "jungle music" in *The Blue Dahlia*. But even though it boasts a Chandler screenplay and has Alan Ladd and Veronica Lake as its key protagonists, the real post-war irony in this film is not the steel plate in Buzz's head but the infidelity of the Ladd character's wife, who stepped out on him while he was off killing the enemy. Whatever the psychological disturbance, whether it's as explicit as the amnesiac ex-Marine George Taylor (John Hodiak) in *Somewhere in the Night* or as subtle as the perpetually sneering Gagin (Robert Montgomery) in *Ride the Pink Horse*, the hardest thing for many returning veterans to face is not what they did in the war but what they missed at home. In that sense the best example I've found is the 1946 *Nobody Lives Forever* (a script by W.R Burnett directed by Jean Negulesco), where John Garfield portrays a pre-war criminal, a gambler whose budding career was stunted by the draft.

The Naked City:
cop meets girl.

A significant side effect of such characterizations is that the occasional and restrained Freudianism of early noir explodes into unrestrained psychosis in such titles as the *The Dark Mirror* and *The Dark Past*, where inky cases of the fantods splatter across film noir like an unrestrained Rorschach. Whatever the feature selection, I usually add as short subject the John Huston documentary *Let There Be Light*, which provides a segue to the next segment.

5. Docu-noir: *The Naked City*

We all know that post-war noir also adapted new technologies: high speed film, faster lenses, smaller cameras and other equipment. Still the "shot on actual location" De Rochement productions at Fox were pretty stodgy affairs, as is *Call Northside 777*, despite James Stewart's performance in it. And should one sit through Lang's *Blue Gardenia* just to comment on its crab dolly work? Fortunately there is a perfect example: *The Naked City*.

Naked City ends with the catch phrase popularized in the TV spin-off of the Fifties: "There are eight million stories in the naked city. This has been one of them." It opens with a voiceover intoned by that most extraordinary of noir producers Mark Hellinger (whose death in 1947 cut short a credit list of noir that already included *Brute Force, The Two Mrs. Carrolls,* and *The Killers*). Over aerial shots of Manhattan, Hellinger solemnly promises that "It was not photographed in a studio. Quite the contrary...the actors, played out their roles on the streets, in the apartment houses, in the skyscrapers of New York itself." Despite the showboating, *Naked City* is remarkably undated (or perhaps has endured beyond that perception). While somewhat intrusive, eventually Hellinger's commentary, which is kept up throughout the film and often slips into second-person mode where he talks to the characters, creates a snide, pseudo-documentary tone that is truly noir. "Take it easy, Garza," Hellinger warns a fugitive, "Don't run. Don't call attention to yourself." The montages of "real" behind-the-scenes events won the big prize for editing in 1948 but seem old hat now after the method became obligatory for so many cop shows. Some examples, such as the PBX board labels tracing the phone calls from the discovery of a body to the notification of the homicide squad, are still effective if no longer novel.

Two excellent alternate choices are by Anthony Mann, *Border Incident* and *T-Men*, both of which were shot by the legendary John Alton, whose lighting of locations yields an eerie blend of the chiaroscuro and the hyper-real.

Possible Additional Reading

Malvin Wald, "The Making of *The Naked City*," reprinted in *The Big Book of Noir*

J.P. Telotte, "The Transparent Reality of Documentary Noir," in *Voices in the Dark*

The shots of the city recall the sardonic freeze-frames of WeeGee the Famous and a compilation book of his photographs is a good addition to the reading list.

6. Fugitive Couples: *Gun Crazy*

"Thrill Crazy, Kill Crazy, Gun Crazy", what more needs to be said? The fugitive couple is a rich tradition in film noir, and Joe Lewis' classic brings it all home. Whether or not a closeted John Dall ever really drooled over Peggy Cummins' gams in black stockings, his heavy-lidded leering makes him the perfect low-budget noir everyman, intoxicated by the pistol-packing con-woman, Annie Laurie Starr. Shot on actual locations (a King Brothers production couldn't afford to build sets), *Gun Crazy* easily cross-refers to docu-noir, B-noir, and even, neo-noir, getting a nod from the 1992 *Guncrazy* and overt homage from the American *Breathless*. The celebrated long take shot from the back seat of the car, as the couple rob a bank while dressed in cowboy costumes, ends with Cummins' post-orgasmic glance over her shoulder. Of course, *Gun Crazy's* car scenes can be strip-mined for over-blown comments such as "The passengers are traveling between two sets of emotional

Contrasting young couples from *The Naked City* (opposite) and *Gun Crazy*. Can you tell by the clothes, decor, and lighting which couple walks on the wild side?

or existential situations...in which the automobile's interior can carry the same charged or claustrophobic atmosphere as the noir city itself." (*Somewhere in the Night*) In plain talk, wherever the spectator is situated, *Gun Crazy* is about the sexual dynamics of mixing guns, gals, and high performance engines.

Possible Additional Reading

Astonishingly the only decent piece out there is Brookover/Silver "What is This Thing Called Noir?" in *Film Noir Compendium*

7. Psychological Melodrama: Auld Lang Noir

Fritz Lang's dry melodramas of hopeless entrapment make him, for many critics, the uber-auteur of noir. Samuel Fuller or Bob Aldrich, he ain't; and the deterministic subtleties of *Human Desire* or *Beyond a Reasonable Doubt* can make the most resolute noir freak nod off. There is certain Yeats-like symmetry to his parables of middle-class mayhem, a sardonic undertone to the impeccably groomed Tom Garrett (Dana Andrews) in *Beyond a Reasonable Doubt* moving smoothly from the world of crime journalism and burlesque joints to courtroom in a double-twist plot. But there's not much "va-va-voom" here.

There are some Lang characters with a lot of intensity, most notably Glenn Ford's relentless cop out for revenge in *The Big Heat* or the small-town Joes (Paul Douglas and Robert Ryan) in *Clash by Night*. But the Langian hero par excellence is Edward G. Robinson and his remarkable performances in *Woman in the Window* and *Scarlet Street*, a double take on obsession with Joan Bennett as the obscure object of his desire. Whether it's the psychology and dream states of *Woman in the Window* or the artist-meets-cons and debasement of *Scarlet Street*, either of these examples probes the melodramatic aspects of noir pretty deeply.

Edward G. Robinson as the hapless Chris Cross buffs and polishes the toes of Joan Bennett's Kitty in *Scarlet Street*.

The alternate choice for "sturm und drang" meets noir is Otto Preminger, not *Laura* but the "Angel" movies: *Fallen Angel* and *Angel Face*. Outside the context of falling in love with a picture, Andrews in the former and Mitchum in the latter are hooked by a bad girl a la Preminger. One survives, the other doesn't.

Possible Additional Reading

Alfred Appel, Jr., "Fritz Lang's American Nightmare" in *Film Comment* (November-December, 1974)

Robin Wood on Lang's *Big Heat* and Aldrich's *Kiss Me Deadly* in *CineAction* No. 21/22

Florence Jacobowitz, "The Man's Melodrama: Woman in the Window and Scarlet Street" reprinted in *The Book of Film Noir*

8. The A's, B's, and Z's of Noir: *Detour* and *D.O.A.*

It's not news that film noir was mostly not mainstream stuff. Still early examples like *Maltese Falcon* and *Double Indemnity* were strictly "A" pictures. There were also "B" studio (RKO) and "B" unit noir films from the beginning. A final post-war effect was the emergence of the "poverty row" noir. But the "Z" grade efforts, made for budgets of less than $150,000, were not limited to PRC and Monogram. As the 1940s ended and the blacklist forced many noir writers to work cheaply for independent producers such as the King Brothers or Harry Popkin, pictures such as *Detour* and *D.O.A.* were made on a shoestring.

The problem with *Detour* as an example is its mannered script and acting. Where else in film noir is there a death as outrageous as that of the hitchhiking Vera (Ann Savage), who ends up strangled by a man pulling on a phone cord from another room. This is, after all, a movie that embodies the fickle finger of fate, and some laughs in that regard from contemporary audiences are unavoidable. For that reason, *D.O.A.*, despite its wacky concept of "luminous toxin," is easier to swallow as an archetype of mischance. The hapless Frank Bigelow (Edmund O'Brien), an accountant away from his small-town girl friend, leering at anything in skirts and kicking up his heels in San Francisco, may be guilty of some mild lechery but does nothing to deserve a fatal dose. Knowing he will shortly die, his relentless pursuit of his unknown killers drips with dark irony without straining the limits of its budget or of credulity in the noir world.

Possible Additional Reading

Paul Kerr, "Out of What Past? Notes on the B film noir" in *Film Noir Compendium*

Andrew Britton, "Detour" in *The Book of Film Noir*

"Hapless Frank Bigelow (Edmond O'Brien)" realizes he's been pumped full of luminous toxin in *D.O.A.*

9. Apocalypse Noir: *Kiss Me Deadly*

It may be that more has been written about *Kiss Me Deadly* than any other film noir, unfortunately much of it is drivel. If Nick the Mechanic were to read about his latently homosexual relationship with Hammer, he'd lay somebody out with a wicked "pretty pow." So Hammer's an asshole, Hammer's a misogynist, Hammer's in the closet, little could Mickey Spillane have suspected that this distorted rendering of his mindless macho divorce dick would become all things to all critics.

In his original *Film Comment* essay in 1974, Alain Silver first suggested that Hammer was on "a quest for a noir grail"; and never have the streets of Los Angeles been more steeped with quasi-mythic, quasi-operatic, quasi-hard-boiled characters who keep popping up as if in some crazed reverse rendering of Twain's *Connecticut Yankee*: damsels in distress, atomic-powered wizards, Lily Carver-cum-Gabrielle-cum-Pandora-cum-Morgan le Fey with a, yes, I'll admit it, phallic roscoe in her hand asking Mike for "the liar's kiss." Perhaps the most phenomenal aspect of *Kiss Me Deadly*, its literally explosive conclusion, recently restored to include long-missing shots of Hammer watching the "great what's-it," his grail, consumed in an atomic inferno, is also the most powerful distortion of Spillane. His pulp endings usually find a snide Hammer watching some treacherous bitch breathe her last. In turning macho myth upside down, Aldrich's Hammer sputters helplessly in the surf, out-smarted, out-gunned and out-classed, hoisted on his own smug petard by some ditzy dame.

Possible Additional Reading

Telotte, "Talk and trouble; Kiss Me Deadly's Apocalyptic Discourse" in *Voices in the Dark*

Silver, "*Kiss Me Deadly*: Evidence of a Style" reprinted in *Film Noir Compendiumit*

Left, Lily Carver/Gabrielle (Gaby Rodgers) decides to give Mike Hammer (Ralph Meeker) a slug in the belly instead of receiving "the liar's kiss." in *Kiss Me Deadly.*

Right, favorite Stanley Kubrick character actor, Timothy Carey, as the deranged sniper-for-hire Nikki Arane in *The Killing*.

10. The Classic Period Ends: *The Killing* and *Touch of Evil*

As Schrader suggested in 1972 and Silver/Ward elaborated in their 1979 introduction for the real big book of noir, *The Encyclopedic Reference*, whether you think it's a movement or a genre or, like David Bordwell, a mass hallucination, noir is not really about auteurs. At the same time, as Schrader was quick to note, a lot of marginal auteurs did their best work in noir. While no one could dispute concluding a survey of the classic period with *Touch of Evil*, my experience has been that, after a steady diet of mainstream noir for so many weeks, *Touch of Evil* can actually end up seeming like a cheesy pastiche. There is a compelling irony to watching a massive Orson Welles lumbering through this film (which was to be his swan song as a Hollywood director) under the full weight of his uncontrolled gastronomy. The manic performances of Welles, Akim Tamiroff, and even Dennis Weaver are an apt coda for noir, a last, Münch-like scream of unfettered, expressionistic excess. But what does *Touch of Evil* really say? There's a new sheriff in town, a drab, play-by-the-rules, poker-up-the-ass detective in a shiny pressed suit, not very noir and not very interesting.

The caper gone nightmarishly awry is not a new concept. But the time-distorted overlay of events in *The Killing* is as compelling as it was over forty years ago. Sterling Hayden's Johnny Clay is a natural progression from his characer in *The Asphalt Jungle*, smarter, meaner, and noir to the core. Kubrick breaks down the archetype and reveals "the skull beneath the skin" with visuals as spare but precise as T. S. Eliot's prose. This is the ultimate evolution of classic noir: surrounded by such icons of menace, psychosis, and exploitation by femme fatales respectively as the hulking Ted de Corsia, the deranged Timothy Carey, and the cuckolded Elisha Cook, Jr., Clay's careful scheme disintegrates. This time when Hayden's character expires there is no ironic allusion in the manner of *The Asphalt Jungle*, but rather the complete dissolution of his life and dreams, blown away like the money from the heist.

Possible Additional Reading

Richardson, "Film Noir in Limbo: *Touch of Evil*" in *Autopsy*

11. TV Noir

While a survey of TV noir is probably not in the cards at those institutions of higher learning where the film snobs rule, the soft-boiled, noir-inspired television homicide squads and private eyes are worth a look. The transition from docu-noir is unmistakable not just in the television series versions of *The Naked City* or *The Lineup*, but in the granddaddy of by-the-book cop shows, *Dragnet*. While the laconic style of creator and star, Jack Webb, may have long ago succumbed under the weight of countless parodies, the style of exposition continues to inspire imitators. It may be four decades later, but it'still just a small step from Sgt. Friday to the protagonists of, where time and location sub-titles and a single ominous chord open every sequence, or the de rigueur hand-held in *Homicide*.

While they may be a little harder to find, besides the ubiquitous *Dragnet*, it's worth tracking down one or two more samples from the 50s, if not *Naked City* or *The Lineup* (both of which hold up quite well), *Peter Gunn*, *Richard Diamond*, or best of all, the remarkable *Johnny Staccato*, created by John Cassavetes before he went for high art. Easier to find and also worth a look are Michael Mann's first forays into neo-noir by way of TV, *Miami Vice* and the very dark, period series *Crime Story*.

Possible Additional Reading

> James Ursini, "Angst at Sixty Fields per Second" in *Film Noir Reader*
>
> Jeremy Butler, "Miami Vice: The Legacy of Film Noir" reprinted in *Film Noir Reader*

12. Neo-noir

Where does this phenomenon begin? Some could argue for Don Siegel's remake of *The Killers* released theatrically in 1964, just six years after *Touch of Evil*, because it was too violent for television. It does feature Ronald Reagan slapping Angie Dickinson; but even with that it seems pretty tame today. *Chinatown*? Richard Jameson was calling that "son of noir" twenty-five years ago. If one is to believe Silver and Ursini in their extended essay on neo-noir in the latest edition of their big book, this phenomenon took off in Hollywood in the 1980s. It's easy to read through their Addendum filmography of nearly 200 titles and cull one's favorite examples, such as *Body Heat*; *The Hot Spot*; *Kill Me, Again*; or *Sea of Love.* In a spin-off article, Silver makes an interesting point about how bloated, star-driven and big budget neo-noirs violate the classic tradition at their peril, often resulting in really bad movies, especially compared to new examples still working in the no-money, B-through-Z picture milieu. So it may be worth sampling one of these under $1 million efforts, such as *Guncrazy, Delusion*, or the strictly micro-budget (hence dear to my heart) *Horseplayer*.

Chances are there will be some high, medium or low-budget neo-noir just released to theaters, cable, or DVD respectively wherever a film noir course is offered. Why not roll the dice and assign one sight unseen as supplementary viewing? I've found that, armed with a deeper perception at the end of so many weeks of study, would-be "filmmakers noir" are quick to discern the cheap and/or superficial knock-off trying to pass themselves off as the genuine article.

Possible Additional Reading

> Silver/Ward/Ursini and divers hands, the "Neo-Noir" section of *Film Noir: An Encyclopedic Reference*
>
> Todd Erickson, "Kill Me Again: Movement becomes Genre" in *Film Noir Compendium*
>
> Alain Silver, "Son of Noir: Neo-Film Noir and the Neo-B Picture" in *Film Noir Compendium*

For many students, particularly mine, the ultimate question is not what noir was, but what it might be. They see film noir as an open-ended experience. Of course, with the short-sightedness of the young, they also see their own times,where slow internet access can be a most grievous fate, as more angst-ridden than any previous. The encapsulation effect, a selective view of the 1940s and 1950s through a noir filter, is not an easy read for those whose parents were not yet born when *Touch of Evil* ended the classic period. Still the through-line of film noir is undeniable and, in what may be the greatest irony, can be exhilarating to perceive for the first time at the turn of millennium.

"Forget it, Jake. It's Chinatown."

Ride the Pink Horse: Pila (Wamda Hendrix) rescues "Lucky" Gagin (Robert Montgomery), who has been left for dead with a knife in his back.

Ride the Pink Horse: Money, Mischance, Murder, and the Monads of Film Noir

Alain Silver

> The holidays
> go around and around
> The merry go-round brings them
> and takes them away.
>
> Federico García Lorca

> Every man takes the limits of his own field of vision for the limits of the world.
>
> Arthur Schopenhauer[1]

The history of film noir is simple enough. Despite occasional squabbling over the identity of the first film noir, it is clear that, after some early prototypes, the classic period of film noir transpired over a mere two decades; but there is certainly no consensus about the philosophy of noir. That the noir phenomenon exists is indisputable. Although some of the critical analyses that have followed in its wake have attempted to muddy the waters, for most commentators film noir is defined, not only by its visual style, but also by its relation to the psychological and philosophical developments of the first half of the twentieth century.

From a simplistic Freudian perspective, the imagery of film noir—its dark corridors, wet streets, and figures lurking in the shadows—reflects the underlying apprehension, even paranoia, of many of its protagonists. Many observers have perceived in the deterministic narratives of film noir a reflection on the concepts of existential anguish and despair. The defining comment of Bradford Galt in *The Dark Corner* (Henry Hathaway, 1946) is cited as a prime example of existential anguish: "There goes my last lead. I feel all dead inside. I'm backed up in a dark corner, and I don't know who's hitting me." These characters who reflect on the uncertainty of their situation, who don't know who's hitting them but must make choices nonetheless, are mired in existential despair. But, as a film cycle or movement that incorporated many generic indicators, film noir is not simply about Freudian or existential motifs, about characters forced to make impossible choices. If there is a noir prototype, it must be approached from a broader base, something more akin to Bateson's analysis of the "transcontextual" double bind: "Exogenous experience may be framed in the context of dreams, and internal thought may be projected into the contexts of the external world."[2] Taken in transcontext, these issues so prevalent in film noir, fate and free will, existential anguish and despair, are not such clear-cut expressions, not instances, as Bateson often noted, of being "just that and nothing more."

There is no clear line from any preexisting epistemology to film noir, not from Freud or Kierkegaard, not from German expressionistic film or American hard-boiled fiction. Being neither philosophy nor aesthetics but fiction, what film noir does take from these sundry influences is a dynamic that uses different character perspectives to create dramatic tension. These differing viewpoints of narrative events are defined with a transcontextual expressive code; that is, some images and events are rendered subjectively using point-of-view shots or voice-over narrative, while others are staged objectively with the camera recording events from the position of a detached observer. Because the aesthetic or system of visual and aural meaning in film noir is fluid or relative, Einstein's paradigm of the railway carriage and the embankment, from which positions observers witness very different behavior from a falling stone, could also apply to the universe of film noir.[3] The problem of

Bradford Galt and of many noir protagonists can be taken as one of perspective. From his dark corner, Galt can see only straight lines; he cannot envision the parabolic narrative arc that has entrapped him.

In his or her quest for the knowledge that promises salvation, the noir protagonist conducts a metaphoric search for an absolute truth, for the thing-in-itself. In an existential or transcontextual world, in any system of values that does not accept the concept of a simple, a priori truth, such a quest is doomed to failure. Despite this, or because of this, most of these figures actually survive their immersion in an unstable noir underworld.

Schopenhauer and *Ride the Pink Horse*

What this essay proposes briefly to consider is *Ride the Pink Horse* (Robert Montgomery, 1947) as a proto-typical noir film and also as an embodiment of aspects of the worldview/aesthetics of Arthur Schopenhauer (1788-1860). In Schopenhauer's major work, *The World as Will and Representation,* revised over the course of four decades, the interplay of will, representation, religion, and aesthetics defines an uncertain universe much like that into which the noir protagonist ventures. As Schopenhauer's first words assert: "The world is my representation: this is a truth valid with reference to every living and knowing being, although man alone can bring it into reflective, abstract consciousness. If he really does so, philosophical discernment has dawned on him."[4] For Schopenhauer, the Kantian thing-in-itself is undiscoverable; but the will to find it is not. What also imperils or destroys any man is not misperception but that same will. Will causes discord, suffering, and evil. Its relentless and compulsive grip on a rational being renders most human action pointless and, ultimately, absurd: "A man can do what he wants, but not want what he wants."[5]

Beyond any philosophical perspective on absolute truth, Schopenhauer's discourses probe the meaning of suffering and suggest that life is substantially without higher purpose. Rather than accept the belief in any absolute, Schopenhauer accepts the world as what each man sees or wills it to be. Ironically for Schopenhauer, although man has free will, he is imprisoned by its pointlessness. The only escapes from will are through sacrifice, through helping others and self-denial, and through an aesthetic experience. In fact, for Schopenhauer, art is more important than knowledge, in that it helps man transcend his situation, for a person listening to music or watching a drama is at moments free from self-consciousness and will.

In the world of film noir, these same contradictions dog the characters. For Schopenhauer, mitigation of will is possible through denial, through the arts, through transcendence, through religious conviction; but, in the end, there is no escape. Action, even self-immolation, is an expression of will that defeats the man who seeks escape. As Schopenhauer noted: "The ancient wisdom of the Indians declares that 'it is Maya, the veil of deception, that covers the eyes of mortals, and causes them to see a world of which one cannot say either that it is or that it is not, for it is like a dream, like the sunshine on the sand that the traveler at a distance takes to be water, or like the piece of rope on the ground that he regards as a snake.'"[6] In film noir, the dream, the mirage, the slightest mistake, are typical expressive factors that embroil its protagonists in the struggle to survive. For Aquinas, Kant, Leibniz, and other rational theists, God and truth exist to prevent man and morality from being meaningless. Hence, a righteous man can navigate a world of shifting monads without fear of running aground on a shoal of misperception. For Schopenhauer, a rational atheist, his answer was plain enough to be frequently co-opted by religion and nowadays is even sold emblazoned on T-shirts: "Compassion is the basis of all morality."

If Schopenhauer believed that truth traveled a bumpy road to validation,[7] he could embrace a Keatsian view that equated truth with beauty.[8] As with most ironic drama, the narratives of film noir revolve around the distinction between belief or perception and truth. It is in that nexus, the place where who people are and what events represent may be confounded, that lines between good and evil, between malice and morality, are blurred and that noir figures grapple with their antagonists for survival.

The postwar film noir *Ride the Pink Horse* is based a 1946 novel by Dorothy B. Hughes. Hughes's main character, known only as Sailor, who travels from Chicago to a fictionalized Santa Fe, New Mexico during a

Opposite, Gagin approaches the *tíovivo* carousel for the first time. At left, Pancho touts his ride. At right, Pila stands with her two taller friends.

fiesta week, is intent on blackmailing his mentor, "the Sen," the former Illinois Senator Willis Douglass. The screenwriters, Ben Hecht and Charles Lederer, had worked individually and as a team on such earlier noir films as *Cornered* (Edward Dmytryk, 1945), *Gilda* (Charles Vidor, 1946), *Notorious* (Alfred Hitchcock, 1946), and *Kiss of Death* (Henry Hathaway, 1947). The star and director, Robert Montgomery, had just finished directing *Lady in the Lake* (1947), adapted from Raymond Chandler's 1943 novel. Together, the filmmakers transformed the thoroughly venal Sailor into Gagin, a war veteran with more ambiguous motives for extorting the petty mobster Frank Hugo. In changing the self-aggrandizing Sailor into Gagin, who is likelier to deprecate himself, and the elitist Douglass into the petty mobster Hugo, whose cynical attitude is almost proletarian, the filmmakers define characters that are prototypically noir.

One striking element of the novel that was retained is the high point of the annual festival in Santa Fe, the burning of Zozobra, a god of anxiety or gloom created by the local artist Will Shuster in 1924. While most of the picture was shot on the Universal back lot—much of it centered around an authentic *tíovivo* or carousel that the studio rented from another New Mexican town, Taos—several scenes were shot on exterior locations in and around the plaza of Santa Fe.

Themes and Characters

Although he is referred to only by his last name during the course of the movie, the lead character, the main title announces, is named "Lucky" Gagin. Gagin himself does nothing to explain his sobriquet. Aside from the burning of Zozobra, whom the carousel owner, Pancho, explains to Gagin is the god of bad luck, the only pointed references to luck, good or bad, come from Pila, the young Indian girl who befriends Gagin. In their first meeting, she gives him a good luck charm, a small carving of Ishtam, to "protect" him. Like Sailor in the novel, Gagin comes to town carrying a gun, and, for him, that is the "best charm in the world. Keeps away the boogeyman." Of course, for Gagin, it is not Pancho's boogeyman Zozobra but Hugo that concerns him. Gagin,

fixated on money and revenge, and taking the limits of his own field of vision as the limits of the world, firmly believes that "you make your own luck." For Pancho or Pila, who cryptically remarks, "It is a sign of good luck when you find a new bucket," one should take what the world offers. For them, fate and irony are as invisible as Leibniz's monads or the shadows at the back of Plato's cave,[9] but beauty and compassion are not.

The interaction of the primitive and the sophisticate is a dialectic that Schopenhauer could endorse. Balancing the willfulness, suffering, and pessimism of Gagin are the suffering and kindness of Pancho. Balancing the rationalism and evil of Hugo are the morality and asceticism of FBI Agent Retz. Transcending it all is Pila, whose instinctive and unaffected behavior epitomizes the selflessness that Schopenhauer valued so highly.

Among the various portraits of weary veterans in postwar film noir, Gagin is most literally devoid of identity. Since "Lucky" is an ironic moniker confined to the main title, he has no real first name. The surname Gagin is clipped, guttural, appropriate to Robert Montgomery's taciturn portrayal. Pancho gives him a sort of epithet when he observes: "That's the kind of man I like, the man with no place." When asked his identity on his first visit to Hugo's, Gagin says: "Just tell him Shorty's pal called and will call again." Gagin comes from nowhere in particular, has no stated destination, and, as he offhandedly remarks to the inquisitive Pila, is "nobody's friend."

Initially, the mise-en-scène supports this self-image. Gagin descends from the bus, and the camera tracks him through the small terminal as he deposits an envelope in a locker, conceals the key, then exits and enters the town proper. The actions are direct enough, but the unbroken moving shot in which they are inscribed riv-

Below, as part of a long take Gagin (Robert Montgomery, center) confronts Hugo (Fred Clark, third from left), while the treacherous Marjorie Lundeen (Andrea King, brightly light left) also listens. The take ends with the attack outside when Gagin is stabbed.

ets the audience's attention. The use of a long take instills suspense in the otherwise ordinary acts. From his silent, methodical activity the concentrated staging also distills for the viewer a sense of the tenacity in Gagin's character. At the same time, the sustained camera "imprisons" the protagonist temporarily within the unattractive limits of the bus depot, giving a subtle hint of some underlying fatality even as he emerges and takes the dusty road to town.

Gagin is not a mere cipher. The typical qualities of the embittered loner in film noir, which the figure immediately evokes through this visual inscription, combine with the narrative development of his hatred for Frank Hugo to create a more complex character. The initial assertion of Gagin's generic identity is grounded in understated conflict with both the environment, in which he is a stranger, and the imminent clash with the unseen criminal presence, Hugo. San Pablo itself offers nothing other than the promise of finding Hugo within its confines, nothing to mollify the alienation that Gagin sports so visibly, no alternate reality to the naturalistic images of the terminal, the town, or the crowded hotel lobby. Only after Gagin's quest to even the score for his dead pal, Shorty, is necessarily suspended because of Hugo's absence does he discover Pancho, Pila, and the *tío-vivo*.

From his demeanor and his statements, Gagin is clearly a willful and determined man; yet, remarkably, all the supporting characters in *Ride the Pink Horse* want him to embrace their point of view. This is expectedly the case with Hugo, who wants the incriminating letter that Gagin holds over him, and with Retz, who wants the same item with which to prosecute Hugo. In their first meeting, Hugo lectures Gagin at length about his own beliefs, about what makes his world turn: "[Shorty] got himself all crumbed up looking for easy money. . . . Don't kid yourself you're doing it for Shorty. You're doing it for you. We eat out of the same dish. You used to think if you were a square guy, worked hard, played on the level, things would come your way. You found that people are interested in only one thing, the pay-off. There are two kinds of people in this world: ones that fiddle around wondering whether a thing's right or wrong and guys like us." At the end of *Rink the Pink Horse*, when an injured and insulted Gagin is on the brink of cooperating with Retz, Hugo offers a last, disdainful assessment of guys like Gagin, who "work all your lives and end up with enough money to buy yourself a hole in the ground."

Compare Hugo's attitude to Schopenhauer's profession: "Money alone is absolutely good, because it is not only a concrete satisfaction of one need in particular; it is an abstract satisfaction of all. . . . Money is human happiness in the abstract; he, then, who is no longer capable of enjoying human happiness in the concrete devotes himself utterly to money."[10] Gagin would likely agree that "money . . . is absolutely good." As he ruefully explains when Pancho asks him why he hangs around with Pila, why he doesn't have a princess with more flesh on her bones: "I've had princesses. I got one now back east, but she's busy with another guy. He's got what it takes: dough." Although at odds with the statements of Hugo and Gagin, Pancho's attitude is also aligned with Schopenhauer's in that he expresses a preference for happiness that is not abstract. In his first meeting with Gagin in the Tres Violetas bar, Pancho intervenes when Gagin pays with a twenty-dollar bill for which the barkeep has insufficient change. In an unselfish manner, Pancho suggests that Gagin take ten dollars and that he and the others drink the rest of his change: "You want to make everybody happy, si?" Later, after he offers Gagin his own bed to sleep in, Pancho refuses additional payment and adds: "Some people only happy when they got money. Me, I'm only happy when I got nothing. Nothing and a friend . . . they can keep everything else. Keep the whole world."

Shortly after he meets her, as she leads him to La Fonda hotel and bumps into a post, Gagin tells Pila: "You should look where you're going." In his unenlightened state, he does not yet realize that he should take his own advice. His hatred of Hugo is matched by his distrust of institutions. Of Retz, who represents social morality and the "government," Gagin contemptuously inquires: "Doesn't the government work for Hugo? It did all during the war." When Hugo's girlfriend, Marjorie, proposes a complicated double cross involving an honest attorney, his derisive retort is: "Hugo buys them all—even the honest ones." He is equally scornful of women, or, rather, of "dames": "They're not human beings. They're dead fish with a lot of perfume on them. You touch them, and you always get stung. You always lose."

While the filmmakers cannot express what goes on inside Gagin's head as directly as can the novelist Hughes, Montgomery's direction and performance go beyond the purely laconic prototype. His reaction to Pila is the cornerstone of his character's development and hints at the perception of which Hughes wrote explicitly: "She was young, young as a kid, and she was old, old as this country. . . . She was unreal, alien; yet she belonged, and he was alien. [There was] something deep and strong and old under the tawdry trapping, under the gimcracks. Something he did not understand because he was a stranger."[11]

Visual Style and Symbolism

While Hughes's novel is not written in the first person, her original prose is imitation Hammett, full of offhanded racism and sexism reflecting the main character's prejudices and fears. Her overt symbolism is restricted to figures such as Zozobra: "Made of papier maché and dirty sheets, yet a fantastic awfulness of reality was about him. He was unclean, he was the personification of evil." But, as Sailor realizes moments later: "The evil was manmade; it wasn't real."[12]

For the filmmakers working with viewer expectations associated with film noir, symbolic construction is much easier. The opening shots of the bus moving along the highway end at the local station where Gagin de-

Marjorie Lundeen brassily interrupts the impromptu and quirky breakfast meeting between Gagin and Pila at La Fonda Hotel.

scends and define a real, that is, nonstudio, environment. Montgomery uses his own presence as the lead actor to draw the audience's focus and then stages his first appearance with the intricate sustained shot already mentioned. Although the viewer may not be aware that there is no cut, the unbroken shot creates both suspense and figurative meaning. Since there is no alternate shot, no sudden shift of angles permitted, the implication is that there is no alternate possible outcome. In the next sequence, Gagin walks alone down a porch toward an open area at upper frame center. He moves down a narrow passageway, hemmed in by a wall on one side and a dark wooden post on the other. Again, besides a sense of visual constriction, the staging makes the pathway at frame center the only one available, the only course to follow.

In their first meeting, balanced against the reaction shots of Gagin is the physical aspect of Pila portrayed by eighteen-year-old Wanda Hendrix. Although she was four years older than the fourteen-year-old Indian girl created by Hughes, Hendrix's aspect, while conforming to a Hollywood stereotype of an Indian, is striking. Because it is a movie, the contrast between that aspect and Montgomery's is visually palpable and makes an immediate impact not possible in Hughes's prose: "scrawny...black fathomless eyes...brown face...strong black hair." At the beginning and end of the film, the black-and-white, Hollywood Pila has a dusky face with black hair, parted in the center and braided on each side; but, after enduring Gagin's jibes, being called "Sitting Bull" and hearing that she should fix herself up to "look like a human being," Pila visits the beauty salon in the hotel and gets her hair done. In the most perilous moments of the movie, she sports an incongruous permanent wave with spit curls across her forehead and a flower on top.

Although the first encounter between the two is on a false exterior—the soundstage containing the carousel set—the next sequence takes them into the veritable Santa Fe plaza, just outside the genuine La Fonda hotel. By using location here and in the night exteriors when Zozobra is paraded to his pyre, Montgomery seamlessly imbues the studio sets with a portion of their reality. Within this noir landscape, under the pull of some predetermined inclination, Montgomery/Gagin goes to the Tres Violetas that first night, and Pila is there waiting in the darkness. How did she know he would come to the bar? And, if she knew, why does she say: "I thought I would never see you anymore"? There is another long take when an inebriated Gagin and Pancho leave the bar. As the drunken men stumble away, Pila comes up, then leaves. When they exit the shot, she returns, crossing in the background to frame center, then coming forward. Although she has offered Gagin a totem and now follows in his wake, Pila feels unable to shield him from the deadly fate that she has foreseen, for, as she later will admit to Retz, she has had a vision of Gagin lying dead.

A last long take is used when Gagin goes to a restaurant to exchange the letter for Hugo's money. En route, Gagin weaves through the crowd of onlookers gathered for the parade and burning of Zozobra, and a dissolve momentarily superimposes the effigy of Zozobra on a close-up of Hugo, revealing the true face of Gagin's god of back luck. Gagin appears at the table like a waiter, asking: "Everything all right, Mr. Hugo?" Marjorie leads Gagin from the table onto the dance floor, and they waltz around the corner to the door. Montgomery ends the long take and cuts as they exit into darkness. Outside, he holds on the silhouetted two-shot as Marjorie's purported warning is revealed as treachery and Gagin gets stung by a dame—that is, knifed in the back.

Despite being wounded, Gagin overcomes his assailants and then Pila leads him back to the sanctuary of the carousel. It is not merely because it gives the film its title that the *tiovivo* is the central image of *Ride the Pink Horse*. Like other havens in film noir, like Rica's apartment in *Thieves' Highway* (Jules Dassin, 1949) or Doll Conovan's place in *The Asphalt Jungle* (John Huston, 1950), the carousel offers refuge to the spiritually and physically wounded hero. But, in *Ride the Pink Horse,* Gagin is never fully at ease around it, never understands the emotional relation between it and its patrons. On his first night there, he insists that Pila have a turn on it, and she asks which horse she should ride. Approaching the merry-go-round, Gagin uncovers the horse nearest and suggests tersely; "Why don't you ride the pink one?" To Gagin it makes no difference which horse is chosen. They are all essentially the same, all traveling in the same circle, all taking their riders nowhere and ending up in the same spot. To Pila, who understands instinctively the significance of choice, it makes all the difference. The carousel is at once one of the most stylized objects in the movie—both by nature as a theatrical "amusement" and also because it is photographed on a soundstage under neutral gray light that differs subtly from the "real world" location shooting—and the one object that is most free of artificial restraints. By its very artifice, by the aspects of ritual that its patrons attach to circling a finite space on the small wooden horses, the *tíovivo* becomes a quintessentially noir set piece. Gagin, who comes to it burdened by the complex codes of behavior imposed by the noir universe, focused on the belief that he must even the score, cannot see its broader dimensions.

The symbolism of the carousel as Lorca and others have perceived it is simple: you go a long way in a circle and end up in the same place as you started, a pessimistic metaphor for life, or, as Schopenhauer observed: "After your death you will be what you were before your birth."[13] On one level, the enclosed world and the totemic horses are somewhat Platonic, idealized representations of the actual universe, as stylized as shadows on a cave wall. On another, more primitive level, the carousel is a wellspring of primordial energy, or, as Lorca elaborated:

> On ponies
> disguised as panthers
> the children devour the moon
> as they would a cherry.[14]

Like ropes disguised as snakes, Lorca's poetic imagery pierces the veil of deception with symbolic language.

While long takes and low angles can underscore a sense of fatalism, Montgomery also used montage for phenomenological effect, which is where the perceptual awareness of the characters relates to the visual style, as in the first meeting between Gagin and Hugo. Both shot selection and set pieces color the process. Hugo is hard of hearing, and, early in the scene, he holds the phone upside down so that the earpiece is next to an oversized microphone/amplifier clipped to his shirt pocket. The symbolism of this unsettling inversion is ambiguous. When Hugo and Gagin are speaking alone, close-ups and over-the-shoulder shots alternately isolate and link the two figures; but Hugo continues to sidestep. "Your pal Shorty wasn't as tough as he thought he was," Hugo ingenuously clarifies.

> GAGIN
> So you had him killed.
>
> HUGO
> Let's just say that he lost the argument.
>
> GAGIN
> To three guys with blackjacks.
>
> HUGO
> Were there three?

Shorty's dead, so what difference does it make how many killers there were? Displacement and indirection are part of Hugo's modus operandi, the warp and woof of his veil of deception. At midpoint in the scene, Hugo even walks around Gagin in a circle, a menacing variant on the movement of the *tíovivo*.

In the narrative progression of *Ride the Pink Horse,* Pila's totem Ishtam overcomes the bad luck god, as Gagin survives his encounter with Zozobra's personification in Hugo. In the symbolic and stylistic progression of the movie, Gagin leaves as he began. Like Nick Garcos in *Thieves' Highway,* who learns to trust based on instinct, or Dix in *The Asphalt Jungle,* who refuses to die until he gets home to the ranch in Kentucky, the lessons learned in the sanctuary are critical. Only after he accepts the *tíovivo* as a beneficent "live uncle" does Gagin begin to comprehend its meaning. Conditioned as he is to living with his estrangement, even taking solace in that emotion as part of his role, Gagin alone cannot resolve his conflict. Only after the sacrifices of Pancho and Pila can he make the right choice, reject evening the score, and save himself in the process.

Perhaps the most telling interaction of the carousel, noir stylistics, and the principles of Schopenhauer is in the beating of Pancho. Moments after he conceals a wounded Gagin next to Pila in one of the *tíovivo* chairs, two of Hugo's thugs arrive. Pancho protects several children aboard the carousel by offering a free ride. Then in several angles, the camera is mounted on the carousel, focused on a young boy and girl, another boy alone, and Pila wearing a blanket over her head like a mantilla with a covered Gagin beside her. While the children's heads turn to watch the men walk up in the background, Pila does not move. As the shadows of horses fly across their bodies, the men stand on each side of Pancho, hemming him in. Their verbal interrogation about the man Pancho met in the bar, the man whose name he does not know, quickly gives way to a more severe approach. As they beat him, Pancho's cries and groans and the dull thud of a clenched fist are mixed with the repetitive carillon sound of the carousel. The cutaways to the moving camera reveal closer shots of the now terrified children, trapped on the merry-go-round, and unable to run away, grimacing and whimpering as the relentless motion of the mechanism takes them past the wall where the men beat the prostrate Pancho over and over. Finally, as Pancho moans, "Oh, my, you hurt Panchito," the thugs relent, convinced he knows nothing.

Pancho crawls over to the lever that starts and stops the *tíovivo,* and, as it slows, the children finally jump off and run away. Although his kindness had already been demonstrated the night before, Pancho is not resentful. Instead, he offers an aesthetic evaluation of the beating that echoes Schopenhauer's belief in validation and redemption through suffering: "They want to know, where is Gagin. Hit me in the nose, I don't know. Hit me in the mouth, I don't know. I fall down, and I don't know." Pancho recreates it vividly, almost gleefully, for Gagin, a man who conversely exemplifies that particularly pointless striving that Schopenhauer believed was the real root of human suffering. Where a simple thank-you would have sufficed, Gagin's response is to offer to cut Pancho in, to give him $5,000—when he gets it. Pancho had already voiced his casual acceptance of violence when he bandaged up Gagin's wound: "Knife is good. More easy to fix. I got knifed three times. When you're young, everybody sticks knife in you." Just as casually, he shrugs off the possibility of a fortune that he doesn't need: "Lots of people gonna get lots of things, but they don't." To Pancho, kindness and friendship are their own rewards.

Thanks to the intervention of Pila (and Ishtam), Agent Retz (Art Smith) arrives in time to rescue Gagin and arrest Hugo.

The Ideal Truth

Gagin's self-deprecating remark to Hugo, "There are a lot of people in this world smarter than me, and they aren't sitting up nights figuring out how to help me," neatly mirrors an observation of Schopenhauer's: "The more unintelligent a man is, the less mysterious existence seems to him."[15] Indeed, the ending of *Ride the Pink Horse* reaffirms that an instinctive behavior can be more effective than a more purely analytic one. The extortion plot is resolved when a dazed and confused Gagin goes to confront Hugo. Pila catches up to him at Hugo's door but cannot prevent him from being captured. After he is slapped and loses consciousness, Pila is beaten. A low-angle close-up frames Hugo leering like Zozobra over the shoulder of a henchmen as he tells him to "keep it up." Then Retz intervenes, and Gagin is saved. In a semicomic "afterword," Gagin worries that Pila will be quite upset when he goes to say good-bye. In a moment that recapitulates his lack of understanding, he awkwardly makes small talk, returns her totem of Ishtam, and is confounded by her easy acceptance of the fact that their relationship is ending.

Two core beliefs of Schopenhauer could arbitrarily be linked to many different movies or other works of art: that the world is a personal representation and that what Schopenhauer calls *unwillful perceptions of art* can help man escape the tyranny of self. But, in many noir films, as in *Ride the Pink Horse,* the characters' attitudes toward money and power, the striving for a needless wealth that Schopenhauer compared to "sea-water: the more you drink, the thirstier you become," reflect a moral alignment between the attitude of the filmmakers and the seminal values expressed in *The World as Will and Representation.*[16]

From both an aesthetic and a philosophical perspective, Gagin remains relatively unenlightened at the conclusion of *Ride the Pink Horse.* His final, puzzled look as he glances back at Pila confirms this. Gagin still takes the limits of his own field of vision for the limits of the world. Pila transforms the moment at the Tres Violetas when she knocked out a Hugo minion with a whisky bottle. As she animatedly recounts it in Spanish and reenacts it for her friends with Pancho standing by nodding his approval, Pila turns that bottle-breaking event into art. As Schopenhauer observed: "The picture or the poem will thus emphasize its idea, and give us that ideal truth which is superior to nature."[17] The final shot of the picture fades out, not on Gagin, but on the smiling face of Pila. As does Pancho, she realizes that the risks that she took and the beating that she endured were the compassionate and moral thing to do—and that a good story shared with friends is all the reward anyone should need.

Notes

1. The epigraphs to this essay are taken from Federico García Lorca, "Tío-Vivo"; translation by Linda Brookover; and Arthur Schopenhauer,"Psychological Observations," chap. 5 of *Studies in Pessimism,* trans. T. Bailey Saunders, in *The Essays of Arthur Schopenhauer*, Champaign, IL: Project Gutenberg, 2004. The text of the Spanish original of the Lorca poem is as follows: "Los días de fiesta/van sobre ruedas./El tío vivo los trae,/y los lleva."

2. Gregory Bateson, *Steps to an Ecology of Mind*, New York: Ballantine, 1972, 272-73. Bateson coined the word *transcontext* to describe a situation in which autogenous or internal perception gives one meaning and exogenous or external factors create another.

3. "The stone traverses a straight line relative to a system of coordinates rigidly attached to the railway carriage, but relative to a system of coordinates rigidly attached to the ground (the embankment), it describes a parabola. With the aid of this example, it is clearly seen that there is no such thing as an independently existing course, but only a course relative to the particular body of reference." Albert Einstein, *Relativity-the Special and General Theory,* trans. Robert W. Lawson, 15th ed., New York: Crown, 1952, 10.

4. Arthur Schopenhauer, *The World as Will and Representation,* trans. E. F. J. Payne, 2 vols., New York: Dover, 1966, 1:3.

5. Quoted in Albert Einstein, "The World as I See It," in *Ideas and Opinions,* ed. Carl Seelig, trans. Sonja Bargmann, New York: Bonzana, 1954, 8: "I do not believe in human freedom in the philosophical sense. Everybody acts not only under external compulsion but also in accordance with inner necessity. Schopenhauer's saying, 'A man can

do what he wants, but not want what he wants' has been a very real inspiration to me since my youth; it has been a continual consolation in the face of life's hardships, my own and others', and an unfailing well-spring of tolerance. This realization mercifully mitigates the easily paralyzing sense of responsibility and prevents us from taking ourselves and other people all too seriously: it is conducive to a view of life which, in particular, gives humor its due."

6. Schopenhauer, *The World as Will and Representation,* 1:8.

7. "At times we fancy that people are utterly unable to believe in the truth of some statement affecting us personally, whereas it never occurs to them to doubt it; but if we give them the slightest opportunity of doubting it, they find it absolutely impossible to believe it any more." Arthur Schopenhauer, *Counsels and Maxims,* trans. T. Bailey Saunders, in *The Essays of Arthur Schopenhauer*, Champaign, IL: Project Gutenberg, 2004.

8. "Beauty is truth, truth beauty,—that is all/Ye know on earth, and all ye need to know." John Keats, "Ode on a Grecian Urn," lines 49-50.

9. Plato's allegory of the cave is described in bk. 7 of *The Republic.* Men cannot see a monad, the elemental or ideal truth from which material truth derives but a semblance; it is as if they were chained inside a cave and able to "see only their own shadows, or the shadows of one another, which the fire throws on the opposite wall of the cave" *Republic,* trans. Benjamin Jowett, Adelaide: University of Adelaide Library Electronic Texts Collection, 2004, bk. 7, lines 515a–b.

10. Arthur Schopenhauer, *Parerga and Paralipomena* (1851), trans. T. Bailey Saunders, excerpted in *The Oxford Book of Money,* ed. Kevin Jackson, Oxford: Oxford University Press, 1995, 317.

11. Dorothy B. Hughes, *Ride the Pink Horse*, Edinburgh: Canongate, 2002, 33.

12. Ibid., 18.

13. Arthur Schopenhauer, "On the Doctrine of the Indestructibility of Our True Nature by Death," essay 10 in *Parerga and Paralipomena: Short Philosophical Essays,* ed. and trans. E. F. J. Payne, New York: Oxford University Press, 1974, 2:268.

14. Sobre caballitos/disfrazados de panteras/los niños se comen la luna/como si fuera una cereza." García Lorca, "Tío-Vivo"; translation by Linda Brookover.

15. Quoted in Tom Morris, *Philosophy for Dummies*, New York: Hungry Minds, 1999, 172.

16. Arthur Schopenhauer, "Property, or What a Man Has," chap. 3 of *The Wisdom of Life,* trans. T. Bailey Saunders, in *The Essays of Arthur Schopenhauer*, Champaign, IL: Project Gutenberg, 2004.

17. Arthur Schopenhauer, *The Art of Controversy,* trans. T. Bailey Saunders, in *The Essays of Arthur Schopenhauer*, Champaign, IL: Project Gutenberg, 2004.

Sharing with friends: Pancho and Gagin at Tres Violetas.

Dark jazz riffs at the New Orleans
night club in *Nightmare*.

Dark Jazz: Music in the Film Noir

Robert G. Porfirio

1. Pre-Noir: Expressionism, Violence, Death and Sexuality

The juxtaposition of jazz in the broadest sense of the term with an expressionistic decor can be detected in the Hollywood musical almost from its inception (*Broadway*, 1929; *King of Jazz*, 1930), especially at Universal where the "Germanic" influence was most pronounced and effected even in a traditional "folk opera" like *Showboat* [Figure 1, from the "Old Man River" montage with Paul Robeson]. Yet the confluence of expressionism and jazz was already inherent in Weimar culture and cannot be easily rationalized in terms of that culture's interest in African "primitivism" or popular Americana. Aside from the romantic mystique attached to its origins, the improvisational nature and affective qualities of jazz were quite compatible with the expressionistic quest for "deeper meanings" that focused upon heightened states and the unconscious in order to probe "the secrets of the soul." Still, jazz, with its sources in the black American demimonde and its unfortunate association with brothels, speak-easies and "dope," did lend itself to sensational popular image that in turn reinforced its association with sex, violence and death, three themes dear to "Germanic" hearts. To no one's surprise, Hollywood capitalized upon these associations, emphasizing the strident and violent aspects of the music over its warm and sentimental side and this emphasis culminated into those popular jazz scores of the mid 1950's that gave aural significance to contemporary urban "problems" (e.g. Elmer Bernstein's score for *The Man with the Golden Arm*). And while an early all-black short like *Black and Tan* (1929 RKO, directed by Dudley Murphy) used Duke Ellington's music as a springboard for a film whose visual expressionism synthesized hallucination, orgasm, and death in a haunting manner, the typical Hollywood musical of the 1930's was much less ingenious in its exploitation, except for a few brief "interludes" such as Berkeley's "Lullaby of Broadway" sequence of *Gold Diggers of 1935*. Surprisingly, the gangster film relied very little on the use of jazz. So it remained for the next generation and particularly for the noir cycle to promote that special relationship between jazz and urban violence.

Even before the cycle began in earnest, Warner's *Blues in the Night* (1941, directed by Anatole Litvak) combined some of the visual marks of the noir style with an older gangster idiom to depict the story of the trials and tribulations of a (white) jazz band. But it was an early entry, *Among the Living* (1941), that used the music's dissonant milieu to prompt one of Paul Raden's (Albert Dekker) homicidal attacks. This association of jazz with disturbed mental states that was made even clearer later in *The Blue Dahlia* (1946), where the amnesiac Buzz (William Bendix) refers to it as "jungle music." Appropriately, it was those entries directed by Robert Siodmak that propelled the triad of jazz, violence and sexuality within the cycle,

1.

most memorably through certain expressionistic interludes in *Criss Cross* (1949), *The Killers* (1946) and *Phantom Lady* (1944). Yet jazz could almost be used to express quieter moments and nostalgic reveries (especially when nudged in the direction of blues); and though Al Robert's remembrance of his songstress fiancée (Claudia Drake) in *Detour* (1945, directed by Edgar Ulmer) was bathed in his warm glow, it was shot in a typically expressionistic fashion [Figure 2].

Coming at the end of the cycle, *Nightmare* (1956, a more stylized version of the earlier *Fear in the Night*, 1947) rather self-consciously deployed its noir conventions, exploiting the bizarre surroundings of its New Orleans locale and casting its victimized hero, Stan Grayson (Kevin McCarthy) in a role of jazz arranger and clarinetist. Grayson's dark odyssey through a succession of Bourbon Street "jazz joints" as he attempts to identify the unusual jazz piece associated with his "nightmare" is particularly blatant in this respect: the collage of discordant sounds, the chiaroscuro lighting, the oblique angles, all heighten the effect of the setting. At one of the "joints" he appears to discover the girl in his "nightmare," his first view of her distorted by that split-mirror effect which by then had become something of a visual cliché [Figure 3]. Though this unnamed blonde (Marian Carr) turns out to be someone else, she is a fitting denizen of this world, capturing its essence with her seductive voice when she tells Stan, "Look around, maybe everyone here has lost their marbles." Finally even the dissonance of jazz is enhanced as an aural effect and not simply by Stan's "blurry" memory, for he discovers that the crucial piece of jazz is actually a familiar tune rendered "strange" by being played back too slowly on a phonograph.

D.O.A. (1950) begins its Germanic bias in its source material (the German Film, *Der Mann, Der Seinen Morder Sucht* [1931], directed by Robert Siodmak and partially scripted by Billy Wilder) as well as in Rudolph Maté's and Ernest Laszlo's expressive use of its authentic locales. Its expressionistic influence, however, is most pronounced in the jazz sequence at "The Fisherman Club" whose Dantesque proportions mark it immediately as the nodal point between the mundane tone of the earlier part of the flashback and the macabre tenor of what is to follow. It also serves as a barometer for the complex ambivalence provoked by jazz; a jaded white bartender describes the frenzied white patrons as "jive crazy," declaring his preference for Guy Lombardo while the black group plays on, sweating in agony as the Fisherman himself thrusts his saxophone in an apparent gesture of defiance [Figure 4, second from left: actually Illinois' Jacquet, known for using the upper register of his tenor sax to produce irresolvable high "hot" notes]. Finally, "The Fisherman" is the major locus for a network of metaphoric associations integral to the structure of *D.O.A.*, not the least of which the association of jazz, sex and death: it represents Frank Bigelow's further descent from the security of the small town of Banning and his fiancée, Paula, into San Francisco's demimonde; the thrill of illicit sex is implicit not only in the milieu but in the person of Jeanie (Virginia Lee), a "jive crazy" blonde whom

Bigelow tries to pick up and whose hip response to everything is "easy"; Jeanie's presence coincides with that of the furtive figure of Halliday (William Ching) who is able to "slip" Bigelow the poisoned drink precisely because Bigelow is distracted by Jeanie; a sporadically audible "blues" tune sung by a female vocalist ("I wanted to kiss you...I tried to resist you...") indexes the sexual potential of Jeanie as well as the lethal potential of the milieu; and as Bigelow recalls a "blurred" variation of this tune on subsequent occasions, it becomes an index to the perverse nature of the whole world.

2. Expressionism and the Libido

The earlier expressionistic obsession with the debilitating effects of the Weimar night life (particularly as it involved the Berlin milieu and the femme fatale) made the emigrés willing exploiters of the popular association of jazz with death, drugs, and sex, while jazz's own improvisational qualities could be conceived in terms of the Freudian "unconscious." Robert Siodmak was probably most prone to this exploitation and it can be observed in many of his noir films, most notably in the "jam session" scene from *Phantom Lady*. Yet here the femme fatale is ironically the innocent heroine, "Kansas" (Ella Raines), posing as a tart to wheedle some information out of the trap-drummer Cliff Milburn (Elisha Cook, Jr.) as part of a last ditch effort to save the life of her employer, Scott Henderson, (Alan Curtis); and it is Milburn who takes her to the late-night jam session. But this situation in turn was borrowed from the original novel of the same name by Cornell Woolrich, easily the most expressionistic writer of the "*Black Mask* School" and one who had already demonstrated an interest in the power of drugs to unleash the passions with such short stories as "C-Jag" (1940) and "Marihuana" (1941). In the novel, Woolrich uses the jam session episode to capture the dangerous eroticism of both drugs and jazz with his own distinctively overwrought prose style:

"The next two hours were sort of a Dantesque Inferno. She knew as soon as it was over she wouldn't believe it has actually been real at all.... It was the phantasmagoria of their shadows, looming black, wavering ceiling-high on the walls. It was the actuality of their faces, possessed, demonic, peering out here and there on sudden notes, then seeming to recede again. It was the gin and marihuana cigarettes, filling the air with haze and flux. It was the wildness that got into them, that at times made her cower into a far corner...."

In Siodmak's version "Kansas" does a good deal less "cowering," and he draws adeptly from his expressionistic arsenal to heighten the erotic and oneiric elements. Since the jazz sequences invariably represent a break in the temporal order, Siodmak exploits this in a manner that would become a characteristic trope: eliminating diegetic dialogue throughout the whole sequence (approximately 3 minutes) in favor of the jazz so that visual, editorial, and acting styles might all benefit from a greater formative range. The

sequence itself begins as Cliff, snapping his fingers in time with the music, leads "Kansas" down a dark alley and then opens the door to the "jazz den," the camera trucking backward ahead of them and then forward slightly to enter the "den" before them. From this point on, the jagged editing and oblique angles serve to defamiliarize the surroundings in accord with the polyphonous music, as Cliff weaves "Kansas" through the band to a chair, before taking his place behind the drums. The phallic power of the instruments, revealed in turn by camera movement or cutting, seems to alternately repel and attract the girl, finally motivating her to rise and pour a drink for Cliff. He pauses just long enough to consume the drink and kiss her clumsily, her displeasure suggested by the subtle gesture of her clenched fist and slight grimace. But it is when "Kansas" attempts to fix her makeup at a mirror which "rocks" with each pulsating beat of the piano that the unreality of the place is marked by the typical Germanic trope, just as Cliff prepares to go into his solo [Figure 5] and the remainder of the sequence (approximately 1 minute) is cut to a tempo that matches Cliff's solo riff with a progression that is unmistakably sexual. "Kansas" nods her approval as he begins [Figure 6] then approaches Cliff to coax him on with periodic thrusts of her body [Figure 7]. The libidinous nature of the jazz is barely veiled in metaphor here, either by the amount of intercutting between the girl and the drummer [Figures 7-12] or by the high-angle shot of him playing a drum between his legs. At one point "Kansas" throws back her head in laughter which is completely masked by the din of the music. As Cliff reaches the climax of his riff [Figure 10] she beckons with her head [Figure 11] and he responds by throwing away his "drum stick" [Figure 12] and following her to the door, bowing to his fellow musicians with a slight flourish before departing. Such a stylized "musical interlude" would seldom be equaled by the Hollywood cinema!

3. Style and Musical Parody

By late 1952, when the "Girl Hunt" ballet sequence in *The Band Wagon* was designed, the cycle's narrative and visual conventions were familiar enough to be gently parodied. Since this was done as a modern ballet it achieved a surreal quality the original lacked: the visual density of the film noir's photographic iconography was reduced to its essentials as painted backdrops and its discursive irregularities were heightened into a series of actions (all danced) which refused to cohere into a story. This quality is evidenced in the sequence's opening shot [Figure 13], a backdrop of a deserted city street which in its austerity is reminiscent of painting by Edward Hopper.

Look carefully at the stairwell which Rod Riley (Fred Astaire) is climbing [Figure 14]. Only the first level is tangible, the rest is a painting which aptly leads nowhere. Close to the end of the sequence when his battles are momentarily over, detective Riley takes out a cigarette and a woman suddenly shows up to light it [Figure 15]; she looks strikingly similar to the other femme fatale (both are played by Cyd Charisse) whom Rod was forced to shoot earlier in the scene reminiscent of *Double Indemnity*. As Rod's voice-over narration again warns of a woman's lethal untrustworthiness, the two walk off into the stillness of the night, disturbed by the shriek of a jazz trumpet which serves as a solemn reminder of the well-known affinity of sexuality and death.

4. Aural Structure and Effects in a Sequence from *The Dark Corner*

The accompanying eight frames were drawn from a rather long (over 9 minutes) and complicated sequence (over 50 separate shots, many of them compounded by moving camera) from *The Dark Corner* whose quintessential "noirness " derives from the manner in which the narrative's central conflict is expressed through its visual and aural forms. The conflict permits the detective-hero, Bradford Galt (Mark Stevens), to be framed for the murder of his treacherous ex-partner, Tony Jardine (Kurt Kreuger), by a hoodlum named Stauffer (Willliam Bendix) according to the plan of Hardy Cathcart (Clifton Webb), a wealthy art dealer jealous of his wife's affection for Tony. It is not my intention to submit this sequence to any sort of reading, but rather to suggest how aural structure complimented visual form in generating that tension-charged atmosphere for which the film noir is duly recognized. My choice here demonstrates specifically how the noir cycle achieved an aural expressionism despite its progressive adherence to conventions of "realism" the latter evidenced by the fact that sequence's sounds are all diegetically motivated. Therefore, while the accompanying frames obviously display the noir penchant for mannered lighting as a means of synthesizing exteriors with studio interiors, they were selected principally to locate its major aural transitions and should not necessarily be regarded as among the most essential or "representative" shots in the sequence under consideration.

The segment itself begins with an exterior scene during which Brad attempts to persuade his secretary Kathleen (Lucille Ball) to wait for him inside a Newsreel theater [Figure 16] for an hour while he returns to his apartment to meet with Stauffer, whom he knows as "White Suit" and from whom he is to buy some information. The only sounds here are some background noises of traffic, trolley bells, and ticket dispenser, aside from the dialogue itself; it is structurally significant that there is no further dialogue until some five minutes into the sequence when these two characters are reunited. As Kathleen reluctantly enters the theater, the scene shifts to Stauffer secretly gaining access to Brad's apartment through an open bedroom window off the fire escape [Figure 17]. Behind his furtive action can be heard the naturalistic noises of traffic, trolley bells and a "honky-tonk" piano playing "Red, Hot and Beautiful" (by

Jimmy McHugh), ostensibly emanating from a nearby arcade whose proximity to Brad's apartment has been indicated in an earlier scene.

While Stauffer cautiously makes his way into Brad's living room a slow orchestral version of "Mood Indigo" begins to fade up, first in counterpoint with the noise of the piano and traffic, then displacing the piano entirely as Stauffer moves toward the entry door at the front of the living room (and, presumably, closer to an adjacent apartment which is its source). Stauffer next removes a handkerchief and a bottle of fluid from his coat pocket and sits in a chair facing the entry door. The scene then shifts to Brad as he walks down a dark street toward his apartment building [Figure 18], behind which are the off-screen noises of traffic interwoven with the sounds of a "streetplayer's" rendition of Brahms' "Wiegenlied" (actually performed by both accordion and violin). The comforting qualities of this familiar lullaby, which escorts Brad into the apartment building (the camera remains stationed outside to continue to motivate the music and as Brad enters the elevator he is viewed through the glass of the building's front door), function at once to connote his guileless vulnerability and to generate an ironic tension in the viewer who is aware of his danger.

A series of intercut shots, Stauffer waits inside the apartment; Brad exits the elevator into the corridor; Stauffer, alerted by the elevator noise, prepares for Brad's arrival by dousing his handkerchief with ether [Figure 19] and positioning himself to one side of the entry door; Brad innocently lets himself in, is waylaid by Stauffer and eventually subdued by the ether, maintains a respectable level of aural "realism," enhancing the volume of "Mood Indigo" on corridor shots, muting it on apartment interiors while fading up the traffic noise and mixing both with the loud sounds of the scuffle. The same aural "realism" prevails in a similar series of intercut shots which follow: Stauffer, alerted next to the arrival of Jardine by the noise of the elevator, positions himself to the side of the door with a poker in his hand while Jardine locates the apartment and rings the buzzer; Stauffer opens the door from the side and the unsuspecting Jardine enters the darkened apartment as the camera pans down to the floor, to indicate Jardine's murder only by his shadow and the sound of the clubbing blows, each followed by a groan: Stauffer then pulls Jardine's body completely into the apartment and shuts the door, once again muting the sounds of "Mood Indigo."

As the scene shifts to the exterior shot of Kathleen waiting anxiously for Brad outside the theatre [Figure 20], there is an abrupt transition to a much louder level of traffic noise that in turn is quickly displaced by the "Mood Indigo" in the following scene during which Stauffer messes up the apartment and places the poker in the unconscious Brad's hand before departing through the window. While Brad awakens from his stupor and begins to realize what has happened, Kathleen's opportune arrival is indicated aurally by the simultaneous sounding of the buzzer and the abrupt displacement of the jazz by Beethoven's "Minuet in G," as if someone nearby was practicing the piano. Since it is Kathleen who will be the stabilizing influence in the life of the oppressed hero, reviving his spirits when they are down and suggesting possible remedies to his predicament, the minuet serves a major paradigmatic function, announcing her presence even prior to her muffled cries for "Brad" and a shot of her outside the door [Figure 21] as she tells him that she intends to stay there all night unless he lets her in.

Brad does open the door, of course, explaining to her how thoroughly he has been framed, rejecting the idea of going to the police, and dismissing her offer of aid while the "Minuet" begins to fade out. For a few moments their dialogue exchanges are without any background noise, but when Brad orders her to go and starts to exit towards his bedroom, dragging Jardine's body after him, a muted orchestral version of a swing piece, "I Don't Care who Knows It" (by Jimmy McHugh) suddenly fades up. It continues to play behind a series of alternating shots during which Kathleen straightens up the living room [Figure 22] and washes the poker in the kitchen sink before returning it to the fireplace while Brad hides Jardine's body under his bed and washes up in the adjacent bathroom [Figure 23]. The choice of that particular tune for its sentimental meaning seems clear enough here for Kathleen, once having coyly resisted Brad's advances, is now ready to commit herself to the full extent of helping him cover up a murder, and this meaning is reaffirmed when Brad re-enters the living room, sees what she has done and kisses her, an act punctuated by a harp glissando that segues into the next swing piece (appropriately titled "Do You Love Me ?"). However, since neither of the last two tunes were widely known at the time of the film's production, one can move beyond the merely affective sentimentalism of the former to consider it as a source of dissonance in conjunction with the visuals behind which it initially appears (and also beyond the purely literary "irony" of its title, "I Don't Care Who Knows It"), a syntagma whose alternations bear the symbolic weight of ritual: Kathleen "gets rid" of the broken glass/Brad "gets rid of the body" and "straightens up" his appearance; Kathleen washes the blood off the poker/Brad washes his hands, etc.

Yet dissonance is operative at the plane of diegesis itself where variations of volume level "placed" the source of the other music (except for the original "honky tonk" piano) near the corridor close by the front of the living room, whereas this piece is recognizably louder in Brad's bedroom and, conjoined with traffic noises, seems to emanate from somewhere outside the same open window through which Stauffer entered [Figures 17 and 23]. Indeed, much of the whole sequence's tension is the product of the dissonant interaction of music, effects and visuals, a tension falsely resolved with the couples' embrace (and the glissando), though they will soon leave on an unsuccessful quest for "White Suit." As one might expect, tension is only finally resolved at the conclusion of the film with the death of Cathcart and the "cleansing" of Brad's reputation, after which Kathleen makes plans for their hasty marriage, "I told you I play for keeps!" while the Cyril Mockridge score moves to the resolution of its finale.

21.

23.

22.

The Big Heat.

Creativity and Evaluation: Two Film Noirs of the Fifties

Robin Wood

In a course during which I screened two films, we discussed at great length the historical antecedents and development of film noir; the somewhat tedious and "academic" question of whether it was a genre or a style; its relation to American (and, more widely, patriarchal capitalist) ideology; its relation to other genres, either precedent or contemporary (screwball comedy, the musical, the horror film, the World War II movie, the woman's melodrama)—the areas of difference and overlap ... All of this proved profitable and important of course, but I found myself, increasingly, wanting to argue for the importance of discrimination between different works on quite traditional grounds that always came back, in the end, to the question of personal authorship: discriminations that drew necessarily on terms like "intelligence," "sensitivity," "complexity"... I have mentioned the vague sense of guilt and uneasiness that this induced. It can be traced, I think, especially, to a fashionably dominant trend in film theory/criticism, the notion that what one should attempt to "read" (or initiate a reading of, the process being by definition interminable) the entire text in all its endless determinations. (John McCullough's article on *The Big Sleep* in *CineAction!*[1] is a useful example.) I think the attempt to decipher texts as cultural products without boundaries, interweaving infinitely with other texts both cinematic and non-cinematic, is very interesting and potentially very profitable; it is not what I personally wish to undertake, but I am certainly not "against" it, on principle. What angers me is the arrogance of the assumption that this is now the "only" way in which we "must" read texts. McCullough's tone, in the article cited, clearly tells us that it was very reprehensible of Michael Walker to offer an "auteurist" reading of *The Big Sleep*: "we" know better now (and, whatever he might have intended, McCullough's "we" sounds suspiciously like the "Royal We" to me.) Why an attempt to read a film in one way for one purpose should invalidate attempts to read it another way for a completely different purpose is a logic that escapes me. We are back with the "either/or" syndrome, or, to take up my earlier comparison, with the desire to replace a lawn-mower with a hair-dryer: if I possess both hair and a lawn I can use both. There remains, of course, the question of what is most important within a given text. I can only repeat that, if a text is alive, it is animated by personal creativity, and it is the text's aliveness that interests me.

One evaluative comparison that arose on the course was between Altman's *The Long Goodbye* and Penn's *Night Moves*; but I have already made what seem to me the necessary points in the essay on Altman reprinted in *Hollywood from Vietnam to Reagan*, and (although it was written 15 years ago) seeing the two films again in close juxtaposition fully reconfirms my judgment then. I turn instead to *The Big Heat* and *Kiss Me Deadly*.

The outcome of the comparison (to avoid any suspense)—that Aldrich at his best was a very interesting director, Lang, when working with congenial material, a great one—will cause little surprise (and will presumably, to semioticians, amount to more than a boring irrelevancy, if indeed it is allowed even to carry any meaning). What seems to me important is the grounds on which it can be based: especially in view of the fact that Aldrich's film is clearly the more "satisfying" (i.e. coherent) of the two.

The comparison rests on the fairly close parallels between the two films. Both belong to the '50s, and are characterized by that period's mounting paranoia and potential hysteria, with the threats of nuclear power and the Cold War in the background (with *Kiss Me Deadly* one might rather say the foreground). They consequently belong to what one might see as the first (partially) revisionist period of film noir, wherein the figure of the investigator (clearly the moral centre of the '40s Hammett/Chandler adaptations) is subjected to scrutiny and criticism. (The second far more drastic, revisionist period is the '70s, with *Night Moves* and *The Long Goodbye* as prime instances). The threat in both films is the greed for power: Lagana in *The Big Heat* wants to control the city; virtually all the characters of *Kiss Me Deadly* are trying to gain possession of "the Great Whatsit," which turns out to be nuclear energy itself, no less. In both, the hero's integrity/moral stature is called into question (ambiguously in Lang, unambiguously in Aldrich), and the criticism of the hero is articulated primarily through the women's roles. The denouement, in each case, involves the downfall of the film's most prominent villain through a woman's violent actions (Debbie/Gloria Grahame revenges herself on Vince/Lee Marvin; "Lily Carver"/Gaby Rodgers shoots Dr. Soberin/Albert Dekker) before the hero intervenes. A crucial step in the early stages of each narrative involves the murder of a woman (Lucy, Christina) precipitated by the fact that she has given the hero information, and made possible by the fact that, because of his contemptuous attitude toward her, he offers her insufficient protection.

One of the most impressive things about Aldrich's film is its relationship to Mickey Spillane's thoroughly obnoxious novel, of which the film constitutes a drastic critique. Spillane's totally unreflecting fantasy-identification with Mike Hammer—there seems no critical distance whatever between author and character—is unambiguously rejected in favor of what amounts to a systematic discrediting of him.

The critique of the hero is clearly central to the progress of both films. In Aldrich this is far more devastat-

Different concepts of domesticity: opposite, "normal," the idealist police detective Bannion (Glenn Ford) with his wife (Jocelyn Brando) and daughter in *The Big Heat* and, below, skewed, the vulgar divorce dick Mike Hammer (Ralph Meeker) with his girlfiriend Velda (Maxine Cooper) at his elbow gets information from his only friend, police lieutenant Pat Murphy (Wesley Addy), in *Kiss Me Deadly.*

ing and uncompromised—but only because the overall vision is altogether simpler and cruder. Lang plainly dislikes Bannion/Glenn Ford, but cannot simply denounce him, as Aldrich can Hammer, because (a) he sees him as necessary to a culture that may not be entirely unredeemable (Hammer/Ralph Meeker is as necessary as a pain in the ass) and (b) he realizes that Bannion's virtues and flaws are inseparable from each other (Hammer has no virtues, he is all flaw). Bannion's virtues and flaws can be summed up in a single word: he is an idealist, always a problem for a pragmatic materialist like Lang. Hammer, on the contrary, is a mere vulgar materialist, like virtually everyone else in the film: the case is as simple as that. He is motivated by a greed that makes him indistinguishable from the nominal villains, and the means he employs are as callous and devoid of human caring as those of the FBI. The extraordinary, irresistible force of Aldrich's film is achieved at a certain cost: the elimination of all complexity of attitude.

In both films the critique of the "hero" is effected primarily through the female characters. It is characteristic of *Kiss Me Deadly* that there this is achieved by direct and explicit denunciation: Christina/Cloris Leachman near the beginning and Velda/Maxine Cooper towards the climax, are both given speeches whose function is in effect to tell the audience what they are to think of Mike Hammer. Neither speech seems very clearly motivated in terms of the characterization and situation of the speaker: Christina has only just made Hammer's

acquaintance, so that her insights into his character, while certainly valid, seem somewhat abrupt and rhetorical; Velda has been thoroughly complicit with him (to the point of prostituting herself at his instigation to incriminate errant husbands in divorce cases), bolstering his egoism, and her only reason for turning on him appears to be her recognition that this time he is involved in something much more dangerous than usual. At least the film never applauds her for "devotion to her man," but it is also clear that the women in the film, although they suffer in various ways and degrees, carry absolutely no moral weight. Both Christina and the false Lily Carver die because, like everyone else, they are pursuing "the Great Whatsit"; as for Velda, what moral substance can we grant a character who devotes herself singlemindedly to the "hero" the film despises and condemns?

The case is very different when we turn to *The Big Heat*. Here, the critique of the hero—itself a far more complex matter: Bannion, unlike Hammer, is a moral crusader from the outset and subsequently motivated by his outrage at Katie's death—is dramatically enacted, not explicitly stated in somewhat arbitrary speeches: the evidence, I would claim, of Lang's far surer, finer, more complex grasp of his theme, the token of a finer mind

Different concepts of honor and violence: below, Bannion beats Vince Stone (Lee Marvin) whom he knows is responsible for the torture of his informant, Debbie in *The Big Heat*. Opposite, Hammer amuses himself by roughing up gunsel Charlie Max (Jack Elam) in *Kiss Me Deadly*.

and sensibility. Consider how our attitude to Bannion is defined (or more precisely redefined: hitherto we have seen only the idealism) in the scene in "The Retreat" with Lucy Chapman early in the film. In retrospect from it, Bannion's automatic readiness to take Bertha Duncan on trust develops a fresh significance (we saw it earlier, I think, simply as an aspect of his moral goodness). With the confrontation with Lucy (for whose death Bannion is clearly responsible—he offers her no protection despite the fact that she has given him "dangerous" information, and treats her with undisguised contempt because she doesn't measure up to his standards of bourgeois respectability) Lang shows us the other side of the idealism, a type of idealism that is usually a "given," an unquestioned positive, but is here subjected to astringent analysis: a self-righteous priggishness, class-based, that judges people purely in terms of their social position, and which blocks Bannion from any finer insights into character. (One might comment here, as an aside, on the perfect casting of Glenn Ford.)

Lucy, shortly after she gives our idealist hero the crucial information he needs to start him on the track, and is summarily dismissed for her pains, is tortured to death. Her fate seals what is already clearly there in the scene in "The Retreat," our detachment from Bannion as an identification-figure: for Lang ensures that we see Lucy very differently from the way in which he sees Lucy. The critique of Bannion is developed through his dealings with and attitude to Debbie Marsh/Gloria Grahame (another instance of perfect casting!). I discussed

Different views of femme fatales: below, Bannion meets with another B-girl with big earrings, neckace and cleavage, Lucy Chapman (Dorothy Green). Opposite, the clean-scrubbed and jacketed Lily Carver (Gaby Rodgers) about to kill her mentor Dr. Soberin (Albert Dekker) in *Kiss Me Deadly*.

this at some length in an article mainly on *Rancho Notorious* in the Film Noir issue of *CineAction!* (No. 13/14), and shall try not to repeat myself more than is necessary for my argument. Consider, however, Debbie's death scene near the end of the film. Earlier, Debbie, in love with Bannion (or, more precisely, in love with his perceived idealism, his moral integrity) has asked him to talk to her about his dead wife Katie/Jocelyn Brando, and Bannion, seeing her as a "fallen woman" contaminated by her involvement with gangsters, in contrast to Katie's flawless, if somewhat artificially constructed, bourgeois purity, has shrunk in revulsion from doing so. At the end, he is able at last to grant Debbie's wish for three reasons: (a) Debbie has murdered Bertha Duncan for him, with the gun he somewhat pointedly left with her, thereby exposing and destroying Lagana; (b) she has been instrumental in the arrest of Vince Stone; and, most important (c) he perceives that she is dying: she can be safely sentimentalized, without the consequences of any awkward involvement or responsibility.

Between the death of Lucy Chapman and the death of Debbie Marsh (for both of which Bannion has a responsibility he never, in his smugness, allows himself to fully recognize, permitting the former by his negligence—Lucy is, after all, just a "B-girl," not a policeman's wife like Katie or Bertha Duncan—and precipitating the latter by insinuating Debbie into performing for him an action he is too "moral" to perform himself) comes the brief but crucial appearance in the film of another female character, Selma Parker/Edith Evanson, the crippled woman who works for Dan Seymour's car-wrecking company. Her one scene (apart from a very brief reappearance when she identifies Lagana's henchman Larry for Bannion) occurs around the midpoint of the film, and provides the narrative with its turning-point. Without the slightest ostentation or underlining of "significance," Lang privileges Selma's intervention. Although she appears briefly in the background of the scene in her boss's office—the image I think everyone retains is of her hobbling on her stick between the rows of

A now disfigured Debbie Marsh (Gloria Grahame), who reveled in her beauty in front of the mirror with Vince Stone (page 406) cannot face Bannion for whom she has sacrificed so much.

wrecked cars toward Bannion, who is on the other side of a chainmail fence. She defends her boss (who, out of fear, has refused to give Bannion information)—he "isn't a bad man," and after all, who else would employ a woman like herself?—before risking her own life (we know that she could easily join Lucy Chapman in the morgue) by telling Bannion what he needs to know. It's an extraordinary little scene—understated, almost thrown away: Selma is the one character in the film whose motives are absolutely pure. Lucy talks to Bannion because she was in love with Tom Duncan; Debbie acts because she is in love with Bannion. Selma has everything to lose and nothing whatever to gain, except self-respect. While Lang admires the other women, I think he invites us to put Selma (and what a little gem of a performance!) in a special category. *The Big Heat*, consistently, reveals a sensitive awareness of the social position of women, and offers a moving, unobtrusive tribute to their resilience, courage and tenacity, that *Kiss Me Deadly* needs, but entirely lacks.

The three female victims of Dave Bannion (if Selma survives, it is not his doing) are roughly paralleled by the three female characters of *Kiss Me Deadly*. If Aldrich's film offers an equivalent for the death of Katie Bannion, it is the death of Nick, Hammer's devoted "best buddy." This points to what is surely the film's most interesting aspect, a dimension lacking from *The Big Heat* and from Lang's work in general: its pervasive suggestion that the American construction of "masculinity" (together with its accompanying paranoia) is built upon the repression not only of the male's "femininity" (which would account for Hammer's hatred of/contempt for women, the film's major debt to Mickey Spillane), but his innate homosexuality. It is a theme that Scorsese was to "realize" fully and magnificently a quarter of a century later in *Raging Bull*; in Aldrich it remains a flickering, tantalizing implication, a "subtext" in the strict sense, yet it is worth recalling that an interest in the ambiguities of gender and sexuality recurs spasmodically throughout Aldrich's work (and never in Lang's; the one apparent exception—the suggestion of homosexuality in the psychopath of *While the City Sleeps*—is treated entirely negatively, as no more than pathological symptom). *The Legend of Lylah Clare*, *The Killing of Sister George*, *The Choirboys*, are overt examples, but even a film like *All the Marbles*, with its "tag team" of female athletes under an "apathetic and non-athletic" manager, is relevant here. Aldrich's treatment of this theme is not notable for much complexity or sensitivity (the sledgehammer sensibility that is both the strength and limitation of *Kiss Me Deadly* prohibits any nuance), but its presence (which is perhaps, in subterranean forms, more pervasive than the few examples cited suggest) is partly responsible for the distinctive quality of his work.

It can certainly be argued (and I shall not dispute it) that *Kiss Me Deadly* is much the more striking of the two films. It has a force, directness and impact that one is never likely to forget, and isn't this the outward manifestation of an intense creative energy? Fair enough: such a description acknowledges the film's undoubted distinction and testifies to its authenticity as a response to the contemporary cultural climate. With it must be considered the film's stylistic progressiveness (beside which *The Big Heat* appears decidedly conservative): "Years ahead of its time, a major influence on French New Wave directors," as Leonard Maltin's TV Movies guide (and indispensable barometer of contemporary taste) succinctly puts it. The influence seems to me unproven: the *Cahiers* critics adored the film, because it demonstrated again what could be achieved within a generally disreputable Hollywood genre, but I can't see that, when they made their films, they learnt much from it directly. It is one of the those films that appears stylistically innovative, because it employs devices that one was not then accustomed to meeting within the general run of "private eye" thrillers. In fact, its pervasive "baroque" rhetoric (deep focus, strikingly extreme low and high camera angles) derives entirely from Welles and Toland: the "innovation" lies in applying it to film noir (from whose world it was never entirely alien). It is certainly an audacious film; I don't think this is a valid reason for preferring it to a movie that is content to utilize (with great intelligence) the shooting/editing codes dominant in the Hollywood cinema. *The Big Heat* proves yet again (how many demonstrations does one need?) that those codes can be put in the service of subversive and radical purposes. Lang at his best (as he is in *The Big Heat*) is among the cinema's subtlest and most subversive moralists; Aldrich's moral sense does not lend itself to the finer discriminations—which, it is worth insisting once again, are as much political as moral.

If both films depict a culture in which corruption is virtually all-pervasive, the world of *Kiss Me Deadly* is just corrupt, and there is little more to be said about it. Hammer is allowed one moment of grace; his grief over Nick's death, as he gets drunk in a bar: a moment that eloquently confirms one's sense that the emotional center of the film is homoerotic (Hammer nowhere evinces this concern over women). Otherwise, the simplicity—the lack of complexity, of delicate exploration—of Aldrich's vision actually makes it much easier to enjoy *Kiss Me Deadly* on the superficial level on which genre movies are generally offered, the level that we call "entertainment." The to-hell-with-all-this, blow-it-all-up attitude to American civilisation actually provides a relatively easy excitement, satisfaction, and exhilaration. (The studio—which added a final shot [Ed. Note: nothing was added. Some shots were excised: see pages 322-324 above] still there is some prints showing Hammer and Velda standing amid the waves, apparently safe—need not have worried: audiences generally seem to derive a lot of pleasure from the fact that Aldrich blows up everybody). Lang's cautious, probing attitude that qualifies every judgment makes an easy satisfaction impossible (we would get no satisfaction from blowing up a civilisation that contains Lucy Chapmans, Selma Parkers and Debbie Marshes). One is left with a sense of discord and disturbance—with the sense of a culture to whose problems there will be no easy solutions: a disturbance crystallized in the film's last line: "Keep the coffee hot."

Notes

1. "Pedagogy in the Perverse Text," in *Cineaction!* (Toronto), Winter-Spring 1990.

Femme fatale Rita Hayworth runs her fingers through an obsessed Glenn Ford's hair in *Gilda*.

Film Noir, Voice-Over, and the Femme Fatale

Karen Hollinger

The period of the 1940s was the golden age of filmic first person voice-over narration, which involves an overt act of communicating a narrative to an audience by a recognized speaker in a film. Most commonly after an initial presentation of a narrating situation in which we see the narrating character begin to tell the story, the film moves into flashback sequences that visually portray the recounted events. We, as viewers, intermittently hear the narrator speaking within the film although we no longer see the narrating situation; thus, the voice seems to come from a time and place distinct from the visual portrayal of events. The first person narrator also plays a part in the story told and refers to him or herself as "I." This type of narration can be distinguished from the third person narrational mode, which involves a narrator who plays no part in the film's diegesis except to narrate the story from the perspective of an uninvolved observer.

By the 1940s the voice-over technique had found wide acceptance in various types of Hollywood films. Critics point especially to its use in popular 40s genre films: war films, semi- or pseudo-documentaries, literary adaptations, and films noirs.[1] The unique quality of the use of first person voice-over in films noirs and its connection to the films' investigation of their female characters, however, deserves further analysis.

In contrast to films noirs, other 1940's genres use voice-over primarily to accentuate the verisimilitude of and to increase audience identification with their narrators' stories. Voice-over is used in war dramas, for instance, to increase viewer identification with the films' heroic soldier protagonists. Semi- and pseudo-documentaries, like war films, employ voice-over most often in the third rather than the first person, to add credibility to their stories. In films adapted from literary sources, the voice-over is most often associated with a recreation of the original novel's authorial narrational voice. Thus, the voice-overs employed in these films are associated with authority, heroism, and power, either authorial, narrative, or both.

Films noirs, however, do not attempt this association; instead, they most often contain weak, powerless narrators who tell a story of their past failures or of their inability to shape the events of their lives to their own designs. Eric Smoodin, for instance, argues that voice-over in film noir represents an aberrant use of the technique, standing in stark contrast to its use in other classical Hollywood films.[2] Smoodin's characterization of noir voice-over narrators as aberrant fits well with established views of film noir as a deviant genre within the classical Hollywood tradition. Films noirs, for instance, commonly are seen as "maladjusted" texts that reflect "the dark side of the screen," the ideological contradictions, disequilibrium, and disturbing imbalance characteristic of the World War II and post-war periods.[3] Because noirs reached their peak of popularity during and after the war, wartime social turmoil has largely been seen as responsible for their "deviant" nature.

A close analysis of first person voice-over noir films, however, yields a number of salient features which their simple categorization as aberrant classical Hollywood reflections of wartime and post-war angst elides. First of all, the genre's use of first person voice-over occurs within a configuration that commonly involves a confessional/investigative mode. The voice-over penetrates into the past of a central male character as well as into this character's psyche in order to arrive at a fundamental truth that is seen as causing an individually and/or socially abnormal or destructive situation. This confessional/investigative arrangement is also typically tied to a vaguely psychoanalytic situation, a Freudian "talking cure" of sorts in which the confessing narrator is somehow relieved of guilt or anxiety by arriving at a sense of truth through confession. In film noir, first person narrators, in fact, frequently offer their confessions to patriarchal authority figures within the film text or to the film audience itself who seem to be asked to grant a kind of absolution and to act as a curative force.

Interestingly, what the confessing male narrators of these films search for in their past experiences or psychological condition is a revelation that involves the truth not so much about masculinity but rather about femininity. Like Freud, these films seem to be concerned with ascertaining "what the woman wants," finding the essential nature of female difference, which often is symbolized in female sexuality, as it was also for Freud. Femininity thus becomes the ultimate subject of the film's discourse. Michel Foucault argues in *The History of Sexuality* that Western society has attempted to control sex by putting it into a discourse which connects it with a search for truth. According to Foucault, this search for the truth of sexuality while seeming to reveal sexual truth, really acts only to mask, deny access to, and assert power over it. The confession is merely one procedure that has been developed for telling a "truth" about sex, which, in fact, masks the very nature of sex itself.[4]

Indeed, the male confessors of film noir do seem determined to probe femaleness in order to capture a hidden "truth" which is the key not only to female but to male nature as well. But like Foucault's conception of the ultimately unrevealing truth of Western society's discourses on sexuality, the truth about women uncovered in film noir often fails to reveal real gender difference or even really to imagine this difference at all. At the same time, the very project of these films, their repeatedly unsuccessful attempts to probe the nature of sexual difference, foregrounds a societal failure to resolve the contradictions inherent in conventional configurations of sexuality and gender difference.

Approached from a psychoanalytic perspective, the male confessing/investigating figures of film noir and the paternal figures who often listen to their stories consistently try to interpret the meaning of femaleness by male standards, from the point of view of the phallus. In these terms, femaleness is always judged as excess or lack from the perspective of male normalcy. The difference is reduced to one of degree, not kind, and the different truth of woman is elided in favor of the single phallic truth of man with the woman becoming either more or less than the male norm. In this phallic economy, femaleness becomes simply insufficiency or excess in comparison to maleness, and real difference is masked under a discourse that approaches understanding only of this limited conception of truth. In this way, the films can soothe castration fears that the notion of sexual difference might raise in the male spectator and that the advances of women out of the home and into the work place exacerbated in 1940's society. By eliding difference, the films can create a unified male spectator untroubled by contradictions within his society that are symbolized in the films by female otherness.

In this sense, films noirs serve a very conservative ideological function, yet their repeated use of first person voice-over narration also opens up, within the films, points of resistance to this ideological conservatism. At first glance, the noir voice-over seems to do exactly the opposite, to establish within the text a single overriding male narrational perspective that appears to dominate all other textual elements. As the films progress, however, this single, dominating point of view does not hold, and the films begin to fracture.

Voice-over creates this fragmenting effect by establishing within the film a fight for narrative power as the narrator struggles to gain control of the narrative events recounted. This battle between the narrator and the film's flashback visuals leads to an extreme tension between word and image. It has been argued that voice-over narration in film noir implicates the spectator completely in the perspective of the film's male narrator and leads this implicated spectator to join with the narrator in his condemnation of the film's major female character, the dangerous and often deadly femme fatale. Mary Ann Doane, for instance, sees the noir voice-over as embedding the figure of the femme fatale in the narrative's metadiegetic level, framing her speech within an overpowering masculine discourse in order to withhold from her access to narration and grant the male narrator control of both her words and image.[5]

While one can point to those characteristics of noir first person voice-over which attempt to subject the female image to male narrational power, this power is not nearly as complete as Doane suggests. As a number of feminist critics have suggested, women in classical Hollywood films have been positioned as objects of spectacle, fixed and held by the male gaze.[6] The femme fatale of film noir is clearly yet another female object of spectacle, defined by her dangerous, yet desirable sexual presence, but she is an object with a difference. Female characters in classical Hollywood films are traditionally portrayed as weak, ineffectual figures safely placed in the fixed female roles of wives, mothers, or daughters and desperately in need of the male hero's affection and protection. Films noirs release the female image from these fixed roles and grant it overwhelming visual power. The iconography of the femme fatale grants these beautiful, provocative women visual primacy through shot composition as well as camera positioning, movement, and lighting.

The freedom of movement and visual dominance of the femme fatale admittedly is presented as inappropriate to a "proper" female role and as igniting sinister forces that are deadly to the male protagonist. Narratively, this dangerous, evil woman is damned and ultimately punished, but stylistically she exhibits such an extremely powerful visual presence that the conventional narrative is disoriented and the image of the erotic, strong, unrepressed woman dominates the text, even in the face of narrative repression.[7]

The male voice-over in film noir, while it may attempt to control the female image, serves instead to pit the femme fatale's dominant visual presence against the male voice, thereby foregrounding ideological battles raging in the 1940s in regard to women's appropriate social role. This situation of embattlement is exacerbated by the voice-over's fragmenting effect with regard to spectator positioning. Susan Lanser, writing on first person narration in literature, and Ellen Feldman, working with its use in film, suggest that various stages of surrogate positioning exist between a narrator or central character and the text's implied author and implied reader/spectator.[8] In films noirs, the relationships among the implied spectator, voice-over narrator, and the agency of the implied author are inscribed in the text in a way that triggers what can be termed a proliferation of point of view, a divorce of the narrator's, implied author's and implied spectator's positions.

Often, within a narrated work, a narrational hierarchy is established in which one perspective, either that of the narrator, implied author, or implied spectator/reader, comes to dominate and enclose all others or the three perspectives merge into a unified whole. In film noir a narrational hierarchy fails to establish itself and a proliferation of point of view dominates the texts. While first person voice-over can act as an authoritative evocation of the power of the text's implied author, when it is combined with certain elements in film noir (the confessional mode, investigative and psychologically penetrating narration, the flashback structure, and most notably the investigation of the femme fatale) it loses control of events that seem inevitably to escape the voice-over narrator's power. As a result, sound becomes dislocated from image, the gap between the planes of the narrative widens, establishing a narrational hierarchy becomes difficult, and finally point of view fragments. Situated within these gaps and torn by this fragmentation, the spectator is placed in a position from which he or she judges between what is shown and the narrator's account of it, attaining a distance from the narrative that allows for meaning to be perceived not as a static quantity to be passively grasped as the single ideologically "correct" position but rather as a battleground for competing perspectives.

Throughout the period of the 1940s, voice-over noir texts evidence such extreme tendencies to fragmentation and proliferation of point of view that any attempt to resolve their investigations of their female characters are rendered hopelessly inconclusive. The following examination of four prominent voice-over noir films demonstrates how the structural aspects of the texts have a resulting effect on spectator positioning that encourages a perception not only of the text's structural contradictions but also of a social failure that lies beneath them, a failure even to begin to comprehend a female nature that, because of women's changing societal roles, seems to have appeared unfathomable.

Laura (Preminger, 1944) is a case in point, which might at first glance seem aberrant in the noir canon. Unlike other first-person narrators, Waldo Lydecker (Clifton Webb), is not victim to the evil designs of an ambitious femme fatale. Instead he reveals himself to be her psychopathic would-be killer. He sets out to murder the film's heroine twice when she tries to break his hold on her by forming an attachment to another man. Yet, in spite of Lydecker's differences from the conventional noir narrator, the effect of his voice-over is indicative of the pattern characteristic of other noir films. His narration encompasses a significant amount of the first half of the film when he is involved in a struggle with Detective McPhearson (Dana Andrews), who is investigating the supposed murder of Laura Hunt (Gene Tierney). Lydecker's voice-over is his attempt to impose his interpretation of Laura's character and of his involvement with her on both McPhearson and the spectator, since his first narrative is addressed directly to the audience and his second to McPhearson. According to his account, he always demonstrated and continues to feel only a fatherly concern for her welfare.

Suddenly, in mid-film, Lydecker's voice-over disappears. This loss of narration has a significant effect on spectator positioning within the text's structure. Lydecker sets himself up as an initial object of spectator identification. He also ties himself to the implied author of the work by announcing at the beginning of his narration his literary pretensions; he tells us that he was just about to begin a written eulogy for Laura when he was interrupted by McPhearson's arrival to question him about her murder. Thus, when his position as a spectator surrogate is repudiated by the loss of his narration and the final revelation in the film's closing scenes that he is, in fact, a murderer, the effect on the spectator is devastating. The film cannot effectively provide another object of viewer identification to replace him. McPhearson would be the logical choice. He serves as the center of the investigation after Lydecker's narration disappears and acts as the film's hero, saving Laura from Lydecker's second murder attempt in the closing scenes. Significantly, however, he never assumes the role of narrator.

In this way, the film is very different from the novel on which it is based. *Laura* by Vera Caspary establishes single unified narrational control even in a multiply narrated work.[9] The novel contains several narratives, each of which is presented by a different narrator: Waldo Lydecker, Detective McPhearson, Laura's fiancé Shelby Carpenter, and Laura Hunt herself all provide accounts of Laura's attempted murder. In the novel, how-

Below, "*Laura*...might at first glance seem aberrant in the noir canon. Unlike other noir narrators, Waldo Lydecker (Clifton Webb), the film's first person narrator, does not fall victim to the evil designs of an ambitious femme fatale." Seen here with Det. McPherson (Dana Andrews) the effete Lydecker tells the story of Laura's life while bathing.   Opposite, Lydecker faints when Laura (Gene Tierney) turns out to be alive.

ever, McPhearson writes a concluding statement in which he identifies himself as the overriding authorial presence in the text. He explains in this conclusion that he accumulated and organized the various narratives. This narrational control is never replicated in the film; instead, the spectator is placed in a position characterized by a complex oscillation between identification with the villain/narrator's position and that of the investigating hero. The film's attempts at its conclusion to realign the spectator with legal authority through an identification with the figure of McPhearson are, thus, seriously compromised.

As a result of this disorienting narrational structure, the film fails to investigate adequately the character of its major female character. It attempts to do so by alternately presenting her through Lydecker's voice-over narration as a possible murder victim or a cold-blooded murderess. McPhearson also sets out to investigate her, yet as the film progresses, his investigation is transformed into an investigation of Lydecker. Laura remains an enigma throughout: Lydecker's attempts to narrate her story end in the sudden disappearance of his voice-over, and McPhearson's investigation brings him only to Lydecker as her attempted murderer. Laura herself remains a mystery, her unknowable nature symbolized by her portrait which hangs prominently over the fireplace in her apartment, overlooks much of the action, and eventually leads McPhearson to become obsessed with her. Like the image in the portrait, Laura presents a beautiful, fascinating surface, but one impenetrable to investigation.[10]

In contrast to *Laura*, other noirs with voice-over narration hold more closely to the formula of the noir hero as the victim, rather than the attempted victimizer, of the dangerous femme fatale. *Gilda* (Vidor) and *The Postman Always Rings Twice* (Garnett), both released in 1946, have criminal narrators who are presented as victims of the machinations of female characters. *Gilda* provides another instance of lost narration similar to that found in *Laura*. It begins, as Richard Dyer points out, as Johnny's story.[11] Johnny Farrell (Glenn Ford) tells in voice-over of his involvement with his male mentor Ballin (George Macready) and Ballin's wife Gilda (Rita Hayworth). Yet, Johnny's voice-over serves primarily to inform the spectator of his negative assessments of Gilda's character and of his disdain for her, rather than to tell us much about Johnny himself. In addition, Johnny's perspective is so immersed in a narrative progression that calls all of his judgments into question that it is difficult to view his commentary from anything but a critical perspective. Johnny, in fact, seems totally unable throughout the film to comprehend the true nature of his feelings for Gilda. The visuals show repeated instances of their mutual attraction, but his voice-over tells only of his disdain for her. For instance, as he contemplates his feelings at one point in the film he comments in voice-over: "I hated her. So I couldn't get her out of my mind for a minute." This remark seems more a product of frustrated sexual attraction than of disdain. Johnny's voice-over also seems curiously unaware of his feelings for Ballin. The film, through the narrative presentation of the strong attachment between the two men, hints at a homosexual involvement between them

Johnny Farrell intercepts Gilda as she returns home escorted by gambler Gabe Evans (Mark Roberts).

that Ford later indicated was obvious to the actors as they fashioned their roles.[12] Yet, Johnny's voice-over totally ignores this aspect of his sexuality.

The film also fails to place Johnny's narration within an introductory or concluding narrating situation. It begins with Johnny's voice-over imposed over the visual depiction of his initial encounter with Ballin. As the narrative progresses, Johnny, as narrator, periodically interjects comments over the action, but his narration suddenly disappears as conflicts are resolved at the film's conclusion. Johnny's voice-over is not only abruptly terminated, completely unmotivated, and stemming from an indefinite time and place of narration, but it is also curiously tied to the emotions and reactions of his character in the flashbacks rather than to those of his narrating persona, who is recounting the story in the past tense. Thus, the voice-over is tied to the conflicts that dominate the text until its conclusion rather than to the attempts at resolution that are made in the film's closing segments.

These concluding attempts at resolution are imposed upon the narrator by an authoritative listener/interpreter, who suddenly appears at the film's conclusion to provide both the narrator and spectator with a suggested interpretation of events. A detective who has been investigating both Johnny and Ballin steps in to analyze Johnny's behavior toward Gilda and advise him of the proper attitude he should adopt toward her. As the detective sees it:

> It's the most curious love-hate pattern I've ever had the privilege of witnessing and as long as you're as sick in the head as you are about her, you're not able to think of anything clearly... How dumb can a man be? I'd hate to see you break down and act like a human being. Gilda didn't do any of those things you've been losing sleep over, not any of them. It was just an act, all of it, and I'll give you credit. You were a great audience, Mr. Farrell.

This interpretation provides Johnny with crucial insight into his past behavior and empowers him to go to Gilda, confess his love, and beg her to take him back. Yet as voice-over narrator, Johnny never recognizes this insight. Not only is his narration tied to his feelings of disdain for Gilda, but by the film's end, the voice-over has completely disappeared. While the detective's perspective seems to offer the implied author's interpretation of events, it cannot provide the spectator with complete involvement in this point of view because it is not accepted or endorsed by Johnny's voice-over.

The film's attempts to explicate the nature of its femme fatale are seriously undermined by this failure. As Foster Hirsch notes, *Gilda*'s ending seems forced.[13] It is tacked on to a text that condemns its femme fatale so strongly through Johnny's narration and the visual presentation of her sexual seductiveness (for example, her "Put The Blame on Mame" musical number) that the film's final recognition of her as a "good woman," an innocent victim of the sinister designs of the evil Ballin and the unfounded suspicions of the self-deceived narrator, rings false.[14] The film's voice-over narrator never seems to determine the true nature of Gilda's character, and this failure renders all attempts to resolve other narrative conflicts inadequate. In its conclusion, the film projects its evil completely onto the character of Ballin, a "foreigner" connected with a Nazi tungsten cartel, and exonerates its American characters, Johnny and Gilda. Yet, the voice-over technique and its failure to close off the questions concerning Gilda's character or to validate completely either Johnny's voice-over perceptions of events or his final non-voice-over insights call this attempted resolution into question. Again, the character of the film's femme fatale is left unresolved and uncontrolled.

The operation of fate in *The Postman Always Rings Twice* serves a purpose very similar to that of the lost voice-overs in *Laura* and *Gilda*. It prevents the film from centering its point of view on its central character's perspective and from resolving its textual conflicts successfully. *Postman* ends with a concluding frame in which the narrator/protagonist proclaims to the audience his belief that fate has taken a hand in engineering his destruction. This fatalistic notion of human destiny seems intended to eradicate all social contradictions raised in the film. The narrator's problems are said to stem not from his inability to find a satisfying place in the social structure but from a malign fate that directed his life to destructive ends. Frank Chambers (John Garfield) declares at the film's conclusion that his unjust conviction for the murder of his lover Cora (Lana Turner)

Above, diffident attorney Kyle Sackett (Leon Ames, center) listens as accused adulterous murderers Cora Smith (Lana Turner) and Frank Chambers (John Garfield) reveal their distrust of each other in *The Postman Always Rings Twice*.

Opposite, from his cell awaiting execution, Frank is the ostensible narrator.

represents divine retribution for their earlier murder of her husband. Yet, throughout the film, Frank's voice-over describes his situation differently. He still views events as out of his control, but he describes himself as trapped not by fate or divine retribution but by Cora's sexual hold over him. As he puts it, "She had me hooked, and she knew it." Cora is presented as responsible for encouraging Frank's sexual desires for her, and thus deliberately luring him into a relationship with a married woman that leads him to murder.

The concept of fate is used very differently in the 1934 James M. Cain novel upon which the film is based.[15] While the film attempts to replicate very closely the novel's first person narration, it does so in a way that destroys the book's identification of its implied author's perspective with a fatalistic notion of human destiny. In spite of the novel's first person narration, its implied author's point of view is clearly delineated from its central character's. Frank's character in the novel, like his filmic counterpart, is driven by a malign fate, but he is completely unaware of this aspect of his situation. The conviction that it is the operation of fate that engineers Frank's doom is aligned in the novel not with Frank's perspective on events, but with the implied author's.

In the film, Frank's final declaration of the divine retribution he sees worked out through his punishment identifies the concept of fate strongly with his individual perspective on events at the moment of his execution, rather than with that of the implied author. The limited nature of this perspective is accentuated by its last minute expression in the concluding frame, by the visual presentation of the unwise decisions made through-out the film by both Frank and Cora as they act to engineer their own destruction, and by Frank's feelings expressed earlier in the film's voice-over narration that he was trapped by Cora's sexual allure. In the novel, the concept of fate permeates the whole structure of the work. It is not expressed as a final judgment by the narrator; instead, it seems intimately connected with the implied author's overriding perspective.

The use of first person narration in the film, rather than drawing together the implied spectator's and implied author's positions through the intermediary perspective of the narrator or uniting them in contradistinction to the narrator's position, acts, instead, both to implicate the spectator into the narrator's perspective and at the same time to call this perspective into question. The sudden revelation of a priest in the closing frame as a hidden narratee further disorients the viewer who had previously identified with the addressee of Frank's narration. In the novel, the text is clearly signaled as Frank's written account of the murder which he gives to a priest for possible publication after his execution. He does not narrate this account to the priest as he does in the film; rather, it is always intended for the reader's consumption.

Postman, like other noirs that use voice-over narration, expresses much more ambiguity in its narrational strategy than is found in its novelistic source. Rather than achieving centralization of point of view through the dominant perspective of a single character or of the implied author in contradistinction to this character, the film defuses point of view, separating the implied spectator's position from both that of the narrator and the implied author. Hence, the film fails to achieve the unification of point of view found in the novel.

This fragmented point of view structure leaves the film's investigation of its femme fatale unresolved in a way that it is not in the novel, where Cora and Frank are both portrayed as puppets of a malign fate. In the film, Frank's narration seems hopelessly confused as to Cora's role in bringing about his doom. We never know for sure if we are to hold her responsible for having trapped him in a web of uncontrolled female sexuality or if fate trapped them both in its inexorable grip and divine retribution punished their sins. As a result, the nature of Cora's character is left enigmatic and unresolved.

In contrast to *Postman, The Lady From Shanghai* (Welles, 1948) attempts to envision a more positive fate for its narrator. Like other noirs employing the voice-over technique, however, it also sets out to connect its flashback visuals to its voice-over narration by extending the narrative battles for control of events within the flashbacks out into the narration. This extension calls its attempts at positive resolution into question. In *The Lady From Shanghai*, Michael O'Hara (Orson Welles) tells the story of his involvement with the beautiful femme

fatale Elsa (Rita Hayworth), her evil lawyer husband Arthur Bannister (Everett Sloane), and her lover George Grisby (Glenn Anders). As Michael describes them, they are "a pack of sharks mad with their own blood, chewin' away at their own selves."

Michael allows himself to get involved with this sinister group through what he describes as his own stupidity and his intense attraction to the beautiful Elsa. He confesses in voice-over just before we see the flashback presentation of his initial meeting with Elsa:

"Sleeping rattlesnake" attorney Arthur Bannister (Everett Sloane) questions Elsa (Rita Hayworth) during her trial in *The Lady from Shanghai*.

When I start to make a fool of myself, there's very little can stop me. If I'd known where it would end, I would have never let anything start. If I'd been in my right mind, that is. And once I'd seen her...once I'd seen her, I was not in my right mind for quite some time.

While he admits that his involvement with these evil characters involved him in a murder plot, he eventually claims to have escaped their designs. Yet, he can never fully exonerate himself from his involvement with the evil they represent. As he puts it at the end: "I'd be innocent officially, but that's a big word, innocent. Stupid's more like it." In his final dialogue with Elsa as she lies dying, he condemns her for having attempted to "deal with the badness and make terms" with it. Michael proposes that he'll never "make terms" with evil again. Elsa in response expresses her cynical belief that one cannot win in a struggle with evil, and he retorts, "But we can't lose either, only if we quit." He then leaves her to die alone.

Michael's final actions indicate that he has won his battle by extricating himself from involvement with the evil that Elsa represents, but he does so only by callously abandoning her in her dying moments, ignoring her pleas for him to stay. Additionally, as he leaves her, Michael's voice-over narration reaffirms the ongoing nature of his struggle:

Well, everybody is somebody's fool. The only way to stay out of trouble is to grow old, so I guess I'll concentrate on that. Maybe, I'll live so long that I'll forget her. Maybe, I'll die tryin'.

As his voice-over narration demonstrates, Michael's battle seems far from over.

While this battle is extended into the narration by Michael's final proclamation that his struggle to extricate himself from Elsa's influence continues, the spectator is not implicated in Michael's perspective by this extension. In comparing the film to the novel upon which it is based, *If I Die Before I Wake* by Raymond Sherwood King, it becomes clear that the novel more strongly encourages its reader to adopt its first person narrator's perspective than does the film.[16] The novel's narrator, like his filmic counterpart, is a common man trapped in a web of conspiracy and murder that he has great difficulty even understanding. Yet, the film's Michael O'Hara focuses repeatedly through his voice-over narration on his stupidity in having gotten involved with Bannister and Grisby and in having fallen so completely under Elsa's spell. The novel's protagonist/narrator, on the other hand, constantly reminds the reader that he was trying desperately throughout his experiences to comprehend the exact nature of the intrigue surrounding him.

The narrator of the novel might never fully gain control of events, but his expressed desire to understand what is going on around him, rather than constantly reiterating his inability to do so, connects his perspective to that of the reader who is also trying to learn the significance of events. The film's emphasis on Michael's stupidity and complete enthrallment by Elsa's beauty have the opposite effect. While the spectator is trying throughout the film to comprehend the nature of the conspiracy surrounding Michael, Michael himself seems unable to distance himself enough from events to achieve any comprehension of their significance. As a result, the spectator's adoption of his perspective is significantly reduced.

The novel also connects its narrator's perspective with that of the work's implied author much more strongly than the film does by having the text conclude with the supposed place of its authorship. The narrative ends with an inscription from Tahiti. In this way, it becomes a personal account that connects its narrator strongly with its implied author. The film also attempts to make this connection by having its star, Orson Welles, also function as its director, but the connection is incomplete because Michael O'Hara with his prominent Irish brogue and repeated attestations to stupidity seems very different from Welles' boy genius persona. The emphasis on the characterological status of the narrator interferes with his identification with the implied author.

Because the film fails to achieve unification in its point of view structure, it cannot resolve the issue of the nature of its femme fatale. Elsa is characterized as a beautiful, enigmatic woman with a mysterious past that is never fully revealed. In the book, while she is initially an enigmatic figure, any mystery associated with her is eventually resolved. The narrator discovers that she is an ex-chorus girl who married Bannister for his money, and in the end a detective involved in the case describes her as the "cleverest, most cold-blooded murderess that he ever heard of."[17]

While the novel's narrator seems to accept the detective's final characterization of Elsa as evil, in the film Michael never fully comprehends Elsa's enigmatic nature. While she does implicate him in a sinister murder conspiracy, her involvement is complicated by indications that she is really as much a victim of Bannister and Grisby's evil designs as Michael is. Described by Michael as a "sleeping rattlesnake," Bannister is clearly portrayed as an evil figure whose physical deformity symbolizes a twisted inner nature. It is not completely certain, however, whether Elsa partakes of his evil or has merely been victimized by it.[18] As Bannister prepares to shoot her, he makes an intimate connection between them: "Course killing you is killing myself, but, you know, I'm pretty tired of both of us." Yet, Michael's final words to Elsa do not portray her as inherently evil but only as having foolishly attempted to compromise with evil:

> You said the world's bad, and we can't run away from the badness, and you're right there, but you said we can't fight it. We must deal with the badness and make terms, and didn't the badness deal with you and make its own terms in the end, surely.

The film's extension of its narrative battles out into its narration lead yet again, as in other voice-over noirs, to its failure adequately to resolve the question of Elsa's true nature. This irresolution places viewers in a position that reduces their unification with narrational and implied authorial perspectives. A sense of closure at the film's end is thus minimized in favor of a recognition of the conflicts and contradictions inherent in the text. In spite of attempts at resolution, the spectator cannot help but question the concluding notion that Michael could successfully divorce himself from evil in a society that seems to validate the actions of the sinister lawyer Arthur Bannister and ally them with the allure of Elsa's captivating beauty, nor are we even sure that Elsa's beauty should be seen as aligned with or abused by that evil. What we are left with is a feeling of irresolution.

In conclusion, films noirs with first person voice-over narration attempt to forge a connection between their flashback visuals and voice-over narration by structuring their texts as narrative battles that extend out into the narration itself. This strategy prevents them from achieving the sense of narrative resolution and unification of point of view that the films seek at their conclusions. The disruptive potential of the voice-over technique and its complicating effect on the investigation of female sexual difference in the films are too strong to allow attempts at closure to have their desired effect. Since noir films focus so strongly on the investigation of their female characters, their failure to resolve the issue of female sexual difference in any satisfying way calls attention to the instability in regard to women's social positioning that characterized the period of the 1940s. The ideological irresolution that dominates the films speaks of a society torn between challenges to its patriarchal social structure and conservative support of the existing status quo. The fragmented nature of the films encourages a questioning of social norms that is muted but never completely shut down as they end by an attempted resolution of conflict.

These films, therefore, cannot be explained away so easily as aberrant representatives of a classical narrative form that employs them merely as safety-valves for wartime angst, alienation, and discontent, nor can they be seen as raising problems inherent in the social structure only to close them off by final narrative resolution and unity. They are structured, instead, as scenes of battle between conflicting aspects of their social milieux. The embattled narrational and resulting ideological structure that the voice-over technique and the unresolved issue of female sexual difference create within the texts points to the conflicted nature of the noir genre in its response to social contradiction and societal change. Specifically in regard to their presentation of

Another angle of Narrator Michael O'Hara (Orson Welles) with the duplicitous Elsa in the funhouse from *The Lady from Shanghai*.

women, they strongly represent, through their narrational structure, the inability of a patriarchal society not only to answer the question of "what the woman wants," but even to understand it.

Notes

1. Sarah Kozloff, *Invisible Storytellers: Voice-Over Narration in American Fiction Film* (Berkeley: University of California Press, 1988), 34.

2. Eric Smoodin, *Voice-Over: A Study of the Narration within the Narrative* (Dissertation, University of California, Los Angeles, 1984), 152.

3. Richard Maltby, "Film noir: The Politics of the Maladjusted Text" *Journal of American Studies* 18 (1984), 73-87; Foster Hirsch, *Film Noir: The Dark Side of the Screen* (New York: Da Capo Press, 1981).

4. Michel Foucault, *The History of Sexuality. Volume I: An Introduction*, trans. Robert Hurley (New York: Random House, 1978), 53-55.

5. Mary Ann Doane, *The Desire to Desire: The Woman's Film of the 1940s* (Bloomington: Indiana University Press, 1987), 54-55.

6. See, for example, Laura Mulvey, "Visual Pleasure and Narrative Cinema" *Screen* 16 (1975): 6-18; and Mary Ann Doane, "Woman's Stake in Representation: Filming the Female Body" October no. 17 (1981): 23-36.

7. Janey Place, "Women in Film Noir," in *Women in Film Noir*, ed. E. Ann Kaplan (London: British Film Institute, 1980), 35-54.

8. Susan Sniader Lanser, *The Narrative Act: Point of View in Prose Fiction* (Princeton: Princeton University Press, 1981); Ellen Harriet Feldman, *The Character-Centered Narrative: A Comparative Study of Three Films Structured According to the Organizing Perspective of a Single Character* (Dissertation, New York University, New York, 1981).

9. Vera Caspary, *Laura* (Boston: Houghton Mifflin, 1942).

10. For another reading of Laura which sees it as much more uncomplicatedly in accord with patriarchal norms see Kristin Thompson, "Closure within a Dream: Point-of-View in Laura" *Film Reader* 3 (1978): 90-105. Maureen Turim, *Flashbacks in Film: Memory and History* (New York: Routledge, Chapman, and Hall, 1989), 185-186, presents a short, but useful, analysis of the complexities involved in Lydecker's narration; and Eugene McNamara, *Laura as Novel, Film, and Myth* (Lewiston, New York: The Edwin Mellen Press, 1992) discusses at length the novel, film, the film's production, and its reception.

11. Richard Dyer, "Resistance Through Charisma: Rita Hayworth and Gilda," in *Women in Film Noir*, ed. E. Ann Kaplan (London: British Film Institute, 1978), 93.

12. Dyer, 99, note 3.

13. Hirsch, 188.

14. For other readings of *Gilda* that focus on the film's portrayal of Gilda's character, see, for instance, Dyer, in Kaplan, 91-99; and Mary Ann Doane, "Gilda: Epistemology as Strip Tease" *Camera Obscura* 11 (1983): 6-27.

15. James M. Cain, *The Postman Always Rings Twice* (New York: Random House, 1934).

16. Raymond Sherwood King, *If I Die Before I Wake* (New York: Simon and Schuster, 1938).

17. King, 295.

18. Other feminist critics, ignoring the ambiguities in her portrayal, have read the film as an unequivocal condemnation of Elsa as an evil character. See, for example, E. Ann Kaplan, *Women and Film: Both Sides of the Camera* (New York: Methuen, 1983), 60-72; and Lucy Fischer, *Shot/Countershot: Film Tradition and Women's Cinema* (Princeton, N.J.: Princeton University Press, 1989), 32-49.

Wendell Corey as assisttant D.A. Cleve Marshall and Barbara Stanwyck as the title character in *The File on Thelma Jordon*.

The Camouflaged Femme Fatale: *The File on Thelma Jordon* and *Pushover*

Elizabeth Ward

One of the enduring ironies of *Double Indemnity*, which is arguably one of the most important noir films of the classic period, is the casting of its principals. In a credit block of stars that included Fred MacMurray, Barbara Stanwyck, and Edward G. Robinson, how many viewers not already familiar with the plot from James M. Cain's novel would have expected the star of *Little Caesar* to be the only good guy? The tough-talking, sometimes shady characters portrayed by Barbara Stanwyck in *The Lady Eve, Meet John Doe*, and *Ball of Fire* were far from shrinking violets, what heroine of Howard Hawks or Preston Sturges could be, but compared to Phyllis Dietrichson in *Double Indemnity* they were choir girls. And long before *Flubber* or *My Three Sons* and also before portraying the craven second mate in *The Caine Mutiny*, Fred MacMurray was more likely to be trading jibes with Claudette Colbert than tossing bodies on train tracks. While it's clear from the recollections of various of the filmmakers that MacMurray was not the first choice for Neff, his casting was ultimately the most inspired in a film whose performances are among the most gripping in film noir.

Film noir is after all about style; and style is, according to Raymond Chandler, co-scenarist of *Double Indemnity*, not only "the most durable thing...the kind of style I am thinking about is a projection of personality."[1] For the directors of film noir, the stylistic layering was never just a visual patina laid over a crime story. While a fog-shrouded street or ominous footsteps from an unseen figure might quickly create suspense, the real shock of film noir came in the behavior of its protagonists. And the easiest way to play with the viewer's head was to cast against type, to work counter to the expectations by creating a core confusion between type of film and type of actor. This piece then is a consideration not just of unintentional femme fatales in two later noir films, but also of the flip side of *Double Indemnity* in that they center on subsequent portrayals of noir figures by Barbara Stanwyck and Fred MacMurray.

As the title character in *The File on Thelma Jordon* (1950, directed by Robert Siodmak), Barbara Stanwyck plays a very different type of femme fatale than Phyllis Dietrichson in *Double Indemnity*, who Thelma nonetheless resembles in method and motivation, as well as inevitably physical appearance. Although she ensnares the innocent Cleve Marshall to ensure the success of a crime to benefit her and another man, Thelma does something usually associated with male criminals in film noir: she falls for her victim. Where Phyllis was emotionally empty, a woman whose profession of love to her co-conspirator Walter Neff came only to avoid being shot by him, Thelma is a confused and reluctant criminal. While there may be contemporary critics such as Jean-Pierre Chartier who thought that, absent Phyllis' predatory sexuality, Walter would not be "responsible" for his actions but merely "a law-abiding young man seduced by a calculating bitch,"[2] this does not jibe with the filmmakers portrayal of Neff. While he may not have ever used his inside knowledge of the insurance business for personal gain, it had clearly crossed his mind before he met Mrs. Dietrichson.

Thelma's patsy is Cleve Marshall (Wendell Corey), who is not only an assistant district attorney, an occupation that, in theory at least, is more dedicated to upright behavior than selling insurance, but is actually guiltless when Thelma enters his life. While he never dumps any bodies on train tracks, shortly after meeting Thelma, Cleve is cheating on his wife and soon thereafter covering up the questionable circumstances of the death of Thelma's wealthy aunt. In a typical noir twist, Cleve does a poor job of concealing the murder, and Thelma is accused of committing it. But Cleve is assigned to prosecute her, and his intentionally feeble attempt to convict results in her acquital.

As conspirators and sexual partners Cleve and Thelma are as guilt-ridden and romantic as Walter and

Above, The File on Thelma Jordon: Cleve helps Thelma make the death of her Aunt Vera (Getrude Hoffman) appear to be other than murder. Opposite, Det. Paul Sheridan (Fred MacMurray) on stake-out with partner Rick McAllister (Phil Carey) in *Pushover*.

Phyllis were calculating and carnal. Whereas Phyllis keeps her little indiscretion with her step-daughter's boyfriend from Walter, Thelma tells Cleve that her shady boyfriend Tony Laredo (Richard Rober) is her estranged husband, something which the smitten Cleve actually believes. The crucial moment that will determine Thelma's unhappy fate in the noir universe is not when she tells that lie and not even when she murders her aunt, but when Cleve confronts her after the acquittal at the mansion she inherited from her aunt. Cleve faces her squarely, like the straight shooter he is or used to be, but his presence in the room is shadowed by Tony Laredo. Literally a man of darkness, with an animalistic sexuality, Tony is irresistable to Thelma, something of an "homme fatal." She cannot break with Tony despite her feelings for Cleve, despite, or perhaps because of, his clean-cut normality and self-sacrificing love for her. As she looks from one man to the other, Thelma knows they are equally bound to her because they both know the truth about her real nature; but she realizes that her deceptions have left her no choice: she belongs in the dark shadows with Tony. Romantically, she attempts redemption when she causes Tony to swerve off the road in a flaming crash and confesses in a desperate belief that her dying avowal may permit Cleve to salvage his shattered life. But Cleve has now become a noir figure, as Thelma's effect on his life has been just as fateful as a life sentence pronounced in a court room. In the end, it is Cleve who walks off into the shadows. "Because of his children and because of the years," he resolves to carry on the sham of his career and his marriage, but without Thelma and without his honor, he is an emotional Sisyphus, bearing the weight of a tragic mistake, toiling uselessly in darkness for salvation.

Pushover (1954, directed by Richard Quine) also resonates back to *Double Indemnity*: it involves murder for money and a cool, beautiful blonde who seduces a man into betraying his profession and his colleagues. In portraying Det. Paul Sheridan, Fred MacMurray reprises key aspects of Neff. Both characters are similarly vulnerable, superficially clever but unwise, concealing romantic disillusionment behind a mask of cynicism. While the use of MacMurray inevitably recalls Neff, but ten years have passed and they have not been kind to face of Neff, who was an ambitious young man in a well-cut suit, glib, attractive, and on the make. Paul Sheridan is slower in movement and less prone to snappy patter, with a puffy face that betrays an inactive and unrewarding life as palpably as a rumpled rain coat. For Neff, it was not just Phyllis but the challenge of the cheat, outwitting his mentor Barton Keyes, a guy who knew all the angles. For Sheridan, the temptation is all Leona McClane. Again the intricacies of noir narrative create the essential irony: Paul is assigned to approach and sweet talk Leona as part of his stake-out because she is the girlfriend of fugitive bank robber Harry Wheeler. Although Sheridan's con is part of his police work, the role playing alters the reality. The final factor, as it was for Neff and his brief time with Lola in *Double Indemnity*, is the age difference between the vibrant young Leona and the veteran detective. Sheridan sees the chance to obtain the missing money as a way to buffer the years between them.

Clockwise from top left, fateful clinches: Fred MacMurrray is willingly ensnared by Barbara Stanwyck's Phyllis Dietrichson, black widow in waiting. As Neff notes about his crime, "I killed him for money and for a woman. I didn't get the money and I didn't get the woman. Pretty isn't it." MacMurray's character makes the same mistake in *Pushover*, above, but is torn between his cop instincts and his desire for Kim Novak's Leona McLane. As Thelma Jordon, without the blond tresses, Stanwyck's character nonetheless get her hooks into Wendell Corey's D.A.

In the police interrogation room early in *Pushover*, Sheridan's younger partner Rick sits pensively by the window and remarks, "money's nice but it doesn't make the world go 'round." Paul's retort: "Don't it?... I promised myself as a kid that I'd have plenty of dough." Sheridan's snort confirms that he knows that "plenty of dough" is not what cops earn. In this context Leona and the missing $200,000 are a last chance that he cannot pass up. Like Walter and Phyllis in *Double Indemnity* the sexual attraction between Paul and Leona helps to sustain viewer identification with the criminal protagonists. While on stake-out Paul is forced to watch Rick pine platonically over Leona's neighbor, Ann, a wholesome brunette. Once he has succumbed to Leona's overtures, so that he betrays his badge and takes both her and the money, Paul is both disdainful and jealous of Rick's innocent infatuation. As a middle-aged man, MacMurray uses the same facial expressions he did as Neff to convey markedly different meanings.

The physical surroundings during Paul and Leona's moments together in his apartment are remarkably similar to those of the Neff/Dietrichson rendez-vous in *Double Indemnity*. The staging in *Pushover* is almost a mirror reverse of the former but significantly less glamorous, despite or perhaps because Leona's naive, breathless sexuality has replaced Phyllis' sophisticated, throaty lust. Unlike their knowing and unknowing counterparts in *Double Indemnity*, this couple do not redirect the tension of their secret and only partially consummated liaison into a betrayal of the other. It is only Paul who believes the money is critical to sustaining

A conflicted Paul Sheridan and Leona are confronted by her neighbor Ann Stewart (Dorothy Malone).

their emotional attachment. When confronted by the police, Leona actually urges Paul to forget about the money. It is not until he is lying in the street grievously wounded that Paul realizes and says "We really didn't need the money, did we?"

Since *Pushover* is a film noir and Leona is a femme fatale by default and she actually does bring doom both to Harry Wheeler, whom Paul kills, and then Paul who is shot by his own partner, she is far removed from the predatory Phyllis Dietrichson or Kathie Moffat. As a young actress, Kim Novak easily imbues Leona with inexperience and captures the confusion of the character's mixed ambitions. Although he initially accuses her of manipulating him and although Leona's physical youth and beauty give her the power to do that, she is too guileless. Having been manipulated herself by Harry Wheeler, she now becomes as much Sheridan's victim as he is hers. While it may be her suggestion, he, in fact, controls all the elements of their criminal scheme and only gives her simple directions which she follows unhesitatingly. One of Leona's few moments of defiance occurs early on when Paul reproaches her for accepting Wheeler's favors. Vehemently refusing to settle for squalor, she turns abruptly from Paul and in a rim-lit medium close shot pointedly affirms that "Money isn't dirty. Just people." Paul's face is visible behind, as it registers weary understanding of what made her compromise between disgust with her prospects and disgust with Wheeler. His expression also foreshadows the self-immolation to which his own lack of prospects will lead as he contemplates destroying his connection with the law and society.

In his noir-defining essay Jean-Pierre Chartier alluded to the "pure young girl(s)" in film noir who constitute "some hope about future generations"[3] That effect is negligible in *Double Indemnity*. While it is well exemplified in the relationship between Rick and Ann in *Pushover*, it it not without some irony of its own. The gradual and reasonable (they are of like age and appearance) development of the attraction between Rick and Ann strongly contrasts with the impulsive connection between Paul and Leona; and the conventional behavior of the career woman and the dedicated police detective reinforces the safety of social values as Paul and Leona are driven to desperation and destruction. But the high moral tone is severely undercut by the aspect of voyeurism in Rick, as he literally window shops for the right woman. Paul and Leona are brought together on orders from his police superior. Rick's intentions may be honorable, but watching Ann without her knowledge is stalking. Ann, though, unquestionably fulfills the purpose to which Chartier alludes. Although Paul has taken her hostage in his attempt to escape and although her lover Rick saves her, she immediately runs not into Rick's arms but to aid her now-wounded captor. If there is a fundamental aspect of women in film noir and their relationship to social values, a conclusion like this embodies it. Ann understands the emotions which Paul has experienced even as he holds a gun on her, even as Rick shoots him down. Rick's view of the patriarchal structures that empower him is inflexible and, even if he were not a police officer, he would be likelier to resort to violence and confrontation to resolve crises. He places his loyalty to those values over his partner's life. Although she is unable to dissuade him and suffers herself as a result, Ann's first allegiance is to the value of human life. Leona and even Thelma share that inclination. Even Phyllis, whom male observers call a "calculating bitch," understands human impulse and empowers herself by exploiting it. Ultimately, what the inobvious femme fatale reveals about noir and its deadly underworld, is that the doomed male is brought down as much by his own ego and his inability to understand the emotional truth—"We really didn't need the money, did we?"—as by any fatal woman's schemes.

Notes

1. Raymond Chandler, letter of March 8, 1947 to Mrs. Robert Hogan, in *Selected Letters of Raymond Chandler*, Frank McShane, editor, New York"Columbia Universuty Press, 1981, page 87.

2. Editor's Note: cf. Chartier's "Americans Also Make Noir Films," page 38 above.

3. Editor's Note: cf. Chartier, page 37 above.

Robert Siodmak directs Yvonne de Carlo and Burt Lancaster in *Criss Cross*.

Notes on Contributors

Sheri Chinen Biesen is professor of Film History at Rowan University and author of *Blackout: World War II and the Origins of Film Noir* and *Music in the Shadows: Noir Musical Films*. Her Ph.D. is from University of Texas at Austin, following M.A. and B.A. degrees at University of Southern California School of Cinema-Television, and has taught film at USC, University of California, University of Texas, and in England. She has contributed to *Film Noir Reader 4, Gangster Film Reader, Film Noir: The Encyclopedia, Film and History, Historical Journal of Film, Radio and Television, Quarterly Review of Film and Video, Literature/Film Quarterly, American Jewish History, The Historian, Television and Television History, Popular Culture Review* and edited *The Velvet Light Trap*. She appeared in the documentaries *the Rules of Film Noir* and *Public Enemies: The Golden Age of the Gangster Film*. Her essay of *Double Indemnity* will appear in the anthology *Film Noir Light and Shadow*.

Linda Brookover has worked extensively in the fields of multi-cultural education and holds two masters degrees in Education (from Texas A&M and U.C.L.A.). She has written on a variety of American Indian/ethnographic subjects for *OneWorld*, an on-line magazine which she co-edited. Previously a corporate communications specialist and electronic toy designer, she now works as a social-science researcher and educator. She wrote the screenplay for the Showtime family feature *Time at the Top* and contributed essays and sidebars to *Film Noir Reader 2, The Noir Style, The Vampire Film*, and *The Zombie Film*.

Todd Erickson is a veteran communications professional by day and a film noir aficionado by night. He coined the term "neo-noir" in the early 1980s while researching for his master's thesis, *Film Noir in the Contemporary American Cinema* (Brigham Young University, 1990) under the mentorship of film historian James V. D'Arc and film noir experts Alain Silver and Robert Porfirio. A condensed version of his thesis titled "Kill Me Again: Movement Becomes Genre" was published in *Film Noir Reader*, ten of his neo-noir title essays appeared in *Film Noir: The Encyclopedia*, and his analysis of *It's A Wonderful Life* is scheduled for the anthology *Film Noir Light and Shadow*.

Philip Gaines has produced a number of low-budget independent features (several of which he co-wrote) and has taught moviemaking and, occasionally, movie history at several local (that is, situated in Hollywood) institutes of technology. His interest in film noir developed when he was a film student and has continued to the neo-noir project he is still trying to produce. He also wrote the production guides *Hollywood on 5, 10, and $25,000 a Day* and *Micro-Budget Hollywood*, a term he coined with co-writer David Rhodes.

Karen Hollinger wrote *In The Company Of Women: Contemporary Female Friendship Films*, *The Actress: Hollywood Acting and the Female Star,* and *Feminist Film Studies*. She co-edited, with Virginia Wright Waxman, a monograph on *Letter from An Unknown Woman* and has published articles in *Film Criticism, Literature/Film Quarterly, The Quarterly Review of Film and Video, The Journal of Film and Video, Studies in Short Fiction* and numerous anthologies such as *Chick Flicks: Contemporary Women at the Movies* and *Genre and Contemporary Hollywood*. Her Ph.D. is from University of Illinois, Chicago and she is professor of film and literature at Amstrong State University in Savannah.

Richard Lippe teaches film at York University, Canada. He continues to contribute to *CineAction*, which he helped to establish more than 30 years ago and has contributed to other print and on-line reviews from *Movie*. (UK) to *Senses of Cinema*. His dissertation topic (York, 1992) was *Cukor, Women and the Melodrama: Close Readings of Four Films* and he has been a contributor/co-editor to *Introduction to the American Horror Film, George Romero Interviews, The American Nightmare: Essays on the Horror Film*, and *Queer Cinema, the Film Reader*, as well as prefatory material to new editions of studies of Penn, Bergman, and the *Apu* trilogy by his late partner Robin Wood.

R. Barton Palmer is Calhoun Lemon Professor of Literature and Director of Film Studies at Clemson University. Among his books on American filmmaking are *Hollywood's Dark Cinema: The American Film Noir*, *Perspectives on Film Noir* (editor), *Joel and Ethan Coen*, *A Little Solitaire: John Frankenheimer and American Film* (with Murray Pomerance), *The Philosophy Of Steven Soderbergh* (with Steven Sanders), and *Michael Mann and Philosophy* (with Steven Sanders and Aeon Skoble), and *Film Noir* (with Homer Pettey). His piece on *Stranger on the Third Floor* is set for *Film Noir Light and Shadow*.

Robert Porfirio began his ground-breaking work on film noir while in the Master's program at U.C.L.A. which culminated in his 1979 dissertation for Yale University, *The Dark Age of American Film: A Study of American Film Noir (1940-1960)*. His articles include contributions to *Continuum, Dialog, Literature/Film Quarterly*, and *Sight and Sound*. He is co-editor of *Film Noir Reader 3* and all editions of *Film Noir: An Encyclopedic Reference*, for which he wrote scores of individual entries, and also contributed essays to *The Noir Style*. He was formerly assistant professor of American Studies at California State University, Fullerton. Our esteemed colleague passed away in 2014.

Alain Silver wrote and edited the books listed on page 2, the earliest of which was based on his U.C.L.A. dissertation. His articles have appeared in *Film Comment, Movie* (UK)*, Wide Angle, Literature/Film Quarterly,* and *Photon* and anthologies on *The Hummer*, Akira Kurosawa, and Crime Fiction, as well as the on-line magazines *Images* and *Senses of Cinema*. His filmed screenplays include *White Nights* (from Dostoyevsky), the Showtime feature *Time at the Top*, and *Nightcomer*, which he also directed. He has also produced more than two dozen independent features, ranging from *Cyborg 2* to the recent *Sacred Blood*—which he scripted—and forty soundtrack albums. His commentaries have been heard and seen on KCET Television, Starz, E! Entertainment Television, Channel Four UK, AMC, Sci-fi Channel, CBC/Ontario and numerous DVDs discussing Raymond Chandler, Robert Aldrich, the gangster film, and the classic period from *Murder, My Sweet* to most recently Criterion Collection releases of *Kiss Me Deadly* and *Ride the Pink Horse*.

Director Howard Hawks (left) rehearses with the cast of *The Big Sleep*.

Vivian Sobchack, Professor of Critical Studies and Associate Dean of the School of Theater, Film and Television at the University of California, Los Angeles, was the first woman elected president of the Society for Cinema and Media Studies. Her essays have appeared in *Quarterly Review of Film and Video*, *Artforum*, *Camera Obscura*, *Film Quarterly*, and *Film Comment*. She has edited two anthologies: *The Persistence of History: Cinema, Television and the Modern Event* and *Meta-Morphing: Visual Transformation and the Culture of Quick Change*. Her own books include *Screening Space: The American Science Fiction Film*, *The Address of the Eye: A Phenomenology of Film Experience*, and *Carnal Thoughts: Embodiment and Moving Image Culture*.

J.P. Telotte is a Professor in the School of Literature, Communication, and Culture at Georgia Tech, where he teaches courses in film history, film genres, and film and technology. Co-editor of the journal *Post Script*, Telotte has authored more than a hundred articles on film and literature, such books as *Voices in the Dark: The Narrative Patterns of Film Noir*, *Replications: A Robotic History of Science Fiction Film*, *A Distant Technology: Science Fiction Film and the Machine Age*, and *Dreams of Darkness: Fantasy and the Films of Val Lewton*, and *The Mouse Machine: Disney and Technology* and edited volumes on *The Cult Film Experience: Beyond All Reason* and *Science Fiction Film, Television, and Adaptation: Across the Screens*.

James Ursini wrote and edited the books listed on page 2 and provided text for the Taschen Icon series on Bogart, Dietrich, Elizabeth Taylor, Mae West, and De Niro. His early study of Preston Sturges was reprinted in a bilingual edition by the San Sebastián Film Festival. Forthcoming as editor is *Film Noir Light and Shadow*. His film noir DVD commentaries (most often with Alain Silver) include *Out of the Past, The Dark Corner, Nightmare Alley, Lady in the Lake, Kiss of Death, Brute Force, Crossfire, The Lodger, The Street with No Name, Where Danger Lives, Kiss Me Deadly* and such other titles as *Hobson's Choice* and limited edition of *The Egyptian* and *The Wayward Bus*. He has been a producer on features and documentaries, wrote and co-directed the independent neo-noir *Nasty Piece of Work* and has lectured on filmmaking at UCLA and other colleges in the Los Angeles area where he works as an educator.

Elizabeth Ward is co-editor of all the editions of *Film Noir: An Encyclopedic Reference*, to which she contributed numerous entries. She co-wrote and co-photographed *Raymond Chandler's Los Angeles* (1987), on which she has also lectured. Additional books with Alain Silver are *The Film Director's Team* (2nd Edition, 1992) and *Robert Aldrich: a guide to references and resources* (1979). Her articles and interviews related to film noir have appeared in *Movie*, the *Los Angeles Times*, and the reference volumes *Survey of Cinema* and *Dictionary of Literary Biography* (on Leigh Brackett). She has worked extensively as a production manager, assistant director, stage manager, still photographer, and costume designer in motion picture and television production. After completing a degree in filmmaking at U.C.L.A., she worked in the Feldman Library at AFI West. Currently she pursues visual arts in the high Sierras.

Tony Williams is the co-author of *Italian Western: Opera of Violence* and co-editor of *Vietnam War Films* and *Jack London's The Sea Wolf: A Screenplay by Robert Rossen*. His numerous books include *Jack London: the Movies*; *Hearths of Darkness: the Family in the American Horror Film*; *Larry Cohen: Radical Allegories of an American Filmmaker*; *Structures of Desire: British Cinema 1949-1955*; *John Woo's Bullet in the Head*; *The Cinema of George A. Romero: Knight of the Living Dead*; and *Body and Soul: The Cinematic Vision of Robert Aldrich*. His articles have appeared in *Cinema Journal*, *CineAction*, *Wide Angle*, *Jump Cut*, *Asian Cinema*, *Creative Filmmaking*, several *Film Noir Readers*, and *The Zombie Film*. He is an Associate Professor and Area Head of Film Studies at Southern Illinois University, Carbondale. He will write about Hitchcock and Welles for *Film Noir Light and Shadow*.

Robin Wood whose numerous books on motion pictures were seminal to English-language film criticism ranging from his early auteur studies of Alfred Hitchcock, Howard Hawks, Ingmar Bergman, and Arthur Penn to such later work as *Hollywood from Vietnam to Reagan* and *Sexual Politics and Narrative Film: Hollywood and Beyond*. He was a long time Professor of Film Studies at Queen's College and York University. Early in his most distinguished career he was a contributor to such seminal journals as *Cahiers du Cinéma* and *Movie* (UK) and a founding member of the collective that edits the film journal *CineAction*. He passed away in 2009.

A lighter moment on the set of *Gun Crazy*: John Dall and Peggy Cummins share ice cream with director Joseph H. Lewis.